INTERPRETIVE
ARCHAEOLOGY

INTERPRETIVE ARCHAEOLOGY

A READER

Edited by
Julian Thomas

Leicester University Press
London and New York

Leicester University Press
A Continuum imprint
Wellington House, 125 Strand, London WC2R 0BB
370 Lexington Avenue, New York, NY 10017-6503

First published 2000

British Library Cataloguing-in-Publication Data
A catalogue record for this book is available from the British Library.

ISBN   0-7185-0191-8 (hardback)
         0-7185-0192-6 (paperback)

Library of Congress Cataloging-in-Publication Data
Interpretive archaeology : a reader / edited by Julian Thomas.
       p. cm.
     Includes bibliographical references and index.
     ISBN 0-7185-0191-8 (HB)—ISBN 0-7185-0192-6 (PB)
     1. Social archaeology. 2. Archaeology—Methodology. 3. Archaeology—Philosophy. I. Thomas, Julian.

CC72.4.I574 2000
930.1—dc21
                                                                    99-089007

Typeset by Ben Cracknell Studios
Printed and bound in Great Britain by TJ International, Padstow, Cornwall

CONTENTS

FIGURES

NOTES ON CONTRIBUTORS

John C. Barrett is Reader in Archaeology at Sheffield University. His research interests include archaeological theory, funerary archaeology and landscape archaeology.

Barbara Bender is Emeritus Reader of Anthropology at University College London. Dr Bender has written on socio-developments within gatherer-hunter societies, past and present, the emergence of inequality, and transitions to farming. She has excavated in many parts of Europe, in the Sudan and in North America, and has taught in the USA. She is currently working part-time on the social construction of landscape and on heritage issues.

Pierre Bourdieu is Professor of Sociology at the Collège de France. He is the author of many books including *Reproduction in Education, Society and Culture*; *Outline of a Theory of Practice*; *Distinction: A Social Critique of the Judgement of Taste* and *Homo Academicus*.

Victor Buchli is Lecturer in Anthropology at University College London. Dr Buchli writes on material culture and social change. His specific interests are architecture, post-socialist transition and the archaeological study of the present. He has conducted field work in Russia and Kazakhstan as well as in Britain. At present he is conducting research on the re-construction of the post-Soviet built environment and is beginning a project investigating notions of physicality and understanding of material culture.

Thomas Dowson is Lecturer in Archaeology at Southampton University. He specializes in rock art in the Americas, Europe and Southern Africa, and the socio-politics of rock art research. He has recently been engaged in projects concerned with using rock art to reconstruct indigenous histories.

Moira Gatens is Associate Professor of Philosophy at the University of Sydney. She is the author of *Feminism and Philosophy: Perspectives on Difference and Equality* and *Imaginary Bodies*.

Joan Gero is Professor of Anthropology at American University, Washington, DC. She focuses her research on gender and power issues in prehistory, especially in the Andean regions of Argentina and Peru. After directing excavations in New England, South Carolina and Labrador, she researched the early administrative centre of Queyash Alto in Peru during the 1980s, while her current co-directed project in the Argentinian Andes involves Early Formative household economies. She writes about the origins of state level society, feminist interpretations of prehistory and the socio-politics of doing archaeology; her many publications include the popular book *Engendering Archaeology: Women and Prehistory.*

J. D. Hill is Assistant Curator of Archaeology at the British Museum. He is a specialist in the archaeology of Iron Age Britain and Northern Europe, archaeological theory and pottery analysis. His previous work has included studies of later prehistoric social organization, ritual and taphonomy/site formation processes. His main fieldwork interests are in south Denmark where he is co-director of the Als archaeological project. His current research is focused on cultural and social change in Iron Age southern England and the social and economic interpretation of pottery, and he is working on the Ceramic Sociology of Iron Age East Anglia project.

Ian Hodder is Professor of Archaeology at the University of Cambridge, and Professor of Cultural and Social Anthropology at Stanford University, California. His research interests include post-processual archaeology, methodological studies of quantitative approaches to spatial analysis, material culture and social structure. His many publications include *Reading the Past* and *The Archaeological Process.*

Tim Ingold is Professor of Social Anthropology at Aberdeen University. Professor Ingold has carried out ethnographic fieldwork among Saami and Finnish people in Lapland, and has published widely on hunter-gatherer and pastoral societies, evolutionary theory and human ecology. He is currently researching environmental perception and the anthropology of technology.

Harald Johnsen works for the Troms fylkeskommune, in Tromsø. He received his master's degree in Archaeology from the University of Tromsø in 1992.

Matthew Johnson is Professor of Archaeology at the University of Durham. His research interests include medieval and post-medieval archaeology of England and Wales, vernacular architecture, landscape history and archaeological theory.

Siân Jones is Lecturer in Archaeology at Manchester University. She specializes in the area of archaeology and identity, in particular the interpretation of ethnic identity from archaeological remains, which is the subject of her recent book, *The Archaeology of Ethnicity* (1997). In the course of her research she has focused on material from the Iron Age and Roman periods in Britain and in the region of Palestine. Alongside this work she has also looked at the role of archaeological knowledge in the construction of modern ethnic and national identities, in particular the intersection of nationalism and archaeology in modern Israel.

Igor Kopytoff is Professor of Anthropology at the University of Pennsylvania. He is a general practitioner in cultural anthropology, with an ethnographic focus on Africa and with some past research in northern Asia. More specifically, his interests, research, and publications deal with social structure, political organization, and religion – and the process of transformation in them. He has also worked and published on slavery as a general cultural phenomenon, with a special interest in indigenous slavery in Africa as a culture-historical phenomenon. He has done fieldwork in the Congo, Cameroon, and the Ivory Coast.

Paul Lane is director of the British Institute in Eastern Africa, Nairobi.

Bruno Latour is Professor at the Centre for the Study of Innovation at the School of Mines, Paris. He is the author of *Aramis, or The Love of Technology*; *We Have Never Been Modern*; *Science in Action*; and *The Pasteurization of France*.

Mark P. Leone is Department Chair in Anthropology at the University of Maryland. He is interested in historical archaeology and interpretation, critical theory, outdoor history museums and African–American archaeology.

Randall McGuire is Professor of Anthropology at the University of New York, Binghamton. His principal interests lie in the development of power relations in the past. He has carried out most of his field work in the US Southwest, and currently is conducting a long-term field project in northwest Mexico. He has also done historical archaeology and oral history research in the northeastern US. He has initiated a project investigating the 1913–14 coal strike in southern Colorado. In addition to historical archaeology, history and ethnology, his interests include quantitative methods, social theory, cultural resource management and archaeomagnetic dating.

Henrietta Moore is Professor of Anthropology at the London School of Economics. Her research is concerned with East and Central Africa, economic anthropology, development, gender and feminist theory.

Bjørnar Olsen is Professor of Archaeology at the University of Tromsø.

Michael Parker Pearson is Reader in Archaeology at Sheffield University. His research interests include later prehistory, funerary behaviour, archaeological theory and ethnography. He has conducted field projects in the Outer Hebrides, Madagascar and south Yorkshire (including Scrooby Top and Scabba Wood).

Linda Patrik is Associate Professor of Philosophy at Union College, Schenectady, New York. She graduated cum laude from Carleton College and received her doctorate from Northwestern University, specializing in European philosophy. She has studied phenomenology, existentialism, hermeneutics and Sanskrit at the universities of Freiburg and Tübingen, and the philosophy of archaeology in Athens. Her research on meditation has taken her to India and her research on archaeology led her to work on a dig in Tunisia. She has published papers on eastern philosophy, phenomenology and the philosophy of archaeology.

Parker B. Potter, Jr received his PhD from the State University of New York at Buffalo, and worked as field archaeologist for the 'Archaeology in Annapolis' Program.

Keith Ray is County Archaeologist for Herefordshire. He received a PhD in Archaeology from Cambridge University for his work on the Igbo-Ukwu assemblage.

Colin Richards is Lecturer in Archaeology at the University of Glasgow. His research interests include Neolithic archaeology, material culture studies and ethnoarchaeology.

Paul Shackel is Director of Graduate Studies in Anthropology at the University of Maryland. He is interested in historical archaeology, industrial archaeology, complex societies, labour history, consumer behaviour, and public history.

Michael Shanks is Professor of Classics as Stanford University. His publications include *Experiencing the Past: On the Character of Archaeology*; *Classical Archaeology: Experiences of the Discipline*; and *Art and the Early Greek City State*.

Anthony Sinclair is Lecturer in Archaeology at the University of Liverpool. His research interests include Palaeolithic and Mesolithic archaeology, Japanese archaeology, archaeological theory, technology and fieldwork in Britain and South Africa. He is Co-director of the Carden Project.

Shirley S. Strum received her PhD in Anthropology from UC Berkeley in 1976. She currently teaches primate behaviour, human evolution and conservation at UC San Diego.

Julian Thomas is Professor of Archaeology in the School of Art History and Archaeology at the University of Manchester. His publications include *Time, Culture and Identity: An Interpretive Archaeology* and *Understanding the Neolithic*.

Christopher Tilley is Professor of Anthropology and Archaeology at University College London. Professor Tilley has research interests in theory and philosophy, material culture and prehistoric Europe, with regional expertise on Europe and New Guinea. He is currently carrying out research in Bodmin Moor, Cornwall on the cultural construction of landscapes and on a project involving the comparative study of museums, ethnicity and tourism in the Pacific. His broader research interests are in the study of theories of representation in relation to material form.

Ruth Tringham is Professor of Anthropology at the University of California, Berkeley. Her research interests include the study of Neolithic and Eneolithic Southeast Europe, gender archaeology and multimedia.

Alison Wylie is Professor of Philosophy at Washington University, St. Louis. Her interests include philosophy of the social and historical sciences, and feminist perspectives on archaeology.

Tim Yates received his doctorate in Archaeology from King's College, Cambridge. He has published on archaeological theory, ethnoarchaeology and the European Bronze Age. He has carried out extensive field research on the rock carvings of Bohuslän, Sweden.

ACKNOWLEDGEMENTS

The editor and publishers wish to thank the following for permission to use copyright material:

Academic Press Ltd, London, for L. Patrick (1985), 'Is there an archaeological record?' from M. Schiffer (ed.), *Advances in Archaeological Method and Theory*, pp. 27–62.

Archaeological Review from Cambridge and the authors for A. Sinclair (1989), 'This is an article about archaeology as writing', *Archaeological Review from Cambridge*, 8, pp. 212–33; and P. Lane (1986), 'Past practices in the ritual present: examples from the Welsh Bronze Age', *Archaeological Review from Cambridge*, 5, pp. 181–92.

Ashgate for J. D. Hill (1993), 'Can we recognise a different European past? A contrastive archaeology of later prehistoric settlements in Southern England', *Journal of European Archaeology*, 1, pp. 57–75.

Berg publishers for C. C. Richards (1993), 'Monumental choreography: architecture and spatial representation in late Neolithic Orkney', in C. Tilley (ed.), *Interpretative Archaeology*, pp. 143–78.

Blackwell Publishers for Randall H. McGuire (1991), 'Building power in the cultural landscape of Broome County, New York 1880–1940', in Randall H. McGuire and Robert Paynter (eds), *The Archaeology of Inequality*, pp. 102–24; H. Moore (1994), 'Bodies on the move: gender, power and material culture', in *A Passion for Difference*, pp. 71–85.

Cambridge University Press for K.W. Ray (1987), 'Material metaphor, social interaction and historical interpretations: exploring patterns of association and symbolism in the Igbo-Ukwu corpus', in I. Hodder (ed.), *The Archaeology of Contextual Meanings*, pp. 66–77; I. Kopytoff (1986), 'The cultural biography of things: commoditization as process', in A. Appaduai (ed.), *The Social Life of Things*, pp. 64–9; Ian Hodder (1982), 'Theoretical archaeology; a reactionary view', in I. R. Hodder (ed.), *Symbolic and Structural Archaeology*, pp. 1–16; and M. Parker Pearson (1982), 'Mortuary practices, society and ideology: an ethnoarchaeological study', in I. R. Hodder (ed.), *Symbolic and Structural Archaeology*, pp. 99–113.

Carfax Publishing Ltd for R. Tringham (1994), 'Engendered places in prehistory', *Gender, Place and Culture*, 1 (2), pp. 169–203.

Cruithne Press for C. Y. Tilley (1991), 'Materialism and an archaeology of dissonance', *Scottish Archaeological Review*, 8, pp. 14–22.

Joan Gero (1993) for 'The social world of prehistoric facts: gender and power in Paleoindian research', in Hilary duCros and Laurajane Smith (eds), *Occasional Papers in Prehistory*, No. 23.

M. Johnson (1989) for 'Conceptions of agency in archaeological interpretation', *Journal of Anthropological Archaeology*, 8, pp. 189–211.

Kluwer Academic Publishers for Alison Wylie (1992), 'On "heavily decomposing red herrings": scientific method in archaeology and the ladening of evidence with theory', in L. Embree (ed.), *Metaarchaeology*, pp. 269–88.

Sage Publications Ltd for S. Strum and B. Latour (1987), 'The meaning of social: from baboons to humans', *Social Science Information*, 26, pp. 783–802; P. Bourdieu (1970), 'The Berber house or the world reversed', *Social Science Information*, 9, pp. 151–70; and J. C. Barrett (1988), 'Fields of discourse: reconstituting a social archaeology', *Critique of Anthropology*, 7: (3), pp. 5–16.

Society for American Archaeology and the authors for M. Shanks and R. McGuire (1996) 'The craft of archaeology', *American Antiquity* 61(1), pp. 75–88; and H. Johnsen and B. Olsen (1992) 'Hermaneutics and archaeology: on the philosophy of contextual archaeology', *American Antiquity* 57(3), pp. 283–302.

Taylor & Francis Books Ltd for I. R. Hodder (1992), 'Symbolism, meaning and context', in *Theory and Practice in Archaeology*, pp. 11–23; T. Yates (1990), 'Archaeology through the looking-glass', in I. Bapty and T. Yates (eds), *Archaeology after Structuralism*, pp. 154–202; S. Jones (1996), 'Discourses of identity in the interpretation of the past', in Graves Brown, S. Jones and C. Gamble (eds), *Cultural Identity and Archaeology: The Construction of European Communities*, pp. 62–80; V. Buchli (1995), 'Interpreting material culture: the trouble with text' in I. Hodder, M. Shanks, A. Alessandri, V. Buchli, J. Carman, J. Last and G. Lucas (eds), *Interpreting Archaeology: Finding Meanings in the Past*, pp. 181–93; T. Ingold (1993), 'The temporality of the landscape', *World Archaeology*, 25, pp. 152–74; B. Bender (1989), 'The roots of inequality', in D. Miller, M. Rowlands and C. Tilley (eds), *Domination and Resistance*, Allen and Unwin, pp. 83–95; C. Y. Tilley (1989), 'Interpreting material culture', in I. Hodder (ed.), *The Meaning of Things*, Allen and Unwin, pp. 185–94; and Moira Gatens (1995), 'Power, bodies and difference', in *Imaginary Bodies: Ethics, Power and Corporeality*.

The University of Chicago Press for M. Leone, P. B. Potter and P. Shackel (1987), 'Toward a critical archaeology', *Current Anthropology*, 28 (1), pp. 283–302.

Every effort has been made to trace copyright holders and to obtain their permission for the use of copyright material. The authors and publishers will gladly receive any information enabling them to rectify any error or omission in subsequent editions.

The editor would like to thank Matt Leivers, Rick Peterson and Julia Roberts who scanned the texts and compiled the index.

1

INTRODUCTION
The Polarities of Post-Processual Archaeology

Julian Thomas

New Archaeologies

In 1972 Mark Leone published a collection of articles under the title *Contemporary Archaeology: A Guide to Theory and Contributions*. In the ten years which had preceded this publication American archaeology had undergone a fundamental revolution, with the emergence of what had come to be known as the New Archaeology. While it had been prefigured by earlier calls for increased conceptual sophistication and problem-orientation (e.g. Taylor 1948), the New Archaeology represented a unified programme for the reform of the discipline. At its core were a demand for robust means of constructing and verifying hypotheses about the past, and a desire to address questions of past social and cultural process, which might or might not articulate with evolutionary approaches. Taken together, these imperatives recast archaeology as a science of material culture. Leone saw his book as a means of demonstrating that a new and powerful body of theory had begun to accumulate, whose coherence and integration were not always evident, since the theorization was dispersed in journal articles or embedded in accounts of fieldwork and analysis. Leone was offering a selection of the canonical statements of the New Archaeology as a handbook or reference source for professional archaeologists (1972, ix). Armed with this volume, archaeologists could go out and *do science*. Beyond this, his concern lay with demonstrating the contribution which archaeology was increasingly making to human knowledge.

This book might be compared with Leone's, in that it attempts to document the principal ideas and approaches which have characterized a particular phase of disciplinary development. Just as Leone had collected together many of the best-known contributions to New or processual archaeology, this volume contains some of the most-quoted examples of post-processual or interpretive archaeology. However, at this point the parallel breaks down. The New Archaeology can be identified as a unitary project, because its practitioners believed that there was a single truth about the past that could be accessed as long as one had the right approach, and did the right kind of science. There were certainly disagreements amongst the New Archaeologists, some of them acrimonious, but they tended to revolve around the identification

1

of appropriate ways of addressing the archaeological record. The ultimate objective of archaeological investigation was generally agreed: the generation of law-like statements covering human social and cultural development. There has never been this degree of conformity over the ambitions of a post-processual archaeology, to the extent that Christopher Tilley (this volume, Chapter 24) argues that there is no such thing as a post-processual archaeology. Similarly, Ian Hodder (1991a: 37) has suggested that we should speak not of a post-processual movement but of a post-processual era. This is not to imply that processual archaeology has become a thing of the past, and is no longer practised. Rather, the period since the early 1980s has seen the development of a variety of perspectives which are either critical of processual archaeology, or build on its foundations in ways which were not originally imagined.

Instead of the development of a single new research programme within archaeology, the past two decades have seen archaeologists beginning to engage with a very wide range of debates which are being conducted within the human and social sciences. Processual archaeology gained much of its inspiration from the natural sciences: ecology, geology, evolutionary biology and the 'spatial science' of human geography. More recent work has simply widened the scope of this interdisciplinarity, so that a greater variety of theoretical materials are now recognized as being relevant to archaeology. What this means in practice is that those archaeologists who are described as 'post-processualists' do not constitute a distinct research community, and may understand their closest affinities as lying with other disciplines: anthropology, philosophy, sociology, cultural studies, art history, technology studies, performance studies, and so on. As a consequence, this book represents anything but the exposition of a 'party line'. What I have chosen to include here is a series of papers, all of which I have found inspiring, in various ways. I do not necessarily agree with everything that is contained in all of the articles, and they very plainly do not agree with each other. But I have found something useful in each of them, and I would recommend any or all of them to my students. In tune with the interdisciplinarity of contemporary archaeology I have chosen to include a number of papers which were not written by archaeologists. Some of these are works that have been repeatedly referenced in archaeological debates, while others are pieces which I believe to have considerable relevance to the discipline (although the authors probably did not have archaeology in mind when they wrote them).

This book, then, is a celebration of the diversity of the ideas which are presently being employed in archaeology. To some it will appear to be a 'post-processual manifesto', but my intention in this Introduction is to draw attention to the differences of opinion which exist within this non-existent school of thought. To that end I will attempt to identify a series of areas within which unresolved tensions can be recognized.

Epistemology: for and against
There is some agreement that recent developments in archaeological theory have resulted in a wider range of issues being addressed within the discipline: gender, power, symbolism, ritual action, personal identity, nationalism, representation, and so on. However, this growing diversity of investigation is continually met with the objection, 'This is all very well, but where is the methodology?' This argument is

extremely beguiling, and it is easy to be seduced by it. Ian Hodder (1991a: 8) notes that post-processual archaeologies have been more concerned with theory than methodology, and indeed that the critique of processualism has been most cogent at a philosophical level. It is tempting to imagine that if one's theoretical framework is more powerful, it should be possible to generate an epistemology which is superior to that of the New Archaeology. However, attempts at founding a 'post-processual method' tend to collapse, in that they generally rely upon some set of presumed universals, whether of human nature, cognitive processing, or the capabilities of the human body. The reason for this failure is easy to discern. The New Archaeology *was* methodology. It was above all an attempt to place epistemology at the centre of archaeological practice, and to establish foolproof ways of determining the veracity of statements about the past. Many of the criticisms of the New Archaeology have been pitched precisely at the poverty of this empiricism: the hypothesis-testing approach attempts to do away with any need to interpret, and to take responsibility for our interpretations (Shanks and Tilley 1987a: 47). The method itself should automatically guarantee truth. Now, if we have already argued that archaeological evidence is theory-laden, and that our observations take place in the context of a series of pre-understandings and prejudices which we cannot evade, it makes little sense to attempt to construct a universal epistemology for archaeology. To do so is to implicitly accept the terms of argument of the New Archaeology. If there is no one definitive knowledge of the past, no single methodology can reveal it to us.

This is not necessarily to argue for the methodological anarchy advocated by Feyerabend (1975). We should be rigorous in our procedures, while remaining realistic about what they can and cannot achieve. We need methods which are context-specific, strategically employed, and designed to elicit particular information from particular sets of evidence. The knowledge that we produce will not necessarily be one from which we can generalize. And as Shanks and Tilley (1987b: 6) argue, our methods should be seen as secondary to and derived from social theories, which help us to understand the conditions under which we conduct our investigation. When epistemology assumes the foundational role that it had for the New Archaeology, particular kinds of knowledge claims can come to be disregarded. One of the most important lessons that feminism has taught archaeology is that there are important things to know about the past which simply cannot be tested. Gender, for instance, has often been completely neglected on the grounds that it cannot be empirically 'found' (Wylie 1992).

Interpretation
The New Archaeology saw hypothesis-testing as a means of confounding one's own assumptions about the past, and allowing oneself to be surprised by the evidence. Many archaeologists have now turned to a conception of knowledge informed by hermeneutics, in which whatever questions and tests we use to confront the material are conducted *within* the interpretive process. The 'hermeneutic circle' is not something which can we can evade; it does not have an 'outside'. This means that we must always take into account the position of the interpreter, who is the means through which any understanding of a situation is to be achieved. Although there are many who are now happier with the tag 'interpretive archaeology' than with 'post-processualism'

(Shanks and Hodder 1995: 5), there remains some debate over the character of archaeological interpretation. For Hodder (1991a: 11) interpretation is a process in which the past and present constitute one another, and the notion that past and present can enter into a dialogue of sorts is accepted by many (Johnson and Olsen, this volume, Chapter 7). Yet while some understand interpretation to be a process in which past meanings are recovered, others hold that it is a contemporary practice which creates a knowledge that is of and for the present (Shanks and Tilley 1989a: 4).

Interpretation makes sense of the archaeological evidence (Tilley 1993: 10), rendering it comprehensible. 'The interpreting archaeologist fills the gaps in the past, but these gaps are always already there. They are not simply a feature of preservation or inadequate amounts of survey or excavation. Like a metaphor the past requires interpretation' (Shanks and Tilley 1987a: 21). But this leaves open the relationship between observation and interpretation (Hodder 1999: 81). Is interpretation an act which we carry out upon materials that we already know in some sense? Does it add a deeper level of understanding to something that we can already grasp through observation? Or is there an interpretative aspect to our apprehension of things? Martin Heidegger (1962) would have argued that we always come to things with a certain pre-understanding, which enables us to comprehend them *as* something in particular. By this argument there can be no fixed distinction between observational knowledge and interpretation: there is interpretation in all knowing.

Cultural and epistemic relativism

Our knowledge of the past is created in the present, through our involvement with archaeological evidence. Because each of us has a different access to power and knowledge, and has a different set of experiences to draw upon, we will each construct the past in different ways. Our understanding of any past world is contingent and incomplete, but so was that of anyone who occupied those worlds. To be able to grasp the full significance of all aspects of the past, or the present, one would have to be gifted with divine omniscience. These arguments have often been rehearsed over the past twenty years, but they still remain troubling to many archaeologists. Aside from the presumed lack of a definitive methodology, it is this denial of a single and entirely knowable past which has provoked the most voluble criticisms of post-processual archaeologies. If there is no definitive past, it is argued, then anything goes: there is nothing to stop us saying anything we like about prehistory (see Yoffee and Sherratt 1993a, for example). UFO enthusiasts and Nazi archaeologists have an equal right to present their own interpretations of the past. So post-processual archaeologies are charged with *relativism*.

Broadly speaking, relativism involves a belief that there are no universal criteria that we can use to compare or judge between values, customs, beliefs and interpretations. However, there are two distinct forms of relativism, both of which can be identified within archaeology. The first is cultural relativism, often associated with the work of the anthropologist Franz Boas. Cultural relativists hold that it is inappropriate to evaluate other societies (including those of the past) according to our own standards, since these have themselves been constructed within a particular set of historical conditions. Ian Hodder's position in *Reading the Past* (1986) comes close to a cultural relativism. Hodder proposes that frameworks of meaning are implicated in all aspects of human life, so that no action can be separated from its cultural context. These frameworks of meaning are not universal, and as a consequence the same act conducted in two different societies may not carry the same significance (*ibid.*, 118). It is therefore impossible to compare the subsistence practices, funerary rites or metalworking techniques of any two communities in abstraction from the systems of meaning which render them comprehensible.

More radical still is epistemological relativism which questions the universality of our knowledge of the world and the means by which we acquire it. Epistemological relativists may be entirely sceptical concerning the existence of universal truths, the possibility of objectivity and value-freedom, and even the existence of a definitive reality, as opposed to a series of equally valid interpretations of existence. However, it is not the case that all forms of epistemological relativism doubt the existence of a real world 'out there'. For instance, Richard Rorty (1989: 5) has suggested that our real problem lies in imagining that we can capture and express the world in language, no matter how real that world may be. The notion of truth as it is commonly understood relies on the belief that statements or sentences can be made to correspond to things in the world. This correspondence theory of truth requires that the world out there should be made up of sentence-like entities which are waiting around for us to label them with words. Having eventually 'labelled' everything, we shall have acquired a satisfactory understanding of reality. Rorty presents an alternative perspective: we use language to describe the world, and our descriptions never entirely correspond with reality. Nor do they ever exhaust all that might be said about any particular phenomenon. He argues that scientists and scholars do not tell truths about things in the world, so much as use language to re-describe things. The language that we have at our disposal is an accident of history, so the notion that our description of some phenomenon is more 'truthful' than that of people living in another time is a nonsense. But what we can do is to attempt new and novel re-descriptions of the world, which allow us a more profound understanding of things.

In *Re-Constructing Archaeology* (1987a), Michael Shanks and Christopher Tilley adopt a form of epistemological relativism, which serves as the basis for a critique of the New Archaeology's avowed scientific objectivity. Shanks and Tilley set out to demonstrate the extent to which the whole philosophy and methodology of the New Archaeology were dominated by the values of contemporary capitalism. The New Archaeology had sought to turn archaeology into a science, but in the process it had come to associate scientific reason with method, with simply following a given set of rules of procedure. Here, truth is connected with objectivity, with being free from biases. Thus the aim of the scientist is to remove all potential forms of distortion from their observations, so that he or she can see the world as it really is. Shanks and Tilley's case is that this kind of value-freedom is an illusion, and that facts and values are always intimately bound up with each other. Their illustration of this point involves the evaluation of a series of the supposedly value-free, objective, scientific methodologies of processual archaeology, showing that each embodies a series of contemporary values. In the first place, the New Archaeology presented 'facts' as if they were isolated and context-free pieces of information, passed from hand to hand like the alienated commodities that circulate in a capitalist economy. Similarly, cultural evolution judges different human communities according to their adaptive success, their efficiency in material terms. Systems theory relies upon conservative values of persistence and homeostasis, and denies that internal conflict or contradiction can ever bring about positive change. Mathematics and quantification in archaeology purport to boil archaeological evidence down into a set of neutral and easily understood patterns, but in practice they dehumanize the past, reducing it to malleable figures in the same way that contemporary capitalism reduces men and women to mere statistics.

However, Shanks and Tilley reject the charge that relativism disables intellectual inquiry by affording equal validity to all interpretations (1987a: 60). One can be pluralistic without being uncritical, and different perspectives can enter into a productive debate. It may be that their truthfulness or falsity cannot always be established, but this is not the only basis for distinguishing between competing accounts of the past. We can make judgements on the basis of the ethical and political values which different archaeologies embody. This, of course, raises a series of further problems.

Archaeology and political commitment

Shanks and Tilley's position is that we can discriminate between different versions of the past, but that the only way of doing so is on the basis of the value systems which lie behind them (1987b: 195). While some archaeology may be written as overt propaganda, the real problem is that we always bring a series of prejudicial assumptions to our study of the past, of which we may not be remotely aware. To be objective is a practical impossibility, since it is our prejudices and our interests which motivate us to act at all, but the aim of a critical archaeology is to make us aware of the reasons why we study what we do. This cannot be achieved by attempting to achieve a position of neutrality, erasing ourselves from the scene of knowledge production. On the contrary, we should conduct our inquiry on the basis of an explicit and honest commitment to a distinct set of values. A similar argument is presented by Leone, Potter and Shackel (this volume, Chapter 27). But significantly they write from a more orthodox Marxist perspective, which lacks the hermeneutic element found in Shanks and Tilley's work. The consequence of this is that Leone, Potter and Shackel consider that a critical archaeology can produce a more secure and even objective knowledge of the past, by removing sources of bias. Shanks and Tilley would presumably object that while critique can provide us with a superior understanding, it is none the less a contemporary knowledge, which must remain radically incomplete.

Drawing as they do on the social sciences, it is unsurprising that many recent varieties of archaeological thought have been alert to the political significance of the past. Yet there is a further point of argument that divides these approaches in a fundamental way. Many authorities are willing to recognize that archaeology is conducted in a political context (for example, Kohl and Fawcett 1995). However, rather fewer are ready to concede that archaeology is itself a political practice. This point of view is ultimately derived from the work of Antonio Gramsci (1971), who argued that all forms of cultural production are implicated in a 'war of position', in which conflicting visions of reality compete in order to secure the support and compliance of social groups. Archaeology can support or dispute conceptions of human nature, or constructions of ethnic and national identity, or accounts of the universality of particular social arrangements. As such it is directly embedded in the political field, and the statements that archaeologists make are always potentially politically active. This is all the more important in a global and multicultural context, where the utterances of archaeologists have direct implications for minority communities, in terms of access to land-rights, sacred sites and human remains (Zimmerman 1989).

Difference and alterity

One of the principal ways in which the past can be political lies in its difference from the present. The recognition that even the most mundane everyday activities have changed over time, and *have a history*, serves to undermine our conviction that the way that we are in the present is the way that humans normally are (Foucault 1984). If nothing about human beings is changeless and eternal, then political change can be recognized as a real possibility: we are not restricted by the fixity of 'human nature'. For instance, a more equitable future seems possible when we recognize that acquisitiveness and the profit motive are not written into the human constitution. Accordingly, a concern with the alterity of the past has been an abiding theme within post-processual archaeologies (see Hill, this volume, Chapter 25).

On the other hand, some authors have been concerned to draw attention to the potential drawbacks of conceiving the past as Other. Such a past can become an exotic fantasy onto which we project our own desires and fears (Hodder 1999: 154). Ian Hodder has also raised the interesting question of how we can ever recognize the difference of the past if it is entirely produced in the present (this volume, Chapter 6). One answer to this would be that while our understanding of the past is a contemporary interpretation, the existence of archaeological remains in the present alerts us to the otherness of past ways of being. In the act of interpretation we come to terms with this alterity and subdue it, but the process is one in which our understanding of ourselves in relation to the past has been challenged.

Cross-cultural generalization and historicism

In one of the most important and influential critiques of processualism, Hodder (this volume, Chapter 3) questioned the utility of the comparative method as it is employed in archaeology. Cross-cultural generalizations were habitually used as the basis for establishing universal laws of culture, but in practice they had the effect of erasing variability, reducing humanity to a set of standardized themes (adaptation, competition, social hierarchy, subsistence practice). Hodder argued that archaeologies which took symbolism and meaning seriously should look back for inspiration to a previous generation of British archaeologists, like Gordon Childe, Grahame Clark, Glyn Daniel and Stuart Piggott. These prehistorians had emphasized the historical contingency of human life, and had understood artefacts to be material manifestations of ideas. While their approach had been 'normative' in presenting material culture as the product of internalized traditions, more sophisticated theoretical frameworks could actually build upon their work to address the specific historical and cultural contexts in which artefacts were produced.

Hodder's advocacy of historicism was consistent with his cultural relativism, and most post-processual archaeologies have followed suit in emphasizing the specificity of contingent circumstances. However, while the uniqueness of cultures is generally agreed upon, there is sometimes a willingness to accept that human universals underlie the construction of these cultures. Hodder, for example, argues that universal principles of meaning allow people to be socialized, and enable them to come to terms with the social world (1986: 124). Similarly, Tilley (1994: 12) discusses fundamental human bodily attunements which facilitate the experience of place and landscape. Do these propositions represent cross-cultural generalizations? We could argue that *being human* is not so much the characteristic of an entity which possesses a series of attributes, as an activity, something which one does. This being the case we could say that being human does not rely upon any foundations or essences, it simply takes a particular form. It involves, for instance, a concern over one's own being (Heidegger 1962). But it is clear that post-processual archaeologists are not agreed on the question of how much is held in common by human beings in different places and times.

Totalization

Just as the generalizing approaches of the New Archaeology have been criticized for homogenizing human diversity, so the system-level analyses of processualism have been attacked on the grounds of their remoteness from human experience. It is undeniably the case that people are commonly embedded in social relationships which extend over enormous geographical distances, and that certain historical processes are pan-continental in scale (Sherratt 1995). However, we should also recognize that these processes were lived through at a more intimate level (Barrett 1989a: 306). Human action and knowledgeability are localized, and it is more likely that we will comprehend historical processes by investigating the ways in which they were worked through 'on the ground' than by instituting a systemic explanation which bears down from above. Moreover, as Foucault (1984) suggests, the willingness to deal in totalized accounts of the past suggests an affinity with totalitarian politics. If we are comfortable for the people of the past to disappear into vast systemic processes, perhaps we will show equally little concern for the disappearances of people in the present.

These arguments have some affinity with the rejection of a unified archaeology with a single methodology that we have already discussed (Tilley, this volume, Chapter 5). If there is no singular past, then there may be many stories which are worth listening to, including those of the dispossessed, the poor, the slaves, the illiterate and the insane. One of the great strengths of archaeology is that it can use material evidence as a means of addressing these 'other histories', and allowing other voices to come to the fore. In this way, archaeology becomes an agent of 'history from the bottom up'. None the less, it is worth suggesting that, although we may reject the idea of a totalized understanding of a given period, we should not allow our accounts of the past to become so parochial that they are unable to contest the large-scale histories and prehistories of conventional archaeology.

Context

The reaction against generalization and the growing emphasis on the localized conditions which render material culture meaningful lead one towards a consideration of the notion of context. For Ian Hodder, 'reading' an item of material culture is achieved by placing it into its context, the 'totality of the relevant dimensions of variation around any one object' (1986: 139). Just as words have multiple meanings but 'make sense' in the context of sentences, so material symbols can be better understood when we encounter them in a particular physical setting. Context is thus a relational concept, and Hodder stresses that each object can be part of the context of other objects (1991a: 15). He argues that the context of an artefact is composed of a number of dimensions of variability: time, space, depositional unit and typology (Hodder 1986: 131). But is the *archaeological* context of a thing (the pit, floor, hearth or ditch from which it is retrieved) comparable with its *historical* or *cultural* context? Or is it more appropriate to say that any artefact will have a variety of different kinds of context, each of which casts a different kind of light on the thing?

Hodder's focus on context serves to define a way of working in which the myriad potential meanings of material things become restricted. The symbolic significance of an object ceases to be arbitrary when it is bounded within its appropriate context (Hodder, this volume, Chapter 6). As a number of archaeologists have pointed out, this leaves open the question of how we define and limit the context itself (Yates, this volume, Chapter 10; Tilley 1993: 9). For Yates, context is an arbitrary means of trying to halt the limitless signifying capacity of material things, while Tilley stresses that the interpreting archaeologist is integral to the context of the artefact. Context is therefore not simply a bounded entity set in the past, but an aspect of the relationship between the past and the present. The notion of a contextual archaeology has been one of the most important developments of the post-processual era, but it may be that we should not think of context as a fixed container that surrounds an object. Instead, we might choose to say that the relationships in which an artefact is embedded are heterogeneous and regioned. The place in which a thing is found, the other things alongside it, the designs with which it is decorated are all places where we can begin our exploration of its significance, but they do not exhaust its potential meanings.

Past meanings, past minds?

In an exponentially growing archaeological literature concerned with interpretation, cognition, symbolism, text and context it is inevitable that the issue of meaning must loom large. What do we mean by meaning? Arguably, two different answers could be given to this question. One is to say that any item of material culture has two kinds of meaning. First, it has a prosaic, denotative or material meaning, connected with its function, use and appearance. An axe *means* a thing for chopping wood; a chair *means* a thing for sitting on. Over and above this the artefact may have a secondary meaning, which is symbolic or connotative. So the axe may be a symbol of exchange relations and gender identity, or the chair may be a throne and carry connotations of royalty and state power. I would suggest that this is the conception of meaning which is most commonly employed within contemporary archaeology. But alternatively, we might say that the meaning of a thing is its significance, the way in which we come to understand it. In this formulation the distinction between primary and secondary meaning breaks down. Recognizing a throne *as* a thing to sit on has no necessary priority over recognizing it *as* a symbol of royalty. The two are entirely bound up with each other in the way in which the chair reveals itself to us.

Ian Hodder has argued that the attempt to interpret archaeological evidence necessarily involves trying to get at the meanings inside the minds of past people (1999: 72). By complete contrast, John Barrett suggests that: 'Instead of attempting to read back from modern archaeological remains to meanings in the past, a better proposal is to explore the implications of particular material conditions for the structuring of specified social relations' (Barrett 1987b: 471). In other words, since the minds of dead people are no longer available to us for scrutiny, we cannot address meaning at all. Instead, we should consider the material mechanisms which made the production of meaning possible, in different ways at different times. Tim Yates (this volume, Chapter 10) objects that this perspective attempts to place materiality outside the condition of meaning. It is as if meaning is an addition to a set of material conditions which we can already know in a transparent way. Yates maintains that as soon as we encounter the material traces of the past, they are meaningful to us. But this meaning is a contemporary one, which cannot be identical with past meanings.

Hodder's search for a past meaning that was contained in the heads of past people seems to me to rely upon the mind/body dichotomy. Meaning is something that exists in the rarefied sphere of thought. By contrast, Barrett wishes to evict meaning from the material world altogether. These are perhaps the two sides of the same coin. My own argument would be that when we encounter the material remains of a past world we engage in a work of reanimating a technology of meaning. We enter into a relationship with that past world because the material things themselves were integral to a past way of life. But we do this in the present. We are not recovering past meanings, but creating new meanings which result from the meeting of past and present.

Ideology

The concept of ideology was of critical importance within early manifestations of post-processual archaeology, as it provided a means of challenging the New Archaeology's belief that archaeological evidence amounts to a reflection of past social relationships (see Miller and Tilley 1984b). The origin of the concept as it is now commonly understood lies with Marx and Engels, in their book *The German Ideology* (1970). In that work, Marx and Engels were interested in the way in which history had come to be written by the German idealists, and in particular Ludwig Feuerbach. Their argument was that this school of historians tended to reproduce the conception of the world that prevailed amongst the dominant classes. Marx and Engels suggested that in any historical epoch, the dominant set of ideas will be those of the ruling class. The population at large is provided with a set of understandings which are taken as fact, and their compliance allows society to reproduce itself without a constant state of class violence existing. That is to say, if the lower orders were aware of their own real interests, and of the way in which they were constantly being exploited by the dominant group, they would tend to struggle against that domination.

Thus, each class that comes to power throughout history tends to represent its own sectional interests in ideal form, as a set of unquestionable and eternal truths that constitute the only universally valid ideas. Because the rest of the community accepts these ideas, their understanding of the world becomes a warped and partial one. Marx uses the image of a camera obscura as a metaphor for this situation: reality is viewed through a lens which inverts it. Since people gain a distorted impression of their own interests and their relationship to the material conditions of existence, they tend to comply with the desires of the ruling class.

As a number of writers have pointed out, Marx and Engels' account of ideology is one which allows space for two different interpretations of the term (Callinicos 1983: 129; Therborn 1980: 3). Firstly, there is what has been described as a *pragmatic* conception of ideology. This suggests that ideology is a *product of lived experience*. Because different people have different experiences of the world, they tend to conceptualize it in rather different ways. Their aspirations and values will vary from person to person, and especially between people whose economic circumstances are different. Simply because different classes live under different material conditions, they will have distinct understandings of the way the world works. Moreover, it will tend to be the understandings of the dominant class that dominate the consciousness of society as a whole.

On the other hand, there is what we might call an *epistemological* view of ideology. According to this way of thinking, ideology is seen as 'false consciousness', a distinct set of *untruths* about the world which are concocted by the dominant class and imposed on the rest of the community. Ideology, then, becomes a pack of lies designed to keep the workers in their place. From birth, the working classes are subjected to a range of propaganda which tells them how to behave, and which emphasizes the value of submitting their will to the common good. These untruths should be distinguished from the real conditions in which people live, and they serve to hide reality from them. They are also quite distinct from the kind of knowledge that is produced by science, which is objective and untainted by ideology. This kind of understanding tends to represent Marxism as a kind of science of social and economic relations, which seeks to expose and undermine ideological notions by building up a true and undistorted picture of the world.

It was a more sophisticated version of this epistemological conception of ideology that was presented by Louis Althusser in the 1960s. In his article 'Ideology and ideological state apparatuses' (1971b), Althusser asks why ideology should exist at all, by considering the process of social reproduction. If a social formation is to maintain its existence from one generation to the next, both material resources and positions of authority must be reproduced. This requires that the labour force must continue to accept its position, and must submit to the established rules of order. So from birth, members of the working class have to be placed in a position of not wishing to question their lot. Althusser contends that societies, or sets of social relations of production, are like great faceless machines which require people to insert themselves into particular roles and positions in order to allow the whole to function. As he puts it: 'the structure of the relations of production determines the places and functions occupied and adopted by the agents of production, who are never anything more than the occupants of these places' (Althusser and Balibar 1970: 180). So capitalism, or any other mode of production, requires that people take up positions on production lines, or in offices, in which of course they are exploited and their labour power is sucked out of them.

The role of ideology is to present a different view of all of this. People *may* only exist to be a cog in a vast process of production, but it is only through adopting these positions, says Althusser, that people gain their sense of self-identity. Ideology makes people believe that the world around them exists for their benefit, rather than that they exist to service the productive process. Ideology sets up an imaginary picture of the way that the world is, and this serves as the basis for people's actions. What this means is that ideology is not just a set of ephemeral ideas, but is a set of real relationships in the world, even if they are in reality articulated to a vision of the real interests and material conditions of people which is illusory. Such an ideological understanding of real relationships is produced and promoted by the dominant class. The fundamental point here is that if people who live under capitalism are to become human beings at all, they have to accept and adopt this ideology. Because ideology infiltrates and permeates all aspects of our culture, it is simply not possible to gain an understanding of the world without ingesting a whole set of ideological notions in the process. Principal among these is the idea that each of us is a free, rational, decision-making individual, who is in control of their own life and is free to do what they like, rather than a mere node in a network, a bearer of relations of production. So ideology actually gives each of us our place in the world.

This notion that ideology is composed not of ethereal ideas but of real relationships is emphasized by Althusser's insistence that ideology exists in and through human institutions. Thus, in modern capitalist society there are a whole series of Ideological State Institutions, through which ideological messages are conveyed from the dominant to the subordinate classes. At each stage in their emergence as distinct human beings, people are constantly bombarded with these messages regarding what is and what is not acceptable behaviour: in schools, the media, public information, the workplace, and so on. Where the Ideological State Apparatuses can achieve the compliance of the workforce without violence, the Repressive State Apparatuses (the police and the army) can be held in reserve. In pre-capitalist society, Althusser suggests that it is the church which serves as the major Ideological Agency, producing an ideology which is concerned with the relationships between the vassal, the lord, the king, and God: an imaginary set of relations which ensures a compliant peasantry. This emphasis of Althusser's on religion as a form of ideology leads on to the use that prehistorians have made of his ideas, in claiming that ritual practice can be seen as a form of ideology (Shanks and Tilley 1982).

As we have noted, the use of the concept of ideology made archaeologists aware that, as a form of signification, material culture could be mobilized to present a distorted image of social reality, or to support sectional interpretations of the world. More recently, some archaeologists have begun to express reservations about the theory of ideology. Some, like Barrett (1994: 77) follow Abercrombie, Hill and Turner (1980) in doubting the capability of structures of ideas to 'dupe' entire populations and secure their compliance. Instead, ideologies may serve as a means of enhancing the solidarity of distinct social groups. Others agree with Foucault (1980a) that the notion of ideology relies upon a distinction between truth and ideological falsehood. Quite apart from the problems inherent in identifying and verifying a single and definitive truth, it is arguable that any form of knowledge (irrespective of its truth value) is potentially active in power relationships. Thus we should concern ourselves less with demonstrating the falsity of ideological messages, and more with how forms of knowledge serve to promote particular interests.

The 'active individual'

As Lynn Meskell has recently observed, 'accessing individuals in the past' has been a recurrent theme for post-processual archaeologies (1998a: 363). But again, there is little unanimity over the possibility or desirability of this objective. For entirely laudable reasons, one of the early criticisms that was made of processual archaeology was that it had lost sight of human beings in its pursuit of adaptive systems and long-term change (Hodder 1986: 6). Personal creativity and intentionality were underplayed. As a corrective, a focus on the active individual was proposed, stressing the dynamic role that people have in historical processes through their strategic use of material culture. This approach was underpinned by the use of the 'practice theories' of Bourdieu and Giddens. According to these perspectives, social institutions are presented as being reproduced through the continual exercise of human agency. It is through practice that structures are carried forward, yet agency is constituted structurally and draws on various resources in order to be effective. However, it is arguable whether 'individual' and 'society' can be conflated with 'structure' and 'agency' (see Johnson, this volume, Chapter 12). John Barrett has complained that Hodder's concern with the active individual actually decontextualizes human beings, by presenting them as entirely free agents who can create social practices in a way that seems to be untrammelled by cultural tradition or processes of subjectification (1987b: 471).

A very different point of view was represented by Shanks and Tilley (1987b: 65), who pursued a series of post-structuralist arguments, under which human subjects are not considered to be the authors of texts and material culture, but the 'effects' of processes of signification. That is to say, language and material culture are not the product or prerogative of any single person: it is the cultural field which constitutes us as beings of a particular kind. In this sense human beings are 'produced' by their cultural traditions, and it follows from this that they may be produced in radically different ways in different times and places. This suggests the possibility of an 'archaeology of subjectification', exploring the mechanisms through which identity and agency are constructed in different epochs.

Of course, if the character of 'being human' is not fixed but culturally variable, it is open to question whether the notion of the active individual is not itself historically situated. Marilyn Strathern (1988) has demonstrated that for many Melanesian communities the notion of a bounded and self-contained individual with an internal world of subjectivity is virtually incomprehensible. Melanesians more often conceive of themselves as 'dividuals', who are at once embedded in relationships of kinship and obligation, and composed of body parts and substances which can be disaggregated. Arguably, the concept of the individual is not a neutral synonym for 'person' or 'subject', but is a way of thinking about human identity which is specific to western modernity. Since the Renaissance, and more thoroughly since the Enlightenment, Western thought has prioritized the exercise of free will and reason by a political subject who is autonomous from cultural tradition and social ties. Indeed, such individuals are not imagined to be the products of societies, but form societies through a contract to their mutual advantage. 'The individual' is at once an ideal to which only some members of society can hope to approximate (male, white, educated, wealthy heterosexuals) and a kind of fantasy. For human beings do not come into the world fully equipped to deal with reality. Language, cultural attunements, and habitual social skills are all the prerogatives of the community, and unless we grow up within such a community we cannot be human at all.

Postmodernity

The suggestion has often been made that in some way post-processual archaeologies have an affinity with postmodernity or postmodern*ism* (e.g. Bintliff 1991; Hodder 1990b; Walsh 1990). This is another point over which I feel that there is some level of disagreement. For some, post-processualism is simply the manifestation of postmodernism within the discipline of archaeology. For others, the two phenomena are entirely unrelated. I would like to suggest that the relationship is a more complicated one than either of these views would allow, and that much of the difficulty rests with the variety of different meanings that can be attached to the term 'postmodern'. This requires a little explanation.

Perhaps the best place to begin is with the contrasting term, modernity. While we are accustomed to using the word 'modern' as a synonym for 'contemporary' or 'up-to-date', in philosophical terms it applies more properly to an era in the history of the Western world that began with the decline of feudalism. Modernity has been the age of capitalism, of mercantilism, of European expansion across the globe, of the emergence of nation–states, and of industrialization in manufacturing. It has also been an era of empires, racism, genocide, and of the industrialization of warfare. All these phenomena were underwritten by a series of what Jean-François Lyotard (1984) refers to as 'metanarratives'. By this he means the understanding that some great, long-term pattern underlies the whole of human history, which can be expressed in a story-like form. These metanarratives would include the rise of the West, the emancipation of the human spirit, universal progress, the development of economies, the growth of democracy, and so forth. As a consequence, modernity has involved a widespread faith in the notion that everything we do contributes to a greater design, which will ultimately lead to a better world. Along with this set of metanarratives came a concern with origins. While the Greeks and Romans had discussed the concepts of evolution and progress, the medieval world was more accustomed to the belief that human capabilities and achievements were in decline, and that a Golden Age had existed at some time in the past (Trigger 1989b: 31). The notion of social evolution, from savagery to civilization, or from stone to bronze and to iron ages only re-emerged in the modern era. Archaeology as a discipline is a product of modernity, and one of its principal tasks has been to investigate the origins of the modern nation-states by tracing the migrations of tribes and races. Similarly, in more recent times, archaeology has concerned itself with the origins of modern humans, the origins of agriculture, the origins of urbanism, and so on, creating a series of metanarratives of its own.

The sets of ideas which most thoroughly characterized Western modernity were those that were associated with the 'Scientific Revolution' of the seventeenth century, and the Enlightenment of the eighteenth. The former was based on the understanding that the universe has a definable structure which obeys a series of invariant laws, and that this structure can be identified through human experience. In other words, we can discover how nature works through scientific experiment. The Enlightenment sought to transfer this vision of an ordered and predictable universe into human society. If the medieval period had been dominated by superstition and religion, the Enlightenment promoted a secular society in which God, and the avoidance of sin, had been replaced by Reason (Gray 1995: 145). What was suggested was that, as superstition lost its grip on humanity, the human will was gradually freed. By acting freely and rationally, people would create an ideal society – and indeed René Descartes argued that a person who acted freely and in a fully rational way would be incapable of sin (Caroll 1993: 122). So the moral void that was left behind by the removal of God from the centre of the universe was filled by a series of moral codes, based upon Reason and human nature (Bauman 1992; 1993: 25). This concept of human nature was of cardinal importance to the Enlightenment project. What was implied was that just as the world of Nature had a fixed character that could be determined by the natural sciences, so Man (and the masculine is intentional) had a nature which was universal and which could be known. It was with the Enlightenment that we can identify the foundation of a series of Sciences of Man, which worked to explain human nature: sciences like economics and statistics, human biology and anatomy, and linguistics (Foucault 1970).

Over the past half century there have been growing indications that modernity, as a human project and as an experience of the world, is drawing to a close. These have taken a number of different forms. First, Lyotard has written of an 'incredulity towards metanarratives' (1984: xxiv). By this he means that in the Western nations there is now little faith in the idea that history can be understood as a unified and directional process leading towards the betterment of humankind. In an era which has seen the battle of the Somme, the Holocaust, Hiroshima, the Khmer Rouge and Bosnia it is very difficult to place any belief in progress. Reason, and technology, seem just as capable of providing us with nightmares as with a perfect world. This need not imply that human existence is hopeless, but it does at least suggest that the world that we live in is infinitely complex, and travelling in a number of different directions at once. There is no one historical narrative: there are many interwoven histories. The postmodern experience involves a sense that there is no one centre defining everything that is going on in the world: it is no longer the case that a global empire can be ruled from a single city.

The second process that we could point to is a fundamental change in the character of capitalist economics. In the early part of the twentieth century, industrial capitalism reached a height of sophistication with what has been called 'Fordism', after Henry Ford's motor company. Fordism involved a production-line system within massive factory buildings, in which every worker had their place, and probably had a job for life. The company provided them with health care, food in a canteen, paid holidays, pensions, child-care, training and sometimes even housing. In various ways, the worker's whole life could be bound up with the company. The company was located in a certain place, and the workers formed a community living close by the factory, or the mine, or the mill. The paradigm of this development would be Cadbury's chocolate factory and company housing at Bournville in Birmingham. The past few decades have seen this pattern gradually eclipsed by what has come to be known as post-Fordism, or flexible accumulation (Aglietta 1980). Under this regime, the larger companies have increasingly become multinational, and are not associated with a single product. They are not located in a single place, and they periodically move their operations around the world as labour costs change. Jobs tend to be short-term and insecure, and markets are international and deregulated. Workers are told that they have to be flexible, accept the going rate, re-skill themselves periodically, and expect to have a series of different jobs in their lifetime (Murray 1989).

All of this is deeply inter-connected with a third tendency, which has been described as the annihilation of space through time (Harvey 1989). This is an apt description of the communications revolution. Over the past two centuries, methods of transportation have changed dramatically, so that people and goods can be moved around the globe at hitherto unthinkable speeds. More recently, however, the speed at which information can be transferred from one place to another has become faster still. In consequence, money, stocks and shares can change hands at terrific speeds, so that we now have a digitized global economy of capital flows. Importantly, this is an economy which the state simply cannot control, as the British Conservative government found to its cost on 'Black Wednesday' in 1992, when billions of pounds were lost in the attempt to prop up the value of sterling on world markets. Speculators and multinational corporations can now move money from place to place at will, ruining regional economies in the process. Economics are no longer bound to locations, and this has begun to have a corrosive effect on the nation–state, the diagnostic political form of modernity. At the same time, we have also seen the state eroded from within by new nationalisms in Eastern Europe, indigenous movements in the post-colonial world, and regional movements in Western Europe (Friedman 1989). The old certainties of economics and political identity are gradually crumbling away.

Another effect of the communications revolution has been the proliferation of television, film and advertising. Throughout the world people are constantly being bombarded with images and messages. Where once people would have had an experience which was bounded by the world that physically surrounded them, now we have a massively expanded knowledge of the world, and yet it is a superficial knowledge generated by electronic images. These are what Jean Baudrillard (1988) calls 'simulacra', experiences that are not real, but consist only of images. These experiences have no real depth, they do not really touch us, and yet they make up the fabric of our existence. In a curious way this recalls Althusser's (1971b) discussion of ideology, which he describes as a real and lived relationship with an imagined set of conditions. Just as we have an electronic financial economy, so we now also have a world-wide economy of images, continually circulating and bouncing off one another, creating new meanings as they go. And of course, we have the cyberspace of the Internet, in which people communicate and form relationships without any physical encounter. All of this creates a depthless existence of images and flows, in which our sense of space and time is gradually eroded. On the one hand, everywhere is increasingly the same as everywhere else – everywhere has shopping malls, McDonald's, Coke and *Baywatch*. The ultimate postmodern experience is the food plaza in a shopping centre, where you can eat dishes from all over the world – and they all taste the same. Because nothing has any depth, because nothing has any attachment to place or tradition, everything is simply a commodity that circulates in the global market. But on the other hand, we crave distinctiveness and authenticity, and these are provided for us in the form of Viking Yorvik, Catherine Cookson Country and the Millennium Dome.

This brings us back to the relationship between the past and the present, and the kind of archaeology that can exist in a postmodern world. Clearly, if our sense of space and time is being diminished, and if images and experiences are increasingly part of a global economy, we have to be very concerned about the development of the heritage industry. If heritage is to be marketed as a leisure pursuit, is it not simply a part of the general commodification of existence? Has our relationship with the past changed, so that instead of a set of traditions that are passed down to us and which give us an authentic place in the world, we simply have a set of images – of cave men, Roman soldiers, knights in armour and penitent monks – which can help to provide an instant fix of gratification? This is certainly the lesson that some people have drawn from postmodern architecture. Postmodern buildings often use elements and details drawn from different periods in a mix-and-match fashion, deliberately clashing references and meanings to striking effect. To some this is deeply worrying, because it suggests that instead of creating something new that genuinely reflects the present, this architecture simply reworks the past. It is an architecture of 'decorated sheds' (Harries 1993). In the same way, we could argue that our culture of heritage is a symptom of a world in which history has ended, and all that is left for us is to draw on groundless images of the past and re-present them endlessly. In this way of thinking, the postmodern era represents nothing less than the final victory of market capitalism, in which the future holds nothing for us but new TV series, new fashions and new kinds of fast food.

This seems to me to be an unduly pessimistic point of view. It relies on the understanding that postmodernity is a single process that can be readily grasped in its entirety (Strohmeyer and Hannah 1992). There has been a tendency to view the cultural and intellectual developments of the past few decades as a mere reflection or product of economic changes (Harvey 1989). In these terms, post-processual archaeologies are a side-effect of the postmodern condition. Like other post-modernisms, they might be expected to deal in pastiche, play, irony and self-conscious intellectualism (Bintliff 1991). What this view overlooks is that the kinds of thought that are conventionally labelled as postmodernist are in many cases the inheritors of a long tradition in the human sciences, which has consistently developed a *critique of modernity*. This tradition has been extremely diverse, both in philosophical and political terms. It has ranged from the romanticism of Hölderlin to the Christian existentialism of Kierkegaard (Blackham 1952), the hermeneutics of Gadamer and the hermeneutic phenomenology of Heidegger, to the conservatism of Spengler and the Western Marxism of Horkheimer and Adorno (1972).

I would suggest that any connection between post-processual archaeologies and postmodernity can ultimately be traced to the entity that they have set out to criticize: the New Archaeology. It is no exaggeration to suggest that the New Archaeology was identical with the Enlightenment project. Like the Enlightenment, the New Archaeology emphasized reason, and optimistically believed that there was no aspect of the past which was inaccessible to scientific method. Like the Enlightenment, the New Archaeology stressed the universality of humankind, and valued quantitative rather than qualitative understandings of reality. This reality was singular, and could be addressed from a singular point of view, whose relative superiority was self-evident. And like the Enlightenment, the New Archaeology was unwilling to accept that other ways of understanding might eventually come to eclipse or supplement it.

Post-processual archaeologies should not be expected to present a uniform view of the past and how we hope to understand it. Indeed, the most important development of the past twenty years has been the collapse of the belief that there can be a single royal road to knowing the past. The post-processual era has not seen the emergence of a new kind of archaeology, so much as a new kind of discourse within archaeology.

PART I

ON THE CHARACTER OF ARCHAEOLOGY

INTRODUCTION

Although many authors are agreed that some fundamental change has overtaken archaeology since the early 1980s, there is very little consensus over the character of this change. As a result, two inter-related questions have preoccupied archaeologists throughout this period. First, what kind of an archaeology do we want to practise? As the discipline adopts new conceptual frameworks and abandons older ones, the kinds of knowledge it produces and the issues that it investigates are irrevocably changed. But this leads on to a more fundamental question: what kind of an enterprise is archaeology? Hitherto, the nature of archaeological inquiry has largely been taken for granted. The presumed objective existence of something called 'the archaeological record' has tended to limit debate to methodological questions: how do we squeeze a knowledge of the past out of the evidence? It is arguable that one of the more significant developments in recent years has been the questioning of the status of the 'evidence', the 'record' itself. For as long as material things were considered to be a passive record of past human action the vision of archaeology as a search for a key to translate the record could be sustained. But the growing recognition that material culture had an active role to play in human social life, and even that material things were intrinsic to social relationships, has meant that an exclusive focus on method and technique could no longer be upheld. Our relationship with our object of study is increasingly 'up for grabs', and this has called for a reconsideration of exactly what it is that we do when we do archaeology. The chapters in Part I present a series of quite different arguments concerning the material world and its investigation, but each of them opens up a range of new possibilities for understanding the past.

One aspect of this re-evaluation has been the outright rejection of certain aspects of processual archaeology. In his contribution, Ian Hodder points to the way in which functionalist thought has imposed a series of limitations on what can and cannot be discussed within the social sciences. By concentrating on relations between population, resources and ecology, functionalism precludes any consideration of meaning, agency and creativity, and promotes a conservative outlook which only values social change as a reaction to external pressures. Moreover, the processual emphasis on explanation prescribes a form of reasoning in which the world can be reduced to a series of separate variables. In opposition to this John Barrett argues here for an approach which emphasizes relationships rather than entities. Our world is composed of social and ecological relationships, from which distinct entities emerge (Strathern 1996). Finally, Christopher Tilley points to the idealism of positivist archaeologies which imagine that we can gain an understanding of the past by simply collecting an ever-growing mountain of observations on material traces that exist in the present. All of these perspectives are couched in critical terms, but in each case the effect is to extend the possibilities open to archaeological interpretation.

If the rote-learning of methods of inquiry and the lawlike explanations of functionalism are no longer viable, interest has increasingly come to focus on the intellectual content and origins of the arguments that we make about the past. If much of the initial inspiration for new conceptions of material culture was drawn from structuralism, this has meant that archaeologists have needed to become accustomed to quite advanced philosophical debate in order to assess its strengths and weaknesses. In turn, a growing acquaintance with a wider range of literature in philosophy and the social sciences has spawned a series of new debates. These have touched on the desirability of totalizing grand theories and the appropriate scale of analysis, and the nature of human history. Perhaps most important of all has been the increasing recognition of archaeology as a cultural product, something which is constructed in the present within given political and cultural circumstances. This is essentially the point which Tilley makes when he insists on the materiality of archaeological practice. Archaeologists and their evidence exist alongside each other in a material world, and the degree of disengagement which would be required to ensure scientific objectivity is a practical impossibility. As Tilley goes on to argue, the consequence of this is that we cannot allow ourselves the luxury of claiming that what we write about the past is the dispassionate product of scientific procedure. On the contrary, we have to take responsibility for our accounts of the past, and hope to understand the influences and prejudices which encourage us to write in the way that we do.

In an extended meditation on the consequences of recognizing archaeology as a contemporary production, Shanks and McGuire employ the metaphor of craft. For them, archaeology is a labour of mind and body which employs theories and raw materials in order to create a form of knowledge that is politically active. As they note, the notion that the past may be 'crafted' in the present may be troubling for some, but this makes it no less real. Describing archaeology draws attention to the various skills which it employs, and which are passed from person to person in various kinds of apprenticeship. Moreover, it acknowledges that archaeologists represent a community of practitioners, in the field and in the academy, who share a vocabulary and a series of habits of working. It is this image of archaeology as the practice of a community which offers an optimistic vision for the future. As Tilley suggests, we should not expect to find agreement over our ways of working or our understandings of the past, but if we think of our work as involving a series of conversations between practitioners it may be that our differences can prove productive.

2

FIELDS OF DISCOURSE[*]
Reconstituting a Social Archaeology

JOHN C. BARRETT

Introduction

Archaeology continues to arouse little or no interest amongst those who work within the neighbouring disciplines of the social sciences. Historians pay it scant regard and anthropologists can be as dismissive (Leach 1973a). It is not so much that the task archaeology sets itself, to understand the human past through material remains, is uninteresting, nor is it impossible to achieve. Rather there exists a crisis in the current practice of archaeology which contributes towards its apparent irrelevancy.

Archaeologists act as if the object of their study is a modern material record of past events. Inferences about the past are drawn from the various procedures which 'read', 'translate' or otherwise give meaning to this record. Linda Patrik characterises the treatment of archaeological evidence as a record in terms of two models (Patrik 1985). The first employs the evidence as a fossil record where direct, mechanical relationships are taken to exist between past processes and their surviving imprints in archaeological materials. The second treats the evidence as a text. Here a more complex connection between past and present appears to exist for the record encodes ideas and meanings which were created in the past.

These treatments of the 'evidence as record' have resulted in an over-riding preoccupation with issues of methodology. These issues concern the way the record can be calibrated, allowing knowledge of the past either to be read from it, or allowing ideas about the past to be assessed against it. As archaeological evidence is a modern phenomenon the procedures required to link process to record are established in contemporary, ethnoarchaeological research (e.g. Binford 1983a; Hodder 1982b).

However, the two perceptions of the archaeological record which Patrik identifies have different methodological implications. If the evidence is treated as a fossil record then it is also assumed that cross-culturally comparable processes will result in comparable patterns in the surviving evidence. This assumption underpins the New Archaeology's attempts to establish highly generalised statements about the human past which are open to cross-cultural verification. On the other hand, if the evidence is

[*]First published in *Critique of Anthropology* (1988), **7**(3), 5–16.

a textual record then it is composed as a 'matter of author's choice and convention' (Patrik 1985: 33). The record's meaning must now be culturally and historically specific and, given this, translation becomes highly problematic. How can we read these exotic texts? It is noticeable that whilst demands for a 'textual archaeology' have arisen from ethnoarchaeological fieldwork, as well as having a deeper theoretical derivation (papers in Hodder 1982a), clearly developed procedures of archaeological translation have yet to be presented (cf. Hodder 1984b). The most successful translations have been achieved in historical archaeology. Here written texts are the means by which the material texts are translated (Deetz 1977; Glassie 1975; Leone 1984).

Patrik's paper is important, not only for the clarity with which she has distinguished between the different concepts of an archaeological record, but also or her concluding remarks. She writes:

> I would like to raise the question expressed in the title of this paper: 'Is there an archaeological record?' For the question hints that archaeological evidence may not form any kind of record at all . . . If neither the physical recording connection nor the recording connection of signification seem exactly right for an appropriate conception of archaeological evidence, if neither seems to capture the actual connection between archaeological evidence and what it is evidence of, then perhaps the whole concept of recording is not appropriate for the evidence.
>
> (Patrik 1985: 57)

With this comment Patrik opens the way to a rethinking of the archaeological evidence. She demonstrates that to speak of an archaeological record carries metaphysical implications which determine the way inferences are drawn from that evidence. Of her two models I wish to leave aside that of the evidence as a fossil record. Within the limited applications which Patrik identifies for it the model is internally consistent. However, the model of archaeological evidence as a text is inadequate. I do not believe that such texts are capable of adequate translation. But more importantly this model does not accurately represent the relationship between human action and material conditions. In offering a reconsideration of our use of archaeological evidence I will argue that we should treat it not as a record of past events and processes but as evidence for particular social practices.

Archaeological evidence

Social archaeology, as currently practised within the entire spectrum of archaeology, attempts to demonstrate that empirically recoverable patterns of archaeological material record the nature of past social organisations, beliefs or ideologies. The recoverable pattern of things is commonly taken to record the adaptive procedures of a particular type of social system including the internal organisation of that system whereby goods, energy or information are stored and circulated. Social practices in the past have therefore appeared to result in a static configuration of archaeological materials (Renfrew 1974). Social institutions, the product of recurrent social practices, similarly appear as static material representations. Archaeological analysis, equating social institutions with the systemic pattern of things, becomes the analysis of lifeless systems.

Functionalism is inherently concerned with statics, and what Renfrew terms 'system thinking', far from 'explaining continuous change', simply allows us to 'describe the society at any given time by a large series of observations or measurements, the observables to be measured are the *parameters* of the system. The changing values of those system variables effectively describe for us the successive system states through time' (Renfrew 1984: 249). 'Parameters' and 'system states' are clearly statics, and subsequent reference to input and feedback within the system does nothing to dispel the original, static formation. This view is entirely consistent with the notion that time is nowhere contained in routine archaeological observations because the material record is only a set of 'observationally static facts' (Binford 1977a: 6). Time, existing in neither an adequately conceived social theory nor in basic analytical observations is expelled from a place central to archaeological practice, a remarkable failure for an historical discipline to display.

Ultimately, questions which might distinguish between liberal and Marxist archaeologies (the way institutional relations work in harmony or in tension as contradictory forces) fail to distinguish between various functional explanations. For example, if conflicts between social groups are expected then a functional integration is achieved via an ideological feedback:

> The social order must be legitimised and the principles upon which control is based justified. One of the most powerful means of achieving this is in the active production of a normative consensus naturalising and misrepresenting the extant nature of asymmetrical social relations so that they appear to be other than they really are.
>
> (Miller and Tilley 1984a: 2)

Social systems cannot be analysed in terms of pre-existing social institutions. Instead it is necessary to confront the issue of human agency by which institutionalised practices are themselves maintained. In current archaeological practice social institutions appear static and history, driven from their very essence, becomes a problem limited to the explanation of periods of change.

If material residues are taken to record or reflect social conditions or meanings then they are immediately isolated from the actual processes of social discourse where that material originally resided as the media of communication and social practice. The result is that the creative process, which constantly brings the social system into being, takes on the appearance of largely abstract forces lying outside the material conditions and the control of social agency.

I wish to develop this argument, particularly in the light of Giddens' theory of structuration (Giddens 1979; 1981). Before doing so, however, I must emphasise that I am seeking not only to break with the functionalism which characterises much of current archaeological thinking, but also with the more recent demands for an 'archaeology of meaning' as propounded by Hodder. In his own attempt to escape functionalist explanations Hodder has shifted the attention of archaeology towards considering the intentions and motivations of human agents. He seems to suggest that through a detailed analysis of the patterns preserved in the material record it should be possible to recover something of the 'ideas in people's heads' (Hodder 1984b: 25). Even if this were possible, and published examples of this kind of reasoning are far from convincing (Hodder 1984a), we are simply moved from a position where social structures govern human behaviour to one that asserts the primacy of the individual.

In the theory of structuration Giddens employs the 'time-space continuum' as the framework within which structured actions of human agents can be observed reproducing the institutionalised form of the social system. 'All human action is carried on by knowledgeable agents who both construct the social world through their action, but yet whose action is also conditioned or constrained by the very world of their creation' (Giddens 1981: 54). Knowledge here extends beyond a discursive understanding of the world and includes the practical knowledge of 'how to go on'. This in turn may be distinguished from unconscious sources of cognition and motivation (Giddens 1979; 1981: 27). Practical knowledge should not be reduced to a set of rules drawn upon to enable participation in the workings of pre-existing social institutions. Instead it is knowledge which is rediscovered and reproduced by action and discourse. It is through this continual process of rediscovery that human subjects define themselves. This is achieved by the agents' ability to monitor the world they occupy, and which they contribute towards constituting as a culturally meaningful resource. Structuration is the rediscovery of those competent methodological procedures employed in structuring particular social practices. Structuration therefore involves a duality for 'the structural properties of social systems are both medium and outcome of the practices they recursively organise' (Giddens 1984: 25).

This duality is of central importance to us, but it is a concept which has received a certain amount of criticism. Smith and Turner argue that:

> the notion of the duality of structure seems to us to involve a vitiating circularity . . . social structures are constituted by human agency as well as simultaneously being the medium of such constitution. We will show that action is taken as a (prior) necessary condition for structure and structure as a (prior) necessary condition for action, so that we are forced into an impossible circle.
>
> (Smith and Turner 1986: 127)

However the circle is broken. Giddens has stated that 'structure exists only as memory traces' (Giddens 1984: 377; cf. Cohen 1986: 126) meaning, I take it that action draws initially upon, and is guided in anticipation by, the subject's memory of previous experience. Important although this point is, an equal, if not greater, emphasis must be placed upon the particular material conditions within which social practices are situated.

The material world acts as a storage of cultural resources, including architectural forms of spaces and boundaries and the temporal cycles of day/night and seasonality in which people pass through and are held in place by, this architecture. The material world therefore acts as a complex series of *locales* within which meaningful and authoritative forms of discourse can be sustained.

There is no contradiction in recognising the essential role material *locales* play in structuring action, and realising them they are in turn sustained by that action. However, this argument is not developed by Giddens, although he does recognise that 'linguistic competence involves not only the syntactical mastery of sentences, but the mastery of circumstances in which particular types are appropriate . . . In other words, mastery of the language is inseparable from mastery of the variety of contexts in which language is used' (Giddens 1987: 79).

If Giddens has not developed a clear understanding of the importance of the material situations occupied by social practices, Bourdieu has. He has argued for example that

> inhabited space – and above all the house – is the principal locus for the objectification of the generative schemes; and, through the intermediary of the divisions and hierarchies it sets up between things, persons and practices, this tangible classifying system continuously inculcates and reinforces the taxonomic principles underlying all the arbitrary provisions of . . culture.
>
> (Bourdieu 1977: 89)

The material world, permanent and decaying, constructed and demolished, exchanged and accumulated, is a potentially powerful system of signification. It is inhabited by actors whose practical understanding of their daily routines is constructed with reference to a material architecture and their temporal movement through those spaces and across their boundaries. This architecture has no single, objective meaning. In Bourdieu's study for example:

> The house . . . is globally defined as female, damp, etc., when considered from the outside, from the male point of view, i.e. in opposition to the external world, but it can be divided into a male-female part and a female-female part when it ceases to be seen by reference to a universe of practice coextensive with *the* universe, and is treated instead as a universe (of practice and discourse) in its own right, which for the women it indeed is, especially in winter.
>
> (Bourdieu 1977: 110)

The material world contains acculturated structures drawn upon and invested with meaning by human action. Archaeological evidence should not be treated as a static outcome of past dynamics (a record). Instead it is the surviving fragments of those recursive media through which the practices of social discourse were constructed. Social practices are the object of our study: archaeology is the empirical examination of material evidence to discover how such practices were maintained within particular material conditions. To facilitate the required reconceptualisation of archaeological evidence we need not further methodological refinements but new intellectual procedures.

The field of discourse

Discourse is a means of communication, it draws upon and reproduces particular structures of knowledge, thus also reproducing relations of dominance between individuals and collectivities (Bourdieu 1979a). In all discourse power is sustained as 'reproduced relations of autonomy and dependence' (Giddens 1981: 50). Such relations involve authoritative demands being recognised through some degree of compliance. Thus control is established over humans and material resources. The authority of the code is signified by the symbols through which the participants know, and acknowledge the validity of, the conditions under which they act. That acknowledgement reproduces the authority of the code, but may transform the conditions under which it is sustained.

In discourse meaning is located in the particular employment of a code; it is grounded in the context of usage (Asad 1979; Giddens 1979: 98). Structured in time-space, Bourdieu has shown that the lapse of time between the establishment and fulfilment of an obligation is part of the practical strategy of discourse. 'To restore to practice its practical truth, we must therefore re-introduce time into the theoretical representation of a practice which, being temporally structured, is intrinsically defined by its *tempo*' (Bourdieu 1977: 8). An authority deriving from hereditary status and age may demand gifts of agricultural produce from the labour of others. These products, returned as food gifts, may further increase that original authority. These temporally separate and irreversible practices transform the meaning of the circulated gift, a point lost when we telescope gift and counter-gift into a timeless 'objective' system of reciprocity. Bauman has also suggested that signs exist in primary or in secondary and derivative contexts in relation to their temporal position in a particular discourse (Bauman 1971: 284). This recognises that the claim of dominance, established by mobilising (as primary signs) an authoritative code, is then acknowledged by reciprocation of compliance (through the mobilisation of secondary signs).

Particular lines of authoritative knowledge are reproduced in discourse. But other forms of knowledge and the means of resistance are not eliminated (Braithwaite 1984). Power resides in the ability of certain agents to maintain an 'authoritative discourse which seeks continually to preempt the space of radically opposed utterances' (Asad 1979: 621). The hegemonic growth of a particular authority involves penetrating increasingly wider ranges of discourse with meanings of a dominant code. Discourse reproduces systems of prestige and rank which include, but are not necessarily reducible to relations of production in the Marxist sense (Ortner and Whitehead 1981: 15). There can be no general theory which specifies the locus of a determinate discourse, for we are dealing with codes particular to their historical and cultural contexts. Dislocation between the various structures of power and prestige are to be expected, and they cannot all be reduced to a single formula of determinacy. Change is possible because of the tensions which exist between alternative forms of discourse and because of changing material conditions under which utterances may come to lose their authority.

The means of conceptualising the occupancy of time-space by situated practices must avoid splitting the analytical procedure into alternative questions of temporal frequency and spatial organisation. It seems to me that Giddens fails to avoid this split in his recent discussion of 'time-geography' (Giddens 1985).

Similarly in current archaeological thinking time and space are merely employed at a descriptive level. They are used to define relationships by patterning atomised units of observation: sequences of stratigraphic units (time), of geographical distribution of artefacts (space). But, as Scholte states 'empirical entities do not create intelligible relationships, relations create entities' (1981: 169).

To move archaeological study away from the patterning of things to the structuring of relationships (i.e. social practice) requires heuristic devices allowing us to think about the way time-space may have been occupied by such practices. I wish to define one such device as the *field of discourse*.

The field is an area in time-space occupied by virtue of the practice of a particular discourse. Such fields 'shade off' in time-space and contain material conditions which contribute towards the structuring of practice. Archaeological evidence is the residue of these various material conditions.

No field is closed, one may encompass another. A number may crosscut at moments of their existence; the same material components may be shared by a number of fields, and the symbolic components of one field may be stored and transformed into the symbolic components of another. The means therefore exist for alternative discourses to challenge authoritative statements or to avoid their domination. And one authority may extend its hegemony into neighbouring fields. It is therefore a matter of priority to consider the degree of co-variance on the axis of time-space between different fields, thus exposing mechanisms central to the history of particular authority structures.

The analytical strength of the field of discourse is threefold: it is concerned with human relationships not material entities; time-space is fundamental to its definition; and it refuses single units of material residues fixed historical meaning. The analytical components of the field are as follows:

a) The temporal frequency within which the field is routinely occupied. This tempo is often likely to conform to cycles of agricultural production, where the seasons of nature are endowed with cultural meaning (Bourdieu 1977). The emergence of the modern world was achieved by breaking with many of these natural rhythms of authority, the clocktime of industrial production extending from the factory to the home (Giddens 1982).

b) The spatial extent of the field. This is the geographical space occupied by the actors involved in a particular discourse. Often of a limited scale involving face to face encounters, examples will include the residential spaces within a household, the spaces occupied by cycles of agricultural production (Pred 1985), or the places of religious observance.

c) The cultural resources which are drawn upon to define and instigate the authoritative demands of discourse, and those resources which, in turn, are chosen to be employed in acknowledging the existence of that authority. These resources may include the architectural settings which structure the orientation of the subjects' bodies, the adornments of dress placed on those bodies, or the items exchanged. These cultural/symbolic resources may often have been stored and transmitted from one field to another. It is through such modes of transmission that certain forms of authority come to be 'presenced' over wide regions of time-space.

d) The transformations which take place in the available cultural resources as the field is reproduced. These transformations themselves reproduce authority and domination in discourse whilst transforming the material conditions of future discourse (the latter may be seen as an unintended consequence of action). Authority only exists in as far as it elicits a response, and it is not possible to propose a means by which cultural resources may have been constituted as authoritative without considering the response evoked which completed the cycle of discourse. The symbolic resources of authority may originate in a restricted locale, but in discourse they have to be mobilised over the same spatial region as that from whence the resources of domination are to be drawn. The two sets of resources are temporally displaced in any discourse, being linked in a cycle of reproduction.

To consider more fully this as an archaeological approach I will take, as a single example, the archaeological analysis of gender. This has raised profound methodological problems for contemporary archaeology.

The archaeology of gender

The feminist critique of archaeology has been one of the signs of an emergent self-critical discipline. As Conkey and Spector state, histories of '*man* and *mankind* are not general, but exclusive' (Conkey and Spector 1984: 2). But archaeology has long worked as if gender were not an issue of history, and where the archaeology of *man* has rendered gender distinctions invisible.

Now that gender has been forced into the historical agenda traditional archaeology is returned to the issue raised by Patrik. Questions of gender in archaeological research appear to flounder upon the methodological question of visibility (Conkey and Spector 1984: 6). If we treat the material evidence as record the question turns on how the evidence records particular gender activities. If we accept, as we must, that gender is constituted in historically and culturally specific ways then we are employing the archaeological record as a text. Specific codes signify the meaning of female and male in particular cultural contexts and we are returned to the question of how such texts are to be read.

Janet Spector has outlined a methodology for gender studies in the fields of ethnoarchaeology and ethnohistory. Her *task-differentiation* framework is intended to identify the dimensions of female and male activity patterns (Conkey and Spector 1984: 24). Tasks are identified and the parameters of performance then mapped in terms of gender and age, size and nature of groups and the individuals involved, the temporal frequency of performance, the spatial dimensions of task differentiation and the mat features associated with each task. Ultimately the aim is to isolate, in a non-androcentric way, the gender-specific features found within the organisation of labour for a given social group.

Whilst such a cataloguing from ethnoarchaeology and ethnohistory will undoubtedly awaken archaeologists to the complexity and the diversity of gender activities within different ecological, economic and social contexts, problems do remain. I am unclear how we will ever reach the point when with 'enough studies of this type, we may begin to approach the archaeological record with sufficient understanding to interpret assemblages in terms of gender' (Conkey and Spector 1984: 27).

It is a requirement of historical analysis that we may discover potentially unique ways by which women and men have defined themselves. But the translation of an 'archaeological text' will require us to impose meanings upon that text, rather than discover meaning from it. I assume, for example, that Spector's approach seeks some form of cross-cultural generalisation by which material residues may be linked to gender-specific activities. But what if there is no continuity between past and present in the cultural expression of gender?

Given this possibility it might be tempting to counter current androcentric assumptions by suggesting radical inversions in gender roles. But the danger is always that myths are created, rather than a critical history of gender conflicts. Rachel Hasted has written:

When we are arguing political conclusions from historical precedents our evidence ought to be investigated all along the line: if we come to believe in myths we may miss a more valuable insight into our own (women's) condition.

It matters to me that as feminists we should share what we find out about women's history with other women honestly, not glossing over our areas of ignorance. It is not in our interests to sell short the complex history we have – in fact we should be telling other historians that their level of awareness on women's history just isn't good enough.

(Hasted 1985: 24)

Gender is constructed as a relationship; it cannot be understood simply in terms of female or male activities. Rosaldo argued that there can be no satisfactory cross-cultural discovery of what constitutes women's experience (Rosaldo 1980). Instead, it is necessary to understand specific historical conditions under which gender categories are brought into being. Those categories are and were produced as a relationship (a discourse) in which women and men are agents who control certain sets of cultural resources (Rosaldo 1980; O'Brien 1982).

A comparison is possible here between Rosaldo's conception of 'gender' and the way Thompson argues that 'class' can be understood neither 'as a "structure" nor even a "category", but as something which in fact happens (and can be shown to have happened) in human relationships' (Thompson 1968: 9).

Gender is therefore structured through various types of discourse. The routine structuring of these relations will be central to many social practices. ' In marrying people "make families" but they also control debts, change residence, stir enmities and establish social bonds' (Collier and Rosaldo 1981: 278).

The archaeological study of gender does not depend upon a methodological breakthrough rendering specific gender activities visible in the 'archaeological record'. It must be founded instead upon the critical realisation that gender relations and conflicts are historical forces. From this position we can recognise that gender discourse is always structured by control over certain human and material resources (cf. Braithwaite 1982; Moore 1982; O'Brien 1982). Gender is therefore produced out of the 'choreography' of human existence (Pred 1977). As people pass through time and space they encounter the complex architecture of an acculturated world. The access they claim to the spaces and resources of that architecture at any moment is determined by, and in turn determines, their authority in this and other forms of discourse. The renegotiation of gender authority will require a renegotiation of these architectural conditions.

As an illustration of this approach I have argued elsewhere that late bronze–early iron age southern Britain can be understood in terms other than those dominated by questions of technological change (Barrett 1989a). Gender and age categories are renegotiated at this time by restructuring the forms of domestic space and inventing new forms of technology concerned with food preparation and its service. The abandonment of traditional funerary practices may also mark a shift in the expression of authoritative systems of inheritance. These changes in social practices laid the foundations for a substantial political emphasis being placed upon the control of agricultural (and probably human) fertility during the iron age of southern Britain. In all this, metal and the adoption of a new technology play a subsidiary role.

Metalwork circulates amongst, and between, gender and age sets which were established by means other than the control of metal itself.

Conclusion

In following the question posed by Linda Patrik, as to whether of not there is an archaeological record, I have argued that an alternative view of our evidence is possible. Indeed I have been concerned to establish that the concept of a record is inadequate to meet the challenge of an archaeology concerned with the history of knowledgeable human agency. In this case the record appears as a text, which I contend can only be translated in our own terms. However self-critical such 'translations' may be, they can never confront the real conditions of authorship by which the text was constructed. Whilst our concerns and motivations in archaeological and historical writing do indeed derive from contemporary conditions (as the study of gender illustrates) we cannot deny the real nature of historical conditions (Thompson 1978). It is those conditions we must confront in a self-critical way. We will not achieve this by continuing with the methodological obsession to give an archaeological record meaning. Here history simply appears as a by-product. We should instead set out to make history. By that labour we will necessarily encounter our evidence, and by working with it we will discover something of its significance within the context of social practice.

ACKNOWLEDGEMENTS

I am grateful to all who have read and commented upon the numerous earlier drafts of this paper, including Kathy Barrett, Steve Driscoll, Pam Graves, Pat Hamilton, Mark Leone, Margaret Nieke, Colin Richards and Robin Torrence. I am particularly grateful to Mary Braithwaite for earlier guidance and criticisms and to Keith Ray for his detailed comments. Lorraine Mepham and Norma Wakeling produced the typescripts, and the faults remain my own.

3

THEORETICAL ARCHAEOLOGY*
A Reactionary View

IAN HODDER

Functionalism is defined as the use of an organic analogy in the explanation of societies, with particular reference to system, equilibrium and adaptation. The New Archaeology is found to be functionalist and a critique of functionalism is put forward, centring on the dichotomies between culture and function, individual and society, statics and dynamics, and on the links to positivism. Criticisms of an alternative approach, structuralism, include the lack of a theory of practice, the dichotomies between individual and society, statics and dynamics, and the paucity of rigour in the methods employed. A contextual or cultural archaeology is described which is based on the notion of 'structuration', and which attempts to resolve many of the difficulties associated with functionalism and 'high' structuralism. The main concern is with the role of material culture in the reflexive relationship between the structure of ideas and social strategies. Similarities are identified with the historical and humanistic aims of an older generation of British prehistorians such as Daniel, Piggott, Clark and Childe. Today, however, the earlier aims can be followed more successfully because of developments in social theory and ethnographic studies.

Functionalism and the New Archaeology
In defining functionalism, a simplified version of Radcliffe-Brown's (1952) account will be used since his approach can be shown to be close to that followed by many New Archaeologists (those who in the 1960s and 1970s were concerned with explanations and approaches of the types outlined by Binford and his associates). Functionalism introduces an analogy between social and organic life. Emile Durkheim (*Règles de la Méthode Sociologique* 1895 [1964]) defined the 'function' of a social institution as the correspondence between it and the needs of the social organism. In the same way that the stomach provides a function for the body as a whole and allows it to survive, so any aspect of a past society can be assessed in terms of its contribution to the working of the whole society. A society is made up of interrelated parts and we

---

*First published in I. R. Hodder (ed.) (1982), *Symbolic and Structural Archaeology*, Cambridge: Cambridge University Press, pp. 1–16.

can explain one component by showing how it works in relation to other components. But these are all very general statements, and there is room for a great variety of views within these general propositions. Indeed, Radcliffe-Brown (1952: 188) stated bluntly that the 'Functional school does not really exist; it is a myth'. Functionalism often appears to be little more than a 'dirty word' used by the opponents of anthropologists such as Malinowski, Boas and Radcliffe-Brown himself, and it may convey little meaning. So if it is to be used of the New Archaeology, a more specific definition needs to be provided.

The concept of function is closely linked to the notion of system. In the middle of the eighteenth century Montesquieu used a conception of society in which all aspects of social life could be linked into a coherent whole. What Comte called 'the first law of social statics' held that there are relations of interconnection and interdependence, or relations of solidarity, between the various aspects of society. It is possible analytically to isolate certain groups of particularly close interrelationships as systems.

According to the functionalist viewpoint as stated in systems theory, societies reach a healthy organic equilibrium, called homeostasis. Plato, in the Fourth Book of his *Republic* saw the health of a society as resulting from the harmonious working together of its parts. The Greeks distinguished good order, social health (*eunomia*), from disorder, social illness (*dysnomia*), while the notion of malfunction and social pathology was a central concern of Durkheim. (In recent systems archaeology, pathologies have been listed and their effects examined by Flannery [1972].)

Pathologies occur during periods when the organic unity and equilibrium are upset as a result of maladaptation. A society can only continue to exist if it is well adjusted internally and externally. Three types of adaptation can be distinguished. The first concerns the adjustment to the physical environment, the ecological adaptation. The second is the internal arrangement and adjustment of components of the society in relation to each other. Finally, there is the process by which an individual finds a place within the society in which he lives. It is through these three types of adaptation that societies survive and evolve. Many anthropologists and archaeologists, however, have discussed change largely in terms of ecological adaptation, the meeting of external constraints. It is an ecological functionalism which prevails today in archaeology.

In this chapter the term functionalism refers to the use of an organic analogy and to the viewpoint that an adequate explanation of a past society involves reference to system, equilibrium and adaptation as outlined above. Although functionalism, and specifically ecological functionalism, were mainstays of the theoretical framework of an earlier generation of archaeologists such as Gordon Childe and Grahame Clark, they have become more widely important as a result of the New Archaeology of the 1960s and 1970s. Indeed, processual and systems archaeology is almost by definition a functionalist archaeology. As Leach (1973a: 761–2) pointed out,

> Binford's remark that 'behaviour is the by-product of the interaction of a cultural repertoire with the environment' may be proto-typical of the 'new' archaeology, but to a social anthropologist it reads like a quotation from Malinowski writing at the time when naive functionalism was at its peak – that is to say about 1935.

This view is too extreme, but Renfrew (1972: 24) also states that to examine connections between subsystems as in systems theory 'is, of course, simply a

statement of anthropological functionalism, that different aspects of a culture are all interrelated'.

The degree to which archaeology has adopted a functionalist conception of society and culture is apparent in the writings of the major figures of the 'new' discipline. Although the archaeological contributions of these writers differ, the notions of organic wholes, interrelated systems, equilibrium and adaptation can all be identified most clearly. For example, in Flannery's (1972) systems model for the growth of complex societies, the job of self-regulation within the sociocultural system 'is to keep all the variables in the subsystem within appropriate goal ranges – ranges which maintain homeostasis and do not threaten the survival of the system' (*ibid*.: 409). According to Binford (1972a: 107) 'we can . . . expect variability in and among components of a system to result from the action of homeostatic regulators within the cultural system serving to maintain equilibrium relationships between the system and its environment'. Similarly, for Clarke (1968: 88), 'the whole cultural system is in external dynamic equilibrium with its local environment'.

> Equilibrium is defined as that state in which dislocation amongst the component variety is minimised . . . Dislocation most frequently arises . . . when different networks independently transmit mutually contradictory information – resenting an anomaly at nodes in the structure of the system. Sociocultural systems are continuously changing in such a way as to minimise the maximum amount of immediate system dislocation.
>
> (*ibid*.: 129)

According to Hill (1971: 407), a set of variables is only a system if their 'articulation . . . be regulated (maintained in steady-state) by homeostatic processes'.

The importance of maintaining equilibrium with the 'environment' has also been emphasised by Renfrew (1972). Indeed, man's relationship with the environment is seen by him as one of the main aspects of systems theory. 'The whole purpose of utilising the systems approach is to emphasise man–environment interrelations, while at the same time admitting that many fundamental changes in man's environment are produced by man himself' (*ibid*.: 19–20). 'Culture . . . is essentially a homeostatic device, a conservative influence ensuring that change in the system will be minimised. It is a flexible adaptive mechanism which allows the survival of society despite fluctuations in the natural environment' (*ibid*.: 486).

Thus it is thought that human sociocultural systems can be described as if they were adapting to the total social and environmental milieu. Renfrew (1972: 24–5) talks of the 'essential coherence and conservatism of all cultures . . . the society's "adjustment" or "adaptation" to its natural environment is maintained: difficulties and hardships are overcome'. A similar view is expressed by Binford (1972a: 20): 'Change in the total cultural system must be viewed in an adaptive context both social and environmental.' Indeed Binford's (1972a: 22) definition of culture 'as the extra-somatic means of adaptation for the human organism' is one of the main tenets of systems archaeologists. 'Culture, from a systemic perspective, is defined . . . as interacting behavioural systems. One asks questions concerning these systems, their interrelation, their adaptive significance' (Plog 1975: 208).

Culture is all those means whose forms are not under direct genetic control . .
which serve to adjust individuals and groups within their ecological communities
. . Adaption is always a local problem, and selective pressures favouring new
cultural forms result from nonequilibrium conditions in the local ecosystem.
(Binford 1972a: 431)

The functionalist and processual emphasis in archaeology aimed objectively to identify
relationships between variables in cultural systems. There was a natural link to an
empirical and positivist concept of science.

The meaning which explanation has within a scientific frame of reference is
simply the demonstration of a constant articulation of variables within a system
and the measurement of the concomitant variability among the variables within
the system. Processual change in one variable can thus be shown to relate to
a predictable and quantifiable way to changes in other variables, the latter
changing in turn relative to changes in the structure of the system as a whole.
(Binford 1972a: 21)

This statement demonstrates the link between functionalism and a conception of
explanation as the prediction of relationships between variables. It is thought that the
relationships can be observed empirically and quantification can be used to assess
the significance of associations. The way is thus open for recovering cross-cultural
generalisations, and 'the laws of cultural process' (ibid.:199). Although Binford
(1977a: 5) appears more recently to have doubted the explanatory value of cross-
cultural statistics, the above attitudes to explanation have at times been developed
into a rigid hypothetico-deductive method based on a reading of Hempel
(e.g. Watson, Leblanc and Redman 1971; Fritz and Plog 1970).

Critique of functionalism

I do not intend to examine the problems of applying systems theory in archaeology
(Doran 1970), nor whether systems theory has really aided archaeologists in their
functionalist aims (Salmon 1978). Rather, I want to consider the criticisms of
functionalism itself. Martins (1974: 246) describes the critique of functionalism as
an initiation *rite de passage* into sociological adulthood, and I have suggested elsewhere
(1981) the need for a wider debate in archaeology concerning the various critiques
of and alternatives to ecological functionalism.

Many of the problems and limitations of the organic analogy as applied to social
systems have long been recognised. Radcliffe-Brown (1952: 181) noted that while
an animal organism does not, in the course of its life, change its form, a society
can, in the course of its history, undergo major organisational change. Other problems
are not inherent to the approach but result from the particular emphasis that is
given by archaeologists, perhaps as a result of the limitations of their data. For example,
a systems approach which assumes that homeostatic equilibrium is the natural state
of things results in the notion that all change ultimately has to derive from outside
the system. Negative feedback occurs in reaction to outside stimuli, and positive
feedback and deviation amplifying processes need initial external kicks. According
to Hill (1977: 76) 'no system can change itself, change can only be instigated by

outside sources. If a system is in equilibrium, it will remain so unless inputs (or lack of outputs) from outside the system disturb the equilibrium.' The result of this view has been to place great emphasis on the impact of supposed 'independent' variables from outside the sociocultural system under study. The favourite external variables have been environmental factors (e.g. Carneiro 1968), long-distance trade (Renfrew 1969) and population increase (Hill 1977: 92), although it is not often clear why the latter is assumed to be an independent variable. Little advance has been made in the study of factors within societies that affect the nature of change (see, however, Friedman and Rowlands 1977a). But Flannery (1972) has shown how the systems approach can be extended to include internal forces of change and those forms of internal adaption within the organic whole which have been described above.

A more fundamental limitation of the functionalist viewpoint centres on the inadequacy of function and utility in explaining social and cultural systems, and on the separation made between functional utility and culture. All aspects of culture have utilitarian purposes in terms of which they can be explained. All activities, whether dropping refuse, developing social hierarchies, or performing rituals, are the results of adaptive expedience. But explanation is sought only in terms of adaptation and function. The problem with such a viewpoint is not so much the emphasis on function since it is important to know how material items, institutions, symbols and ritual operate, and the contribution of the New Archaeology to such studies is impressive. It is rather the dichotomy which was set up between culture and adaptive utility which restricted the development of the approach .

In archaeology the split between culture and function took the form of an attack on what was termed the 'normative' approach. In Binford's (1965) rebuttal of the 'normative school', he referred to American archaeologists such as Taylor, Willey and Phillips, Ford, Rouse and Gifford who were concerned with identifying cultural 'wholes' in which there was an ideational basis for the varying ways of human life within each cultural unit. Such archaeologists aimed at identifying the normative concepts in the minds of men now dead. Binford more specifically criticised the normative studies which tried to describe the diffusion and transmission of cultural traits. It is not my concern here to identify whether the normative paradigm, as characterised by Binford, ever existed. Certainly, as will be shown below, European archaeologists such as Childe were already able to integrate a concern with cultural norms and a notion of behavioural adaptability. But in Binford's view, the normative approach emphasising homogeneous cultural wholes contrasted with the study of functional variability within and between cultural units. The normative school was seen as historical and descriptive, not allowing explanation in terms of functional process. So he moved to an opposite extreme where culture, norms, form and design had only functional value in, for example, integrating and articulating individuals and social units into broader corporate entities. In fact Binford suggested that the different components of culture may function independently of each other. Functional relationships could thus be studied without reference to cultural context, and regular, stable and predictable relationships could be sought between variables within social systems. As a result, an absolute gulf was driven between normative and processual studies. 'An approach is offered in which culture is not reduced to normative ideas about the proper ways of doing things but is viewed as the system of the total

extrasomatic means of adaption' (Binford 1972a: 205). More recently (1978a) Binford has still more clearly separated the study of norms from the study of process. He has attacked the historical and contextual emphasis of Kroeber and Kluckhohn (ibid.: 2). On the one hand (ibid.: 3), artefacts are the reflections of the mental templates of the makers and these ideas in the minds of men cannot adapt intelligently to new situations. On the other hand, cultural variability is simply the result of adaptive expedience. He could ask (1979a: 11), 'do people conduct their ongoing activities in terms of invariant mental templates as to the appropriate strategies regardless of the setting in which they find themselves?' Indeed, his Nunamiut ethnoarchaeology is introduced as an attempt to identify whether faunal remains could be studied as being 'culture-free'. Cultural bias can only be identified (1978a: 38) when an anomaly occurs; when the adaptively expedient expectations are not found.

The dichotomy set up between culture and function limits the development of archaeological theory because 'functional value is always relative to the given cultural scheme' (Sahlins 1976: 206). All actions take place within cultural frameworks and their functional value is assessed in terms of the concepts and orientations which surround them. That an item or institution is 'good for' achieving some end is partly a cultural choice, as is the end itself. At the beginning of this chapter Durkheim's definition of the function of a social institution as the correspondence between it and the needs of the social organism was described. But the needs of the society are preferred choices within a cultural matrix. It follows that function and adaptation are not absolute measures. All daily activities, from eating to the removal of refuse, are not the result of some absolute adaptive expedience. These various functions take place within a cultural framework, a set of ideas or norms, and we cannot adequately understand the various activities by denying any role to culture. An identical point is made by Deetz (1977) in his comparison of cultural traditions in two historical periods in North America.

The above discussion is particularly relevant to the functionalist view of material items. As already noted, Binford assumes that culture is man's extrasomatic means of adaptation. According to David Clarke (1968: 85) 'culture is an information system, wherein the messages are accumulated survival information'. In this way material culture is seen as simply functioning at the interface between the human organism and the social and physical environment in order to allow adaptation. It has a utilitarian function (Sahlins 1976). The result of this view is that cultural remains are seen as *reflecting* in a fairly straightforward way, what people do. Even work on deposition and post-depositional processes (Schiffer 1976), while adding complexity to the situation, still assumes that material culture is simply a direct, indirect or a distorted reflection of man's activities. This is a continuation of earlier views of material culture as 'fossilised action'. As Fletcher (1977b: 51–2) has pointed out, material culture is seen simply as a passive object of functional use; a mere epiphenomenon of 'real' life. But there is more to culture than functions and activities. Behind functioning and doing there is a structure and content which has partly to be understood in its own terms, with its own logic and coherence. This applies as much to refuse distributions and 'the economy' as it does to burial, pot decoration and art.

Linked to the separation of function and culture has been the decreased emphasis on archaeology as an historical discipline. If material items and social institutions can

be explained in terms of their adaptive efficiency, there is little concern to situate them within an historical framework. The evolutionary perspective has emphasised adaptive relationships at different levels of complexity, but it has not encouraged an examination of the particular historical context. However, it is suggested here that the cultural framework within which we act, and which we reproduce in our actions, is historically derived and that each culture is a particular historical product. The uniqueness of cultures and historical sequences must be recognised. Within the New Archaeology there has been a great concern with identifying variability. But in embracing a cross-cultural approach, variability has, in the above sense, been reduced to sameness. Diachronic sequences are split into phases in which the functioning of systems can be understood in synchronic terms as instances of some general relationship. The dichotomy between diachrony and synchrony is linked to the split between culture and history on the one hand and function and adaptation on the other. The resolution of the culture/function dichotomy which is sought in this book will also reintroduce historical explanation as a legitimate topic of concern in archaeology.

Another limitation of the functionalist perspective of the New Archaeology is the relationship between the individual and society. The functional view gives little emphasis to individual creativity and intentionality. Individual human beings become little more than the means to achieve the needs of society. The social system is organised into subsystems and roles which people fill. The roles and social categories function in relation to each other to allow the efficient equilibrium of the whole system. In fact, however, individuals are not simply instruments in some orchestrated game and it is difficult to see how subsystems and roles can have 'goals' of their own. Adequate explanations of social systems and social change must involve the individual's assessments and aims. This is not a question of identifying individuals (Hill and Gunn 1977) but of introducing the individual into social theory. Some New Archaeologists have recognised the importance of this. 'While the behaviour of the group, of many individual units, may often effectively be described in statistical terms without reference to the single unit, it cannot so easily be explained in this way. This is a problem which prehistoric archaeology has yet to resolve' (Renfrew 1972: 496). The lack of resolution is inherent in the functionalist emphasis in archaeology.

Further criticism of functionalist archaeology concerns the emphasis on cross-cultural generalisations. After an initial phase in which ethnoarchaeology was used largely to provide cautionary tales and 'spoilers' (Yellen 1977), the concern has been to provide cross-cultural statements of high predictive value. Because of the preferred hypothetico-deductive nature of explanation, it became important to identify rules of behaviour and artefact deposition which were used regardless of cultural context. As already noted, such an approach was feasible because the particular historical and cultural dimensions of activity were denied. Different subsystems were identified, such as subsistence, exchange, settlement, refuse disposal and burial, and cross-cultural regularities were sought. Since the role of cultural and historical factors was not examined, it was necessarily the case that the resulting generalisations either were limited to mechanical or physical aspects of life or were simplistic and with little content. Some aspects of human activity are constrained by deterministic variables. For example, it is difficult for humans to walk bare-footed on spreads of freshly knapped flint, or to work or sit in or near the smoke of fires (Gould 1980; Binford

1978b). Certain types of bone do hold more or less meat or marrow, and they fracture in different ways (Binford 1978a; Gifford 1981). The seeds sorted by wind during winnowing depend partly on wind velocity and seed density (Jones, pers. comm.). Smaller artefacts are more difficult for humans to hold and find than large artefacts and so the patterns of loss may differ (Schiffer 1976). Cross-cultural predictive laws or generalisations can be developed for these mechanical constraints on human behaviour, and ethnoarchaeology has been most successful in these spheres, but attempts to extend this approach to social and cultural behaviour have been severely criticised as is shown by the debate over the hypothesis put forward by Longacre (1970), Deetz (1968), and Hill (1970) (e.g. Stanislawski 1973; Allen and Richardson 1971), and the result has been the frustration implied by Flannery's (1973) characterisation of Mickey Mouse laws. As soon as any human choice is involved, behavioural and functional laws appear simplistic and inadequate because human behaviour is rarely entirely mechanistic. The role of ethnoarchaeology must also be to define the relevant cultural context for social and ecological behaviour.

Linked to the emphasis on cross-cultural functional laws is the idea of 'predicting the past' (Thomas 1974). The percentages of modern societies in which women make pots (Phillips 1971) or in which size of settlement is related to post-marital residence (Ember 1973) are difficult to use as measures of probability for the interpretation of the past because modern societies are not independent nor do they comprise a random or representative sample of social forms. More important, however, is the lack of identity between prediction and understanding. It is possible to predict many aspects of human behaviour with some accuracy but without any understanding of the causal relationships involved. Equally, a good understanding of a social event may not lead to an ability to predict the outcome of a similar set of circumstances. Levels of probability and statistical evidence of correlation are no substitute for an understanding of causal links and of the relevant context for human action. The use of mathematical and statistical formulae which provide good fits to archaeological data leads to little understanding of the past. My own involvement in spatial archaeology, a sphere in which statistical prediction has been most successful, has shown most clearly that prediction has little to do with explanation.

The embrace of the hypothetico-deductive method and prediction in relation to interpretation of the past has allowed the definition of independent levels of theory. A distinct 'middle range theory' has been identified because it has been assumed that objective yardsticks or instruments of measurement can be obtained for the study of past systems and their archaeological residues (Binford 1978a: 45). We have general theories of social development and lower level theories concerning the formation of the archaeological record. Similarly, Clarke (1973a) suggested that pre-depositional, depositional, post-depositional, analytical and interpretive theories could be distinguished despite the existence of overall controlling models. This separation of levels or types of theory is partly possible because of a model of man which separates different functional activities and sets up predictive relationships between them. Thus, depositional theory can be separated from interpretive theory because artefact deposition is adaptively expedient and can be predicted without reference to wider social theories. The hypotheses concerning social institutions and social change are thought to be different in nature from the hypotheses concerning the relationship between society and material culture. But both material items and their deposition are actively involved in social relations and we cannot separate independent levels of theory. Frameworks of cultural meaning structure all aspects of archaeological information. Leone (1978) has shown most clearly how data, analyses and interpretations are inextricably linked. The different theoretical levels should be congruent, and beyond natural processes there can be no instruments of absolute measurement.

The aim of the New Archaeology was to show the rationality of institutions with respect to their environments. The main criticisms of this general approach as described above are as follows. (1) The dichotomy set up between cultural form and objective functional expedience is misleading, and material items are more than tools holding survival information. (2) The functionalist viewpoint is unable to explain cultural variety and uniqueness adequately. (3) Social systems become reified to such an extent that the individual contributes little. (4) The cross-cultural generalisations which have resulted from functionalist studies by archaeologists have been unable to identify valid statements about social and cultural behaviour because the relevant context is insufficiently explored. (5) Different levels or types of hypothesis have been identified, but in fact all hypotheses are and should be integrated within a coherent social and cultural theory. This volume [*Symbolic and Structural Archaeology* (Hodder 1982a)] seeks to respond to these criticisms by developing alternative approaches. I wish to begin by considering various definitions of 'structure'.

Structure as system pattern and style

In the preceding discussion of functionalism, reference has been made to the adaptive utility of material items and institutions within social and cultural systems. Subsystems (pottery, settlement, social, economic, etc.) can be identified and discussed in cross-cultural perspective. Within each socio-cultural system a particular set of systemic relationships is produced in order to meet local needs at particular moments in time. In the analysis of such systems, the words 'system' and 'structure' are interchangeable. The system (or structure) is the particular set of relationships between the various components; it is the way the interrelationships are organised. Within New Archaeology, then, structure is the system of observable relations. Structure is the way things are done and it, like individual items and institutions, is explained as the result of adaptive expedience.

The functionalist view of structure is apparent in discussions of social organisation, social relations or social systems, none of which are distinguished from social structure. The term social structure is used by New Archaeologists to refer to bands, tribes, chiefdoms, states, as well as to reciprocal, redistributive and prestige transactions. Social structure is observed directly in burial and settlement patterns where the visible differentiation in associations and forms is seen as reflecting roles and activities organised in relation to each other. The structure of social relations as a whole is organised so as to allow adaptation to such factors as the distribution of environmental resources (uniform or localised), the availability of prestige items or valued commodities, and the relationships with neighbouring social groups.

In such systemic studies the close relationship between the terms 'structure' and 'pattern' is apparent. In identifying social and economic structures various patterns are analysed. These patterns include the distributions of settlements of different sizes and functions across the landscape, the distributions of artefacts and buildings in settlements, the distributions of resources, the distributions of artefacts among graves in cemeteries, the regional distributions of exchanged items and the regional distributions of artefacts in interaction or information exchange spheres or 'cultures'. These various patterns are 'objective' and are immediately susceptible to statistical manipulation, quantification and computerisation. The concern with pattern allows the legitimate use of a wide range of scientific software, including numerical taxonomy and spatial analysis.

The identification of pattern and the implementation of 'analytical archaeology' is extended to studies of arrangements of attributes on individual artefacts, where 'pattern' is often equivalent to 'style'. The analysis of pottery and metal decoration, and of the form of artefacts, leads to the definition of 'types' based on the association of attributes. Artefact styles are interpreted as having utilitarian or non–utilitarian functions; they are technomic, sociotechnic or ideotechnic (Binford 1972a). Style is involved in the support of group solidarity (Hodder 1979) and the passing on of information (Wobst 1977).

In functionalist archaeology, structure is examined as system, organisation, distribution, pattern, or style. It is produced by people attempting to adapt to their environments. Like any artefact, structure is a tool for coping. If culture is a tool acting between people and the environment, and if the term 'culture' describes the particular adaptive organisation produced in each environmental context, then structure is also similar to culture. A culture is seen as the way material bits and pieces are assembled and associated in a geographical area in order to allow human adaptation.

Structure as code

In this chapter I wish to distinguish between system and structure (Giddens 1979), by defining structure not as system, pattern or style, but as the codes and rules according to which observed systems of interrelations are produced. Several archaeological studies have made a contribution to the analysis of structure as code, and some examples are discussed here.

Within studies of Palaeolithic cave art, Leroi-Gourhan (1965) has made specific interpretations of signs as male or female and has suggested various codes for the combination and relative placing of the signs within the caves. Marshak (1977) identified specific interpretations of symbols as dangerous and he related the structure associated with the meander in cave art to the general flow and participation in daily life. Conkey (1977) identified general aspects of the rules of organisation of Upper Palaeolithic art, such as 'the non–differentiation of units', and did not attempt to provide a specific meaning in terms of social organisation. All these analyses were concerned to identify codes or rules, but the nature of the interpretation of these structures and of their relationships to social structures varied.

Studies of later artefact and pottery design have often tended towards a still more formal emphasis in that little attention is paid to the social context in which structures are produced. The linguistic model has been developed fully by Muller (1977) in his analysis of the grammatical rules of design. His work, and Washburn's (1978) definition of different types of symmetry, do not result in any attempt at translating cultural meaning and symbolism. Rather Washburn uses symmetry simply as an additional trait for the discovery of population group composition and inter-action spheres. Such analyses can be, and have been, carried out without any major change in functionalist theories of society.

Some of the work on the identification of settlement structures has also involved little criticism of the New Archaeology. Clarke's (1972b: 828, 837) identification of structural transformations (bilateral symmetry relating to male/female) in the Iron Age Glastonbury settlement appears as a peripheral component of a systems analysis. A clear link is made between the generative principles of the settlement design and the social system. Isbell's (1976) recognition of the 3000-year continuity in settlement structure in the South American Andes, despite major discontinuities in social and economic systems, raises more fundamental problems for systemic studies since structure is seen to continue and lie behind adaptive change. Fritz's (1978) interesting account of prehistoric Chaco Canyon in north western New Mexico shows that the organisation of houses, towns, and regional settlement can be seen as transforms of the same underlying principle in which west is symmetrical to east, but north is asymmetrical to south. This study is concerned to link the organisation of social systems to underlying structures. The structuralist analysis of a Neolithic cemetery by Van de Velde (1980) has related aims. Fletcher's (1977a) work on the spacing between 'entities' – posts, walls, door posts, pots and hearths – in settlements is concerned less with social strategies and more with ordering principles which carry long-term adaptive value. Hillier *et al.* (1976) have identified a purely formal logic for the description of all types of arrangement of buildings and spaces within settlements.

The above examples are drawn from prehistoric archaeology but structural studies have an important place in historical archaeology (Deetz 1967; Ferguson 1977; Frankfort 1951; Glassie 1975; Leone 1977). While many of the prehistoric and historic archaeology studies explain structure in terms of social functions and adaptive values, they also introduce the notion that there is more to culture than observable relationships and functional utility. There is also a set of rules, a code, which, like the rules in a game of chess, is followed in the pursuit of survival, adaptation and socio-economic strategy. In an ethnographic analysis of the Nuba in Sudan, it has been shown that all aspects of material culture patterning (burial, settlement, artefact styles) must be understood as being produced according to sets of rules concerned with purity, boundedness and categorisation (Hodder 1982b). Individuals organise their experience according to sets of rules. Communication and understanding of the world result from the use of a common language – that is, a set of rules which identify both the way symbols should be organised into sets, and the meaning of individual symbols in contrast to others. Material culture can be examined as a structured set of differences. This structured symbolising behaviour has functional utility, and it must be understood in those terms. But it also has a logic of its own which is not directly observable as pattern or style. The structure must be interpreted as having existed partly independent of the observable data, having generated and produced those data.

The concern with material culture as the product of human categorisation processes is described by Miller (1982a). It is sufficient to emphasise here that the various structuralist analyses of codes can be clearly distinguished from functionalist studies of systems. Both structuralists and functionalists are concerned with relationships and with the way things and institutions are organised. In other words, both are concerned with 'structure' if that word is defined in a very general way. But there is a difference in that the logic analysed by functionalists is the visible social system (the social relations) which exists separately from the perceptions of men. For Leach (1973b, 1977, 1978), structure is an ideal order in the mind. For Lévi-Strauss (1968a), it is an internal logic, not directly visible, which is the underlying order by which the apparent order must be explained. But for Lévi-Strauss, the structure often appears to lie outside the human mind (Godelier 1977). Structuralists, including Leach and Lévi-Strauss, claim that adequate explanation of observed patterns must make reference to underlying codes.

Criticisms of structuralism

The problems and limitations of the different types of structuralism are discussed by, for example, Giddens (1979), and in this chapter only those criticisms will be examined which are particularly relevant to the themes to be debated in this book. A major problem concerns the lack of a theory of practice (Bourdieu 1977). The structuralism of Saussure, which uses a linguistic model, separates *langue* as a closed series of formal rules, a structured set of differences, from semantic and referential ties. The formal set of relationships is distinct from the practice of use. Similarly, Lévi-Strauss identifies a series of unconscious mental structures which are separated from practice and from the ability of social actors to reflect consciously on their ideas and create new rules. In both linguistic and structural analyses it is unclear how the interpretation and use of rules might lead to change. How an individual can be a competent social actor is not clearly specified. As in functionalism, form and practical function are separated.

The failure within structuralism and within structuralist analyses in archaeology to develop a theory of practice (concerning the generation of structures in social action) has encouraged the view within functionalist archaeology that structuralism can only contribute to the study of norms and ideas which are epiphenomenal. The gulf between normative and processual archaeology has been widened since, on the one hand, structuralist approaches could be seen as relating to ideas divorced from adaptive processes while, on the other hand, it was thought by processualists that social change could be examined adequately without reference to the structure of ideas. Some of the structuralist studies identified above, such as those by Muller and Washburn, make little attempt to understand the referential context. The notion of a 'mental template' can be criticised in a similar vein because it envisages an abstract set of ideas or pictures without examining the framework of referential meaning within which the ideas take their form. In other, more integrated studies, such as those by Fritz and Marshak, the social and ecological contexts of the structures identified are examined, but the link between form and practice is insecure and no relevant theory is developed. On the other hand, work such as that of Flannery and Marcus (1976), which fits better into the functionalist mould, relates all form to function and structural analysis is limited. Few archaeological studies have managed to provide convincing accounts of the relationship between structure as code and social and ecological organisation.

Other limitations of structuralism can be related to the above. As in functionalism, the role of the individual is slight. In functionalism the individual is subordinate to the imperatives of social co-ordination. In the structuralism of Lévi-Strauss the individual is subordinate to the organising mechanisms of the unconscious. The notion of a 'norm' in traditional archaeology implies a structured set of cultural rules within which the individual plays little part.

The dichotomy between synchrony and diachrony, statics and dynamics, exists in structuralism as it does in functionalism. Structural analyses can incorporate time as a dimension for the setting up of formal differences, but the role of historical explanation is seen to be slight in the work of Lévi-Strauss, and there is little attempt to understand how structural rules can be changed. Structures often appear as static constraints on societies, preventing change. Structuralism does not have an adequate notion of the generation of change.

While the main concern of reactions to structuralism is to develop an adequate theory of practice (Bourdieu 1977; Piaget 1971, 1972; Giddens 1979), other criticisms have concentrated on the methods of analysis. Structures, because they are organising principles, are not observable as such, and this is true whether we are talking about anthropology, psychology or archaeology. They can only be reached by reflective abstraction. Thus, structures of particular kinds could be said to emerge because the analyst is looking for them, trying to fit the data into some expected and hypothetical structural pattern. But how can such hypotheses ever be falsified (Pettit 1975: 88)? For structuralism to be a worthwhile pursuit, it must be possible to disprove a weak hypothesis. However, Pettit (ibid.: 88–92) feels that rejection of structuralist hypotheses is impossible, at least in regard to myths, for a number of reasons. For example, the initial hypothesis in structuralist analysis often is necessarily vague so that the analyst can give himself room to shift the hypothesis to accommodate the new transformations. Also, because there are few rules on the way in which structures are transformed into different realities, one can make up the rules as one goes along. By using sufficient ingenuity, any two patterns can probably be presented as transformations of each other.

Thus the structural method of Lévi-Strauss 'is hardly more than a licence for the free exercise of imagination in establishing associations' (ibid.: 96). There is certainly a danger that archaeologists may be able to select arbitrary aspects of their data and suggest a whole series of unverifiable transformations. These criticisms are discussed in detail by Wylie (1982). Here I wish to note that Pettit's attack is directed at those formal and structural analyses which take little account of the referential context of social action. Within a structuralism in which a theory of practice has been developed, Pettit's criticisms have less force because the structural transformations must 'make sense' as part of a changing and operating system. Abstract formal analysis must be shown to be relevant to a particular social and historical context, and it must lead to an understanding of the generation of new actions and structures through time.

All the above criticisms of structuralism have concerned the need to examine the generation of structures within meaningful, active and changing contexts. The criticisms of both functionalism and structuralism centre on the inability of the approaches to explain particular historical contexts and the meaningful actions of individuals constructing social change within those contexts. Archaeology in particular has moved away from historical explanation and has tried to identify cross-cultural universals concerning either the functioning of ecological systems or (rarely) the human unconscious. There is a need to develop a contextual archaeology which resolves the dichotomy evident in functionalism and structuralism between cultural norm and societal adaptation.

Archaeology as a cultural science

The approaches developed by the majority of the authors in *Symbolic and Structural Archaeology* (Hodder 1982a) are not structuralist in that they take account of the criticisms of the work of, for example, Leach and Lévi-Strauss, made by various 'post-structuralist' writers (Harstrup 1978; Ardener 1978). Yet the insights offered by structuralism must be retained in any adequate analysis of social processes, and it is for this reason that I have not deleted the term structuralism from the papers in *Symbolic and Structural Archaeology* (Hodder 1982a) (e.g. Wylie 1982; see also the term 'dialectical structuralism' used by Tilley 1982). Even if structuralism as a whole is generally rejected, the analysis of structure has a potential which has not been exhausted in archaeology.

Structural analyses involve a series of approaches described by Miller (1982a). Important concepts which can be retained from structuralism include syntagm and paradigm. Syntagm refers to rules of combination, and to 'sets' of items and symbols. In burial studies it may be noted, for example, that particular 'costumes' can be identified which are associated with particular sub-groups within society. The rules of combination describe the way in which items or classes of item (e.g. weapons) placed on one part of the body are associated with other classes of item on other parts of the body. Similarly, sets of items may be found to occur in settlements. Syntagmatic studies can also be applied to the combination of attributes on artefacts, and Hodder (1982e) rules for the generation of Dutch Neolithic pottery decoration are described. Paradigm refers to series of alternatives or differences. For example, in the burial study, a brooch of type A may be found worn on the shoulder in contrast to a pin or a brooch type B placed in the same position on other skeletons. Each alternative may be associated with a different symbolic meaning.

But in all such structural analyses the particular symbol used must not be seen as arbitrary. 'High structuralist' analyses are directed towards examinations of abstract codes, and the content or substance of the symbol itself often appears arbitrary. However, the symbol is not arbitrary, as is seen by, for example, the placing of a symbol such as a crown, associated with royalty, on the label of a bottle of beer in order to increase sales. The crown is not chosen arbitrarily in a structured set of differences. Rather, it is chosen as a powerful symbol with particular evocations and connotations which make its use appropriate within the social and economic context of selling beer in England. The content of the sign affects the structure of its use. Barth (1975) has demonstrated elegantly that material symbolisation cannot be described simply as sets of categories and transformations, however cross-cutting and complex one might allow these to be. Culture is to be studied as meaningfully constituting – as the framework through which adaptation occurs – but the meaning of an object resides not merely in its contrast to others within a set. Meaning also derives from the associations and use of an object, which itself becomes, through the associations, the node of a network of references and implications. There is an interplay between structure and content.

The emphasis on the symbolic associations of things themselves is not only a departure from purely formal and structuralist analyses. It also breaks with other approaches in archaeology. In processual analyses of symbol systems, the artefact itself is rarely given much importance. An object may be described as symbolising status, male or female, or social solidarity, but the use of the particular artefact class, and the choice of the symbol itself, are not adequately discussed. Similarly, traditional archaeologists use types as indicators of contact, cultural affiliation and diffusion, but the question of which type is used for which purpose is not pursued. The symbol is seen as being arbitrary. In this book an attempt is made by some of the authors to assess why particular symbols were used in a particular context. For example, in Hodder (1982e) the shape of Neolithic burial mounds is seen as having been appropriate because the shape itself referred back to earlier houses, and such references and evocations had social advantage in the context in which the tombs were built.

The structural and symbolic emphases lead to an awareness of the importance of 'context' in interpretations of the use of material items in social processes. The generative structures and the symbolic associations have a particular meaning in each cultural context and within each set of activities within that context. Although generative principles such as pure/impure, or the relations between parts of the human body (see Shanks and Tilley 1982), may occur widely, they may be combined in ways peculiar to each cultural milieu, and be given specific meanings and associations. The transformation of structures and symbols between different contexts can have great 'power'. For example, it has been noted elsewhere (Hodder and Lane 1982) that Neolithic stone axes in Britain and Brittany frequently occur in ritual and burial contexts, engraved on walls, as miniatures or as soft chalk copies. The participation of these axes in secular exchanges would evoke the ritual contexts and could be used to legitimate any social dominance based on privileged access to these items. In a study of the Neolithic in Orkney (Hodder 1982b) it has been suggested that the similarities between the spatial structures in burial, non-burial ritual, and domestic settlement contexts were used within social strategies to legitimise emerging elites.

So far, it has been suggested that material items come to have symbolic meanings as a result both of their use in structured sets and of the associations and implications of the objects themselves, but that the meanings vary with context. It is through these various mechanisms that material items and the constructed world come to represent society. But what is the nature of representation in human culture? In particular, how should social relations be translated into material symbols? For New Archaeologists these questions are relatively unproblematic since artefacts (whether utilitarian, social or ideological) are simply tools for adaptive efficiency. Symbols are organised so as to maximise information flow and there is no concept in such analyses of the relativity of representation. It is in studies of representation that concepts of ideology play a central role, and although there is considerable divergence of views within this book (Hodder 1982a) on the definition and nature of ideology, it is at least clear that the way in which structured sets of symbols are used in relation to social strategies depends on a series of concepts and attitudes that are historically and contextually appropriate. I have demonstrated elsewhere (1982c), for example, that social ranking may be represented in burial ritual either through a 'naturalising' ideology in which the arbitrary social system is represented as occurring in the material world, or through an ideology in which social dominance is denied and eradicated in artefacts and in the organisation of ritual. This example demonstrates two extremes in the representation and misrepresentation of social relations, but it serves to indicate that all material patterning is generated by symbolic structures within a cultural matrix.

Burial pattern, then, is not a direct behavioural reflection of social pattern. It is structured through symbolically meaningful codes which can be manipulated in social strategies. Archaeologists must accept that death and attitudes to the dead form a symbolic arena of great emotive force which is employed in life. Similar arguments can be made in relation to other activities in which material culture is involved (Hodder 1982b). Throwing away refuse and the organisation of dirt are used in all societies as parts of social actions (see, for example, the use by Hippies of dirt and disorder in the 1960s and 1970s in western Europe and North America). Equally, the preparation of food, cooking and eating have great symbolic significance in forming, masking or transforming aspects of social relations. Pottery shapes and decoration can be used to mark out, separate off or conceal the social categories and relationships played out in the context of food preparation, storage and consumption. There is no direct link between social and ceramic variability. Attitudes to food and the artefacts used in eating activities play a central role in the construction of social categories (as is seen, for example, in the use by Hippies and Punks of natural 'health' and unnatural 'plastic' foods in contemporary western Europe). Similar hypotheses can be developed for the wearing of ornaments on the body, the organisation of the production of pottery and metal items, and the organisation of space within settlements and houses. Before archaeology can contribute to the social sciences, it must develop as a cultural science. The concern must be to examine the role of material culture in the ideological representation of social relations. Excavated artefacts are immediately cultural, not social, and they can inform on society only through an adequate understanding of cultural context.

Material symbolisation is not a passive process, because objects and activities actively represent and act back upon society. Within a particular ideology, the constructed world can be used to legitimise the social order. Equally, material symbols can be used covertly to disrupt established relations of dominance (see Braithwaite 1982). Each use of an artefact, through its previous associations and usage, has a significance and meaning within society so that the artefact is an active force in social change. The daily use of material items within different contexts recreates from moment to moment the framework of meaning within which people act. The individual's actions in the material world reproduce the structure of society, but there is a continual potential for change. The 'power' of material symbols in social action derives not only from the transformation of structures between different contexts or from the associations evoked by particular items or forms. It resides also in the ambiguous meanings of material items. Unlike spoken language, the meanings of material symbols can remain undiscussed and implicit. Their meanings can be reinterpreted and manipulated covertly. The multiple meanings at different levels and the 'fuzziness' (Miller 1982a) of material symbols can be interpreted in different ways by different interest groups and there is a continuing process of change and renegotiation. It is essential to see material symbols as not only 'good to think', but also 'good to act'. Artefacts, the organisation of space and ritual are embedded in a 'means-to-end' context. The effects of symbols, intended and unintended, must be associated with their repeated use and with the 'structuration' of society. Symbolic and structural principles are used to form social actions, and they are in turn reproduced, reinterpreted and changed as a result of those actions.

The dichotomy between normative and processual archaeology is thus by-passed by the notion that symbolic structures are in a continual state of reinterpretation and change in relation to the practices of daily life. Because of the emphases on context and on the continual process of change which is implicated in material practices and symbolisation, archaeological enquiry is of an historical nature. Artefacts and their organization come to have specific cultural meanings as a result of their use in particular historical contexts. The examples of the crown and the Neolithic barrows have been provided above. The enquiry is also historical because the intended and unintended consequences of action affect further action. They form a setting within which future actors must play.

The approaches explored in *Symbolic and Structural Archaeology* are neither idealist nor materialist. They attempt to bridge the gap between these extremes. On the one hand, it is hoped that the major criticisms of structuralism, as outlined above, are avoided. The aim is not to identify cognitive universals. It is not intended to encourage the notion that material items are simply reflections of categories of the mind, nor to develop abstract linguistic analyses of material symbolism. Archaeology is seen as an historical discipline concerned with the active integration of cultural items in daily practices. Structures are identified in relation to meaning, practices and change. Verification is aided by the use of models concerning the ways in which structures are integrated in action. The models identify the components which make up cultural contexts. They suggest relevant causal relationships within adaptive systems.

On the other hand, attempts are made to answer the various criticisms of functionalism described earlier in this chapter. It is clear that the approaches outlined here can be described as extensions of the New Archaeology in that there is a continued concern with social processes and with the use of material items in those processes. Since processual studies in archaeology have been so closely linked to functionalism it is necessary to indicate that the suggestions made here can avoid the various criticisms of that school. A significant development is that the culture/function and statics/dynamics dichotomies are denied since meaning and ideology are inextricably tied to daily practices. In addition, attempts are made to locate the individual as an active component in social change, since the interests of individuals differ and it is in the interplay between different goals and aims that the rules of the society are penetrated, reinterpreted and reformed. The cross-cultural generalisations which are to be developed are concerned less with statistical levels of association in summary files of modern societies and more with careful considerations of relevant cultural contexts. Finally, all aspects of archaeological endeavour become infused with the same social and cultural theories, the same models of man. Theories concerning the relationship between material residues and the non-material world are placed within overall theories of society and social change.

The historical context of a symbolic and structural archaeology

The above outline of various aspects of a structural (but not structuralist) and symbolic archaeology are expanded in the other chapters in *Symbolic and Structural Archaeology* (Hodder 1982a). While the ideas put forward here can be seen to provide an extension of the New Archaeology, an asking of additional questions, it would be misleading to claim that the aims of a contextual or cultural approach are altogether new. The views are reactionary in the sense that they have certain similarities to the attitudes of an older generation of British prehistorians. Writers such as Childe, Clark, Daniel and Piggott placed a similar emphasis on archaeology as an historical discipline, they eschewed cross-cultural laws, and they saw material items as being structured by more than functional necessities. They saw artefacts as expressions of culturally framed ideas and they were concerned primarily with the nature of culture and cultural contexts.

Many traditional archaeologists acknowledged that artefacts were ultimately expressions of ideas specific to each cultural and historical context. These archaeologists were 'normative' in the sense described by Binford. But British prehistorians often found it difficult to apply their aims in practice since the ideational realm was seen as being unrelated to the practical necessities of life. Daniel (1962: 129) asserted that, although prehistory used scientific methods, it was a humanity (an art or human science) partly because it was concerned with man as a cultured animal, with a transmittable body of ideas, customs, beliefs and practices dependent on the main agent of transmission, language. Thus, artefacts such as Acheulian handaxes 'are cultural fossils and the product of the human mind and human craftsmanship' (ibid.: 30). On the other hand, archaeologists have access only to the 'cutlery and chinaware of a society' (ibid.: 132), not to its ideals, morals and religion. Since 'there is no coincidence between the material and non- material aspects of culture' (ibid.: 134–5), prehistorians cannot speak of social organisation or religion. It is this belief in the lack of integration between the different aspects of society and culture which prevented a development of the humanistic aims that Daniel had set up. There was no theory according to which the structure and cultural form of all actions within each context could be considered.

Similar problems were accepted by many British archaeologists. Piggott (1959: 6–11) agreed with Hawkes (1954) that it was difficult for archaeologists to find out about past language, beliefs, and social systems and religion. He used megalithic burial in western Europe as an example of the limitations of archaeological data (ibid.: 93–5). An archaeologist can reconstruct the ritual such as successive burials, making fires at entrances to the tombs, the offerings of complete or broken pots placed outside the tomb, the exposure of the corpse before internment, the moving aside of old bones. But having reconstructed the ritual, noted its distribution, and suggested that the dispersal could indicate a common religion, 'it is at this point we have to stop' (ibid.: 95). While it is certainly true that the detailed beliefs connected with the ritual are unlikely to be recoverable archaeologically, it is not the case that no further inference can be made about the place of the described megalithic ritual in Neolithic society. The chapters by Tilley and Shanks, Shennan and Hodder in the last part of this volume [of the original work] use generalisations from ethnographic and anthropological studies to link Neolithic megalithic ritual into other aspects of archaeological evidence. Piggott was prevented from following his historical and humanistic aims by a lack of theory linking idea to action.

The difficulties encountered by Hawkes, Piggott and Daniel in their pursuit of an historical and humanistic discipline concerned with culture and ideas resulted from a lack of theory concerning the links between different aspects of life – the technological, economic, social and ideological rungs of Hawkes' (1954) ladder. Grahame Clark and Gordon Childe had similar aims, but also employed theories concerning the relationships between the different subsystems. Their work could less easily, I think, be described as 'normative' in Binford's sense.

By 1939 Clark was already employing an organic analogy for society which has continued in to his more recent writings. In 1975 material items were described as parts of organic wholes adjusting within an environment. Every aspect of archaeological data 'forms part of a working system of which each component stands in some relationship usually reciprocal, to every other' (1975: 4). Man and his society could be seen as the products of natural selection in relation to the natural environment. But this ecological and functional stance has, throughout Clark's writings, been coupled, sometimes uncomfortably, with an awareness of the importance of cultural value within historical contexts. He was at pains to emphasise that the economic organisation of prehistoric communities was not conditioned by but was adjusted to available resources, and could not be understood outside the social and 'psychic' (1975) context. 'Most biological functions – such as eating, sheltering, pairing and breeding, fighting and dying – are performed in idioms acquired by belonging to historically and locally defined cultural groups . . . whose patterns of behaviour are conditioned by particular sets of values' (1975: 5). Clark's greater willingness to discuss social and 'psychic' aspects of archaeological data is consonant with, but also contradicts, his use of a functional theory. Unlike Daniel, for example, he saw the material and non-material worlds as functionally related. On the other hand, it was difficult to see how a generalising and functionalist approach could be used to interpret specific historical contexts and cultural values.

Clark, like Daniel and Piggott, accepted that artefacts were not only tools of man, extensions of his limbs, 'they were also projections of his mind and embodiments of his history' (Clark 1975: 9). Gordon Childe was prone to make similar statements. Also, and again like Clark, he began with a functionalist view of the relationship between ideas and economies. But during his life he questioned whether an anthropological functionalist approach based on general laws of adaption could be used to explain particular historical sequences.

In the 1920s, Childe had already espoused the view that culture was an adaptation to an environment. By 1935 and 1936 he could state clearly that culture could be studied as a functioning organism with material culture enabling communities to survive. Material innovations increased population size and so aided selection of successful communities. Magic, ideas, and religion could be assessed in terms of their adaptive value (1936). But Childe also criticised natural and organic models and he acknowledged the importance of cultural styles and values. In his earliest work particular patterns of behaviour were seen simply as innate characteristics of specific peoples. Thus in Germany there had been a 'virile' Stone Age, European cultures had 'vigour and genius', and 'stagnant; megalithic cultures were not European' (Trigger 1980a: 51).

But in *Man Makes Himself* (1936) Childe began to give more careful consideration to the structure of ideas and its relationship to social action. He noted (ibid.: 238) that the achievements of societies are not automatic responses to environments, and that adjustments are made by specific societies as a result of their own distinctive histories. The social traditions and rules, shaped by the community's history, determine the general behaviour of the society's members. But these traditions can themselves be changed as men meet new circumstances. 'Tradition makes the man, by circumscribing his behaviour within certain bounds; but it is equally true that man makes his traditions' so that man makes himself. Yet at times in *Man Makes Himself* ideas act only as a constraint on social change. A functional/non-functional dichotomy is set up and ideas do not take a full part in the practice of economic and social actions.

In later writings Childe further resolved some of the contradictions between an ecological functionalist stance and a concern with the form and content of cultural traditions. In 1949 he emphasised that different conceptions of the world framed archaeological evidence in different terms. He began by saying that the meaning that is given to the outside world, and one's perceptions of it, is socially and culturally determined. The environment of man is not the same as the environment of animals since it is perceived through a system of conventional symbols (1949: 7). Man acts in a world of ideas collectively built up over thousands of years and which helps to direct the individual's experience (ibid.: 8). If the environment of man can only be understood by reference to his mind, so too must past 'laws' of logic and mathematics be studied as part of culturally variable worlds of knowledge. Geometrical pattern in space and concepts of space vary in different societies and 'any society may be allowed its own logic' (ibid.: 18).

Even basic distinctions between mind and matter, society and nature, subject and object were seen by Childe as having varied through time. In Neolithic Europe these distinctions were not made. For example, the ritual burial of animals and the use of miniature axes and amulets were seen as suggesting mental attitudes which did not separate society and nature, practice and ritual (ibid.: 20). This conceptual separation of man from nature was envisaged (ibid.: 20) as being first apparent in the writings of Egyptian, Sumerian, and Babylonian clerks. But nature was still personal; it was an I–thou not an I–it relationship. Social relations were projected onto nature. It was only with the arrival of the machine age that causality could become fully depersonalised and mechanistic; our own distinctions and views are part of this latest stage.

Thus, 'environments to which societies are adjusted are worlds of ideas, collective representations that differ not only in extent and content, but also in structure' (ibid.: 22). While it could be claimed that Childe never developed these various components of a general theory so that they could be used successfully in archaeology, and while he never developed structural analyses, never gave the individual sufficient place in social theory and never gave an adequate account of the recursive relationship between norm and practice, he did, more than any other archaeologist, recognise the contextual nature of social action and material culture patterning. He tried to develop a non-functionalist conception of man and his culture by emphasising the relative nature of functional value and by concerning himself with historical contexts. 'Whether Childe saw beyond the New Archaeology or mere mirages in the Promised Land remains to be determined' (Trigger 1980a: 182). While there are clear differences between the work of Childe and the viewpoints put forward in *Symbolic and Structural Archaeology*, the papers do develop many of the themes he espoused.

Whatever the other differences between traditional British prehistorians, all claimed archaeology as an historical discipline. 'Archaeology is in fact a branch of historical study' (Piggott 1959: 1). 'Prehistory is . . . fundamentally historical in the sense that it deals with time as a main dimension' (Clark 1939: 26). In both these quotations archaeology is referred to as historical simply because it is concerned with the past. Daniel, however, gave additional reasons why prehistory should be viewed as part of history (1962: 131). Prehistory suffers from all the problems found in historical method – the difficulty of evaluating evidence, the inability of writing without some form of bias, and the changing views of the past as the ideas and preconceptions of prehistorians alter.

But the term 'historical' can be used to refer to more than the study of the past or the subjective assessment of documents. Prehistoric archaeology and history are idiographic studies which provide material for generalisation about man (Radcliffe-Brown 1952). Historical explanation describes an institution in a society as the end result of a sequence of events forming a causal chain. Of course, generalisations are used in this type of explanation, but the particular and novel structure of the cultural context is emphasised (Trigger 1980a). Within such a viewpoint there is no absolute dependence on cross-cultural generalisations and laws, and Childe did not see archaeological inference as a deductive process.

Childe was wary of the use of cross-cultural laws and he rarely referred to ethnographic generalisations. Daniel (1962: 134) also doubted the possibility of identifying immutable laws concerning man, his culture and society and he denied the deterministic use of ethnographic data. Indeed the only traditional British prehistorian who has frequently used ethnographic data, Grahame Clark, is the one scholar who has accepted most readily the functionalist stance and has referred to cross-cultural laws of adaption and selection.

If archaeology was to be accepted as being concerned with historical explanation, the viewpoint of most traditional archaeologists that cross-cultural ethnographic correlations should be used with caution was correct. But ethnographic analogies could be used if the relevant context for the comparison could be specified. Childe did use ethnographic analogies when he thought that the total context was comparable (Trigger 1980a: 66) and in his later writings he emphasised the importance of close links between archaeology and ethnography. But the general paucity of detailed studies of particular ethnographic contexts severely hampered the development of historical explanation by traditional prehistoric archaeologists. There were few analogies and little general theory concerning the use of material symbols in social action and within different ideologies. It will be possible to reuse the traditional definition of archaeology and prehistory as history if contextual ethnoarchaeology continues to expand and if a general theory of practice is further developed. The use of analogies associated with an emphasis on a general understanding of the nature of the links between structure, symbolism and action allows the idiographic aspect of historical explanation to be retained, in line with the viewpoints of traditional archaeologists, without accepting the existence of immutable behavioural, ecological or functional laws.

There is some evidence that the contextual and cultural archaeology proposed here and that of some traditional British prehistorians have a common direction, at least in comparison with the deterministic functional laws and positivism of much of the New Archaeology. But traditional prehistorians such as Childe found difficulty in pursuing their aims, partly because the careful collection of large amounts of primary archaeological data and the resolution of chronological issues had only just begun. But their work was also hampered by the lack of an adequate theory of social practice wherein the role of material culture in the relation between structure, belief and action could be described. In pulling archaeology 'back into line', it is necessary greatly to expand, alter and develop the earlier approaches.

Conclusion

The theory discussed in this chapter is reactionary in that it accepts that culture is not man's extrasomatic means of adaptation but that it is meaningfully constituted. A contextual or cultural archaeology is also reactionary in that it sees archaeology as an historical discipline. Man's actions and his intelligent adaptation must be understood as historically and contextually specific, and the uniqueness of cultural forms must be explained. It is only by accepting the historical and cultural nature of their data that archaeologists can contribute positively to anthropology, the generalising study of man. The papers in *Symbolic and Structural Archaeology* also react against the rigid logico-deductive method that has become characteristic of much New Archaeology. Explanation is here not equated solely with the discovery of predictable law–like relationships but with the interpretation of generative principles and their coordination within relevant cultural contexts.

In this chapter I have attempted to demonstrate that archaeology could profitably explore the notion that the severe and absolute rejection by some New Archaeologists of many traditional emphases hampered the development of a mature discipline. In particular, the dichotomies set up by Binford and various of his associates between culture and function, norm and adaptation, history and process, altogether impeded an adequate understanding of the very aim of their enquiry – social and economic adaptation and change. I have tried to show that the New Archaeology can be extended by a reconsideration of the issues outlined by traditional and historical archaeologists, and that culture, ideology and structure must be examined as central concerns.

Symbolic and Structural Archaeology (Hodder 1982a) outlines some avenues of exploration, but it would be incorrect to suggest that a single viewpoint is here espoused or that we have got very far along the road. There are many differences of opinion concerning, for example, the nature of ideology, the degree of determinacy in social change, the types of structure that should be analysed, and the value of any reference to structuralism. There is disagreement about epistemology and about whether positivist approaches should be used. But the variety of different views indicates the importance and breadth of the questions being asked by the authors in this volume and by the Cambridge seminar. While little more than a beginning has been made in answering the questions, the fact that they have been raised at a theoretical level is encouraging for the development of archaeology as a discipline integrated within the social sciences.

In addition to the general theory and the epistemology it is necessary to build models that can be applied in a rigorous archaeology. Because so little is known of the generative principles used in the production of material residues, of the relationships between material culture and ideology, of the discursive and non-discursive dimensions of material symbolisation, or of the ways by which material culture is structured within and yet structures daily practices, the main response to the new questions has naturally been to turn to ethnoarchaeology. It is desired to develop a theory of practice in which culture and function are integrated and which provides analogies and models which are usable in archaeology. Information must be provided which allows the testing of structural analogies in that a large amount of different types of archaeological data (economic, settlement, burial, pottery decoration, refuse, etc.) can be seen as being meaningfully constructed in relation to each other within each cultural context as part of social processes.

Archaeology can be defined as a distinct discipline both in terms of its concern with the material world constructed by man and in terms of the long periods of time to which it has access. A symbolic and structural archaeology investigates both these components and thus realises the full strength of archaeology as an independent discipline, contributing to and being well integrated into the social sciences. Our concern must be with cultural studies, today and in the past.

4

THE CRAFT OF
ARCHAEOLOGY*

MICHAEL SHANKS AND RANDALL H. McGUIRE

Anglo-American archaeology today appears to be in a state of disarray, rent by a host of splits and divisions and troubled by doubts and uncertainties (Bintliff 1993; Flannery 1982). In the theoretical arena ongoing debates pit processualists against post-processualists, scientists against humanists, evolutionary theory against history, and an interest in generalizing against an interest in the particular (Preucel 1991; Yoffee and Sherratt 1993a). Many scholars have difficulty moving from these polemical controversies to the doing of archaeology; they are plagued by doubt as to the relationship between theory and practice. There is uncertainty about how to connect academic archaeology, rescue archaeology, and cultural resource management, or how archaeology should relate to the public interpretations and uses of the past (Barker and Hill 1988; Chippindale 1986; Chippindale *et al.* 1990; Leone *et al.* 1987). Witness the lack of dialogue and lack of institutional connection between academics and field-workers (Athens 1993; Duke 1991; Hunter and Ralston 1993; Schuldenrein 1992). Archaeologists debate the nature of the relation between past and present, and these debates take on political significance in the issues of reburial and ownership (McBryde 1985; McGuire 1992). Should a universal archaeology-for-all, based on an objective knowledge of the past, be sought? Or should scholars build local archaeologies relative to the interests of different archaeology, and cultural resource management, and often contentious social agendas (Gathercole and Lowenthal 1989; Layton 1989a, 1989b)? At the base of this disarray lie fundamental questions concerning the character of the discipline, questions that seem to leave us with many incommensurable archaeologies.

The aim of this paper is to offer a new point of view on these questions. We seek to rethink these polarizations in a more productive and less polemical way than we, and others, have considered before. We do not propose another new archaeology. Nor do we seek to mark yet another set of oppositions to bedevil the field. Instead we want to look at what it is that archaeologists actually do and to ask how they might make more of it.

---

*First published in *American Antiquity* (1996), **61**, 75–88.

Archaeologists take what's materially left of the past and work on it intellectually and physically to produce knowledge through reports, papers, books, museum displays, TV programs, whatever. In this archaeology is a mode of cultural production or technology with a raw material (the fragmented past, result of formation processes) and with theories and methods that allow (or indeed hinder) the production of what archaeologists desire, whether it is an answer to a research hypothesis, general knowledge of what may have happened in the past, or a tool in a political armory in the present. We will consider the character of such modes of cultural production.

We will look at archaeology as a human activity that potentially links human emotions, needs, and desires with theory and technical reasoning to form a unified practice, a 'craft of archaeology'. Our argument is not that archaeology should be a craft, but that good archaeology has always been a craft: a socially engaged practice which is not alienating, which edifies and provides diverse experience. Our intention is therefore not so much to draw an analogy as to outline those structures which, if given more importance, would make of archaeology a richer and more edifying practice.

Craft and its connotations

The term 'craft' invites caricature. Comfortable middle-class people in smocks expressing themselves in activities that once were the livelihood of the working class and known as trades. Housewives sitting at the kitchen table in their Colonial Revival homes lovingly painting wooden geese, cows, or pigs in country-home correct, Sherman–Williams milk-paint colors. These crafts are arty, complacent, conservative, and safe. Craft has undertones of regressive ruralism – getting back to the securities of pre-industrial village life and community, the creation of James Deetz's (1977) communal, natural, *Small Things Forgotten* way of life in the suburbs. People surround themselves with crafts to create the illusion of a simpler traditional life. They may take up crafts as hobbies or pastimes: physical activities with clear untaxing guidelines in which they can lose themselves and escape.

It is for these reasons that craft work may not be taken seriously. Traditional and safe, homely and affirmative, craft work is not considered challenging, avant-garde, and critical, such as the work in the fine art galleries and the great art museums. In the discourse of 'fine art', craft does not speak of the genius of an individual that has broken the bounds of convention and stretched the horizon of creativity. Rather, it comforts us with familiar forms executed with skill and technique to be judged by price and decorative appeal. The artist is envisioned in the studio making art in creative bouts and seemingly effortless flurries of activity. We see the craftsperson in the workshop patiently absorbed in the manufacture of objects. The identity of the artist lies in creativity, the identity of the craftsperson in labor. Art is intellectual and singular; craft is practical and everyday. Craft and art both create things of beauty, and share in the quality that we call creativity, but craft remains somehow less than art. This division of art and craft is partly institutionalized in the distinction between 'fine' and 'applied' arts, a decidedly western and post-Renaissance categorization (Dormer 1988, 1990, 1994; Fuller 1990).

Archaeology often is not taken seriously, both by the general public, which sees it more as recreation than work, and by colleagues in other scientific disciplines, who see it more as a technical skill than a discipline, more as craft than art. The physicist stands by the chalkboard locked in thought and then in a flurry of equations and a shower of chalk dust discovers a new principle. The archaeologist digs patiently in the dirt, absorbed in labor until slowly the discovery emerges from the earth. We associate most scholarly disciplines with a subject: biology with the study of nature, geology with the study of the earth, math with the study of numbers. and physics with the study of the laws of nature. Archaeology is most often associated in popular literatures with an activity: digging in the earth. Most of the sciences are defined in terms of an intellectual program, archaeology in terms of a type of labor. Although prehistoric archaeology in Britain has a sense of identity, at least according to its practitioners, still the usual image associated with the discipline is the excavator on site, an occasionally romantic figure, snatching pieces of the past from irrecoverable loss in a muddy ditch. In the United States archaeology is usually part of anthropology, but like craft to art, it is often thought of as the lesser part.

Archaeology was traditionally defined in terms of its practice. You were an archaeologist if you did archaeology by digging in the earth (Flannery 1982). Some scholars, such as Gordon Willey and V. Gordon Childe, wrote great summaries that synthesized what the field archaeologists had found but rarely did they do the actual digging. The New Archaeology of the 1960s challenged this equation of archaeology with technique. It sought to make archaeology more legitimate as an intellectual pursuit; a nomothetic science we could all be proud of. New Archaeologists wanted it to be more than a set of techniques, and they elevated theory to a pursuit that directed fieldwork. This desire considerably inflated one of the divisions that we live with now – particularly the separation of the theoretical from the dirt-digging archaeologist.

Consider the following set of divisions. They do not precisely coincide, but they are at the heart of an alienated division of labor that has been so important in the development of our western society. This division of labor separates thinking from doing and segregates those who think from those who do in a hierarchy of labor (Braverman 1974; Hounshell 1984; and Noble 1984 provide standard histories; Ollman 1971 is a powerful philosophical critique; Harding 1986 and Haraway 1989 contribute feminist positions on the issue).

art	craft	cognitive	affective
theory	practice	intellect	emotion
reason	execution	knowledge-that	knowledge-how
decision	implementation	masculine	feminine
creativity	technique	scientific research	management
truth	beauty		

Science and fine art are here (paradoxically) united in that each claims the intellectual high ground in opposition to what is considered the more practical pole of the duality.

It is in this system that the division between theoretical and rescue archaeology, for example, finds its roots in western political economy.

Humans must think to act, and action invokes thought. The alienation of art from craft, reason from action, and theory from practice breaks apart those things that are naturally joined in human action, and makes one pole of the unity less than the other. Thus this system of oppositions may be described as ideological.

The Arts and Crafts movement at the turn of the century sought to restore the unity of thinking and doing. The practitioners constructed craft as an aesthetic, a philosophy, in opposition to this alienation. A. W. Pugin and John Ruskin had established earlier in the nineteenth century a strong link between ethics and design. The movement is particularly associated in England with the work and writings of William Morris as a reaction against factory manufacture and the industrial revolution. Arts and Crafts guilds were set up by A. H. MackMurdo, C. R. Ashbee, William Lethaby, and Walter Crane. Visionaries such as Gustav Stickley and Elbert Hubbard brought the movement to the United States. In their guilds and companies they championed craft and workshop-based labor where tools served the craftsperson, as opposed to the machine-based labor of industrial capitalism where workers served machines. Arts and Crafts communities of workers such as the Roycrofters of East Aurora, New York, sought to break down the opposition of management and workers, designers and laborers. Craft was to be art in society, art not separated from life (Institute of Contemporary Arts 1984; Thompson 1977a; Tillyard 1988).

We suggest that the notion of craft that developed in the Arts and Crafts movement mends those rips in modern archaeology: reason from execution, theory from practice. It focuses our attention on the labor that unifies all the different archaeologies as craft. Craft unifies theory and practice; in this unity neither pole can be the lesser. Thus craft erodes notions of hierarchy in archaeology including those that lead to inequalities based on gender. We will also show how it redefines archaeology in a way that escapes the gender-stereotyped images of the archaeologist as either a discoverer or a puzzle-solver. In the discovery image the hero, usually male, risks life and limb to discover or uncover archaeological knowledge in exotic and dangerous lands (Gero 1991b: 2). In the puzzle-solving image the archaeologist, again usually male, takes the pieces, the facts about the past provided by secondary specialists, often female (Gero 1985), and assembles these pieces to solve the puzzle of the past.

Craft: a sketch of positive cultural production

Craft is productive work for a purpose: it is utilitarian, and avoids a separation of reasoning from the execution of a task. Craft is holistic. Craft resists this separation of work from what is produced because it is opposed to labor that separates reasoning from execution (as in management and workers) and divides activity into discrete tasks (as on an assembly line). Craft involves a rediscovery of subjugated knowledge, the recovery of practices made marginal in the rational organization of productive routines. The potter at the wheel must conceptualize the form desired even while pulling that form up from the lump of clay. The reasoning and labor of making pottery combine in the craft of throwing the pot and are embodied in the pot. The throwing of pots is at once an abstract intellectual activity and a concrete labor.

Craft is located within productive relations, both economic and cultural. It crucially involves a dialogue with its 'client' or community, whose interests the craft serves. The potter serves clients who want certain items, yet shapes those wants by expanding on the needs and aesthetics found in the community. To do this the potter must be part of and participate in the life of the community to gain the knowledge, awareness, acceptance, and opportunity necessary for such a dialogue.

Craft involves an immediate and practical unity of the intellectual or cognitive and the emotive or expressive. The pot must first be created as an abstraction in the mind but throwing the pot is a sensuous activity that is emotive and expressive. For the transformation of the pot from an abstraction to a concrete object to succeed, the craftsperson must respect and understand the properties of the craft material and incorporate an aesthetic – this is the interpretation of purpose and material within 'style'. The potter must understand the elasticities and limitations of the clay, master a set of techniques, and be able to use an aesthetic sense to apply these techniques to the clay and make a pot. Craft is a process of interpretation and involves taste and the judgment of quality; it is a process of design.

The judgment of craft involves criteria that are social, technical, and aesthetic. Craft items are utilitarian: they serve needs, and these are social needs. Our social position and background help determine which vessel forms we will need for our table, in what number, and for what purpose. A finished teapot can be judged on technical criteria – is it free from cracks; does the lid sit level on the teapot; and does the tea flow freely from it? But it must also meet some sense of aesthetics, be pleasing to the eye and to the hand. The complex terms imposed by interpretation and taste apply to these judgments on the labor and products of craft. To conceive archaeology as craft invokes these aspects of this sketch: a labor both cognitive and expressive, which involves reason and execution and which applies to social and practical interests, whether these are addressed or not.

Archaeology as craft

We believe craft is latent within archaeology – a potential that is already with us and that we need to recognize.

A craft of archaeology manufactures archaeological knowledge. Archaeologists are not heroes who overcome great adversity to discover facts about the past; nor do they merely act as detectives gathering the facts of the past and assembling them like so many pieces of a puzzle. Rather archaeologists craft facts out of a chaotic welter of conflicting and confused observations: they modify them and reformulate them out of existing knowledge. Here we refer to the considerable and growing body of work in the sociology and philosophy of science, which contends that facts, objectivity, and scientific truth are social achievements and are the result of what scientists and archaeologists do. Objectivity and truth do not exist as abstract attributes of the material world, but are real, material, and located in our (scientific) relationship with the world (Gero 1991b; Haraway 1989; Harding 1986; Knorr-Cetina 1981; Knorr-Cetina and Mulkay 1983; Latour 1987; Latour and Woolgar 1979; Lynch 1985; Pickering 1992; Wylie 1991a). The crafting of archaeological knowledge, like any scientific enterprise, requires great skill and creativity. The discipline of archaeology – method, theory, and philosophy – cannot be reduced to a set of abstract rules or procedures that may then be applied to the 'real' world of archaeological data. We do not simply 'discover' the facts, a single story, or account of the past, and the pieces of the puzzle do not come in fixed shapes that only allow a single solution. The craft of archaeology involves application of discipline to particular purpose: it is a logic of particular archaeological situations. The craft of archaeology is the skill of interpreting purpose, viability, and expression.

Purpose

Purpose refers to the social and other significance of archaeological projects. Archaeological knowledge, we contend, is made rather than discovered or assembled. This making entails a relationship with a client or customer for whom the craft-worker labors. It necessitates a dialogue with that community so that the work will fit the need. Archaeological knowledge, as the product of archaeological practices, is utilitarian and incorporates purposes that may be established in dialogue with others and in the interpretation of need. These purposes and needs relate to specific communities that the craft of archaeology may serve: the government, the academy, a local village community, a city council, a Native American nation. This is an application of interests, in every sense of the word. Different interests may involve different archaeological products. In most cases the archaeologist must serve more than one community, and a single project may entail or require multiple products. Such an interchange between archaeologist and client community is not one way. Archaeologists are not simply to accept the terms and interests of the client. A good work of craft enhances, alters, and creates new possibilities of experience, however modestly.

The work of the potter is a mediation or reconciliation of various spheres of interest and need. To produce work that is irrelevant to a community may be an expensive indulgence, even while perhaps adhering to a notion of avant-garde art. Yet to create something which simply panders to the supposed interests and fancies of the market can be an empty consumerism. There is also the community of fellow potters within which craftspersons ponder all aspects of the production of works in clay. Some of these musings are perhaps esoteric and of little interest to wider communities.

The most respectable and edifying work of craft, we suggest, is one produced when the potter takes the needs and interests of the 'client' or customer and interprets these in a way that answers purpose while giving something more. The new teapot serves its purpose and pours tea, but the skill of the potter may succeed in providing it with a surface and form that enhance its use. It may be entertaining perhaps. It may provide satisfactions or vicarious experiences, and refer also to distinctive 'styles'. The potter's skill in making such an edifying teapot has many origins. One is certainly the character of the dialogue within the community of potters: the debate and polemic around styles, form, and surface, as well as more mundane information exchange.

So too with archaeology. A discipline that simply responds to its own perceived needs and interests, as in the idea of an academic archaeology existing for its own sake ('disinterested knowledge'), is a decadent indulgence. But it is important nonetheless to respect the autonomy of the discipline and the community formed by archaeologists, if only *de facto*. The academy may well be a valid community served by the archaeologist; or it may not be. It depends on the dialogues within, their character, range, and creativity. And, of course, it is in the interests of archaeologists to enable dialogue as a context for creative work. Such liberal and democratic values of and within an autonomous academy are worth restating, especially given the pressure to wholly accommodate archaeological practice to external interests.

So a craft of archaeology challenges a consumerist approach to archaeology. We commonly see such an approach in some cultural resource management in the United States and in the 'heritage movement' more generally. Archaeologists define the consumer of archaeological knowledge either in terms of limited but powerful interests (such as companies and firms needing to comply with legislation) (Fitting 1978) or in broad sweeping generalizations (such as the general public) that obscure and deny many varied interests (DeCicco 1988; Hills 1993; Knudson 1989). In the first case the archaeologist is called on to produce a very limited product to minimize the costs for the client, and in the second the archaeologist is asked to package what we have learned so that it will appeal to a mass market. Craft archaeology fosters an active dialogue between the discipline and those that it serves. A craft archaeology should find its clients among the diversity of communities and interests that it studies, works in, lives in, and draws funding from (Potter 1990).

Viability

Whatever the craftworker wishes to do, the work must be viable and practical. Craft of necessity responds to the raw material, which dictates much of what the craft product will be. The archaeologist also needs a good technical understanding of the past and a respect for material objectivity. The facts of archaeological knowledge are created from observations of a reality, and the archaeologist must recognize that reality and master the technical aids that assist or allow us to observe it. But this does not mean giving absolute primacy to the object past. In the interplay between archaeological craftworker and object, both are partners in the final product. The archaeologist gains familiarity through working with the artifacts from the past, which defy this familiarity through their resistance to classification and categorization. The archaeological record can never quite be captured or pinned down – there's always more.

Is this not also the experience of the potter? Even after a lifetime's work with clay, familiarity seems so partial and superficial. There is always so much more in the inert mineral body. Tight control of processing can achieve predictable results, as in industrial production. But this is a deadening and alienating of the craft encounter with clay. In the genuine dialogue the clay always replies somewhat unpredictably, perhaps in the response of the body to firing, spectacularly in the varied response of surface finishes and glazes. Much of the craft is in interpreting and channeling the quality of response, the resistance.

We might ask why so much of the archaeological work done under the headings of cultural/archaeological resource management or rescue archaeology seems so wooden, uninteresting, and simply boring, especially when it has not always been this way. In the early 1970s many creative individuals struggled with the new imperatives of this work to craft an archaeology that served a mix of new and old interests. Those early years witnessed many exciting successes, and an equal number of dismal failures, that led to a call for a uniformity of product (McGimsey and Davis 1977). As a result, the craft was lost in much of this work and replaced by standardized procedures, evaluative criteria, and the routinized practice of industrial production

(Paynter 1983; Raab *et al.* 1980). The extent to which organizations such as the Institute of Field Archaeologists (IFA) in the United Kingdom (founded in the early 1980s), with its Board of Trade approval and codes of practice (IFA 1988, 1990), escapes such routinization is a debated point. Interesting, exciting, and valuable research survives only where individuals resist the alienation of industrial work and struggle to do craft.

Should the ideal of archaeological work not be a craft ideal – the notion of apprentices working with their teachers to master the doing of archaeology? The current reality of archaeology seldom fits this ideal because managers have broken apart tasks, and they expect individuals to specialize in a particular activity. The end result of this deskilling is that only those individuals managing or directing the work understand and can control the whole process (Paynter 1983). Rewards are differentiated according to imposed levels of task: interpretation over recovery, for example, with project directors reserving for themselves or controlling what is considered the more prestigious. The workers themselves are placed at the bottom of a top–down control hierarchy that seeks to maximize efficiency and profit instead of guiding apprentices to mastership. This is where the lessons of the Arts and Crafts movement are important. Unlike our analogy to the lone potter, that movement sought to integrate groups of workers and managers performing specialized tasks in a craft production. This was accomplished by cross-training individuals in various tasks, involving all in the decision-making process, and giving each individual control of their own segment of the work process. In this craft production knowledge and skills were shared, individuals contributed to the design and decision-making process in terms of their levels of skill and involvement, and individuals managed their tasks rather than the tasks managing the individuals. We suggest this approach should be applied to archaeological practice in order to confront the reality of an industrialized archaeology.

Expression

Archaeologists have largely down-played or even denigrated the expressive, aesthetic, and emotive qualities of archaeological projects over the last three decades as they sought an objective scientific practice. Yet most of us cherish the experience of holding a just-recovered artifact, contemplating its beauty, feeling the tactile pleasure of its shape, and pondering the minor flaws and the unique peculiarities of form that reflect the person that made it. Many of us prize the solitude and oneness with nature that we experience on a survey transect through farmland or the desert, or the physical and emotional feeling of well-being, material accomplishment, and deserved rest we experience at the end of a day of excavation. In popular imagination archaeology is far more than a neutral acquisition of knowledge; the material presence of the past is an emotive field of cultural interest and political dispute. It is this that motivated most of us to be archaeologists, maintained us through the toil and struggle of becoming archaeologists, and sustains us as we do the myriad of other things we must to do to make a living as archaeologists. Archaeological labor is social as well as personal; it relates to the social experiences of archaeological practice and of belonging to the archaeological community and a discipline of academic discourse.

It is mainly the expressive and emotive dimension of archaeology that attracts wider communities. Expression and emotion are what makes archaeology such a (potentially) significant feature of cultural politics. We clearly see this in the experiences of the World Archaeological Congress (WAC) in Southampton, England, in 1986 and Delhi, India, in 1994. Issues of academic freedom and apartheid greatly shaped the Southampton congress (Ucko 1987), and extraordinary scenes of violence erupted, partly over religious difference, at the end of the Delhi congress.

Craft is essentially creative: taking purpose, assessing viability, working with material, and expressing interpretation to create the product that retains traces of all these stages. The creative element in craft contains an aesthetic of skill and of workmanship. Craft's expressive dimension is also about pleasure (or displeasure) and is certainly not restricted to the intellectual or the cognitive. The genuine craft artifact embodies these emotions, and the response to it is a multifaceted one. Pleasure is perhaps not a very common word in academic archaeology, but a craft archaeology must recognize its role and embody it in the product we make. This means addressing seriously and with imagination the questions of how we write about the past, how we address our activities as archaeologists, and how we communicate with others (Hills 1993; Hodder 1989a; Hodder *et al.* 1995; Tilley 1990).

Designing archaeologies

In the craft of archaeology the past is designed, yet it is no less real or objective. Some archaeologists fear a hyper-relativism. They think that if knowledges of the past are constructed then anything may be done with the past. They worry about how the past can be constructed when its reality happened in its own present. Recognizing that we as archaeologists craft our knowledge of the past is not, however, the same as saying we make up the past. The realities of the past constrain what we can create, just as the clay constrains the potter when she makes a teapot. We do not worry if a teapot is real or not because it was created by human hands. We are more commonly concerned with whether it is pleasing to the eye, and if it works or not.

Hence the question of archaeological design is 'What kind of archaeology do we want, and will it work?' The craft object, the product, is both critique and affirmation; it embodies its creation, speaks of style, gives pleasure in its use, solves a problem perhaps, performs a function, provides an experience, signifies, and resonates. It may also be pretentious, ugly or kitsch, useless, or untrue to its materials and creation. In the same way each archaeology has a style; the set of decisions made in producing an archaeological product involves conformity with some interests, percepts, or norms. As with an artifact, the judgment of an archaeological style involves multiple considerations. We need to consider its eloquence, that is, how effective and productive it is. We should also make an ethical appraisal of its aims and purposes and possible functions. Technical matters are implicated, of course, including how true it has been to the material past, and the reality and techniques of observation that it uses to construct facts. Judgment refers to all these aspects of archaeology as craft: purpose, viability, and expression.

In the skill of archaeology, hand, heart, and mind are combined; it is an embodied experience. In such a skill know-how is as important as know-that. Archaeology as craft implies notions of apprenticeship and mastery, rather than the application of (cognitive and abstract) method. Formalized method can never substitute for skill. This is also to recognize the importance of experience (in every sense) and of subjective knowledge and familiarity with archaeological materials. Important also is the social and political character of the archaeological community, the context for mastering these skills. Craft values wisdom more than technical knowledge, more than the right, or correct, answer. Wisdom involves knowledge, insight, judgment, and a wise course of action.

A unified discipline

We propose that archaeology could form a unified discipline in its craft. Archaeology's craft is to interpret the past. The archaeologist is one of contemporary society's storytellers. Archaeologists forge interpretations that provide systems of meaning between past and present in order to help orient people in their cultural experiences. This skill is the basis of the archaeologist's authority, but everyone has not mastered the craft of dealing the past archaeologically. The craft of archaeology unifies the discipline through its practice, both in terms of uniting the activities of archaeology and in terms of divisions that appear to divide us.

We use the present tense here, but a hierarchy of archaeological practice presently exists giving the highest position to those who discover the knowledge, assemble the puzzle, or instruct us in how these things are to be done (Gero 1985) – the 'archaeological theorists.' Lower positions are accorded those who support the discoverer, and provide the pieces of the puzzle to be assembled. In this scientific mode of commodity production the higher levels of analysis each appropriate the products of the lower in their practice so that the theorist is accorded greater renown than the prehistorian, the field director a higher position than the laboratory assistant, and the synthesizer more attention than the faunal analyst. We divide the practice of archaeology into those of us who manage and sit on committees, synthesize, generalize, and theorize and those of us who sort, dig, and identify. As Gero (1991b) points out, this hierarchy does more than just rank activities; it has a more profound social dimension.

Embedded in this hierarchy of practice is a gender division of labor that relegates women's knowledge and production or practices gendered feminine to the lower rungs of the hierarchy of practice thus depreciating them as real contributors.

There is also another mode of scientific production centered around a growing class of 'archaeological engineers', scientific technicians whose standing is related to their control of scientific analysis, usually of materials. Much central and university funding has been invested in Great Britain in this form of archaeological science, and special funds exist in the U.S. National Science Foundation to equip such research. The distinction between the two forms – theorists and engineers – of archaeological science is analogous to that between physics and engineering (Latour 1987).

We would contrast the modern hierarchy of practice with a unified practice of archaeological craft where there is a range of endeavors from the interpretive to the technical, to the practical, to the creative. Each of the different activities necessary to craft archaeological knowledge embodies some mix of these endeavors, labors of the hand, heart, and mind. There is no single correct route to the final product – the archaeological work. There is no hierarchy of archaeological practices, from washing sherds to theory building; the craft involves both theory and more modest operative functions. The skill and the experience accord both significance and respectability. All archaeological activities can be reconciled in terms of their contribution to unalienated practice and their relation to the elements of archaeology's craft: purpose, viability, and expression. All archaeological activities are subject to judgment and critique on this basis.

The craft of archaeology unifies all archaeologies but does not reduce them to a single thing. Archaeology as craft must lead to multiple archaeologies and diverse archaeological products as it enters into dialogues with different interests and communities. As such, archaeology has a practice, a topic, and obligations, but no necessary methodology. The craft of archaeology has particular responsibilities to both past and present, rooted in the character of archaeological experience and not in an archaeological rule book or cookbook (Shanks 1995).

To celebrate a creative diversity of archaeological results that attend to different needs automatically opposes those impulses to get on with doing archaeology and opposes the impulse to cut out the critical reflection. By celebrating the diversity of archaeological research addressing different needs, we are resisting the impulse to simply get on with 'doing archaeology' and to reflect critically about our profession. What is there to fear from an examination of our practices, the interests and desires they attend, and the emotive worlds they serve?

To the question 'What is archaeology?' we would answer that it is archaeology's craft – the skill of interpreting archaeological experiences and situations – that makes us archaeologists and not sociologists or historians. It is archaeology as a craft, a mode of cultural production, that makes archaeology different from digging ditches.

The political economy of archaeology

Much of what we have said in this essay concerns the political economy of archaeology, the discipline, its organizations, and its practices. We hope we have made it clear that such matters are inseparable from the structure of contemporary society. Our following remarks are brief, intending to sketch fields of debate rather than provide definitive comment.

The oppositions that bedevil archaeologists are not foibles peculiar to our discipline and practice; rather they originate in the pervasive alienation of contemporary capitalism. The separation of reason from action and theory from practice found in archaeology is at the root of modern life. The maximization of profits dictates that complex crafts be deskilled, or broken down into constituent parts, enabling minimally trained individuals to complete work rapidly. This deskilling divorces knowledge from practice: each worker comprehends one small piece of production while high-level managers oversee and understand the entire process. This factory model of production permeates most aspects of our lives and consciousness. In Christmas movies even the elves work on an assembly line with Santa Claus as the benevolent manager. The shifts in the United States and United Kingdom to a 'Post-Industrial' or 'Information Age' have only furthered this alienation as the training and technical know-how to control 'knowledge' has increased and the need for the skilled craftsperson declined (Bell 1974; Grint 1991; Touraine 1974).

Our discussion also provokes debates on the cultural politics of higher education and its institutions. Thinking about archaeology as a technology of cultural production forces us to consider the proper role of university courses in archaeology, and of the research efforts of academics. The traditional home of archaeology has been in the academy, but today the vast majority of archaeologists do not work in the academy. Instead they are employed in some aspect of contract or rescue archaeology, or in public planning. It remains the case, however, that all archaeologists pass through the academy to receive the credentials needed to practice archaeology. The academy has always had an ambiguous position in the United States and the United Kingdom. On the one hand, it ultimately derives from an ecclesiastic model of the life of the mind aloof from the grubby realities of day-to-day life. On the other hand, public monies finance the academy, and with this funding comes the expectation that the academy will pragmatically serve society (Giamatti 1988; Kerr 1964; Rosovsky 1990). Current conservative educational policies tend to champion this expectation.

The academy has always resisted the factory model of production and sought itself a community of scholars. This community models itself on medieval guild principles of long apprenticeship (graduate school and junior faculty status) to be followed by master status (tenure). Scholars, having proven themselves through an arduous process, are granted security and freedom to pursue their intellectual interests freely. Students embrace a liberal education freeing their minds to explore, and to connect with others in a search for truth (Giamatti 1988: 109). This model is, of course, the ivory tower, and it implies an academy estranged from society.

In the public universities of the United States, and in the tradition of the red-brick universities of England, the community-of-scholars model persists alongside, and often in conflict with, the principle that the university exists as a business to serve society (Kerr 1964; Giamatti 1988). National and state governments fund the academy to further economic development and address the needs of the state. Universities do this by training professionals (doctors, lawyers, teachers, engineers, military officers, and others) and by conducting research related to the technical advance of farming, manufacturing, and war. The public tends to regard the university as another level of education necessary for children to enter the middle class. Governments in Great Britain and the United States have responded to the general economic decline that began in the mid–1970s by stressing the public service obligations of the university. They have put greater emphasis on business models to structure the university. In the United States university administrations have become enamored with management models such as 'Total Quality Management'. These models treat the university as a business marketing a product to consumers (the students) and demand more accountability from faculty as to their time and effort.

Neither of these models is conducive to archaeology as craft. The self-indulgence of the ivory tower leads us not to the discovery of truth, but rather to the creation of esoteric knowledge of interest to a few. In the last decade a profusion of authors have arisen to denounce the academy as wasteful, and the professorate as lazy, and to call for universities that serve the public interest (Bloom 1987; Sykes 1988). They wish to reduce the university to a factory that efficiently produces uniform, dependable, monotonous products: practical knowledge to advance industry, and uncritical, technically trained students to staff it (Lynton and Elman 1987).

The factory model has firmly taken hold in contract or rescue archaeology. Increasingly in the United States, competing profit-taking private firms dominate this realm of archaeological practice. In the United Kingdom archaeology has been opened up to developer funding (Department of the Environment 1990; Welsh Office 1991).

The largest arena of archaeological practice has largely abandoned the apprentice model in favor of the factory approach.

The traditional scheme of archaeological fieldwork was an apprentice structure where students learned through participation under a master (Joukousky 1980: 27). Archaeologists undertook fieldwork with two fundamental goals: to gain knowledge of the archaeological record and to train students to become masters. While contract and rescue archaeology began in this idealistic setting, it did not always serve this type of archaeology well; there were a number of spectacular failures, such as the New Melones project in California, that led to calls for a more businesslike approach (Cunningham 1979; Walka 1979). By the late 1970s apprenticeship had given way to the scientific management models of factory labor.

The scientific paradigm of the New Archaeology aided in this transformation. The New Archaeologists were (and many remain) openly contemptuous of the mastery model (Flannery 1982; Redman 1991). They advocated instead a 'scientific' approach based on specialist teams. This encourages a hierarchy of both effort and reward.

Today contract and rescue archaeology exist in a highly competitive realm that exaggerates the importance of efficiency. The factory model of production maximizes efficiency by standardizing the product, and by breaking tasks down into component activities (Paynter 1983). Efficiency maximizes profit and leads to greater top–down control. Once the task of archaeology has been broken down into its components, only the managers at the top can control the whole process. In both the United States, and in the United Kingdom, national and government institutions now audit archaeological services, and dictate the form and content of reports (Cunliffe 1982; Cunliffe 1990; Department of the Environment 1975; English Heritage 1991; Society of Antiquaries of London 1992). While there are strong arguments, of course, for quality control and standardization, the negative results have included a degenerative homogenization of the archaeological product, and in many arenas the dulling of creativity and satisfaction in the work.

Ultimately issues of the sociology and politics of education, and of the organization of archaeological practices, should be placed within the context of large-scale changes in society. These may be summarized as the shift to economic structures of flexible accumulation from managed 'Fordist' economies (Harvey 1989; Rose 1991). The considerable debate over the character of postmodernity deals with the effects of these changes (Shanks 1992a; Walsh 1992). Obvious features of the changes in archaeology are the rise of the heritage industry, the commercial exploitation of the material past, and the tying of academic effort to outside interest. Floating labor forces servicing contract archaeology, competitive bidding (tendering) (Swain 1991), and the rise of archaeological consultants (Collcutt 1993) are further aspects of this new political economy of archaeology.

The politics of craft

We cannot think a craft archaeology into existence, or create it through some act of pure will. Nor can we with a wave of our hand transform the larger political and economic structures that archaeology exists within. In this section we will gather some comments about the implications of a craft archaeology.

A first step, however, must be to critically discuss and debate what the goals of archaeology should be. Through such debate we can consider alternative practices for archaeology and learn how to 'do' a craft archaeology. We face the same problems as the Arts and Crafts movement of a hundred years ago. We may do well to look at the successes, and the ultimate failure, of this movement as a place to start.

We would begin with the realization that a craft archaeology is subversive, in that it requires us to resist the dominant structures that shape contemporary archaeological work. We have commented that work done in a contract or rescue context is often dull and uninspired. Yet this is not always the case; there are many examples of exciting, interesting, and creative research done in these contexts. In all of these cases, however, the archaeologists had to resist the pressures for routinization, and work beyond the specifications of contracts and laws. They either sacrificed efficiency and profit, or put in extraordinary efforts over and above what they were paid for. Such exciting work does not result from the structure of the enterprise but rather in spite of it.

Breaking hierarchies of expertise and managerial authority may involve new management structures, and new project designs. There is a need for the 'experts in the trench' – archaeologists who bring technical and scientific specialized knowledge to the point of the trowel, rather than delegating technical reporting as a post-excavation task. Computerization already allows for much of what happens in the lab or research office to occur on-site, and in the hands of those who excavate. Data collection should not be so radically separated from analysis and interpretation because we may search for methodological strategies that allow flexible renegotiation of project aims and objectives in the light of finds in the field (Shanks and Hodder 1995).

Fundamental to an archaeological craft that recognizes itself as cultural production is the relative positioning of communities of workers and their publics. It is people who practice and 'consume' archaeology, and there is need to take careful, and sensitive, account of the characteristics of their communities. This brings us to a most important aspect of archaeological craft: our obligation to take responsibility for what we do and produce. A craft archaeology cannot hide its interests behind a notion of knowledge for its own sake, detached from the needs and interests of contemporary communities.

Conclusions

As craft, archaeology can be both science and humanity. The place of science is that of technical understanding of the material past and of opening archaeological awareness to the empirical richness of the things found – from the mineral inclusions and character of a clay fabric revealed in petrological examination, to the variability within a ceramic industry explored in statistical analysis.

But analogy with craft also shifts concern away from epistemology and methodology (which pose the question of how to achieve a true and objective image and explanation of the material past and have been the focus of so much attention in the last 25 years). Judgment of archaeological work need have little to do with method and adherence to a particular epistemology of how to achieve 'knowledge' – of the past. Judgment and assessment occur according to contribution to an archaeological practice that is not alienated.

The shifts from epistemology and method can also overcome the split between the subjective and objective elements of archaeology, the empirical and expressive, in

69

that the labor of craft is a constant dialogue between archaeologist and material, archaeologist and community – an expressive and interpretive experience within which the past is created.

To conceive archaeology as craft is also to confirm the importance of theory, but not so much as an abstract model of procedure, belief, explanation, or description. Archaeology is now familiar with the format of many papers: they begin with a theoretical statement, premise, or argument that is then 'applied' to a body of material. Being theoretically aware, however, is less about this 'top–down' application. It is rarely good to make pots by beginning with an abstract aesthetic and then applying it to a piece of clay. Theoretically informed practice is simply being reflective, applying critique (aesthetic, philosophical, ethical, political, whatever) to the practice at hand. Looking at pottery decoration may also require examination of ideas such as style, ideology, indeed, art and craft, which inform an interpretive and creative understanding of material.

Finally, the analogy with craft points to the importance of recent developments in archaeological work, calling for a more humanist discipline which accepts the place of subjectivity and the affective. But rather than splitting the discipline into objectivists and relativists, scientists and historians, processualists and postprocessualists, we can effect a reconciliation and dialogue, and a unity of diversity through the concrete sensuous practice we experience as archaeology.

ACKNOWLEDGEMENTS

A number of people assisted us in the formulation of our ideas and in the preparation of this paper and they deserve our thanks. Randy McGuire would like to thank his colleagues, Al Dekin and Sharon Brehm, at Binghamton University who discussed the place of the academy in modern US life with him and loaned him many sources.

5

MATERIALISM AND AN
ARCHAEOLOGY OF DISSONANCE*

CHRISTOPHER TILLEY

Some of the major criticisms directed against an 'object' referred to as post-processual archaeology by defenders of so-called 'scientific' approaches have been that it embraces a hopeless relativism and a rampant subjectivism thus destroying the very possibility of a serious study of the past (e.g. Binford 1987, 1989; Earle and Preucel 1987; Schiffer 1988; Renfrew 1989). Such a reaction was perhaps only to be expected. The aim of this paper is to demonstrate that underlying many of the new approaches that have developed over the last decade (see e.g. Hodder 1982a, 1986, 1990a; Miller and Tilley 1984a; Shanks and Tilley 1987a, 1987b; Tilley 1990; Bapty and Yates 1990; Tilley 1991) resides a deeply materialist philosophy running counter to extreme forms of epistemic relativism, while simultaneously advocating the need to recognize and embrace cultural and contextual *difference*. Nine points of difference are drawn between the epistemological and ontological structure of 'post-processual' archaeology on the one hand and scientific archaeology on the other. Turning the tables, as it were, I shall argue that scientific archaeology embraces a hopeless idealism and leads us to an impasse in which we simply cannot hope to make sense of the past. The idealism embraced by scientific archaeology, while referring to itself as a materialism, has to be replaced with a fresh kind of materialism capable of coping with the complexities of trying to make sense of the past. The future of an adequate philosophy of archaeology lies in a revised materialist position accepting some of the basic tenets of a Marxist dialectical materialism perspective while going substantially beyond the views of Marx himself to include a number of ideas drawn from post-structuralist thought.

The death of grand theory and the birth of dissonance
For 'scientific' archaeology, resting on the twin pillars of functionalism and positivism, a true knowledge of the past was felt to reside in following delimited sets of procedural rules such as the hypothetico-deductive method linked to an explanatory theory stressing 'systemness' and notions of material culture as constituting a means of societal adaptation to particular sets of ecological and social circumstances. More generally

---

*First published in *Scottish Archaeological Review* (1991), **8**, 14–22.

the aim of philosophy in archaeology was seen as a way of adjudicating between competing knowledge claims and producing a harmonious relationship between archaeologists and their data. Ideally there would be *a* philosophy of archaeology, a methodology of archaeology, and a set of concrete results of investigation which would eventually be built up in a systematic knowledge of the past in a manner analogous to the knowledge embodied in a medical textbook concerned with human physiology. What was lacking, and what was required was a theory of the formation of the archaeological record (middle-range theory) linked to higher level interpretative theory and lower-level empirical observations. Archaeologists would be striving for a general theory of material production and use linked perhaps to a general theory of the social. Behavioural links would be set up between particular patterns of social action and particular sets of material remains. This is clear enough in the work of Binford and others who conceive of a body of archaeological knowledge as being in some ways equivalent to that found in a dictionary. If you don't know the meaning of a word you simply look it up; in the archaeological middle-range dictionary, eventually to be published, clues could similarly be found to understand particular deposits. Whatever the details of the projects of individual archaeologists, the aim has been to strive towards a systematic knowledge of and study of the past linking together in a cosy way a community of investigators with shared aspirations and (hopefully) shared theories and methodologies.

For 'scientific' archaeology this has always remained a goal rather than a reality. Diversity of opinion and debate, however muted at times, has always been present. This striving for a grand theory that could both explain everything and unite all participants in a quest to understand the past is hardly unique to archaeology. The natural sciences have always been united at some basic level which, of course, has shifted historically. History, by contrast, with its deep distrust of the general has always been short on grand theories, while the history of sociology and anthropology has been a succession of attempts to produce the synthesis that will finally unite the world and produce understanding of it. From Spencer and Kant to Weber, Durkheim and Marx to Parsons to Lévi-Strauss to, most recently, Bourdieu and Giddens. A notion of totality has always provided the key concern – society as in some fundamental sense a holistic unity that can hopefully be appropriated by a totalising body of theoretical knowledge. Recipes and panaceas: systems theory, structural-Marxist base-superstructure model; structuration theory. All these and many more provide simplistic remedies to what in reality are very complex problems concerned with an entire nexus of relations to do with the construction of social identity, material culture production, use and meaning.

'Structural-Marxist; Cognitive; Dialectical-Structuralist; Symbolic; Structuralist; Contextual; Radical; Critical; Relativist; Idealist; Post-Structuralist; Hermeneutic; Leftist; Marxist; Reactionary; Nihilist; Soft-Focus . . .'. These are just a few of the labels attached to 'post-processual' archaeology by its equally eager proponents and detractors over the past years. One reaction to all this is may be that it merely signifies a group of confused people who tend to change their ideas expediently every five minutes and a series of opponents who don't really have much idea of what is precisely going on. I want to suggest that all these labels, brands of archaeology, have much more fundamental significance. What we are witnessing today is the break-up of grand theories, both of the social totality, and ways to acquire knowledge of 'it'. The pretence that there might be one way of properly studying the past has been exploded. While we can to a certain extent describe what *a* 'scientific' archaeology is (was?) there is no such entity as post-processual archaeology. This development might be described as a kind of archaeological *glasnost* moving us away from the Stalinist one party state of functionalist empiricism. Instead we have a process of democratization, argumentation, debate. Archaeology is becoming a discipline that no longer aims to provide for its practitioners the solace of a cosy, conceited unity. The comfortable world which 'scientific' archaeology hoped to provide has been turned upside down. The plurality of different approaches we have today changes both the terms on which we debate and the way which we think about the past.

What we have are a whole series of competing and different perspectives that we can label in various ways with cross-overs and differing linkages between them. The most important of these labels today appear to be: structural/semiotic approaches; hermeneutic approaches; post-structuralist approaches; Critical Theory approaches; Marxist approaches; and Feminist approaches. Each may be and is combined with parts of one or more of the others. All reside in an uneasy and contradictory relationship. I happen to believe there is much of value in all of them. Equally, any desire to combine them all into a new-found unity is both impossible and undesirable. What we can do is use the vast variety of perspectives now at our disposal to play with empirical evidence and specific problems in different ways. These frameworks provide alternative ways of looking and approach. Each will highlight some elements of the social while neglecting others. Some other archaeologist will, of course, wish to situate themselves more deeply within one of these thought traditions. They will have their choice; I will have mine and an exciting and productive exploration of the past and the present can begin.

How has this development towards plurality taken place and what wider significance has it? First, it reflects a much wider trend in the social sciences as a whole, of which archaeology has now become, belatedly, firmly a part. Second, it appears to signal a sea-change in the social sciences in the English-speaking world, particularly highlighted in Britain. Sceptical empiricism and a deep distrust of theoretical abstraction have often been claimed as a fundamental part of the British 'national character'. Such ways of thought have been traditionally associated with our distrusted continental neighbours. A flood of translations during the past two decades has exposed a British and an American audience to a mass of competing authors and views from Sartre to Gadamer to Derrida and Foucault, setting the scene for our current debates. By contrast, and to give an opposed example, I read with amazement that Foucault had only heard of the Frankfurt School of Critical Theory a few years before his death. In Britain we appear to have been peculiarly open to all the translations of the continental schools and this has provided a unique opportunity for the kinds of debates going on today and a radical diversification of approach. The end of grand theory which I have described, is rooted in these material conditions.

It is also a movement in a *materialist* direction because it involves a realization that to think we can capture *everything* in one model or framework of thought is a sheer idealism that reduces the complexity of the social to a simplistic pattern that has no basis in reality. The analyst or defender of the framework being proposed, of course, may acknowledge that this is the case. He or she is inevitably reduced to the tactic of claiming that the model, framework, or whatever has isolated the truly essential aspects of the real and that left out is trivial or unimportant. Such inclusionary and exclusionary reasoning has, of course, provided the very stuff of sociological debate. But rather than adopt this position or strive towards the (forever delayed) grand synthesis, the materialist alternative I want to advocate is to explore the tension, feel the friction.

This has the radical effect of creating a massive arena for creative debate and argumentation which has been sadly lacking in archaeology. The ultimate, unrealistic, and idealist goal of all archaeologies produced to date is one in which we should all be striving to produce consensus, shared aspirations, ways of working, frameworks for understanding. The harmony to be fostered by the Stazis or thought control police of 'scientific' archaeology has given way to what might be termed an archaeology of *dissonance*: clashing cymbals, a cacophony of competing sounds, contradictory perspectives in tension.

As already made clear it is only too easy to claim that unbridled relativism has thus been spawned and embraced. In the social context of late capitalism, in an age of the 'post-modern' we have simply lost our faith, our belief in anything. Truth, rationality, knowledge, have been discarded to be replaced by a babble of voices which have no basis, no purpose, other than to make themselves heard. The result: incommensurability, a neverending proliferation of equally valid pasts. The effect: impotency, sterility, a sapping of purpose and confidence. Such a view is a regressive one in which the terms of the debate, and therefore the conclusions to it, have already been set by the *idealism* of positivist 'science'. The alternative to this is a kind of rejuvenated materialism in archaeology that is sufficiently subtle to capture the actual day-to-day practice of archaeological research. Lying behind what I have termed the archaeology of dissonance is a materialist kernel running contrary to any form of idealism and the background notion that one past is as valid as another.

Varieties of materialism

Materialism is a particularly tricky term to use because virtually all archaeologists today are happy to refer to their work of theoretical position as being 'materialist' in one sense or another. To be a materialist for many archaeologists goes no deeper that to make reference to the fact that 'data', 'material' is being studied. Others advocate a 'cultural materialism' in which the social is simply considered to be a second nature. This position, at the heart of much scientific archaeology, is an idealism because it is incapable of recognizing the difference between communities of plants and animals and human societies. The notion of materialism has a much deeper sense in the Marxist positions of 'dialectical materialism' and 'historical materialism', the former referring to a particular way of working with the external world via the concept of the dialectic, the latter referring to a theory of history in which 'social being determines consciousness'. History has to be understood as an effect of the changing material conditions of life as mediated and transformed through technology. The forces of production provide a spur for social change. The materialism I wish to advocate accepts that knowledge is to be derived from studying a real object world existing independently of mind (the reverse of this position is an extreme idealism) and that the Marxian concept of the dialectic provides a useful way of proceeding. But it is a materialism which aims to extend beyond the object to include the investigating subject, his or her sociopolitical context, and notions of truth and knowledge. It embraces a number of interlinked theses which, for the sake of ease, I will unpack.

1. Argumentation as a material process

From a materialist perspective the relationship between theory and data is a dialectical one. Each stands apart and has effects on the other and simultaneously helps to constitute this other. This is a process in which it is realized that knowledges are made, not found. This emphasis on the production of knowledges inevitably refers us to the determinate social conditions in which the 'making' takes place and moves us away from an over-emphasis on the external object world. Because theory and data help to form each other without simply collapsing *into* one another, there can be no question of an external process of testing out theories against data. This is an idealism failing to recognize the manner in which we constitute the 'real', the 'external' in thought before working further on it. A materialist explanation cannot ground claims to truth in a notion of a solid bedrock of fact standing outside the archaeologist simply deflecting his or her hypotheses through a testing process. A materialist explanation intimately involves the subjectivity of the archaeologist and therefore involves *choice*: deciding what to write and what not to write, how to conceive of the past. This burden of choice between alternative pasts cannot be simply removed by an idealist reference to a supposedly concrete object world standing apart from the archaeologist and passing judgement on his or her subjectivity. Archaeological evidence provides resistances to theoretical appropriation. A materialist perspective demands that we respect the evidence without supposing it has the final say. We need to be empirical without being empiricist. 'Scientific' archaeology is idealist because it supposes that the archaeologist has no effect on the form and nature of that which is being investigated.

2. Taking responsibility

So a materialist explanation is one that has to be actively argued for and against. This means taking responsibility for what we say and do not say. It makes doing archaeology intensely *personal* involving defence or attack on various positions. 'Scientific' archaeologists, while always acting to the contrary, like to tell us that their theories are not like children, their relationship to what they say and do is impersonal and distanced. References to a positivist science involve the relief of any burden of responsibility – the data simply decides for us what is right or wrong, true or false. This is an irresponsible idealism – there is a *material* connection between what we believe, do and produce. The data never decides and we must learn to do so and then defend what we have managed to say.

3. The materiality of writing

An anecdote:

> No man is equipped for modern thinking until he has understood the anecdote of Agassiz and the fish:

A post-graduate student equipped with honours and diplomas went to Agassiz to receive the final and finishing touches. The great man offered him a small fish and told him to describe it.

Post-Graduate Student: 'That's only a sunfish.'

Agassiz: 'I know that. Write a description of it.'

After a few minutes the student returned with the description of Icthus eliodiplodokus, or whatever term is used to conceal the common sunfish from vulgar knowledge, family of Heliichthinkerus, etc., as found in textbooks of the subject.

Agassiz again told the student to describe the fish.

The student produced a four-page essay. Agassiz then told him to look at the fish. At the end of three weeks the fish was in an advanced state of decomposition, but the student knew something about it.

(Ezra Pound, 1961)

The idea here is that the eye, our gaze, captures the world outside it. All we have to do is stare long enough and hard enough and the secret meanings inhering in the artefact will reveal themselves to us. Our gaze, the gaze of the post-graduate student, is supposedly theoretically innocent and when we write we simply put down our acquired knowledge in the form of words on a page which transparently represent the world beyond the text. A double idealism, a double innocence, thus pervades 'scientific' archaeology. It believes it can know by simply looking harder and that the text, the medium for expression does not matter. But our seeing is never unmediated. In the anecdote from Pound the student was not simply learning about 'reality', the sunfish, but a way of approaching that reality – a discourse bound up in a particular thought tradition (empiricism). The plurality of different archaeologies and their theoretical apparatuses mean that today we have a whole variety of different discourses that will produce different realities. All these have to be written and the movement from things to text transforms. Meaning is created in the text. It does not reside outside it. Writing is a *material* process actively creating meaning and the reality of that which we investigate.

4. Power-knowledge-truth as material relations

For 'scientific' archaeology, truth and knowledge do not have anything to do with power. They remain *ideal* states standing apart from all human beings and untainted by them. We strive to reach these things – certainty in our knowledge which provides us with the satisfaction of making true statements. A materialist position, by contrast, regards power as investing knowledge and truth. Power decides what is true or false, what can count as knowledge. This firmly situates archaeology in a sociological field and underlines the fact that all speech, all knowledge, all truths are bound up with the social institutions and the individuals within them producing the past and particular sets of validation procedures (never the only ones) giving a measure of self-confidence that we are capturing the real in our discourses. Archaeologists always make 'true' statements and these truths, curiously enough, change from day to day, week to week. Today's truths are tomorrows falsehoods. Rather than setting up an asocial ideal of truth and continuously finding it doesn't exist, a materialist archaeology will shift the focus of the debate and examine the network of power, tradition, authority – all determining what can be said and what must be left unsaid.

5. The materiality of subjective experience

A 'scientific' archaeology fears the subject – his or her values, politics, ethics, intentions and aspirations. The person doing the investigation should be screened out. In a sense the *ideal* archaeologist would be a programmed machine with no feelings, no identity, no sociological background. This *ideal* archaeologist would attain the *ideal* of true knowledge through a stripping away of context and tradition. In addition his or her *ideal* knowledge would be the production of generalities transcending particular archaeological contexts (sites or regions). Such an ideal archaeologist has never existed and will never exist. Any striving towards attaining such an ideal moreover would mean the archaeologist could not speak or write. It is only through accepting the *materiality* of our social context, where we are at and where we are going, that any archaeology is possible. Rather than decrying subjectivity we rather need to celebrate it. This does not mean a relativism in which each archaeologist is locked into producing his or her distinctive past. What is implies, rather, is working with our subjectivity to understand something outside it through a dialogic encounter – asking questions of the past and evaluating answers. The questions we ask are, of course, crucial because our answers are dependent on them. The questions themselves come from the community of investigating archaeologists and their competing theoretical and conceptual apparatuses.

In thinking about questions and answers we need to distinguish between two senses of relativism. Cultural relativism is an assertion of the importance of context, the material conditions of life. What goes on in London and Port Moresby will not be the same. It is simply irrational and idealist to reject this. The cross-cultural generalization of much 'scientific' archaeology represents an idealism because it either does not respect context or selects from it in an unacceptable manner. If you take a series of foreign coins, grind them down, erase the valuations, faces, etc. they all become the same – pieces of metal. But what was important about them is, of course, lost. Abstracting in this manner 'science' in archaeology simply produces worthless base metal. A defence of cultural relativism does not mean we have to accept epistemic relativism – that all the statements we make have equal value and that we cannot decide between them. This also represents an idealism in supposing that anything goes, that archaeology does not form a field of debate in which positions are put forward, attacked and defended and that these statements have little or nothing to do with evidence. Without working on evidence we would have nothing to say.

6. The materiality of time–space

Time and space are fundamental concepts involved in all archaeological work, for the 'scientific' archaeology they are simply dimensions. Space provides co-ordinates for mapping sites and artefacts, time provides a medium for looking at how the spatial co-ordinates alter. A 'scientific' archaeology reveres the distribution map on which sites are reduced to dots and, of course, one dot (representing, say, a megalith) is exactly equivalent to another. The aerial photograph provides another medium for inspection, the archaeological gaze. This vision of time and space as *abstractions* divorced from the social: time as a series of dates and space as a vacuum, a container of events and social practices is quite clearly *idealist*. Social conceptions of space and time have not been and are not always the same. The manner in which people situate themselves in a *particular* time and a *particular* space has material effects on the entire gamut of social practices. Time and space, in a materialist conception, are recursively related to the social and cannot be divorced from it. They are not abstractions, dimensions, but form part and parcel of social life. The factory clock provides a medium of, for and in capitalist production. A time of memories and social tradition has a fundamentally different effect on production and social relations in pre-capitalist social forms.

The archaeologist, with the eye of the eagle, peering at the distribution map or the aerial photograph 'knows' everything but such a knowledge is idealist in that it does not attempt to accommodate itself to the real, does not appreciate the fundamental fact that, for example, the megalith builders did not know where *all* (or most) of the other megaliths were and certainly did not regard them with a relation of equivalence. Thomas (1990a) has recently made this point strongly – megaliths and other structures funnelled movement, helped to construct social relations. To appreciate this simple fact we need to return to the ground, simulate movement and the effects of architecture in an hermeneutic appropriation of space. This is certainly not an 'objective' practice like studying the distribution map because it requires the infusion of our subjectivity in a *material* relation with that being studied. Such a practice permits us to speak. Dots on a map are ideal for statistical manipulation but such a knowledge always remains an abstraction and does not lead us very far to an appropriation of meaning. The dot *divests* meaning in the asocial co-ordinate space of the map. Equivalence becomes substituted for difference.

7. The materiality of the body and its desires

For a 'scientific' archaeology, *ideally*, the relationship of everyone to the past is an equivalent one. This permits scholarly communication and the transmission of knowledges. Such a position is inadequate. Our gender, our race, our social context dramatically effect our relationship with the 'Otherness', the foreignness of the past and what we want out of it. This idealism of 'scientific' archaeology has two main consequences: (i) there can logically be no place for a feminist archaeology or an archaeology rooted in the experience of a particular class or culture; (ii) it always tends to produce the past in the image of the present. An extension of the notion of an equivalent relationship between all scholars and the past is found in the very conception of past social actors. Palaeolithic and neolithic peoples, we are told over and over again, behaved just like us, rationally exploiting their environments. This is sometimes referred to as 'uniformitarianism'. A pan-human form of rationality has to be presupposed. A materialist position understands, by contrast, that human agency is always constituted and this process of the formation of subjects and their desires alters according to time, space and circumstance.

8. Relationality and materiality

Meaning for the 'scientific' archaeologist generally resides on the surface of things. It almost always stems from a process of functional identification. A pot is a pot, and an axe is an axe. The attribution of a function to an object becomes the primary way of investigating meaning. A materialist position, by contrast, is one that does not in an *idealist* manner *pre-judge* the issue. It remains open to the *materiality* of the object. A pot may not just be a pot; its meaning may be of an altogether different significance. A materialist perspective realizes that the social world is one made up by a networking of signs that inhere in things. Analysis attempts to go beyond the surface to look at relationships generating meaning, what we actually see. Depth knowledge is substituted for surface knowledge. Knowledge of the tangible and the observed flows from the unobserved. This involves a process of the mediation of the object through the subject. It begins from the object in context. This object is considered not as a thing to which *automatically* a function is to be attributed but as a signifier. Understanding the object as signifier requires a process of dissemination: tracing links between it and other objects (signifiers), links which can only be made through the operation of a theoretical and conceptual labour. This labour materially works on the object as signifier until the moment when it is made to speak through the text. The archaeologist *presences* the past, draws it out of its shell through the materiality of his or her relationship with it.

9. Contradictions and the plurality of meaning

A 'scientific' archaeology wants harmony, agreement, a place for everything and everything in its place, a total and totalizing documentation of the past. It wants a firm body of knowledge to convey about the past and to speak with *authority* to the non-archaeologist. It wants to foster disciplinary autonomy (a distinctive body of archaeological theory and knowledge). It always wants to resolve disputes, search for consensus. It cannot bear contradictions either in a text or between positions. It believes at heart that there is a meaning in the past, to material culture which we all ought to try and approach. Again, this is an *idealism*. Perhaps there is one thing that we can be certain about life, living and working, and that is the fact that human social existence is riddled with aporias, contradictions, uncertainties. Rather than be surprised by contradictions between positions, within ourselves as persons in our lived relation with the world, this is the very stuff of human life. Imperfection rather than perfection, meanings not meaning. To suggest that material culture has a meaning which we should try to capture in our discourse results from the idealism in supposing that people are separate from what they produce and use. The meaning of material culture inheres in subject–object relations and these are always changing from the past to the present. Meaning is created and read into things in the past and the present from different sets of subject–object relations. The polysemy characterizing all material culture resides in the very materiality of object–subject relations; that subjects work on objects to produce meanings which change according to the circumstances of the subject.

Conclusions

It might be argued by some that, despite protestations to the contrary, some glimmers of a 'grand theory' are being proposed in the nine strands of what has been claimed to be a 'revised materialism'. But this is not the intention. The points are meant to constitute a series of proposals framing an arena of debate at an exciting and productive time for archaeology. I have no right whatsoever to tell anyone what they ought to be doing. What I want to do by proposing these strands of materialism is to explode the myth of 'scientific' archaeology, lift the shackles of the dominant discourse which would say: 'Do as I do or you cannot be taken seriously'. To be taken seriously the 'scientific' archaeologist always tries to claim that he or she is a materialist opposed to a wishy-washy idealism. What I have tried to do is show that their position is in fact an idealism, masquerading as a materialism, and providing no realistic (materialist) entry point into the past and its relation to our present.

The decline of grand theories means that we can no longer set up massive theoretical frameworks and then attempt to apply them to the past. Instead we need to relate theory much more intimately to evidence. In so doing we will realize that the entirety of archaeology becomes a series of differing theoretical practices in which theory dialectically arises and changes from linkages with the object world. The way forward in reconstructing the past from the standpoint of the present may be in the production of archaeological ethnographies in which we actively use our competing subjectivities to presence the past and make the life-blood flow in its veins. Archaeology will become much more daring and bold, a series of experiments with conceptualization and writing producing alternative linkages, alternative ways of understanding. A gallery of the past full of different pictures, a flood of meanings which can be debated and discussed.

ACKNOWLEDGEMENTS

This paper, or rather a version of it, was originally presented at a conference organized by the Glasgow University Archaeological Society in February 1990. I am grateful to the organizers for the invitation to speak and to have a material trace of that event published in SAR. At the conference I did not present a prepared paper, a formal document to be read out. In preparing this paper I have tried to re-capture some of the spontaneity of the conference event by reducing a 'scholarly' apparatus of reference and quotation to a minimum and trying to write as if I were speaking. Whether this exercise has been at all successful the reader can judge.

PART II

INTERPRETATION, INFERENCE, EPISTEMOLOGY

INTRODUCTION

For the New Archaeology, epistemology was central to the project of creating a reliable knowledge of the past. As we have seen, much of the unity of the New Archaeology derived from its belief that there were universal principles of investigation and repeatable methodologies which could be applied irrespective of cultural and historical context. As Linda Patrik argues here, the optimism of the early New Archaeology was vested in a particular understanding of the material evidence, whereby static traces were linked in a lawlike fashion to the human actions that produced them. If the relationship between dynamics and statics really were this straightforward, then archaeology could be reduced to the simple matter of finding the right method for reading the evidence. And presumably, there would be only one right method. However, later and more sophisticated forms of processual archaeology disrupted this picture of action and its record, arguing that more complex inferential mechanisms were needed to render the evidence meaningful (e.g. Binford 1983a; Schiffer 1972a). These approaches none the less continued to adhere to the notion of a 'science of the archaeological record', albeit a more flexible form of science than was envisaged in the first flush of enthusiasm for hypothesis-testing. Yet as Alison Wylie points out, rhetorical references to 'the scientific method' can still prove limiting once we start to come to terms with the complexities of the relationships that exist between people and the material world.

Linda Patrik's argument is that one of the principal distinctions which can be drawn between processual and post-processual archaeologies lies in the ways in which they conceptualize 'the archaeological record'. While the former broadly consider the evidence to be the equivalent of a fossil imprint, for the latter it is more like a written text, which implies that it is in some way encoded. If the record is composed of material symbols its significance may be culturally relative, and the 'messages' which it conveys may be ideologically distorted, and may mask the past 'reality'. Much of Ian Hodder's work in the 1980s and 1990s can be seen as an attempt to step back from the potential chaos which a textual model of the archaeological record threatens. For him material culture is meaningfully constituted, and the meaningful character of things renders them powerful in social strategies. Thus the material world is not a passive product of social life, but an active element of day-to-day practice. As Patrik and Barrett (this volume, Chapter 2) imply, these arguments start to do damage to the understanding that archaeological evidence is a 'record' in any sense at all, for material culture is evidently integral to the very processes it supposedly records. Hodder rejects the universal logic of the hypothetico-deductive method, but argues that something like a post-processual methodology can be founded on the notion of context.

While any object, like any word or sound, can have a virtually limitless range of meanings, Hodder suggests that these meanings are limited by the context in which the object occurs. Just as we can pin down the meaning of a word by looking at the sentence and the paragraph in which it is deployed, so an artefact's significance depends upon its material associations: the other objects it is found with, and the grave, house-floor or pit in which it is located. This means each object is part of the context of other objects, so that where such an analysis begins and ends must be somewhat arbitrary. Despite this, Tim Yates objects that context places an artificial limitation on the signifying potential of material culture. If we are to define context as 'the totality of the relevant environment' surrounding an object, someone must define what is and is not 'relevant', drawing a distinction between an inside and an outside. In place of a contextual archaeology which he sees as domesticating the limitless productivity of material symbols, Yates advocates an exploration of difference which will never finally come to rest. Clearly, this takes us still further away from any idea of an approved method that can lead us to a point of rest where our questions about the past have finally been answered.

But what kind of a knowledge is it that archaeology is trying to produce? Hodder's answer is unequivocal: if we are interested in the meaning of material culture, then we are necessarily concerned with the ideas that were in the heads of past people. It was for this reason that Hodder reassessed the historical philosophy of R.G. Collingwood, who had advocated a mental reliving of historical events from the point of view of the protagonists. In this way, it might be possible to appreciate the 'inside of the event', the cultural significance as opposed to the outward appearance of a happening. In their paper, Johnson and Olsen suggest that this position is rather close to that maintained by the early German hermeneutic historians, Humbolt and Droysen. The implication is that archaeology is increasingly moving away from the natural scientific model of *explanation*, in which the causal relationships between a series of discrete variables are identified, and toward *interpretation*, which assesses the contextual significance of phenomena. For Droysen and Dilthey this distinction between *Erklärung* and *Verstehen* provided the ground for appropriate methodologies for the natural and human sciences, respectively. However, such a division has the effect of enshrining the split between culture and nature, implying that two separate realms exist which are to be investigated in entirely different ways. It might be more helpful to suggest that explanation and interpretation represent two different modes of investigation which can be applied equally to human and non-human phenomena, and which might be expected to produce different kinds of understanding.

Johnson and Olsen suggest that archaeologists should progress beyond the early, romantic hermeneutics to consider the philosophical hermeneutics of Hans-Georg Gadamer. Gadamer denies the possibility of leaving our own historical context behind and getting inside the skin of past people. Indeed, it is the very set of assumptions and prejudices which we acquire through living in a particular place and time that make us *care* what the past was like at all. We cannot produce a knowledge of the past which is identical with that which past people themselves would have written, but we can enter into a conversation with a past cultural horizon in which we gain some kind of enlightenment. Our engagement with the past produces a knowledge which is of and for the present.

6

SYMBOLISM, MEANING AND CONTEXT*

IAN HODDER

For many people, one of the most fascinating aspects of archaeology is that it straddles the gulf which separates the arts from the sciences. More specifically, it brings together the 'softer' humanities and social sciences with the 'harder' physical and natural sciences. The underlying reason for this link is the dual character of material culture. The artifacts studied by archaeologists tell us about history but not in the language of the historian. The archaeologist deals in things and not words. Material culture is both the product of human purpose and yet it is material following the laws of the non-human world. The term itself captures the duality of 'material' and 'culture'.

Archaeologists increasingly use a battery of scientific techniques to deal with the material side of this duality. In the 1960s and 1970s, however, so-called New Archaeologists tried to extend a natural science approach into all areas of the discipline. Even cultural issues were thought to be accessible using a philosophy derived from the natural sciences, emphasising general laws, hypothesis testing and independence of theory and data. This approach was most successful in areas of cultural life such as subsistence which were more closely integrated with the natural environment. It paid little attention to the social world and even less to symbolic and ideological issues. Using the metaphor of the natural sciences, archaeology was seen to be dealing with only one hermeneutic. By this I mean that archaeologists and the data they studied were thought to be within one framework of meaning, one hermeneutic, called western science.

But it is also possible to view material culture as part of cultural expression and conceptual meaning. It is possible to go beyond the immediate physical uses and constraints of objects to the more abstract symbolic meanings. In this case, understanding material culture is more like interpreting a language because it is dealing with meanings which are only loosely, if at all, connected to the physical properties of objects. These symbolic meanings are organised by rules and codes which seem to be very different from culture to culture and which do not seem to be strongly determined by economic,

*First published in I. R. Hodder (1992), *Theory and Practice in Archaeology*, London: Routledge, pp. 11–23.

biological and physical matters. Faced with this historical indeterminacy, the natural science model for archaeology breaks down. Using the metaphor of the humanities and social sciences, archaeology can be seen to be dealing with a double hermeneutic. As well as the framework of meaning of western science within which archaeologists work, there is also the framework of meaning, perhaps constructed very differently and according to different rules and principles, of the culture being studied. The problem then becomes one of how to translate from one hermeneutic to the other.

In *Symbols in Action* (Hodder 1982b) and 'Burials, houses, women and men in the European Neolithic' (Hodder 1984a) (hereafter 'Buildings, houses . . .'), the point is made that material culture has to be interpreted within its own hermeneutic. However, at the time they were written I had not recognised the problem of translating from one culture to another. Indeed, I had not even recognised the world of western science within which I worked as *cultural*. My aim was simply to show the inadequacy of a universalising natural science approach which treated objects as if they were only products of the physical world. As a result of detailed ethnoarchaeological work undertaken in Africa and published in *Symbols in Action* (1982b), I wanted to make three points (see also Hodder 1986).

First, material culture is meaningfully constituted. I understand this to mean that there are ideas and concepts embedded in social life which influence the way material culture is used, embellished and discarded. All human action is meaningful not simply because it communicates messages to other people. Information-processing approaches have the danger of reducing the meanings of objects to 'bits' of information which are studied simply in terms of their effectiveness in conveying messages. But whether material culture is functioning as a tool or as information, it is organised by concepts and ideas which give it meaning. While I would now doubt that these concepts are necessarily rigidly organised into 'codes' and 'sets' and 'structures', I take the line in *Symbols in Action* that some form of structuralist analysis is appropriate. In 'Burials, houses . . .', on the other hand, the organising scheme that 'tombs mean houses' derives from, although it cannot be reduced to, a specific social and economic context and is not seen as being organised by abstract structures. Whether one thinks that our concepts are deeply structured by binary oppositions and the like (the approach taken in *Symbols in Action*) or whether the meanings are closely tied to a specific social context (as is attempted in 'Burials, houses...'), the claim is made that material culture is constituted within frameworks of conceptual meaning.

Although material culture is always meaningfully constituted, it can be given conceptual meanings in different ways. For example, it is important to distinguish meaning from intention. At one level, it is to ask questions about intentions such as 'What was the purpose of the shape of that ditch?', 'Why is this wall made of turf and that of stone?', 'Why does this tomb look like that house?' Merriman (1987) has shown that prehistoric archaeologists can answer questions about even the most abstract intentions. He shows that a wall built in Iron Age central Europe was built like examples in the Mediterranean in order to gain prestige by association with the exotic Mediterranean civilisations. Indeed, archaeologists routinely argue that certain items have high value, indicate high status or give prestige. In all such cases, the archaeologist must be assuming that to some degree the participants in the culture being studied purposively gave prestige connotations to the objects concerned. After all, it would be difficult to see how an object could give prestige if nobody at the time recognised it as such. Even if the initial producer of an artifact did not intend it to have prestige, a prestigious object would normally be used intentionally.

But the intentions do not exhaust the meanings of the objects. This is because there may be conceptual meanings which are not recognised by the makers and users of objects. Unrecognised and unintended meanings can perhaps be distinguished. *Unrecognised meanings*: on the one hand, there are the realms of meaning of which actors are unconscious or only dimly and infrequently conscious. We are able to act effectively without calling up into our conscious minds all the cultural meanings of the things we do. For example, I might show a visitor to my house the living room and dining room but not the bedroom and kitchen without realising that I am using a code common in England which separates public from private in a particular way. *Unintended meanings*: on the other hand, different people will read different things into actions. The producer or user of an object is always to some degree uncertain about how the object will be given meaning by others. Different people might link the same object to different conceptual schemes. With speech, it is possible to some degree to monitor the effects of what one is saying and then emphasise, recapitulate, rephrase a sentence so that the intended meaning is got over. But with writing, and with much material culture, the text and the object become separated from the author and producer. Over space and time, distant from their production, texts and objects can be given numerous meanings in different contexts. One has only to look at the different meanings which have been given to Stonehenge (Chippindale 1983) to appreciate the way in which archaeological objects, enduring for millennia, can be given new interpretations.

Because of these unrecognised and unintended areas of meaning, and because different groups in society can give their own, often contrasting, meanings to the same objects, the emphasis placed in *Symbols in Action* on structured 'wholes' needs to be tempered with a fuller understanding of socially embedded, conflicting meanings. In other words, conceptual schemes and symbolic meanings need to be related to practice. In the practices of daily life, whether they be primarily economic, social or ideological, actors draw upon conceptual schemes and resources, but they do so differently depending on their economic, social and ideological position and intentions. In the Nuba case discussed in *Symbols in Action*, it is quite possible that deeper study would have shown that men and women viewed the pure/impure = cattle/pig = male/female oppositions differently (see Hodder 1986). Barrett (1987b) has pointed out in relation to the study presented in 'Burials, houses . . .' that no account is given of whether tombs meant houses to all or just some people. It may of course be the case that the different meanings given by groups within society are in some sense subsets of a larger 'whole', but such integration needs to be demonstrated rather than assumed.

The second general point that resulted from writing *Symbols in Action* followed on from the first. If material culture was meaningfully constituted, and if the conceptual meanings were at least partly arbitrary, then material culture had to be studied contextually. The notion of arbitrariness needs some clarification. I have argued above that the abstract and symbolic meanings of material culture objects cannot be reduced to their biological and physical properties nor to the uses to which they are put. For example, there is no intrinsic religious significance in two pieces of wood nailed together in the form of a cross. To say that the meanings of material culture objects are partly arbitrary is to say that those meanings cannot be determined from cross-cultural scientific study of the material properties and functions of objects. While material culture meanings may be historically arbitrary in this sense, they are not arbitrary in another sense. Any use of an artifact depends on the previous uses and meanings of that artifact or of similar artifacts within a particular historical context. However fast that context is changing the meanings of artifacts at time t are not arbitrary because they are partly dependent on the meanings of artifacts at time t-l.

The symbolic meanings of artifacts are thus not entirely arbitrary because they are bounded within contexts. For the archaeologist wishing to understand past meanings of objects it is thus essential to define the context within which an object has associations which contribute to its meaning. I will discuss the definition of context more fully in a further paper (Hodder 1992). For the moment, I would define context as the totality of the relevant environment (Hodder 1991b: 143). The context of an archaeological 'object' (including a trait, a site, a culture) is all those associations which are relevant to its meaning. This totality is of course not fixed in any way since the meaning of an object depends on what it is being compared with, by whom, with what purpose and so on. There is thus a relationship between the totality and the question of relevance. The definition of the totality depends on perspective and interest and knowledge. In addition, there is a dynamic relationship between an object and its context. By placing an object in a context, the context is itself changed. There is thus a dialectical relationship between object and context. The context both gives meaning to and gains meaning from an object.

Contextual archaeology thus involves 'thick description' (Geertz 1973a) in the sense that it emphasises the need to understand the meanings of an object by placing it more and more fully into its various contexts. But on the other hand, as is made clear in *Symbols in Action*, any such contextualisation depends on generalities. Any account of the past involves translating the 'other' into 'our' terms. We cannot even begin to make sense of the archaeological data without making general assumptions. But the danger has been in archaeology that these generalisations have been applied without sensitivity, without recognition of that aspect of human culture which is historically non-arbitrary. It is necessary to interpret generalisations in relation to specific contexts. As such, a contextual archaeology is not relativist. By this I mean that it accepts the ability to move between cultural contexts, using generalisations, in order to understand the 'other'. But it does argue that these generalisations have to be accommodated to the 'other' context in sensitive and 'thick' ways. The generalisations are, in the process, themselves transformed. The movement between generalisation and context, like that between context and object, is continual and unstable.

The third main point that resulted from *Symbols in Action* was that material culture is active, not passive. This essential point underlies the first two. It argues that material culture is not a passive by-product of human behaviour. In essence an argument is being made here against a mechanistic view of society. With the attempt to see societies and human culture through approaches championed in the natural sciences, archaeologists had come in the 1960s and 1970s to emphasise predictable relationships between behaviour, material culture and environment. Thus we were told with statistical precision that settlements with a certain floor area would contain a certain number of people, or that burial complexity related to social complexity in some direct manner. In fact, of course, societies are not made up of people doggedly following ahistorical rules. Groups in society have different goals and strategies for attaining them and they give different meanings to the world around them. As a result, individuals face some degree of uncertainty in applying historical rules in social action. Because of the unrecognised and unintended meanings and consequences of action, monitoring and interpretation of action are continually needed. All human action is thus creative and interpretive. General rules have to be interpreted in relation to context in the same way that archaeologists have to interpret generalisations in relation to the contexts they are studying. In both cases the meanings are not self-evident. They cannot be passively absorbed. They have to be actively constructed.

Verification

The three points discussed above raise a host of difficult questions. For example, if material culture is meaningfully constituted, how can archaeologists reconstruct the different meanings given to objects by long-dead people? If meanings are contextual, how do we know what the relevant context in the past was? If material culture is active and the meanings constructed, how can we use generalisations? Is not the whole attempt to get at 'their' meanings doomed? How can we hope to get into 'their' minds?

Some archaeologists find these questions so difficult that they prefer to throw up their hands and argue that we should not try to get to 'their' meanings. Clearly there is a view, which I will discuss in Chapter 11 [of the original work], that we should simply accept that archaeologists cannot reconstruct the past. All they can do is construct it, impose our meanings on the data and leave it at that. In Chapter 11 [of the original work] I will reject this view as too extreme. I will argue that we can to some extent accommodate our constructions to an understanding of 'their' meanings. But for those who do aim to reconstruct rather than just construct the past, what I do find totally incomprehensible is the view that we can do this without getting at 'their' meanings. Many people seem to accept that human culture is meaningful and purposive and yet at the same time they seem to convince themselves that human culture can be studied without recourse to meaning.

Originally, the idea that it was difficult for archaeologists to gain access to past symbolic meanings was encouraged by an empiricism and scepticism expressed in Hawkes' (1954) ladder of inference. According to this ladder it was possible for archaeologists to reconstruct past technologies and economies with relative ease in comparison with past social organisation and ideas. This separation of the material and the cultural has often been associated with a materialism, from Childe to Binford, according to which it is possible to infer the social and ideational from the material. Many archaeologists would today reject such approaches and would accept that material culture is both materially and meaningfully constituted. But because of the hangover from empiricism, positivism and materialism, such archaeologists, in the same breath, deny the possibility of getting at past minds. For example, Earle and Preucel (1987) accept the importance of symbolism but say we cannot get at the minds of prehistoric people. The same is true of Bintliff (1990: 13). But what would be the point of interpreting past symbols (as symbolising prestige, status, inside or outside) if we did not think they had those meanings to 'them'?

Binford has often argued that it is necessary to avoid making interpretations of the role of mind and symbolic meanings in understanding both archaeological and 'actualistic' data. But then he suggests the following generalisation that 'if one plans to occupy the site for some time and *does not care* to have the debris from one activity inhibit the performance of another, one develops special use areas peripheral to the domestic area' (1989: 256, my italics). At the heart of this generalisation is a belief or perception which 'they' held: 'one does not care to'. At the core of all generalisations about discard are such assumptions about 'their' minds.

As another example, Barrett (1987b) argues that it is dubious and unnecessary to claim that we can understand 'their' world. He says we can study discourse without discovering ideas in people's heads, and that we can reject a 'text' model for material culture even though he sees social action as meaningful, as constructed, as active. 'I do not believe that such texts are capable of adequate translation' (Barrett 1987a: 6). Yet his whole approach to discourse accepts that material culture does not have single objective meanings (ibid.: 9), that the material world is used to give signification, and that it is invested with meaning. He asserts that authoritative codes are signified by symbols through which 'the participants know' (ibid.: 10) and accept the validity of the conditions under which they act. Since Barrett seems to reject a naïve materialism, he must, in order to apply his approach, interpret meanings in 'their' heads, despite his rhetoric to the contrary. And this is indeed abundantly clear in his own applied work. For example, he has stated the need to get at the 'subjective geography' of how people 'perceived' their landscape (Barrett 1989b: 122–3). He has interpreted the location of a cemetery on the edge of agricultural fields as being determined 'by the acts of growth and fertility' (ibid.: 124). For this interpretation of how the burials gave authority to people in the past to make any sense at all, it must be assumed that, at some level, the ideas of growth and fertility were in 'their' heads.

Willy-nilly, Barrett has, like the rest of us, found himself interpreting conceptual meanings in 'their' heads. I have never read an archaeological text in which some interpretation of what 'they' were thinking has not been a necessary part of the argument, however much it might be denied by the author. When I call some remains on a site a house or dwelling I must mean that 'they' used it and recognised it in a house-like way. Otherwise, presumably would call it a storage facility or something else. Of course, I can claim that the term 'house' is a neutral label but I suspect that the analysis would proceed rather differently, with different conclusions if I were to give the remains other supposedly neutral labels such as shrine, cattle byre, or even dance floor or gambling den! Similarly, interpretations of what things meant to 'them' underlie 'neutral' labels such as settlement, wall, pit. If 'they' did not see the settlement as settlement-like and therefore did not use it in a settlement-like way, it would be meaningless to talk of it as a settlement. Even when I reconstruct an economy from animal bones on a site I must at least be assuming that 'they' thought of the animals from which the bones derive as useful for food, clothing, etc. When Renfrew (1982a) reconstructs an ancient system of weights and measures, we must assume that 'they' understood the system themselves. Otherwise, how could it have worked? I have already given the example of artifacts which archaeologists designate as prestigious or of high or low status. How could an object have had prestige or have given status if 'they' did not perceive it as prestigious or of a particular status?

In my view, the idea that archaeologists can get away without reconstructing ideas in the heads of prehistoric peoples is pure false consciousness and self-delusion. It derives from an earlier commitment to empiricism, positivism and materialism and from a narrow view of what scientists do. It should be clear, however, that the ideas that archaeologists reconstruct are not necessarily the conscious thoughts that would have been expressed if we could travel backwards through time and talk to people in prehistory. As I made clear above, there is a difference between meaning and intention. No social actor can be aware of all the extent and levels of meanings within a particular context. For the ethnographer as for the time-travelling prehistorian, what is said can never exhaust all the levels of meaning. On the whole, archaeologists will often concentrate on larger and longer-term scales of context, which help to frame meanings of which 'they' may rarely have been consciously aware.

If it can be accepted that archaeologists do indeed attempt to reconstruct past conceptual meanings which are in some sense in 'their' heads, the onus is on us to try and get as close as possible to those past meanings. But how are we to know how close we have come to getting it right? And if another archaeologist comes up with a competing theory, how can we verify our different claims? An important initial step in answering such questions is to return to the dual nature of material culture. As much as artifacts are organised by conceptual schemes, they are also made to do something in the world. They are real objects which people made; held, used, exchanged, buried, discarded, etc. We need also to return to the idea that conceptual meanings exist in relation to social, political and economic contexts. They are not purely abstract. They are embedded in real world contexts. The emphasis on symbols in action is that conceptual meanings both give meaning to and derive meaning from action. Theory and practice are in a relation of dependence and tension.

Conceptual schemes thus have effects on the material visible world. They contribute to the patterning of the material world and they are themselves constrained by that world. Although heavily transformed by survival and recovery factors, the patterning of material remains is recovered by archaeologists. The associations of artifacts of different types in layers and pits, in sites and regions, in cemeteries and landscapes, retain a trace of an original patterning which was itself produced by actions informed by conceptual schemes.

It would be wrong to claim that the surviving archaeological patterning can be interpreted in a simple and objective way. We cannot hope to avoid dealing with the problems raised by the double hermeneutic. Rather, we have to accept that, in order to make sense of the patterned remains, we have to approach them with questions and a relevant general anthropological and historical understanding. As noted above, archaeologists sometimes approach the search for and interpretation of patterning by placing too much emphasis on the universality of their ideas and measuring devices. Indeed, in the study presented in 'Burials, houses . . .' (Hodder 1984a), I made a number of invalid cross-cultural assumptions about women, labour and land. These ideas were simply imposed on the data in ways that were typical of much processual archaeology (cf. Barrett 1987b), I made no attempt to understand the tomb-house link in terms of particular strategies as I was later to do by using the concept of the domus (Hodder 1990a). In other cases, too, I had too much hope in universal 'objective' links between material culture and its meanings. For example, I assumed that material culture was organised by a universal 'language' (Hodder 1986). While it clearly is the case that we need to use generalisations and that we need to work on refining them and understanding how they work in different contexts, they can never be claimed to be neutral or objective. The more universal a relationship, the more likely we are to have confidence in it, but in the end we always have to accept that the past may have been different. If they did things differently there, we always have to interpret our generalisations in relation to those differences.

While now embarrassed by the processual aspects of 'Burials, houses . . .', it is useful in demonstrating another aspect of the verification procedure that archaeologists routinely use. As well as referring to generalities to support their arguments, they also try to find as much of the evidence that they can account for in their theories. The more data that can be accommodated by a particular theory, the more likely we are to find it preferable. In 'Burials, houses . . .' the claim that tombs meant houses is a claim about prehistoric meanings which at some point and at some time were in some people's heads. This claim about an historically non-arbitrary and contextual meaning is supported by the fact that this 'thought' was translated into physical evidence by making the tombs look like houses. The claim also uses generalities which allow us to label evidence 'houses' and 'tombs'. But no claim is made in this work that tombs mean houses cross-culturally. Neither is it argued that in certain social and economic conditions tombs are universally built like houses. Rather an attempt is made to support the theory that tombs meant houses by looking for internal links and associations. This interpretation is plausible because a good number of specific formal links can be made between the houses and the tombs and because of temporal and spatial overlaps between the occurrences of the two types. Similarly, the interpretation of the Orkney evidence in *Symbols in Action* is supported by the repetition of the same schemes within different categories of material.

I do not think that it would be possible to 'verify' these interpretations in any absolute or final sense. Indeed I doubt whether one can reach this type of certainty with any but the most banal of archaeological statements. But I do think it is clear that further evidence could be collected which would either strengthen or weaken the interpretations made. For example, in the cases of the European tombs and houses, further evidence might show a considerable gap in time between the houses and tombs, thus weakening the hypothesis that the tombs copied the earlier houses. Or else, further evidence might show that the internal ordering of space in the two types of monument is clearly different.

One of the reasons for reviewing *Symbols in Action* and 'Burials, houses . . .' is that since they were written new material has been excavated which confirms rather than weakens the suggested meanings. In my undoubtedly partisan view the hypotheses have been positively 'tested' by new evidence. Take for example the hypothesis that tombs meant houses in 'Burials, houses . . .', and take the eight points of similarity. Some of these now seem ruled out (Hodder 1990a). For example, it is now clear that the pits along the sides of the houses are an early feature and thus cannot be compared with the ditches along the sides of the later tombs. And there seems to be little evidence for the use of decoration in the houses. But in other ways the points of similarity have been increased. Both Midgley (1985) and Bogucki (1987) have argued that the Polish tombs are like houses in that they tend to form clustered patterns similar in form to the Kujavian 'villages' of houses. Perhaps the strongest evidence, however, is that in many areas in northern Europe the tombs seem to be located directly over earlier settlements (Midgley 1985) and over dumps of domestic rubbish. There does seem to be a close association between the tombs and houses.

Other supporting evidence has come from excavations which have shown links between the Danubian cultures which built the long houses and the construction of the tombs (Hodder 1990a). For example, the trapezoidal tomb of Les Fouaillages in the Channel Islands has pottery from a late Danubian tradition (Kinnes 1982). In Burgundy, at Passy, a series of linear funerary monuments associated with Danubian material culture shows the appearance of the idea of linear tomb burial even within cultures associated with long houses (Thevenot 1985). Indeed, the evidence for a link between houses and tombs was recently seen to be strong enough for Sherratt (1990) to suggest a general interpretation for the processes of transformation in north and west Europe.

It is not necessary to assume that builders of burial monuments throughout northwest Europe 'remembered' their derivation in central European houses. But it is possible to argue that the tradition that tombs represented houses was a long one, as is suggested by the frequent siting of tombs over settlements or houses. Further evidence to support a local link between tombs, other ritual monuments and houses in Orkney, as argued in *Symbols in Action*, has come from recent excavations at Barnhouse (Richards 1992). Here Structure 2 (Figure 6.1) has close similarities to the tombs, with six recessed chambers (as at Quanterness) or rooms placed around a central area with hearth. Structure 8 allows parallels to be drawn between houses, tombs and the henge at the nearby Stones of Stenness. Richards (1991; 1992) emphasises the common use of similar types of central hearth. Despite the chronological difficulties with the arguments presented in *Symbols in Action* (see Sharples 1985), new evidence, which could easily have undermined the interpretation of meaning, has in fact supported it.

I do not conclude from these examples that I have in some ultimate way been proved right in my interpretations of these meanings in the heads of prehistoric peoples. I fully expect other interpretations to be suggested which overthrow or transform my own. This must always be the case with any historical or anthropological reconstruction. But I do conclude from these examples that it is possible to make statements about past meanings which can be strengthened or weakened by consideration of the evidence. On this basis it is possible to prefer one hypothesis, which fits the data better, over another. Of course, archaeologists also have other grounds for preferring one particular hypothesis. And it is undoubtedly the case that the data themselves can be redefined to favour preferred hypotheses. Much as they may seem to be, the data are not 'set in stone'. And yet, however subjective it may be, the patterning in the data is real and there is only so much that can plausibly be distorted. There is a very real sense in which my hypothesis that tombs meant houses in Neolithic Europe will have to stand the test of time, both as perspectives and theories change and as more data are collected and old data re-examined.

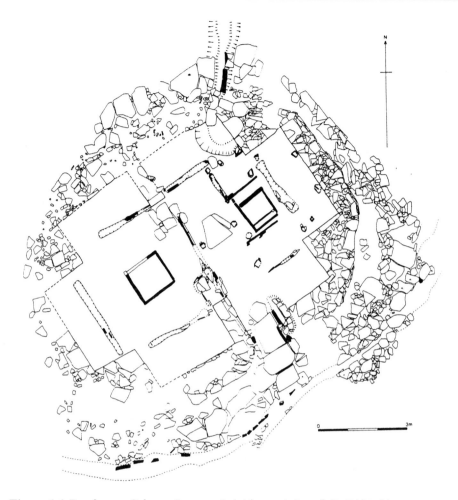

Figure 6.1 *Barnhouse, Orkney, Structure 2 (with permission of C. Richards)*

A final aspect of the strengthening of interpretation of meaning is to provide a plausible social and economic context within which the meaning can be situated as discourse (Barrett 1987b). After all it is only by showing how the meaning worked in practice that we can say we have properly provided it with a context. The attempts to provide such a context in the following chapters are relatively unsuccessful, especially in 'Burials, houses . . .' where, as already mentioned, there was too much dependence on cross-cultural hypotheses based on inadequate social theories. A fuller account (see Hodder 1990a) would interpret the tombs as often providing a stable 'home' in a dispersed and relatively mobile settlement pattern. In a northwest European context without long-term stable houses or villages, the tombs provided the only focus for stable long-term social structures which were needed in an agricultural system increasingly based on delayed returns for the input of labour.

Symbols in Action and 'Burials, houses . . .', then, present a contextual approach to past symbolic meanings. They demonstrate the potential for interpreting specific, not general meanings. Unlike most other approaches in archaeology, the contextual approach, close to thick description, seeks to ask questions such as 'Why was this particular shape or decoration of pot used rather than any other?', 'Why were the tombs this shape?', 'What specifically did the tombs mean?' It is only by asking such questions that we can understand the way in which material culture was socially active and was involved in long-term change. What these works do not do, however, is adequately consider the social context, incorporate different and competing 'voices', and explore the relationship between 'their' and 'our' contexts.

7

HERMENEUTICS AND ARCHAEOLOGY*

On the Philosophy of Contextual Archaeology

HARALD JOHNSEN AND BJØRNAR OLSEN

From the late 1960s to the early 1980s, theoretical positions within Western archaeology were dominated by the idea that the objectives and logic of archaeology are more or less the same as those of natural science. Indeed, these were the only acceptable objectives if the discipline was to be classified as scientific at all. To become a proper science, archaeology was to model its practice on the natural sciences, a strategy the proponents associated with hypothesis testing, formulations of law-like assumptions, and an unquestioned faith in the cumulative growth of scientific knowledge (e.g., Binford 1972a, 1983b, 1987; Clarke 1968; Fritz and Plog 1970; Schiffer 1976, 1988; Watson et al. 1971).

During the last decade, however, this naturalist conception of archaeology has fragmented. Various critics, whose critiques are often lumped together under the heading 'postprocessual' (Hodder 1985), have strongly challenged the positivistic foundation of the preceding 'new' or 'processual' archaeology (e.g., Barrett 1987a; Hodder 1982d, 1986; Leone 1982b; Miller and Tilley 1984a; Patterson 1989; Shanks and Tilley 1987a, 1987b, 1989a).

Central to this development is the so-called 'contextual' archaeology proposed by Ian Hodder (e.g., 1982b, 1982d, 1986, 1987f, 1990a, 1991a, 1991c), in which archaeology is focused on as an interpretative practice. This 'interpretative turn', which at first sight seems to be a *verstehen* antithesis to the explanatory framework applied by the new archaeology, constitutes the background of the present paper, which is a critical discussion of contextual archaeology in relation to its hermeneutic–philosophical background.

It is remarkable that there has been little or no reference to the German hermeneutic tradition in these attempts at establishing an interpretative archaeology. Instead, the English historian and philosopher R. G. Collingwood has frequently been cited as Hodder's main source of inspiration (e.g., Hodder 1986, 1987e: 353; see also Melas 1989: 143). It is quite understandable that Collingwood's approach to history, an approach that can be described as not so much concerned with the

---

*First published in *American Antiquity* (1992), **57**(3), 419–36.

explanation of external phenomena as with their internal significance, was attractive to dissenters to the processual school because it strongly challenges the naturalistic conception of historical causality. However, Collingwood's philosophy of history represents well-known hermeneutic positions that have been widely debated and criticized within Continental philosophy and historiography. Thus, we argue that Hodder's position would have been clarified, enriched, and probably altered had he considered this long debate. Hodder's latest papers on interpretive archaeology support the validity of this argument (Hodder 1991a, 1991c). We shall consider his latest turn in more detail in the final section of this paper.

The main aim of our paper is to show the significance of philosophy to the present archaeological debate, or more specifically, of hermeneutics to archaeological interpretative theories. The concerns of hermeneutic philosophy intersect with a fundamental concern in the epistemology of archaeology: What are the (pre)conditions for our understanding of past human society? The hermeneutic question is not so much what we understand as how we understand: What conditions make understanding of otherness, past or present, possible? Unfortunately, in archaeology, as in many other social and human sciences, these conditions have often been dismissed as subjective and unscientific prejudices to be eliminated (or concealed) through the application of rigorous scientific methods through which objective knowledge can be obtained. However, our aim is not to propose hermeneutics as a superior 'method' for understanding the past (or as a method at all). What is important to us is an examination of the epistemological 'problems' inherent in the task of understanding past traces in a present context.

This paper is in three parts. First, we give a brief introduction to early hermeneutics from Schleiermacher to Dilthey. Then we discuss the work of Hodder and Collingwood in the light of this tradition. Finally, we discuss parts of Gadamer's philosophy and his critique of early hermeneutics in relation to the contextual archaeology proposed by Hodder.

Before we start we should state that we are well aware of the limitation of the present paper. We have deliberately left out several areas of clear relevance to the present thematic, such as the critical hermeneutics of Habermas (1986) and Apel (1986), the 'structural' hermeneutics of Ricoeur (1981), and the radical theories provided by French poststructuralism (Tilley 1990). By choosing a more limited approach we want to distance ourselves from what we see as a worrying trend of 'intellectual potlatching' in the current theoretical debate in archaeology. In this debate it often seems to be more important to cite as many (new) philosophical and theoretical works as possible, than to seriously discuss some of the fundamental problems raised in one or two of those works (not to say considering some of the contradictions between them). Since we find it more fruitful to conduct a thorough discussion of a limited hermeneutic field than to provide a superficial account of all interpretive theories, we have resisted the temptation to include the above-mentioned approaches in this paper.

Part one: early hermeneutics
The term hermeneutics derives from the Greek word *hermeneuein* (to interpret or understand) and is etymologically connected to Hermes, the messenger god of the

Greeks (Wind 1976: 7). Today, the term is associated with a theoretical orientation, which in very general terms can be referred to as the *verstehen* approach, used in various disciplines in the human and social sciences such as philosophy, sociology, ethnography, history, and literary criticism.

Modern hermeneutics grew out of two fundamental intellectual movements at the turn of the eighteenth century in Europe: on the one hand Romanticism and its nostalgia for the past, and on the other hand the *Aufklärung* (Enlightenment) and its struggle against prejudice (Ricoeur 1981: 66). In earlier, pre-Romantic conceptions of interpretation hermeneutics was regarded mainly as a technical-interpretative method ensuring the proper and correct interpretation of past texts.

This pre-Romantic quest for validity was questioned by Friedrich Schleiermacher (1768–1834), who is regarded as the founder of modern hermeneutics. According to him, hermeneutics is used to illuminate the conditions for the possibility of understanding and its modes of interpretation (Mueller-Vollmer 1986: 9). His famous and influential doctrine for a proper (textual) understanding is formulated in the following claim: 'Before the art of understanding can be practised, the interpreter must put himself both objectively and subjectively in the position of the author' (Schleiermacher 1986: 83). To put oneself objectively in the position of the author is to know his or her language as completely as possible. If one is able to speak a language (i.e., to master the grammar), one is also able to understand its utterances. A shared linguistic competence bridges the gap between the speaker and the listener, or between the author and the interpreter. This is the grammatical or technical mode of understanding. However, a complete understanding requires a psychological positioning too. Thus, the interpreter must know the unspoken assumptions and intentions of the author's thought, his or her internal or mental history, as well as the life context (including the standards and norms of the society) in which he or she was situated (Schleiermacher 1986).

In their attempt to introduce the hermeneutic dimension into the study of history and into historical understanding, a similar approach was advocated by German historians, such as Wilhelm von Humboldt (1767–1835). Understanding is founded in language and, as for Schleiermacher, speaking and understanding are connected by a shared linguistic competence in the speaker and the listener: 'One can understand a word which one hears only because one could have spoken it oneself', Humboldt wrote (Mueller-Vollmer 1986: 14). According to Humboldt, historical understanding is ensured by a similar correspondence between subject and object: the historians can understand history because they themselves are part of the historical process they are studying. Humboldt called this bond between history and the historian investigating this history 'the pre-existing basis of understanding'. In certain respects this echoes Giambattista Vico's claim that humans can only have true knowledge of what they themselves have made, i.e., we can have true knowledge only of history and not of nature (Vico 1961). This distinction also forms the philosophical background for the claim made recently in sociology by Anthony Giddens. He asserts that the primary difference between the natural sciences and the social sciences is that the latter is involved in a 'double hermeneutic'. The social sciences cannot be kept insulated from their 'object world', they are themselves part of the society they are studying (Giddens 1987: 30; see also Shanks and Tilley 1987a: 108).

This insight laid the ground for the famous and influential distinction made by Johann Gustav Droysen (1808–1884) between 'understanding' (*Verstehen*) and 'explanation' (*Erklärung*). Verstehen refers to the nature and method of the historical or human sciences as opposed to the causal explanations identified with the natural sciences. According to Droysen, historians are able to understand historical things because they are dealing with nothing alien: 'The possibility of this understanding arises from the kinship of our nature with that of the utterances lying before us as historical material' (Droysen 1986: 121). This kinship is expressed in the notion of intentionality. Historians study the intentionality of actions, and Droysen stressed the point that such intentions cannot be depicted from causal analysis in the manner of the natural sciences. The intention of an action can be grasped only through an understanding of the concrete situation (or context) in which the action takes place. Following Schleiermacher's conception of textual understanding, Droysen asserted that the only appropriate approach to history is a hermeneutic one relating the whole and its parts: 'The part is understood within the whole from which it originated, and the whole is understood from the part in which it finds expression' (Droysen 1977: 35). As historical interpreters, we must break into this hermeneutic circle and make an intuitive leap in order to share the understanding being explored. We can then explore the dialectical relations that exist between the parts and the whole.

Droysen and Humboldt are considered representatives of the so-called 'Historical School' traced back to Johann Gottfried Herder (1744–1803). These historians regarded historical evolution as an organic process: cultures are born, grow, and finally die (Johannessen 1985). Following Schleiermacher who advanced the conception of the organic unity of a text, these historians conceived all cultures as organically and internally coherent. Each culture should be considered as an independent unity bound together by a spirit, the *Volksgeist*. These views were developed into ideas about the nation in the Romantic period, which led to the widespread interest in tracing the lineage of the *Volk*, a quest that motivated early archaeological research as well (Trigger 1989b). The contributions of this historicism to historical research are summarized in the following points (Johannessen 1985: 61):

(1) All understanding is historical understanding, which provides a guideline for any understanding of texts, art, and actions.
(2) Historical understanding requires sympathetic identification (*Einfüllung*) with a distant period or person. This method of 'empathy' can be followed only if historians erase their own time and person in favor of that of their subject matter.
(3) The knowledge objects of historians are not so much the concrete traces of the past as such, as the consciousness of those who produced them.
(4) Every period has its own values and historians must avoid judgements based on values and moral concepts drawn from their own time. They should describe, analyze, and interpret without any prejudices.

Wilhelm Dilthey

In the German hermeneutic tradition, the work of Wilhelm Dilthey (1833–1911) is both the culmination of Romantic hermeneutics and a starting point for the twentieth-century turn leading to Heidegger and Gadamer. In response to the rise of positivism as a philosophy, Dilthey set as his project the following: to provide the human and social sciences (the *Geisteswissenschaften*) with their own philosophical foundation, distinct from, but with a status comparable to (and as respectable as) that of the natural sciences (Ricoeur 1981: 49). Dilthey contended that Kant's epistemology, concerned with the explanation of external phenomena, is valid only for the natural sciences. Following the distinction employed by Droysen between the human and the natural sciences, Dilthey turned to hermeneutics to secure the epistemological basis of the *Geisteswissenschaften* in the concept of understanding: 'understanding introduces procedures which have no analogy in the methods of science. For they rest on the relationship between expressions and the inner states expressed in them' (Dilthey 1986: 163).

Contrary to preceding hermeneuticians such as Schleiermacher, Dilthey did not ground understanding as a methodological concept in language or linguistic competence. For him, understanding is rooted in the experience of human life itself: it is primarily a 'category of life' (*Lebenskategorie*) (Mueller-Vollmer 1986: 25). The basis for our understanding of other persons in other historical situations is to be found in our own experience of life, the world as we live it. Through this experience we have already achieved the categories for thinking about human beings (Dilthey 1986: 149; Waterhouse 1981: 10). In Dilthey's view, all human beings have to 'understand' their social and cultural environment. This 'elementary form of understanding' of a 'lived experience' (*Erlebnis*) is reflected in our actual behavior, it is manifested (or objectified) in a 'life expression' (*Lebensäusserung*). This manifestation of human life is what we as human scientists understand. The source of a 'life expression' is the 'lived experience', and we understand its expressed meaning in the form of an experience 'lived again' (the process of 'recreating' or 'reliving') (Dilthey 1986: 153-159; Mueller-Vollmer 1986: 20–26).

Dilthey's life philosophy based on the life experience of the individual is contradicted by his adoption of Hegel's theory of the 'objective mind' or spirit (*Geist*) (Dilthey 1986: 155–156). This adoption was an attempt to solve the problem of bridging the distance between the individual's self-understanding and historical and social-scientific understanding of permanently fixed life expression (Gadamer 1975: 198; Warnke 1988: 30). Influenced by Hegel and the early writings of Husserl, Dilthey found the ultimate answer in the objective mind, an overarching and intersubjective consciousness in which 'what individuals hold in common has objectified itself in the world of the senses' (Dilthey 1986: 155). Dilthey (1986: 155) locates our possibility of historical understanding in the existence of this objective mind:

> In this objective mind the past is permanently enduring present for us . . . It is the medium in which the understanding of other persons and their life-expressions takes place. For everything in which the mind has objectified itself contains something held in common by the I and Thou. Every square planted with trees, every room in which seats are arranged, is intelligible to us from our infancy because house planning, arranging and valuing – common to all of us – have assigned a place to every square and every object in the room . . . Thus the individual orientates himself in the world of the objective mind.

Dilthey's movement from the experiences of individuals to those of the species is achieved through the attainment of an objectivism according to which the possibility pertains of historians and social scientists transcending their own historical position to attain purely objective and unconditioned knowledge of the life and experiences of others. Paradoxically, having criticized Kant for ignoring the historicity of 'reason', Dilthey himself proposes a conception of knowledge that has no traces of the historical, contextual, and partial (Gadamer 1975: 205–210; Warnke 1988: 33).

Part two: archaeology and hermeneutics

Archaeology can be defined as a discipline in which archaeologists interpret past societies by reading the 'traces' or 'life expressions', those societies left behind. In a similar way, hermeneuticians are concerned with understanding or interpreting textual manifestations without the immediate presence of, or access to, the societies in which the texts originated. This has been noted by Anthony Giddens who writes:

> If there are two disciplines, then, whose intersection concerns the limits of presence, they are surely those of archaeology and hermeneutics: archaeology because this is the subject *par excellence* which is concerned with relics or remains, the bric-a-brac washed up on the shore of modern times and left there as the social currents within which it was created have drained away; hermeneutics, because all survivals of 'a conserved past' have to be interpreted, regardless of whether they are pots or texts, and because this task of discovering is conceptually and methodologically indistinguishable from mediating the frames of meaning found in coexisting cultures.
>
> (Giddens 1987: 357)

Despite the obvious conjuncture of objectives and aims in archaeology and hermeneutics, and regardless of the influence of hermeneutics on historical research, sociology, and anthropology, its direct influence on theoretical positions within archaeology has been limited. During the 1980s, however, its incognito influence on the archaeological scene can be traced through the works of Ian Hodder. Other than a superficial reference to Dilthey (Hodder 1986: 91), Hodder never refers to the German tradition in his works from the 1980s, and he does not use the term hermeneutics at all in relation to his own approach. (Most recently, however, he has recognized this tradition (Hodder 1991a, 1991c). We shall return to this 'discovery' in the final section of the paper.)

Since the early 1980s Hodder has consistently emphasized how the role of the individual as well as the interpretive position of the archaeologist have been ignored in explanations and explications of prehistoric societies. The individual perspective is neglected not only in the ecological functionalism of the new archaeology, but also in Marxism and in what he terms 'high' structuralism (Hodder 1982d: 6). The alternative Hodder proposes is 'contextual archaeology', an interpretative strategy based on the claim that all understanding is historically and culturally situated.

Although the sources of his contextual archaeology sometimes seem to be mixed, Hodder (1987e: 353) has claimed himself to be 'a child of Collingwood'. This close kinship is further revealed through such assertions as 'history in the sense intended here involves . . . getting at the inside of events, at the intentions and thoughts of subjective actors' (Hodder 1986: 77), and, 'it is only when we make assumptions about the subjective meanings in the minds of people long dead that we can begin to do archaeology' (Hodder 1986: 79). These assertions clearly echo his proclaimed intellectual ancestor, who wrote that 'All history is the history of thought' (Collingwood 1946: 15).

We now explore aspects of Hodder's archaeology during the 1980s in relation to Collingwood's philosophy of history and situate both within a broader tradition of early hermeneutics.

History vs. nature: the inside and the outside of the event

One of the most central themes in Collingwood's philosophy of history is the rejection of the idea that historical reasoning should be modeled on an analogy to the natural sciences. In accordance with the conceptions advanced by the Historical School and by Dilthey, he maintains that the past, consisting of particular events located in specific historical contexts, cannot be comprehended by the tools of a science in which this situating is irrelevant (as is the case for the objects of mathematics). Moreover, natural-science knowledge is verified through observation and experiment, while the historian's ideas of the past never can be tested that way (Collingwood 1946: 5). In Collingwood's view, natural and historical processes should not be confused. Their differences are exemplified by comparing the work of a paleontologist with that of an archaeologist:

> The archaeologist's use of his stratified relics depends on his conceiving them as artifacts serving human purposes and thus expressing a particular way in which men have thought about life; and from this point of view the palaeontologist, arranging his fossils in time-series is not working as an historian, but only as a scientist thinking in a way which can at most be described as quasi-historical.
>
> (Collingwood 1946: 212)

According to the Historical School, historical understanding is the understanding of things 'inner' by means of their outward expressions. Von Humboldt (1986) asserted that every concrete work of the past, written or material, contains an inner idea or essence that constitutes its real truth. In his philosophy of history Collingwood develops this into a basic distinction between 'the inside' and 'the outside' of an event, which separates the concerns of history from that of the natural sciences. The outside of an event is everything 'which can be described in terms of bodies and their movement', in other words, the concrete physical characteristics of what happened at a particular place at a particular time. The inside of an event is 'that which can only be described in terms of thought', in other words, the thoughts and intentions behind the event. The unity of the inside and the outside of a past event constitutes the action, which Collingwood (1946: 213) claimed is the historian's proper object of study. Thus, while both the natural scientists and historians are concerned with events, only historians are concerned with those that are the outward expression of thought:

> His work may begin by discovering the outside of the event but it can never end there; he must always remember that the event was an action, to discern the thought of its agent.
>
> (Collingwood 1946: 213)

I take it to be the role of history to understand human action, rather than events. To get at action is to get at the subjective meanings, at the *inside* of the events. There is thus a close link between history and idealism.

(Hodder 1986: 79; emphasis in original)

In Hodder's work, this dichotomy between the inside and the outside of an event reappears as a distinction between two main types of (contextual) meaning (Hodder 1986: 121–122): the structured system of functional interrelations and the structured content of ideas and symbols. The first is achieved through knowledge of the human and physical environment. Here the objects are given meaning by studying how they function in relation to factors such as ecological conditions, subsistence activities, the organization of labor, social and economic exchange, etc. According to Hodder, processual and Marxist archaeologists have contributed significantly to these areas, which more or less correspond to what Collingwood denoted as the outside of events. The second type of meaning, i.e., the content of ideas and symbols, involves more than saying 'this fibula functions to symbolize women'. Rather, it implies asking question such as 'what is the view of womanhood represented in the link between female skeletons and the fibula in graves?' (Hodder 1986: 121).

Such contextual meaning represents an abstraction from the symbolic function of material objects to reach the meaning content behind them. The question to be asked is how we can reach this level of meaning, or, to put it another way, how to reach the inside of the events, 'to grasp the intentions, values and organisational schemes within human action' (Hodder 1987f: 2).

Reenactment, meaning, and intention

According to Collingwood, there is only one way in which a historian can discern the thoughts of past agents: by rethinking them in his or her own mind. This is his essential concept of reenactment. 'The history of thought, and therefore all history', Collingwood (1946: 215) wrote, 'is the reenactment of past thought in the historian's own mind'. Even if there is considerable ambiguity in Collingwood's concept of reenactment (Saari 1984), a plausible interpretation is that it implies discovering an agent's intention by asking ourselves what questions he or she was trying to solve with a given action. Thus, to understand the actions of Julius Caesar within politics and warfare implies envisaging the concrete situation in which Caesar stood, the strategic problems he was trying to solve, and the possibilities that were open to him (Collingwood 1946: 215). According to Hodder, in archaeology this reenactment of the past implies such questions as 'why should anyone want to erect a building like that, what was the purpose of the shape of that ditch, why is this wall made of turf and that of stone?' (Hodder 1986: 94). It is obvious that the topics to which such questions can be addressed are quite limited. One would hardly ask questions such as 'why should anyone want to construct a social system like this?' However, the main problem with this approach is that it presupposes that the course of history conforms to the intention of the individual actors. Because many consequences of actions clearly are unintended they cannot be adequately understood within this framework of reenactment (Barrett 1987b: 469).

In more general terms, the meaning of any product of the past, lying in front of us as historical material, is equated with the intention of the producer/author. This is explicitly formulated by Collingwood (1946: 282):

> When a man thinks historically, he has before him certain documents or relics of the past. His business is to discover what the past was which has left these relics behind it. For example, the relics are certain written words; and in that case he has to discover what the person who wrote those words meant by them. This means discovering the thought . . . which he expressed by them.

A line of connection runs here from Collingwood via Dilthey to Husserl. In his phenomenology, Husserl established that mental life is characterized by intentionality. Mental life, as such, cannot be grasped, but we can grasp the intention through the intentional product, 'the objective and identical correlate in which mental life surpasses itself' (Ricoeur 1981: 50).

In a similar vein, Hodder conceives the meaning of past material culture as the one intended by the producer/user. Thus the primary goal of Hodder's contextual archaeology is to understand prehistoric peoples on their own terms and to develop tools for recapturing their conception of the world:

> In the constitution of the cultural world, all dimensions . . . already have meaning associations. An individual in the past is situated in this historical frame, and interprets the cultural order from within its perspective. The archaeologist seeks also to get 'inside' the historical context, but the jump is often a considerable one.
>
> (Hodder 1987b: 7)

> Rather than translating the text into something other than itself, the aim is, as far as possible, to understand it in its own terms.
>
> (Hodder 1987f: 8)

> By 'contextual', I mean an analysis which attempts to 'read' or interpret the evidence primarily in terms of its internal relations rather than in terms of outside knowledge. In particular an emphasis is placed on internal symbolic relations rather than on externally derived concepts of rationality.
>
> (Hodder 1990a: 21)

> Interpretative approaches at least try to understand the other in its own terms in that they look for internal rather than external criteria of plausibility in order to support their arguments.
>
> (Hodder 1991a: 15)

Methodologically, to get at the meaning of an object we have to know its context as fully as possible. Since our concern has moved from the outside to the inside of events, 'to understand material culture adequately, in its meaning context, will involve long-term participation in the cultures studied' (Hodder 1986: 103). This, however, is an unobtainable condition for an archaeologist studying the past. Thus, the solution is to get to know 'the totality of the relevant dimensions of variation around any object' (Hodder 1986: 139). Hodder is aware, of course, of the problems involved in defining the relevant dimensions of contextual relations among artifacts:

> There seems to be no easy answer to this problem, except that it is important to know all the data as thoroughly as possible, and gradually to accommodate theory to data by trial-and-error searching for relevant dimensions of variation, cross checking with contextual information and so on.
>
> (Hodder 1986: 141)

Because the meaning of past material culture is equated with the one intended or thought by the producer/user, the only way to grasp it is to know the relevant context as completely as possible, relating the whole and the parts in a hermeneutical circle. Consider the following statement by Schleiermacher (1986: 84):

> The vocabulary and the history of an author's age together form a whole from which his writings must be understood as a part, and vice versa. Complete knowledge always involves an apparent circle, that each part can be understood only out of the whole to which it belongs and vice versa. All knowledge that is scientific must be constructed in this way. To put oneself in the position of the author means to follow through with this relationship between the whole and the parts.

Even if Hodder does not explicitly articulate his understanding as early hermeneuticians did, he clearly shares their conception of a proper understanding. By putting oneself in the position of the author, one is able to understand the bits and pieces of the text in light of the contextual wholeness of the author herself or himself. In accordance with this tradition, the relevant contextual relations are limited to those in effect when the past material originated and do not include those in which the archaeologist is situated. Further, the dialectical nature of this material itself, as present traces of the past, is ignored.

Contexts: past and present

Against this view, one can argue that Hodder actually discusses contextual relations on two levels. He is concerned not only with the context of the archaeological record itself, or more precisely, the context in which it originated, but also with our contemporary contexts, i.e., the historical and cultural location of the archaeologist. Discussing our own context, Hodder (1986: 106) urges us to be self-critical in the imposition of meaning, to avoid 'intellectual colonialism', and he asks if the meaning we impose on the past is particular to our own cultural and social background (Hodder 1986: 122). He postpones the answer to this question, and when he eventually attempts to deal with it, his conclusions remain vague and contradictory. On the one hand, Hodder (1986: 170) asserts that 'there is a dialectical relationship between past and present: the past is interpreted in terms of the present.' On the other hand, however, he claims that 'the subjectivity of other objects can be comprehended without imposing our own "objective" subjectivities' (Hodder 1986: 170). He repeats this claim in his latest major work where he asserts that his contextual archaeology is an attempt to 'interpret the evidence primarily in terms of its internal relations rather than in terms of outside knowledge' (Hodder 1990a:

21, see also Hodder 1991a: 13, 15). (There is a similar ambiguity in Collingwood's (1946: 247–248) work.)

Hodder considers the main task of archaeological interpretation to be the recovery of buried or lost meaning. This implies giving essential importance to the 'original context', and subordinating the contextuality of the archaeologist in achieving the meaning of an object. This priority is evident in statements such as 'an object out of context is not readable' (Hodder 1986: 141), where original context is clearly meant:

> [A] symbol painted on a cave wall when there are no deposits in the cave, when there are no deposits in the region that contain other depictions of the symbol or other objects, and when there are no graves containing the symbol, is scarcely more readable. It is partly for this reason that historical archaeology is an 'easier' approach . . . In prehistoric archaeology, the further one goes back in time, so that survival rates diminish, the more difficult it becomes to ground hypotheses in data . . . In many areas contextual archaeology can hardly begin until more data have been collected.
>
> (Hodder 1986: 141–142)

In this very explicit statement the conditions for readability or understanding are clearly limited to the past. The context in which the symbol originated exclusively enables one to understand its meaning (see Hodder 1986: 51). One's present context, and experiences from living and reading in the present, are irrelevant to this understanding. Hodder may of course argue that he is concerned with methodology not with epistemology (see Hodder (1991a, 1991c) for statements on this), but this escape is hardly a good solution, since there are no 'methods' outside of epistemology. We still have to ask: Why is the original context given priority? It seems to us that this can be only because meaning is equated with intention. Thus, when one reads a book, one has to know the context of its production, to grasp the intention of the author, in other words, the meaning of the text. The author and the original context become the only entrance to a proper interpretation of the text. This position seems to be a basic point in Hodder's contextual archaeology, at least the way it was presented until the beginning of this decade.

However, in some of Hodder's works from the late 1980s this advocacy of historical 'empathy' is contradicted by radical approval of 'free reading'. Consider, for example, his reply to Bell's (1987) critical review of *Reading the Past*: 'The book is real but different readers give it different realities' (Hodder 1987g: 87). In relation to the arguments referred to above, the following conclusion is rather confusing (Hodder 1987g: 91):

> I do not want to argue that my interpretation of 'my own' book is right and that Bell is wrong. The book is divorced from me. Its meaning does not depend on the author but on the reading of it that is given. I do not wish for any authority in relation to the text.

This, of course, is a legitimate theoretical point of view, associated with the poststructuralist position in literary theory and philosophy (Hodder 1989e: 68–70; Olsen 1990; Yates 1990a). However, serious problems arise when it is held simultaneously with the historicism of early hermeneutics that is embedded in his contextual approach. At least Hodder should explain why the way his own book is interpreted should be kept epistemologically distinct from the way past cultures are interpreted. Such serious inconsistencies appear even in less marginal parts of his work (e.g., Hodder 1986, 1989c, 1989e, 1990a).

Contextuality and universality

Similar to the contradiction inherent in Dilthey's philosophy, Collingwood's idealism of grasping the intention of historical agents is contradicted by his attempt to give thought a universal status that denies time:

> Acts of thought certainly happen at definite times . . . but they are not related to time in the same way as mere feelings and sensations. It is not only the object of thought that somehow stands outside time; the act of thought does so too.
> (Collingwood 1946: 287)

According to Collingwood, historians cannot apprehend an individual act of thought 'in its individuality'. What they apprehend of that individual act of thought is only something others might have had and which the historians themselves have had: 'It is the act of thought itself, in its survival and revival at different times and in different persons; once in the historian's own life, once in the life of the person whose history he is narrating' (Collingwood 1946: 303). Accordingly, to be a proper object of historical study, an event must have a universality and possess a significance valid for all people at all times (Collingwood 1946: 303). Thus, the task of getting inside the past event is realized by obtaining a universal or objective thought.

Hodder seems to arrive at a similar conclusion. We can grasp the particularity of the past 'because historical meanings, however "other" and coherent to themselves, are nevertheless real, producing real effects in the material world, and they are coherent, and thereby structured and systematic' (Hodder 1986: 154). In other words, because historical meaning is manifested in a 'life expression', it has become an objectified expression of human life comprehensible for all of us. Note that this emphasis on the 'objectified thought' comes close to the view of Childe, who himself disclaimed the possibility of reenacting in our own minds the thoughts and motives of the agents:

> In practice the separation of subject from object is transcended. Real thoughts of the past have issued in action. Real thinking has already been objectified. To study a past society there is no need to turn real thoughts into objects, for that has already been done. The relics and monuments studied by archaeologists are patently objects, and need no translation into an alien conceptual framework.
> (Childe 1949: 25)

The objectivism expressed in Childe's materialism is at least theoretically coherent. He is a determinist who does not pretend to take hold of the subjective intentions of the prehistoric agents. However, the contradiction between particularism and universalism is embedded in the very foundation of Hodder's archaeology.

Although he does not formulate it very explicitly, Hodder seems (at least partly) to ground the possibility of historical understanding in our own life experience. Discussing Collingwood's conception of universal meanings Hodder (1986: 124) states that 'The universal principles of meaning which I wish to suggest lie behind such experiences are only those followed routinely by all of us as social actors, and by archaeologist in interpreting the past.' In another work he argues in a similar vein that 'The archaeologist . . . uses the same methods and assumptions to reconstruct past cultural orders as were used to construct and live within them' (Hodder 1987b: 10). Thus, Hodder's solution to the problem of historical understanding follows the one adopted by Dilthey and Collingwood, namely, the introduction of an objective mind capable of bridging the distance between the intentional meanings of past individuals, permanently fixed life expressions, and our own understanding in the present (see Hodder 1986: 170).

According to Hodder (1986: 123), another basis for such universals of meaning is the assumed similarity between past material language and our contemporary verbal language, 'that there are some very simple rules underlying all languages'. Even if these ideas are clearly drawn from Saussurian linguistics and structuralist theory at large, they are also concordant with the attempts made by Schleiermacher to ground understanding in language. Each human being has a basic linguistic disposition, and this competence enables one to understand utterances by others. Even if Hodder is aware that we translate the meaning of 'the Other' into our language, he makes the *a priori* assumption that 'our language is flexible and rich enough to identify and perceive differences in the same way words are used in different contexts' (Hodder 1986: 170). Situated in a non-English linguistic context, we are not quite sure what Hodder puts into such terms as 'our language'. However, one of the many problems with this assumption is that if 'our language' were not flexible and rich enough, how could we ever be aware of it?

Conclusion: contextual archaeology and early hermeneutics

We have shown how Ian Hodder's contextual archaeology of the 1980s, an approach he himself describes as an attempt at 'filling in and extending Collingwood's account' (Hodder 1986: 119), is closely linked with early hermeneutics. Their common ground is articulated in the conception of understanding primarily as a methodological concern, that interpretation is the understanding of things 'inner' by means of their outward expression, that the aim of understanding is primarily a reproduction of an original production and could be gained through a reliving or reenactment of the forces and motivation that led to that particular manifestation. The equation of meaning and intention, context and origin, reveals further dimensions of this nostalgic project. Furthermore, the retreat to a universal mind or an objectified thought is a common solution adopted by Dilthey, Collingwood, and Hodder to the problems inherent in this project. Finally, we have pointed out that the theoretical ambiguity in Hodder's writing makes both *Reading the Past*, and some of his later works (see Hodder 1987b, 1987e, 1987f, 1987g, 1989c, 1989e, 1990a) seem bewilderingly confused between this 'historicist' position and poststructuralism.

The very term 'contextual' archaeology is redundant. After all, can approaches to understanding be anything but contextual (see Yates 1990a: 271)? The main task is rather to specify which contextual relations are central to our understanding. In Hodder's archaeology of the 1980s, 'context' is used in a deterministic and narrow sense to reduce any possible signification of an object to its immediate condition of origin. To take this approach is to ignore the dialectic between past and present embedded in past material culture itself that lies before us as present traces of a past. This dialectic between the 'no more' and the 'still' strikes the very core of archaeological epistemology, but is nevertheless ignored in most theoretical reasoning in archaeology.

Part three: contextual archaeology revisited

We now move from tracing the genealogy of Hodder's contextual archaeology to explore Gadamer's critique of early hermeneutics and his own proposals for historical understanding. Apart from judging Gadamer's work to be an important critique and corrective to the epistemological foundation of contextual archaeology (as Hodder (1991a, 1991c) recently has acknowledged), we also use it to start a discussion regarding the relevance of hermeneutics to the epistemology of archaeological understanding and to the present theoretical debate in archaeology more generally. This also moves the debate on analogy and inference in archaeology beyond its present methodological level.

The hermeneutics of Hans–Georg Gadamer

The philosophy of Martin Heidegger in *Being and Time* (1962) marks a turning point in philosophical hermeneutics. Understanding is no longer to be a textual concern or to be conceived as a method for securing a sympathetic identification with a distant reality. It is to be primarily a concern with life itself. Rather than being outside reality, a subject vs. an object, understanding is a way of being in the world. In *Truth and Method* (1975), Hans-Georg Gadamer developed the dense thinking of Heidegger into a more accessible interpretation. Like earlier hermeneuticians, Gadamer takes the art of interpretation of texts as his starting point, and he conceives of it as a model for the experience of life itself (Lindseth 1981: 9). According to Gadamer, his hermeneutics is an attempt

> [to] clarify the conditions in which understanding takes place. But these conditions are not of the nature of a 'procedure' or a method, which the interpreter must of himself bring to bear on the text, but rather they must be given.
>
> (Gadamer 1975: 263)

For Romantic hermeneuticians, hermeneutics was considered as a set of necessary methodological tools for overcoming the historical distance between the interpreter and the historical phenomenon. This distance in time, they argued, causes misunderstanding due to the changes in the meanings of words, world views, and modes of perception. Thus, the meaning of a text or an object must be recovered by a disciplined reconstruction of the historical situation or life context in which it originated (Gadamer 1977: 7; Linge 1977: xiii). 'Starting from the documents, artifacts, action and so on that are the content of the historical world, the task of understanding is to recover the original life-world they betoken and to understand the other person (the author or historical agent) as he understood himself' (Linge 1977: xiii–xiv).

The context of the interpreter affects the interpretation in a negative way by being a source of prejudices and distortions. Thus the achievement of a correct interpretation depends on the interpreter's ability to free himself or herself from prejudices. Despite the assertion made by early hermeneuticans such as Schleiermacher and Dilthey about the finitude and historicity of humans, they 'continue to pay homage to the Cartesian and Enlightenment ideal of the autonomous subject who successfully extricates himself from the immediate entanglement of history and the prejudices that come with that entanglement' (Linge 1977: xiv). This, what Linge (1977: xiv) calls 'the methodological alienation of the knower from his own historicity', is precisely the focus of Gadamer's criticism of early hermeneutics. Following Heidegger in asserting our own historicity as an ontological (rather than methodological) 'existential', Gadamer conceives the interpreter's own historical location and the distance separating him or her from his or her object as a productive precondition of understanding:

> Time is no longer a gulf to be bridged, because it separates, but it is actually the supportive ground of process in which the present is rooted. Hence temporal distance is not something that must be overcome. This was rather, the naïve assumption of historicism, namely that we must set ourselves within the spirit of the age, and think with its ideas and its thoughts, not with our own, and thus advance towards historical objectivity. In fact the important thing is to recognise the distance in time as a positive and productive possibility of understanding. It is not a yawning abyss, but is filled with the continuity of custom and tradition, in the light of which all that is handed down presents itself to us.
>
> (Gadamer 1975: 264–265)

One of the most controversial points in Gadamer's philosophy is the concept of prejudice. The negative connotation that is attached to this concept today is, he claims, a product of Enlightenment thinking, 'the prejudice against prejudice itself' (Gadamer 1975: 240). Originally, it meant a prejudgement, a judgement given before all elements determining a situation are investigated. Gadamer sees prejudices as the very condition for experience and understanding; they are 'biases to our openness to the world. They are simple conditions whereby we experience something – whereby what we encounter says something to us' (Gadamer 1977: 9). In this sense, prejudices are the precondition for any experience of the past and the present, and should be regarded as productive rather than repressive.

The past plays an essential role in Gadamer's concept of understanding, a role he felt was ignored by philosophers before Heidegger. The role of the past is not only to supply the material or events that constitute the object of our interpretation: 'As prejudice and tradition, the past also defines the ground the interpreter himself occupies when he understands' (Linge 1977: xv). Understanding the past is not simply reconstruction, an attempt to grasp the past in itself; it is rather a mediation or translation of past meaning into the present through which the past already functions in and shapes the interpreter's present horizon (Linge 1977: xiv–xvii). Each interpreter encounters the past with a particular set of prejudices. Thus understanding and interpretation are not an historical quality, but an effect of history: 'Understanding is essentially an effective-historical relation' (Gadamer 1975: 267).

When we as archaeologists try to understand a historical phenomenon, we are already subject to the effects of history, including the history of research and our personal biographies. These determine in advance both what seems to be worth inquiring about and the objects of investigation. Thus, history is not just something we interpret as an object divorced from us, but is actively involved itself in shaping this understanding. This ignorance of the effect of history and tradition in our own

111

encounter with the past is a main failure of the historical objectivism advocated by archaeologists of the processual school (e.g., Binford 1983b, 1987; Schiffer 1988):

> Historical objectivism, in appealing to its critical method, conceals the involvement of the historical consciousness itself in effective-history. By the method of its fundamental criticism it does away with the arbitrariness of cosy-recreations of the past, but it preserves its good conscience by failing to recognise those pre-suppositions . . . that govern its own approach to understanding.
>
> (Gadamer 1975: 268)

Effective-historical consciousness does not imply a final state of self-knowledge. As historical beings, we are always 'on the way' to self-knowledge that can be achieved only in the dialectical interplay with the 'other' (Bernstein 1983: 143). Thus, for Gadamer, the interpreter's present situation loses its privileged position and 'becomes instead a fluid and relative moment in the life of effective history' (Linge 1977: xix).

The reflexivity of this position is explicated by use of the concepts of 'horizon' and 'fusion of *horizons*'. Gadamer (1975: 269) defines a horizon as 'the range of possibilities that can be seen from a particular vantage point'. Living within a horizon does not imply a closed and limited existence. Rather, a horizon is essentially open, enabling us to look beyond it, not to look away from it, but to see it better within a larger perspective. Just as the individual does not exist only in himself or herself, but always is involved with others, the closed horizon of a time period or culture is a false abstraction, too. As such, a horizon is 'something into which we move and that moves with us' (Gadamer 1975: 271). In other words, when a historical conscious person places himself or herself in a historical situation this does not imply that he or she moves out of his or her own horizon. It is rather a question of constructing a comprehensive horizon which the limited horizons of the text and the interpreter fuse:

> There is no more an isolated horizon of the present than there are historical horizons. Understanding, rather, is always the fusion of these horizons which we imagine to exist by themselves . . . . In a tradition this process of fusion is continually going on, for there old and new continually grow together to make something of living value, without either being explicitly distinguished from the other.
>
> (Gadamer 1975: 273)

Returning to the problem of the proper interpretation of the meaning of a historical text, we briefly recapitulate that for the early hermeneuticians, this task was identified with grasping the subjective act of authorial intention. Understanding is a transaction between the creative consciousness of the author and the receptive or reconstructive consciousness of the interpreter (Linge 1977: xxiv). Against this, Gadamer holds that the meaning of a text cannot be identified with a preconceived intention. A received text gains meaning, becomes understandable, only when presented and applied in new historical contexts. People in every historical period have to interpret a text in their own way: 'The meaning of a text surpasses its author not occasionally, but always. Thus understanding is not a reproductive procedure, but rather always also a productive one' (Gadamer 1975: 280). The text outlives both the author and the various interpreters, and none of them has any privileged 'last word'.

Gadamer has produced an essential critique of the early hermeneutic project, a criticism that also reveals some of the epistemological limitations (as well as methodological alienations) of Hodder's contextual archaeology. However, Gadamer's own hermeneutics have been subject to serious criticism, so we end this section by posing some of the critical questions.

One critical point is Gadamer's notion of fusion of horizons: How can one know when a fusion of horizons take place? In other words, how do we distinguish such a fusion from a mere projection of our own worldview on an alien culture? Further problems are related to his notion of authority as a norm for distinguishing between 'legitimate' and 'illegitimate' prejudices (Warnke 1988: 107–138). This authority is claimed to be both personal ('that the other is superior to oneself in the judgement and insight and that for this reason his judgement . . . has precedence over one's own . . .. It rests on the recognition that others have better understanding' [Gadamer 1975: 248]) and transpersonal ('That which has been sanctioned by tradition and custom has an authority that is nameless, and . . . has a justification that is outside the arguments of reason' [Gadamer 1975: 249]). It is obvious that this part of Gadamer's philosophy runs into serious difficulties when confronted with the question of the role of power and ideology in sustaining and legitimating tradition (cf. Habermas 1986).

Paradoxically, Hodder's latest major work, *The Domestication of Europe* (1990a), can be used to exemplify this criticism against Gadamer. In contrast to his earlier work, Hodder now appeals to an effective historical consciousness that seems inspired by Gadamer's work (even if he does not refer to Gadamer). He does this by claiming that we think about the past through structures determined by the past itself:

> At the same time as contextualizing past events, I have been trying to make those past events probable and plausible to us in the 'present'. In doing so I have tried to erode the idea of a separate present and have focused on the degree to which our thoughts and actions are *created through the past* . . . I have tried . . . to show that *those interpretations are themselves logically constructed over the long term.*
>
> (Hodder 1990a: 279; emphasis added)

Hodder maintains that the interpretation he derives at is at least partially constructed by European (pre)history itself in a continuity extending back not only to the Neolithic period, but even to Lower Paleolithic time (Hodder 1990a: 283–293). Partially he legitimizes this view by using old IndoEuropean concepts such as *domus*, *foris*, and *agrios*. These concepts, he suggests, helps him to think of the European past in its own terms (Hodder 1990a: 45–46, 130, 275). As an unintended(?) effect, his interpretations achieve an authority that is nameless; they are, to borrow a Gadamerian term 'sanctioned by tradition'.

Hodder then (re?)writes a metahistory in which the essence is that the desire to control and domesticate a dangerous wilderness determined the course of European prehistory. These desires were constructed as early as in the Lower Paleolithic period when

> the objectification of a culture-nature distinction within stone tools allowed the creation of a symbolic order in which the 'wild' could be constructed in relation to 'cultural.' From then on, basic emotions, fears, and desires were increasingly played upon in order to generate a social order.
>
> (Hodder 1990a: 288; see also Hodder 1990a: 293)

However, the critical question to be posed is: From where do Hodder's thoughts about wild and domesticated derive? Hodder never discusses from which cultural and historical period he has learned to think in terms like 'joy of life', 'comfort of the home', or 'the danger of the wild' (see Hodder 1990a: 28–29). However, *we* have a suspicion that he might have learned this from the effective history of his own English society as it developed since the seventeenth century, and from late Western history at large. From this perspective Hodder's fears and emotions toward the wild are both 'natural' and 'historical'.

Thus, Lentricchia's critical comments on Gadamer's notion of the authority of tradition may even be valid for Hodder's account of the European past:

> The long temporal unity of historical consciousness, the very basis of shared tradition and the bond of a community of meaning: are these determinations of established power and the effects of massive repression?
>
> (Lentricchia 1983: 154)

The lack of a notion of power is clearly a serious limitation of Gadamer's philosophy. Moreover, the danger that his problematic notion of authority may be transposed into moral legitimation of repressive politics poses questions that no serious students of his work can avoid. On the other hand, we oppose those who use these limitations in Gadamer's work as a reason for dismissing the rest of his philosophy.

Conclusion

The (post-)positivist debate in Western universities during the 1970s involved challenges of many of the theoretical foundations of most human and social sciences. However, while the positivistic conception of historical and social causality was questioned and more or less rejected by most sociologists, social anthropologists, and historians, archaeologists were more than ever attracted by the explanatory and scientific framework supplied by the natural sciences (Kohl 1981). Not until the 1970s was the naturalism associated with the new archaeology challenged by postprocessual archaeologists. So far though, no *verstehen* approach has been proposed in archaeology comparable to that of Winch (1963) in sociology and Geertz (1983b) in anthropology. One reason might be that while sociology and anthropology are highly informed philosophically, archaeologists seem to be unfamiliar with much of the philosophical debate outside that of the logical-empiricist conception of the natural sciences to which their scientific aspirations have been tied.

We have given a brief introduction to hermeneutic philosophy to situate the contextual archaeology of Ian Hodder within this tradition. Although the theoretical foundations of his archaeology are mixed and can be located in philosophical positions as varied as Marxism, structuralism, and post-structuralism, his interpretative approach during the 1980s was closely related to that of early hermeneuticians such as Schleiermacher, Droysen, and Dilthey. As we have shown, the English historian and philosopher R. G. Collingwood constitutes Hodder's link to this philosophical tradition (see Hodder 1991c).

The historicism of Hodder's approach derives from his conception of understanding as primarily a reproduction of an original production, a creation and reliving of the inner forces and motivations of past events. This position contains both an idealism and an objectivism. The claim that Hodder's archaeology is *idealist* is a well-known characterization and common to most critics and commentators (e.g., Barrett 1987b; Binford 1987; Trigger 1989b). This is due to his setting the task of getting inside or reliving the past event ('It is only when we make assumptions about the subjective meaning in the minds of people long dead that we can begin to do archaeology' [Hodder 1986: 79]). However, what is generally overlooked is that this approach contains simultaneously an *objectivism*. It implies that an archaeologist can transcend his or her own historical and cultural location to attain a privileged vantage point outside the constraints of histories and cultures, 'where the subjectivity of other objects can be comprehended without imposing our own "objective" subjectivities' (Hodder 1986: 170). This attempt to make oneself contemporary with the 'total' history is in fact attainable only if one has an 'objective mind' (Hodder 1986: 124, 154, 170).

To conclude, we return to the problem with which we began this paper: What is the relevance of hermeneutic philosophy to archaeology?

First, archaeological interpretation, as any other interpretation, always takes place from the vantage point of the present. As Dilthey foresaw, such understanding is primarily a 'category of life'. Instead of disregarding the present as the appropriate context for understanding the past, we should acknowledge it as the very precondition for making this understanding possible. The failing of Romantic hermeneuticians was that they dismissed this temporal distanciation by making the subjective intentionality of the author the ultimate standard of valid interpretation. We have identified a similar shortcoming in the most elaborated archaeological interpretative theory, the contextual archaeology of Ian Hodder. The failure of his theory as it was advocated during the 1980s derived from his emphasis on limited horizons, where priority is given to the past horizon in which the past material text once originated (even if this priority is sometimes collapsed into the horizon of the present reader).

Despite its open reflexivity, a main argument against Hodder's contextual archaeology is that it reflects his disregard for the fact that understanding is essentially dialectical, that 'a new concretization of meaning . . . is born of the interplay that goes on continually between the past and the present' (Linge 1977: xxvi). Rather than regarding past and present horizons as immovable bedrocks, we should explore their dialectical relation, in which understanding the otherness of the past is more like dialectic than observation. However, this dialectical relation should not be confused with a simplistic notion of question and answer, where intentionality or any other 'determining structures' (Wylie 1989d) can be used to discover a final meaning. This dialectic is rather a never-ending process where new meanings are continuously produced as the past text enters new historical contexts. In this way, and keeping parts of Gadamer's hermeneutics at a distance, we think that a notion of changing, intersecting, and reacting horizons is more useful than a idealistic notion of 'fusion of horizons'.

Second, this dialectic character of archaeological understanding tells us that we can also learn something about ourselves from studying the past. Trying to elicit what is unique to this Otherness (in the sense of discovering its difference, even its incommensurability), we can come to a sensitive and critical understanding of our own biases and prejudices. Discovering our own incapacity to understand prehistoric features within a frame of instrumental reason may be a good lesson for us. We may learn that our own utilitarian conception of the world is not a 'natural' feature of humanity, but a culturally and historically situated phenomena. Living in a world heavily burdened by the cultural hegemony of our own Western societies, this knowledge is undoubtedly valuable. On this point we totally agree with some of the views proposed recently by Hodder (Hodder 1990b: 15). However, in this understanding we must avoid the 'two extremes' referred to by Bernstein:

> The extreme of a type of romantism that assumes that what is alien is necessarily superior, and the ethnocentrism of thinking that there is nothing more to the world than lies within our own 'philosophy' – that is, our own well-entrenched beliefs, attitudes, standards, methods and procedures.
>
> (Bernstein 1983: 91)

Our third conclusion is that hermeneutics, and especially Gadamer's philosophy, can contribute to some of the most central theoretical issues in contemporary archaeology because it points to the situated character of historical, social scientific, and even natural scientific understanding. By illuminating the inadequacy of the idea that objectivity can be obtained via a restricted set of simplistic methods (e.g., Binford 1983b: 47–49), it makes any claim of 'objective' and 'value-free' conceptions of the past or of the scientific process impossible. Archaeology itself, its objectives, observations, criteria for evaluation of data, etc., is a product of effective history that refers to tradition, semantic fields, and prejudices. However, this effective historical consciousness has to do with ontology. It concerns more *how* we understand than *what* we understand. Thus, it cannot be used as a method for a proper understanding of the past as Hodder is proposing in some of his latest work (Hodder 1990a, 1991a, 1991c).

Finally, our general conclusion is that archaeologists can learn something from the debate that began in Continental philosophy more than 200 years ago. Such knowledge will help us avoid some theoretical pitfalls, and to develop more fruitful approaches to archaeological interpretation than they have done so far. To obtain this knowledge will need hard work, and one cannot expect to accomplish it within the deadline of one's next paper or book. However, it will pay out in the long run.

Postscript

All publishing involves a certain time lag between submittal and appearance. Sometimes this creates problems. After your paper is submitted to a journal, something else that should have been considered is published. This is annoying and frustrating, but nevertheless an inevitable part of communication through the publishing system. After this paper was submitted to *American Antiquity*, Hodder published two papers where he, for the first time, deals explicitly with hermeneutics and Gadamer's philosophy. Having declared himself as a 'child of Collingwood' in 1987 (Hodder 1987e: 353), Hodder (1991a: 7) now dismisses Collingwood's view as 'outdated' – in that it 'fails sufficiently to examine the relationship between past and present' (Hodder 1991c: 34). He also finds this to be a weakness of his own account (Hodder 1991c: 34).

Due to the above-mentioned circumstances we have not been able to adequately include Hodder's 'new' approach in our discussion. We still find our paper worth publishing for two reasons: First, Hodder's work during the 1980s is a real product that still has an important impact on theoretical discussions in archaeology. Second, although we regard his latest contributions as a positive turn, we still find his account of hermeneutics insufficient (Hodder 1991a: 1–11, 1991c: 33–34). This even counts for his (self-)criticism of Collingwood which is superficial (Hodder 1991c: 34). Even if we do not intend to start a new discussion here, we shall end this added section by spelling out some of our disagreements with Hodder's (new) account of hermeneutics.

Hodder discovers hermeneutics in a search for a proper postprocessual *method* (Hodder 1991a: 1–12). Thus, his account of hermeneutics and the philosophy of Gadamer is placed in a section titled 'some comments on method' (Hodder 1991c: 33). In his fight against a dangerous and reactionary relativism, Hodder claims 'a guarded objectivity of the past' (Hodder 1991a: 10) and that 'the organized material has an independence' (Hodder 1991a: 12). However, since the 'objectivity' of the data is hidden, in the sense that 'things are not what they seem' (Hodder 1990a: 307), Hodder needs some transformation rules, e.g., a method. His advocacy of hermeneutics therefore boils down to a quest for a new method that can secure a proper interpretation of the past. However, while early hermeneutics clearly was concordant with this aim, the late hermeneutics of Heidegger, Gadamer, and Ricoeur clearly is not:

> The hermeneutics developed here is not, therefore, a methodology of the human sciences, but an attempt to understand what the human sciences truly are, beyond their methodological self-consciousness, and what connects them with the totality of our experience with the world.
>
> (Gadamer 1975: xii)

We would also like to state that Hodder runs into serious problems when he tries to give his notion of a 'guarded objectivity of the past' a moral justification by arguing that this 'allows subordinate groups to use the archaeological past to empower themselves through the evidential aspects of archaeology' (Hodder 1991a: 15). This moral argument for an objective past (and for a method that can ensure its proper interpretation) may seem acceptable when related to specific cases such as South Africa. Here it is possible to show unambiguously that indigenous black communities inhabited the area before the arrival of white settlers, and that an 'objective' past can serve progressive politics in the present. However, in other contexts (and we know several ones) such simplistic objectivity can be used as part of reactionary politics; e.g., as a means to repress ethnic groups arriving later to a region than the 'original' population. Thus, the political 'progressiveness' of an 'objective' past is subtle and can even prove dangerous. However, this problem illustrates the basic argument of our paper: that the interpretation of the past, the meaning we give it, and the way we receive it cannot be kept insulated from our present being in the world.

ACKNOWLEDGEMENTS

Various people have read and commented on earlier drafts of this paper. We especially express our gratitude to John Barrett, Narve Fulsås, Bryan Hood, Mark Leone, and Inger Storli. The paper has also benefited significantly from the comments of four *American Antiquity* reviewers: Ian Hodder, Richard Watson, and two others who wished to remain anonymous.

8

IS THERE AN
ARCHAEOLOGICAL RECORD?*

LINDA E. PATRIK

> It has become clear that every archaeologist has thoughtfully or unthinkingly
> chosen to use concepts of a certain kind.
>
> (David L. Clarke 1973a)

Archaeology is coming of age as a rigorous science in its methods and explicit
commitment to the testing of results and hypotheses. Important theoretical work
in archaeological epistemology has also been undertaken that clarifies archaeological
inference and the utility of various strategies and analytic models. There are, however,
certain problems in archaeology that fall under David Clarke's heading of archaeological metaphysics: 'Archaeological metaphysics is the study and evaluation of the
most general categories and concepts within which archaeologists think; a task long
overdue' (Clarke 1973a: 12–13).

These problems are perhaps more hidden than problems of methodology, inference,
and analysis – and probably more pervasive – because these metaphysical problems
do not plague ordinary archaeological practice, and thus can be ignored in the day-
to-day, hard work of archaeology. Instead, these metaphysical problems are the burden
of archaeological theory; they concern basic concepts and basic assumptions used
by archaeologists when they conceptualize the entire *Gestalt* of their field, and how
their work connects with reality.

Some of these metaphysical problems are packed into the very language of
archaeology in a way that is difficult to extricate without unduly alarming those
archaeologists, who are even more partial to the language of archaeology than to
its theories. The phrase *archaeological record* is certainly one of these favorites in
archaeological language, but it is not without its problems. First among them is
ambiguity: the concept of the archaeological record is used by different archaeologists
in different ways, and thus lacks rigor as a theoretical concept within the discipline
as a whole. A second set of problems concerns the concept's status as a model of
archaeological evidence: as a model, it brings metaphysical implications to

---

*First published in M. Schiffer (ed.) (1985), *Advances in Archaeological Method and Theory*, 8, New
York: Academic Press, pp. 27–62.

archaeological theory and suggests strategies for drawing inferences on the basis of archaeological evidence. In the following pages, some of the metaphysical implications of the concept of the archaeological record are outlined to show that there are actually two different models of archaeological evidence as a record, each with its own conceptual and methodological implications.

The reason for focusing on the concept of the archaeological record is to clarify some of the issues in the current debate between 'New' Archaeologists and structural or contextual archaeologists (Hodder 1982a; Leone 1982a, 1982b). This debate concerns basic metaphysical assumptions made by archaeologists about their evidence, as much as it concerns different methodological approaches to this evidence. Looking closer at this debate, one discovers that even though both sides conceive of archaeological evidence as 'the archaeological record', they mean radically different things by the concept: New Archaeologists conceive of the archaeological record along the lines of a fossil record, but the structural archaeologists conceive of the archaeological record along the lines of a text, that is, a record composed of material symbols. Behind their different conceptions of the archaeological record is their more fundamental disagreement about the formation processes that have produced the record, especially those processes involving human behavior: new archaeologists emphasize adaptation and cross-cultural laws, whereas the structural archaeologists emphasize social action and culturally specific rules by which meaning is encoded in symbols. These basic differences are reflected in two distinct models of the archaeological record, as the following pages show.

What is the archaeological record?

The archaeological record is an insufficiently defined, catch-all concept, that postulates a unified and practically inexhaustible reservoir of archaeological evidence. The concept is used by archaeologists as a model for their evidence, because it implies something about this evidence that is not directly observable – namely, that the evidence records something. What archaeological evidence records and even that it records are not observable facts; the former is inferred from the evidence, the latter presumed as a basic hypothesis for the purpose of inference. The question is, however, do all archaeologists construct the same model of their evidence when they call it the 'archaeological record'?

Many archaeologists speak with confidence about doing something to or with the archaeological record. But what they do varies from archaeologist to archaeologist: for example, applying scales to it (Binford 1968: 25); giving meaning to it (Binford 1982a: 129); extracting, obtaining, or eliciting information from it (Watson et al. 1971: 25, 112); testing hypotheses against it (Renfrew 1972: 18, 44); and making observations on it (Schiffer 1976: 17). Most of these 'treatments' suggest that the archaeological record is objective and accessible. Other archaeologists speak of it, perhaps not with less confidence, but with the conviction that it is malleable by the present (Leone 1973: 131, Leone 1981a). Leone (1982b: 751), for example, warns that the archaeological record can be misunderstood because of subjective biases held by archaeologists. Hodder (1985) emphasizes how meaning is given to the archaeological record in terms of current cultural paradigms.

These same archaeologists, along with a number of others, also speak knowingly about what is in the archaeological record. Here is just a short list: there are 'differences and similarities in the archaeological record', sometimes called 'variability in the archaeological record' (Binford 1968: 26, 27); 'past human behavior as it is preserved in the archeological record' (Watson et al. 1971: 161); 'materials . . . – artifacts, features, residues – [that] are no longer participating in a behavioral system' (Schiffer 1976:27–28); 'ethnic groups . . . "hidden", in the archaeological record'(Hodder 1982b: 187); 'the idea of the individual (Leone 1982b: 755); as well as such concrete contents as 'battered pieces of stone, lumps of corroded metal, fragments of indestructible pottery, shapeless banks of earth and amorphous hollows in the ground – axe-heads without handles, whorls without spindles, hinges without doors and unfurnished rooms' (Childe 1956a: 12).

A further complication is that archaeologists refer to different things, or different stages of archaeological evidence (by my count, at least five), when they use the phrase, archaeological record. These are usually referred to collectively as the archaeological record, but sometimes a single thing or one member of a population is referred to individually as an archaeological record. These five things or populations are (1) what exists prior to deposits as a receptacle for them (i.e., the ground), (2) material deposits, (3) material remains, (4) archaeological samples, and (5) archaeological reports.

1. The archaeological record is a kind of preexisting receptacle for material deposits:

> *Predispositional and depositional theory* – covers the nature of the relationships between specified hominid activities, social patterns, and environmental factors, one with another and with the sample and traces which were at the time deposited in the archaeological record . . .
>
> (Clarke 1973a: 16)

2. Material deposits, collectively, comprise the archaeological record:

> The loss, breakage, and abandonment of implements and facilities at different locations, where groups of variable structure performed different tasks, leaves a 'fossil' record of the actual operation of an extinct society.
>
> (Binford 1964: 425)

3. Material remains, collectively or singly, comprise the archaeological record:

> the durable objects constituting the archaeological record – pottery, metal, obsidian, emery – offer only a small part of the possible range of commodities traded. Much evidence for early trade has perished . . . slaves, wine, wood, hides, opium, lichens even . . . make up a considerable repertoire of traded materials which are only rarely recorded archaeologically. The range and volume of trade could thus have been far greater than the record now documents.
>
> (Renfrew 1972: 441)

> Although the humans themselves are long dead, their patterned behavior can be investigated by the hypothetico-deductive method of science because archaeological remains and their spatial interrelationships are empirically observable records of that patterning.
>
> (Watson et al. 1971: 22)

4. Archaeological samples, collectively, comprise the archaeological record:

> The aim of this book is therefore to explain how archaeologists order their data to form a record and how they may try to interpret them as concrete embodiments of thoughts.
>
> (Childe 1956a: 1)

> In order to achieve this representative assessment [of the range of surviving archaeological traces] it is first necessary to appreciate the factors which cause variability in cultural systems (e.g., land use potential), and in the archaeological record itself (e.g., selective recovery by field-workers).
>
> (Cherry et al. 1978: 11)

5. Archaeological reports constitute archaeological records:

> [I]s not the archaeologist's most urgent task the actual research into the ground for new evidence, carried out with all necessary precautions and the most modern techniques, so that no data escape his scrutiny? It is an equally important task to re-evaluate, in highly critical mood, the results of the most notable excavations made in the past. This is the only short route towards providing a larger number of archaeological records of dependable value.
>
> (de Laet 1957: 81)

Considering the variety of such statements about the archaeological record, it seems that archaeologists are familiar with what the archaeological record is – familiar enough to know what methods to apply to it and what kinds of data can be expected from it. But at the same time, this wide variety of statements suggests that in the discipline as a whole, there is no working consensus on what the concept really means, and no explicit definition of it as a theoretical concept. The concept of the archaeological record is certainly one of the most basic concepts used by archaeologists; it is not only used frequently in theoretical writings, but is also taught to, and taken for granted by, students of archaeology as part of their enculturation in the discipline. But the widespread acceptance and use of the concept should not be grounds for leaving it unexamined. On the contrary, the widespread use of the concept in such a variety of ways is a clear symptom that the concept is in need of philosophical examination. As David Clarke remarked, 'the more fundamental the metaphysical controlling model, the less we are *normally* inclined to rethink it' (Clarke 1973a: 14; original emphasis).

The archaeological record as a scientific model

From a Kuhnian perspective, the concept of the archaeological record can be viewed as part of archaeology's disciplinary matrix (Kuhn 1970: 184, 1977: 297). Such a matrix includes a variety of cognitive, methodological, and evaluative elements, the most important being the symbolic generalizations, models, and exemplars that are the common possession of the community of specialists comprising the discipline. It would appear that the concept of the archaeological record is part of such a disciplinary matrix because it expresses the shared commitment of archaeologists to a model of archaeological evidence, namely, the model of a record. According to Kuhn:

> Models . . . are what provide the group with preferred analogies or, when deeply held, with an ontology. At one extreme they are heuristic: the electric circuit may fruitfully be regarded as a steady state hydrodynamic system; or a gas behaves like a collection of microscopic billiard balls in random notion. At the other, they are the objects of metaphysical commitment: the heat of a body *is* the kinetic energy of its constituent particles, or, more obviously metaphysical, all perceptible phenomena are due to the motion and interaction of qualitatively neutral atoms in the void.
>
> (Kuhn 1977: 297; original emphasis)

Whether the concept of the archaeological record is a metaphysical or heuristic model, it functions by drawing archaeological evidence into a comparison with other kinds of records. It is beyond the scope of this essay to examine the roles of analogies and models in science, especially because this topic has received extensive treatment by philosophers of science and archaeological theorists (e.g., Black 1962; Clarke 1972a; Hesse 1966; Salmon 1982a, 1982b). But a few points can be drawn from these discussions to indicate some of the possible theoretical and methodological problems raised by the concept of the archaeological record in its function as a model.

According to these discussions, a model does not simply compare two phenomena, one to the other, but relates these phenomena in a more complex way that brings the different systems of ideas associated with each phenomenon (e.g., the system of ideas about sound and the system of ideas about waves) into a mutual interaction (Black 1962). The result of this interaction is that any system of ideas comprising a scientific theory will be pervasively altered by the introduction of a new model or by radical change of the prevailing model (Black 1962: 25, 219). Now when a model is rigorously defined and applied, it is tied into a theory so that the theory's logical consistency, explanatory force and predictive capacity are preserved and actually furthered by the model. But because a scientific model is so closely woven into the theory's entire system of ideas, if that model is flawed, ambiguous, or unclear, it can afflict the entire theory with its 'disease' and weaken the theory's overall cogency. Thus it is important to analyze the model of the archaeological record for its wider metaphysical implications for archaeological theory. This is especially crucial if there happen to be two models, each embedded in a different theory. For without such analysis, the metaphysical implications of the two models may easily be confused, and their corresponding theories hopelessly tangled.

A second point concerns the methodological applications of models. When scientific models assimilate one phenomenon (e.g., sound) to another phenomenon (e.g., waves), they do not simply express the known similarities between the two phenomena, that is, the positive analogies. Instead, they also include what the philosopher of science, Hesse, calls 'neutral analogies' – namely, possible but yet unknown or untested similarities. It is Hesse's view that one of the greatest advantages of using models in science is the promise that the neutral analogies of models hold for making new kinds of predictions (Hesse 1966: 8). Thus, depending upon exactly what the model of the archaeological record implies for archaeological evidence, it may include neutral analogies that could open up new areas for future research. If, however, there are two distinct models of the archaeological record, different avenues for research might be projected by the models. Without a careful analysis of what each model means for archaeological inference and research, proponents of the two models may be headed off in different directions without knowing why, or the same archaeologist may end up bounding first in one direction, then the other, like a ping-pong ball.

For these reasons, the following section undertakes a philosophical analysis of the concept of the archaeological record and discovers that the model, as it is currently used by archaeologists, actually comprises two models – the physical model and the textual model. Consequently, the concept of the archaeological record brings two distinct sets of metaphysical and methodological implications to archaeology, corresponding to the current split in archaeological theory between New Archaeology and structural, or contextual, archaeology.

The physical and textual models of the archaeological record

Although the dictionary definitions of *record* include meanings that range from document to Olympic record, from phonograph record to court record, there are two meanings that seem more appropriate for archaeological evidence. One of these definitions of record would draw the archaeological record into a comparison with static, physical things that are the causal effects of what they record. The other meaning would compare the archaeological record to a text, comprised of material symbols that signify what they record.

Examples of the first meaning of *record* are fossil records. They record past animals and plants because of physical processes that transform organic bodies into static, patterned physical marks in rocks; these marks are the physical effects of the original bodies and of other natural processes (Shipman 1981). In the case of fossil records, the recording connection between the record and what it records is a strict causal connection, maintained in a physical medium. Given sufficient knowledge of the laws governing this causal connection, the original organic body can be inferred from the fossil record. Such inferences require the uniformitarian principle, which 'might be called the first law of taphonomy and paleoecology' (Shipman 1981: 11). Finally, a physical record (e.g., a fossil record or phonograph record) is 'passive' in the sense that it records its causes by preserving the static effects of these causes; its recording occurs simply because it bears an imprint.

In contrast, the meaning of 'record' included in 'historical record' implies a far more complicated connection between the record and the event it records – a connection that involves the encoding of ideas as much as it involves the causation of marks on pages. Human authors, not physical processes, produce historical records and establish the language code by which these documents actually record past events. This is true both of records that describe events that have already occurred and of records that embody the event itself (e.g., the Declaration of Independence). Although the physical actions of the authors (e.g., how the muscles in their hands function) and the physical properties of the texts themselves are determined by causal laws (e.g., laws of human anatomy, laws of gravity determining how ink flows out of pens), this is not true of all the formation processes of historical records. Because the writing of historical records is also a matter of author's choice and cultural conventions of discourse, historical records vary from culture to culture, and from author to author: style. Kinds of evidence used, argument structure, language, and other relevant elements of historical records are not determined by cross-cultural causal laws. Moreover, an historical record does not simply bear a physical imprint, but it comprises a body of signs that encode ideas and information about past events. In a certain sense, historical records are 'active', because they actively communicate messages and information that may transform the reader's ideas or behavior: they may even be used as part of an educational or political strategy to shape social structures. A final feature that distinguishes historical records from physical records is that textual records may lie, exaggerate, or mask the truth, either through deliberate or unconscious choice on the part of the author.

These two different definitions of *record* are used by the disciplinary neighbors to archaeology, paleontology and history, for their own basic evidence. But this is not surprising because paleontology initially derived its concept of the fossil record from the metaphor of an historical record: the fossil record is like a book that holds in its strata, as a book holds in its pages, the story of the earth, ancient organisms, and their evolution. The metaphor originated with the belief that a divine creator was responsible for the formation processes of the fossil record: just as authors produce texts, the divine creator produced the earth and creatures on it. (This general view still echoes in Cuvier's 1812 theory of divine intervention in the earth's history [Rudwick 1979: 379–383].) The gradual change in geology and paleontology to a nontextual interpretation of the fossil record involved a different theory of its formation processes (Gillispie 1959). Instead of a creator's choices, physical and biological processes were now held responsible for the formation of earth's strata and for the fossilization of the creatures captured within them; instead of being evidence of a divine plan, the patterns in the fossil record were now attributed to causal laws. Presently the fossil record is a theoretical model by which paleontological evidence is conceived as a physical record, not a textual record.

But the case is slightly different for the archaeological record. Because archaeological evidence is presumably the product of both natural processes and behavioral processes, rather than the product of either one of these alone, there is disagreement amongst archaeologists over what kind of record archaeological evidence forms: Is it more like a fossil record or an historical record? On the one hand, it is like fossils, because it comprises the enduring physical effects of past physical objects, events and residues; it is also similar in some of its formation processes. But archaeological evidence is also like historical evidence because it has been produced by human activity, and much of it has been distributed spatially through behavior that was regulated by convention. Because many of these conventions were culturally specific, they are more like rules of grammar, which guide the ordered distribution of words in sentences, than like the natural laws that determine fossilization processes of organic bodies.

In this debate, most new archaeologists follow Binford in identifying the archaeological record as a kind of fossil record: 'The loss, breakage, and abandonment of implements and facilities at different locations, where groups of variable structure performed different tasks, leaves a "fossil" record of the actual operation of an extinct society' (Binford 1964: 425). Many historical archaeologists also conceive of archaeological evidence along the lines of a fossil record, rather than an historical record. South, for example, adopts Binford's general view of the archaeological record (South 1977: xiii. 277, 296–299), as well as Binford's advice to historical archaeologists to tackle historic sites in ways that can test general hypotheses about 'the processes responsible for the formation of the archaeological record' (Binford 1972c: 123, South 1977: 14–17). Deagan (1982) presents another belief shared by many historical archaeologists about the difference between the archaeological record and historical records. She argues that there may be inaccuracies in historical records that could be detected and even corrected by the information gained from the archaeological record because the latter is more objective (Deagan 1982: 171).

On the other side, Wylie's recent discussion of structural archaeology (Wylie 1982) suggests that the structural or contextual archaeologists are working with the possibility of treating the archaeological record as a text. Wylie also recognizes that this textual or linguistic model has important metaphysical implications concerning the formation processes of the archaeological record:

> This argument [given by Leach for the structural approach] establishes that the archaeological record is at least a potential subject for a linguistic type of analysis: that it is reasonable to attempt to disembed the underlying ideas, or at least the principles of articulation by which ideas effectively structured the materials encountered in the archaeological record. In fact, however, it establishes considerably more. It introduces the linguistic source model as, in effect, a metaphysical theory which claims to have brought a crucial and otherwise overlooked dimension of the phenomenon into view, namely, that it is meaningful in the sense that systems of meaning are instrumental in its formation.
>
> (Wylie 1982: 41)

Because of these two very different meanings of record a clearer distinction should be drawn between the two corresponding forms that the model of the archaeological record takes in theoretical archaeology: I call them the physical model (Model$_p$) and the textual model (Model$_t$) (Table 8.1). Since one function of a model is to bring out the similarities between the properties of a model and what is modelled on it, each of these models emphasizes certain properties of archaeological evidence over others. Some of the important differences between these two models have been sketched in Table 8.1, which is based on Hesse's schema for outlining the positive, negative, and neutral analogies between a model and what is modelled upon it (Hesse 1966: 57–60). These analogies are charted horizontally and marked by: + (positive), − (negative), or 0 (neutral). Certain properties of archaeological evidence that seem more debatable are indicated in parentheses, followed by a question mark.

In essence, the two models differ in how they describe the basic components of the archaeological record, how they define what is recorded, and how they construe the formation processes of the present features and spatial order of these components.

Table 8.1 Analogies packed into the two models

Model$_p$: properties of fossil records		Archaeological evidence: properties of archaeological evidence	Model$_t$: properties of historical records	
+	Physical marks	Primarily physical remains or features	−	Linguistic signs
0	Past organic bodies and traces	Past human artifacts and residues; (behaviour?)	+	Past human actions, ideas, and events with human import
+/0	Physical laws	(Correlates, c− and n− transforms? symbolic principles?)	0	Author's choice, rules of grammar, and conventions of discourse
+	Excavated and analysed	Excavated and analysed; (decoded?)	0	Decoded, read, and analysed
0	Passively bear imprint of past, living organisms	Used to draw inferences about past behaviour	0	Communicate ideas and information
0	Not deliberately deceptive	Reflects past behaviour (or can disguise it?)	0	Can lie, mask, or exaggerate the truth
+	Excavated only once; can be analysed again	Excavated only once; can be analysed again	−	Can be read and analysed again
+	Cannot be exactly duplicated	Cannot be exactly duplicated	−	There may be copies
+/0	Loss, fragmentation, diagenesis	Loss, fragmentation, disorder, intervening transformation processes; (loss of code?)	+/0	Loss, fragmentation, disorder; loss of code so that records cannot be translated

Table 8.2 summarizes these basic differences. Where the two models do not differ is in their implication that there are patterns in the archaeological record that can be accounted for by regularities in the processes forming the record. But Model$_p$ attributes these regularities to causal laws alone. Model$_t$ on the other hand, attributes many of these regularities to codes or rules that regulated human behavior, but did not determine it causally. Such rules function as grammatical rules do, guiding, but not dictating, language use. They usually form the unconscious, skeletal structure of behavior, which is fleshed out by individuals' own behavioral strategies, in the way that grammatical rules are unconsciously manipulated by an author and fleshed out by the author's chosen

words. And like grammatical rules, behavioral codes undergo change over time. Model$_t$ also allows a place for individuals' idiosyncratic actions, creativity, or protest; just as some authors break new ground (and perhaps break a few grammatical rules in the process), so, too, certain individuals produce, use, or discard material items (in Hodder's (1985) words, they 'bring things off') in unique, unpredictable ways.

Table 8.2 Basic differences between the metaphysical implications of the two models

Metaphysical implications of Model$_p$	Metaphysical implications of Model$_t$
The record consists of physical objects and features that are static effects of past causes.	The record consists of physical objects and features that are material signs or symbols of past concepts.
What is recorded are physical objects or processes.	What is recorded are human actions, ideas, and events of human importance.
The features and spatial order of the record's components are due to physical and behavioural processes that exhibit causal regularities; these regularities can be expressed as universal or probabilistic laws.	The features and spatial order of the record's signs are due to behavioural processes that exhibit creative strategies and rule-guided regularities, in addition to the causally determined processes covered by Model$_p$, the rules guiding behavioural processes can often be expressed as culturally specific conventions.

Notice in Table 8.2 that Model$_t$ does not completely exclude causal laws in accounting for the present physical composition of the archaeological record. Because signs and their spatial ordering are, in one sense, also physical effects of behavioral and physical causes (e.g., any letter on this page is a physical mark, which is the physical effect of such causes as the printing machine and my own typing behavior), all signs have a material dimension formed in accordance with causal laws. But to these causal laws Model$_t$ adds three things: (1) It attributes a special sign or symbol function to archaeological evidence, over and above any causal connection between this evidence and what it is evidence of. (2) It postulates culturally specific sets of behavioral rules as well as the more flexible behavioral strategies of individuals, by which these signs were created, ordered, used, and deposited; these rules are not, strictly speaking, causal laws, primarily because they are not invariable in time and space. (3) It attributes a 'non-passive' power to material signs: it emphasizes the creativity of (some of) the individuals who produced or used these material signs, the dynamic integration of material signs within social action, and the active transformation of social structures through human use of such signs.

The two models in the current debate

It is interesting that New Archaeologists are some of the most frequent users of the phrase, the archaeological record. In general, they are committed to Model$_p$ because it is considered necessary for the justification of archaeological inferences. Their basic argument is that laws are required in scientific inference; hence, behavioral laws, as well as natural laws, are sought in order to formulate, test, and confirm archaeological inferences in a rigorous, scientific way. (See Salmon [1982a] for a thorough discussion and critique of this general argument.) Because Model$_p$ of the archaeological record includes the implication that all archaeological evidence has been formed by processes determined by causal laws exclusively – laws of human behavior as well as of nature – Model$_p$ provides a preliminary description of archaeological evidence that coincides with the New Archaeologists' program of making the inferences based on this evidence scientific.

Model$_p$ also coincides with New Archaeology's optimism about all that can be discovered about the past through archaeological evidence (Binford 1968: 21–23). Consider Binford's famous statement, 'The formal structure of artifact assemblages together with the between element contextual relationships should and do present a systemic and understandable picture of *the total extinct* cultural system' (Binford 1962: 218–219; original emphasis).

In terms of Model$_p$, archaeological evidence is determined by invariant universal or probabilistic laws. These laws are not simple, unilinear, causal laws, but complex laws that determine systemic relations between multiple variables. Viewing archaeological evidence in this way, Binford and other New Archaeologists regard the archaeological record as 'a faithful remnant of the causal conditions operative in the past' (Binford 1981b: 200) and regard their own task as understanding those causal conditions. Although New Archaeologists generally dispute the Pompeii promise, which would cast the archaeological record as a distorted record of a cultural system stopped in time, they do at least regard the archaeological record as a static context that is causally linked to dynamic cultural systems of the past. Their hypothesis, then, is that the linkages between dynamics and statics are lawlike, and thus allow one to draw deductive inferences. Armed with this basic hypothesis and systems theory, New Archaeologists feel justified in extracting information about nonmaterial aspects of culture from the archaeological record (Binford 1968: 22). This methodological principle is related to Model$_p$'s implication that archaeological evidence, in its spatial distribution, does not merely record 'lifeless' material culture, but records past living behavior, in the way that a fossil bears the imprint of a past living organism. Thus archaeological evidence is presumed to be potentially informative about past behavior and social structures, those nonmaterial aspects that gave 'life' to past societies.

> Proponents of the new approach concentrate on the positive aspects of the archeological record by emphasizing the systematic order of the surviving remains. This order is related to pre-historic activities and events in ways the archeologist can ascertain. Thus, he can obtain from the archaeological record information on many aspects of an extinct cultural system.
>
> (Watson et al. 1971: 112)

128

Thus Model$_p$ attributes two very important features to archaeological evidence: it has been formed by law-determined processes, and it records its causes in the way that a fossil records a past living organism. These features have not been proven to be true of archaeological evidence, but are only neutral analogies of Model$_p$. They have important implications for archaeological theory and practice, but cannot be taken for granted yet.

Recently many archaeologists have criticized New Archaeology's emphasis on cross-cultural laws and its ecological functionalism. Some have even embarked upon alternative approaches, which draw upon structuralist or Marxist theories developed in the other social sciences. (See Hodder 1981: 10–11, 1982a, 1982b 1982c, 1982d, and this volume [of the original work]; Kohl 1981; Leone 1982a, 1982b; Renfrew 1982b, for some indications of the ferment amongst the critics of New Archaeology.) There are important differences between the theories of these 'postprocessual' archaeologists, such that it would be an oversimplification to say that they all have exactly the same model of archaeological evidence. But many of the structural, symbolic, or contextual archaeologists do lean towards the textual model of the archaeological record, without explicitly formulating it as their basic theoretical model of archaeological evidence.

Hodder, for example, uses the phrase, 'archaeological record', infrequently, yet he makes implicit use of Model$_t$ throughout his most recent work. Hodder may stop short of outright adoption of Model$_t$, but Hodder's theory does incorporate some of the most basic features of this model. Hodder's regard for archaeology as an historical discipline draws archaeological evidence into a comparison with historical evidence (Hodder 1982d: 4), and his criticism of cross-cultural laws of human behavior and his emphasis on specific cultural contexts can be viewed in terms of Model$_t$'s implication that the formation processes of archaeological evidence include behavior that is regulated by culturally specific rules (Hodder 1982d: 5). But clearly most important is his general discussion of material symbols, and of structures as codes or rules, because these points imply the kind of recording connection packed into Model$_t$. According to Hodder, artifacts, architectural structures, residues, graves, etc. are not merely products of people's response to their environment – they are material symbols that encode meaning. Moreover, the structures that ordered these symbols are not the observable systems, patterns, or styles, postulated by various functionalist and systems theory approaches (Hodder 1982d: 6–9); consequently, these structures might not be captured by multivariate analysis of observable traits and spatial distributions of finds. Instead, Hodder speaks of these structures as the underlying logic by which material symbols are given meaning and combined. His emphasis on ideational structures and his treatment of archaeological evidence as material symbols imply that the connection between this evidence and what it is evidence of is the signification connection of Model$_t$, not the physical recording connection of Model$_p$.

Besides Hodder, other archaeologists have recently moved towards Model$_t$, some of them explicitly recognizing their use of a more linguistic model (e.g., Glassie 1975). But because structural, symbolic, or contextual archaeology is somewhat new, the exact formulation of its model of archaeological evidence is still in the making. Most archaeologists working in this field seem to be exploring their new paradigm (Hodder

1982d: vii) rather than dictating all of its implications. But from the theoretical discussions and general direction of research taken by those who align themselves with structural archaeology, their model of archaeological evidence is shaping up along the lines of Model$_t$, not Model$_p$.

The difference in how these archaeologists conceive of archaeological evidence, as compared to New Archaeology's conception of the evidence in terms of Model$_p$, is related to the different set of theories forming the background of their thinking. Instead of drawing heavily upon the philosophy of science (e.g., Hempel, Kuhn, Popper, and Salmon), many 'postprocessual' archaeologists have been focusing on theories in anthropology that have been influenced by linguistics, for example the theories of Lévi-Strauss, Leach, Douglas, Bourdieu, and Sperber, to mention just a few. Because this theoretical background may be unfamiliar, let me sketch the textual model's roots in structuralist and semiotic theory, and then some of the model's theoretical implications for structural archaeology. After this elaboration of the textual model, the following section returns to Model$_p$, and discusses some of its implications for archaeological inference.

The textual model: its theoretical roots and its implications for archaeology

Because Model$_t$ represents archaeological evidence as a body of material symbols, the model relates archaeological evidence to semiotics, the general study of signs, and to recent theories of symbols. Peirce (1955), Saussure (1966), Barthes (1968), and Eco (1976) provide the standard works on semiotic theory; also see Hawkes (1977) for a bibliography of semiotics, and Culler (1976) for a summary of Saussure's theory. Recent theoretical works on symbols or symbolic behavior include Douglas (1970), Sperber (1975), and Bourdieu (1977); see Schwimmer (1978) for a collection of essays on symbolic anthropology. Semiotics is closely related to structuralism, which is the study of the underlying unconscious structures of ideas embodied in human language, artifacts, and activities (Lévi-Strauss 1963: 18–25, 62, 87; Piaget 1970; see Leach [1974] for a summary of Lévi-Strauss' theory; see Pettit [1975] for a critique of structuralism). These structures are held to represent the mind's most basic rules of categorization, its most elementary symbolic schemes (Leone 1982b: 742–743; Lévi-Strauss 1963: 46–51, 202–204, 206–231; Lévi-Strauss 1966; Piaget 1970: 52–73). Though related, semiotics and structuralism differ from one another slightly in that semiotics focuses on the actual products and behavior of humans, treating these as signs (e.g., Barthes 1968; Baudrillard 1968). Structuralism focuses on the mind's processes of categorization, treating sign production as a basic categorizing operation (e.g., Leach 1971: 124–136; Lévi-Strauss 1966, 1969, 1970; Miller 1982a).

Both semiotics and structuralism analyze material artifacts, rituals, gestures, images (e.g., advertising, films), and other nonlinguistic things as sign systems (Barthes 1968, 1979; Leach 1976: 10; Peirce 1955). In addition, both use analytic techniques and models that have either been drawn from linguistics, or been developed so as to be applicable to nonlinguistic as well as linguistic signs (Barthes 1968: 9–12; Lévi-Strauss 1963: 31–80, 364–365). Although this linguistic bent has been criticized recently by some of the theorists working on symbols (Bourdieu 1977; Sperber 1975), semiotics and structuralism are still generally recognized as providing the theoretical background for the analysis of symbols. Thus, anthropologists and archaeologists who have been influenced by any of these approaches tend to speak of the 'symbolism' and 'grammar' of artifacts and behaviour (Conkey 1980, 1982; Deetz 1977: 108; Douglas 1970; Glassie 1975: 17–18; Hodder 1982b; Leach 1976: 10) in the shared belief that nonlinguistic things can be (1) as symbolic of meaning as words are, and (2) as well-ordered in larger cultural systems of artifacts and behavior as words are in sentences.

The above two points are central to Model$_t$, of the archaeological record and distinguish structural, symbolic, or contextual archaeology in important ways from new archaeology. Because these points draw archaeological evidence into a comparison with linguistic signs and other symbols, they imply that archaeological evidence is not merely a body of physical effects of past causes, but is a body of signs that encode and communicate past human ideas, actions, and events. Thus Model$_t$ and Model$_p$ imply radically different views of the recording connection between archaeological evidence and past artifacts, human behavior, events, residues, etc. This difference is important for archaeological method, because it is precisely this connection that justifies drawing inferences from archaeological evidence (i.e., the record) to past artifacts, behavior, and events (i.e., what it presumably records). For Model$_p$, the recording connection is a causal connection between physical effects and their causes. For Model$_t$, the recording connection is a signification connection between material signs and the meanings they encode and communicate.

Most structuralists and semioticians argue that the signification connections between signs and their meanings cannot be reduced to causal connections, because if they were causal, they would be fixed and thus invariant in all times and places. Although they range widely in their arguments, they generally follow Saussure (1966: 65–70), one of the founders of modern semiotics, in arguing for the arbitrariness of signs (cf. Hodder 1982d: 9; Lévi-Strauss 1963: 88–96). *Arbitrary* here does not mean chaotic or lacking associative content – it means that the signification connections of signs and their meanings are 'not necessary', 'not caused naturally', 'not law determined'. For example, Leach makes use of Saussure's argument about the arbitrariness of signs in his outline of different kinds of communication, including nonlinguistic communication through behavior and artifacts (Leach 1976: 12–16). Hodder also draws upon Saussure's argument when he claims that 'The ability of material objects to have different meanings in different contexts is a common characteristic of all symbols' (Hodder 1982b: 202).

Hodder extends this argument about the arbitrariness of signs in his discussion of the evocative power of material symbols and the contextual meaning of such symbols. Because a material symbol is arbitrary in Saussure's sense, the connection between a material symbol and its meaning is not fixed by causal laws: there are no cross-cultural, psychological, or behavioral laws that determine which meaning must go with which symbol, at all times and places. Instead, there is great flexibility in how humans create, use, and interpret specific material symbols (for a similar argument about language, see Chomsky's [1959] critique of Skinner.) Hodder takes this basic point further with his argument that the connection between a material symbol and its meaning is not fixed in any one-to-one relation, even by convention. Instead, the meaning of a material symbol is 'evoked' out of the wide range of practical uses and implicit associations of the symbol, when that symbol appears in active use. Evocation is a flexible signification connection that cannot be codified in a 'dictionary' giving the meanings of material symbols. Evocation draws upon implicit meanings, it relies upon people's memories of past associations, it expands through improvisational manipulations of symbols so that there can be generation of new meaning, and it is always contextual. From this it follows that the meaning of any material symbol is ambiguous without sufficient knowledge of the implicit values and associations of the symbol, as well as knowledge of the social actions by which that material symbol is manipulated as an active instrument in a social context.

Although the signification connections of material symbols are flexible and evocative rather than fixed and formularized, the meanings of these symbols within a particular culture are recognizable and roughly consistent for the people within it. The reason is that there are rules or codes, usually implicit, that regulate the patterning of the traits and combinations of material symbols. These rules or codes are like grammatical rules, mutually accepted by members of a group and passed down between generations, so that, on the one hand, there are design traditions and accepted production methods for material symbols (Deetz 1977: 108–117; Glassie 1975), and on the other hand, there are ordered ways in which material symbols are combined with other symbols and with behavior in active use.

Semiotic theory accounts for this double patterning of material symbols by arguing that symbols, like words, are always units within larger sign systems, such that their meanings depend upon their systematic relations to other signs in these larger systems (Hodder 1982b: 212; Lévi-Strauss 1968a: 31; Saussure 1966: 111–122). There are two dimensions in which each sign can be said to exist within a larger sign system (Saussure 1966: 122–131). (1) The first is the dimension of all the possible, alternative signs available for encoding meaning; that is, the paradigmatic or associative dimension. In archaeology, this dimension comprises the available range of traits or behaviors from which a social actor chooses; this is also the dimension in which signs show analogy of form or show contrast to one another. (2) The other is the dimension of all the signs and behavior actually combined together by social actors; that is, the syntagmatic dimension. By virtue of this dimension, no bit of archaeological evidence can function effectively as a material symbol when isolated from its patterned context. Hodder provides an example of an archaeological analysis that distinguishes these two dimensions of material signs. In his study of Dutch Neolithic pottery, he charts the possible decorative motifs available to potters (Hodder 1982e: Figure 16, adapted from Van de Velde) as distinct from the actual combinations of motifs in real pots (Hodder 1982e: Figures 3, 4, 6, 9–14, 17). These two dimensions are systems in the sense that a code, or underlying set of rules, orders signs within these two dimensions (Hodder 1982d: 7).

According to an argument advanced by Hodder and other structural archaeologists, these codes or rules are not cross-cultural causal laws, nor can they be reduced to purely adaptive mechanisms, because they distinguish the cultural life of humans from the kind of life that other organisms have in the same ecological conditions (Sahlins 1976: 55–125). (This point contrasts sharply with Binford's [1962: 218] acceptance of White's [1959: 8] definition of culture as 'the extrasomatic means of adaptation for the human organism'.) And even though these rules or codes regulate the creation, manipulation, and discard of material signs, there is also great leeway in the human behaviour by which signs are made, used, and deposited. This is primarily because material signs are not simply used for adaptation within a certain environment, but are used creatively as a part of individuals' strategies for wielding, gaining, or subverting power. Bourdieu (1977) and Hodder (1982b) have both analyzed the ways in which individuals construct architectural spaces or manipulate artifacts for the purposes of negotiating their power within a group or of indicating their opposition to other groups. As Hodder (1985) puts it, 'The effective use of material symbols is thus part of the negotiation of power. It has no set lines and everything is to be played for.'

Summarizing the metaphysical implications that Model$_t$ brings to bear upon archaeological evidence: (1) The components of the archaeological record are not merely the effects of past causes, but are signs that encode and communicate certain meanings (Hodder 1982b: 186). (2) No component of the archaeological record can function as a sign in isolation from its patterned context, but each requires a contextual reading in order to be a functional and meaningful sign (Hodder 1982b: 217). (3) The patterning of material signs, both in their traits and spatial distribution, derives from three interrelated sources: culturally specific behavioral codes, which have functioned like grammatical rules; individuals' strategies for plying and fleshing out these codes; and causally determined behavioral and natural processes. These metaphysical implications may be viewed as neutral analogies of the textual model; they may prove fruitful for extending the explanatory capability of the model and for opening up new areas for archaeological research. On the other hand, these implications may prove to be too disanalogous to the features of archaeological evidence and thus be limitations of the textual model – this can only be decided by archaeologists themselves after more theoretical and practical work with Model$_t$.

Recall that two basic metaphysical implications of Model$_p$ were that the archaeological record has been formed by law-determined processes, and that it records its causes in the way that a fossil records a past living organism, that is, through a physical recording connection. These implications contrast with the above three implications of Model$_t$, in ways that are important for the methodological applications of the two models. For the two models do not merely represent archaeological evidence differently; they also imply different principles for archaeological inference based upon this evidence. In the following sections, discussion focuses on how the two models imply different principles and raise different problems for archaeological inference.

The physical model and its implications for archaeological inference

Hand-in-hand with New Archaeology's adoption of Model$_p$, has been their emphasis on the Hempelian deductive-nomological model of inference (Binford 1968; Fritz and Plog 1970; Salmon 1977; Watson et al. 1971). New Archaeology's approach to archaeological inference includes the demand for laws in the premises of archaeological arguments, and Model$_p$ provides the theoretical service of representing all archaeological evidence as collectively comprising a physical record, which was formed by processes determined by causal laws. With the conception of archaeological evidence presented by Model$_p$, a certain optimism about what can be inferred from the archaeological record arises, because everything in the record is not only modeled as predictable by the Hempelian model of inference, given the proper hypotheses, but is also modeled as recording the past in a strict, lawlike way.

If archaeology relied on the Hempelian model of inference alone, it would not be justified in deductively inferring the past causes of the record, because you cannot deduce a cause from an effect, even on the basis of knowledge of the causal laws determining the formation of the effect. This would be the fallacy of affirming the consequent, that is, the fallacy of deducing p from the two statements, 'If p, then q' and 'q'. (An instance of this fallacy is, 'If an animal is pregnant, then it is female. This animal is female. Hence, it is pregnant.') Philosophers and theoretical archaeologists have readily acknowledged the fallacy as a pitfall to be avoided, yet have also sometimes discovered that it has not always been avoided by practicing archaeologists (Morgan 1973: 270; Stanislawski 1978: 29).

But when $Model_p$ is used for all archaeological evidence a way around this fallacy opens up, because the model makes archaeological inference from q to p justifiable. It works this way. The hypothetico-deductive method of verification is explicitly used in New Archaeology. In terms of this method, any evidence in the record would be an explanandum (i.e., an item to be explained). It would be deducible or predictable from (true) premises stating established or hypothetical causal laws that determined the formation processes of the record, and hypothetical premises stating what the past materials and events were that initiated these formation processes (i.e., statements of general laws and of antecedent conditions are the explananas, that is, the items that do the explaining). If archaeological excavation and analysis turn up evidence that conforms to such predictions, the hypothetical premises stating laws and those stating the conditions of past materials and events again support (Salmon 1975, 1976; Watson 1976: 61); they are not actually verified, but they are at least tested in this way and strengthened in their hypothetical possibility.

What $Model_p$ does is add a further hypothesis that facilitates archaeological inference: the model implies that there is not merely a causal connection between archaeological evidence and past materials and events, but a physical recording connection. A recording connection of the kind implied by $Model_p$ involves a tighter fit between cause and effect, so that the effect is conceived under this model as an unambiguous indicator of its cause. This additional hypothesis of a tight, unambiguous recording connection is essentially what Binford has recently argued for: he states that archaeologists 'must develop a theoretical understanding of certain properties of the archaeological record that will *have unambiguous referents in the past and will be uniformly relevant to the past*' (Binford 1982a: 131; original emphasis).

There are three kinds of physical recording connections that link present physical things to 'unambiguous referents in the past' – in other words, these connections make the effect an unambiguous indicator of its cause: (1) the recording connection of physical remains (e.g., skeletons); (2) the recording connection of what is substantially equivalent to something (e.g., fossils); and (3) the recording connection of unique, nomological traces (e.g., fingerprints).

A skeleton is sufficient and unambiguous evidence of the existence of the body, of which it is the physical remains. Although a skeleton may be ambiguous about certain features of that body, it is at least unambiguous in indicating that there actually was a body, and that whatever features this body had, these features must be consistent with those implied by the skeleton. In a sense important for logic, a skeleton is materially equivalent to the body: if the body exists, its skeleton must also exist; if the skeleton exists, the body had to exist at one time. Much the same is true of a fossil. Because a fossil retains the imprinted form of at least some part of an organic body, although not always – its matter (Moore *et al.* 1952), a fossil is the inorganic, substantial equivalent of that organic body. Not all organic bodies cause fossils, but if a fossil does exist, the organic body it records had to exist at one time. (Paleontologists distinguish body fossils from trace fossils: the former represent body or plant parts, whereas the latter only represent behavior of animals e.g., tracks, trails, burrows, and other activities [Frey, 1975]. Generally, the latter do not provide as hard evidence for the existence of animals as the former do [Finks 1979: 328; Hantzschel and Frey 1975], but they do provide more potential evidence about animal behavior [Seilacher 1967].) Finally, a fingerprint is a patterned trace, whose singularity of patterning indicates only one finger as its cause. If the fingerprint exists, the finger causing it also had to exist.

Work by paleoecologists, taphonomists, and other paleobiologists have shown that skeletons, fossils, and unique nomological traces all undergo deterioration or complete destruction through natural and cultural processes (Behrensmeyer 1978; Behrensmeyer and Hill 1980; Gifford 1981; Shipman 1981; Thomas 1971). Consequently, the stratigraphy, quantity, or features of these physical records at a site cannot be used to make direct inferences about species population, duration of occupancy, co-occupancy, habitat, or other features of paleocommunities (Olson 1980: 5–19; Shipman 1981: 3–9). But these problems affect inferences about paleocommunities, not inferences about whether or not a single animal or plant existed, made on the basis of its own skeleton, fossil, or unique nomological trace. This is because the recording connections assumed for each of these physical records make possible direct inferences about the existence of their causes.

Skeletons, fossils, and fingerprints are all effects q of past causes p. In their case, the effect q is conceived as an unambiguous indicator of its cause p, because it is presumed that q could only have been caused by p, thus q is sufficient evidence for p. This means that there is a tight logical connection between q and p, that warrants the deduction of the cause p from the effect q. Once you find a skeleton, you do not treat it as simply confirming the hypothesis that there once was a body – you immediately conclude that there was a body of which the skeleton was part, and do not think it necessary to seek further corroborating evidence for this conclusion. Body fossils and fingerprints are treated as evidence that is almost as strong. Given certain basic hypotheses about lawlike, natural processes occurring in fossilization (Finks 1979) and in taphonomic events (Behrensmeyer 1978), or generalizations about the uniqueness of line patterns on fingers, one also deduces p from q in the case of fossils and fingerprints.

Because Model$_p$ represents archaeological evidence as a physical record that records its causes in the way that fossil records do, Model$_p$ implies that archaeological evidence has the same kind of physical recording connection. So just as a fossil, skeleton, or fingerprint points back to what it records as an unambiguous indicator, archaeological evidence by Model$_p$ presumably points back to its causes in the same way. This tight recording connection implied by Model$_p$ may even be conceived as warranting the deduction of the cause from the effect, in the way that a body can be deduced from a skeleton, an organic body from a fossil, and a finger from a fingerprint. Thus Model$_p$, especially when combined with the Hempelian inference model, raises the possibility (one might say the optimism) of inferring past causes from their effects, of inferring past materials and events from their archaeological record, without falling prey to the fallacy of affirming the consequent.

The logic of archaeological inference, and its apparent susceptibility to the fallacy of affirming the consequent, can be sketched as follows (derived from Morgan 1973). A valid hypothetico-deductive inference would have this basic structure:

I.

1. In C, if p, then q.	In certain antecedent circumstances, if a certain (past) cause p has occurred, then a certain effect q occurs in the archaeological record. Hypothetical causal law.
2. C	Archaeological hypothesis that certain circumstances occurred.
3. p	Archaeological hypothesis that the cause occurred.
4. therefore q	Archaeological prediction of effect to be found in archaeological record.

In contrast, the fallacy of affirming the consequent would have the following structure:

II.

1. In C, if p, then q.	(Same as I.1 above)
2. C	(Same as I.2 above)
3. q	Archaeological evidence found in the archaeologial record (effect).
4. therefore p	Archaeological conclusion about the occurrence of past cause.

However, if Model$_p$ implies a physical recording connection between p and q that is like the recording connection of fossil records, then q unambiguously records p in a way that justifies deducing p from q. Just as there is a concrete material equivalence between an animal and its skeleton, and just as there are tight, indexical connections between organic bodies and their fossils, and between fingers and fingerprints, there is presumed to be a similar connection between the archaeological record and what it records. Insofar as archaeologists use Model$_p$ and accept its metaphysical implication of a physical recording connection between archaeological evidence and items or events in the past – a connection that is like a fossil's recording connection – they make use of this implication as an additional, albeit implicit, assumption in their inferences. Because of this additional assumption, Model$_p$ basically cancels out the fallacy of affirming the consequent because the inference now works this way:

III.

1. In C if p, then q.	(Same as above)
2. C	(Same as above)
3. If q, then p.	Recording connection between q and p; metaphysical implication of Model$_p$

4. q	Archaeological evidence found in the archaeological record effect
5. therefore p	Archaeological conclusion about the occurrence of the past cause

Thus Model$_p$ has important consequences for archaeological inference. Its metaphysical implication of a physical recording connection between archaeological evidence and past items or events – a connection that is like that of fossil records, skeletal remains, or unique nomological traces – allows for the inference of these past items or events from their archaeological record. Model$_p$ justifies the inference of cause from effect, while avoiding the fallacy of affirming the consequent. But certain questions must still be faced: Is the physical model of the archaeological record a ruse by which archaeologists skirt the fallacy of affirming the consequent? Or have archaeologists actually identified certain features of their evidence – that it can record its causes through an unambiguous physical recording connection – so that, in truth, there is no fallacy inferring these causes from the evidence?

Rethinking the physical model

New Archaeology has not been without its critics, even amongst its progeny, and some of the recent debate over its basic premises can be viewed as a critical rethinking of its adoption of Model$_p$ as the exclusive description of the archaeological record. Some of these critiques borrow phrases that derive from Model$_t$; others explore some of the implications of Model$_t$ without adopting the model as a whole.

Gould, for example, criticizes the attempt by New Archaeologists to read the patterns and regularities in archaeological evidence as 'the basis for general laws of human behavior' (Gould 1980: 40). Yet Gould's own attempt to forego laws in favor of 'general *propositions* about human behavior that posit relationships that are invariable in time and space and are susceptible to testing without assigning them the exalted status of law' (Gould 1980: 42; original emphasis) still misses the logical difference between statements (call them laws or propositions) that are invariable in time and space, and statements that express behavioral rules that function like grammatical rules (Gould 1980: 116–137). The crucial expression here is 'invariable in time and space'. By retaining the status of invariance in time and space, Gould's general propositions about human behavior are still laws, just redubbed. Because Gould ignores this logical difference, he finds no problem in 'leapfrogging' (the term is Tringham's 1978: 172) from behavioral rules to behavioral laws:

> Thus the empirical attitude of the ethnoarchaeologist in studying anthropological processes leading to human residues enables him to move from his discovery of 'rules' of behavior as they occur in particular human societies to the possibility of discovering in residue formation 'laws' of behavior that are universal to mankind.
>
> (Gould 1978b: 8)

In his own ethnoarchaeological studies, Gould seems to recognize that Model$_p$ is too narrow, with its implication that all the patterns exhibited in archaeological evidence are due to uniformitarian causal laws (Gould 1978a: 250–259, 1980: 36–42). In *Living*

Archaeology, he even toys with Model$_t$ when he employs such textual metaphors as 'the archaeological signature', 'the grammar of lithic technology,' and 'the grammatical structure of material relations' (Gould 1980: 115, 121, 137). In the end, however, it is clear that he is committed to Model$_p$, when he holds out for general principles of human behavior that are not conventional, but ecological (Gould 1980: 48–53). Such principles relate human behavior, including the use of symbols (Gould 1978b: 6), to ecological conditions in ways that are presumably valid for any human society, given the same conditions. This, however, makes these principles laws, not 'grammatical' structures or rules.

> The results of this approach so far in Australia are promising, and living archaeology now is clearly applicable to the study of general principles that determine material relations in *any* human society [emphasis added]. It even offers the opportunity of making reliable discoveries in the real or ideational behavior. As long as living archaeology addresses problems related to general principles in human residue behavior, it will serve as the baseline for archaeology as a social science.
>
> (Gould 1980: 251–252)

So although Gould uses phrases that seem to be derived from Model$_t$, ('the grammar of lithic technology', 'the grammatical structure of material relations'), his general theory does not provide the overall conceptual framework for these phrases – they remain mere metaphors without Model$_t$ to back them up. Michael Schiffer also attempts to rethink some of the basic premises of New Archaeology, among them the concept of the archaeological record (Schiffer 1972a,b, 1976, 1983; Schiffer and Rathje 1973). His work is a clear attempt to recast the concept of the archaeological record into a more rigorous form, so that it can stand as a scientific model, tightly integrated into an overall theory of formation processes (Schiffer 1972b, 1976). Instead of simply presuming, as many archaeologists do, that archaeological evidence forms a record, Schiffer tries to show how this evidence has been formed into a record, and what processes have intervened between the record and the past artifacts, features, and residues it records. He rejects the principle that archaeological remains, in their present spatial distribution and material condition, directly record patterns of past behavior and social organization. For in many cases, these remains have been altered by natural and cultural processes between the time that they were output materials, deposited by a past cultural system, and the time that they are excavated and 'read' as a record by archaeologists:

> If we desire to reconstruct the past from archaeological remains, then these [cultural and natural formation] processes must be taken into account, and a more generally applicable methodological principle substituted for the one that asserts that there is an equivalence between a past cultural system and its archaeological record.
>
> (Schiffer 1976: 11–12)

What makes Schiffer's theory interesting for the present discussion is that it verges upon archaeological semiotics, not by the usual route of French structuralism, but by its own analysis of the distortions introduced into the archaeological record by intervening cultural and natural formation processes. Schiffer approaches the textual model without actually adopting it when he treats archaeological evidence as a record that can be read once the complex code that structures that body of evidence is deciphered and purified of distortions. Yet he is not committed to all of the metaphysical implications of the textual model or to all of the theoretical baggage of structuralist theory, because he uses this model only to analyze distortions in the archaeological record, not to describe the evidence comprising the record itself. In Schiffer's theory, correlates, C-transforms, and N-transforms are treated as archaeological tools of translation, needed to decode (or to borrow a term from poststructuralism, 'to deconstruct') the archaeological record. It is as though he is reaching for a notion of textual distortion without having to buy the whole textual model of the archaeological record.

> The more realistic principle is that the structure of archaeological remains is a distorted reflection of the structure of material objects in a past cultural system. Such distortions are caused by cultural and noncultural formation processes. These distortions are taken into account and corrected by constructing appropriate conceptual and methodological tools to act as lenses through which the structure of the past can be perceived by observing the structure of the present. Just as all information needed to produce a sharp print is encoded in even the most poorly focused negative, the information for reconstructing the past is encoded in the structure of the present – but instead of applying holographic restoration techniques, we apply c-transforms, n-transforms and justifiable stipulations to eliminate the distortions introduced by formation processes.
>
> (Schiffer 1976: 42)

Schiffer's work on the distortion introduced by intervening formation processes also raises several interesting questions about archaeological inference. For according to Schiffer, these intervening processes do not simply disturb, erase, or distort patterns in the components of the archaeological record; they are not merely a kind of entropy that diminishes patterns. Instead they are regular in a way that can be expressed by laws (i.e., C- and N-transforms), and thus they create new patterns of their own within the archaeological record (Schiffer 1983). Thus in order to make inferences about past behavioral systems, it is first necessary to identify which kind of processes are responsible for the identifiable patterns in the evidence – past behaviour processes or intervening formation processes.

But notice that Schiffer alters the model of the archaeological record slightly, because what is recorded by the components of the record could be the past behavioral system, the intervening processes, or both. In other words, most other archaeologists speak of the archaeological record as a record of past behavioral systems only. Schiffer has shifted the model so that the archaeological record is understood as a record of everything that has occurred up until the present, including all of the intervening processes (also see Sullivan 1978). To use two analogies, the archaeological record would either be like a taped radio broadcast that has been distorted by noise, gaps, and other disturbances, but still remains a record of music or of someone speaking. Or it could be like a sign that has been covered with layers of graffiti, so that it is a record not only of the original message, but also an accumulated record of all the intervening graffiti messages as well. It seems that Schiffer's theory of formation processes has led to an implicit redefinition of the concept of the archaeological record, so that the scale is tipped towards the latter analogy: like the sign covered with graffiti, the archaeological record is a record of intervening processes as well as past behavioral systems.

This redefinition is to be expected and can be justified by recalling the nature of a scientific model. A model is so much a part of scientific theory, that any alterations in the theory will be likely to affect the model, and vice versa. Because Schiffer's theory is one of the few archaeological theories that tries to transform the concept of the archaeological record from a metaphor into a rigorous scientific model, the physical model inherited from new archaeology was bound to change in Schiffer's hands. This shift in $Model_p$ broadens the sense in which the archaeological record is a record, but the model may still need to be rethought. For there may be some problem with the very concept of a record if there is no distinction between what distorts the record and what is recorded by the record.

Another look at the textual model and its implications for archaeological inference will make it clear that $Model_t$ has its problems, too, so that neither $Model_p$ nor $Model_t$ can presently claim archaeology's uncritical acceptance. Perhaps a mutual understanding of the problems with the two models will lead to a synthesis of the two or even to a completely new model of archaeological evidence, rather than leading to battlelines drawn firmly around each model by its respective camp.

The textual model and its implications for archaeological inference

Structural archaeologists face their own problems of inference – some inherited from French structuralism, others arising out of their own emphasis on a contextual, historical approach. Most of these problems are recognized by Hodder and the other archaeologists exploring this approach (Hodder 1982a). The problems are basically four, all of them methodological in a broad sense: (1) the problem of how to discover the unobservable, underlying codes that structure material symbols (the problem of paleopsychology); (2) the problem of never having archaeological access to the complete material, behavioral, and social context of any material symbol (the problem of incomplete context); (3) the problem of attempting generalizations about a culture from fragmentary material symbols, which may have belonged only to an elite, to certain classes, or to a certain gender (the general problem of history); (4) the problem of relying upon material symbols that may have been used to mask or subvert the power relations in past cultures (the problem of ideology). Without trying to resolve these problems, I think that a few brief comments can show why these problems are theoretically important.

The first problem might be considered insuperable by new archaeologists (e.g., Binford 1982a, 1982d), but it is assumed as a justifiable task by archaeologists who aim for a more complete picture of specific cultures than can be provided by strict scientific method (e.g., Glassie 1975: 185). The problem is to discover the structures or symbolic principles, by which meaning is encoded in material artifacts, even though these are not observable patterns but underlying codes. Ardener (1978) discusses this general problem by distinguishing 's-structures' (the observable patterns) from 'p-structures' (the underlying codes). He argues that when the calibrations of these two different structures do not exactly match up, the analytic methods used for studying observable patterns will not reveal the underlying codes (Ardener 1978: 306–307). The code itself is 'either inaccessible – a black box – or unfalsifiable' (Hodder 1982d: 8), or a projection of the archaeologist's own cultural code (Ardener 1978: 310).

The second problem is that all material symbols require a contextual interpretation because their meanings are a function of the specific associations they evoke in a culture and of the actual ways they are combined with other symbols and behavior. Because the complete context of material symbols includes many items, social actions, and natural events that do not survive as archaeological remains, archaeological research is at a greater disadvantage than ethnographic research in its access to the contexts that make material symbols meaningful. Further, ethnographic analogies, which cut across cultural contexts, have little, if any, use in the interpretation of the meanings of material symbols because these analogies downplay the uniqueness of specific cultural contexts in order for the analogy to be seen. Even if there are certain basic structures or principles, common to all humans, 'they may be combined in ways peculiar to each cultural milieu, and be given specific meanings and associations' (Hodder 1982d: 9).

The third problem is that not all important human behavior gets encoded in language or material symbols. Even if one managed to 'crack the code' of a past material culture and were able to 'read' its material symbols accurately, one would still not be able to infer everything archaeologists want to infer about past human behavior. (Even though classicists know ancient Greek and can read ancient Greek texts, they are still in the dark about a great deal of ancient Greek behavior.) Deetz (1977) provides another angle on the problem when he notes that historians face the problem of reconstructing the past from evidence left by a literate elite, but archaeologists have access to 'small things [used and] forgotten' by those who make up the vast majority of the population. Still, material symbols can be as tightly controlled and as rarefied as literacy; not everyone in a culture can use all symbols. Such differences in the rights to own or manipulate certain symbols usually indicate important political differences in the population, and these can be revealed archaeologically, for example, in graves (however, also see Hodder 1982c: 152–153). But just as there is a silent, illiterate majority in history, so there are large numbers of people in the past who had minimal access to material symbols.

Finally, the fourth problem is the possibility that material symbols, like written and spoken language, can be used to mask, exaggerate, or even disrupt the true behavior or power relations in a society (Braithwaite 1982; Leone 1982b: 749). The artifacts found by archaeologists do not come stamped with a guarantee of their sincerity. Consequently, any archaeological interpretation of their meanings will involve the kinds of hermeneutic problems attendant upon any attempt to discover the 'true' meanings behind the manifest ones (Ricoeur 1970, 1974). Further, an archaeology that focuses on the power relations behind material culture, instead of limiting its attention to the symbols themselves, will require ideology critique (Althusser 1971a, 1976, 1977a; Habermas 1971; Meltzer 1981; Shanks and Tilley 1982).

These four problems are not unique to structural or contextual archaeology, because they arise for historians and anthropologists as well. They need not obstruct the development of this approach in archaeology, but they do deserve theoretical consideration by all who enter this field: Can the underlying code of past symbols be recovered? Can material symbols mean much outside of their original cultural context? Can material symbols expose enough of the truth about past cultures?

Conclusion: can there be a synthesis of the two models?

To conceptualize archaeological evidence as an archaeological record is to adopt a model of this evidence that has important implications for archaeological theory. When that model is Model$_p$, it supports the optimism of the New Archaeologists about discovering laws of human behavior, invariant in time and space, that would make archaeological inference sufficiently rigorous to qualify archaeology as a science. In contrast, construing archaeological evidence in terms of Model$_t$ promotes a structural, symbolic, or contextual approach. Because Model$_t$ includes recognition of individual ingenuity and of culturally specific rules, it de-emphasizes the role of laws in archaeological inference.

Further implications of the two models evince other important contrasts. Model$_p$'s physical recording connection means that archaeological inference should move from material components of the record to material phenomena in the past. Model$_t$'s signification recording connection means that archaeological inference should move from material phenomena to mental phenomena, from material symbols to the ideas and beliefs they encode. As a final point, Model$_p$'s overall comparison of archaeological evidence to fossil records lends itself to New Archaeology's emphasis on adaptation: past artifacts are treated like past organisms, adapted to their environment. Model$_t$, on the other hand, compares archaeological evidence to historical records and thus makes theoretical discussion of individuals' strategies for manipulating cultural codes more likely than discussions of adaptation.

Clarifying their positions in a recent set of papers, Binford and Hodder have made the following remarks, which point up some of the contrasts mentioned above:

> We do not have to try to study mental phenomena. In fact we study material phenomena.
>
> (Binford 1982d: 162)

> [H]ow material culture relates to society depends on the ideological structures and symbolic codes.
>
> (Hodder 1982c: 153)

> Thus the behavioural and adaptive interrelations, and the self-regulation, take place within a framework of ideas. The objects found by archaeologists are not just functional tools but must be treated 'always and exclusively as concrete expressions and embodiments of human thoughts and ideas'.
>
> (Childe 1956a: 1; Hodder 1982c: 151)

> We do not find 'fossilised' ideas, we find the arrangements of material which derive from the operation of a system of adaptation culturally integrated at some level. I don't have to know how the participants thought about the system to investigate it as a system of adaption in a knowable natural world.
>
> (Binford 1982d: 162)

Considering all of their disagreements over cross-cultural laws, material and mental phenomena, and ecological functionalism, I think that the differences between their positions cannot be overemphasized. Their adoption of different models of archaeological evidence coincides with more far-reaching theoretical differences that cannot be bridged by a simple synthesis of the two models.

Nonetheless, I venture the following suggestions for allowing both models their place in archaeological theory. I must confess to qualms, however; a philosopher should not tread where only an archaeologist can stand. But because my own philosophical orientation inclines me towards the structural approach, I do not want to see it dismissed by American archaeologists. If the following remarks simply provide food for thought, so that archaeologists reflect upon bridging the two models or inventing a completely new one, then these remarks will serve their intended function.

Perhaps the two models apply to different levels of archaeological evidence: the physical model seems more appropriate for archaeological remains, and the textual model for the original material artifacts in use and as deposits. They could be synthesized by treating one as the temporal, causal consequence of the other: archaeological evidence conceived in terms of $Model_p$ is itself the record of archaeological deposits conceived in terms of $Model_t$. Archaeological evidence is like a fossil record of a past body of material symbols; when these symbols were produced, actively manipulated and deposited, they were composed like a textual record.

In terms of Binford's 'simple' scheme of archaeological tasks (Binford 1982d: 160), $Model_p$ describes what the world is like now – it applies to archaeological remains as they presently exist, and compares these remains to a fossil record. $Model_p$'s explanatory value lies in its account of why archaeological remains are in their present state and spatial distribution: causal laws connect the present state and distribution of archaeological remains to past material artifacts, features, and residues, as well as to intervening processes. $Model_t$ describes what the world was like then – it applies to past material artifacts, features, and residues, in use and in deposit, and compares these to a textual record composed of material signs. $Model_t$'s explanatory value lies in its account of why these past 'material phenomena' were formed and combined in specific ways: namely, because they were material symbols of 'mental phenomena', structured by underlying codes and manipulated by individuals in social actions.

This way of distinguishing the two models accords with the theoretical interests of New Archaeologists and of structural or contextual archaeologists. Binford and especially Schiffer concentrate on methods for justifying inferences from present materials to past material culture, taking into account all distortions introduced through intervening processes. Hodder and other structural archaeologists focus on material symbols in active use; they say less about justifying inferences from present, lifeless, material fragments. Hodder's contextual theory really applies to manipulable objects when these were whole and in use, not to sherds, flakes, and other scanty materials.

This way of synthesizing the models suggests that New Archaeology's methods for inferring past material culture from presently existing materials may be regarded as preliminary steps to structural or contextual archaeology's interpretation of the meaning of past material symbols. Before the past textual record of material symbols can be decoded, it first has to be reconstructed and purified of distortions: New Archaeology focuses on the latter task, structural archaeology on features that

143

functioned as material symbols: its inference can also show which cross-cultural laws provide the boundary conditions within which cultures differ; its analyses can show the past natural conditions to which people had to adapt. Structural or contextual archaeology draws inferences beyond those of New Archaeology, moving from 'material phenomena' to 'mental phenomena', analyzing artifacts and behavior in terms of culturally specific codes, and studying individuals' symbolic and social strategies for living in groups and for tackling the environment in creative ways.

Stepping back onto more familiar philosophical ground, and leaving the archaeological field to those who not only tread it but dig it, I would like to raise the question expressed in the title of this paper: 'Is there an archaeological record?' For the question hints that archaeological evidence may not form any kind of record at all, even though it is presently conceived as a record (or as two kinds of record) by virtue of archaeologists' choice of concepts – really their choice of concepts through their choice of words. If neither the physical recording connection nor the recording connection of signification seem exactly right for an appropriate conception of archaeological evidence, if neither seems to capture the actual connection between archaeological evidence and what it is evidence of, then perhaps the whole concept of recording is not appropriate for the evidence. After all, even if paleontologists are still working with an old metaphor – the fossil record – there is no need for archaeologists to do the same. And if material symbols cannot, in the end, be analyzed on a linguistic model; then they need not be compared to textual records. Might there be a new model of archaeological evidence that does not borrow at all from the concept of a record?

ACKNOWLEDGMENTS

I wish to thank Michael B. Schiffer, who commented on earlier drafts of this essay, supplied me with one of his unpublished papers, and encouraged me to discuss structural archaeology. My thanks also go to Merrilee Salmon, Robert Baker, Jan Ludwig, Felmon Davis, and Stanley Kaminsky for their critical comments. In acknowledging the help I gained from these critics, I do not mean to burden them with any responsibility for the errors or omissions in the paper.

I would also like to express my gratitude to the American School of Classical Studies in Athens, especially to its former director, Henry Immerwahr, for allowing me to use its library for research. I also benefited from discussions with John Overbeck, Elizabeth Schofield, Tucker Blackburn, Jack Davis, Galewood Overbeck, and Miriam Caskey at the site of Kea. Finally, an old debt of gratitude is owed to Margaret Alexander.

9

ON 'HEAVILY DECOMPOSING RED HERRINGS'[*]

Scientific Method in Archaeology and the Ladening of Evidence with Theory

Alison Wylie

Oppositional debate

These are difficult times for philosophy in archaeology. On the one hand, there is a vast and increasing constituency within archaeology that would be happy to see the last of all who insist on the importance of questions about the epistemic status and the limits and aims of inquiry. And on the other, the tenor of debate among those who do take such issues seriously has been so acrimonious, so deeply adversarial and so sharply polarized, that there is often very little constructive engagement of the issues raised. Indeed, the attacks and counter-attacks frequently seem simply to miss each other; adversaries joust with such gross caricatures of opposing views they can hardly be taken seriously, and then reinscribe in their own platforms the very contradictions they mean to transcend.[1] Not surprisingly, a recurrent charge is that critics or opponents have simply failed to see what is *really* important, that their positions turn on irrelevancies, that red herrings abound.

Two such charges are especially intriguing, they work so completely at cross-purposes. Binford inveighs against the 'big red herring' of over-extended claims about the theory dependence of observations which he finds 'basic' to the relativist, anti-science positions he attributes to Hodder and, indeed, to all 'yippie' ('post-processual') archaeologists (1989d: 35). In direct opposition to this pro-science (processualist) position, Shanks and Tilley enjoin Renfrew to 'dispose of his heavily decomposing scientific red herring', to 'stop wafting . . . in front of our noses' the 'myth, mirage, obfuscation' of appeals to a reified and simplistic conception of scientific method. In what follows, I want to examine the concerns that lead some to take these red herrings seriously and others to dismiss them as inflammatory irrelevancies. And I want to argue, in this connection, that the highly charged rhetoric now typical of debate obscures considerable common ground between processualists and anti/post-processualists.[2]

---

[*]First published in L. Embree (ed.) (1992), *Metaarchaeology*, Dordrecht: Kluwer, pp. 269–88.

Scientific method vs. theory ladenness

Where the red herring of scientific method is concerned, I find I have considerable sympathy for Shanks and Tilley's insistence that abstract ideals of 'science', as sometimes invoked by Binford and by Renfrew, should be problematized (1989b: 43). The close historical and sociological analyses of scientific practice spawned, in the last several decades, by the demise of positivism have seriously undermined any presumption of a unity of scientific method – or of a coherent body of 'techniques, now well established . . . for the investigation of the natural world', to use Renfrew's terms (1989: 38) – that could be appropriate to all the various disciplines we call 'science' and that differentiate them clearly from various forms of 'fringe' and non-scientific practice.[3] Indeed, Renfrew's own (parenthetic) acknowledgement that the techniques of science are 'always evolving', and Binford's frequent description of science as a process of 'learning how to learn' (1989: 230, 250, 487), suggest that the hallmark of the traditions of inquiry we commonly call 'scientific' is precisely their flexibility (their adaptive responsiveness, as it were) under complex and diverse conditions. It would seem to follow that any boundaries between science and non-science, any criteria of demarcation or conception of what counts as 'scientific', must be enormously plastic – both across fields and over time.[4] This is not necessarily to endorse Feyerabend's argument that the *only* principle of practice which holds across the board is that any rule can be transgressed: 'anything goes' (Feyerabend 1988, revised edition of 1975). But it does suggest that Shanks and Tilley are right to object that appeals to 'science', or the 'scientific method' are, at best, unhelpful in determining how to proceed when a return to the innocence of 'empiricist' ideals is no longer tenable.

On the other hand, where the red herring of theory-ladenness (or, paradigm dependence) is concerned, the position of anti/post-processualists is exceedingly paradoxical. They have made good use of contextualist (specifically, Kuhnian) arguments to establish that even the identification of archaeological data, and certainly the construal of data as evidence, is inevitably mediated by some interpretive theory. In a typical passage, Shanks and Tilley argue that 'what makes the archaeological data speak to us, when we interpret it, when it makes sense, is the act of placing it in a specific context or set of contexts' (1987a: 104). They go on to argue, on this basis, that there is, therefore, no foundational 'realm of fact' that can serve as a final, autonomous, basis for judging the 'truth' or credibility of 'theory' (1987a: 111). In this spirit, Hodder once insisted that archaeologists simply 'create facts' (1983: 6; see also 1984b), while Shanks and Tilley conclude that there is 'literally *nothing independent of theory* or propositions to test against' (1987a: 111).

And yet, even as anti/post-processualists endorse a 'radical pluralism' according to which 'any interpretation of the past is multiple and constantly open to change, to re-evaluation' (Shanks and Tilley 1987a: 109), they have been eager to distance themselves from those forms of relativism that enforce an 'anything goes' tolerance of all imaginable constructs. In recent discussions Shanks and Tilley declare, quite simply, that they 'don't accept any view of the past' (1989b: 50). This is by no means a new theme. In *Re-constructing Archaeology* they were quite clear on the point that, if archaeology is to fulfil its potential as a basis for critique of, and active intervention in, the present, the threat of an 'anything goes' relativism must be resisted: 'we cannot afford the essential irrationality of subjectivism or relativism as this would be cutting the very ground away from under our feet' (1987a: 110). Given this, it would seem incumbent on Shanks and Tilley to give some further account of how, exactly, archaeologists are to judge the relative credibility of evidential, as well as of interpretive and explanatory claims, to say how archaeologists are to 'be empirical' rather than 'empiricist'.[5] And yet, as their critics, and even some of their fellow travellers, point out, it is unavoidable that they, and anti/post-processualists generally, have failed to give any very satisfying account of how archaeologists can (or do) make and justify judgements about the credibility of competing claims about the past.

This is a point Hodder has made at length in a recent discussion of the approach he now advocates, which he terms 'interpretive' archaeology (1991a). He objects that, in their reaction against the failure of processual archaeology, anti/post-processual archaeologists remained too exclusively preoccupied with theoretical questions. They were primarily concerned to theorize the 'internal', meaningful aspects of the cultural subject that processualists had left out of account but in the process, failed to come to terms with what amount to methodological questions about the nature and practice of interpretation. While this call for closer and sustained attention to these issues is welcome, the critical assessment on which it is based seriously underestimates the centrality of epistemological concerns in anti/post-processual discussions since the early 1980s (see, for example, contributions to Hodder 1982a). And it has to be said that, in setting the agenda for 'interpretive archaeology', Hodder himself offers few concrete suggestions as to how such issues might be addressed, beyond endorsing a 'guarded commitment to objectivity' (1991a: 10), and invoking philosophical hermeneutics as a promising source of insights about interpretive practice.[6]

It might seem illegitimate to require of Shanks and Tilley a methodological programme, given their principled stand against the alleged methodolatry of processualism, the preoccupation with abstract, 'mechanistic procedures of so-called scientific or objective analysis' (1989a: 2), with 'predefined methods' (1989b: 45) capable of assuring that, in Binford's terms, 'we [will not be] led to construct a false past' (Binford 1989: 39). However, accounts of method need not be arbitrary or prescriptive in the ways Shanks and Tilley find objectionable; there seems a perfectly good sense in which the reflexive dimension of practice that they endorse could, and should, include the 'hammering out' – the articulation and critical appraisal – of flexible, provisional principles of method that are emerging in practice. Indeed, they themselves seem to recognize this when they insist on the need to address the question, 'what are the most fruitful strategies' for inquiry, for 'reading and writing' the past into the present (1989b: 44).

The challenge Shanks and Tilley face, given their insistence that 'the entire world is always already a vast field of interpretive networks' (1989a) and that objects of inquiry are always theorized objects, is to explain how some types of theoretical construct can constrain the construction of others, such that some are properly regarded (for some purposes, and at some moments in the process of inquiry) as 'objects' or as evidence – 'as a network of resistances to theoretical appropriation' (1989b: 44) – while others function as tools of appropriation. This will not be a distinction that ascribes any permanent status to specific components of discourse; those claims that function as resistances, that are treated as 'objects' at one juncture, are always open to reassessment as interpretive or explanatory or generalizing constructs at another. So part of the task at hand is to explain how and why, under what constraints or with what warrant, the status of various kinds of constructs changes. This will require a nuanced account of how archaeological data – facts of the record – are constituted as evidence, how they are 'laden' with theory such that they can have a *critical* bearing on claims about the cultural past and can, in turn, sustain what Shanks and Tilley call a 'particular and contingent objectivity' (1989b: 43). Whether or not this is properly termed a theory of 'testing', or constitutes an analysis of 'scientific' (or 'systematic') inquiry, seems to me a semantic quibble, a genuine irrelevancy.

It is here that I see the convergence between the interests of processualists and anti/post-processualists. While polemical appeals to 'science' as a model of practice are surely a red herring, these by no means exhaust the response of processualists to their critics. In particular, Binford's long preoccupation with the 'question of accountability' (1989: 34), specifically, the question of how archaeological 'inferences' are, or can be, 'justified' (cf. Binford 1989: 3, 10, and throughout), is quite explicitly motivated by a concern to show that it is possible to sustain what *he* calls 'relative objectivity' (Binford 1989: 230, with reference to 1982a), in face of the threat of complete cognitive anarchy that he finds implicit in the 'open relativism' of anti/post-processualism (e.g., Binford 1989: 34). Although he is vehement in denying that general questions about theory-ladenness have any relevance to practice (1989: 34), the middle range practices he advocates of building and exploiting 'source side' resources (Wylie 1985a) are, in a quite straightforward sense, strategies for securing, or rendering systematic, the 'inferences' by which archaeological data are laden with theory. And in this Binford actually provides many of the resources necessary for dealing effectively with the problem of method – for determining 'the most fruitful strategy of inquiry' (Shanks and Tilley 1989b: 44) – faced by anti/post-processualists like Shanks and Tilley.

In arguing this I reject Binford's own disclaimers to the effect that 'seeking middle-range research opportunities does not address itself to the bogeyman of paradigm dependence' (1989: 38); on the contrary, substantive work on the 'theory' that is to laden evidence would seem absolutely fundamental to any responsible treatment of problems or circularity and nepotic theory-dependence. I would also qualify Shanks and Tilley's claim that 'vital philosophical and social questions of the theory dependence of "data" . . . are glossed over in the archaeological literature in general' (1989b: 43). Because they reject processual analyses out of hand as dependent on a naïve conception of 'science' and scientific method, I believe they fail to see the relevance of many of the specifics of analyses like Binford's to the problem of understanding how 'data' can be both theory-laden – itself a construct, and constructed as evidence – and also a source of 'resistances' to theoretical appropriation. And finally, in recognition of a shared concern to come to grips with these problems, I would question Binford's insistence that no one but he takes seriously the 'fundamental' epistemological problem of establishing 'how . . . we have confidence in or render secure the inferences and descriptions of the past offered by virtue of our study of artifacts' (1989: 10), how we go about 'developing reliable means for inference justification' (1989: 3). He underestimates the persistence of these concerns historically (see Grayson 1986) and, faced with inflammatory critical claims about paradigm dependence, fails to recognize the constructive elements of anti/post-processual responses to them in contemporary contexts.

Common ground

In the spirit of exploring this common ground, let me first identify three points on which there is now grudgingly consensus, and then sketch an account of how archaeological observations are constituted as evidence such that, despite being richly 'theorized' – indeed, undeniably a 'construct' – they do routinely turn out differently than expected, and can play (at least provisionally) a constraining role in the formulation and evaluation of knowledge claims about the cultural past.

By now all parties to the debate accept, by way of a first point of agreement, that neither data nor evidence are given, stable, or autonomous of theory. Although processualists resist its more extreme formulations, this is a point they have been prepared to accept since at least the early 1980s. It is central to Binford and Sabloffs' lengthy discussion of 1982, and is acknowledged in Renfrew's more recent observation that 'post-positivist philosophers of science . . . agree that the material record can only be studied and data elicited by working within some kind of theoretical framework: the data can never be entirely free of the theoretical framework which produces them' (1989: 39).[7]

Second, by extension of this, all recognize that the identification of archaeological data and their constitution as evidence relevant for understanding the cultural past depend, inevitably, on some body of linking principles: 'source-side' or background knowledge; middle-range 'theory'; mediating interpretive principles.

Finally, all seem agreed that, although archaeological data and evidence are radically constituted – they are richly 'theorized' constructs – the process of 'ascribing meaning' (to use Binford's terms) is not necessarily viciously circular; the dependence on linking principles by no means guarantees that the resulting evidence will conform to expectations. The main reason for this, on which Binford has commented extensively and which Shanks and Tilley, among other anti/post-processualists, routinely exploit in practice, is that the ladening or linking theories on which archaeologists depend are enormously diverse and disjointed they often derive from contexts that are wholly unrelated to any of the theoretical presuppositions (or interests) that inform the choice of archaeological questions, the selection of descriptive categories, or the explanatory and interpretive models of the past that are to be evaluated in the course of inquiry. In short, the 'theory' that ladens observations or data is rarely monolithic or all-pervasive (Wylie 1989c). Moreover, these theories are themselves at least potentially subject to evidential constraint; they are by no means *necessarily* a body of knowledge, an 'edifice of auxiliary theories and assumptions', that '*archaeologists have simply agreed not to question*' (Hodder 1983: 6; emphasis in the original). The result is that archaeologists can, and routinely do, make quite closely discriminating empirically and conceptually reasoned judgements about the relative credibility of claims about the evidential significance of archaeological data; these are by no means certain, but neither are they entirely arbitrary.

A concern to make sense of the considerations that shape these judgements as they figure in the natural sciences has been a central preoccupation, in the last decade, in philosophical contexts, especially in post-positivist philosophy of science. Dissatisfaction with the perceived excesses of social constructivist accounts of science takes a number of forms. Many object that the reaction against positivism has simply inverted positivist priorities, privileging theory or interests over observation (see, for example, Galison 1987: 7–9) and is no more adequate than the manifestly problematic (positivist) theories they displace. The result is a range of positions which provide, at best, 'partial insights into the character of observation' (Galison 1987: 12) and which are, in consequence, unable to make sense of the difficulty of doing science, or of cases in which scientific practice shows little of the instability and arbitrariness of construction on which some of the stronger Strong Program sociologists of science (among others) have insisted. In response to this impasse, there has been considerable interest among historians and philosophers of science in reassessing what it means to say that observations are theory laden. This is one concern that informs the recent philosophical work on experimental practice (e.g., as described by Galison 1988, and Hacking 1988). And it is evident in Shapere's analysis of the role played by 'prior information' in determining what will count as an 'observation' in physics (Shapere 1982: 505). He insists that although nothing can provide observation an 'absolute guarantee' of efficacy (Shapere 1985: 22, 36), it is simply not the case that observational beliefs are all (equally) doubtful or unstable; the analysis he gives of why this is the case is extended in important ways by Kosso (1988, 1989) and by Hacking (1983). Comparing these analyses with those emerging in archaeology at the intersection between contested positions, I am struck by some persistent similarities in the factors found to be crucial in stabilizing and warranting evidential claims. To be specific, I discern two categories of factor – security and independence – as especially relevant for understanding how evidence-constituting inferences are established in archaeological contexts (see Wylie 1992).

First, in both contexts, the key to stabilizing evidential claims is very often taken to be the security of the sources on which is based the imputed linkage between a surviving archaeological record and the antecedent contexts, conditions, events, or behaviours presumed responsible for it. But security is a complicated matter. On one hand, what counts is security in the sense of 'freedom from doubt' (Shapere, 1985: 29), or entrenchment, in the source fields from which linking principles are drawn, a judgement which concerns both the credibility of the source field and the degree to which the appropriated 'theory' is uncontested. On the other hand, however, an important consideration in archaeological contexts has to do with the *nature* of the imputed link, viz., whether or not, or to what degree, the background knowledge in question establishes an exclusive and determinate connection between archaeological remains (whether these be classes of artifactual material or structural features of the record) and the specific antecedent conditions or processes thought to have produced them.[8] The ideal of security in this sense is realized when the available background or source knowledge supports a biconditional linking principle to the effect that a surviving archaeological trace could have been produced by only one kind of antecedent condition, event, or behaviour.

This is, of course, the 'deductivist' ideal once endorsed by Binford and still implicit, despite his recent repudiation of strict deductivism (1987 reprinted in 1989: 242, 261; 1989: 17), in his tendency to privilege the sort of middle-range theory that captures systemic and ecological determinants; these are areas in which source-side inquiry is seen to promise unconditional, 'uniformitarian' linking principles. Ironically, this ideal also figures in Hodder's appeals to universal principles of meaning-constitution when, for example, he finds in Collingwood the 'implicit' conclusion 'that a universal grammar exists when he [Collingwood] suggests . . . that each unique event has a significance which can be comprehended by all people at all times', and then subsequently appeals to 'universal principles of meaning which . . . are followed by all of us as social actors' (1986: 124). The suggestion that such reliable structural, cognitive principles might underwrite inferences from material remains to the intentional dimension of past human lives was a key component of Hodder's argument that archaeology can and should take into account the 'insides' of human action and cultural contexts. More closely controlled and qualified assessments of security in this sense figure in Shanks and Tilley's analyses of Swedish tombs and grave goods (Shanks and Tilley 1982, 1987a, and Tilley 1984), for example, in their analysis of 'structural homologies' operating across categories of material associated with these tombs (Tilley 1984: 136), and in the arguments they give for referring these to structuring principles underlying the social relations and systems of control operating in prehistory (Shanks and Tilley 1982: 150). In a similar vein, I have argued that the judicious use of analogical inference turns on systematic empirical assessments of the degree to which it is plausible to impute, to the subject context, what Weitzenfeld describes as 'determining structures' (1984) – a nexus of causal, intentional, or functional processes and mechanisms that may not, in fact, be literally determining – which link compared and inferred properties with some specified degree of reliability (Wylie 1988).

There is, finally, a third sense of security relevant to archaeological assessments of evidential claims which has to do with the number and complexity of the linkages required to connect some body of archaeological material to those dimensions of the cultural past that are of investigative interest. It is assessed in terms of something like the considerations of directness, immediacy, and amount of interpretation or degree of 'nesting' of inferences described by Kosso in amplification of Shapere's analysis of observation in physics (Kosso 1988: 455; Shapere 1982, 1985). In archaeological cases there can be no question of literally 'interacting in an informationally correlated way' with the cultural past, such as is relevant in discussions of experimental practice in physics and biology; in this sense any direct measure of 'immediacy' is otiose. Nevertheless, the length and complexity of the causal chain by which archaeological remains are produced (i.e., the number of interactions and of different kinds of factors involved) are clearly a relevant analog of the 'directness' and degree of 'nesting' (or, amount of interpretation) that Kosso finds crucial to the credibility (*qua* potential objectivity) of physically mediated observation. Clearly, when you depend on linking principles that postulate probable, or incompletely determining, antecedent causes – the typical case, where you lack strictly biconditional linking principles – the possibility of error in a judgement of evidential import increases exponentially as you expand the number of such links on which you depend. I take it that Schiffer's interest in delineating the range of interacting 'transform' processes (cultural, natural, depositional and so on) that work together to produce what survives as an archaeological record (e.g., Schiffer 1983) is at least in part motivated by a concern to improve security (or, to mitigate insecurity) of this sort.

There are, then, (at least) three sorts of security at issue in archaeological assessments of evidential claims: security as a function of the entrenchment or freedom from doubt of the background knowledge about the linkages between archaeological data and the antecedents that produced them; security which is due to the nature of the linkages, specifically, the degree to which they are unique or deterministic; and security that arises because of the overall length and complexity of the linkages involved.

In addition to considerations of security, Binford has famously insisted on the importance of 'independence'. Appeals to independence take at least two general forms in his recent discussions and, significantly, in the interpretations that anti/post-processualists have used to illustrate the fruitfulness of their alternative approaches to the archaeological record. The first, and perhaps the most straightforward sense of independence is between the linking principles used to constitute data as evidence and any of the theoretical presuppositions involved in framing the explanatory and interpretive models of the past on which this evidence is meant to bear. For example, Binford urges that archaeologists base their 'ascriptions of meaning' on principles that presuppose background knowledge about 'processes that are *in no sense dependent* for their characteristics or patterns of interaction upon interactions [that constitute the subject of the reconstructive hypothesis under evaluation]', in this case, interactions between 'agricultural manifestations or political growth' (Binford 1983b: 135; see also Binford and Sabloff 1982). In this Binford appeals to exactly the sort of independence that Hacking (1983: 183–185) and Kosso (1988: 456) find crucial in determining whether an observation can stand as evidence for or against a given test hypothesis in experimental contexts (mainly in biology and physics). It is an independence between the constituents and the conclusions of an inference that runs along what amounts to a vertical axis from some element of a given data base, via claims about how it may or must have been produced, to conclusions about its significance as evidence of some aspect of the cultural past. It is this sort of independence, as exploited in micro-biology, physics, and astronomy, which leads Hacking to declare that, although observations are clearly 'loaded with theory', it is very often theory which has no connection with the subject under investigation, on current understanding of the relevant subject domains (Hacking 1983: 185).

A second sort of independence, operating on a horizontal dimension, arises when a number of *different* linking principles are used to constitute data as evidence of the cultural past. In some archaeological cases, this is analogous to the independence Hacking finds exploited by the makers and users of microscopes, where completely different physical processes -different interaction chains, and different bodies of ladening 'theory' – are used to detect the same microscopic bodies, or structural features of these bodies. This independence serves to underwrite a localized 'miracle' argument to the effect that it would be highly implausible that independent means of detection should converge if the body or structure under 'observation' did not exist (Hacking 1983: 202). As Kosso puts this point, 'the chances of these independent theories all independently manufacturing the same fictitious result is small enough to be rationally discounted' (Kosso 1989: 247).[9]

Certainly this sort of triangulation on a single aspect of an archaeological subject is sometimes possible and important. It is perhaps part of what Binford has in mind when he argues the value of varying the descriptive categories in terms of which analyses of patterning inherent in a given body of data are carried out (Binford 1989: 242), and it is what makes the use of different methods of dating compelling in determining the antiquity of an archaeological feature or record. But in addition, there is the horizontal independence that arises between lines of inference when diverse resources are used to constitute evidence of quite distinct aspects of a past context, cultural system, or series of events. On the assumption that these are interconnected, the requirement that they yield a coherent model of the past context, taken as a whole, sets up a system of mutual constraints among vertically constituted lines of evidence. And these can be as important in determining the credibility of any given bit of evidence as are security (in any of the senses described) or independence between the individual linking principles and any broader claims they may be used to support or refute. This seems the sort of independence Binford means to exploit when he argues the need to use 'alleged knowledge warranted with one set of theory-based arguments as the basis for assessing knowledge that has been warranted or justified in terms of an intellectually independent argument', to set up 'an interactive usage of our knowledge . . . to gain a different perspective on both sets of knowledge' (1987 reprinted in 1989: 230).

The significance of this final consideration is that, when independently constituted lines of evidence fail to converge, assumptions thought unproblematic may suddenly be thrown into question; they expose an area of 'ambiguity', to use Binford's most recent terminology (1989: 224, 230; this is reminiscent of Gould's proposal of a 'method of anomaly', 1980). As Shanks and Tilley argue, this strategy of setting up lateral constraints can make clear ways in which the past context in question is different from, and often more complex than, standing assumptions had allowed (Shanks and Tilley 1982). It is, in fact, dissonance between (independent) lines of inference and analysis that originally led anti/post-processualists to insist on the need to consider 'internal', 'ideational' or 'cognitive' dimensions of the cultural past, a point which some processualists have accepted (e.g., Renfrew 1989). When independently constituted lines of evidence do converge, they provide much more compelling support for the model(s) of past systems or activities with which they are consistent than any individual line of inference could do. As Tilley argues, with reference to the analysis of parallel formal and temporal structures emerging in a number of lines of evidence related to Swedish megalithic tombs – e.g., the orientation and structure of tombs, the distribution of grave goods in association with them, the (divergent) elaboration of ceramic design both in association with tombs and settlement sites – it is the demonstration of 'links between different aspects of the material-culture patterning' that 'lends some credibility to the (interpretive) arguments presented' (1984: 144).

Conclusion

What emerges as common ground in the current debates is, first and foremost, a commitment to some form of *mitigated* objectivism. Although Shanks and Tilley reject all abstract, universalistic conceptions of objectivity, they do maintain that the interesting question is not whether objectivity 'exists', but 'what it is' (1989b: 43), and they explicitly endorse what they describe as 'a particular and contingent objectivity' (1989b: 43); they even conclude that it is meaningful to 'speak of the *final primacy of objectivity*' (1989b: 44). There are striking parallels here, not only with Hodder's recent promotion of a 'guarded commitment to objectivity' (1991a), mentioned above, but also, ironically, with Binford's post-positivist notion of 'relative objectivity' and Renfrew's argument, in comment on Shanks and Tilley, that 'it is not necessary to claim that the data must be in some absolute sense "objective" . . . in order to propose their use in the evaluation of truth claims' (1989: 36). Thus, even the strongest advocates of 'science' in archaeology abandon claims to epistemic absolutes where the stability and autonomy of evidence are concerned, while their critics have substantially qualified their original rejection of any notion of objectivity as incoherent and radically unobtainable, and seem prepared to countenance it, in mitigated form, as a regulative ideal that is crucial to archaeological practice.

In addition, I find substantial convergence in how this mitigated objectivity is understood, at least in outline. Where evidence cannot be treated as a stable, foundational given, the crucial factors affecting judgements of objectivity, in this sense, have to do with the inferences by which, and the grounds on which, archaeological data are ascribed 'meaning' as evidence. Mitigated objectivity is achieved insofar as the ladening theory − the body of middle range, linking principles − used to constitute archaeological data as evidence is, itself, secure in the various senses described, and independent along vertical and/or horizontal dimensions. It is a fine irony, where independence is concerned, that what lends archaeological evidence some credibility on this account − what secures for it, and the claims based on it, a degree of 'relative' or 'particular and contingent' objectivity − is precisely the disunity of the sciences, the fact that archaeologists, like physicists or biologists (the common objects of philosophical attention in the parallel discussions I have been citing), cannot expect to find in the theories orienting their labours all the resources they need in order to bring their data to bear (as evidence) on these theories.

Finally, I am intrigued by a further irony that would seem to reveal another important point of convergence. Despite disclaiming any concern with the 'red herring' of paradigm dependence, Binford does recommend that, to control for the residual blinkering effects of such dependence, archaeologists should deliberately shift frameworks; they should bring into play 'multiple perspectives' (1989: 486). It is important, he argues, to seek 'some external frame of reference with respect to which we can appreciate [the] content [of our own paradigms] . . . another paradigm is a good frame of reference, a different base from which to view experience' (1989: 486). With this, it would seem, Binford advocates just the sort of pluralism that Shanks and Tilley have tried to promote *as a means of enhancing the potential 'objectivity' of archaeological knowledge*, in the newly 'relativized' and fallibilistic sense endorsed by all parties to the debate. I conclude, then, that far from being antithetical to 'scientific' modes of practice, recent manoeuvrings in the debate between processualists and their critics make it clear that pluralism and theory-ladenness are essential to it. And with this, the red herrings brandished on both sides of the current divide decisively lose their rhetorical force.[10]

NOTES

1 Binford asks whether debate is worth it and observes that 'antagonists rarely perform at very admirable levels' (1989: 486). More specifically, he bewails the prevalence of *ad hominem* and

ignoratio elenchi (straw man) fallacies (1989: 4, 78), but indulges in them with evident glee (see 1989: 9), formulating such crude caricatures of the positions he rejects it is hard to describe them as anything but 'straw men'. I have in mind his 'field guide' to archaeological positions (1989, chapter 1) and his seemingly more serious (and repeated) attribution of empiricist commitments to every party to the debate but himself and, it would seem (ironically) Dunnell. I say ironically because of Pat Watson's characterization, which I think accurate, of Dunnell as the only consistent empiricist currently engaged in the debate (1986: 446).

Likewise, Shanks and Tilley insist that they have 'a duty to engage in constructive dialogue and to take our critics seriously' (1989b: 42), and declare that the 'adoption of rhetorical strategies . . . does not free us from the responsibility of dealing directly with the issues vital to the development of our archaeology' (1989b: 48). But despite this they reaffirm the value of engaging in quite deliberate rhetorical provocation for the purpose of unsettling the orthodoxy of archaeological (and other) conventions (see their discussion of Chapter 1, *Re-Constructing Archaeology*, 1989a: 8). And, as noted by virtually every commentator who contributed to the *Norwegian Archaeological Review* forum on Shanks and Tilley's work, this has resulted in a programmatic stance riddled with 'serious contradictions' (e.g., Bender, Hodder, Trigger, Renfrew, 1989) or, at least, 'incompatibil[ities]' (Olsen 1989). Shanks and Tilley retain, at the heart of their own position, substantial elements of most of the orthodoxies they reject: they continue, in some contexts, to privilege evidence and related (empiricist and realist) presuppositions of foundationalism (Trigger 1989a: 29, Olsen 1989: 19); they embrace various structuralist assumptions (Bender 1989: 13); their critique of the 'subject' is compromised by a failure to fully incorporate the insights of post-structuralism (Hodder 1989d: 16); and their political stance exploits, or leaves unchallenged, many aspects of their own privilege and location within institutions of the establishment (Bender 1989: 12; Olson 1989: 20).

2 Renfrew (1989) has objected that the positions identified by Hodder and others as 'post-processual' (Hodder 1985) do not, in fact, displace or transcend processual archaeology, they are, more accurately, 'anti-processual'. Because I want to articulate some common ground between the divergent views represented by this terminology, I will refer to the former positions as 'anti/post-processual' in what follows.

3 Certainly, Renfrew's appeal to Popper is unhelpful, given that Popper's criteria of demarcation and falsificationism have proven seriously problematic, both descriptively and explanatorily, as a general account of scientific practice.

Binford does not invoke any specific philosophical models or conceptions of science in recent discussions, but rather presupposes what seems a vernacular conception of science and 'the scientific method'. In this connection, he frequently objects that 'post-processualists' put inappropriate demands on scientific method; these are likened to the hypothetical demand that science should provide an understanding of 'life after death' by a group that thinks this crucial to the completeness of our knowledge and well-being, and that rejects scientific method when it proves not to serve these goals (1989: 27–28). The point of this allegory seems to be that the failure of 'science' to provide access to the intentions and beliefs of past agents – to 'internal' and ethnographic dimensions of the cultural past (Hodder 1991a) – cannot be taken seriously as grounds for concluding 'that science is useless', and that it should be abandoned as 'a learning *strategy so far as the world of experience is concerned*' (my emphasis, Binford 1989: 27). Presumably the goals of inquiry should be revised so that they are amenable to investigation by 'scientific method', i.e., so that they concern only claims referable to 'experience'. Elsewhere, when differentiating processual archaeology from both its traditional antecedents and the 'post-processualism' that presumes to supersede it, Binford identifies, as the major problem to which processualists have responded, the need to systematically 'evaluat[e] the utility and accuracy of ideas'; 'the method [for effectively meeting this problem]', he says, 'was science' (1989: 17).

4   A central point of contention in which the question of boundaries figures centrally in the *Norwegian Archaeological Review* discussions of Shanks and Tilley's post-processualism, has to do with the worry that Shanks and Tilley's anti-objectivism must entail complete abandonment, or erosion, of any distinction between archaeological discourse (as scientific) and pure fiction. Renfrew challenges Shanks and Tilley to demonstrate that this is not a consequence of their position, clearly assuming that it is manifestly untenable; in effect, he charges that anti/post-processualism is threatened by a *reductio ad absurdum*. The general failure of all attempts to establish a coherent and plausible demarcation theory suggests, however, that we need a thorough rethinking of what it would mean to distinguish scientific from fictional discourse. As Helen Longino observes, 'the novelists among us might remind us that if there is a fiction in the discourses of truth, so there is a truth in the discourses of fiction' (1990a: 174). Surprisingly, however, Shanks and Tilley seem to share Renfrew's conviction that such boundaries must hold, as when they argue that 'there is no simple choice to be made between a subjective or an objective account of reality unless one is to abandon science altogether and write novels instead' (1987a: 110).

5   This is a paraphrase of Shanks and Tilley's declaration, both in *Re-Constructing Archaeology* and in response to comments in the *Norwegian Archaeological Review* discussion, that archaeologists should recognize a distinction between 'being empirical and being empiricist' (1989b: 50; see also 1987a: 115, point #5).

6   Hodder appeals, more specifically, to Gadamer and post-Gadamerian theorists (especially Ricoeur), as offering analyses that have the special virtue of explicitly dealing with the problem of a disabling relativism which he now finds implicit in the advocacy of pluralism. His main concern, in this connection, is to secure a 'boundary between an open multivocality where any interpretation is as good as another and legitimate dialog between science and American Indian, black, feminist, etc. interests' (1991a: 9). To this end, he advocates an 'interpretive position' which 'give[s] science a context in archaeology as methodology', thereby avoiding an 'ungrounded undermining of knowledge claims by interested groups and . . . a subsuming of the past within a homogenized theoretical present' (1991a: 10).

7   Renfrew hastens to add that 'when the chips are down, however, it is the data which have the last word' (1989: 39). He then cites Braithwaite (1953) to substantiate this claim: not a notably post-positivist discussion!

8   Well entrenched background knowledge which suggests that the linkages in question are radically unstable or idiosyncratic will obviously undermine, rather than secure, any inference which relies on them, so security in the first sense never functions alone.

9   Although Kosso is mainly concerned with arguments that exploit the independence between the background knowledge used to constitute observational evidence and the claims this evidence is used to support or refute – he develops a formal measure of independence of this sort – he also considers the role played in stabilizing evidential claims, and thus securing their objectivity, by the use of multiple lines of evidence that bear on a single subject. It is perhaps significant that, when he makes this point, he refers to the way in which evidence is used to establish claims about 'ancient history'. Although this is presented as an extension of Hacking's discussion of multiple methods for detecting the same entity or determining the value of a constant, my argument here is that there is, in fact, an important difference between cases in which the variety of evidence is mutually reinforcing because it bears on the *same* entity or aspect of the subject domain, and cases where it bears on different aspects of a subject domain presumed to be interdependent in some specific way. This is the case I consider below as a second, distinct sort of 'independence' consideration.

10 This paper was written while I was a 'visiting scholar' in the Department of Anthropology, University of California at Berkeley, and with the support of a research grant awarded by the Social Sciences and Humanities Research Council of Canada. I gratefully acknowledge the generosity of both institutions, and especially their commitment to support interdisciplinary research which does not fit easily within standard disciplinary categories.

A draft of this paper was presented at the 1991 annual meeting of the Society for American Archaeology (New Orleans, April 1991); it is dedicated to Dr. James F. Pendergast who received an SAA Distinguished Service Award at those meetings. He was responsible for my early exposure to archaeological field work, from which has grown my continuing fascination with the discipline as a whole.

10

ARCHAEOLOGY THROUGH
THE LOOKING-GLASS*

TIM YATES

We have only to understand the mirror stage *as an identification*, in the full sense that analysis gives the term: namely, the transformation that takes place in the subject when he assumes an image . . . This form would have to be called the Ideal-I, if we wished to incorporate it into our usual register, in the sense that it will also be the source of secondary identifications, under which term I would place the functions of libidinal normalisation. But the important point is that this form situates the agency of the ego, before its social determination, in a fictional direction . . . I am led, therefore, to regard the function of the mirror stage as a particular case of the function of the *imago*, which is to establish a relation between the organism and its reality.

(Lacan 1977a: 2–4)

Framing the past

In some way yet to be determined, a genuine historicity is possible only on condition that this illusion of an absolute present can be done away with, and the present opened up again to the drift from the other ends of time.

(Jameson 1972: 187)

Narcissism and the text

The dominant metaphysical conceptualisation of the 'archaeological record' in post-processual archaeology is that of the text. As defined by Ian Hodder – the archaeological text is a web of similarities and differences from which is built up the network of meaningful associations through which we know the past. The concept of the text, of course, serves to denote the epistemological shift away from the identity (passive) of the 'record to the networking (active) of differences. The emphasis is placed upon the chains of signifiers, making any particular item or artefact

* First published in I. Bapty and T. Yates (eds) (1990), *Archaeology after Structuralism*, London: Routledge, pp. 154–202.

referent to the other signifiers with which it is articulated. The artefact, studied in isolation by the functionalists, is engulfed in a system of difference, which locks it into a framework of ever-shifting reference.

But Hodder perceives that it is necessary to suspend this movement, for otherwise the boundaries of the text will never appear and we will be led off into a labyrinth from which no return is possible. A 'text', as such, ought to have borders, boundaries (covers, chapters, spine . . .?) to hold it together. At the conceptual level, therefore, the chains must be closed (at the practical–interpretative level, they are already closed, as we shall see) and the signifiers will have to be fixed by returning them to points which are stable and no longer shift. The theory of context which has consumed all structuralism under a common banner, steps into the breach formed by the disappearance of the signified. Context operates to close these chains of signifiers, allowing us to conceive of a totality – a 'text' – once again, a totality which produces definable, stable relationships between the signifiers of the differential matrix, and allows us to pass down, once more, to the signified. 'The totality of the relevant dimensions around any one object can be identified as the context of that object' (Hodder 1986: 139). The meaning of a particular signifier, 'X', is contextually determined, in its relationship to 'all those aspects of the data which have relationships with "X" which are significantly patterned' (Hodder 1986: 139). Thus the context of a burial would be the edges of the grave, which determine what is within it and what is to be conceived as outside, as part of the exterior. At the borders of context, the shifts and exchanges of difference are no longer possible.

Hodder introduces the concept of context at a crucial point, therefore, in order to reintroduce into the radical horizontality of Saussurian structuralism, at least as it is mediated within post-structuralism by Derrida (and, in a different way, Lacan), the notion of depth, the vertical relationship as the passage back to a signified, which will never have been wholly absent. He endorses the notion of the differential signifier, and recasts the archaeological record as a web of similarities and differences which are constructed in the process of interpretation, arranged in order to form meaningful associations. However, there have to be, for this process to take place, points which escape the play of differences which a reading of Saussure's work must force us to accept. Conceptually, the notion of context operates to close down the chains of signifiers and to forestall difference, the effects of which would be too unsettling if let loose to play out their will through the domain of an archaeology. What this amounts to is the delimitation of practice around an object rather than a domain, though it is now to be called context rather than 'the past'. We decentre the archaeological text, rendering its component parts only differential marks within a system of differences, only to panic at the prospect and to recentre that text on an element that escapes this movement – for context cannot, to perform its promised function, itself be a part of the movement it serves to forestall. If it is to be a part of these differences, then it cannot, at the same time control them. The *arche* is dispatched on a journey by Hodder along a signifying chain, meeting on the way politics, the present, androcentrism, whatever, and then returned to its place at that moment when, seeking to stabilise the forces that this interest in Saussurian theory has set loose, context is defined non-differentially, non-contextually. Context is allowed to become transhistorical and, in the process, to cease to signify – the borders of the text take place in 'lack', in the absence of any significant (signifying) differences and similarities (1986: 139), a point without significance, without difference, without text.

Thus far, the function of context has been purely conceptual. It amounts, in fact, to a systematic exploration of the limits of the paradigm, but it succeeds only in recasting the paradigm in new terms, to modify certainly, but not to change it beyond recognition. We have lost signifieds, opened outwards onto a surface apparently without features, and been saved by these points outside of signification which no longer signify. The problem becomes that of locating these functions. Context reassures the archaeological structure that there is the possibility of a distant presence waiting to be discovered or rediscovered, of a return to the vertical. To do this, and in order to set it to work to recover this *arche*, we must dispense with any further flirtation with the concept of difference. 'The abstract analysis of signs and meanings is particularly a problem in archaeology which is primarily concerned with material culture' (1986: 47). What archaeology seeks to do is to discover how non-arbitrary meanings 'come about', and to do this, evidently, we require that our theories be centred. And to centre them on the outside of difference, we must centre them on that which escapes the rule of the sign – on the materiality of material culture.

The role of context cannot, of course, be kept at a purely conceptual level, for it needs to be located within the terms of analysis. It is therefore placed within its *material* dimensions, material being defined as that which does not signify, as that which is meaning-less. Structuralism would thus appear to have come full circle with the reintroduction of the referent which had, from the very beginning, been written out of its frames of reference, bracketed off. Thus for John Barrett, whose work represents a different emphasis but nevertheless still parallels that of Hodder, the 'architecture' of the material world is reciprocally related within a dialectics of structure/action, but is nevertheless still more permanent and stable than the mere memories of past experience (Barrett 1987a: 8). Unable to refind the signified directly, and so to reintroduce the vertical passage to the *arche*, the referent is returned to its place, on the outside of the text, and the polarity ideal-material is reified. The problem of the horizontality of structure or, in Derrida's phrase the *structurality* of structure, which the whole elaboration of context has sought to solve, is finally by-passed by refinding that which, since ever there was an archaeology, has named its terrain, its cipher, mute and silent but containing the codes of the past:

> Even though written language may have the same basic principles as material culture language, a written language is always very difficult to decipher even when much of it survives. This is partly because it is very complex, designed to express complex ideas and thoughts, and has to be fairly precise and comprehensible. But there are no grammars and dictionaries of material culture language. Material culture symbols are often more ambiguous than their verbal counterparts, and what can be said with them is normally much simpler. Also, the material symbols are durable, restricting flexibility. In many ways material culture is not a language at all – it is more clearly action and practice in the world. In so far as it is a language, it is a simple one when compared to spoken or written language. For these various reasons, material culture texts are easier

to decipher than those written documents for which we do not know the language.

(Hodder 1986: 123)

Material culture as a sign is turned against itself, such that the *materiality* of artefacts acts to break the flows of difference. Referentiality is tamed in the face of the referent. But, because we have already adopted these terms of discussion, and because this materiality, as the site of the absent context, cannot be outside the text without being, at least partially, 'inside' (which is to say that context has a *thickness*), the referent is indistinguishable from this function of context as the signifier outside of signification. Where processualism has proposed and maintained the identity and ontology of the signified – the unmediated passage to the signified of an object, namely its 'function' – post-processualism overturns the hierarchy and rests upon the perceived ontology of the signifier, where stability is offered to the structuring of meaning by the 'lack' that is context and which is filled by the material world which intervenes from the outside in order to break the flows of differing and reference.

Hodder's context and Barrett's field of discourse, both coupled to this materiality, are conceived on the basis of a signifier without a signified, without any necessary requirement having been placed upon it to mean, since its function is to perform this break in flow which threatens to carry off, once and for all, the objects of archaeological study (as the institution still defines them, and guards them, jealously), *linearly*, *horizontally*, and without return.

For what is the alternative? The flows must be broken, for otherwise we will drown in the flood that will break over the institutional practices and rituals of this science. The present would be opaque and we would be trapped within it, like a prisoner. And it is precisely the *arche*, the ontology of the origin, that is at stake. The radical difference and horizontality that holds structuralism together as an epistemological challenge is shocking because it threatens to overturn the conventional metaphor which requires that we conceptualise our work vertically as a return to the origin or to the originary point. Excavation promises to pass from surface to depth, absence to presence, present to past. We all *know* that archaeology is not just about digging up the past from the plough-soil, but we still think it possible for us to excavate – by induction, by deduction, by strategies of reading through context(s) which break up and divide this featureless plain of the signifier. We still think in terms of the passage from the manifest to the hidden.

So, for instance, context is resolved around two poles, one of the past and the other of the present, a conceptualisation that is anticipated in the division between primary and secondary evidence and which, to a greater extent than is recognised, it repeats. It reproduces this 'original' distance and spacing, only now we want to try to think them in terms of each other, in terms of a single context. Conceptually, neither has priority, and the intervention into the chain of signifiers that is necessary to write the past is structured by a dialectic between production and reproduction, construction and reconstruction, *telos* and *arche*, present and past. But this is not enough, it cannot be sufficient, to make us overlook that this writing is still an intervention, the chain has still been broken, the past has still been produced.

Someone has had to decide what to put into the context and what to exclude, and this cannot be forgotten. If context is to contain the past and the present, then we know that these poles are not complete, for chains have been rearranged and fixed around the enclosure, in order to prevent this context from being carried off linearly.

This structure therefore, still reassures the *arche*, the ontology of the past, precisely because it attempts to stabilise all that signifies with this context. In order to allow the *arche* to confront the present from a position of relative autonomy, from its outside, Hodder *already* has to decide what form this past will take. What matters here only appears on the outside, that which determines every configuration of the structure, starting with what is chosen to be placed within it and which prevents it from following off in a spiral of supplementary significations along chains of differences of which past and present, subject and object and so on are only spacings on the level. The emphasis upon the already-interpreted, upon the irreducibility of interpretation, is a strategic blow against empiricism and positivism, but it offers us no escape from the system which holds us and imprisons us in the present, despite the *supposed* relative autonomy of the past.

It is not a question of a failure within context, of a component part which can be added or subtracted in order to guarantee the function. It is a question of the difference of the past *failing* to arrive because it has been prevented from appearing *before* it is given the option of a contextualised arrival. Difference here means not only a space, a spacing of the past from the present, but also a structural incompatibility, a contradiction – so we may say that context, to which we would now have to append a great deal that calls itself hermeneutics, protects the present from the past. Universalised categories are inserted into the past through context – the domestic, for instance, becomes a structuralised difference (it is *already* a signified) to be compared across cultures and genres, such that the frame for the past is already set, its form dictated in *advance*, so that all that remains for the archaeologist is to fill this frame with a landscape, the elements of which will be permitted to signify through this prefix. The structure of male/female is a similar problem, where a radical division between form and content allows Barrett (1987a) to be vociferous in his opposition to the notion of material culture as 'text', because the past can only signify in its own terms, while at the same time preserving the hope that unique structures can still be identified. We ought first, surely, to have thoroughly diagnosed the problem, but instead the past becomes only a reflection of the present, where it is no longer clear where the forms with which we wish to populate the past originate.

The past is therefore claimed to have a relative autonomy, for the *arche* is not dismantled (context, in fact, situates the *arche* in order only to reassure it), but we remain trapped within the present, which takes on the form of an inevitable and irresistible super-ego (to use Freud's term for that which guarantees obedience to the social and cultural laws of the present). The present sets the rules for interpretation, and no possibility is offered for reflexivity with respect to these categories. Sørensen's (1987) framework has two poles, male and female (where do they come from? what are they? how do they function? – these questions should have been considered), which are set to work through a space in the Late Bronze Age (but where are they really going?). Within this framework, no further dissent is possible, because *there is no longer anything left to question* – these questions belong to the outside of context (this dialectic of past and present) which is not recognised as such. Like Narcissus gazing into the pond, we mistake what is actually our own image for that of another, the self for other, out of a desire to break with that which imprisons us – within our own bodies, which is always our own space and our own time. Reading these accounts of the Neolithic, the Bronze and the Iron Ages, we should emphasise the colonisation, by a hoard of little Oedipuses, carrying with them the message that some things are outside of meaning, outside of history and beyond question – that some things just never change.

The past, to which hermeneutics and contextual archaeology claim to assign a relative autonomy, is already silent, already unable to respond, dispute or debate, to enter into a discussion with the present. The prison house of difference, which carries off the *arche* along chains of signifiers, is recovered by context only as a distant mirror, endlessly reflecting back our own image. Context becomes not only the point of incision into a signifying chain but the point of entry for this narcissism. What we want to do is not peer through or beyond the mirror – for there is no space into which we may pass beyond the shiny surface which is not already a mirror, an illusion; no space from which we may confront the present as it were *from the outside*, and by believing that any of these possibilities are open we will continue to run the risk of mistaking the same for other, identity for difference. We do not and cannot gaze beyond, for this beyond is infinitely veiled, preluded by a limitless hall of mirrors. *We must shatter the looking-glass, open outwards and sideways, never back or down.*

In order to conduct this rethinking of the past on the inside of the present, to build beyond context, and to release the radical differentiality of the past, its challenge to and against the present, the metaphor must be shifted back from depths to surfaces, back from the signified to the signifier, from all that holds us to the context of the past at the expense of its form, back to the past *in the present*. This means reasserting the horizontality or structurality of structure and the signifying chain, by which the past is active in the present only as a trace, and is effective through the processes and powers of the unconscious. What we need to theorise, to elaborate, is a means of breaking out of the cycles of reproduction and production, of pasts and presents, to break with this security, and to mix strategy with adventure. We need to theorise this silence, the silence of the border and the voicelessness of context. What I propose here is to rethink the difference between past and present, silence and voice, self and other, within the terms or supplementary significations of the unconscious/conscious, *in the present*.

> This is why it seems useful and legitimate to ask of every production what it tacitly implies, what it does not say. Either all around or in its wake the explicit requires the implicit: for in order to say anything, there are other things *which must not be said*. Freud relegated this absence of certain words to a new place which he was the first to explore, and which he paradoxically *named*: the unconscious. To reach utterance, all speech envelops itself in the unspoken.
>
> (Macherey 1978: 85)

On the unconscious

> Let us therefore compare the system of the unconscious to a large entrance hall,
> in which the mental impulses jostle one another like separate individuals.
> Adjoining this entrance hall there is a second, narrower, room – a kind of
> drawing room – in which consciousness, too, resides. But on the threshold
> between these two rooms a watchman performs his function: he examines
> the different mental impulses, acts as a censor, and will not admit them into
> the drawing room if they displease him . . . But even the impulses which the
> watchman has allowed to cross the threshold are not on that account necessarily
> conscious as well; they can only become so if they succeed in catching the
> eye of consciousness. We are therefore justified in calling this second room
> the system of the *preconscious*.
>
> (Freud 1917: 336–7)

Freud's spatial and topographical model for the structure and operations of the psyche
has, to a certain extent, become sedimented within the conventions of western culture,
although certainly more sympathetically in Europe than in Britain. It is fairly
commonplace to speak of an unconscious, in the sense of something unintended or
not anticipated, but this is much less specific and more diluted than Freud's own usage.

The human mind does not, of course, function homogeneously in Freud's model
of consciousness. From his work with Breuer on hysteria, making use of hypnosis
in the clinical research, Freud had been led to postulate the existence of other kinds
of consciousness and motivation. 'The possibility of giving a sense to neurotic
symptoms by analytical interpretation is an unshakeable proof of the existence –
or, if you prefer it, of the necessity of the hypothesis – of unconscious mental
processes' (1917: 13). The symptom is the result when these unconscious thoughts
and impulses make their appearance in the conscious system (though their significance
remains in the unconscious). From the quotation above it should be clear that the
conscious is not a thing or an identifiable space – it is not a separate room. What
is conscious for Freud is that which is being thought at any one time. The fundamental
distinction, therefore, is not between conscious and unconscious but between
thoughts *available* to consciousness and thoughts not so available. The conscious
has no space within the terms of this metaphor, but is rather like the host wandering
around the drawing room, engaging with those whom the doorman has allowed
access. The conscious takes place within the pre-conscious, which is divided from
the unconscious by the operations of a censor, who acts to *repress* all impulses
originating there and prevent them from becoming available to consciousness.

What is of interest here is the way in which unconscious material becomes available
to consciousness, and is manifested consciously by evading the repressive threshold and
adopting a form which is acceptable to the censor. In *The Interpretation of Dreams* (1900),
Freud draws a distinction between the manifest content of the dream, which is what
it appears on the surface to mean, and the latent dream thoughts, which are the real
motivation for the dream, its proper, correct unconscious meaning. Between the
two is the action of the dream work which, by processes of condensation, displacement
and secondary revision, forms out of the latent dream thoughts the manifest content.
So the original impulse can lose some of its elements, having diverse meanings

concentrated onto single symbols, *condensed* from many to a few; it can have its centre *displaced* and its symbols replaced by others which are apparently without connection; and its lacunae will be revised in order to form an apparently complete narrative structure. All this creates a path whereby the cathexis of energy imputed to the unconscious material can gain conscious release via a detour. 'The dream, in short is one of the detours by which repression can be evaded' (Freud 1905a: 44).

The same processes of psychic distortion account for the formation of the symptoms that form neuroses. Thus, in Breuer's treatment of Fraulein Anna O, a 21-year-old woman suffering from various forms of hysteria, the shock and disgust felt at seeing a friend allow a dog to drink from a glass of water was distorted into an hysterical thirst and an inability or refusal to drink (Freud and Breuer 1895).

> The formation of the substitute for the ideational portion has come about by *displacement* along a chain of connections which is determined in a particular way . . . The result is fear of a wolf, instead of a demand for love from the father.
> (Freud 1915a: 155)

This latter is, of course, a reference to the 'Wolf-Man', who was the subject of Freud's most celebrated case history, in which an obsession with a particular symbol took the place, by displacement, of the original emotional and ideational content of the neurosis.

If we look at another of the case histories, that of Little Hans (1909), we see exactly how distortion operates. Hans was a five-year-old boy living with his parents in a suburb of Vienna, and his neurosis arose within what Freud called the Oedipus or Castration complex. It originated in his own personal obsession with his penis, which was prominent among his erotogenic zones, and the threat of castration for masturbation, which attaches itself to an object remote from the original meaning but in some way connected to it. This object performs the role of substituting for the original symbol. According to Freud's interpretation Hans tried to repress his love for his mother and his desire to masturbate by his fear of horses, the latter becoming the symbol for his father in his unconscious. The choice of this symbol was not random, but was 'determined' by certain points of similarity between the horse and his father, and by his not-too-distant childhood games where he would ride on his father's back. In the neurosis, therefore, certain points became of significance and acted as these points of contact – the emphasis on the black around horses' mouths (muzzle) was linked to his father's moustache, so also the blinkers worn by drays were connected in Hans' mind to his father's glasses. The distortion operating between the latent and manifest content of the neurosis was the means by which repression was bypassed.

Freud emphasised that repression is not a part of the process of substitution of content by symbols, since the aim of repression is only a withdrawal of the cathexis of energy from unconscious material. What repression does is to create a *substitutive formation* – it leaves behind traces of the original meanings, the symptoms. So symptom-formation is a part of the process of repression via substitutive formation, but where the repressed has been allowed to return to consciousness, to cross back over the threshold that separates the entrance hall from the drawing room.

What is clear here is the similarity of these processes to the linguistics that launched structuralism into cultural analysis. Thus repression works linearly- so that displacement is a movement along a chain of signifiers, so that the place of the father can be taken by that of a horse or a wolf. Psychic distortion is part of the processes that articulate the signifying chains of meaning. Thus a symptom is not a single signifier connected to a signified that exists only in the unconscious. Writing about the case of Ida Bauer – to whom Freud gave the pseudonym Dora – a young hysteric, Freud emphasised that '. . . at least one of the meanings of a symptom is the representation of a sexual fantasy, but . . . no such limitation is imposed upon the content of its other meanings' (1905a: 80; 1910: 37). The connection between the manifest and the latent meanings, the dynamics studied by psychoanalysis, can thus be linearised, so that they are linked as different points of focus along a signifying chain. These shifts and focuses constitute the dream symbolism, which – although the emphasis is upon the individual history of a neurosis – need not always be personal, as is underlined in Freud's description of the symbols found in dreams, where many of the connections derive from mythology, folk stories and fairy tales (Freud 1900: 466ff; 1910: 64; 1917: 186ff). Indeed, Freud depicted the field of psychoanalysis as extending, necessarily, beyond medicine to the humanities and social sciences (1926: 351ff).

It is Lacan who most particularly pursues this potential for reading Freud in the terms of Saussure. To a certain extent, he had been prefigured by Freud himself who, as far back as 1900 had begun to conceive of the necessity of a linguistic metaphor for the unconscious. Opening Chapter Vl of *The Interpretation of Dreams*, on the dream work, he comments that the apparently nonsensical content of dreams can be solved if, instead of trying to take the dream as a whole, 'we try to replace each separate element by a syllable or word that can be presented by that element in some way or another' (1900: 382). Many of the dreams analysed by Freud contain similar uses of a linguistic analogy.

For Lacan, the dream symbol becomes the signifier, and it is precisely this linguistic structure that allows us to read dreams. It is 'the very principle of the "significance of the dream", the *Traumdeutung*', (Lacan 1977a:159). Thus the movement of displacement and condensation that is fundamental, not only to the manifestation of the dream but also to its interpretation, and therefore to the hypothesis of an unconscious, can be approached linguistically, as (following Roman Jakobson) *metonymy* and *metaphor*. Displacement becomes metonymy, a relation which exists only in 'the *word-to-word*' (Lacan 1977a: 156), that is, between signifiers, without involving the signified as a determinant factor, since it is (for Lacan as for Derrida) always divided from the signifier by a barrier resisting signification. Metaphor, which now describes the movement of condensation, articulates the appearance of the signified only as one signifier taking the place of another signifier – the function of two equivalent signifiers combining into a relation such that one appears to become the signified for the other.

The processes of signification/consciousness are therefore detached from the mythical vertical dimensions in which they had been contained –

$$\frac{\text{signifier}}{\text{signified}} \quad \text{as} \quad \frac{\text{conscious}}{\text{unconscious}}$$

or, as in the dream symbolism –

$$\frac{\text{manifest}}{\text{latent}}$$

and forced into a horizontal structuring in which what moves are the relations of difference amongst signifiers. It is thus possible to account for the unconscious and its effects wholly at the level of the signifier. Thus Lacan allows the content of the unconscious to float, as the signified floats, under the barrier which prevents it from surfacing by connection to a signifier. Reading Edgar Allan Poe's short story 'The Purloined Letter' (Lacan 1988), the content of the letter, which is a metaphor for Lacan for the contents of the unconscious, are never revealed to us, as it moves from point to point, engaging with different supplementary signifiers and significations attracting different meanings. However, it is still returned to the point from which it started out and its meaning as ontology is assured. 'At every moment each of them [the characters in the story], even their sexual attitude, is defined by the fact that the letter always arrives at its destination' (Lacan 1988: 205). Lacan insists on the non-differential status of the phallic signifier, Lacan's name (drawn from the Freudian concept of the Oedipus/Castration complex) for the point where the signifiers of the signifying chains are determined. It is this that, like the letter/unconscious which in the story is displaced, determines its return to its proper place.

It is at this point therefore that Lacan compromises by insisting on the status of the unconscious as a veiled and virtual presence, something that can be located and isolated and whose meaning-effects can be returned to where they belong. So Dupin the detective in the story, recovers the letter and fulfils his contract. Just when the unconscious appears to become on the level with consciousness.

> Lacan leads us back to the truth, to a truth which itself cannot be lost. He brings back the letter, shows that the letter brings itself back to its proper place via a proper itinerary . . . the signifier has its place in the letter, and the letter refinds its proper meaning in its proper place.
>
> (Derrida 1988b: 436)

Derrida's reading focuses upon the status of the phallic signifier which, by being the point at which difference as references ceases, is the point where the symbolic order is established. It refers, of course, to the Oedipal triangle (Mama-Papa-Me) where the chains of the symbolic are arranged around the hierarchy of the presence/absence of a penis. Lacan, however, emphasises that the concept of the phallus refers to many things as well as the organ in this myth. It is the means by which the subject (ego) is produced and against which the pre-symbolic self (the Id) appears only as a negative.

The proper place to which the letter is returned, therefore, is the place of the phallus, the place of the Oedipus or Castration complex – 'woman as the unveiled site of the lack of a penis, as the truth of the phallus, that is of castration' (Derrida 1988b: 439). But where Lacan emphasises the singularity and indivisibility of the letter/phallus, thus determining the unconscious and the symbolic through the point of closure of the Oedipal triangle, Derrida emphasises the differential status even of this signifier, its belonging to difference and to text, such that, where before the letter's arrival appeared guaranteed, its status is now open to question:

167

Its 'materiality' and 'topology' are due to its divisibility, its always possible partition. It can always be fragmented without return, and the system of the symbol, of castration, of the signifier, of the truth, of the contract, etc., always attempt to protect the letter from this fragmentation . . . Not that the letter never arrives at its destination, but it belongs to the structure of the letter to be capable, always, of not arriving . . . Here dissemination threatens the law of the signifier and of castration on the contract of truth. It broaches, breaches the unity of the signifier, that is, of the phallus.

(Derrida 1988b: 444)

By taking apart the status of the phallic signifier (the signifier that is not a signifier because difference/reference at that point are no longer possible) Derrida's reading insists on the horizontality of signifying relations, such that the unconscious as a defined place, a present signified, is no longer possible. 'The irreducibility of the "effect of deferral" – such, no doubt, is Freud's discovery' (Derrida 1978: 203). The textual metaphors found throughout Freud's work – as in, for instance, 'A Note upon the "Mystic Writing Pad"' (1925) where the occurrence of memories existing only in the unconscious is addressed – are taken to their fullest extent. The conscious or manifest dream text is not a transcription of a latent meaning:

because there is no text *present elsewhere* as an unconscious one to be transposed or transported . . . The text is not conceivable in an originary or modified form of presence. The unconscious text is already a weave of pure traces, differences in which meaning and force are united – a text nowhere present, consisting of archives which are *always already* transcriptions. Originary prints. Everything begins with reproduction. Always already repositories of a meaning which is never present, whose signified presence is always reconstituted by deferral.

(Derrida 1978: 211)

In place of that space to which Freud gave a thoroughly metaphysical name (that is, one invoking surfaces and depths, signifiers and signifieds, manifest and latent meanings . . . etc.), Derrida has only 'a certain alterity':

. . . the unconscious is not, as we know, a hidden, virtual, and potential self-presence. It is deferred – which no doubt means that it is woven out of differences, but also that it sends out, that it delegates, representatives or proxies; but there is no chance that the mandating subject 'exists' somewhere, that it is present or is 'itself', and still less chance that it will become conscious . . . the unconscious can no more be classed a 'thing' than anything else; it is no more a thing than an implicit or muted consciousness . . . With the alterity of the 'unconscious', we have to deal not with horizons of modified presents – past or future – but with a 'past' that has never been nor will ever be present, whose 'future' will never be produced or reproduced in the form of presence.

(Derrida 1973: 152)

The unconscious becomes, we may say, not a space to be discovered beneath consciousness, but a spacing *within* consciousness, within consciousness as writing and consciousness as text. The id is neither the being-present that Freud seems to suggest not the being-absent of which Lacan writes. The id is not to be conceived on the basis of presence or absence, but as difference. If the pre-symbolic is all that does not appear in the symbolic, then we may align the unconscious with all that the symbolic – in the form of the ego, the subject and the super-ego – seeks to repress. The id would contain all that must be excluded from the symbolic/the present in order for them to exist. The id is 'primitive and irrational' (Freud 1933: 107) without being the simple negation of consciousness: 'There are in this system no negation, no doubt, no degrees of certainty: all this is introduced by the work of the censorship between the Unconscious and the Preconscious' (Freud 1915b: 190). The unconscious, removed from the metaphysical function given it by Freud and retained by Lacan, becomes all that, inside the symbolic and cultural order, is also its outside, that which threatens from the inside (there is no outside) but cannot be contained there.

Archaeology through the looking-glass

> In the multiplicity of writing, everything is to be *disentangled*, nothing *deciphered*; the structure can be followed, 'run' (like the thread of a stocking) at every point and at every level, but there is nothing beneath: the space of writing is to be ranged over, not pierced.
>
> (Barthes 1977a: 147)

Archaeologists, despite many of their claims, are fetishists. They eschew antiquarianism (the very antithesis of science), the sheer possession of objects regardless of meaning, but our museums continue to overflow with artefacts. They try to lend theoretical legitimacy to this preference. Binford denounces structuralism as idealist, but his materialism and functionalism rest upon the idealism of the sign conceived as an immediate and tangible unity. A clever deception. Hodder dissents, but only to renew the contract (albeit in a modified form) after a circuitous detour through structuralist logic. He rejects the notion of the arbitrary sign, because what is of concern is *material* culture. Barrett endorses this view, and despite attempts to suspend material and ideal dialectically, still valorises the difference by preferring the former as a vessel to limit and contain the latter. The material world maintains discourse because of its materiality. After the sign, after the signified, after difference, post-processualism arrives at the signifier without signification, without a signified, without difference – a material culture that is no longer divisible through or by difference. *Material* culture is related to meaning and the sign as the *indivisible* is related to the divisible. Its very properties signify permanence, the raw, the hard, the physical, the tangible. Where Saussure threatens to carry us off sideways, laterally, along the horizontal chains of signifiers leading off everywhere at once, Hodder restores the signifier to its place (the place from which it had been deferred, *purloined*) and reintroduces the depth and the truth that assures us of a contract with the signified, an intelligible descent to the *arche*.

Saussure, like the minister in Poe's short story, purloins the signifier and with it the *arche*, and takes it from its place, diverts its course. The past is forced back into signification, and in this flat and featureless plain of difference, we choke. We've got signifiers everywhere, cloaking the horizon, and none of us know which way to turn or what to do with them. We don't know where the past is any more, all we've got are these signifiers. The archaeologist is sought out and contracted. Hodder pursues it, and returns it to its place, its proper context, *the* context out of which it would not have been readable (1986: 141) – which is to say that there are contexts and there are contexts, and we must establish the *proper* context and return the signifier (*arche*) to its place. He leads us back, back from the spectre of structuralism released (by Derrida) even from the limits set it by Saussure, back to the truth of archaeology and back to David Clarke's indivisible disciplinary identity ('Archaeology is archaeology is archaeology') which assures and reassures this truth, back to the material culture with which archaeology has always been concerned. Back to the context without which it could never have operated and which functions ultimately to protect structuralism from subversion by its own logic. Materialism without (proper) context is antiquarianism; materialism with (proper) context is archaeology (Hodder 1986: 120). An obvious sigh of relief; the horizon clears, the signifiers dissipate. Someone spots the *arche*, it is found and returned. An archaeology becomes possible once again.

Context is indispensable. To divert the signifier (the *arche*) from its context is to dispense with archaeology, to break with its rules and its truth. The signifier, forced through difference into a labyrinth of referential traces (in which the *arche,* too, would be carried off) is returned to its proper place, is 'contextualised', and the verticality of the signifying relationship re-established. 'To affirm the importance of context thus includes reaffirming the importance of archaeology as archaeology' (Hodder 1986: 120). The *arche,* diverted and purloined by an unfettered and structuralist logic, is refound through a *material* culture that intervenes (has intervened) to foreclose the difference of difference and the structurality of structure.

Material culture is indivisible. We can talk therefore of the *phallusy* of context for, like Lacan's concept of the phallus (which performs the same function) it operates on the singularity and indivisibility of the letter/signifier, which breaks through the shifting chains of discourse in order to lock them in place and in order to recover the identity, possibility and stability of presence and truth. At this point, through the phallic law of the indivisible signifier, an archaeology becomes practicable, because it is precisely this truth and the potential for this truth that will have been protected and preserved.

But the materiality of the signifier is not the identity and integrity of its form, but its ever possible partition, through difference that works along a line that runs between the signifier and itself. This phallus/material culture is broken up by 'the delicate levers that pass between the legs of a word, between a word and itself' (Derrida 1988b: 78). Post-processualism articulates material culture as text, as writing, but makes of this graphic metaphor only a further fetish, a further identity that reassures the *arche.* 'But the pen, when you have followed it to the end, will have turned into a knife' (Derrida 1981: 302). The signifier in material culture is cut up, the *arche* dissected, by difference, and set loose to wander again, a nomad in an infinite plain without points that can be fixed or mapped out in advance.

Beyond context as/and the rule of the phallus, beyond this version of materiality, there is the horizontal structure, through which excavation works laterally not vertically. The past is to be disentangled in the present, not deciphered. No *arche,* no marginal text, no original meaning. No context can deliver. Nothing is hidden any more, everything is on the level and is in this sense *manifest*. It is a question of connecting signifiers on a horizontal plain, pursuing traces of difference and identity through difference. Past and present are bound on this surface, out of which we do not pass. There is no beyond, no beneath into which the archaeologist can pass, no 'before' to be made present, no potential presence for the past. There is only and always difference. Only a chain of signifiers articulating a further chain of signifiers: there are only, everywhere, differences of differences and traces of traces.

Where contextual archaeology (the last gasp of the old order and the first breath of the new) sought to presence the *possibility* of the *arche* through a glorious, ontological signifier, to assert the radical horizontality of archaeological production is to open archaeology onto a discourse no longer concerned with the past or present as alternatives – as if it were possible for them to rise and separate, for us to choose one and not the other, for one to become present and the other to be made absent. All these perspectives – past not present, object not subject, etc. – are founded upon a mutual exclusivity which forms the topography of an innocence so ingrained within archaeology that it is not so much 'merely' in the name, in its etymology, as a part of the walls and foundations which enclose the institution. We are beginning to break down the barriers which enclose the *arche* from the outside. When the horizontality of the signifier and the signifying chains is asserted, the past cannot appear without the present, and the *arche* as pure signification is delayed indefinitely. It forces us to abandon a project centred on the past or the present and commits us to a practice firmly spaced within difference. Without the various ontological centrings that have protected the fortress, our historical labour shifts to being focused upon differences rather than identity, on the dividing line between identity and non-identity, subject and object, presence and absence, surface and depth, past and present, conscious and unconscious and to what opens these binaries onto a signifying chain.

> It was never our wish . . . to transform the world into a library by doing away with all boundaries, all frameworks, all sharp edges . . . but that we ought rather to work on the theoretical and practical system of these margins, once more, from the ground up.
>
> (Derrida 1979: 84)

A systematic discourse on the borders and margins.

But these borders and margins will not be those immediately of the past and present. The hermeneutic project will always have reassured identity lent to it a stability and put the *arche* back in place. The relative autonomy of the past can only be thought, first of all, from the present. Like the unconscious, the past is 'structured like a language'. The *arche* is produced as a space or spacing in a horizontal surface of signifying traces. It is a question of the present displacing itself onto this space now called 'the past' and distanced from the present rhetorically, horizontally. And it is a question of condensation, of the elements of this writing representing many other elements, a *dialogism* to use Bakhtin's term. Age is a measure of lateral distance, and 'the past' is a rhetorical signifying space, a space in a horizontal chain. It is a 'contemporary' space, a space contemporaneous with the present in which the utterance takes place, a space in the present.

171

What we use to measure this space – a radio-carbon date, for example – does not launch us into the past. It is no more the past than a railway timetable. They are part and parcel of a rhetorical system of writing designed to create a regulated and controlled spacing on a horizontal signifying plain and to give to this space, thereafter, the associated meanings of past and present. The designation 'X number of year BP (before present)' is a rhetorical gesture designed to distance the remarks hung on it from the present and provide them with a different stage, one spaced from me, the present and the conditions of my writing. It should not be allowed to deceive me into thinking that the referentiality of these remarks is anything other than contemporary. Don't think that chronology has anything to do with temporality, with being outside the present, with anything we might call 'history'. The spatial representation of time is not enough to establish distance but, because of the nature of this writing, this would be its rhetorical function. All it does is to create the effect or impression of distancing (from the present) through a process of regulation and ritualisation within signifying effects articulated on a horizontal surface.

The effect of depth, the signified, is thus produced on this horizontal surface, amongst signifiers and signifying chains arranged laterally. Lacan's formula for describing metaphor expresses this succinctly:

$$f \frac{(S') \ S}{(S)} = S \ (+) \ s$$

(Lacan 1977a: 164), which can be described as the function of two signifiers combining in a relation such that one appears to take the place of the signified for the other.[1]

It should therefore be possible to account for the production of the past in archaeology wholly on the level of the signifier. The *arche* is differed and deferred, displaced and condensed – it is no more than a signifying trace, an effect, which is not a virtual presence or a presence to be placed (discovered, rediscovered, reconstructed) in a context. It has to be thought on the basis of difference, not a difference (past/present) already prescribed in advance, but of difference from the present. The past, produced in this way, is the experience of difference, but it is not a foreign country, it is a little England, a home from home. This narcissism is assured at every moment because rhetorical and formal strategies and the sedimented symbolism of archaeology create the impression of space on a signifying chain as temporal remoteness. Thus contextual archaeology is caught up in these cycles of specular identification of self as other and finds, not the relative autonomy of the past mediated by the present but the doorway that opens onto a hall of mirrors.

What we need is a means of breaking with the present, in order to find the past from the inside of the codes and regulations that protect and guarantee the present. The past appears and has value, therefore, not as a reconstruction of the past but as a deconstruction of the present, the strategies of which explicate 'the relationship of the work to itself' (Derrida 1986: 124). Like the unconscious, the past only appears when a rupture of the present can be effected, when the 'thetic' (to use Julia Kristeva's term), which originates in the mirror stage and is completed in the full inauguration of the symbolic, is broken through. We should, therefore, align ourselves with the Id, with Kristeva's semiotic, which 'constantly tears it [the symbolic] open, and this transgression brings about all the various transformations of the signifying practice that are called "creation" . . . what remodels the symbolic is always the influx of the semiotic' (Kristeva 1984: 62). So, to paraphrase Sollers' comments on the novel, the past is the way in which society speaks to itself, and it signifies the ways in which the subject must live in order to be accepted there. It provides the codes of instinctive reference, the exercise of its power, 'the key to its everyday unconscious, mechanical, shut' (quoted in Laing 1978: 99).

And yet it is possible to use the resources of this signifying practice to explore the present, to chart its limits and work through its fissures, to explore the real, the possible, the tangible. The present is not the prison it appears to be, and we are not necessarily condemned to be contained within its walls: 'There is a crack there. Construction and deconstruction are breached/broached there. The line of disintegration, which is not straight or continuous or regular . . .' (Derrida 1987a: 132).

Writing is not a discovery, or a rediscovery, of something located elsewhere, 'It is something newly raised up, an addition to the reality from which it begins' (Macherey 1978: 6). It is not passive with respect to reality, but it adds and produces and changes the real. An emphasis upon production ruptures the unidirectionality of our epistemologies. From a critical knowledge of our present we can start to explore that unconscious that sustains the present through the mirror of the past, in order to release another unconscious which is capable of remoulding and reshaping the present. The 'past' is only of any value if it can break out of these cycles of projection and introjection, and this must involve an identification of the past with the unconscious – with all that lies 'outside' the present (while always being 'inside'), with all that is forbidden, with that forged on the difference between the intelligible and the possible, the spoken and the silent.

The 'distant mirror' must be shattered, not pierced. No passage across boundaries but their fragmentation. It is in the difference between the conscious/spoken/ intelligible and the unconscious/unspoken/silent in the present, rather than in the simple difference between the past and the present that we find the space of our writing. Our task as archaeologists is not to administer the scene in order to locate the past (the *arche*) here, there or wherever, but to work the scene in order to break with the present and to allow 'the past' to wander through its corridors unfettered.

Reading the unconscious

No 'theory,' no 'practice,' no 'theoretical practice' can intervene effectively within this field if it does not weigh up and bear upon the frame, which is the decisive structure of what is at stake, at the invisible limit at (between) the interiority of meaning (put under shelter by the whole hermeneuticist, semioticist, phenomenologist and formalist tradition) and (to) all the empiricisms of the extrinsic which, incapable of either seeing or reading, miss the question completely.

(Derrida 1987a: 61)

Cambridge, 1989

(framing)

Otherwise we miss the question completely.

What becomes of concern in context, therefore, is the thickness of its walls, the silence of its borders, the function of the frame, the dividing line (always active, never passive) that wedges between interior and exterior, forcing them apart.

We always try to forget about this frame, Kant reduced the parergon (hors d'œuvre, accessory, supplement, addition) to a secondary status with respect to the ergon, the essence of the aesthetic, beauty itself. The drapery on the body of the statue, the ornamental frame that surrounds the painting, the columns of the classical building – all are parerga, secondary, detachable, and we would lose nothing if we were to discard them. Always, we must know what belongs on the inside, and what is therefore to be valued, and what remains external, on the outside, what can be removed from our attention and disregarded.

It is precisely the strategic legitimacy of this move that is at stake.

'No text,' Umberto Eco writes, 'is read independently of the readers' experience of other texts' (Eco 1981: 21). There is only a radical intertextuality where everything is text, is already text. Every text is a multiple reading head for further, other texts. 'An apocalyptic super-imprinting of texts: there is no paradigmatic text. Only relationships of cryptic haunting from mark to mark. No palimpsest (definitive unfinished-ness). No piece, no metonymy, no integral corpus' (Derrida 1979: 136–77).

What is important then is the marginal and the question of the marginal. And perhaps we should also say that what is of interest is less of the form of a context than of a 'reading formation', which 'would be the question of studying texts in the light of their readings, readings in the light of their texts' (Bennett 1987: 74). A question always of refusing to separate the reading of an archaeological text from my experience of other texts, from experience as text itself.

Vienna, 1905

(posing the question)

Psychoanalytic research is most decidedly opposed to any attempt at separating off homosexuals from the rest of mankind as a group of special character. By studying sexual excitation other than those that are manifestly displayed, it has found that all human beings are capable of making a homosexual object-choice and have in fact made one in their unconscious . . . On the contrary, psychoanalysis considers that a choice of an object independently of its sex – freedom to range equally over male and female objects – as it is found in childhood, in primitive states of society and early periods of history, is the original basis from which, as a restriction in one direction or the other, both the normal and the inverted types develop. Thus from the point of view of psychoanalysis the exclusive sexual interest felt by men for women is also a problem that needs elucidating and is not a self-evident fact based upon an attraction that is ultimately of a chemical nature.

(Freud 1905b: 56–7)

The framework of heterosexuality is not natural or originary, but a secondary development. It is already a parergon. The choice of sexual object could go either way, and 'normality' – heterosexuality, my heterosexuality, for example – appears as the child takes on the rules and regulations of culture, and learns to structure not only its thoughts, attitudes and actions but its whole being around these provisos. Stephen Frosh writes – 'heterosexual genitality is not a natural organisation of sexual instinct, but a channelling of, or restriction on, potential to be found in the child' (Frosh 1987: 46). Normality is a work of repression, passing through a series of stages, but the perverse character of human sexuality remains within the subject, repressed and subdued, but capable of breaking out of the unconscious to form, in conscious life, the parapraxes, the dreams, the neuroses and their symptoms. Although I am a heterosexual I am still capable, Freud tells me, of making a homosexual object-choice in my unconscious. I have *already* done so, and thus everything depends upon how well I keep these forces walled up there. The 'unity' of the unconscious-conscious/preconscious is, therefore, a bisexual unity. 'And I am accustoming myself to the idea of regarding every sexual act as an process in which four persons are involved' (Freud 1954: 289). I am not one; I am divided, dissipated, my maleness is distributed on all sides: I am already a crowd.

No rigid division can thus be drawn between normal and abnormal sexuality. Normality is not a function of reproduction, but, on the contrary, the elevation of reproductive sex to a position that condemns all else to a position from which, henceforth, they will always be described as deviant or perverse. The 'natural' state of libido – if it makes sense to think of it in this way – would be the free combination and articulation of desire (see Nordbladh and Yates, chapter 8 [of the original work]).

What we seem to be incapable of understanding is the extent to which the organisation of our lives, down to the most intimate aspects and preferences of our ego, is cultural and historical. And this is, of course, a major problem in a science which (processual or post-processual) is attempting to understand culture before the emergence of a Christian morality, let alone those more recent developments which have precipitated on our doorstep the concept of 'Man', upon which so much now depends.

We have to read sexuality always as a supplement, always as an addition, always as a parergon – something without a point of origin, a point of presence. This takes away from anything an immunity to the question. Freud understood it: that we must explain the normal as much as that which deviates from its rules; we must account for its appearance, its conditions, and its functions.

Bohuslän, Sweden, 3000 BP

(becoming a sexed body in the Bronze Age)

If one were to describe the problematics of the Bronze Age – or, indeed, any periodisation in archaeology – then it could be put like this: (1) it ought to be possible to isolate proper identities, and – as a corollary – (2) it ought to be possible to arrange them properly – i.e. normally – so that they obey some expected regularities, fall within established borders, arrange themselves around a recognised and recognisable centre.

The material of concern here is the rock carvings of northern Bohuslän, situated on the west coast of Sweden, abutting on the Norwegian border. I want to discuss this material in a very preliminary fashion, in a marginal manner, suspending questions of chronology, typology, spatial analysis, structural analysis, as I will suspend the question inaugurated by context along with all the regulated symbolism. What is at stake here is not an interpretation, but what may be put into an interpretation, what is inserted into the past through the thickness of context – the pre-contextual (as we would have to call it in Hodder's formula), the 'absolute presents' which, as Jameson stresses, bar the way to a genuine historicity. It is necessary to suspend these questions because, first, these are derivative of a certain organisation of which we are only very dimly aware, and it requires examination and, second, because until we have diagnosed the situation, we do not know what status or value these strategies deserve.

We begin with the marginal, because we recognise it as the displaced centre, as the point where we must begin if we are to attempt to *know* the centre. We begin not with what is said so much as what is not said, with the journey to silence which is the hidden history of the work, its prehistory. These are insidious questions, those which come from behind.

Let me start, then, by describing the rock carvings as a structure of signifying chains whose circuit remains to be completed. In so far as this rock art is 'the sign of the past' it confronts us today as a potential crisis of the Oedipal. For what is absent in the rock art, as always in an unfamiliar semiotic system, is precisely this triangulation, this third term which enters to determine the signifying chains, the Name-of-the-Father as Lacan calls the phallic signifier which determines and establishes the codes of normality.

What is absent from the rock art is precisely this authority, and so it is this authority that must be added whenever there is a requirement, less to say something than to prohibit it, to render a possibility, a possible or potential arrangement or configuration, impossible. Proper identities become through a proper framework, which rests on a division between what is permissible amongst a set of signifiers and what is not permissible – a division which determines for a generative structure what combinations are and will henceforth be possible (the possible always being inseparable from sanction).

Interpretation is an Oedipalisation – the rewriting of a signifying chain according to a grand code whose contingency is hardly perceived, and whose status appears to be natural, ordained, governed from without. It is the territorialisation of the drives which set up over an unformed sexuality the division which will force conformity to a norm and confirm all other organisations as, by comparison, both polymorphous and perverse. Confronted by a chain of signifiers that intrude into the present, the first step of an archaeologist is to territorialise these chains, to execute an occupation of the signifying space. The past cannot be allowed to roam in the present unattended, going where it will – it needs a chaperon, it must be located, given a place, a name, a neighbourhood. Interpretation is always the conflict of the sedentary with the nomadic.

And yet we meet our first hermeneutic problem – although it is really more of an inconvenience. We cannot in the rock art identify properly (i.e. as binary exclusivity) male and female figures. Bohuslän has the highest proportion of human figures in all the rock carvings of northern Europe (Malmer 1981), and yet we cannot,

Figure 10.1 *Being male*

as our point of contact with this origin, locate those two poles which will give us access to this 'otherworld', a point of entry into its symbolic codes. All that we can do is determine whether the figures are phallic or whether they are non-phallic – whether or not they are depicted with erect penises. The phallus is what tends to the signifier (the figure as signifier) a substance – sexlessness reterritorialises around this point, this attribute. Men are there to be found, and they rise up out of a mass of undifferentiated (unsexed) bodies, erect and proud (Figure 10.1). Women, on the other hand, elude the eye. They cannot be identified by any code of reference that we are capable of recognising. Females have become invisible – for their sexual organs offer us that horror of there being nothing to see, nothing to represent (the horror of the castration threat fulfilled):

> A defect in this systematics of regulation and desire. A 'hole' in its scoptophilic lens. It is already evident in Greek statuary that this nothing-to-see has to be excluded, rejected, from such a scene of representation. Women's genitals are simply absent, masked, sewn back up inside their 'crack'.
>
> (Irigaray 1985a: 26)

A whole artistic and social tradition separates us, not simply from the past – the Bronze Age, etc. – but (and this is what we really mean) from the possibility of representation in a different way. The artist, then, looked upon the male and, in common sympathy with us, found an organ to represent, something worthy of attention, but looked upon the female and found no such organ and – in its absence – nothing to represent.

And this would provide us with a topography of 'the Bronze Age' cultural lens, a snapshot of the land refracted through it. It would be composed, on the one side, of figures which are 'incontrovertibly' male, and on the other of figures whose sex is, strictly speaking, indeterminate – they may or may not be female, for we cannot rule out the possibility that these non-phallic figures are – to use Gro Mandt's (1987) delicate little expression – not as 'potent' as the others – an expression which converts the phallic–non-phallic couple into the binary active–passive, always reserving the possibility that this division may be located a little more specifically on a subsequent occasion. It is into this latter class that women disappear.

Thus the phallic/active equation becomes signified as 'male', while the non-phallic/passive equation becomes, by default, female or a passive male. Man as the presence of the phallus, the engorged organ (which need not, we should remind ourselves, follow the more modest dimensions of reality) and woman as the figure without *the* organ, the site of the absence of the penis, the state of 'phalluslessness'. Woman becomes as the non-male, not as a species of being in her own right. Woman possesses – and Freud is as much in line with this opinion as anyone else – not so much a genital as the absence of a genital, not a vagina but a not-penis, the non-presence of the 'proper' organ. A little boy submits to the symbolic order in Freud's account of the Oedipus complex because he fears castration, a becoming-female; the little girl, however, submits because, in this valuation, she is *already* castrated, already a castrato, a submissive, and so no alternative strategy is offered.

So, in what we call 'the Bronze Age' and in this art which we assign to that space, we would be confronted with a twofold sexual system, the phallic and the non-phallic, which need not be strictly equivalent to that of male and female, but which is perhaps beginning to signify these identities through an association with the active–passive couple. The absent phallus could still be signifying male, and anyway this structure remains homosexual because, however great the signifying opportunities open to interpretation, however heterogeneous the divisions active: passive/erect: flaccid/ present: absent appear, they are always referent to the male organ, the identity of which is never open to question, and find their territory defined from that point.

The symbolic world of the carvings is, therefore, divided into a realm of sexual certainty, the phallic/active/male, and a secondary (and therefore derivative) realm of sexual ambiguity, the non-phallic/passive/malefemale. The feminine world of the Bronze Age therefore takes place and is played out in the absence of identity, identity always rising up erect and proud in the form of the male organ with which it is always synonymous. If we were to formalise an anatomy of the sign, as a geography of the body, then it would look something like this:

> PRESENCE: absence
> PHALLIC: non-phallic
> POSITIVE: negative
> POTENT: passive
> IDENTITY: ambiguity
> MALE: 'female'

A fairly typical collection of structural oppositions. All very neat. 'Female' is still suspended within quotation marks because it is a provisional assignment depending upon some cultural supplementations. Interpretation aligns itself with the side of presence, with the molar/male, and attempts to fuse or graft on to it, from a position of (phallic) identity, all that is to be related within the same context and to be determined from that point. Man becomes in the rock art through the identity of his phallus, while, because she is lacking, woman is denied this opportunity, and becomes only as an uncertainty, an incompleteness, the conceptual and cultural absence of the male. It is the task of the archaeologist to forge from this absence an identity and a stability. From a position of certainty established on the basis of a single and exclusive erotogenic zone, a whole principle of hermeneutic method is to be elaborated.

And yet, the indeterminacy of the female almost strikes a familiar note in a society (today) which offers women a discourse based on the values of inadequacy, inconstancy, inferiority and relative irrationality. Women don't know their own minds, they are fickle, inconsistent – whereas to be a man (we are brought up to believe) is to be solid, fixed, like a rock. Does not our own culture arrange its signifiers around these phallic/active: non-phallic/passive dichotomies, and while woman is taught to identify with the latter side, men live with the threat of passing over and joining them. A male can be caught up in a discourse of non-phallic passivity which can precipitate him into the processes of cultural elaboration connected up to a feminine-becoming. It is part of the codes by which patriarchy establishes control not only over women but over any form of dissent from its own ranks. The ideals of the active and erect phallus are also the ideals around which contemporary male peer groups are organised, 'the "strongest" being the one who has the best "hard-on", the longest, the biggest, the stiffest penis, or even the one who "pees the farthest" (as in little boys' contests)' (Irigaray 1985a: 25). Is not impotence, for instance, a betrayal of male identity, an act of infidelity to the gender, a sign that marks the passage from identity to process, from a being-male to a becoming-female? And there are many other means of such a betrayal.

Thus also a man who breaks away from the presumed unity and identity of the male world, who dissents over adopting the regulated symbolism that conditions masculine identity – he drifts from the security and culturally acceptable 'being a male' (ontology) into a shady world of ambiguous or uncertain significations. He produces contradictory signs to which society, rigidly normalised (Oedipalised), finds enormous difficulty in assigning a place within the symbolic order of things. Those who mix the accepted norms of representation – Boy George might be one such example – are condemned to a world of shadows and uncertainties, to a liminal territory in which there is no real ontology, no 'proper' identity. A 'gender bender' has, for that very reason, ceased to signify his phallic/active/masculine identity and is rationalised as no longer *being-male*, but a *becoming female*. Félix Guattari writes:

> To understand homosexuals better we tell ourselves that they are somewhat 'like a woman', and even some homosexuals join in this convention to help normalise the situation. The feminine-passive/masculine-active couple thus remains a kind of obligatory model, dictated by authority, to enable us to situate, localise, territorialise and control the intensities of desire.
>
> (Guattari 1984: 234)

The topography of the rock art, as it is manifested as interpretation (and interpretation as supplementation) takes on a field of signifiers organised only by difference, but it is already a form of inheritance, since this topography is already territorialised. Each signifier here, each body, becomes the focal point of an intensity of desire, a libidinal tension, and it falls to the archaeologist, not so much to interpret as to patrol the territory and survey the scene. S/he who paints a picture of Bronze Age sexuality, provides the body with a frame, such that interpretation is always already a frame-up.

Tanum, c. 1000 BC

(the marriage ceremony at Vitlycke)

When it comes to humans in the rock carvings, it is almost only men that are represented. They often have strongly emphasised sex organs, but this is not marked all the time. Of course, they are found in the scenes, the marriage pictures, where even women are depicted, characterised by their long hair . . .

(Almgren 1975: 73–4; my translation)

Figures of women occur rarely amongst the rock pictures . . . Where a woman is identified, it is in most cases quite certain. That holds especially for the rather dispersed 'marriage scenes'; there one clearly sees that it is a man and a woman that are depicted. The woman is drawn with long hair, the man with a phallus and sword.

(Elverheim 1986: 8; my translation)

This territorialization of sexuality is effected, performed, carried out. A certain combination of figures, perceived in a particular way, are described as belonging to marriage scenes, which strikes us as familiar, proper even appropriate.

Of these scenes. the most famous is located at the top of the large panel at Vitlycke (Figure 10.2), in the heart of Tanum and a few miles south of the town from which the parish takes its name. It is composed of two figures, apparently locked in an embrace and sealing their attachment with a kiss, watched over by a larger, phallic figure who carries a sword and holds an axe above the couple. This latter figure is often described, cautiously, as the priest, which matches the convention that the union here occurring is a legitimated one. The priest would, therefore, be blessing a union between partners in marriage (a union which, we cannot fail to suspect, is already in the act of being consummated).

'The marriage scene'. This descriptive appellation does not belong on the inside and yet neither can we think it wholly on the outside. It stands in an ambiguous

Figure 10.2 *The marriage ceremony*

Figure 10.3 *Being married*

relation to the picture it depicts, neither inside nor outside. It is the addition that bridges the differences and explodes the border. It is the supplement. It is added because it must be added, because there has never been anything without the supplement. Take one away and there would still be supplements, because the ergon is always preceded by a lack, which overturns the hierarchy and installs the parergon in its place. No metacommentary can exhaust this lack, nor could we go back so far as to find a text without a commentary. Discourse multiplies infinitely.

So the verbal appellation could not be either secondary or primary with relation to the origin – it is both at the origin and spaced from it. If we were to represent this by the formula

$$\frac{\text{signifier}}{\text{signified}}$$

then it would only be to accept that the signified appears only by foreclosing a chain of signifiers – the frame intervenes – while, at the same time, being no more than a signifier. 'The marriage ceremony' cannot be judged from any external object-space (no 'past'), it can only be taken apart from within, read for the frame, through the frame, by the frame. It is not the past that must be made to appear, but the parergon that anticipates all statements, all significations, all signifying production. It is the difference of the signifier, a line which passes through 'the marriage ceremony' as a line of force, that offers itself up as an opening for reading.

> 'The marriage ceremony' What is a version? What is a title? What borderline questions are posed here? I am seeking here merely to establish the necessity of this whole problematic of judicial framing and of the jurisdiction of frames.
>
> (Derrida 1979: 88)

A further seventeen scenes follow essentially the same pattern, depicting the figures more or less schematically than at Vitlycke – although the priest would appear to be an optional extra, a walk-on part, since it is depicted at only one other site (see Figure 10.3 for eight of the scenes).

Again, conventional attitudes have dictated the way in which these scenes have been approached. At Vitlycke, the figure on the right is described as the male, with a sword and penis, while the figure on the left becomes, *de facto*, female, lacking either sword or penis, but depicted with long hair (Elverheim, 1986, considers this feature the one certain indication of female sex). Length and style of coiffure are not, of

Figure 10.4

course, universal, cross-cultural and transhistorical sexual symbols (they are not even stable gender signs in our own culture, as the fashion of the last thirty years amply demonstrates), and so it is worth looking at the scenes a little more closely. Only three of the nine 'females' who appear in these scenes actually have long hair – in two cases the heads of the figures are, or are no longer, visible, while in the remaining four examples the 'female' would be indistinguishable from the male on the basis of this feature. It is, indeed, only clear in two cases (Figure 10.3–1 and 10.3–2) to which figure the penis actually belongs (and then only because the artist has troubled to depict the testicles). Thus, we must also note, there are cases where long-haired figures are depicted with weapons (Figure 10.4), an attribute which would, if we had accepted the conventional view, distinguish male from female. Indeed, in the same example, one figure with long hair is quite clearly phallic.

According to P. V. Glob, whose monumental work (1969) on the Danish rock carvings of the same period devotes space to a consideration, and formalisation, of these relationships, the cup mark (small, circular depression), which is found between the legs of human figures on carvings in Denmark and right the way up the Swedish west coast as far as Østfold in Norway, is a female symbol, indicating her genitalia (this argument is repeated *ad infinitum* in the literature, most notably by Burenhult 1978 and Mandt 1987). It is found with figures with long hair, as in Bohuslän (Figure 10.4–5), including the adorant figure from Aspeberget (Figure 10.4–6), but it is not confined to those alone. It is found with figures which otherwise lack any distinguishing or characteristic marks (Figure 10.4–1;10.4–2). There might be a certain logic to this argument – if the penis is depicted by a line or a stroke protruding from the front of the figure, then the vagina, as the opposite of the penis, its absence might well be depicted by a dot, denoting the opening. But this proves as difficult to sustain as the other diagnostic markings. Firstly, the cup mark is not only found with figures whose sex is otherwise uncertain, but with those which are indisputably male – either in front of the figure proximal to the penis (Figure 10.5–1) or between the legs of the figure in what we are told is the 'feminine' position. Similarly, at Aspeberget, a few hundred metres from Vitlycke, the cup mark is found associated with the male bulls which process across the top of the central panel. If it does in any way designate anatomy, then the cup mark would indicate, not simply the hole that is the vagina but that which forms the urethra and the anus as well.

Indeed, if we look back to the embracing figures at Vitlycke, we must note that the marriage couple are accompanied by a cup mark, but beneath the feet of the male, phallic figure, not those of the 'female'. The cup mark cannot be tied down to a self-identical and fixed sexuality, therefore, be it male or female.

The problems involved with these positions and interpretations, and their delicate but by no means uncontradictory choreography, are well illustrated by the blatant circularity of Glob's argument: 'It [the "female" cup mark] is thus seen in the carving at Rished in Bohuslän under a woman standing beside a phallic man . . . .. As cups are not otherwise found in this scene, the location of the cup-mark cannot be fortuitous' (Glob 1969: 306). The cup mark floats, engaging with many different types of figure. It is what we might call a floating signifier, one that travels the signifying chains, traversing the differences that articulate their components. It

Figure 10.5

'becomes' a female sex indicator only if we first presume that the figure it accompanies is female, and if there is, first and foremost, and certainly not interior to the rock art, the necessity of assigning a figure a determinate identity, a determinate sexual identity, particularly a determinate female identity.

What is interesting here is not simply that this designation has taken place – that, of course, might seem to be reasonable – so much as why it has occurred. Why is it necessary to depart from that model which accepted the ambiguity of the non-phallic figures in the rock art in order, now and here – in these particular scenes – to draw determinacy out of indeterminacy? It can only be out of a desire to close off that possibility that at Vitlycke and the other eight scenes are depicted, not a man and a woman in a sexual embrace, but a man and a man. What a shocking possibility! The model of the phallic:non-phallic and active:passive suggests to our cultural eye that there ought to be a woman here, the counterpart for the engorged male organ, but in scenes as suggestive as these it becomes necessary to close off the latent but nevertheless possible signification. As soon as we find a woman here, we have already passed under a prohibition. The possibility that these are homosexual scenes cannot be left open. Therefore (and it is principally at these points, the marriage scenes) the monolithic system of sexuality – already homosexual because it recognises the presence of only one organ, one sex, the phallic male – is displaced to make room for the appearance of woman, in order to prevent another but different form of homosexuality. Under these specific circumstances, Bronze Age woman becomes determinate, is dragged into presence.

But not for her own sake. She appears, we note, only when a set of sexual prohibitions is brought to bear upon the range of possible significations. *The marriage scene.* Women have use value for men (pleasure) but are also a commodity which has exchange value (prestige) amongst men. If, then, this is to be a marriage scene, then we should expect to find a woman here, at the locus of the ceremonies by which she is circulated and exchanged between patriarchal heads. Especially if there is to be a kiss, an act of copulation, then there must be a woman.

Always, we read, she is a commodity, necessary for exchange, necessary for reproduction, necessary when the male requires a space into which he may plug his penis. This we cannot forget. Woman only becomes necessary when something threatens the phallic directionality and unity of the male. She is not a subject, not an individual with an identity, she is no more than a prop, one that post-Oedipally takes the place of the hand which is forbidden by taboo from continuing to gain satisfaction auto-erotically: 'The vagina is valued for the "lodging" it offers the male organ when the forbidden hand has to find a replacement for pleasure-giving' (Irigaray 1985a: 23). Woman appears, therefore, in interpretation only as a structural necessity, as the recognised object of the drives and the correct locus of desire, the regulated destination of the semen. 'She' is not a person, not a 'subject': she is part of the process by which ideology patrols the territory of masculine identity, she is needed to *validate* that identity.

But this sudden determinacy cannot be maintained. Glob notes two scenes from the rock carvings of Denmark that are comparable to those in Bohuslän. The first, which he claims as a marriage scene, is too stylised and too schematic for us to distinguish either sexual partner. The other, which is carved on the Maltegård stone from northern Zealand (Figure 10.5–5) depicts a male figure on the left, with an erect penis depicted by a line, and a 'female' (*sic*) figure on the right, her genitals apparently indicated by a vertical line between 'her' legs. This time the convention that establishes the formula VAGINA = HOLE = CUP MARK is abandoned, and the vagina is to be represented in the same way as the phallus, by a single straight line. 'Undoubtedly we see in this unique piece a depiction of the "sacred" wedding, the May wedding, known from classical lands and recent folklore' (Glob 1969: 294). And yet this scene and its execution are by no means as unique as Glob suggests. What strikes us here is that the apparently 'female' figure is depicted with what would otherwise, under different circumstances, have been described as a phallus–depictions of non-erect phalluses in just this way are by no means unheard of amongst the carvings of southern Scandinavia. Depicting the penis passively rather than as 'potent' (erect) is a means of representation which, while not as common as the erect or non-phallic figures, is found all the way up the east coast of the Skaggerak/Kattegat (e.g. Figure 10.5–4), and in these cases it seems a little unlikely that anyone would not regard these figures as male.

For what we would otherwise have to face is the possibility that the scenes identified in Bohuslän at eighteen sites and, crucially perhaps, on the Maltegärd stone from Denmark, represent not heterosexual but homosexual coitus. The coupling of erect (active) and non-erect (passive) figures is certainly to be maintained, but by examining the circumstances by which these have become, in interpretation, 'women', we must be led to seriously doubt the frameworks within which we have worked. There is no reason to assume that both these figures are not male, nor is there any contemporary reason why they should not be so. In any case, we must accept that there is an ambiguity that is not undesirable but in fact as original as the identities we think we see, which allows these scenes to signify either form of sexuality, and to perform upon the present a deterritorialisation of the rules and structures, the codes and signs, the signifying production, of desire.

The action of making women 'appear' in the otherwise 'homosexual' structures of praxis is only motivated in opposition to this threatening possibility – is only in order to exclude and so deny it, to make women appear in order to make this unspeakable 'other man' disappear. Always there is a kind of male, a certain male, but only under circumstances that it is possible to describe does there become a female: *interpretation is traversed by a line of socio-psychic repression*. She appears, not for herself, not to find herself in herself, as her own identity, but as the portable vagina to be deployed strategically whenever masculine self-identity is threatened or brought into question. The designation 'the marriage ceremony', which delimits this process, teems with significations which should become the object of an archaeology.

> The fact is that women are the only authorised repositories of the process of becoming a sexed body. If a man breaks away from the phallic rat race inherent in all power formations, he will become involved in various possible ways in this sort of feminine becoming. Only then can he go on to becoming animal, cosmos, words, colour, music.
>
> (Guattari 1984: 234)

no place, no date

(becoming human)

> I am convinced – as the experience of psychoses and serious neuroses makes clear – that, beyond the ego, the subject is to be found lying in scatters all over the world of history.
>
> (Guattari 1984: 27)

> If we descend to the least evolved societies . . . Here, the individual himself loses his personality. There is a complete lack of distinction between him and his exterior soul or totem. He and his 'fellow animal' together compose a single personality. The identification is such that man assumes the characteristics of the thing or animal with which he is united. For example, on Mabuiag Island

people of the crocodile clan are thought to have the temperament of the crocodile: they are proud, cruel, always ready for battle . . . The Bororo sincerely imagines himself to be a parrot: at least, though he assumes the characteristic form only after he is dead, in this life he is to that animal what the caterpillar is to the butterfly.

(Durkheim and Mauss 1973: 6–7)

Gregor Samsa woke up one morning to find that he had become a gigantic insect. What shocks us, perhaps, is that the criteria for being-human have been torn back and a metamorphosis has taken place. Such an event should not, strictly, be allowed: man may have been an ape, but he is now (being) that which is absolutely prohibited from mixing with other forms, especially that of the insect. And so, in the end, Gregor is sacrificed in order to preserve the rules of existence, the Oedipalised codes of ontology and of the family (Bogue 1989: 111–12).

But – and presuming from the start that the two are separable rather than internal to each other – we might say that fact is stranger than fiction. If Gregor abandons being for a becoming (and there was never any question of choice), then this horror of a becoming-other is by no means confined to the imagination of literature. Stephen D., for instance, dreamt one night that he was a dog, and woke to find that the transformation of which he had received a premonition was already complete. He awoke to find himself

in a world unimaginably rich and significant in smells, the becoming-animal here marked by the sudden ascendancy of one sense over the others. 'I had dreamt I was a dog – it was an olfactory dream – and now I awoke to an infinitely redolent world – a world in which all other sensations, enhanced as they were, paled before smell . . . I see now what we give up in being civilised and human. We need the other – the "primitive" – as well'.

(Sacks 1985: 149–51)

And it is this becoming-other which we fear as the absolute deterritorialisation of the human. Gregor had to be destroyed less because he had ceased to be human than because he had ceased to be anything in particular – he does not turn into an insect, for he remains Gregor Samsa. He remains a man-becoming-insect, between ontological realms, and so outside of the liberal values that would protect the hallowed space of the human individual.

The body-ego is not fixed and inviolable. It is not something upon which we can rely and assume to be the basis – fundamental and unquestionable – of all experience. The notion of a knowable body-self – which is without doubt an historical one, and therefore one that is socially and culturally determined – cannot confront the transiency and arbitrary nature of the ego and its alliance with the conception of the complete and homogeneous body. From Lacan and the formulation of the mirror stage we know that the vision of the homogenised-body is a specular image with which the ego identifies in order to become signifiable. Fold back the ego (the ego which humanism continually reifies and reproduces) and you find a very different organisation, a whole kaleidoscope of possibilities. Christina, perhaps, whose mind separated one day from her body, or the man whose legs detached themselves and were replaced by those

187

of another man, which would not obey any of his commands (Sacks 1985: 42ff; 53ff). Beyond the ego we start by finding only that which we regard as abnormal or deviant, the unusual, denoting a certain alienness to our society, a lack of fit within our ontologies and their recognised identities. Beyond the egos and the super-egos that dominate our perspectives, our sanctioned literature, our official histories and prehistories, there is the fragmentation of that unity which has dominated western thought since classical times. Do we forget that, if this science of man is a recent development, then the concept of man is scarcely of any greater antiquity? A different relationship existed before the dominance of this ideology – a dialogue, for instance, between madness and reason (Foucault 1973), but certainly a madness always within reason, on the inside – today, as much as in all those yesterdays.

We experience the folding back of 'the real' today only in the terms of what clinical psychology and psychoanalysis (already from positions charged with upholding the tyranny of the normal) call illness, psychosis, neurosis, paranoia, schizophrenia, insanity – all the terms which seek to stabilise the situation by normalising the cracks in the ego's surface. Explorations of alternatives, which attempt to explode the identity of men – becoming-animal in Kafka, becoming-mineral in Beckett – become neutralised by being regarded as 'mere metaphor', since this becoming-other-than-it-appears-to-be is strictly prohibited by the identity, and most particularly by the self-identity, of the ego. And yet all these 'disorders' remind us that the ego is fragile, that it is traversed by lines of stress and strain, by cracks and fissures, and that it is within this fragmentation that history is to be found within the science of man. History shines through these tears and rips in the surface of the body-ego, and beneath the smoothness and pristine quality of the homogeneous and homogenising skin of the antique statue, the self shines through as the lived experience of a Picasso or a Munch. Why shouldn't Gregor turn into an insect? Why shouldn't Stephen D. enter a course that precipitates him in a becoming-dog one which although (or perhaps because) not complete is mourned. *Homo sapiens* opens on to history only as it bursts at the seams – the zoomorphisation of the body and its organs, so that the anus can become wolf, or a rat which is already also a penis, already the worm that burrows as the rat would burrow into the anus of the victim. And, before either of these processes will have taken place – before we speak, following Freud, of a Wolf-Man or a Rat-Man (analysis formalising the transformation as it seeks to reverse it and bring the man back out of the animal) – before the becoming-animal of the body there is already a becoming-female, an unbecoming-male.

> Everyone, even the most unembodied person, experiences himself as inextricably bound up with or in his body. In ordinary circumstances, to the extent that one feels one's body to be alive, one feels oneself to be alive, real and substantial. Most people feel that they began when their bodies began and that they will end when their bodies end.
>
> (Laing 1969: 66)

But what, we must ask, after all, is a body? This image, this contemporary experience of myself and my body, is the image reflected to my ego for its own purposes. When shaken a bit (and it doesn't take a lot) it proves to be a mirage and a chimera. Daniel Paul Schreber – to speak only of an obvious case – 'lived for a long time without a stomach, without intestines, almost without lungs, with a torn oesophagus, without a bladder, and with shattered ribs, he used sometimes to swallow part of his own larynx with his food, etc.' (Freud 1911: 147). When the body in question reformed, the judge awoke from one neurosis only to find that he was now a woman, possessed of the structures that 'give the female skin its peculiar softness' and with 'nerves of voluptuousness' that envelop the whole body producing on his chest (periodically) female breasts, and covering his entire body with those feelings of sensual pleasure 'such as are found only in the genital region in men' (Schreber 1955: 204–6).

Beyond the ego, then, we find a wholly different world, which reminds us how much our ontologies coincide with our ego's and our body ego's – the fragmentation of the body, the involvement in a series of becomings (becoming animal, mineral, female) which would threaten to articulate man with all that we are used to thinking of in opposition to him. Beyond the ego and the limits it imposes upon signification, beyond its controls, regulations codes and taboos, anything is possible – 'Man' ceases to be the centre of meaning and becomes merely an arbitrary signifier, floating and engaging with other signifiers. The body can be experienced in different ways, it can be conceptualised and reconceptualised in chains of production that are as limitless as the signifying units that compose them. The molar identity of man is shattered, and it no longer makes any sense to attempt to understand history on the basis of a monolithic category of the person – 'the science of man' is a theatrical farce, 'the antiquity of man' a charade: games we play in front of the mirror. Beyond the ego/*cogito* which inaugurate the modern period – as the state of being – there is only a state of becoming and unbecoming. If we are to approach prehistory, which must begin at the edges of this modern period, then we must abandon the science of man and work to obliterate his memory. We may read Kafka or Beckett instead of Descartes or Giddens. It is not sufficient to erase Being as does Heidegger any more than it is sufficient to attempt to define it. We must conceive it on the basis of difference, on the basis of equivalence with all the other signifiers of the meaning system. It is in disturbing identity, and the identity of 'man' as exclusivity and as something specifiable in advance and applicable in all times and places, it is in disturbing these cycles of production and reproduction that govern our own image and our own self-image, our time, our place, that history is to be found.

And yet these are not mere dreams or fantasies, these becomings that cut across and dissect the body of 'man'. Respond in this way and you miss the point, you will already have begun on a path that leads back to ontology via a total destruction of history. They are perfectly real, since what is at stake here is always the specular identity of identity. Doesn't deconstruction differ from classical (Hegelian) dialectics precisely because it insists upon the non-identity of identity? That things differ from themselves:

> . . . it is clear that the human being does not 'really' become an animal anymore than the animal 'really' becomes something else. Becoming produces nothing other than itself. We fall into a false alternative if we think you either imitate or you are. What is real is the becoming itself, the block of becoming, not the supposedly fixed terms through which becomes passes.
>
> (Deleuze and Guattari 1988: 238)

You must comprehend the difference, for if identity must be iterable in order to be identified, then we will always already have ruptured the conditions of ontology (Derrida 1977). The becoming-other of being ruptures its self-circuit – the becoming always lacks a subject, a point of pure reference, since that space, too, 'is' not without also and at the same time being caught up in various becomings.

Juxtapose fact and fiction, subject and object, ideal and material, and you will never comprehend the movement of a becoming. When it comes to a becoming, no further separation between fact and fiction is possible – or, rather, the becoming produces at once both fact and fiction, it is a material force. In Andalusia in 1977 no one doubted any of these possibilities:

> If masculine behaviour, for the men of San Blas, has its conceptual focus in the male genital region, then feminine behaviour is concentrated linguistically on the anus. Men show themselves to be constantly aware that the anus can be used in homosexual encounters, in which case the passive partner is perceived as playing the feminine role, and indeed of being converted symbolically into a woman. It is this sexual transformation that men fear.
>
> (Brandes 1981: 232–3)

Do not suppose that because the transformation is symbolic that it is therefore, in some sense, less real than the real. The symbolic not only represents but, because the real is lacking in anything more, it also performs. Of course, the cuckold does not really sprout *cuernos*, the horns, and there will be nothing visible, no physical transformation resulting from the infidelity of the wife. And yet the metamorphosis is still as real:

> To be cuckolded is to be transformed symbolically into a woman. The horns, originally associated or belonging to the woman, are placed on the head of a man, thereby feminizing him. The cuckold not only wears horns but also simultaneously becomes symbolically converted into a *cabron*, or super-goat.
>
> (Brandes 1981: 229)

And this transformation is irreversible, the male is 'forever branded with this female symbol'. A man-becoming-horned (-becoming-goat-) becoming-feminine.

It is as real as the being-male or the being-female. In Samoa, a man must guard his behaviour and appearance against the ever present possibility of becoming *fa'afafine*, like a woman, a latent potential within every male (Shore 1981: 209–10). We have to get outside ourselves (our time, our place) in order to appreciate the difference – the Californian man-becoming-bear, for example, which is a culturally recognised category (Kroeber 1952: 315; Whitehead 1981: 101), could not be comprehended in a society which imposes an absolute taboo on the mixing of the category 'human'.

And so 'the marriage scene' produces an endless stream of ontological significations, and it is these that we need to question. It adds to the rock art not simply what is necessary or sufficient to make it intelligible, but an interpretative excess. To talk of humans as beings, of human-beings, makes a claim upon libidinal organisation that extends far beyond the accredited concepts of 'male' and 'female', forcing its signifying production into little territories, into self-limiting circuits. The marriage scene protects and preserves identity and ontology by conferring upon it legitimacy – by forcing out the possibility of a homosexuality, which is more generally the possibility of breaking with ontology and precipitating man on a course of becoming-passive/becoming-female. Legitimacy, here, is the buttress of identity, and it is without doubt to legitimate and validate the identity of man that woman is called into existence.

So that all these categories of 'being' – subject, ego, *cogito*, agent, as also man, woman, animal – all these designations, presuppose a certain organisation of libido, using the 'concept' to refer to that force which charges a body and its organs in relation to other bodies, without presupposing that there need be any particular unity, hierarchy or axiology. All these signs in the rock art, all signs and all significations, are charged with libido – they offer the possibility of 'man' becoming articulated in a series of becomings that relate humans to all that would lie outside their bodies, and it is this possibility that interpretation has always foreclosed.

Re-examining the production of signs and their relationships as essentially the production of libido,[2] we can begin to re-examine the ways in which the self and body – the body-ego – were signified in what we call (as though it were a place) 'the Bronze Age'. As is clear from what was said above, 'the marriage scenes' cannot support the notion of a rigid and exclusive organisation of the sexual drives than may

Figure 10.6
Becoming animal

191

be generally the case in western societies today, but libidinal deterritorialisation is extended much further to directly assault the integrity of human identity (as we recognise it). Thus the sex organ can be used for copulating with animals (Figure 10.6–1 and 10.6–2) such that the division that separates nature from culture, man from animal, is torn down. The phallus loses its transcendent status, its unimpeachable self-identity. It becomes a weapon, a bow, or an axe that is already, at the same time, the head of an animal (Figure 10.6–6). The penis can integrate the body within an architecture – the boat, as the prow of a ship, which is already signifying an animality (Figure 10.6–3 and 10.6–4). Indeed, so acutely does this masculine ontology come into question that the male can become fully integrated, in the act of copulation, into the body of a deer (Figure 10.6–5). Human and totem as one.

What we see here is the incision, right into the heart of the masculine/phallic principle of identity, of those values which have hitherto been regarded as belonging to a subsidiary 'feminine'/non-phallic discourse within the reading formation that has been analysed here – the values of ambiguity, flow and process- that offers itself, in the marriage scenes, as potentially subversive. It speeds up signification, forcing it forward and shifting it out of the molar and through the molecular. At Källsangen (Figure 10.7) there are only becomings – these are neither man nor animal but something between terms and between these alternatives, something between 'man' and 'animal' and therefore unnameable. These are, at one and the same time, both men and birds, a man-becoming-bird or a bird-becoming-man (who knows from which place to start?). We do not know what to call these unfamiliar figures, but the fact of being unnameable does not alter the fact of the becoming. Nor does it matter that these creatures are not 'real', since nothing can alter the power of the

Figure 10.7 Becoming animal

192

becoming, of representation and presentation. Man articulates with animal – they share features – and if the becoming animal is always incomplete, it still remains more real than the being-human.

(In historical work we ought to be able to say that anything can happen. The value of the past ought to be its potential to untangle the threads that hold us, anchored, to the present.)

But what would be at stake here would be the parergon of the human, the parergon of the body, the body as parergon. For there is no doubt that the body is framed – by the sex organs that shift us into a gender system, by the concept of 'being-human' and its subsiduaries being-male, being-female, being-animal, etc., so that everything that would claim to be the ergon or to represent the ergon man is implicated in a system of lateral restriction. The ergon is characterised by lack, so it must be framed, prevented from following off in every direction. Because of the lack which calls forth the parergon, we go so far back into the body in our attempt to isolate this ergon that there is nothing left – it is not simply the drapes or the hoods that are removable, for everything is detachable and there would still be more. The ergon is occupied only by absence, the absence of being. The body is always a part of the signifying chain, and this phallic/molar/symbolic level as the principle for the interpretation of rock art discourse and for an ontology 'in the Bronze Age' is problematic.

At the level of the semiotic (approaching the rock art not on the basis of the symbolic dimension but only according to relations of difference amongst signifiers) the whole principle that seemed to converge around the phallus as the discourse of identity, subjected to taboo and regulation, collapses in upon itself. Designs (signifiers) can be recombined without any restriction placed upon their possible combinations. Thus, taking only the most common motifs, a ship can be articulated with a man, an animal, a disc, a foot, as each design opens and closes in multiple relations with its others. Not only combinations of two signifiers, but four, five or more motifs are conjoined. And not only combinations of whole signifiers, but an exchange of parts – the legs of a man seed off and become those of a disc, an animal head leads a ship. Although pure or basic figures still outnumber these combinations, it is nevertheless important that, in terms of what signs can be conjoined, all possible permutations appear to be equivalent and none is prohibited. The structure of libidinal production, which convention has sought to force into the directionality and legitimacy of 'marriage' as the only sanctioned combination of motifs, the only permitted signifying union, is blown open, and man combines freely with all the other signifiers and points of focus within the system.

At Kyrkestigan (Figure 10.8), there are various becomings: the warp and weave of identity and identification, the clutter and process of deterritorialisation and reterritorialisation. Where you may see men and animals, ships and circles, I see only the free production of signs, into which man as we know him would disappear, since there would be nothing left against which he could validate his identity, and something new emerge. I see man-becoming-beast, becoming-mineral (becoming-ship, becoming-wood), man-becoming-abstract (becoming-disc), animal-becoming-ship, and so on. I see the rupture of exclusivity and the opening up of new possibilities, the liberation of self, the historicisation of man predicated upon his deconstruction.

Figure 10.8 *Various becomings*

Rather than being based upon the symbolic dimension which would claim for a certain signifier an essential and indispensable status, and fail to realise that these are already caught up in a system of value which organises the range of possible combinations, the rock art signifies according to a more molecular and semiotic structure. Each sign, each apparent state-of-being, is no more than a punctuation point in chains of signifying production, which indicate a relationship of the body to external objects, and therefore to itself, that persists within a less territorialised system of libidinal investment. The identities that occur in the rock art are libidinally charged, but they are not regulated in the way that we, in our society, would recognise as 'natural'. It is not that the discourse is unfixed or without points of identity and an 'organisation', not that we have moved beyond into a space beyond structure, but that the dividing line between fixity and lability is no longer clear. Signifying production is so many becomings as deterritorialisation and reterritorialisation of ontological flux.

(Instead of a) conclusion

not yet

(beyond man)

Writing has the aim of unleashing these becomings from ontology, a fracture of the image in the mirror (stage), of man. It is man, with all his self-limiting production, that must be destroyed. An act of liberation and of infidelity to the present, a destruction of the ego, a deconstruction and a destroying, a complete scouring of the unconscious, of identity and its structures. An intervention within man, within the regime of signs that 'he' names.

> Nietzsche said: man has imprisoned life, the superman is he who will liberate life *within man himself* – to the profit of another form . . . What is the superman? It is a formal composite of forces within man with these new forces. It is the form which flows from a new relation of forces. Man tends to liberate life, work

and language within himself. The superman is, according to the formula of Rimbaud, man laden with the animals themselves (a code which can capture the fragments of other codes, as in the new schemes of lateral and retrograde evolution). It is man laden with the rocks themselves, or the inorganic (where silicon reigns) . . . As Foucault would say the superman is much less than the disappearance of existing men and much more than the change of a concept, it is the advent of a new form, neither God nor man, let us hope that it will not be worse than the two preceding forms.

(Deleuze 1986: 139–141)[3]

ACKNOWLEDGEMENTS

This chapter was originally two papers. The first was presented in different forms to the Society for American Archaeology Annual Meeting in Phoenix, Arizona, April 1988, and then subsequently to the Cambridge Seminar on Poststructuralism and Archaeology in June 1988. The second was written for a one-day seminar on iconography held in Cambridge in May 1989. Both papers were modified and presented at the Institutionen för Arkeologi, Göteborgs Universitet, in October 1989. I wish to thank all those at these sessions and elsewhere who have helped it to develop: Grant Chambers, Knut Helskog, Mike Shanks, Chris Tilley, and especially Ian Hodder and Jarl Nordbladh.

NOTES

1   Lacan's gloss is as follows: '. . . the metaphoric structure indicating that it is in the substitution of signifier for signifier that an effect of signification is produced that is creative or poetic, in other words, which is the advent of the signification in question. The sign + between () represents here the crossing of the bar – and the constitutive value of this crossing for the emergence of signification' (Lacan 1977a: 164).

2   I anticipate the criticism that these interpretations are underdetermined. The point here, however, is not to establish a definitive claim upon what this material 'meant' or 'means' but what it can mean – to establish a different way of reading and therefore of seeing man, one that has been concealed by the ontologies with which 'history' has been approached.

3   The problems of finding a new name for this form when it emerges are obvious – 'Man' is self-evidently inadequate, but we must beware that, by a simple change of nomenclature, we think the problem solved.

I am grateful to Grant Chambers for drawing my attention to Deleuze's work, and for providing a suitable translation.

FIGURE REFERENCES

All figures redrawn by the author from the following sources:

Figure 10.1:   Almgren, 1927, Fig. 73; Baltzer, 1911, pl. xiv-xv.

Figure 10.2:   Almgren, 1927, Fig. 75; Baltzer, 1911, pl. xix.

Figure 10.3   1, 2: Almgren, 1927, Fig. 79; Baltzer, 1881, pl. 51/2.
             3: Baltzer, 1881, pl. 4/16.
             4: Baltzer, 1881, pl. 56/5.
             5: Baltzer, 1881, pl. 56/5.
             6: Almgren, 1927, Fig. 81; Baltzer, 1881, pl. 41/3.
             7: Baltzer, 1881, pl. 3.

             8: Baltzer, 1881, pl. 3.

Figure 10.4   1: Glob, 1969, Fig. 104.
             2: Glob, 1969, Fig. 104.
             3: Almgren, 1927, Fig. 52; Glob, 1969, Fig. 10.
             4: Marstrander 1963, pl. 20.
             5: Baltzer, 1881, pl. 50/8.
             6: Almgren, 1927, Fig. 55a; Baltzer, 1881, pl. 24.

Figure 10.5   1: Svarteborg, site 17/1 (Ancient Monuments Register) – redrawn from unpublished photograph.
             2: Fredsjö, Nordbladh and Rosvall, 1981, No. 182.
             3: Almgren, 1927, Fig. 73; Baltzer, 1911, pl. xiv-xv.
             4: Fredsjö, Nordbladh and Rosvall, 1981, No. 91a.
             5: Glob, 1969, Fig. 102.

Figure 10.6   1: Almgren, 1927, Fig. 75; Baltzer, 1911, pl. xix.
             2: Baltzer, 1881, pl. 54/5.
             3: Fredsjö, Nordbladh and Rosvall, 1971, No. 283.
             4: Fredsjö, Nordbladh and Rosvall, 1981, No. 180.
             5: Fredsjö, Nordbladh and Rosvall, 1981, No. 158.
             6: Fredsjö, Nordbladh and Rosvall, 1981, No. 91b.

Figure 10.7:   Fredsjö, Nordbladh and Rosvall, 1975, No. 75.

Figure 10.8:   Fredsjö, Nordbladh and Rosvall, 1971, No. 241.

PART III

SOCIAL RELATIONS, POWER AND IDEOLOGY

INTRODUCTION

While much of the reaction against the New Archaeology was concentrated at the level of epistemology, an equally important development has been the reconsideration of the kinds of social relationships which may have existed in the past. For the most part, processual archaeology has been dominated by a variety of forms of functionalism, in which societies are conceived as bounded entities within which people and sub-groups have set roles to play, contributing to the success and survival of the whole. This stress on social function articulates in various ways with evolutionary or ecological concerns, so that the goal of human activity may be understood in terms of adaptation or the normalisation of relations with the environment. Under these conditions, a central concern has been 'complexity', the degree of internal differentiation and hierarchy identifiable within social formations. This has tended to encourage the categorisation of past communities according to a series of ideal types: bands, tribes and chiefdoms, or egalitarian, ranked and stratified. Necessarily, this promotes the impression that social units are relatively fixed in their internal structure, and that social change is a reaction to external stimuli. Successive social types enable energy, information and matter to be processed more efficiently, so that increasing social differentiation is identified with the management of resources. As Barbara Bender argues here, the consequence of this view of social evolution is that changes in subsistence practice are identified as a correlate of social complexity.

The earliest direct challenge to these arguments within archaeology came from Marxism: either the anthropological structural Marxism which was practised in the 1970s at University College London (e.g. Friedman and Rowlands 1977b), or the critical Marxism which developed within American historical archaeology (Leone 1978). Above all else, Marxist archaeology demonstrated that societies – even so-called 'egalitarian' societies – are neither homogeneous nor harmonious. Social relationships involve tensions, coercion and inequality, and these can themselves represent the sources of social transformation. This fundamental point has been taken up in a variety of different ways by 'post-processual' archaeologists. Ian Hodder (this volume, Chapter 2) and Matthew Johnson (this Part) have emphasised the importance of the individual as an active constituent of the historical process. In stressing the adaptive behaviour of the social whole, processual archaeology was claimed to have played down human agency and creativity, creating a de-humanised past. Other archaeologists (e.g. Barrett

1987b; Shanks and Tilley 1987b) were more anxious to see people positioned within a set of historically specific social relationships. This perspective manifests itself variously. Some have turned to the sociologist Anthony Giddens (1979, 1984), who stresses the connection between social structure and human agency, such that people are 'created' in a particular way by their social and historical circumstances, yet institutions are only carried forward by human action. Others have preferred Michel Foucault's emphasis on power, which offers the possibility of transcending any opposition between 'individual' and 'society', phenomena which are better seen as products of history than given entities. In this section, two analyses inspired by Marxist thought are presented. Randall McGuire discusses the development of the cultural landscape of Broome County in New York State as a manifestation of social tensions generated under industrial capitalism. Barbara Bender, in contrast, looks back to the European Palaeolithic, and argues that the emergence of art and artefactual elaboration can be identified with developing social asymmetries.

It is arguable that the most important concept which post-processual archaeologists have derived from Marxism is that of ideology. As we have seen, the early New Archaeology relied heavily upon the notion that the archaeological record could be correlated directly with human behaviour in the past. This is nowhere so clearly identifiable as in a series of contributions which discussed the significance of mortuary practice as a means of group adaptation (Binford 1971; Saxe 1970). The gist of these arguments is that funerary activity constitutes a form of communication in which information concerning the social identity of the dead person is conveyed to the living members of the community, so that they can collectively adapt to the loss. This same information can be read from the record by the archaeologist, who can then use the degree of differentiation (in terms of body treatment, grave goods, and interment facilities) as an index of social complexity. However, as Parker Pearson argues in his paper, there is good reason to doubt that mortuary practice provides us with such a clear and undistorted image of past social relationships. Marx and Engels (1970) originally argued that people often do not rebel against social inequality because their understanding of their own circumstances is obscured by ideology. As Althusser (1971b) puts it, ideology is a real relationship with an imagined reality. Our everyday doings in the world are always conducted in the context of an imperfect (and even warped) understanding of how things are. Parker Pearson's suggestion is that mortuary ritual is likely to be a form of representation which is ideological in character, expressing not so much the reality of social relationships as the way in which they are understood within the particular set of dominant ideas that existed at the time of burial.

One of the more recent tendencies in archaeology has been a growing willingness to question the usefulness of the category of 'the society'. This takes us still further away from the functionalist model of the social as a machine or an organism with set roles for its constituent parts. Marxists have long argued that rather than society objectively existing, it has to be continually reproduced. In their article, Shirley Strum and Bruno Latour present a more radical proposal: society has to be 'performed'; people do not dwell within a society but continuously struggle to define one for themselves. This shifts the focus away from 'society' as an object, and toward 'the social' as a field of relationships within which personal identities (such as 'the individual') and collectivities are defined, but remain unstable.

11

THE ROOTS OF INEQUALITY*

Barbara Bender

A major concern of recent work has been to elucidate the different ways in which the term 'complexity' has been constructed, and how these relate to specific historically and socially defined perceptions and preoccupations.

Other authors have discussed the intricacies of the lineal, 'progressive' notion of complexity that has been in vogue in Europe and America since at least the late 19th century. I want to focus on something that indirectly relates to this, which is the almost universally held and taken for granted assumption that the starting point for 'complexity' (however defined) was the development of farming. If gatherer-hunters are mentioned it is as a foil, a counterpoint, to the discussion. This way of dichotomizing things means that somehow the discussion and definition of 'complexity' make little reference to 2 or 3 million years of hominid evolution.

I want to analyse why it is that farming is construed as a necessary condition for the development of 'complexity', which, for my purposes here, I simply define as involving a degree of institutionalized social inequality – and why divisions in gatherer-hunter societies are desocialized and therefore ignored. I shall use an example taken from the south-west European Upper Palaeolithic to show how social inequality might be inaugurated and institutionalized within a gatherer-hunter milieu.

Farming as a precondition
What is it about farming that makes it appear to be both a precondition and an attribute of 'complexity'? Food production per se is a technological innovation that lies at one end of a spectrum of plant and animal manipulation (Higgs 1972). It can be, and often has been, simply a minor element in an otherwise wild procurement existence. When, and if, it becomes a more significant subsistence strategy, it makes certain demands on social practice. It often requires a degree of sedentism; it requires labour inputs on which there are delayed returns; land clearance and agricultural practices mean that one generation quite literally feeds off the labour of an earlier

---

* First published in D. Miller, M. Rowlands and C. Tilley (eds) (1989), *Domination and Resistance,* London: Unwin Hyman, pp. 83–95.

generation, and this tends to reinforce generational bonds (Meillassoux 1972; Bender 1985). This generational debt becomes a potential source of inequality – junior service, senior authority. The fact that land takes on value and therefore becomes something material, something that can be possessed, something to which access can be restricted and the products of which can be controlled, again creates conditions for inequality. Moreover, farming permits a control over nature which, at the cost of high labour inputs, yields greater returns, and these are also open to manipulation. Thus, the assumption is that technology (farming) is the tail that wags the social dog (complexity). Such assumptions have been present across a wide spectrum of social theorizing for a long time. Engels (1972: 117) wrote: 'the dominance of animals . . . developed a hitherto unsuspected source of wealth and created entirely new social relations', and Morgan (1963: 19) pronounced: 'It is accordingly probable that the great epochs of human progress have been identified more or less directly with the enlargement of the sources of subsistence.' In this century Childe continued to stress the significance of changes in the forces of production. The Neolithic Revolution permitted 'the escape from the impasse of savagery' (Childe 1942: 48), and the more ecologically minded 'schools' have been content to accept these readings. In recent years a slightly different version emerges. Woodburn (1980) contrasts the immediate return system of most gatherer–hunters, which is associated with egalitarian social relations, with the delayed returns of some gatherer–hunter groups that technically mimic farming practices and thus have similar social configurations.

This very widespread acceptance of a technological prime-mover or, at least, a technological precondition, must in some part relate to our own embeddedness within heavily industrialized societies in which the very process of industrialization seems to act as a significant force for change, and in which technological change and increased complexity become almost interchangeable concepts. This recourse to farming as prime-mover seems also to legitimate and naturalize concepts of property and control by relating them to the exigencies of subsistence practices. Social phenomena are brought into line with nature, creating a form of environmental legitimation of 'the scheme of things'.

'Natural' divisions in gatherer-hunter societies

This 'naturalization' of social complexity created by tying it to subsistence requirements is echoed in the explanations offered for the development of gatherer-hunter societies. The lack of complexity, the supposedly egalitarian nature of gatherer-hunters, is linked to the inability to control resources, the inability to prevent access, etc. Social differentiation – as opposed to inequality – is acknowledged and linked to age and gender, both of which are then linked to the mode of subsistence. Elders have power because they have experience and are the repositories of knowledge on how to do things. To that extent they have some control over juniors. In many accounts this is adjudged to be only a temporary 'inequality', for juniors will eventually become seniors. As O'Laughlin (1977) pointed out, a wonderful myopia creeps in, for the seniors tend to be male, and the juniors on their way to becoming seniors are also male, so only one half of the population is involved in this inoffensive social progression.

This Eurocentric (indeed more widespread) bias which only discusses 'power', or lack of it, in terms of male activities, also permeates the discussion on gender division. It has become much clearer in recent years how, unconsciously, the reconstruction of early hominid societies has been used to naturalize gender divisions within our own societies (Conkey and Spector 1984). For example, it is assumed that a characteristic of early hominids, something that set them apart from other primates, was a division of labour. A division in which the male, endowed with greater strength and unencumbered with infants, was the hunter, taking on the dangerous 'outside' world, and woman was the child-rearer and localized plant gatherer, centred on the domestic sphere. A 'macho' version of this scenario in which the men got credit for inventing tools and weapons, and for promoting the complex sharing strategies that put a premium on intellectual development, was set out by Washburn and Lancaster (1968); a more *gentle*-manly version by Isaac (1978) still maintained the division of labour, but gave full credit to the women for being the more reliable foragers and for being the probable inventors of carrying equipment. Feminist protestations notwithstanding, this insistence on the naturalness of the division of labour was iterated in a recent article which was presumably meant to be taken seriously (Quiatt and Kelso 1985). The authors insisted that the early hominid division of labour was the most 'natural' way of going about things, since the women would be 'house-bound' (3 million years ago, in the middle of the African savannah!). There would be pair-bonding because it made food-sharing easier, the family would be nuclear - 'child serving and child centred' – and the juveniles would baby-sit and run errands and, in the process, would learn 'the complex routines of bulk food collecting, transporting and processing' (clearly such juveniles would do as well, if not better, in the jungles of New York or London).

Interestingly, the feminist critiques written in the 1970s by Slocum (1975), Tanner (1971) and Zihlman (1981) did little more than reverse the scenario – 'Man the Hunter' (the title of the 1968 symposium) is replaced by 'Woman the Gatherer' (Dahlberg's symposium, 1981). They stress that gathering is more important than hunting in the early time ranges and, while both males and females gathered, it was the females that began the process of sharing, for they would have shared food with their increasingly dependent offspring. Moreover, sharing required collecting as opposed to gathering, and this too, with its associated technology, would have been inaugurated by women. In this scenario the division of labour remains intact and, moreover, current notions of child-rearing are accepted as the norm – that women succour, carry, and provide for their own infants. Indeed, it reads like a legitimation of the one-parent family.

In reality none of these divisions or obligations is written into nature. There are plenty of societies where women succour babies that are not their own, or where child-rearing is communal. There is recent evidence from the Philippines of Agta women who hunt large game on a regular basis, who stop hunting for a couple of weeks prior to giving birth, and take it up again a month later, leaving their infants to be suckled by other women at the camp (Estioko-Griffen and Griffen 1981). It may be that males do have some advantages over females as hunters, in terms of size and body weight and because of their more extensive foraging range, but these are not sufficient advantages to enforce a sexual division of labour; that division, when it occurs, has much more to do with social distinctions and social taboos. On quite pragmatic grounds it seems most likely that early hominids – small and highly vulnerable, in no position to hold onto game in the face of determined opposition from carnivores – would have been opportunistic scavengers, and the sharing would have been equally opportunistic. Shipman (1986) notes that the African savannah of 3 million years ago would have had more game – both prey and predator – than today, and that the form of cut- and gnaw-marks on animal bones found in the early deposits suggests a 'cut-and-run' strategy, possibly linked with a retreat to the treetops, rather than a hunting-home base existence. Hamilton (1984) points out that the strong sexual dimorphism found in early hominid populations may not only indicate the polygynous nature of the males, but a female adaptation which permitted a reduced calorie intake and thus a reduced foraging range. The need for such a physiological adaptation would suggest that females were not significantly dependent upon the males for food. It seems probable that, rather than divisions of labour, flexibility would have been the key to survival. The increase in types of foods consumed, the volatility and complexity of relationships among these ranging, foraging, scavenging, vulnerable groupings, with dependent offspring, with rudimentary technological skills to be passed on, would from the outset accentuate the need for social interaction and communication.

There have been some moves towards the scavenging model for early hominids (Leakey 1981), but this has simply meant that the introduction of a 'natural' division of labour and of ensuing changes in social organization are pushed forward in time. The Mark II version of Man the Hunter moves on to the Middle Palaeolithic, around 200 000 years ago, and the emergence of *Homo-sapiens*, or even the Upper Palaeolithic (*c.* 35 000 years ago) and *sapiens sapiens*. In this version it is suggested that groups adapting to the rigours of the European climate under extreme glacial conditions had to depend upon big-game hunting. This required skill and co-operative action by unencumbered males. Increased co-operation required a more systematic network of contacts which ran counter to an earlier pattern of open breeding networks and forced a degree of social closure. A precondition for such closure was a reasonable density of population, which was not attainable until the Middle to Upper Palaeolithic. Social closure created tensions, since those on the periphery of the network were at a disadvantage compared with those at the centre, and these would be relieved by increased ritual, emphasizing social solidarity between and within groups (Wobst 1976). Social closure and ritual are the hallmarks of culture, so, once again, men, because they are the big game hunters, set the evolutionary process in motion.

The resilience of the Man the Hunter–Woman the Home-maker model is really quite remarkable, yet, again on pragmatic grounds, it has little to recommend it. Europe, during parts of the Upper Palaeolithic, undoubtedly suffered severe climatic conditions, but big-game hunting was by no means the only response. For example, in Cantabria in the earlier Upper Palaeolithic, base-camps in the upland areas exploited a range of animals including red deer, roe deer, ibex, chamois and horse. In the later Upper Palaeolithic a dispersed pattern of small sites is associated with a greater reliance on red deer and on a wider range of resources, including shellfish and small game (Freeman 1973). As Gilman (1984) points out, Upper Palaeolithic techniques were so advanced that groups could and would either exploit a wider range of species or specialize in a single species 'as conditions rendered either strategy more cost effective'. Many of these strategies would not have required co-operative tactics. Undermining the big-game hunting hypothesis still further are the findings that in other parts of the Old

World, unaffected by the glacial advances, and with varied subsistence strategies, there is again evidence of social closure and ritual in the Middle and Upper Palaeolithic.

The purpose of this long exegesis is to demonstrate how the explanation of social phenomena, be it the division of labour, age-sets or potential inequalities in both gatherer-hunter and early farming societies, have tended to be naturalized and made law-like by stressing the dominance of techno-environmental/alias subsistence forces. We legitimize the division and inequalities in our own societies by making them the inevitable outcome of inevitable forces. This use of history is part of our dominant ideology, just as alternative 'histories' are often part of an attempt to undermine or demote aspects of contemporary social relations. If we want to understand the roots of social differentiation and social inequality, we will have to look at quite specific prehistoric and historic social configurations and see how it is that in some societies ideology and practice – including, no doubt, past history – was used to create, maintain or subvert sets of social relations that are by no means written into nature or subsistence. I am not suggesting that the level of technology does not impose constraints upon forms of social relations, but it does not explain change or variability. Farming of itself does not create the necessary surplus to underwrite more hierarchized positions; surplus is relative and is initiated by society: 'There are always and everywhere potential surpluses available. What counts is the institutionalised means of bringing them to life' (Parker Pearson 1984a). I want to consider the way in which such 'institutionalization' might occur and social differences and inequalities might be promoted in the context of certain prehistoric gatherer-hunter societies living in south-west Europe towards the end of the Ice Age. It is, at most, a partial analysis concentrating only on a limited aspect of social relations.

An example from the Upper Palaeolithic of south-west France

The cave and mobile art of north-west Spain and south-west France have been extensively analysed and explained. Leaving to one side the structural analyses of Leroi-Gourhan and Laming, much recent theorizing emphasizes that this art must be seen as an aspect of social action. Both Conkey (1978) and Gamble (1982) equate art with 'style', and 'style' with the signalling of social identity. Conkey recognizes that style is not simply a 'reflection' of social action and ritual, but rather 'it IS ritual communication' (Rowntree and Conkey 1980). Nevertheless she views it as reflexive in an adaptive sense. It is 'an information regulator', a 'parsimonious response to stress' (Conkey 1978). Conkey has undertaken an interesting analysis of stylistic variation in the portable art at the great cave of Altamira in northern Spain, and has quite convincingly demonstrated that a number of local groups must have come together at the site and that it was the locus of regional interaction. She suggests, following Johnson (1982), that such aggregation creates scalar stress which has to be met with shifts in social organization towards a sequential hierarchy, shifts which are formalized and negotiated through ritual. The explanation for both aggregation and ritual remains, again, techno-environmental. In earlier writings Conkey tended to view aggregation as a response either to the need to congregate in order to pool information about the environment, or as a response to demographic circumscription. More recently she seems to see it as a response to subsistence needs – the salmon are running, the deer congregating (Conkey 1985). The resultant stress is dealt with by a temporary shift in social strategy, mediated by ritual. When the groups disaggregate, the ritual goes away. Whereas Conkey's recent writings shade off towards less adaptive modelling, Gamble continues to provide a more straightforwardly environmental-demographic explanation (Gamble 1982; Champion *et al*. 1984: 84–7). He ties 'style' to alliance networks, and alliance networks to problems of resource predictability. Jochim, too, proposes a stress model. He suggests that extreme glacial conditions between 25 000 and 17 000 years ago led to the abandonment of northern and much of central Europe, and the consequent retreat into south-west Europe created population pressure (Jochim 1982). These 'stress' scenarios sit uneasily with the empirical evidence. The major period of cave art was from 18 000 to 8000 years ago. It coincides at most with the end of the glacial advance. From 17 000 BP climatic conditions were ameliorating, and large tracts of northern central and northern Europe were being colonized (Champion *et al*. 1984: 54–7). It is difficult to get a realistic notion of population densities, but one estimate suggests that in Cantabria site densities were around 0.2 per millennium in the Mousterian (Middle Palaeolithic), 1.2 in the Aurignacian-Perigordian (Early Upper Palaeolithic), 11.00 in the Solutrean, 11.7 in the early Magdalenian and 12 in the Late Magdalenian (Straus 1977). White (1982) believes that population increases in Perigord were of the same magnitude, but stresses that the figures for the later periods may well be 'inflated' by better site preservation. He suggests that there was a very gradual population increase, and this would accord more readily with Bordes' famous description of south-west France as 'a human desert swarming with game', than with Jochim's more extreme scenario (Bordes, cited in Leakey 1981).

An alternative reading requires that we re-socialize art, and in the process re-socialize gatherer-hunters. Art, then, is part of what Wolf (1984) has called 'insistent signification' part of the ideological imprinting. It is 'the coercion of a fan of potential connotations into a few licensed meanings'; part of a process of institutionalization, not only of what is to be said and thought, but how it is to be said and who is to say it – part, therefore, of an on-going process of negotiation and renegotiation of social relations.

With art, ideology takes material form. In kin-based societies, as Munn (1970) and Weiner (1985) have so elegantly shown, objects are not 'property' in our sense of the word, they are 'inalienable'. Among the Walbiri or the Maori – and surely among late prehistoric gatherer-hunters – objects 'belonged to particular ancestors, were passed down particular descent lines, held their own stories and were exchanged on various memorable occasions' (Weiner 1985, cited in Rowlands 1987b). They are 'inalienable' and related to specific sets of relations, to particular groupings in particular contexts. They 'anchor' and celebrate a 'socio-moral' order in which authority runs from the ancestor to the senior to the junior in an unending process (Munn 1970). The generational ebb and flow may or may not be gender-specific. Among the Walbiri ritual objects anchor an authority that runs from father to son. Women are acknowledged – in myth and ritual – as 'begetters', but their fecundity is socially appropriated by the males (Miller 1987).[1] It is the process of such appropriation that can dimly be perceived among certain societies in the later Upper Palaeolithic of south-west Europe.

While I shall continue to use the term 'art', and to concentrate upon Upper Palaeolithic cave and mobile art, it must be acknowledged that this reflects the reification of 'art' in our own societies, and sets up a false division within the gamut of material culture. Upper Palaeolithic art must be seen as a facet, no more, of ideological and ritual expressiveness. It reiterates and elaborates concepts that permeate every material and non-material aspect of life. At El Juyo in northern Spain we almost catch the ephemeral action: the creation and recreation of mud 'rosettes', the construction of small pits and hummocks, the precise placement of needles and bone points, the location of a rough stone carving placed so that from one position the human face is visible, from another the feline face (Freeman and Echegaray 1981). Further afield, at Mezhirich on the Central Russian Plain, we see very clearly how house form is another expressive medium: the tents were encased in layer upon layer of mammoth mandible and long bone, carefully arranged in patterned and often mirrored formations (Soffer 1985). At Gönnersdorf, near Cologne, hut floors were covered with schist plaques with rough female engravings on the undersides. In the Ukraine six different musical instruments made of mammoth bone have been found and two six-hole flutes from Russia and France again extend the range of expressive media. We only have the durable remains. The faint traces of paint found on some of the figurines hint at other, non-durable, forms (Marshack 1987).

Not only is there material reiteration, but also social action is confirmed, given depth and continuity by re-use and invocation. Material objects show signs of long usage, of touch and wear; the sculptures, engravings and paintings of objects and on cave walls are touched and retouched over and over again, the animal representations are splattered with markings (Marshack 1977, 1987). Within the caves earlier representations are re-incorporated and, no doubt, re-interpreted (cf. Lewis-Williams and Loubser 1986). The actual durable, immovable fabric of cave and rock-shelter again creates a sense of continuity and makes them part of the process by which the landscape is socialized and 'claimed' (Layton 1986; Miller 1987). We can be fairly sure that artefact, cave and landscape demarcate a ritual rather than an economic homeland. As Munn (1970) puts it: 'the importance of these sacred countries is not economic in the sense that it does not define the limits over which those who reside may forage . . . Rather [it is] a symbol of stability'. Yet this sense of stability and continuity remains an ideological construct, and it masks the process by which social relations are subtly re-evaluated and re-aligned. For example, when an earlier painting is re-incorporated, it both cross-references the past, and takes on new meaning (Layton 1986).

To get a sense of this process of re-evaluation and alignment – and thus of change – we need also to keep in mind the immense timespan within which this cave and mobile art occurs (Conkey 1985; Marshack 1987). Within a 20 000-year span (35 000 to 10 000 BP) the 'domains of discourse' must vary very greatly. For long millennia social relations may have been such that the 'signification' of these material expressions was open to all members of the group, forming part of the process of socialization from birth to death. Objects made of imported shell or fine stones, small sculpted or engraved animals and female figurines, annotated objects, are found in habitation sites right across Europe. Form, distribution and significance changed at different times and places. For example, Marshack (1987) noted that it is only towards the end of the Palaeolithic that there are engravings that have quite specific seasonal connotations. Nevertheless, however varied, this repertoire has in common that it is visible and found in domestic contexts. It is accessible (Hahn, cited in Conkey 1985; Marshack 1987). Personal adornments were often placed in burials, and the lavish endowment of some children's graves (for example, at Sungir in Russia) would also be an expression of communal ritual, since the children can have attained little in their own right. However, there are times, and places, when part of the art and ritual becomes circumscribed, when there is a degree of social closure – by gender, age or status. Access to social knowledge is curtailed and thereby inequalities, however minor, are institutionalized and legitimized.

In the earlier part of the Upper Palaeolithic, entrances to the caves of south-west France and northern Spain were often used as habitations, and entrances, accessible passages and chambers were painted and engraved. Socialization and ritual seem wide open. At some time after 17 000 BP the pattern changes.[2] Certain caves, such as Altamira, Castillo, Lascaux and Pech-Merle, become the foci of regional aggregation and ceremonial activity. In Perigord four of the 86 known Magdalenian sites (Laugerie-Basse, La Madeleine, Limeuil and Rochereil) have 80 per cent of the embellished artefacts (White 1982, cited in Conkey 1985). In Cantabria two of the eight Early Magdalenian have 60 per cent, and in the Late Magdalenian one has 30 per cent. In the Pyrenees, Isturitz and Mas d'Azil stand out. As the arena of ritual and ceremony, such sites would have been associated with intense activity. Things would have to be collected together, made and exchanged. There had to be provisioning for feasting as well as for everyday subsistence. In this later Upper Palaeolithic, the number of paintings in the big caves increases enormously, but part of the ritual now moves inwards. The large, accessible chambers, at Lascaux or Altamira, with their great tableaux, may have remained 'open', but small side chambers and passages show a much more intensive retouching of animals and innumerable 'annotations' (Marshack 1987). At Tuc d'Audoubert in the Pyrenees the ceiling of a small chamber has an engraved horse's head, surrounded by 84 P signs, made in various styles with various tools, and sometimes renewed. An almost identical configuration is found in the neighbouring cave of Trois Frères (Marshack 1987). Often the paintings and engravings are placed far from the cave entrance (Rouffignac 2 km from the entrance; Niaux between 500 m and 2 km; Tuc d'Audoubert and Trois Frères about the same), access is difficult, and the space cramped. Exclusivity can take other forms – at El Juyo in Spain the roughly sculpted stone placed near the entrance reads from the outside as a man's head, but from inside the cave it becomes a feline (Freeman and Echegaray 1981).

Who, then, is being excluded? A strong possibility is that these secret places were an arena for the initiation of young males, and the 'capturing' of the animals in the painting was part of the capture of hunting as a male preserve. They become part of the process by which the 'female controlled biological power of reproduction is subsumed by male cultural control over social reproduction' (Miller 1987). There is – as was noted earlier – no reason in nature for the sharp gender divisions found in many gatherer-hunter societies, they have to be created by proscription and taboo, they have to be 'naturalized' through ideology and ritual.

Other aspects of the later Upper Palaeolithic art of this region, both cave and mobile, may substantiate this notion of increased exclusiveness. Although the animal representations have received most of the attention, there are, in reality, many more geometric signs in the caves. These signs are less frequently found on mobile art, they fall into fairly well-defined classes and have tight regional groupings – there is none of the widespread dissemination associated with mobile art (Leroi-Gourhan 1977–8). They increase in number and variety and become more abstract in the later Upper Palaeolithic. They are often used to 'annotate' animal representations (Marshack 1977). Increased abstraction permits increased ambiguity, creates a code that is harder to crack – an individual sign may carry different meanings depending upon the context of use and specific juxtapositions (Munn 1973). There can be a multiplicity of codes that are differentially available to groups within groups. Layton (1986) notes how a North Arnhem Land artist explained that if he were representing the subject matter in an exclusive male context rather than an open camp, he would use 'geometrics'.

Another interesting feature is that not only are there very high concentrations of decorated pieces at the large sites in Perigord, the Pyrenees and Cantabria, but certain artefacts – spear-thrower, shaft-straightener, harpoon and rod – begin to be highly embellished (Bahn 1982). We seem to be witnessing part of the process by which symbolic representation extends and engulfs the surface of other media, to which access is again limited. Munn (1973: 213) noticed such a development in the male iconography of the Walbiri. Such artefacts have tight distributions; they move in constrained spheres of exchange, available only to socially designated partners.

Social differentiation hinges, in the first instance, on differential access to social knowledge. However, this can be 'converted' into more material control. There is the possibility of exclusive exchange, there are the demands made on people's labour as part of the whole process of ritual, of material creations, of display and feasting. The labour of elder or shaman, young initiate or uninitiated male or female appears, both to us and to the people involved, as a form of communal appropriation. This 'ideology' of communality disguises the way in which the labour is called into being and used by only a limited number of people within the society.

It would seem that the social configuration of areas of south-west France and northern Spain during parts of the Upper Palaeolithic was different from that of contemporary groups, and that the art was part of a process of social negotiation, part of a symbolic 'naturalization' of increased social differentiation. No doubt the seasonal aggregations at the great sites in Perigord, Cantabria and the Pyrenees were made possible by their optimal locations for culling herds or catching salmon, but their ecological setting does not explain the size of aggregation or the intensity of ritual. People came together to celebrate, and they chose locations and seasons that permitted such congregations. No doubt they intensified their subsistence strategies to meet their temporary needs – just as Australian aborigines dug artificial eel runs to permit large ceremonial gatherings (Lourandos 1980). It may even be that the emphasis on reindeer hunting was as much a response to a demand for antler to make into fine artefacts as a demand for meat (White 1982). No doubt such seasonal aggregations permitted the pooling of much practical information, but it also permitted the control rather than dissemination of social knowledge. The ceremony and ritual of the great caves was part of a process of social reproduction which need not have been to the advantage of each and every member of the society.

It is obvious that the developments charted above are still immensely crude. With tighter control of the evidence it may be possible to chart cyclical developments within the different regions. There were perhaps times when the demands made on labour and resources became too great, and a more egalitarian configuration re-emerged.

Conclusions

Marx once exclaimed: 'Man's innate casuistry'! To change things by changing their names. And to find loopholes for violating tradition while maintaining tradition, when direct interest supplie[s] sufficient impulse' (cited in Engels 1972: 120). I have tried to suggest that to understand the emergence of social divisions and inequalities we need to examine the way in which ideological constructions, material and immaterial, promote change. I have not, in this chapter, taken up the question of how such constructions mesh with other aspects of evolving social relations, particularly those of alliance and exchange (but see Bender 1978, 1985). Binford (1982b) has said:

> one of the greatest confusions to have plagued the social sciences is the confusion between regularities in the internal dynamics of cultural systems (synchronic and internal-functional) and the nature of the dynamics which conditioned changes in the organization of systems themselves and in their evolutionary diversification and change (diachronic and external-ecological).

One purpose of this chapter is to stress that no such internal:functional adaptive/external: ecological causative dichotomy is permissible. Societies attempt to reproduce themselves – as societies, not as biological units. The strategies employed may seem adaptive to the participants, they may even be adaptive in the short term, but they are frequently less viable in the longer term. Thus, they hold the seeds of their own destruction, or rather, since human societies are immensely flexible, of change.

Ideological representations are integral to relations of power and control. In some instances these relations make demands on labour and on production, and these demands may, in turn, promote technological developments. The beginnings of inequality do not start with the onset of farming, or with any other ecological input, they lie far back in the varied social configurations and ideologies of gatherer-hunter societies.

NOTES

1 Munn (1970) describes a Walbiri myth which gives a sense of the social appropriation of female fecundity. At the behest of the son, the father snake emits a design-marked board which changes into women with digging sticks. The women move from place to place creating water-holes with their digging sticks, into which their progeny go. They are followed by men who pick up the women's faeces and turn them into sacred boards which they make into head-dresses. Then they dance. When they go into the women's camp they leave the boards outside so that the women cannot see them. In this myth the women are portrayed as life-givers and providers (digging sticks-water-holes-progeny), but this natural fecundity is 'socialized' and pre-empted by the male. In the first instance the ancestral male (snake father) is transformed into a cultural artefact (decorated board) which 'creates' the female. The female then creates in nature, but her (natural) products, her faeces, are taken by the male and re-socialized (into boards and head-dresses) which are then used in ritual. Artefacts and ritual are then kept outside the female domain. The myth also shadows the process whereby the young male is removed from the female 'hearth' and joins the domain of the male initiates.

2 Layton (1986) contrasts the 'open', communal and person-orientated art of some Australian aboriginal groups and the southern African San, and the 'closed', hieratic art of other, totemic, societies in Australia and Upper Palaeolithic groups of south-west Europe.

12

CONCEPTIONS OF AGENCY IN ARCHAEOLOGICAL INTERPRETATION*

MATTHEW H. JOHNSON

As I was going up the stair
I met a man who wasn't there.
He wasn't there again today.
I wish, I wish he'd stay away.

(Hughes Mearns, 'The Psychoed')

Introduction

Much of the polemical literature associated with 'postprocessual', 'contextual', or 'structural and symbolic' archaeology has placed great emphasis on the role of 'the individual' as active social agent in promoting historical change, and the inadequacy of a holistic interpretive framework that denies, bypasses, or ignores such agency. Yet it is the contention of this paper that this problem has not been remedied in the case studies accompanying such polemical statements. The individual has been triumphantly reinstated at the centre of the stage in theory, but quietly relegated to the wings, or written out of the script altogether, in practice.

This paper attempts to trace the origins and development of this concern with archaeological thought, and endeavours to demonstrate how the individual has been 'lost' by consideration of several avowedly 'postprocessual' case studies. It will proceed, not through some fresh theoretical formulation, but by consideration of an issue raised in the author's own fieldwork: the interpretation of a particular episode of sudden change and diversity in material culture where a combination of archaeological and documentary evidence can be brought to bear on the questions of social formation and structure, human intentionality, and so on. In conclusion, the implications of this study for historical and prehistoric archaeology as a whole will be discussed. The approach taken throughout is a deliberately informal one, preferring to assess the way a standpoint or opinion seems to work in practice rather than spending time teasing out its finer theoretical points.

---

*First published in *Journal of Anthropological Archaeology* (1989), **8**, 189–211.

It is worth stressing at the outset two important points. First, the category of the individual or person is not a straightforward concept. Notions of what constitutes individuality, the 'category of the person', vary widely across time and space (Carrithers *et al.* 1985) and no commonsensical, cross-cultural definition can be put forward. It is not the purpose of this paper to explore this concept at length, but to note its absence in any real form, however defined, from much of the literature. Second, it is an oversimplification and a misconception to confuse the search for human agency with the archaeological identification of individuals. The former is a theoretical concern, to fill a gap in our understanding of the cause of material culture variability: it is the proposition that we cannot understand such variability without reference to active agency. The latter, on the other hand, is a practical concern with those superficially exciting moments, present particularly in historical archaeology where one can identify 'real people' and relate them to traces in the archaeological record. This paper has nothing to do with the latter project (for this see Hill and Gunn 1977).

However, it does propose that in a situation where both the material traces and the social context of an individual can be outlined in some detail using a combination of written and archaeological sources, a fascinating empirical study of agency could be conducted. In other words, it expects that the use of 'individuals' known through the documents offers one *means* of attaining the *end* of tackling the theoretical question of 'the individual'. As will be explored below, this has not been the case.

History

As with so many elements of current thinking, stress on human agency can be traced back directly to reactions against the major tenets of the New Archaeology in the late 1970s and early 1980s. In particular, Hodder attacked the holistic nature of systemic interpretation, identifying it in general as functionalist and specifically as allowing no place for social action in its stress on interactions between functionally related variables: 'individuals are not simply instruments in some orchestrated game and it is difficult to see how subsystems and roles can have "goals" of their own. Adequate explanations of social systems and social change must involve the individual's assessment and aims' (Hodder 1982d: 5).

Two related strands lie behind this attack. One is empirical: any form of social explanation which does not include some account of human agency is often seen to be patently inadequate when applied to a concrete historical event, for example in the case of Punks (Hebdige 1979), the 18th Brumaire (Marx 1977), or any account of political history (the objection that these are all 'surface events' and that longer-term processes can be studied without reference to such factors will be dealt with adequately elsewhere: see for example Shanks and Tilley 1987b: 122). In archaeology, this empirical dissatisfaction was raised with reference to stress on environmental/adaptive explanations of cultural phenomena, a dissatisfaction never totally masked by the rise of the 'social archaeology' school. As one member of the latter put it, 'while the behavior of the group, of many individual units, may often be effectively described in statistical terms without reference to the single unit, it cannot so easily be *explained* in this way. This is a problem which prehistoric archaeology has yet to resolve' (Renfrew 1972: 496).

The second is more fundamental, with its roots in the social sciences as a whole. The structure/agency question did not arise in specific terms while 'Anglo-Saxon' social theory was dominated by the functionalist legacy of Durkheim and Malinowski: no successful integration of the Weberian and Parsonian theory of social action with holistic models was ever achieved (Cohen 1968: 49).

It is clear that the problem could be painstakingly traced back in broader terms through methodological individualism (Bell 1987: 79) to Weber (1947) and beyond to Hobbes, but this is not necessary. The sea change in social theory of the 1970s produced at least one coherent statement of a theory of 'the knowledgeable social actor', namely that of Giddens (1979: 49–95). Giddens proposed an analytical framework within which the social actor was assumed to know a great deal about the way in which society operated, and to be more or less capable of reasserting, manipulating, or transforming those rules within a given social situation.

It is worth emphasising, however, that even in this avowedly nonstructuralist conception of social action the actor can only pursue such a strategy with reference to some pre-existing and 'external' 'structure' or *habitus* at any given moment in time, even if historically that structure or *habitus* is constantly shifting and fluid. The implications of this point will be followed up below. It is clear, incidentally, that Giddens owes a great debt to Bourdieu (1977) and also to Weber (1947) in this work.

A brief acknowledgement of Marxist thought should be made at this point, though a full historical study of this aspect would fill another paper. Marx himself clearly does not deserve the accusations often levelled that his actors are pawns in the grip of 'vast impersonal forces', emphasising that 'men (*sic*) make their own history, but . . . under circumstances directly encountered, given and transmitted from the past' (Marx 1977: 300). At the same time, in the hands of many later Marxists, particularly Althusser to whom we shall return, historical materialism becomes an inexorable process capable only of halting by specific historical conjunctures. However, elements of Marxist thought, particularly its stress on social formation, conflict, and more sophisticated versions of its theory of ideology, clearly have a role to play in exploring the question of agency: Shanks and Tilley for example build on Althusser's Marxist conception of social formation when considering these issues in the context of Neolithic burial practices (Shanks and Tilley 1982), while Hodder acknowledges the use of such concepts in his 'contextual' model of archaeological interpretation (Hodder 1986: 118).

The most coherent statement to date in archaeological thinking is that put forward by Shanks and Tilley in their volume *Re-constructing Archaeology* (Shanks and Tilley 1987a: 116–134). They argue that 'individuals are competent and knowledgeable while at the same time their action is situated within unacknowledged conditions and has unintended consequences' (Shanks and Tilley 1987a: 116). Rejecting functional explanation of social action as 'manifestly inadequate', they attempt to deny the dualism usually set up between individual and society and subject and structure. Rather, the agent is an active decentered subject, and his/her actions are conceived of as purposive, determined, and knowledgeable at least at the level of practical consciousness (Bourdieu 1977). Structure in this conception is constituted by 'principles and resources orientating social conduct' (Shanks and Tilley 1987a: 130), including the cognitive ordering of the world, and can embrace contradictions and noncorrespondences: it is underlying, visible only through its effects as translated into social action.

There are several problems with this account of structure and agency. In particular, it is unclear exactly how Shanks and Tilley have transcended the 'disabling dualisms' (Shanks and Tilley 1987a: 120) they attack, and it is difficult to square their emphasis on the active subject engaged in 'a realisation of teleological positioning' (in other words purposive action) with their insistence that all social action is overdetermined by structures, encapsulated in the notion of 'structuration'. One can also argue with their insistence that the cognitive ordering of the world can embrace contradictions. Nevertheless, the relevant point for this discussion is that Shanks and Tilley have raised the conception of agency in archaeological theory to a sophisticated level, and integrated it with corresponding notions of structure, system, contradiction, and so on.

Examples

The proof of the pudding, however, is in the eating: how, in practice, do postprocessual interpretations of material culture make use of these notions? I shall consider Shanks and Tilley's analysis of Swedish and British beer can design from the same volume.

Shanks and Tilley take a systematic sample of Swedish and British beer cans and bottles and subject their design to a statistical analysis. They elegantly demonstrate that the Swedish cans show far more design complexity than their British counterparts in the number and style of words used and in the images presented. Related differences are also seen in the sample of beer advertisements presented.

These differences are understood in terms of different ideological resolutions of the contradiction within capitalist society between the profit gained in the development of production of alcoholic drink and the need to maintain a sober, disciplined workforce. This contradiction is resolved in different ways due to the particular antecedent historical conditions pertaining in the two countries: in Britain, the early development of urban capitalism and the attendant rise of working-class public houses as places of leisure and sociability gave the consumption of beer an integral place in the reproduction of a disciplined labour force. In Sweden, however, beer is both less easily classified as a drink (Shanks and Tilley 1987a: 238) and is predominantly consumed in the home. It was therefore more vulnerable to the attacks of the temperance movement and is more readily problematised by the welfare state today. The can designs and advertisements act to gloss over these tensions and contradictions and, since these are more apparent in Sweden than in Britain, their imagery, wording, and symbolism are more elaborate.

This argument is a scholarly and rigorous one, but it is difficult to see how the active social agent fits into it, decentered or not. Ultimately the beer can variability is explained with reference to its *function* in masking various contradictions within British and Swedish class systems. The main protagonists depicted are social classes, and the main dynamic forces are the social and ideological concomitants of economic change, in particular the contrasts between Britain and Sweden in the particular historical trajectory of nineteenth-century industrial capitalism. Within this explanatory framework social action, as seen in the tangible result of beer can design, is really no more than the execution of a strategy (or even grammar?) narrowly dictated by the position of that class within the social configuration.

Nowhere, indeed, do we even see a subordinate social class acting in any way as an active group: the British public house as a place where working-class consciousness is developed is briefly mentioned (Shanks and Tilley 1987a: 190) but this interesting point is never developed, despite its relevance as part of the antecedent conditions to can design. Nor is the reaction of the working class either to past and present alcoholic restrictions in Sweden or to the images presented in beer advertisements in both countries explored.

In other words, Shanks and Tilley's agents are no more than what Giddens criticises as Althusser's 'cultural dopes', with the 'meat' of the explanation residing in the places and functions that the agents, when aggregated into social groupings, occupy. And even the active social groupings are those at the top of the social scale: here it is implicitly the British and Swedish bourgeoisie attempting to maintain a disciplined labour force.

A second example, this time drawn from historical archaeology, is Leone's discussion of the Paca Garden in Annapolis, Maryland, where Leone is able to reconstruct the complex design of a Georgian garden, the property of one William Paca, merchant and lawyer (Leone 1984: 32). Leone discusses the layout of the garden, relating its spatial organisation, choice of shrubs, and so on to a wider set of attitudes and perspectives on the world also manifested in Georgian architecture and other classes of material culture. These attitudes and perspectives are in turn seen as an ideology, a set of beliefs simultaneously masking the inequality of power and wealth in later eighteenth-century Chesapeake society and making it appear part of the natural order. This ideology, Leone continues, is asserted with greater emphasis as the social order it legitimates comes under increasing strain.

Supplementing this account is a good deal of information about the personal circumstances of William Paca himself. As a prominent lawyer and exponent of rational argument, Leone shows that Paca's life and circumstances exemplified the tensions and contradictions he is seeking to demonstrate in Chesapeake society at large. Paca was prominent at and before the Revolution, arguing with all his legal and logical powers for universal principles of human freedom and equality: yet he himself owned a hundred slaves. The garden thus emerges as his personal 'glossing-over' of the contradictions in his own life.

At first sight this argument encapsulates all that is best in 'postprocessual' archaeology; and indeed, it remains one of the most elegant and convincing demonstrations yet of the Marxist view of ideology. But on closer critical reading one encounters problems. Leone explicitly derives his concept of ideology from Shanks and Tilley's critique of Althusser (Leone 1984: 26; Shanks and Tilley 1982: 13–133). He fails to consider, however, their chief contribution, namely that a given ideology is not a monolithic entity, 'duping' the vast majority of the oppressed in any straightforward or unproblematic fashion (Shanks and Tilley 1982: 131). Nowhere does Leone discuss, consequently, how those who viewed the garden interpreted it, and how their interpretations differed according to their class, gender, ethnicity, or other interests – in short, their goals as active social agents.

Second, Paca's life is treated by Leone as an exemplification of the trends he is discussing, rather than as a unique conjuncture. Paca's particular circumstances are treated as those of the ruling classes in general writ small. His particular strategy in the design of the garden, therefore, is seen as no more than the blind execution of what everyone else is doing. In short, we are back yet again with Althusser's 'cultural dopes'.

A prehistoric study should be discussed to complement these points. In a study of the Dutch Neolithic, Hodder (1982e) presumably aims to follow up his earlier assertion in the same volume that the active individual must be taken account of (Hodder 1982d: 5). He relates changes in pottery decoration, in particular an increase in contrasts and oppositions, to developments in battleaxe and burial variability. The tombs are seen as representing corporate groups, legitimating both rights to place and lineage heads, and acting to mask emergent tensions between age and gender groups. The tombs also place emphasis on the ancestors at a time of shifting, short-term settlement.

It is difficult to see any place given to agency in this interpretation. Indeed, at one point the pots themselves take over this role: 'there is less concern in the LBK-Rossen pottery with symbolically marking out and forming social categories and the boundaries between them' (Hodder 1982e: 175). As with both the studies discussed above, there is no account of how subordinate social groups reacted to the ideology presented, in this case by the tombs and pottery decoration. Again, the dynamic for change, the understanding of the variability, resides in what Hodder sees as emergent contradictions arising from social structure and settlement organisation as a whole.

The transformation of the medieval house

Rather than propose some new theoretical reformulation of an old problem, I want to explore the issue less formally through the use of a case study drawn from my own fieldwork. This is part of a contextual study of vernacular houses in western Suffolk, England, A.D. 1400–1674 (Figure 12.1). To simplify a little for the purposes of this article, this period can be divided into three phases, based on typological analysis

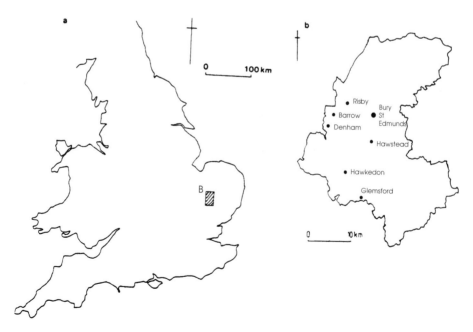

Figure 12.1 Location of area discussed

of the spatial layout of the houses: houses of 'medieval' plan-type, *c.*1400–early sixteenth century; the dominance of fully 'postmedieval' plan-types after *c.*1580; and a 'transitional' period between these two. (It should be noted that these terms apply only to the Old World context and that there is no straightforward relationship with, for example, Deetz's (1977: 39) use of the term 'medieval'.)

Our concern here is with the central, 'transitional' phase in this sequence. This is remarkable in two ways. Quantitatively, it marks a peak in housebuilding in Suffolk over the three centuries. So far, 85 buildings have been surveyed, of which at least 35, and probably more, were either built or substantially altered during this 50-year period. Most areas of England experienced a 'great rebuilding' somewhat later than this, some commentators putting the height of rebuilding around 1580–1630 (Hoskins 1953) or even later (Machin 1977: Graph One; Johnson 1986).

Spatially, the houses of this period are even more remarkable. Medieval houses, as we shall see, have a narrow range of subtypes, and the same is broadly true of postmedieval houses. Yet the transitional period displays a wide range of combinations of old and new forms, including a few very conservative houses whose arrangements barely differ from the medieval antecedents, and several whose plan form alone would be judged fully postmedieval.

Why this sudden upsurge in building? And why this wide variation in adoption and rejection of old and new forms? It is a truism to state that the forms of houses must represent, though not in a reflective or straightforward form, the social strategies and ideologies of their owners (Moore [1986] has provided a full discussion of the relationship between the organisation of space, ideology, and social reality). Let us start by discussing the preceding *habitus* available to 16th century house owners and builders: the form of, and system of values and meanings associated with, the medieval house.

Houses and meanings in the fifteenth century

The conventional typological definition of a 'medieval' house, as a vernacular standing structure, is that it has at least one room, invariably the hall or central living-space, open to the roof (Mercer 1975: 19). The conventional reason given for this is that before the advent of chimney-stacks at the vernacular level, an open hearth had to be used, and therefore space was needed for the smoke to disperse among the rafters of the roof or to be let out through a louver at one of the hipped ends. On one side, or more frequently both sides, of this room, further rooms with ceilings dividing them into two storeys were placed.

At one end the 'parlour' or 'upper' end of the house would provide space for the master and mistress of the household, while at the other the 'service' or 'lower' end of the house provided space for service and kitchen functions.

Within the central hall itself this categorisation of upper/lower: master/service can be seen in microcosm, and is emphasised by the use of fixed architectural features and of movable furniture. The 'upper' end of the hall next to the parlour was frequently placed on a raised dais, particularly in larger buildings such as Oxford and Cambridge colleges: before it stood the open hearth, while on the other side stood symmetrical, opposed doorways to the outside world and access to the service area (Figure 12.2).

Literary references indicate some of the ways in which this arrangement of space was used to enforce social distinction, particularly at mealtimes in the hall. Langland

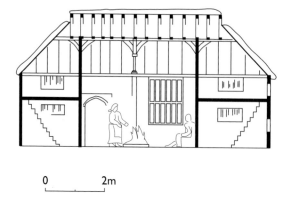

0   2m

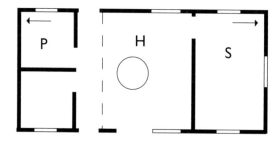

Figure 12.2 Plan and reconstruction of a medieval farmhouse: based on Popples Farm, Brettenham.
S: service/lower end;
H: hall;
P: parlour/upper end

makes reference to the way in which members of the household and guests were placed at the upper or lower ends, or towards the centre or sides of the hall, according to their status and value (Burrell 1931).

Architectural details confirm this picture: the facade of the parlour/hall partition, marking the 'upper end' of the hall and backing the area where the master sat at mealtimes, is often elaborately treated, with extravagantly wide pieces of timber being used to brace the walls and often canopies (Mercer 1975: 90). The roof structure is often unnecessarily elaborate, with a highly ornamented 'crown-post' directly over the centre of the hall above the open hearth forming a central feature. Again, in larger buildings, the upper or 'dais' end is lit by a large bay window, making the organisation of space within the hall visible from the outside (Wood 1965: 112).

The variation around this norm is quite small. A few buildings have only one storeyed end, but these are generally early and very rare by *c*.1450. Many more have, instead of a rectangular shape, a cross-wing at parlour, service, or even both ends, giving extra space and again marking out the internal arrangement of the house from the outside by providing opportunities for impressive projecting jetties and gables. As one would expect, these wings are more usually found at the 'upper' than the 'lower' ends, and are more highly decorated and project forward more boldly at the upper/parlour end. In all these cases, the tripartite division with a central hall as the dominant architectural feature is never varied.

It is clear that the organisation of space within such buildings relates to the organisation of the family and household they accommodate, and that this relationship is far more than being a merely functional one. The role of the master of the house as provider is emphasised by his position at head of the hall, while the careful gradation of those lower down is emphasised by their relative seating at mealtimes and in their position at the 'lower' end as a whole. At the same time, the lack of physical barriers within the hall acts to obscure the inequalities of master/servant and gender relationships attested by social historians (Laslett 1965) by appearing to be nonsegregated space (hence Langland's indignation at the master and his mistress failing to uphold this piece of ideology by eating in the parlour [Burrell 1931: 138]). The metaphor of the family is extended to cover the wider household, a metaphor seen in Langland, implied by commensality and more clearly perceived in later periods (Kussmaul 1981: 8).

Such buildings are notoriously difficult to date in any absolute way within the century (Mercer 1975: 5): even tree-ring dating can prove problematic, since many houses have a high proportion of reused timbers that are often difficult to detect. Some are even likely to be early 16th century; other writers have generally taken the 'medieval' tag to refer to pre-A.D. 1530 structures (Mercer 1975: 21). But this difficulty in dating may be interpreted to our advantage. If plan forms remained stable to the point of identity for over a century, the question of why the sudden change after c.1530 becomes even more acute.

Tradition and transition

The 'transitional' buildings identified fall into two categories: new buildings and conversion of earlier, medieval structures. The latter will be put to one side for the time being. Of the former category, many houses have been so heavily altered since the period of interest that their original form is hopelessly problematic. This leaves a total of 19 houses meriting further consideration, of which only a few will be discussed.

It would be easy to interpret these houses in both a normative and a fetishistic way, seeing each particular house as an oscillation or unhappy compromise between 'medieval' and 'postmedieval' ideals or mental templates, or to see their peculiarities as the result of 'faulty' or 'imperfect' execution of such an ideal. Rather, I want to regard these houses as intentional creations of their owners, as unique conjunctures of their goals as social agents and the limitations and constraints imposed by the wider social, ideological, and technical systems. First, I will consider particular houses and their owners before relating these to wider problems.

Langley's Newhouse and Wolfe Hall

Archaeologically, Langleys Newhouse, Hawkedon, can be dated to the mid 16th century on typological grounds. This is confirmed by the attribution to Sir John Langley, who was rector of Hawkedon from 1554 to 1560 (Pleydell-Bouverie 1980: 15). This attribution is first mentioned in an indenture of 1794[1] and may alternatively be a corruption of the topographical description 'Long-Leys', but the similarity in date between the house and Langley's occupancy at Hawkedon makes this unlikely.

Langleys Newhouse is one of a class of houses (including Wolfe Hall, Denham Priory, and Black Horse Farmhouse) standing in an unusually isolated position. Though it is an impressive site, claimed to be the highest house in Suffolk and standing on a rise commanding views both to the west and overlooking the village and church at Hawkedon about 1 km to the south, it is one at variance with the medieval preference for sheltered sites in low positions near water; the present owners inform me that the house is exposed, cold, and rattles in the winter gales. In addition, one would expect the rector Langley to choose a site closer to the church and the village community for convenience. We may therefore infer that display of his new house was important to Langley, and that he was not unduly concerned about either distance from his vocation or spatial distance from other members of his congregation and community.

Concern for display is also seen in the orientation and architectural detail of the exterior of the house. It stands facing northwest, squarely into the full force of the prevailing wind but at a point of maximum visibility from the road running *c*.30 m away: the studding (close setting of timbers for partly decorative purposes) on the front of the house is closer than that at the back. Finally, the chimney-stack is one of the most impressive of its kind, a 'Tudor' arrangement with four flues, each with a different moulded brick design.

The ground plan and three-dimensional form of Langley's Newhouse (Figure 12.3) are a combination of old and new features. It comprises two rooms on the ground floor, separated by an internal stack with back-to-back fireplaces. There may have been a third room at the lower end of the hall, but on balance this is unlikely. The fireplaces are elaborate: that in the hall is very large, while those in the parlour and the room over this have fine plastered brick arches. The hall and parlour fireplaces also had coloured plaster friezes overhead, with vineleaf patterns and motifs. Next to the hall fireplace was sited a bread oven.

Langley chose to arrange his hall according to a 'medieval' pattern with opposed doorways at the lower end, but replaced the central hearth and open arrangement to the roof with a ceiling and stack. He also placed a stair next to the stack giving access to the upper floor, complete with 'husband-step', one step a few centimetres higher than the others, placed according to Suffolk oral tradition so that a wife engaged in adultery in the chamber over the parlour would be warned of her husband's impending appearance by his stumble on the stairs. The arrangement of

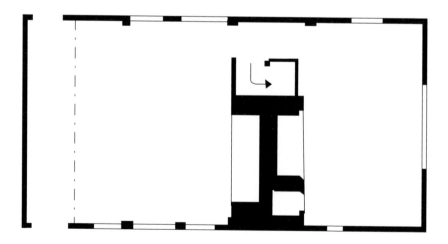

Figure 12.3 Langleys Newhouse, Hawkedon, c.1550: simplified ground plan

the upper end of the house, in particular the back-to-back fireplaces, the site and form of the stair, and the ceiled hall, are all new features, as is the provision of upstairs accommodation; the lower end, with its opposed doorway and provision for cooking facilities in the hall rather than as later in the service range, is old.

Some features appear to evoke old values of emphasis on the hall as a central area of social interaction, particularly at mealtimes, but to use new signifiers to do so. For example, the elaborate ceiling in the hall shows that this room continued to be an area for symbolic display, though the ceiling replaced the former open roof as a means for so doing. Again, the colourful ornamentation round the fireplaces, and the large scale of the fireplace in the hall, stresses the centrality of the hearth area as before, though this hearth is now housed in a brick stack.

Above the ground floor is a full storey with at least one heated room, above which again is a range of attics. The clasped-purlin roof structure is of a type introduced around this time, technically efficient but less ornate than the earlier crown-post system, and clearly not an object of visual display.

The new forms found in Langley's house are not major innovations: the chimney stack had been used in 'polite' architecture such as castles since their inception (Platt 1978), while ceilings were present in medieval houses (see above). It was the use of the stack at this social level and the rearrangement into back-to-back fireplace and continuous ceiling that were novel.

From these details, we can reconstruct a hypothetical picture of Langley's goals, and the way in which he pursued these through the medium of material culture. Langley chose to cut himself off from the nucleated hamlet of Hawkedon, away from the nuclei of his own parish church and the manor house of Hawkedon Hall (Rotherham 1887: 88), itself a formerly medieval building rebuilt around c.1500. He was anxious to display and confirm his status through an impressive house with ornate stack and close studding at a time when concepts of status, particularly that of the clergy, were under considerable threat (Brigden 1984: 94–96).

Most significantly, he used a combination of features evoking elements of the medieval system of values already discussed, particularly around the hall and lower, service end of his house where the activities of the other, inferior members of the household took place. This is not to say that his servants necessarily accepted the ideology most explicitly seen in the organisation of space: they may have had other readings. These are difficult to explore given lack of direct documentation of social classes below the middling level, but reports from this period of resentment and lack of active cooperation in servants (Kussmaul 1981: 44–8) and the petty physical sanctions often needed and used by masters (Stone 1977: 167) show that such classes were far from being blindly 'duped' by the values of family and loyalty. At the same time, the nature of the institution of service as an age class, a stage of transition between childhood and adult life, as well as the inequality between male and female servants (Kussmaul 1981: 37, 71–93), probably militated against the formation of a coherent or at least explicit 'alternative' perspective at this time.

Just as Langley's servants may have had alternative readings, so also may have the women of the household. Distinctive female perspectives on the social order of the time are attested empirically, though these are visible only indirectly through the writings of men (Roberts 1985: 122–4). These are difficult to see directly, however,

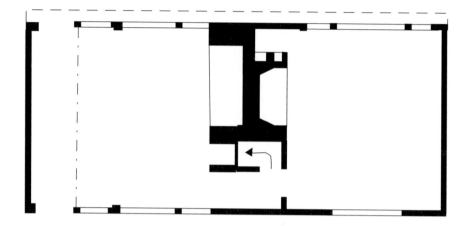

Figure 12.4 Wolfe Hall, Barrow, c.1550: simplified ground plan

in the spatial structuring of the household, since that structuring, as argued above, relates primarily to master/servant relations. Just as inequality among servants probably militated against a coherent status/class perspective at this time, so the class divisions between women probably hindered the development of a coherent female perspective.

A striking similarity can be seen between the siting and spatial organisation of Langleys Newhouse and that of Wolfe Hall, in the parish of Barrow, some 10 miles to the north (Figure 12.4). Though we know the builder with less certainty here, we do know from the annotation of a tithe map of 1594 (reprinted in Gage 1838: 17) that the house was then owned by the Warner family. The Warner householders are mentioned in the tax records of Barrow throughout the sixteenth century (Hervey 1909: 257, 1910: 340) and it is reasonable to suppose that one of this family built the house. Archaeologically the house may be dated to the mid-sixteenth century: the architectural detail is no later than c.1570, while the stack incorporates reused moulded stonework, probably from the Abbey of Bury St Edmunds 6 miles away, dissolved in 1539.

From their valuation in the tax records, the Warners appear to have been upwardly mobile. Like Langleys, their new house combined old and new elements of plan, and was placed in an isolated but commanding spot about a mile south of the village. There are the remnants of a moat to the north of the house, probably an indication of former medieval occupation of the site, and again the framing is more elaborate on the facade of the house facing the village.

Inside, the novel two-room plan with back-to-back fireplaces and stair next to the stack is again combined with opposed doorways at the lower end of the hall, an ostentatious hall ceiling and emphasis on ornamentation of the fireplaces. The posts of the fireplaces are, as mentioned, made of reused ecclesiastical moulded columns, a practice religious conservatives of the period shied away from (Howard 1987). When this evidence is coupled with the sober religious text inscribed over the fireplace we may speculate that the Warners were religious radicals.

Socially, we can see that the Warners situated themselves carefully within Barrow as a parish. Their siting of Wolfe Hall away from the village can be seen in general terms as a spatial metaphor for the rejection of the values of the medieval village community, but also in particular terms, if our ascription of religious (and therefore political) radicalism is correct, as a rejection of the prevailing influence within the village: that of Sir Clemment Heigham, whose great moated house stood in the centre of Barrow and who was nationally known as a religious and political conservative (Macculloch 1986).

As an upwardly mobile family, and arguably as religious radicals, the Warners in their interests and social goals show similarity to those of Langley. We can see their common solution to the questions involved in building of a new house to express and approach those goals. At the same time, variations in approach show that each house is a unique conjuncture rather than simply an exemplification of the trends under discussion. So their strategies, though obviously similar and related in some sense, are not identical. The Warners probably chose an old moated site for their house, another means of invoking aspects of medieval values for their own purposes. Langley's site was a new one, as far as can be ascertained without excavation. Langley chose to decorate his fireplaces with friezes of vine/hop designs and roundels; the Warners chose an improving, Protestant religious text. In each case the reasons for such variations can be partially traced back to wider conditions (for example the reuse of an older site at Wolfe Hall may be related to the unusual landscape and manorial structure within which it stands in relation to the parish as a whole) but must ultimately rest on the choices made by the protagonists as active agents pursuing particular strategies.

Back to structure

The discussion of two houses so far could be extended, given the space, in several directions. First, other plan variants of this period could be discussed in similar terms, as conjunctures of old and new plan elements, conjunctures formulated to meet the demands of particular social strategies. Several larger houses, for example, combine a novel hall ceiling, placed impressively high, with the usual tripartite division into hall, parlour, and service, and stacks and staircases projecting in wings off to the rear (see for example Hawkedon Hall) (Figure 12.5). These appear conservative in plan for their date: their builders appear to wish to reaffirm more strongly the traditional medieval set of social relationships placing them at the head of the parish social structure, while attaining the relative practical comfort and lessened risk from fire of a smoke-free hall. Also, 'compromise' arrangements such as smoke-bays, or smoke-hoods, where the smoke from an open hearth is channelled into a narrow area of the roof rather than a brick stack, can be discussed in these terms.

Second, the complicating additional factor of what the skilled craftsmen could actually build, and how far their technical limitations and interests conditioned the final result, needs to be considered. There are several houses, for example, where the chimney stack is either awkwardly placed at the end of the building (No. 39, Pages Lane, Higham) or, despite a continuous ceiling and therefore no provision for an open hearth, all stacks appear to be 'inserted' (Block Farmhouse, Bradfield Combust, and Greyhound Cottage, Egremont Street, Glemsford). These appear to be conflicts between the client's demand for a ceiled house and the craftsmen's inability or lack of willingness to build one.

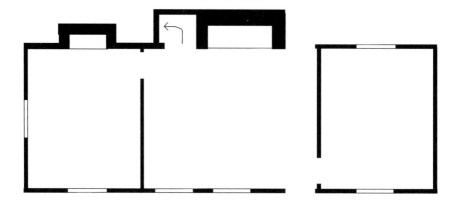

Figure 12.5 Hawkedon Hall, Hawkedon, c.1550: simplified ground plan

Lack of space, however, makes a full discussion of these topics impossible here. What does need to be outlined, however, is how this diversity of strategies in the mid-sixteenth century cohered into a fresh structure by *c.*1580, namely the two- or three-cell farmhouse, ceiled throughout and in Suffolk usually with back-to-back fireplaces. This retained the three-cell medieval structure and with it some of the system of values, but with much higher emphasis on privacy, with the parlour now a heated room, free circulation at both ground and upper floor levels, and lack of direct entry into the hall, an entry now giving access to a lobby giving access to hall, parlour, and stairs (as at Majors Farmhouse, Chedburgh) (Figure 12.6).

This plan form is present from the 1540s, Quays Farmhouse, Risby for example being of this form, but reached striking domination of all other forms parallel to that of the medieval open-hall house only in the later sixteenth century. Its rise from the earlier diversity can be seen in parallel with the rise of a more settled social order, in particular the much-debated rise of the gentry and yeoman classes (Stone 1957). This is not an extreme holistic explanation. Rather, as society became more stable, the interests of both gender and class groups became more clearly articulated and individual social strategies therefore became more clearly and closely determined by society at large.

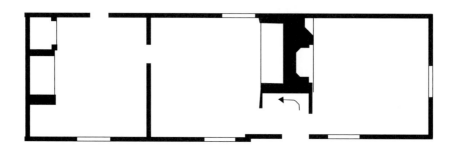

Figure 12.6 Majors Farmhouse, Chedburgh, c.1620: simplified ground plan

The rise of these classes, in houses with a greater emphasis on privacy in general and segregation from servants in particular, functional differentiation between work and domestic areas, greater material comfort in terms of architecture and movable goods (Garrard 1982), can be seen in conjunction with the rise of 'rural capitalism': the breakdown of the communal ties and restrictions of the medieval village community, the notion of land as a more alienable commodity, and the practice of farming for profit (Williamson and Bellamy 1987). So the structuring quality of the organisation of space in Langley's house and other houses played its part ultimately in the formation of early modern and industrial society.

Implications and conclusions

In the first part of this paper, the individual was seen as 'the man [sic] who wasn't there': in postprocessual explanation, the active agent present in a variety of theoretical forms but absent in practice. In the second part, I have tried to help remedy this fault by briefly outlining individual agency in a case study. This has been done by considering some isolated examples of individual housebuilders, but only, it is worth reiterating, as a means to an end: we need not have known who Langley was, merely inferring his social and economic position from the house he built, or have outlined the general circumstances of housebuilders at this time from contextual evidence.

In reaction to the studies discussed at the beginning, I have tried to emphasise the way these actors creatively manipulated existing structures of ideas, that these are not simply reducible to their places and functions within wider social changes, and to include consideration of possible subordinate perspectives on the ideology set up. I have also tried to show how decisions made at a small-scale level relate back in an active way to wider social and economic changes, rather than simply being instances of those changes.

Perhaps the central conclusion to be drawn is that a study of agency cannot be separated from a study of structure: that agency is a manipulation of an existing structure, a structure that is external to the individual in the Durkheimian sense and appears to that agent as a synchronic construct, as something to be drawn upon. Thus, to the mid-sixteenth-century housebuilder and owner, the antecedent house forms could be seen in a very normative way as described above. These forms, and the values they signified, could be drawn on and manipulated.

Two implications flow from this point. The first is that when seeking to understand human agency, the archaeologist must be prepared to describe the antecedent historical conditions, the *habitus* from which the actor draws, in a synchronic and normative way in order to gain understanding of those actions. Parallels may be drawn here with certain themes in social history. For example, Isaac's (1982) discussion of changes in eighteenth-century Virginia is set against a backdrop of an 'ethnography' of the area in the mid-eighteenth century, an ethnography described as a synchronic, stable moment. Of course, such a description is an analytical procedure rather than a description of 'reality', since that moment is itself the product of changing historical forces.

The stance taken towards a particular period will therefore depend on its position relative to the period of interest. In discussing the antecedent conditions of the mid-sixteenth century, I discussed medieval houses in a very normative way, making no mention of their own places as products of social action, or the way in which subordinate social groups reacted or reinterpreted the ideology they represented. This was a deliberate omission for heuristic purposes. If my problem had been to discuss agency in the context of medieval houses, a different stance would have been taken: the social strategies pursued by the middling classes in the late medieval countryside would have been the focus of attention, with the early medieval period being seen as the preceding *habitus*.

It would then have been valid to see the rise of late medieval standing buildings as a novel expression of permanence at a vernacular social level, and to tie this expression into social strategies adopted by yeoman farmers and the lower gentry. These strategies would be interpreted as denying the: feudal lord/vassal: permanence/ impermanence: power/dependence links in values and ideas set up through material culture in the preceding early medieval period. These links would again be described and explicated in a normative way as the antecedent historical conditions for this particular problem.

The second point counterbalances the first: that such a normative outline is not necessarily a repressive, prescriptive one. While to the social agent it appears to be a coherent body of values, it is one to be drawn upon selectively, manipulated and even inverted: sixteenth-century house-builders felt free to invoke medieval values towards their inferiors at the lower end of the hall while modifying those values in other contexts. Thus, norms should be seen as 'tools' for fulfilling strategies rather than necessarily as prescriptive devices (a point made in more detail by Swidler 1986).

Another implication is that agency and structure are analytically distinct but nevertheless intertwined: each is the product of the other when seen from different points within the flow of history. It is difficult therefore to see how the study of one can be separated from the other, as for example Bailey seems to imply in his assertion that different timescales should be subjected to different modes of analysis, each irreducible to the other – 'time perspectivism' (Bailey 1983, 1987: 18). Long-term structures in history do exist (Braudel 1958). This paper has argued, however, that in order to explain their persistence one has to look at the conditions of their replication at the level of the individual and of day-to-day social interaction (as is done, for example, by Lane 1987).

It is perhaps a little simplistic to analyse agency and structure in this way. Some consideration needs to be given to social groupings, such as classes in the Marxian sense or gender or age groups, which may act on a level over and above the individual (Shanks and Tilley's classes are a good example) but still operate as active entities within the social structure as a whole. Such active groupings cannot replace the individual at a conceptual level, since the concern still arises as to how they come to articulate individual interests and why social actors choose to affiliate to a particular group. At the same time, they clearly interact with agency: for example, the probable lack of a coherent perspective of women and servants on Langley's ideology was understood in terms of the divisions within these groups as not allowing a coherent alternative perspective to be articulated.

So an unavoidable dualism remains between individual and society, though it is mediated by intervening groups (Heller 1984: 28–40). The particular form in which dualism will appear in a society will also vary according to that society's conception of the person (Carrithers *et al.* 1985).

Finally, at a methodological level it is interesting to note that the search for agency seems best to be conducted using small-scale studies as representatives of wider changes, in both a temporal and spatial sense. The transformation of sixteenth-century Suffolk architecture is but part of a much wider change embracing Western culture as a whole over the last six centuries and even beyond (Glassie 1975: 193). Again, this technique is one commonly used in historical analysis (Boyer and Nissenbaum 1974; Le Roy Ladurie 1979; Thompson 1977b are but three examples).

I have tried to demonstrate that the questions arising from the search for agency involve much wider theoretical problems, in particular a parallel concern with structure, and that further thought is needed before these wider problems are resolved. This thought should include further consideration of the long term along the broad lines laid down by Hodder (1987f), a rethinking of our conceptions of social structure and system, but above all more case studies of areas where the contextual information and temporal clarity afforded by the archaeological evidence are detailed enough for us to explain variability in these terms, while at the same time with enough time depth to be able to link the substantive conclusions gathered to wider, long-term structures and changes. Such opportunities arise most frequently in historical archaeology: in such contexts, the combination of documentary and material culture evidence may finally allow the shadowy figure on the stair to descend and be recognised.

ACKNOWLEDGEMENTS

I thank Dr Ian Hodder for several stimulating discussions on this topic and much help with earlier drafts of the paper and also Andy Black, with whom I have discussed these issues over many pints.

NOTE

1   Held at Suffolk Record Office, Bury St Edmunds, Accession No. HD.976.

13

BUILDING POWER IN THE CULTURAL LANDSCAPE OF BROOME COUNTY, NEW YORK, 1880–1940*

RANDALL H. McGUIRE

In the first two decades of the twentieth century, capitalism in the United States faced a crisis born of the inherent contradictions in the system and the resistance of labor to existing class relations. In the political arena progressives and yellow journalists attacked the capitalists, and Congress legislated previously unheard of controls on business. Labor was militant and the black flags of anarchy and the red flags of socialism hung in many union halls. Most fundamentally, capitalism faced a realization crisis manifest in the great depression of the 1890s and the declining rate of profit in the last decades of the nineteenth century.

The crisis of the early twentieth century did not result in the long hoped for socialist revolution nor in a radical transformation of capitalism. Rather, capitalism evolved into a more mature form of monopoly capitalism which we still labor under today (Mandel 1978; Amsden 1979: 15–17; Brodhead 1981). Important aspects of this transformation were the advent of consumerism and the renegotiation of capital–labor relations. This renegotiation preserved the essential capitalist relations of production while co-opting the socialist goals of labor. Integral to the transformation was the formulation of a new ideology of class relations which, rather than naturalizing class inequalities, denied the existence of class. The creation and modification of the cultural landscape in Broome County, New York both reflected and participated in this process of ideological transformation.

Late nineteenth-century capitalism

Capitalist production in late nineteenth-century America was based on the extraction of absolute surplus value (Amsden 1979: 13). As was discussed by Marx (1906), increasing absolute surplus value involves the intensification of labor and the lengthening of the working day. Integral to the maintenance and intensification of this type of extraction was the existence of a dynamic reserve army of the unemployed which was constantly replenished by immigration from Europe. One of the main

---

*First published in R. McGuire and R. Paynter (eds) (1991), *The Archaeology of Inequality*, Oxford: Blackwell, pp. 102–24.

characteristics of this factory work-force was extremely high turnover averaging 100 percent a year (Slichter 1919: 16; Nelson 1975: 85–6). With the exception of a limited number of skilled workers the capitalist regarded labor as a replenishable resource to be consumed just as his factories consumed coal. Craft workers thus gained power and special status because of the skills which the capitalist required and they controlled. Unions gained real strength and permanency only among these aristocrats of labor. With the combined force of skills and organization, craft workers attained benefits which granted many of them the trappings of a middle-class lifestyle (Guerin 1979: 57–61; Walkowitz 1978: 102–10). The capitalist, however, constantly sought to deskill production and the proportion of skilled workers in the labor force declined throughout the late nineteenth century.

In addition to the reserve army of unemployed and the high turnover rates which worked against the organization of non-craft workers, coercion was central to the capitalist control of labor. The capitalist hired foremen to drive the workers on the shop floor through a combination of threats, abuse and often physical violence. The foreman hired the worker, fired the worker, supervised the work and in many cases could set the level of compensation (Nelson 1975: 34–54). Capitalists did not hesitate to employ violence in the handling of strikes, and cases like the Homestead strike of 1892 where management fortified the mill and fought pitched gun battles with the strikers differed only in degree from the usual tactics for strikebreaking.

The nineteenth-century capitalist reaped enormous profits but little of this reached the mass of workers. Throughout the later half of this period most workers lived in conditions of poverty working 10 to 16 hours a day and sending their children into the mills and factories to survive (Walkowitz 1978: 102–7; Tentler 1979; Guerin 1979). Workers could afford few of the products of their labor and maintained very low levels of consumption, especially of durable goods (Ewen 1976; Matthaei 1982: 235).

The class relations of the late nineteenth century were rationalized (for the elite) and obscured (from the workers) by an ideology that equated society with nature and derived the apparent inequalities from the characteristics of individuals. The writings of authors such as Conwell (1905) and Sumner (1963) proclaimed this ideology of Social Darwinism and the gospel of wealth. Social Darwinism provided a model for the social world derived from the natural world. Life was a struggle for survival and success and only the fittest would survive: in the natural world this led to the improvement of the species, also a desirable process in society. Success was attainable by all. Its determinates lay in the characteristics of the individual: hard work, thrift, intelligence, sobriety, cleanliness and a little luck guaranteed success. Failure resulted from a lack of these qualities or, more importantly, their opposite: laziness, extravagance, stupidity, slovenliness, and drunkenness. The 'gospel of wealth' proclaimed that wealth was the emblem of success, the reward of a good life and personal ability.

The forms and appearances of late nineteenth-century reality reinforced and validated this ideology. Clear material differences delineated those who had succeeded and were the most fit from those of lesser character and ability who had failed. The failures lived in squalid quarters, possessed little or nothing of value, wasted what little they earned on strong drink, frequently were without work and violated the sanctity of the home by sending their women and children into the mines, mills, and factories.

The ideology both originated in the stark material differences between classes and perpetuated these differences.

The cultural landscape figured prominently in this ideology. It was both a model of and a model for social action. It fulfilled the expectations of the ideology and guaranteed the continuance of the relations which created the reality. Even in the paternalistic company towns, where the capitalist installed his workers in clean, family-oriented dwellings for their own betterment, the form, substance, and spatial relationships of homes and other edifices clearly reflected each individual's position in the factory order (Nelson 1975: 90–5; Walkowitz 1978: 48–75).

The maturation of capitalism in the early twentieth century

The workers of the late nineteenth century did not bend to their yoke willingly but resisted in violent strike after violent strike. Three main periods of labor unrest stand out, the late 1870s, the early 1890s and finally after the turn of the century from 1905 to 1919. By the early 1900s the distinct segregation of classes, abuse of workers, and conflict with capitalists had produced the strongest and most radical militancy in the history of American labor (Amsden 1979; Guerin 1979).

During the first two decades of the twentieth century unions called not only for the improvement of working conditions, increased wages, and shorter hours but also for the establishment of a socialist economy. When the Industrial Workers of the World (IWW) won the American Woolen Company strike in Lawrence Massachusetts, in 1912, the strikers celebrated by singing the Internationale (Guerin 1979: 79). The Bolshevik revolution in 1917 further radicalized workers and for the first time the capitalists were faced with the reality of a socialist revolution. Radicalism peaked in the strikes of 1919 when both the railroad workers and the United Mine Workers called for the nationalization of their respective industries. These strikes were brutally put down with the arrest, deportation, imprisonment, and execution of suspected radicals.

The industry of the late nineteenth century had been built primarily on the production of the means of production and secondarily on the production of consumer goods for the middle and upper classes (Ewen 1976: 24; Mandel 1978: 184–92). By the end of the century these markets had been saturated and capitalism faced a realization crisis. The industries of the USA, in order to survive, had to produce far more than the market which existed for their products. This crisis revealed itself in the great depression of 1893 and the falling rate of profits from 1873 to the 1890s (Mandel 1978: 83, 120–1).

Resolution of the crisis of the early twentieth century lay in two interrelated movements which altered the system of production in the United States without compromising the essential relations of capitalism (Brodhead 1981). The first of these is what Antonio Gramsci called 'Fordism', marked by the introduction of assembly line mass production and a shift to the extraction of relative surplus value. The second movement was an ideological movement which sought to restructure production in the form of an industrial democracy.

In 1910 Henry Ford reorganized his Highland, Michigan plant along an assembly line and by 1914 had cut the assembly time for an automobile chassis from 12.5 hours to 33 minutes (Chandler 1967: 26–7; Meyer 1981). Mass production involved the use of highly specialized single purpose machines with equally highly specialized and easily trained workmen to produce goods at rates that seem astronomical when compared to late nineteenth-century production (Ewen 1976: 23–4). The capitalist extracted increasing amounts of relative surplus value by replacing skilled workers with machines. Mass production dehumanized labor while offering workers greater material benefits for their labor. Principles of scientific management sought to fully integrate the worker with the machines so that human and machine worked in perfect synchronization (Nelson 1975: 55–79). The worker became little more than an extension of the machine in this ultimate dehumanization of the productive process. Ford drew workers to his plants with the famous promise of $5.00 a day and, more importantly, he sought to make products for consumption by the workers, thereby transforming them into consumers (Ewen 1976).

This transformation of the productive process also necessitated a renegotiation of the relationship between capital and labor. Capital no longer depended on the workers solely as a source of human energy; it now also depended on them for markets (Ewen 1976: 23–39; Edsforth 1987: 19). Capitalists expressed this new relationship in terms of a functionally integrated circle beneficial to all: 'They [workers] have time to see more, do more and incidentally buy more. This stimulates business and increases prosperity, and in the general economic circle the money passes through industry again and back into the workman's pocket' (Ford 1929: 17).

For the worker to consume, the material conditions of the working class had to be modified (Ewen 1976). Consumption required the worker to have leisure time and therefore a shorter working day. Higher pay rates would give the worker more to spend and time payment plans and credit would stretch that buying power further. The capitalist stressed home ownership by workers to increase consumption, and modern advertising techniques were developed to encourage and educate the workers in their new role. These innovations co-opted some of the demands of the nineteenth-century labor movement, such as the eight-hour day; they also required a transformation of the highly mobile, erratically employed labor force of the late nineteenth century into a stable, continuously employed population.

This transformation of the relationship between capital and labor and of the material conditions of labor created the new markets required to overcome the realization crisis but it also undermined capital's traditional means of controlling labor. Scientific management centralized hiring in personnel departments and reduced the power of the shop foreman (Nelson 1975: 55–101). Having a vast reserve army of the unemployed would be counter-productive because its members would not have the money to be consumers. Violent actions against labor engendered bad feelings toward companies and alienated consumers. All in all, these changes favored a shift in labor control from coercion to manipulation (Ewen 1976: 26; Filene 1924; Carver 1926; Edsforth 1987).

The ideological basis for this shift lay in the notion of an industrial democracy. John Leitch (1919: 1) wrote, 'Have we not talked rather too much about working people as a class and too little of them as human beings?' The concept of an industrial democracy reformulated the mystification of the capitalist relationship by denying the reality of class stratification. The industrial reformers of the early twentieth century blamed the abuses, poverty, violence, and exploitation of the nineteenth century not on capitalism, but on deviations from the democratic principles which had founded the United States (Carver 1926; Allen 1952).

Not only were labor and capital functionally and beneficially linked in the economy, but also a social revolution was afoot (Allen 1952). 'It is a revolution that is to wipe out the distinctions between laborers and capitalists by making laborers their own capitalists and by compelling most capitalists to become laborers of one kind or another' (Carver 1926: 9). These reformers preached that success in industry required that the capitalist do away with the social and material differences that set him apart from his workers. They also called for the creation of worker councils and company unions. These later reforms did not secure widespread favor but did enhance the ideological shift.

The advocates of industrial democracy drew the form and substance of their new ideology from the past. The late nineteenth century was portrayed as a short-term quirk in the democratic growth of the country. Thomas Nixon Carver (1926: 261–2), a Harvard economist, wrote: 'To be alive to-day, in this country, and to remember the years from 1870 to 1920 is to awake from a nightmare.' The prophets of an industrial democracy remade the colonial past in places like Colonial Williamsburg to sanctify their vision and avidly advocated the Colonial Revival movement in architecture and design. The imagery of a naturally set order was replaced by a vision of a mythic past. However, this new ideology did not abandon all the conceptual baggage of the late nineteenth century; the cult of individual achievement remained a key facet of the mystification. Success and failure still sprang from the abilities of individuals, but the definition of success changed. In a democratic society, where all were partners in industry, success was a relative phenomenon. Whereas in the tenets of Social Darwinism all men had the opportunity to succeed, in the industrial democracy all men could gain some degree of success.

The ideology of industrial democracy both arose from and created the reality of the 1920s. The identification of success with conspicuous consumption was inherited from the past. With the spread of mass production conspicuous consumption became possible for much of the working class. A form of commodity fetishism had been created which confused material things with human relations: once the availability of things changed, the illusion of change in human relations was created (Edsforth 1987: 35). In *Middletown* of the 1920s working-class housewives described how, in their childhood, classes had existed in the community because only the rich had cars, washing machines, and their own homes, but now everyone had these things and only differences of degree remained (Lynd and Lynd 1929: 82–3). Class had seemingly melted away. The cultural landscape was an active participant in the creation of this new ideology. The Colonial Revival movement in architecture and design begat a new metaphor for the wealthy, a metaphor that downplayed ostentatiousness and reinforced the mythic past of the industrial democracy. The capitalist aided the illusion of classlessness by modifying the landscape to create the image of equality and continuous gradation. In the industrial democracy the fetishism of commodities, which replaced relations of stratification with things, became the answer to the socialist alternative. In 1934 a delegation of Soviet shoe producers toured the Endicott-Johnson shoe factories in Broome County, New York. A company history published the next year noted that the Soviets were shocked by the number of workers' automobiles surrounding the factory and they exclaimed 'All these belong to workers? . . . Impossible! in Russia only officials have cars' (Inglis 1935: 111). At that moment, in those factories, men, women, and teenagers labored as extensions of specialized machines doing one small task in the shoe-making process over and over again, several hundred times a day.

The transformation of the cultural landscape in Broome County

The ideological shift that ensued in the early twentieth century is clearly visible in the cultural landscape of Broome County, New York. The contributions to the landscape by two of the most prominent capitalists in the history of the county, Jonas M. Kilmer and George F. Johnson, provide a basis for looking at how that landscape served as both a model for and a model of social action.

The cultural landscape of Broome County was not just a passive vessel collecting meaning, from the action of people. The elites of Binghamton consciously used the landscape to reinforce their view of the world and to give reality to that view. The opacity of the reality so created gave form and substance to the ideology. However, it affected the day to day experience and consciousness of the working class in ways never intended by its creators: in ways of resistance. The landscape also provided the physical environment structuring interaction. Physical proximity has a strong effect on the extent and nature of interaction between individuals and groups. The landscape can be manipulated to invite interaction between groups in some contexts and discourage it in others; it can be used to link the activities of the home with those of work or to sharply split them. The landscape is not simply backdrop and props, it is the stage of human action.

In the history of Binghamton no one ever totally rebuilt the cultural landscape. People sought (and still seek) to shape it to their purposes, but at no time did anyone have the means to totally destroy what had gone before and replace it with their own vision. Each new addition to the landscape entered into a dialogue with the past, a dialogue which reinterpreted the past in terms of the new ideal. The opposition between the new forms and the old creates a tension and a continuing dynamic not totally controlled by those who create the landscape.

The industrial history of Broome County reflects well the general trends seen in the nation as a whole. Manufacturing grew to be the main economic activity in the county after the Civil War. The largest city in the county, Binghamton, became a center for cigar production along with a variety of other industries; among them, glassblowing, metalworking, furniture making, and patent medicines were also present. Most of these industries experienced wild fluctuations in prosperity during the late nineteenth century and few firms lasted more than a decade (McGuire and Osterud 1980).

Through the nineteenth and into the early twentieth century the Irish and migrants from rural Pennsylvania made up the majority of the work-force. Turnover in the plants was great and the work-force highly mobile: less than 50 percent of the people counted in the 1880 census appear in the 1890 census. Wage levels were relatively low with an 1880 average annual wage of $351 for all workers, both manufacturing and white-collar: Walkowitz (1978: 103), in his study of the upstate New York town of Troy, estimated that in 1880 a yearly income of $365 would be needed to support a family of four.

During the late nineteenth century labor became more and more militant in Binghamton. The glassblowers' union struck often and in 1890 the cigar workers walked out of every factory, paralyzing the community (McGuire and Osterud 1980). By the start of the twentieth century many saw Binghamton as a center for the radical union, the Knights of Labor, and a hotbed of labor unrest.

Jonas M. Kilmer came to Binghamton in 1878 after 18 years as a merchant in New York (Bothwell 1983: 68–72). He became a partner with his brother in the production of Dr Kilmer's Swamp Root Cure and in 1893 he bought his brother out, taking on full ownership of the company. He also expanded his ventures by publishing a newspaper, the *Binghamton Press*, and establishing a bank. At the turn of the century he was probably the wealthiest man in the county. He died in 1912 passing on a sizeable financial empire which his son consolidated and expanded through the first half of the twentieth century. The *Binghamton Press* ran a full front page obituary for him and proclaimed his occupation as 'capitalist'. A few old people in the community today remember Jonas Kilmer and he lives on in a handful of myths. All of the tales relate to the power and opulence of his life. Rooms in his mansion were wallpapered with tooled elephant hide and in the last decades of his life he is said to have walked the streets with a riding quirt in his hand.

In the 1880s Kilmer built a new factory for the production of the swamp root cure (Figure 13.1). He located it prominently on one of Binghamton's main streets in a position where it dominated the view from the passenger depot for the railroad; thus one of the first things a visitor to the community would see was Kilmer's industrial palace. Kilmer had the plant faced and embellished with granite. A bank of large, bronze framed, display windows, now bricked up, pierced the first floor. Behind this ornate

Figure 13.1 *Jonas Kilmer's Swamp Root Cure Factory, Binghamton, New York (photograph by R.H. McGuire)*

Figure 13.2 The Binghamton Press Building, Binghampton, New York (photograph by R. H. McGuire)

Figure 13.3 The Jonas Kilmer mansion, Binghamton, New York (photograph by R. H. McGuire)

facade lay a rambling assortment of brick buildings which housed the activities of several hundred workers.

In 1904 Kilmer still retained control of his financial empire and in that year his son ordered the erection of the 12-storey Binghamton Press building as a lasting memorial to his father (Figure 13.2). Located in the center of town this ornate tower was the most prominent building in Binghamton, validating Kilmer's claim to fame in the community. Local legend says that the Kilmers held up construction of the building until the nearby Security Mutual building was completed; they then added several floors to their building to make it taller than the new Security Mutual building. The Binghamton Press building dominated the city's skyline until the 1960s when a state office building rose to compete with it, and it still dominates the horizon from many vistas.

Kilmer built his mansion on the west side of the Chenango River, away from his factory, businesses and workers (Figure 13.3). The house sat at the end of a mansion row near the Kilmers' extensive horse farm. Built of stone in a late Victorian chateau style the building confronted people approaching it from town with two massive towers, giving the air of a fortification. Facing the horse farm the roof falls off in a much more gentle country style. The mansion holds many stained-glass panels and has bas-relief carvings on its face. The structure is even today a grand expression of opulence, power, and success in late nineteenth-century America.

The working class of nineteenth-century Binghamton lived in housing markedly different from Kilmer's castle. They occupied multiple family houses and tenements across the river and downtown from the homes of Kilmer and other local capitalists. The majority of these buildings were overcrowded wooden fire traps lacking in basic comforts (Figure 13.4). There could be little doubt in nineteenth-century Binghamton as to who were the fit and the unfit. The squalor and crowded condition of the working-class neighborhoods clearly showed why their occupants had failed in the struggle for success.

Kilmer had prepared well in advance for his death in 1912. In 1893 he had a major part in the founding of a new rural cemetery in Binghamton, Floral Park. Here the new wealthy manufacturers of Binghamton could create a landscape where their positions and power would endure for the millennium. Equally important, the cemetery was a park where the masses could view the social relations of their world sanctified for eternity (McGuire 1988). On the highest point in this cemetery Kilmer built his mausoleum (Figure 13.5). This building is the grandest mortuary monument erected in Binghamton and larger than the apartments in which many of Kilmer's workers would have lived.

In his manipulation of the cultural landscape of Binghamton Kilmer realized and reinforced the late nineteenth-century ideology of class relations. He and his fellow capitalists built a city clearly divided into class boroughs. The conditions in these boroughs were the reality that the ideology of Social Darwinism demanded. Kilmer's factory and the Binghamton Press building were status offerings in Kilmer's competition with other capitalists and the fact that no others raised comparable structures cemented Kilmer's position as the leading capitalist of his time. Finally in the cemetery, Kilmer gave form to a landscape that he hoped would perpetuate his success and the class relations of his day for eternity.

Figure 13.4 *Late nineteenth-century tenement building, Binghamton, New York (photograph by R.H. McGuire)*

Figure 13.5 *The Kilmer mausoleum, Johnson City, New York (photograph by R.H. McGuire)*

The segregation of the working class into their own boroughs facilitated class solidarity. Men and women from the same households worked side by side on the shop floor; at the end of each day they returned to a common neighborhood, so that class, work, and family networks all overlapped. In 1890 the working class of the community united when the cigar workers, all on the same day, walked out of every cigar factory in town. They turned the ideology of Social Darwinism on its head. They protested that wages had decreased to the point that they were *forced* to send their wives and daughters into the factories. These workers did not belong to a union and the solidarity of the strike sprang from the informal networks of family and neighborhood (McGuire and Osterud 1980: 61). The unions that followed the strike built on these networks.

In 1881 George F. Johnson came to Binghamton as a foreman in the Lestershire boot and shoe factory where he rose to the post of assistant superintendent. In 1890 the company moved its plant to farmland west of the city of Binghamton and away from the labor turmoil of that community. In that same year the company went broke and one of its creditors, Henry B. Endicott, took control of the factory. Endicott had no interest in running the plant and he put George F. Johnson in charge of the operation. In 1897 Johnson became a partner and in 1899 the company was renamed the Endicott-Johnson company. Endicott died in 1919 leaving Johnson in full control of the company, and Johnson set about to realize his vision of an industrial democracy in Broome County.

From the early 1900s until the 1930s the Endicott-Johnson company boomed. By 1934 it had 29 factories in Broome County employing 19,000 people, over 60 percent of the Broome County manufacturing work-force (Inglis 1935). The company engaged in all stages of the shoe manufacturing and marketing process from the tanning of the leather to the retail sale of the shoes.

Johnson brought his family into the operation starting in the 1890s: first his two brothers, Harry L. and Fred, and then in the early 1900s he put his son in charge of the tanning plant and his nephew Charles in charge of the shoe factories. The Johnsons lived amongst their workers, went by their first names and mixed with the workers at picnics and sporting events. The Johnson family provided a metaphor for the company; all workers were told that they were part of the Endicott-Johnson family.

Throughout its history the Endicott-Johnson company sought to forestall worker unrest and unionism. The original Lestershire factory had been built to the west of Binghamton to remove workers from the influence of Binghamton's union work-force. After World War I the company had to deal with high turnover rates and demands for higher wages; it reacted to these problems by instituting a system of welfare capitalism designed to keep wages at low levels, to build worker loyalty to the company and to maintain a stable, dependable, work-force in Broome County (McGuire and Osterud 1980: 78; Zahavi 1983). The welfare system had several facets. The company provided free medical care, inexpensive cafeterias for noon meals, and public farmer's markets; it made many highly visible donations to the communities in the county, among them, parks and carousels. To encourage a stable labor force the company bought up broad tracts of land in the county, hired contractors and built large numbers of single-family homes which were then sold back to the workers, priority in these sales being given to workers with large families (Zahavi 1983). The company's policies were built around the image of the family and encouraged workers through company propaganda, free maternity care and other means to have large families.

As the company grew during the early 1900s Johnson built two industrial villages west of Binghamton. These sites removed the workers from the union influence of Binghamton but, more importantly, they allowed Johnson to construct a new cultural landscape, to create the surface reality necessary for his industrial democracy. Johnson built these communities with a definite image in mind: 'my picture of a real factory was the shop out in the open country, with the homes of the workers around it in a little village' (Inglis 1935: 25). He argued that workers and employers should live as friends and neighbors in a community of mutual interest (Inglis 1935: 97); he thus created a cultural landscape that mystified the reality of class relations at Endicott-Johnson by denying the existence of class differences and class interests.

The first of these communities, eventually named Johnson City, grew up around the original Lestershire factory, while the second, Endicott, was located about four miles further west. The map of Johnson City shows how Johnson integrated the factories, parks, churches, workers' homes, and the homes of his own family in a single whole (Figure 13.6). No clear spatial distinction was made in the community between work and home, boss and worker, or industry and leisure. Endicott was even a truer rendition of this plan because Johnson controlled more of the construction in this town.

Although not visible on a map, the community was split into ethnic enclaves. At least a third of the company's work-force were immigrants and the children of immigrants, and most of the rest were migrants from rural Pennsylvania. A total of more than 18 ethnic groups were present and most of these had their own neighborhood or block. Johnson favored this division through the use of zoning ordinances, by building churches and halls for ethnic associations and by encouraging ethnic floats and the wearing of ethnic dress in company parades and celebrations.

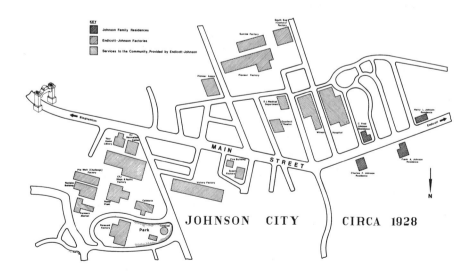

Figure 13.6 *Map of Johnson City, New York (photograph by R. H. McGuire)*

However, the company did not group workers by ethnicity on the shop floor (the only exception to this pattern occurred in the tannery where most of the workers were Italians). In the shoe plants work groups were multi-ethnic and workers spoke English; when they returned to their neighborhoods they lived with fellow ethnics and spoke their native tongue.

Every working-class family had multiple members, men, women, and teenagers, in the factories (McGuire and Woodsong 1990). The jobs in the factories were segregated by sex, however, so that men and women did not work together.

The cultural landscape of the Endicott-Johnson (EJ) villages united all workers in the EJ family and maintained highly visible differences only within the work-force itself. The networks of home, neighborhood, and work intersected but by and large did not overlap. The spatial and conceptual locus of this intersection was the EJ family.

The factories themselves were utilitarian buildings set back from major roads (Figure 13.7). The company built each factory so that the output of one plant passed as directly as possible to the next. Production inside was scientifically organized to minimize any wasted motion and maximize the flow of the product. All of the EJ plants differ markedly from Kilmer's industrial palace.

Johnson erected a variety of buildings as part of his welfare capitalism scheme, many of which remain in use today: these include the Ideal Hospital in Endicott, Your Home Library in Johnson City, and Recreation Park in Binghamton. Johnson left no monument to himself in the form of an elaborate building and, after the factories, the largest edifices he built were for the welfare capitalism program. But many monuments to Johnson do exist in Broome County: in Recreation Park the city of Binghamton erected a bronze statue to Johnson at the dedication of the

Figure 13.7 An Endicott-Johnson shoe factory, Johnson City, New York (photograph by R.H. McGuire)

Figure 13.8 The Endicott-Johnson arch, Endicott, New York (photograph by R. H. McGuire)

park, and EJ workers placed a bronze plaque on a granite boulder near Your Home Library in Johnson City. The most prominent monuments are two granite arches erected by the EJ workers at the eastern boundaries of both Johnson City and Endicott (Figure 13.8).

These monuments are in fact complex statements of social relations which the appearance, and surface perception of the monuments mask. The EJ company often maneuvered workers to gain expressions of worker loyalty and appreciation to the company. In 1916, when Johnson introduced the eight-hour day, the workers staged what the official company history referred to as a massive spontaneous parade through Endicott to Johnson's home (Inglis 1935: 158). The company provided the paraders with a souvenir pamphlet published at company expense. Johnson encouraged shop supervisors to pass around loyalty petitions when he expected worker unrest (Zahavi 1983: 615). In the early 1920s shop supervisors also initiated the construction of the granite arches in Johnson City and Endicott, soliciting funds from workers on the shop floors (Bothwell 1983: 75).

George Johnson's home no longer stands in Endicott but the company history described it:

> The house is of frame construction, of generous size, in plain Colonial style, with a broad porch, well shaded, and it is painted in Colonial Yellow tint. Wide beds of flowers surround it. Compared with the mansions of most captains of industry, this home of the chief of a $36,000,000 corporation is of Spartan simplicity. The establishment is a model of comfort, without a trace of show, a sort of big brother to the many E. J. Workers homes that lie close at hand.
>
> (Inglis 1935: 118)

Figure 13.9 *The Charles F. Johnson home, Johnson City, New York (photograph by R. H. McGuire)*

Figure 13.10 *Endicott-Johnson workers' homes, Endicott, New York (photograph by R. H. McGuire)*

The homes of several of the other members of the Johnson family still stand including that of Charles F. Johnson Jr, the nephew of George, Vice-President of the company and supervisor of all the shoe manufacturing plants. This home, on the main street of Johnson City, is also a Colonial Revival style house (Figure 13.9). It differs from the homes sold to the EJ workers primarily in its size. Most of the EJ workers' homes were craft style bungalows and box-like four-by-fours but many also were simple Colonial Revival structures, the Johnsons' homes in smaller scale (Figure 13.10). The Johnsons chose the styles and plans for the workers' housing. In company photographs and descriptions these working-class dwellings looked solidly middle-class. They had neatly manicured lawns and a car in every drive. The company literature did not show the large gardens and pens for geese, goats, or rabbits that lay in each backyard. The workers turned their backyards into small farms because their wages did not allow them to meet all of their needs (McGuire and Woodsong 1990). To partake of the consumer society they had to engage in subsistence production on their 50 x 150 foot city lots.

When Johnson built his new industrial villages he also provided for a cemetery, which would recreate for eternity Johnson's industrial community. In the center was an area reserved for the Johnson family and the resting place of George F. Johnson himself (Figure 13.11). Johnson's welfare programs included provisions to help workers purchase plots in this cemetery, and markers, so that Johnson lies resting today surrounded by the graves of his workers (Figure 13.12) – the beneficially integrated community preserved for eternity.

The cultural landscape that George F. Johnson created entered into a dialogue with that left by Jonas Kilmer and the other capitalists of his time, a dialogue which validated the new ideology. Even though Johnson located his industrial democracy outside of Binghamton, in part to obtain a *tabula rasa* upon which he could leave his mark, Binghamton remained close at hand and in sharp contrast to his industrial villages.

One of the major messages of industrial democracy to the working class was that the socialist revolution was not needed because industrial democracy had already wrought a revolution in the United States. The company history said of George Johnson: 'Karl Marx urged labor to take capital by the throat and seize its rights; George F. Johnson has taken labor by the hand and led the way to their mutual welfare' (Inglis 1935: 288). No stronger validation existed in Broome County for this statement than the contrast between the tenements of the east side and the EJ workers' bungalows, or between the castle of Jonas Kilmer and the Colonial Revival homes of the Johnsons. But what this contrast and apparent change masked was the lack of any real change in the capitalist nature of relations in the factory. The material demands of the late nineteenth-century labor movement had been met to the advantage of capital, but labor had lost far more than it had gained. Mass production meant a dehumanization of labor, as workers became little more than extensions of their machines. Workers lost control of their actions on the shop floor, and their actions off the shop floor were increasingly manipulated by the welfare policies of their bosses or by advertising which sought to redefine their most basic perceptions of self (Ewen 1976; Edsforth 1987).

The Endicott-Johnson company's policies succeeded in forestalling strikes and union activity until the late 1940s; workers did, however, resist authoritarian

Figure 13.11 *The grave of George F. Johnson, Endwell, New York (photograph by R. H. McGuire)*

Figure 13.12 *Endicott-Johnson workers' graves, Endicott, New York (photograph by R. H. McGuire)*

supervisors and changes in work discipline. When grievances arose the multi-ethnic shop floors were quite capable of shutting down the floor and demanding to talk to one of the Johnsons. The workers used EJ's welfare capitalist philosophy to negotiate with the company, turning the company ideology back on itself so that the company had to either give in or openly deny the ideology (Zahavi 1983). For example, in the depth of the depression the company laid off workers in the tannery. The president and officers of an Italian fraternal and beneficial organization, the Sons of Italy, went to George Johnson. They said: 'Padron, when we came here you promised us a square deal. If we worked well for the company the company would take care of us. The men you laid off have families and you must keep your part of the deal to care for them.' These Italian workers had incorporated the company philosophy into their own ethnic framework and used the reciprocal implications of the philosophy to resist a company action. The men in question were called back to work, but a general work slowdown was imposed in the tannery.

However, the EJ workers' power to use the company's ideology to resist and negotiate their wants with the company did not give them the power to alter the company's position in a world economy. During the depression the company started to slowly dismantle the welfare programs of its founder. A multinational corporation bought the company in the 1940s; in the 1950s the company started losing production to the Orient and by the end of the 1960s EJ had shrunk to only a handful of manufacturing plants in the county.

14

MORTUARY PRACTICES, SOCIETY AND IDEOLOGY*
An Ethnoarchaeological Study

MICHAEL PARKER PEARSON

Introduction

In the last ten years there have been many developments in the reconstruction of past social systems from the material remains of mortuary rituals. There have been several attempts to provide linking principles between the material culture associated with mortuary practices and the form of social organisation (Saxe 1970; Binford 1972b; Brown 1971; Shennan 1975; Goldstein 1976; Tainter 1977; Peebles and Kus 1977). Although there is no 'cookbook' on the derivation of social information from burial remains, certain major assumptions are generally shared by workers in burial studies. Firstly, the deceased is given a set of representations of his or her various social identities or roles when alive so that their status or social position may be given material form after death (e.g. grave goods, monuments, place of burial etc.). Secondly, the material expressions of these roles may be compared between individuals. Thirdly, the resulting patterns of role differentiation may be ranked hierarchically as divisions existing within the society under study. Consequently, the social organisation of any society may be reconstructed and that society can be placed within a larger evolutionary framework according to its degree of organisational complexity. This procedure is very clearly illustrated by Saxe (1970) who uses role theory, componential theory, systems theory, information theory, and evolutionary theory to devise a set of hypotheses linking social complexity with mortuary practices. Studies of available ethnographic information on differentiation between individuals in death do seem to confirm the relationship between dimensions of disposal and the form of social organisation (Saxe 1970; Binford 1972b; Goldstein 1976; Tainter 1978). The basic principles originally outlined by Saxe have been modified by later workers; Goldstein (1976) has considered the value of a spatial framework in the interpretation of mortuary differentiation; Tainter (1978) develops Saxe's quantitative measure of social complexity and introduces the notion of energy expenditure on deceased individuals for determining rank gradings; in their study of the archaeological correlates of

---

*First published in I. Hodder (ed.) (1982), *Symbolic and Structural Archaeology*, Cambridge: Cambridge University Press, pp. 99–113.

'chiefdom' societies, Peebles and Kus (1977) integrate the burial evidence with other archaeological forms (settlement hierarchy and placing, craft specialisation and society-wide mobilisation); O'Shea's study of nineteenth-century Plains Indians and Early Bronze Age communities in Hungary (1979) emphasises the importance of the specific cultural context and suggests that mortuary studies are most sensitive in the analysis of ranked societies (between egalitarian and advanced chiefdom/state societies).

The reconstruction of social organisation through the identification of roles (whether in burial, craft specialisation, settlement hierarchies etc.) can be challenged by the theoretical stance that social systems are not constituted of roles but by recurrent social practices.

The theoretical position adopted here comes from a tradition of social theory which considers power as central to the study of social systems. Social relations between humans take the form of relations of dominance and influence between groups of individuals who share mutual interests. These regularised relations of interdependence between individuals or groups constitute social practices. Practice is made up of individual actions which reflexively affect and are affected by explicit or implicit rules of conduct or structuring principles (which themselves are constantly being modified and changed).

These structuring principles, within which systems of domination are formulated, are legitimated by an ideology which serves the interests of the dominant group. Ideology hides the contradictions between structuring principles by giving the world of appearances an independence and an autonomy which it does not have. Larrain puts this simplistically but clearly when he states that 'In capitalist societies class differences are negated, and a world of freedom and equality re-constructed in consciousness; in pre-capitalist societies, class differences are rather justified in hierarchical conceptions of the world. In both, ideology negates contradictions and legitimates structures of domination' (1979: 48).

Ideology is a term which has proved remarkably hard to define. It can be seen as a system of beliefs through which the perceived world of appearances is interpreted as a concrete and objectified reality. It is the way in which humans relate to the conditions of their existence; their 'lived' relation to the world as opposed to their actual relation to the world (Althusser 1977a: 252). As Hirst has pointed out, ideology is not false consciousness or a representation of reality but people's 'imaginary', lived relation to the conditions of their existence (1976: 11). In perceiving and explaining their surroundings, humans develop concepts which articulate with systems of signification (both verbal and non-verbal). Ideology is a form of signification, a 'pure ideographic system' where the signifier becomes the very presence of the signified concept (Barthes 1973: 27–8). That signification is carried out through a signifier (word, object etc.) connotating a signified concept.

The notion that material culture (defined here as man's transformed environment – portable artefacts, food, fields, houses, monuments, quarries etc.) is a part of human communication and signification is by no means new in archaeology – Childe stated that artefacts should be treated 'always and exclusively as concrete expressions and embodiments of human thoughts and ideas' (1956b: 1). Material culture can thus be seen as a form of non-verbal communication through the representation of ideas (Leach 1977: 167). It is externalisation of concepts through material expression, a supposedly autonomous force which acts reflexively on humans as they produce it and is thereby instituted as a form of ideological control. It must be stressed that material culture is not a somehow 'objective' record of what is actually done as opposed to what is thought or believed (as in literary evidence or the testimony of the native subject); it does embody concepts but in a tacit and non-discursive way, unlike writing or speech. Archaeologists can study incomplete systems of material culture communication (which itself is fragmentary since it is all that is left of a fuller system of verbal and non-verbal communication) since the relationships and associations embodied by material culture can be reconstructed into a system of relationships between signifiers (see Sperber 1979: 28).

It is generally accepted that the context of death is one of ritual action and communication as opposed to everyday practical communication. Mortuary remains have to be interpreted as ritual communication if we assume the existence of ritual in all societies of Homo Sapiens (and probably even before). The definition and explanation of ritual have long concerned anthropologists; it can be very simply defined as stylised, repetitive patterns of behaviour (Keesing 1976: 566) in which a society's fundamental social values are expressed (Huntingdon and Metcalf 1979: 5). There is no clear boundary between ritual activity and other types of action, although ritual does have a peculiar fixity since it is clearly and explicitly rule-bound (Lewis 1980: 7); it is not necessarily 'irrational' and non-technical behaviour (Lewis 1980: 13–16) and may constitute the communicative aspects of any action. Ritual can be seen thus as a kind of performance in the same way as a play where there is a prescribed routine or expression (Lewis 1980: 10–11 and 33). Recent views have challenged the traditional explanation of ritual as the communication of social values which are expressed as unambiguous and believable statements. Bloch sees the formalisation of ritual action as resulting in a rate of change slower than other social actions with a consequent loss of propositional meaning and an increase in ambiguity (Bloch 1974); for Lewis, what is clear about ritual is how to do it but its meaning may be clear, complicated; ambiguous, or forgotten in different societies – it may mystify or clarify depending on cultural context (Lewis 1980: 8, 10–11, 19 and 31). Whether or not the meaning of the performance is clear to the participants, mortuary ritual is a time when roles are clearly portrayed (Goody 1962: 29; Bloch 1977: 286): 'rites of passage are the rare occasions when it is possible to hear people giving lists of rights and duties, and even quite literally to see roles being put on individuals as is the case of 'ceremonial clothing or bodily mutilation' (Bloch 1977: 286). In ritual communication time is static and the past is constituted in the present:

> The presence of the past in the present is therefore one of the components of that other system of cognition which is characteristic of ritual communication, another world which unlike that manifested in the cognitive system of everyday communication does not directly link up with empirical experiences. It is therefore a world peopled by invisible entities. On the one hand roles and corporate groups . . . and on the other gods and ancestors, both types of manifestations fusing into each other . . .
>
> (Bloch 1977: 287)

The roles that are portrayed in death ritual are expressions of status which must be seen as relating to, rather than 'reflecting', social position. Roles and corporate groups are, to Bloch, 'invisible halos' which must be appreciated within their specific context of death ritual rather than the wider framework of social hierarchy.

In any rite of passage the subject passes through a 'liminal' stage (Turner 1969) between two socially ascribed roles; in any analysis of status among the dead, the role of those individuals as members of the dead, as apart from the living, must be considered. Goody found that the Lodagaa dressed the corpse in the apparel of a chief or rich merchant, regardless of the person's social position in life (1962: 71). Among the Merina of Malagasy individuals are automatically classed as ancestors once dead. Status is expressed through membership of one of three 'castes' (nobles, commoners and slaves) and is manifested in the size and location of family tombs. However, the significance of this form of ranking is severely diminished in social life (slavery was abolished in 1896, while the power of the nobles is not political but exercised through minor ritual privileges; Bloch 1971: 69–70) and it has been replaced by a capitalist-influenced economic and political system. The old traditional roles are maintained in death as part of a reaffirmation of the past although the structure of power has shifted and new roles are economically important. Thus in death ritual it is not necessarily the case that the actual relations of power are displayed. It does not follow that those social identities which embody the greatest degree of authority will always be expressed (*contra* Saxe 1970: 6); however, it is important to understand why certain roles are expressed in death as well as in other spheres of social life (e.g. house form, dress, display of material possessions etc.), and also to understand the extent to which they are used as social advertisements between competing social groups.

The use of the past to orientate the present has long been recognised in social theory: 'men make their own history, but they do not make it just as they please; they do not make it under circumstances chosen by themselves, but under circumstances directly encountered, given and transmitted from the past' (Marx 1970: 96). The past, especially through ritual communication (including the context of death), is often used to 'naturalise' and legitimate hierarchies of power and inequality which would otherwise be unstable. The dead are often an important part of the past in the present especially in the form of ancestors, deities and other supernatural beings. The construction of visible monuments, commemorating them collectively or individually, is one means of giving them material expression and recognition in the affairs of humans. The dead are consequently susceptible to manipulation by certain groups to maintain or enhance their influence over others. This can be done by idealising certain aspects of the past through the dead. Within this framework mortuary ritual, along with other aspects of tradition, ritual and custom, must be accommodated in theories of social and cultural change. The following case study of contemporary British mortuary practices and their development since the Victorian period attempts to place the treatment of the dead in such a framework.

The case study

This two-part study of British mortuary practices was based on data for Cambridge 1977, and involved 270 deceased individuals out of 3000 in that year in Cambridge and the surrounding area (15 km radius). Temporal variation in patterning could thus be controlled and connections between status among the living and status after death could be investigated. In the second part of the study these results were placed within a framework of social change over the last 150 years. Without the historical perspective the correlation could not be understood as relationships which had developed through time between mortuary practices, material culture and social trends.

A random stratified sampling strategy was used with stratification designated by the undertaker hired. In this way a cross-section of different funeral establishments, different disposal areas and the complete social spectrum in Cambridge could be analysed. The records of four funeral establishments were used to provide information on individuals relating to occupation, religion, rateable value of property, age, sex, notification of the death in the mass media, number of cars hired for the funeral, type of coffin and fittings, style of dress and treatment of the corpse, whether inhumed or cremated, place of inhumation or disposal of the ashes, and finally the construction, if any, of a monument. Unfortunately, the data on wreaths and flowers were incomplete and could not be included in the analysis.

Although a scale of income groupings has been devised for classifying professions within Britain (see Goldthorpe and Hope 1974), this could not be applied since the records of the profession of the deceased only permitted a two-fold division between males into blue-collar and white-collar workers. The funeral directors' information was given in the strictest confidence and I was expressly asked not to make enquiries with the bereaved families; consequently any more complete information on job and family background was unobtainable. There are a number of ways in which status may be expressed: through ownership of private wealth, type of occupation, family background and accent, and through material expression such as type and number of cars, size and location and internal decoration of houses and style of dress. In other words status should be regarded not as an innate quality inherited or achieved by individuals but as a collection of different forms of social expression and advertisement between groups as well as between individuals. For example, there need not be any correlation between class accent and ownership of private wealth yet both are important expressions of status. The most reliable measure of status which could be used in this study was another form of material expression – rateable value of private residential property. This is a measure of house size, type of neighbourhood and range of internal amenities. There were certain problems in relating this measure to 'status' – influential families might shun the ostentation of living in a large residence, elderly people might move into smaller, more manageable properties than those they had been living in, certain individuals might own several residences, and type of property owned might be different for different age groups.

The information gained from funeral directors, the council rates office and from graveyards and cemeteries was encoded as twenty-one variables which were divided into three groups; social position of the deceased, the form and expense of the funeral and the form and expense of the memorialisation of the deceased. These variables were cross-tabulated using the SPSS statistical package (Nie et al. 1975).

However, there were very few correlations between the twenty-one variables. In correlating property value with funeral cost, memorial cost and total cost, r^2 equalled 0.002, 0.018 and 0.005 – there was no correlation at all, with rateable value accounting for little or none of the variance (Figure 14.1). Although the use of

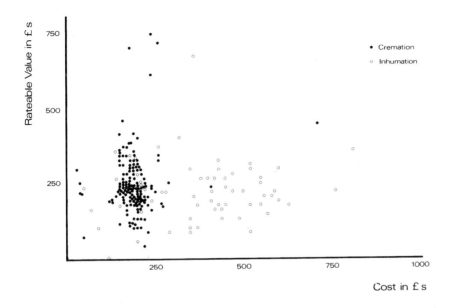

Figure 14.1 The cost of funerals in Cambridge in 1977 as compared with the rateable value of residential property inhabited by the deceased

only one measure of status cannot be relied upon too heavily, this evidence ties in with statements made by funeral directors and other investigators regarding the simplicity and lack of ostentation involved in the purchasing of a 'funeral package'. Undertakers do not always agree on which classes of clients spend most on a funeral – one Cambridge funeral director denied any class differentiation (supporting the results above) and other undertakers have stated that members of the lower class often spend most on a funeral (Farthing 1977; Toynbee 1980: 8). Since it was considered that Cambridge might not be a representative sample, interviews were carried out with members of a London undertaker's firm who also stated that expenditure at funerals and on monuments did not correspond with social position.

There were, however, certain indications of class differentiation. Different funeral establishments catered for different classes of people even though fees were very similar – this was confirmed by the location of these establishments within certain areas of the town. One dealt with clients from the university and also with people from the more select areas of town. Two dealt mainly with middle and middle/upper class housing areas and two with the lower and lower/middle class housing areas on the east side of Cambridge (see Figure 14.2). Although the same basic materials were used by all funeral services (coffins, coffin furniture, hearses) and monumental masons (gravestones), there were certain differences in their use. One of the establishments in a lower class area apparently maintained the distinction of more 'delicate' O-ring coffin handles for women and bar handles for men. In 70 per cent of the cases handled by establishments associated with the upper classes cremations took place, while these only accounted for 50 per cent of cases handled by one of the firms employed by lower classes (in 1977 the national average of deceased

251

Figure 14.2
*Class distinctions
in the choice of
undertaker by
households in
Cambridge.*

● *Residence using
services of
middle/upper class
undertaker.*

▦ *Residence using
services of middle class
undertaker.*

✿ *Residence using
services of lower/middle
class undertaker (a).*

○ *Residence using
services of lower/middle
class undertaker (b).*

Figure 14.3 The Roman Catholic part of the Cambridge City cemetery

cremated was 62 per cent). This would suggest at least some degree of class distinction in choosing between cremation and inhumation, although that relationship has become more complex and blurred. Financial outlay probably had little influence on this decision since at the time cremation was no cheaper. However, it would be more likely with inhumation to place a monument over the final resting place of the deceased and therefore to incur extra expense.

Religious affiliation did not directly match any class groupings although certain ethnic and religious minorities tended to go to certain undertakers and live in the less affluent areas of town (according to undertaker's remarks). Whereas all Roman Catholics have RIP inscribed in their nameplates and a crucifix attached to the lid, those Catholics that were members of the Polish, Italian and Irish communities in Cambridge displayed certain idiosyncratic characteristics; cremation was rare and burial monuments often ornate and expensive. The stone type selected was mainly polished black or grey granite (two of the most expensive types) and decorative motifs were either religious 'pictures' cut into the stone or small marble angel statuettes (under 60 cm in height). Italians and Poles might also mount a small photograph of the deceased on the stone. Catholics, Jews and Moslems were buried in certain areas of the city cemetery which were separated from the main area (Figure 14.3). Moslems are also buried on a different orientation (northeast–southwest), diagonal to the closely packed, well-ordered rows of graves. Burials of members of nonconformist churches are not spatially differentiated within the city cemetery although certain graveyards separated from their churches in the rural centres around Cambridge were specifically for nonconformists (e.g. Melbourne URC burial ground, Cottenham Dissenters' burial ground; see Figure 14.4).

Within the city cemetery there were two groups of monuments which were not physically bounded from the other graves but were easily distinguishable by the style

Figure 14.4 The Nonconformist cemetery at Cottenham near Cambridge

Figure 14.5 *A gypsy monument in the Cambridge City cemetery*

Figure 14.6 *The showmen's monuments in the Cambridge City cemetery*

of monument. These were the gypsies and showmen (the latter are fairground owners and workers, often with kinship links to gypsies). They are generally recognised as occupying the lower levels of the British class system despite their often considerable accumulation of money stored as ready cash or converted into moveable valuables such as Rolls Royces, expensive china, large caravans and brasses (see Okely 1979). Both groups use brick-lined graves and vaults for interment (only very rarely are they cremated although this will increase now that vaults may no longer be built). One showman's vault was decorated with bath tiles. Showmen and their families favoured the distinctive and expensive polished red granite monuments standing up to two metres high in cross or block form (Figure 14.6). The gypsies commemorate their dead with large white marble angels which also stand to two metres or more (Figure 14.5). These groups hold the most expensive funerals in Cambridge with funeral director's fees and monument costs sometimes amounting to over £3000 (expenditure above £500 by anyone in Cambridge is rare). Costs of flowers, food and drink may also be more substantial than other Cambridge funerals. They are some of the few groups in our society where death is regarded as an acceptable area for overt, competitive display between families.

Class differences are also reflected to a certain extent in variation between burial areas. St Giles' cemetery is strongly connected with members of the university while the city cemetery holds the majority of the deceased town dwellers. The surrounding village churchyards and their extensions now contain the remains of many commuters and retired people who have moved into the countryside. This movement by wealthier elements of the urban population has resulted in major changes in the structure of village communities; in the nearby village of Foxton only 25 per cent of the community are still residents from birth (Parker 1975: 234). The class differences are also apparent in the undertakers' use of different churchyards and cemeteries. The two firms associated with the lower classes carried out thirty-four of the fifty-eight inhumations in the city cemetery as opposed to nine out of thirty-eight inhumations by the upper class establishment.

The majority of the Cambridge population are cremated (64 per cent in the 1977 sample, just higher than the national average of 62 per cent for that year). In 1979 at the Cambridge Crematorium, out of 2943 cremations, 2255 were scattered in the grounds, thirty were interred at the crematorium, four were placed on shelves in the Columbrarium, one was placed in a temporary deposit and 655 were taken away for burial or scattering elsewhere. By 1969 one tenth of Catholics in Britain were receiving cremation rites (Ucko 1969: 274), six years after the ban was lifted by the Pope in July 1963. The decision to cremate or inhume the deceased is not as arbitrary as has been suggested elsewhere (Clarke 1975: 51–2). The trend in cremation since the Second World War has been one of extremely even growth (see Figure 14.7) with a rate of increase of 1–2 per cent p.a. Furthermore the cremation movement has spread to a large extent as a class-associated phenomenon through the emulation of upper class preferences in the twentieth century.

There are very few studies of modern western death rituals. Gorer's study of death, grief and mourning (1965) is useful for his attention to religious observance as well as to the treatment of the dead. His questionnaire survey covered the whole of Britain with a sample of 359 cases and was aimed at understanding how people coped in

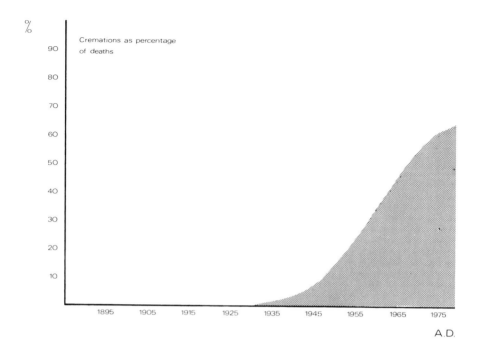

Figure 14.7 *The gradual increase in cremations in the twentieth century*

mourning their dead rather than how status and other factors might account for variability in funeral ritual. One study was carried out thirty years ago in America and was specifically concerned with the manifestation of status in funerals (Kephart 1950). Although he had little quantitative data relating to status during life, Kephart noted that in Philadelphia there were class differentials in the relative cost of funerals, frequency of cremation, elapsed time between death and burial, viewing the body, flower arrangements, public expression of grief, mourning customs and placing within the cemeteries (Kephart 1950: 639–43). Despite funeral cost being status-related, he suggested that a reversal was taking place, with display in death becoming more and more a dwindling upper class phenomenon (1950: 636). This, and the frequency of cremation and placing within cemeteries, seems to match the Cambridge data for 1977, but cost of funerals in Britain is no longer a clear indication of social position.

Trends in mortuary ritual in the nineteenth and twentieth centuries

Changing material culture forms, and relationships between these forms, are here divided into four categories; the siting of burial areas, the placing and marking of burials within these areas, cremation and subsequent treatment of the ashes, and the material culture associated with the funeral and treatment of the corpse. This is an essentially 'archaeological' description which will be followed by a 'social' explanation of these patterns as relations between living and dead and social relations between the living.

The growing industrial and urban centres of the eighteenth and nineteenth centuries used churchyards of parishes subsumed under urban growth for the burial of the majority of the population. These churchyards had been grossly over-crowded since the seventeenth century (Curl 1972: 33). By the nineteenth century, the crowding and filth of living conditions in industrial towns and cities resulted in cholera outbreaks and a high mortality rate (Morley 1971: 7–10 and 34–40). The construction of larger burial grounds in areas of open ground on the outskirts of cities from the 1820s until the early twentieth century was part of a massive onslaught against the insanitary conditions which existed (Curl 1972: 22, 131 and 139–40; Morley 1971: 48; see Chadwick 1843; General Board of Health, 1850). These cemeteries were planned as large parks for the public to use as leisure areas in which the achievements of the dead were glorified and consequently where the moral education of all classes could be improved (Morley 1971: 48; Rawnsley and Reynolds 1977: 217). Whereas members of the upper classes, had been buried on their estates (Curl 1972: 359) or within churches, the Public Health Act of 1848 disallowed intra-mural interment and consequently traditional members of the gentry and aristocracy, as well as new members of the upper classes, shared the new burial areas with the rest of the population. The dead were no longer buried at the centre of society but removed from their immediate association with the church to a location separate from the focus of the community. In the new burial grounds space was allocated according to accessibility and view (Rawnsley and Reynolds 1977: 220). Consequently spatial patterning within the cemetery was a visual representation of the emerging hierarchy. This was further enhanced by the types of memorials constructed over the graves.

The most magnificent monuments were mausolea – actual houses of the dead. There was a myriad of changing fashions in smaller monumental forms: urns on pedestals, broken columns, obelisks, crosses, sarcophagi and caskets, and the more common and more traditionally English horizontal or vertical slabs. Interestingly, archaeology was a major factor in the design of funerary architecture (Curl 1972: 23) with Classical, Ancient Egyptian and Gothic styles copied for all sizes of monument. This re-interpretation in miniature of the huge monuments of man's past can be seen as an association with the dignity and splendour of past civilisations and an implicit legitimation of the current social order in terms of those values.

There appear to be few regional variations in funerary monuments today although styles have changed in several major ways. The amount of individual variation has always been large but reducible to several common themes. The major trend has been one of the simplification and reduction in size – monuments were replaced by headstones with stone kerbs delineating the grave plot (mainly between the 1910s and 1960s) and recently monumentalisation has become restricted (in both cemeteries and churchyards) to small headstones without kerbs. This latest phenomenon, the lawn cemetery, was introduced in Cambridge in 1957 and allows easier maintenance of the cemeteries since bereaved families can no longer be relied upon to maintain their individual plots. Since the First World War styles have been simple, plain and 'modern', without any of the fancifulness of Victorian monuments. There have been a number of associated changes in gravestone fashions. Traditional English building stone has been replaced by foreign white marble and red, black and grey granites. In the last twenty years the cheaper Portland Stone and white marble have become less popular than the more expensive granites, although the association of taste with simplicity helps to explain the new trend in plain slate or sandstone headstones. It is extremely rare to find the profession of the deceased mentioned on gravestones in the last fifty years but this was quite a common occurrence among the upper and middle classes of Victorian society. Today the epitaph symbolises the role of the nuclear family member although designs on the stone can represent profession, hobby, manner of death or religious affiliation. In the 1977 study there were six religious scenes and eighteen flower designs out of seventy-nine headstones – the former were generally associated with Catholics and the latter with Anglicans. No other design symbolism was apparent on any of the other stones.

The construction of bricked graves and vaults was banned by the Cambridge City Council in 1978. The wealthier company owners abandoned their family vaults after the Second World War and have since opted for cremation (Wilson, pers. comm.). The showmen and gypsies were among the last to keep up the use of vaults or bricked graves. Before 1974 the burial plots in Cambridge could be sold in perpetuity but now the Council plans the recycling of cemetery land within the next hundred years with 99 per cent of the population being cremated by the year 2000, thus making cemeteries redundant. Apart from the religious and ethnic divisions apparent in the cemetery, there is a distinction between privately owned and Council owned graveplots. The latter may not have any markers on the grave and are reused every fifteen years. They were traditionally for the poorest section of the community after the cemetery was opened in 1902 but that distinction has since become blurred. The stigma of a pauper's grave has largely vanished and been replaced by the desire for simplicity and lack of ostentation in death among all classes, although welfare burials are still arranged and financed by the Council for those too poor to pay. The giving of bodies to anatomy schools was legalised in 1832 (Polson and Marshall 1972: 613) and has become a growing trend in the last 30 to 40 years. In the 1950s and 1960s this was connected with members of the upper and middle/upper classes but has since spread to all classes (Hindley, pers. comm.). Until the 1970s most anatomy donations, after use, were buried in the 'poorer' area of the cemetery but now most are cremated at no expense to the bereaved. The marking-off of the 'paupers' area' is similar to a tradition found in churchyards of the seventeenth and eighteenth centuries where the south side was generally preferred for burial and the north side reserved for the bodies of murderers, suicides and unbaptised children (Johnson 1912: 335 and 350–1). Today there are no distinctions in death for the mentally ill, criminals, suicides or still-borns, despite the Victorian tradition of burial in the prison or asylum, or outside the burial ground or even in certain parts of the churchyard (where they still remained 'out of sanctuary'; Johnson 1912: 359).

Cemeteries have outlived their Victorian function as leisure amenities for the display of the achievements of the dead and have become storage areas for the disposal of dead bodies; graves are tightly packed in well regimented ranks and oriented east–west or north–south to make maximum use of space. This is summed up by Polson and Marshall writing on laws relating to the disposal of the dead in Britain:

> In principle, ground consecrated for burial or unconsecrated ground, set apart for burial, may not be used for any other purpose. Considerable modification of this principle has become inevitable during the present century, owing to the growing demands of an increasing population for living space. Land in cities

and large towns is at a high premium. The community cannot afford to ignore the potential uses to which disused burial grounds can be applied and the needs of the living have priority over consideration for the dead.

(1972: 247)

The development of cremation was in direct opposition to the Christian doctrine of the resurrection of the body. The campaign for cremation was started in Britain in the early 1870s primarily to introduce a more sanitary precaution against disease and also to make funerals cheaper, keep the ashes safe from vandalism, have the ceremony completely inside and to prevent premature burial (Anon, Cremation Society Pamphlet 1975: 1). Early cremations were placed in caskets and buried under small memorial tablets within the crematorium grounds. In the 1920s and 1930s ashes were stored in the Columbrarium and marked by small plaques. After the Second World War the numbers of cremations greatly increased and ashes were strewn in the crematorium's Garden of Remembrance to save space. At first, trees, shrubs, birdbaths and sundials were set up as memorials to the deceased individual. These were followed by small bronze plates but now the only feasible means of memorialisation is considered to be commemoration of the name in the Book of Remembrance kept in each crematorium (Polson and Marshall 1972: 192–4). In 1972 65 per cent of cremations were strewn in the Gardens of Remembrance and 12 per cent were taken away for burial or strewing in a churchyard or cemetery, scattering at sea or in the country. Interestingly, in Cambridge in 1977 many more ashes were scattered or interred in local churchyards rather than in the city cemetery. There are over 200 crematoria in Britain, centralised disposal areas turning over 400,000 corpses each year, pulverising and then scattering the ashes or collecting them in plastic containers. Crematoria have been criticised for their poor design (Curl 1972: 186); many look more like suburban houses with outsize chimneys rather than places of religious ritual (Figure 14.8). The emphasis is very much on disposal rather than on ceremonies of remembrance and respect to the dead. The whole disposal sequence associated with modern crematoria allows for the saving of space for the

Figure 14.8 A crematorium in Yorkshire. Note the plain and 'functional' style of the architecture

living, with the remains of the dead closely concentrated in an area of 1–8 hectares well away from residential areas and with a minimum of memorialisation for the individual or even collective dead.

The pomp and ceremony of the Victorian funeral has recently attracted great interest from historians (e.g. Curl 1972; Morley 1971). Much greater a percentage of personal income was spent on funerals then than today. In 1843 the average cost of a funeral was £15, a considerable sum for many people, with the most lavish costing £1500 and the cheapest £5 (Morley 1971: 22). The funeral was a conspicuous display of wealth consumption, and expenditure was closely graded according to one's social position (Morley 1971: 22 and 112–13). Families competed with each other so as not to be outdone in respectability (directly equated with wealth and with salvation; Morley 1971: 11). This social competition was manifested by all classes and even the poor would spend comparatively large sums of money on a funeral rather than suffer the shame and loss of dignity connoted by a pauper's burial (Lerner 1975: 99–100; see Bosanquet 1898). The specialist profession of undertaker (along with associated trades of monumental masons, cabinet maker and draper) developed in the early nineteenth century both making possible and encouraging such lavish expense. Formal mourning costume (crepe and black jewellery) and all the paraphernalia of death (black ostrich feathers, large ornate horse-driven hearses, 'mutes' or attendants accompanying the procession, a solid wood coffin, expensive handles and plates, mourning cards) were part of the huge quantity of material culture produced specifically to honour and remember the dead. In the twentieth century, despite the undertakers and stonemasons having a strong economic interest in maintaining the role of the funeral, there has been a gradual but marked decline in the ceremony of death ritual. Even as early as the 1840s and 1850s funerals were made more simple (Morley 1971: 27–31) and today only royalty and major national heroes and some ethnic minorities receive expensive ceremonies in death. The minorities are the only groups that can still be said to actively compete between themselves in death ritual. Although undertakers have received some criticism for their commercial and exploitative attitude (Mitford 1963: 186–7), it must be remembered that the change in public attitudes towards the celebration of death has made funerals appear as unnecessary expense when previously much more was expected to be spent on them. No longer is the context of death a platform for overt self-advertisement between family groups.

The First World War was a watershed between Victorian and 'modern' funerals (Lerner 1975: 91). The massive scale of death, the government decision not to bring bodies home and the large number of unidentified corpses were major factors in bringing this about. Mourning clothes and elaborate processions became more and more unfashionable. Monuments became smaller and more regimented and more simple in decoration, and the coffin and coffin fittings were increasingly of much poorer quality. Although coffins are a major part of the undertaker's bill (on average £100 out of £200) they are mostly chipboard with oak or elm veneer. Traditional styles of handles and plates are retained but these are of thin brass, chrome plastic or plastic, a far cry from the ornate gold, silver and brass decoration of Victorian coffins (Curl 1972: 2). Coffins were considered luxury items not available to the poorer classes until the seventeenth century (Cunnington and Lucas 1972: 156–7). By the Victorian period they were universal objects for display as well as containers for preserving their contents as long as possible (Curl 1972: 29). Since then they have become temporary receptacles for corpses before final removal from society. One funeral director commented on this change:

> Strangely the public accept the veneered coffins quite happily, the desire for a simple and inexpensive funeral overcoming any traditional thought of a solid oak or elm coffin. It is a personal observation that where traditional thoughts as to the coffin occur, these are frequently found in the less well-off section of the community who will spend more on a funeral than the affluent.

There have been a number of changes in the treatment of the body. Embalming has become more and more common as a temporary means of arresting decay – about 75 per cent of corpses are embalmed in London (W. G. Garstin & Sons, pers. comm.) although under 30 per cent in Cambridge receive this treatment (embalming is a process where a formalin-based red liquid is substituted for the blood and a green solution is pumped into the stomach). The corpse's shroud is very similar to a nightdress – the same basic form since the nineteenth century. Among European immigrants (Poles, Greeks, Ukrainians, Italians), gypsies and showmen there is a tradition for burial in best clothes although this is less strong than it used to be. Until just after the Second World War, toys were sometimes placed in children's coffins and females were dressed in their best clothes with jewellery in northern England (Hindley, pers. comm.). In the rural parts of the British Isles in the nineteenth century, beer mugs, jugs, bottles, candles and coins might be placed in the grave (Johnson 1912: 294–5) but this tradition seems to have long died out.

In conclusion, the funeral can be seen as changing from its role as a celebratory rite of passage into more of a consumer package deal where low expense is a major factor in deciding the nature of the funeral. This is clearly highlighted in the magazine *Which?* for February 1961, pages 43 to 45, which gives advice on funerals purely as commercial products where cheapness is a major concern.

Towards an explanation of British mortuary practices

It has been suggested that two interconnected relationships have to be investigated in order to explain the symbolism of mortuary ritual. The first is the categorisation or 'placing' of the dead by the living. The second is the way in which the dead may be used as one of many modes of social advertisement between competing groups. Mortuary practices should be regarded not as a microcosm of social organisation but as the material expression and objectivation of idealised relationships formulated about the dead by different individuals or groups within society.

All archaeological evidence is made up of relationships or associations within different symbolic systems. These associations, expressed in material form, are social constructions of category classification. In any society symbolic links are expressed as specific associations between material forms. The treatment of the dead can be studied in terms of these relationships. Some of these can be outlined as follows: the spatial and topographical positioning of the dead in relation to the living (what kinds of boundaries exist to separate the places of the living and the dead – not just rivers, fences etc. but also spatial distancing, e.g. burial under the settlement, burial on a hill overlooking the settlement); the relation between the physical abodes of the living and the dead (the place of the dead in the form of a bed, a house, a settlement, a rubbish pit; how much energy is invested in the places of the dead as opposed to those of the living); differentiation among the dead (what groups and roles are expressed and idealised in death ritual and why (e.g. why might all dead have the status of chiefs?); what artefacts are expressly associated only with the dead, what artefacts from the living are 'hidden' with the dead (e.g. why might weapons be buried but tools inherited?); the relation of disposal contexts to other forms of death-related expression (e.g. ancestor shrines, cenotaphs). All of these factors will affect the way in which death is seen as the context for social advertisement; which social groups compete against each other (families, sodalities, neighbourhoods etc.) and in what ways is that competition acceptable (how does it compare with other expressions of personal wealth or power such as house design, clothing and jewellery, ownership of possessions etc?)?

Some of these issues have been explored in the previous section but an explanatory framework is still needed to interpret the changes in the symbolism in mortuary ritual. Our changing relation to the dead can be explained in terms of the replacing of traditional agencies of social control, notably religion, by the new agencies of rationalism, science and medicine within the frameworks of modern capitalism. The reduction of ceremony and monumentalisation as well as the increase in cremation may be partly explained within this framework. Available studies of patterns of religious belief indicate an increase in secular ideologies of death; no assumptions need to be made about life after death (in 1965 50 per cent of Britons were likely not to believe in or to be uncertain about an afterlife; Gorer 1965: 33) and the corpse is seen more and more as an unwanted piece of matter which should be disposed of in as hygienic and efficient a way as possible. Many writers have commented on the effect of this attitude in causing psychological problems among the bereaved who are unable to cope effectively with the death of their loved ones without the aid of imposed ritual sanctions (Curl 1972; Hinton 1972; Kastenbaum and Aisenberg 1972; Parkes 1975; Gorer 1965; Schoenberg et al. 1975). The dead are no longer seen to exist in the material world of the living. Cremation in our society solves two supposedly uncontentious problems; the efficient and hygienic disposal of the dead and prevention of any wasting of space in the storage of those disposed remains. However, it is just as hygienic to inter a corpse in a cemetery as it is to burn it (see Curl 1972: 167). Also the notion of saving the land for the living presupposes a shortage of land yet there is plenty available for leisure activities. In 1951 a mere 0.13 per cent of the land surface was used for burial – hardly a massive use of space (Curl 1972: 162).

In the Victorian period public health and hygiene, sanitation and medical services became integral features of every day life and became incorporated with religion and scientific and technological progress as a means of power legitimation. There was a direct equation of class with hygiene, health, cleanness and neatness of residence (Morley 1971: 7–10); the dirtiest members of society were naturally the lowest. Victorian attitudes to hygiene and health have been well documented elsewhere (see Dubos 1965; Salt and Elliott 1975; Sigerist 1944, 1956). Interestingly, The approval of cremation came at a time when major advances were being made in drainage and water supply, refuse and sewage disposal and production of frozen and tinned foods (see Salt and Elliott 1975: 37–8, 42, 56–7 and 60). There have been numerous studies of the role of medicine as a form of social control (see Ehrenreich 1978; Illich

1975; Navarro 1976, 1978; Zola 1975). Death can be said to have been appropriated by the medical profession since hospitals and nursing homes are the main places of death, with doctors as important as undertakers and clergy. In their attempts to prolong life as long as possible, doctors are involved in a self-frustrating war against death. It has become a medical failure rather than a natural process. Death is invariably associated with old people who are increasingly removed from their family environments. Most deaths occur in hospitals or nursing homes (c. 60 per cent) and the likelihood of deaths of children or young people has become far more remote. What was in the Victorian period a natural process of transition is now the end of a living person whose recognition after death is more and more slight.

These changes have reduced the power of the dead as symbols manipulated by the living, and we are losing a language of death celebration (Curl 1972: 337). A further factor in this change is the general context of social advertisement in twentieth-century Britain. The Victorian conspicuous consumption and display of wealth was not limited to burial ritual but occurred in other rites of passage, dress, housing, diet and all forms of social interaction. The reason for such ostentation in death has been interpreted as the result of mass urban migrations and the development of a new mode of production with its re-ordered social structure. In this 'world of strangers' the demonstration of financial power was achieved through conspicuous consumption both at the funeral and in the monument construction (Rawnsley and Reynolds 1977: 220). During the twentieth century the expression of social position seems to have become less overt in all spheres. In our post-industrial technocratic society the upper classes define themselves less by property and money ownership and more by education and managerial control (Giddens 1972: 346; Tourraine 1974 : 41 and 206). The symbols of class allegiance are progressively less clear and less numerous (Tourraine 1974: 37) while the managerial classes shy away from conspicuous consumption, controlling by manipulation rather than imperiousness (Tourraine 1974: 49). In a society of supposed equality of opportunity there are large differences in inherited and earned personal wealth ownership. In 1960 12 per cent of British adults owned 96 per cent of the personal wealth of Britain (Revell 1966); the identification of the members of this elite is not an easy task, with symbols of class often being ambiguous and confusing. Various attempts have been made to recognise this elite; the monarchy, members of Parliament, directors of large firms, top civil service officials, the heads of the military, TUC council members, bishops and archbishops, directors and large shareholders in mass media, vice-chancellors of universities and judges have all been listed as belonging to this group (Giddens 1972: 361). With the exception of the monarchy and some MPs, these individuals do not make themselves socially conspicuous as public figures to the mass of society. Indeed it is only the monarchy and certain individuals of national acclaim who still receive a ceremonial funeral of major proportions. Instead of symbolising the hierarchical differentiation of British society, these state funerals are symbols of national identity to the people of Britain and to the rest of the world. The fact that state funerals are lavish and well-attended does suggest that the relationship between living and dead does not completely account for the decline in death ceremonialism but that changing attitudes of social display are also important.

A major class of memorials commemorating the dead are the war memorials – the Cenotaph in London and cenotaphs scattered all over Britain. They are similar in style and design to other kinds of twentieth-century funerary architecture and yet are not disposal contexts for corpses. They are foci of ceremonies held annually to commemorate the British dead of two world wars. The war dead are commemorated as 'warriors' who died fighting for their country and the ideals of freedom and equality which it enshrines. Nationalism as an ideological means of control is thus legitimated through remembrance of the war dead of Britain (as opposed to the dead of all countries involved in the World Wars). The fact that the soldier buried in Westminster Abbey is named the 'Unknown Warrior' further advances the cause of nationalism since he is related solely to his country, transcending all kinship, regional and class connections.

In summary, two main processes can be held to account for the major changes in mortuary practices in nineteenth- and twentieth-century Britain. The social context of death affects the way in which it is used as a platform for social advertisement – what is considered 'tasteful' is no longer directly related to expenditure of monument size since religious beliefs and medical and hygienic attitudes have changed the status of the dead as a part of our society. Also there is some evidence that social advertisement is no longer accomplished through such conspicuous wealth consumption as was the case in Victorian Britain. In this way class categories as represented and objectified through all forms of material culture may be less pronounced.

Conclusion

This study has been concerned with deriving theories of material culture associated with death ritual from a wider perspective of social theory and an ethnoarchaeological investigation of changing practices and their social correlates. It is hoped that the results can be used in studying societies where only the material culture exists or be re-examined in further ethnoarchaeological analysis.

A number of propositions can be advanced:

(1) The symbolism of ritual communication does not necessarily refer to the actual relations of power but to an idealised expression of those relations.

(2) Relations between living groups must be seen as relations of influence and inequality where deceased individuals may be manipulated for purposes of status aggrandisement between those groups. Ideology as manifested in mortuary practices may mystify or naturalise those relations of inequality between groups or classes through the use of the past to legitimise the present.

(3) The relationship between living and dead should be integrated in studies of mortuary practices; in particular the new role of the deceased individual and the context of death as a platform for social advertisement must be accounted for.

(4) Social advertisement in death ritual may be expressly overt where changing relations of domination result in status reordering and consolidation of new social positions.

Proposition (4) is similar to a rule developed by Childe which is worth quoting in full here:

> in a stable society the gravegoods tend to grow relatively and even absolutely fewer and poorer as time goes on. In other words, less and less of the deceased's real wealth, fewer and fewer of the goods that he or she had used, worn, or habitually consumed in life were deposited in the tomb or consumed on the pyre. The stability of a society may be upset by invasion or immigration on a scale that requires a radical reorganization or by contact between barbarian and civilized societies so that, for instance, trade introduces new sorts of wealth, new opportunities for acquiring wealth and new classes (traders) who do not fit in at once into the kinship organization of a tribe.
>
> (Childe 1945: 17)

Exceptionally wealthy tombs are cited as support for this argument since Childe notes that they occur at the transitional stage of early state formation in Early Dynastic; Egypt, Shang China, Mycenaean Greece, Late Hallstatt Europe and Saxon England.

In conclusion, the ideological dimension of mortuary practices must be considered as a major line of enquiry in studies of all human societies. For the contemporary British material more needs to be done on the relationships between capitalism, nationalism, secular beliefs and attitudes to medicine and hygiene as ideological principles manifested in the material culture associated with death. Secondly, material culture from other contexts (transport, residences, personal possessions, dress, food etc.) should be integrated in a broader study of the degree and direction of social advertisement. Mortuary ritual can no longer be treated as a field of archaeological enquiry which is based on intra-cemetery variability since the treatment of the dead must be evaluated within the wider social context as represented by all forms of material remains. In this way the archaeologist can investigate the social placing (or categorisation) of the dead as constituted through the material evidence of the archaeological record by developing general principles which relate material culture and human society.

ACKNOWLEDGEMENTS

This work could not have been undertaken without the kindness and help of the manager of the Cambridge crematorium, Mr Wilson, and the following members of the Cambridge funeral establishments, Messrs Fuller, Hindley, Sargent, Stebbings and Warner. The National Association of Funeral Directors and the Cremation Society of Great Britain also provided valuable information. I would like to thank those people in the departments of Archaeology, Anthropology and Social and Political Sciences at Cambridge University who showed interest in these matters. My particular thanks go to Dr John Pickles for his help with Victorian burial customs and to Dr Ian Hodder who was responsible for directing my interests in contemporary mortuary practices.

15

REDEFINING THE SOCIAL LINK*
From Baboons to Humans

SHIRLEY S. STRUM AND BRUNO LATOUR

This paper was presented at an interdisciplinary symposium on 'Political Behaviour as a Primate Social Strategy', organized by Glendon Schubert and Shirley Strum at the Xth Congress of the International Primatological Society in Nairobi, Kenya, 24 July 1984. Three articles of the Symposium series have already appeared in the journal *Social Science Information*: James Schubert, 'Human Vocalizations in Agonistic Political Encounters', 25 (2) 1986: Glendon Schubert, 'Primate Politics', 25 (3) 1986, and Nicholas G. Blurton-Jones, 'Tolerated Theft, Suggestions about the Ecology and Evolution of Sharing, Hoarding and Scrounging', 26 (1) 1987.

In the last decade, a wealth of data on human and non-human societies contain a hidden challenge to existing ideas about the nature of society and the social link. The ambiguities and discrepancies in these data have completely swamped earlier attempts to define society in simple terms. Are these incongruities and inconsistencies merely the result of 'practical difficulties' that will be eliminated with more data, better methodology and better insulation of scientific endeavours from ideology and amateurism? In this paper we will not take this conventional position but rather offer a different way to approach the problem.

What if the discrepancies are real and the frame of reference is wrong? In order to explore the implications of such a shift in framework, we will first consider alternative paradigms of society and then take a specific case: the history of ideas about baboon society. Next we will investigate the consequences of adopting a different meaning of social for our ideas about the evolution of the social link. We conclude by suggesting the usefulness of our new framework in resolving several existing problems in human and non-human sociology including the evolution of 'politics'.

Redefining the notion of social
Sciences of society currently subscribe to a paradigm in which 'society', although difficult to probe and to encompass, is something that can be the object of an ostensive

*First published in *Social Science Information* (1987), **26**, 783–802.

definition. The actors of society, even if the degree of activity granted them varies from one school of sociology to the next, are *inside* this larger society. Thus, social scientists recognize a difference of scale: the micro-level (that of the actors, members, participants) and a macro-level (that of society as a whole) (Knorr and Cicourel, 1981). In the last two decades this ostensive definition of society has been challenged by ethnomethodology (Garfinkel, 1967) and by the sociology of science (Knorr and Mulkay, 1983), especially of the social sciences (Law, 1986) and the sociology of technology (Latour, 1986a). In the light of these studies, the conventional distinctions between micro- and macro-levels become less clearcut and it is more difficult to accept a traditional definition of society. Instead society is more compellingly seen as continually constructed or 'performed' by active social beings who violate 'levels' in the process of their 'work'.

The two positions, the ostensive and the performative model, differ in principle and in practice, with crucial consequences for how the social link is characterized. These two views can be summarized as follows.

Ostensive definition of the social link

1   It is, *in principle*, possible to discover the typical properties of what holds a society together, properties which could explain the social link and its evolution, although *in practice*, it may be difficult to detect them.

2   These properties or elements are social. If other properties are included then the explanation of society is economic, biological, psychological, etc.

3   Social actors (whatever their size – micro or macro) are *in* the society as defined in 1. To the extent that they are active, their activity is restricted because they are only part of a larger society.

4   Because actors are in the society, they can be useful informants for scientists interested in discovering the principles of society. But because they are only *part* of society, even if they are 'aware', they can never see or know the whole picture.

5   With the proper methodology, social scientists can discover the principles of what holds society together, distinguishing between actors' beliefs and behaviour. The picture of society as a whole, thus devised, is unavailable to the individual social actors who are within it.

According to the traditional paradigm, society exists, actors enter it adhering to rules and a structure that are already determined. The overall nature of the society is unknown and unknowable to the actors. Only scientists, standing outside of society, have the capacity to understand it and see it in its entirety.

'Performative' definition of the social link

1   It is impossible, *in principle*, to establish properties which would be peculiar to life in society, although, *in practice*, it is possible to do so.

2   A variety of elements or properties contribute to the social link as defined by social actors. These are not restricted to the purely social and can include economic, biological, psychological, etc.

3   *In practice*, actors (no matter what their size – macro or micro) define, for themselves and for others, what society is, both its whole and its parts.

4   Actors 'performing' society know what is necessary for their success. This may include a knowledge of the parts and of the whole and of the difference between beliefs and behaviour.

5   Social scientists raise the same questions as any other social actor and are themselves 'performing' society, no more and no less than non-scientists. They may, however, have different practical ways of enforcing their definition of what society is.

According to the performative view, society is constructed through the many efforts to define it; it is something achieved in practice by all actors, including scientists who themselves strive to define what society is. To use Garfinkel's expression (1967), social actors are transformed, in this view, from 'cultural dopes' to active achievers of society. This shifts the emphasis from looking for the social link in the *relations between actors* to focusing on *how* actors achieve this link in their search for what society is.

Going from the traditional to the performative framework creates two sets of inverse relationships, one that reveals a strange symmetry among all actors and another that points out a new asymmetry. The first inverse relationship is the following: the more active the actors, the less they differ from one another. This shift in definition is tantamount to saying that actors are fully fledged social scientists researching what the society is, what holds it together and how it can be altered. The second inverse relationship is this: the more actors seen to be equal, *in principle* the more the *practical* differences between them become apparent in the means available to them to achieve society. Let us now see how we can apply these principles in the case of baboon societies.

Baboons: history of ideas

When Darwin wrote that we could learn more from baboons than from many of the western philosophers, he knew very little, in fact about baboons (Darwin, 1977). It was the Darwinian revolution that initiated the modern scientific study of the behaviour and society of other animals.

Pre-scientific folk ideas about baboons claimed that they were a disordered gang of brutes, entirely without social organization, roaming around at random (Morris and Morris, 1966). A picture of an orderly society emerged with the first 'scientific' studies. The early laboratory studies of monkeys (Kempf, 1917) and studies of captive baboons (Zuckerman, 1932) incorporated only a very small amount of knowledge about the behaviour of the animals in the wild (Marais, 1956, 1969; Zuckerman, 1932). Despite this, the studies did demonstrate that baboons had a society, albeit very simply organized. Sex and dominance were the primary factors at work (Maslow, 1936; Zuckerman, 1932). Sex held society together, or rather the desire of males for sexual access to females. Baboons were thus both the earliest and the most classic representatives of the orderly and simple society of primates.

The modern baboon field studies initiated in the 1950s (DeVore, 1965; DeVore and Hall, 1965; Hall, 1963; Washburn and DeVore, 1961) were among the pioneering attempts to understand primate behaviour in its natural, hence evolutionary, setting (Washburn and Hamburg, 1965; Washburn et al., 1965). The data suggested that society was not based on sex; the social structure was, instead, provided by the effects of male aggression and the dominance hierarchy it created. Social not sexual bonds held the group together. Comparing their results, Washburn, DeVore and Hall (DeVore and Hall, 1965; Hall and DeVore, 1965; Washburn and DeVore, 1961) were impressed by the similarity of their baboons, although three species were involved and the different populations lived from a hundred to thousands of miles apart. Not only were baboons paragons of orderly social life but they persisted in that same society regardless of geography or even species distinctions.

As primate field studies proliferated in the 1960s and 1970s, so did studies of baboons (e.g. Altmann and Altmann, 1971; Ransom, 1984; Rowell, 1966, 1969; Stoltz and Saayman, 1970). Some observations of baboons in a variety of habitats challenged accepted ideas about baboon society. Forest-living baboons in Uganda (Rowell, 1966, 1969) lacked a stable male dominance hierarchy and a variety of 'adaptive' male behaviours documented earlier. Kinship and friendship appeared to be the basis of baboon society (Ransom, 1984; Ransom and Ransom, 1971; Strum, 1975a, 1982) rather than the male dominance order. These new discoveries were made possible by new methods which included following individually recognized animals over long periods of time. Soon, each baboon troop under observation diverged from the norm, and variations in its behaviour undermined both the nice species pattern and its evolutionary interpretation.

One way out of the dilemma of intra-species variability, a way to eliminate the accumulating discrepancies (and, by implication, the increasing unpredictability of baboon behaviour), was to reject data and the views of the observers. A common position was this: other baboons did not behave differently, they were just inaccurately studied. Baboon social structure did exist in a stable way underneath the variety of observations.

Yet the amount of variation documented among baboons (and for other primate species) eventually subdued, to a degree, the methodological argument. Scientists accepted the idea that both behaviour and society were flexible (e.g. Crook, 1970; Crook and Gartlan, 1966; Eisenberg et al., 1972; Gartlan, 1968; Jay, 1968; Struhsaker, 1969). The difficulty was to find principles that governed the variability. The best candidates at that time were ecology and phylogeny but only the socio-biological approach of the mid–1970s (Wilson, 1975) provided a new synthesis. This revamped evolutionary framework supplied a compelling solution to the question of the principles of society. Stable properties were not in the social structure itself but rather in individual genotypes. Groups were not selected, as earlier evolutionary formulations had implied, individuals were. The society itself was a stable but 'accidental' result of individual decisions, an Evolutionary Stable Strategy (ESS) and ESSs varied with circumstances (Maynard Smith, 1976; Maynard Smith and Parker, 1976; Maynard Smith and Price, 1973).

The socio-biological solution left moot the question of the proximate means by which society could be achieved. Smart gene calculators might be appropriate actors in an 'ultimate' scenario but whole individuals coexisted, competed or co-operated as real participants in society. It is the most recent stage of baboon (and primate) research which had addressed this proximate level. The information comes primarily from long-term studies of baboons in the wild (field sites: Kenya – Amboseli, Gilgil/Laikipia, Mara; Tanzania – Gombe, Mukumi; Botswana – Okavango).

The recent research is of great interest to our argument. The trend has been in the direction of granting baboons more social skill and more social awareness (Griffin, 1981, 1984) than the socio-biological 'smart biology' argument allowed. These skills involve negotiating, testing, assessing and manipulating (Strum, 1975a, b, 1981, 1982, 1983a, b, c, in press; Western and Strum, 1983). A male baboon, motivated by his genes to maximize his reproductive success, cannot simply rely on his size, strength or dominance rank to get him what he wants. Even if dominance was sufficient, we are still left with the question: how do baboons know who is dominant or not? Is dominance a fact or an artefact? If it is an artefact, whose artefact is it – is it the observer's, who is searching for a society into which he can put the baboons? (Even in the classic dominance study, the investigator had to intervene by pairing males in contests over food, in order to 'discover' the dominance hierarchy.) Or is it a universal problem, one that both observer and baboon have to solve?

If baboons are constantly testing, trying to see who is allied with whom, who is leading whom, which strategies can further their goals, as recent evidence suggests, then both baboons and scientists are asking the same questions. And to the extent that baboons are constantly negotiating, the social link is transformed into a process of acquiring knowledge about 'what the society is'. To put it in a slightly different way, if we grant that baboons are not *entering into a stable structure* but rather negotiating what that structure will be, and monitoring and testing and pushing all other such negotiations, the variety of baboon society and its ill fit to a simple structure can be seen to be a result of the 'performative' question. The evidence is more striking in reverse. If there was a structure to be entered, why all this behaviour geared to testing, negotiating and monitoring (i.e. Strum, 1975a, b, 1981, 1982, 1983a, b, c; Boese, 1975; Busse and Hamilton et al., 1981; Hausfater, 1975; Kummer, 1967, 1973, 1978; Kummer et al., 1974; Nash, 1976; Packer, 1979, 1980; Popp, 1978; Post et al., 1980; Rasmussen, 1979; Rhine, 1975; Rhine and Owens, 1972; Rhine and Westlund, 1978; Sapolsky, 1982, 1983; Seyfarth, 1976; Smuts, 1982; Stein, 1984; Walters, 1980, 1981; Wasser, 1981)? And baboons are not alone among the non-human primates (e.g. Bernstein and Ehardt, 1985; Chepko-Sade, 1974; Chepko-Sade and Olivier, 1979; Chepko-Sade and Sade, 1979; DeWaal, 1982; Drickamer, 1974; Gouzoules, 1984; Kaplan, 1978; Kleiman, 1979; Parker and MacNair, 1978; Seyfarth, 1977, 1980; Silk, 1980).

We can summarize the baboon data and argument as follows: first, the traditional, ostensive definition of baboon society has been unable to accommodate the variety of data on baboon social life. As a result, some information has been treated as 'data' and other information as discrepancies to be ignored or explained away. Second, more recent studies demonstrate that baboons invest a great deal of time in negotiating, testing, monitoring and interfering with each other.

A performative definition of society allows us to integrate both sets of 'facts'. Under this definition, baboons would not be seen as being *in* a group. Instead they would be seen as striving to define the society and the groups in which they exist, the structure and the boundaries. They would not be seen as being *in* a hierarchy, rather they would be ordering their social world by their very activity. In such a view, shifting or stable hierarchies might develop not as one of the principles of an overarching society into which baboons must fit, but as the provisional outcome of their search for some basis of predictable interactions. Rather than entering an alliance system, baboons performing society would be testing the availability and solidity of alliances without knowing for certain, in advance, which relationships will hold and which will break. In short, performative baboons are social players actively negotiating and renegotiating what their society is and what it will be.

The performative version of society seems better able to account for the longitudinal data from one baboon site than can the traditional model. This is true when examining predatory behaviour (Strum, 1975b, 1981, 1983a), male interactions (Strum, 1982, 1983a, b), agonistic buffering (Strum, 1982), social strategies (Strum, 1982, 1983a, b, in press), the evolution of social manipulation (Western and Strum, 1983), and the fission of the main study troop (Strum, in press). Baboons 'performing' society might also allow a more consistent interpretation of the cross-populational data and data from other species of monkeys and apes.

Social complexity and social complication

When we transform baboons into active performers of their society does this put them on a par with humans? The performative paradigm suggests an important distinction. What differs is the *practical* means that actors have to enforce their version of society or to organize others on a larger scale, thereby putting into practice their own individual version of what society is.

If actors have only themselves, only their bodies as resources, the task of building stable societies will be difficult. This is probably the case with baboons. They try to decide who is a member of the group, what are the relevant units of the group that have to be considered, what is the nature of the interaction of these other units, and so on, but they have no simple or simplifying means to decide these issues or to separate out one at a time to focus upon. Age, gender and perhaps kinship can be taken as givens in most interactions. To the extent that dominance systems are linked to kinship, dominance rank may also be a given (Chapais and Schulman, 1980; Hausfater *et al.*, 1982). But even age, kinship and kinship-linked dominance may be the object of negotiation at critical points (Altmann, 1980; Cheney, 1977; Chepko-Sade and Sade, 1979; Popp and DeVore, 1979; Trivers, 1972; Walters, 1981; Wasser, 1982; Wasser and Barash, 1981). A profusion of other variables impinge simultaneously. This is the definition of *complexity* 'to simultaneously embrace a multitude of objects'. As far as baboons are concerned they assimilate a variety of factors all at once.

For the rest of our discussion we will consider that baboons live in *COMPLEX* societies and have complex sociality. When they construct and repair their social order, they do so only with limited resources, their bodies, their social skills and whatever social strategies they can construct. A baboon is, in our view, the ideal case of the *COMPETENT MEMBER* portrayed by ethnomethodologists, a social actor having difficulty negotiating one factor at a time, constantly subject to the interference of others with similar problems. These limited resources make possible only limited social stability.

Greater stability is acquired only with additional resources; something besides what is encoded in bodies and attainable through social skills is needed. Material resources and symbols can be used to enforce or reinforce a particular view of 'what society is' and permit social life to shift away from complexity to what we will call *complication*. Something is 'complicated' when it is made of a succession of simple operations. Computers are the archetype of a complicated structure where tasks are achieved by the machine doing a series of simple steps. We suggest that the shift from complexity to complication is the crucial *practical* distinction between types of social life.

To understand this point better, we might look at what baboon-watchers do in order to understand baboon social life. First, individuals are identified and named, and the composition of the group is determined by age, sex and kinship, and perhaps also dominance rankings. Items of behaviour are identified, defined and coded. Then attention is consciously focused on a subset of individuals, times and activities, among the variety of interactions that occur simultaneously. Of course we could interpret this procedure as merely a rigorous way of getting at the social structure that exists and informs baboon societies. This interpretation of the scientific work fits nicely with the ostensive definition of society. In our view, however, the work that human observers do in order to understand baboon societies is the very same process that makes human societies different from baboon ones. Modern scientific observers replace a complexity of shifting, often fuzzy and continuous behaviours, relationships and meanings with a complicated array of simple, symbolic, clear-cut items. It is an enormous task of simplification.

How does the shift from social complexity to social complication happen? Figure 15.1 illustrates how we imagine this progression. The first line represents a baboon-like society in which socialness is complex, by our use of that term, and society is complex but not complicated because individuals are unable to organize others on a large scale. The intensity of their social negotiation reflects their relative powerlessness to enforce their version of society on others, or to make it stick as a stable, lasting version.

The second line positions hypothetical hunter–gatherers who are rich in material and symbolic means to use in constructing society compared to baboons, although impoverished by comparison with modern industrial societies. Here language, symbols and material objects can be used to simplify the task of ascertaining and negotiating the nature of the social order. Bodies continue their social strategies in the performation of society, but on a larger, more durable, less complex scale. Material resources and the symbolic innovations related to language allow individuals to influence and have more power over others thereby determining the nature of the social order.

Line 3 represents agricultural societies where even more resources can be brought to bear in creating the social bond. In fact, the social bond can be maintained in the relative absence of the individuals. These societies are more complicated and more powerful than hunter–gatherer groups and the performation of society is possible on a larger scale because negotiations at each step are much less complex.

Modern industrial societies are depicted by the fourth line on the diagram. Here individuals are able to organize and 'mobilize' others on a grand scale. According

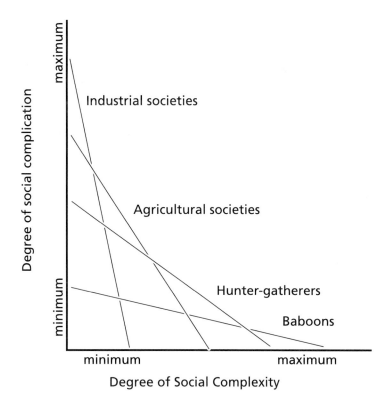

Figure 15.1 *Complexity versus complication: the trade-off*

to our scheme, the skills in an industrial society are those of simplification making social tasks *less complex* rather than making them more complex by comparison with other human and animal societies. By holding a variety of factors constant and sequentially negotiating one variable at a time, a stable *complicated* structure is created. Through extra-somatic resources employed in the process of social complication, units like multinational corporations, states and nations can be constituted (Latour, 1987). The trend as we have sketched it, is from complex sociality, as found among baboons, to complicated sociality as found among humans. Starting with individuals who have little power to affect others, or enforce their version of society, or make a lasting social order, we encounter a situation where individuals employ more and more material and 'extra-social' means to simplify social negotiations. This gives them the ability to organize others on a large scale, even when those others are not physically present. By using additional new resources, social actors can make weak and renegotiable associations, like alliances between male baboons, into strong and unbreakable units (Callon and Latour, 1981; Latour, 1986a).

The evolution of the performative social bond
Our use of a performative framework produces two important permutations. First, it grants full activity to all social participants. Individually and together they create

273

society and, in theory, they are all equal. But, secondly, new asymmetries are introduced when we consider what practical means actors have to enforce their own definition of the social bond and to organize others according to individual views of what society is.

This suggests a novel way to examine the evolution of the social bond. What follows is really a classification of meanings of social which may have implications for an evolutionary scenario.

We can begin with the common definition of social – 'to associate'. But how does an actor make the social link hold? Some associations are weaker while some are stronger and longer lasting. Our comparison of complexity and complication, from baboons to humans, suggests that resources play a role in the construction of society and in social stability.

The etymology of the word social is also instructive. The root is seq-, sequi and the first meaning is thus 'following'. The Latin 'socius' is a fellow sharer, partner, comrade, companion, associate. 'Socio' means to unite together, associate, to do or to hold in common. From the different languages, the historical genealogy of the word 'social' is construed first as following someone, then enrolling and allying and, lastly, having something in common. These three meanings are quite appropriate for baboons. The next meaning of social is to have a share in a commercial undertaking. 'Social' as in the social contract is Rousseau's invention. 'Social' as in social problems, the social question, is a nineteenth-century innovation. Parallel words like 'sociable' refer to skills enabling individuals to live politely in society. As is clear from the drift of the word, the meaning of social shrinks as time passes. Starting with a definition which is coextensive with all associations, we now have, in common parlance, a usage that is limited to what is left after politics, biology, economics, law, psychology, management, technology and so on, have taken their own parts of the associations.

The performative framework we are advocating, in effect, gives back to the word 'social' its original meaning of association. Using this definition we can compare the *practical* ways in which organisms achieve societies. Figure 15.2 summarizes our views about the possible evolution of the performative social bond. We focus on the types of resources that actors have with which to create society and to associate, but we do not restrict the idea of 'resources' in any sense.

Aggregations of conspecifics is the first meaning of social in various accounts of the origin of society (see Latour and Strum, 1986 and references included there). However, most accounts fail to distinguish between this aggregation and the origin of social skills. Once aggregation occurs, whatever its cause (e.g. Alcock, 1975; Hamilton, 1971), two different strategies are possible in our model. The first is for the actor to depart, fleeing others as soon as possible. This option generates asocial animals who exist alone except for brief reproductive interludes and temporary associations.

The second option is of greater interest. If the aggregated individual is not going to flee, he or she must adapt to a new environment of conspecifics. This is the meaning of social most common in the animal behaviour literature: to modify one's behaviour in order to live in close proximity to others of the same species. Acquiring the skill to create society and hold it together is then a *secondary* adaptation to an environment made up, in large part, of conspecifics. In order not to be exploited

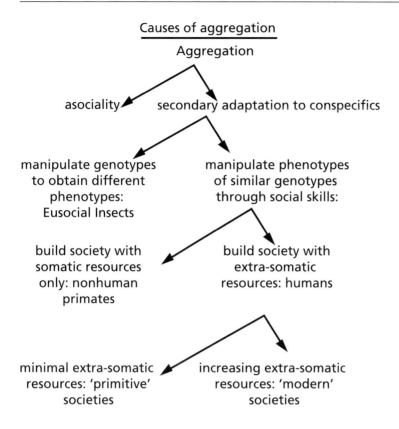

Figure 15.2 *The evolution of the performative social bond*

by their new social environment, individuals must become smarter at manipulating and manoeuvring around each other.

Once the social option has been chosen, two other possibilities appear. In the first, it is the genotypes that are modified until they are socially distinct. Insect societies are an example where the actors' own bodies are irreversibly moulded. In the second possibility we find a different meaning of social. In this case the genotypes produce similar phenotypes. These phenotypes are then manipulated by the ever-increasing social skills of individuals. This option also branches into two alternatives.

Baboons provide an example of the first. Social skills are necessary to enroll others in the actor's definition of what society is. But baboons have only 'soft tools' and can build only 'soft' societies. They have nothing more to convince and enlist others in their definition than their bodies, their intelligence and a history of interactions built up over time. This is a *complex* task and only socially 'smart' and skilful individuals may hope to be successful in baboon society.

The second possibility is to acquire additional means of defining and strengthening the social bond. Here we have the human case where the creation of society uses material resources and symbols to simplify the task. Social interactions become more *complicated* but not more complex. Much of the skill necessary to achieve society in the other, baboon-like, option now resides in the creation of symbolic and material bonds. The result is that actors, rather than appearing to create society, now appear to be inserted into a material society that overpowers them (the traditional paradigm discussed earlier).

For human societies there is an additional branching: 'primitive' societies are created with a minimal amount of material resources; increasing such resources produces 'modern' societies. Thus technology becomes one way of solving the problem of building society on a larger scale. In this sense even modern technology is social. It represents a further resource in the mobilization of individuals in the performation of society.

To summarize our theoretical model, once individuals are aggregated and choose not to avoid each other, there must be a secondary adaptation to a new competitive environment of conspecifics. Two strategies are possible: manipulate the genotypes to obtain different phenotypes (eusocial insects) or manipulate the phenotypes of similar genotypes through increasing social skills. Similar bodies adapting to social life have, themselves, two possibilities: build the society using only social skills (non-human primates) or utilize additional material resources and symbols, as necessary, to define the social bond (human societies). In the human step different types of societies are created depending upon the extent of new resources that are used.

Politics

What relevance does our exploration of the meanings of social have for politics? The answer depends, of course, on how politics is defined (Mackenzie, 1967). At the simplest and broadest level, politics is simply that which is characterized by policy, of 'sagacious, prudent, shrewd persons' or of 'expedient, skilfully contrived actions' (*Oxford English Dictionary*). Schubert (1986) proposes a definition of politics that would allow cross-species, evolutionary comparisons. For him, politics is the manner in which individuals seek to influence and control others who are not closely related to them but live together in large social groups. In these groups there are subgroups that co-operate or compete for control over the policy that determines the group's cultural rules.[1]

Both our approach and Schubert's suggest that the ability to influence and control conspecifics is an important aspect of political behaviour. In shifting to a performative definition of social, we conceive of the social link as an *active* exercise in negotiation and control. What is different, between different species and between different human groups, is the scale on which others can be organized, mobilized and influenced. In our model, material resources and symbols play a significant role in creating the difference between a 'soft' society with limited stability, where individuals have minimal power to influence others, and a 'hard' and stable society, where others can be influenced without even being present.

Can we identify the beginnings of political behaviour in the beginnings of socialness, as we have redefined it and traced its development through our version of the evolution of the social bond? Certainly the traditional view that individuals are relatively passive and enter into a society that overpowers them would lead us to believe that political action begins when individuals become 'actors', taking the initiative in determining 'what society is'. In this view such initiative comes very late in the evolutionary time-scale. But if all social actors 'perform' society to some degree, are active participants from the *beginning*, probing and investigating, negotiating and renegotiating, where would we comfortably place the beginnings of political behaviour? Should we exclude the eusocial insects because the major negotiations occur before the phenotypes appear? Should we exclude non-human primates because their sphere of influence is limited by the extent of their material and symbolic resources?

While the thrust of Schubert's 'biopolitical behavioralist' definition is to urge caution when attributing political behaviour to non-human primates, at least as some recent animal studies have done (e.g. DeWaal, 1982), the thrust of our argument is to draw a closer parallel between what we call 'social' and what has been defined as political. These efforts do not erase the significant differences between ants, baboons and, for instance, the technocrats of the Pentagon. Rather they highlight the source of those differences in a new way: the resources used and the practical work required in mobilizing them. In our definition of resources, genes, power, language, capital and technology, for instance, are all seen as strategic means of enhancing one's influence over others in increasingly more durable ways. Politics is not one realm of action separated from the others. Politics, in our view, is what allows many heterogeneous resources to be woven together into a social link that becomes increasingly harder and harder to break.

NOTE

1   Until recently, 'cultural rules' might have excluded non-human animals, *a priori*. Now the evidence is striking for animal 'mental models' (e.g. Griffin, 1981, 1984).

PART IV

FEMINISM, QUEER THEORY AND THE BODY

INTRODUCTION

In the Introduction to this volume, I suggested that the 'post-processual era' in archaeology has been defined by a willingness to explore the radical theoretical perspectives which are current in the humanities as a whole. It is the implication of most of these approaches that as well as studying the past we should also reflect on the present circumstances within which we conduct our archaeology. However, some of the most powerful and critical strands in contemporary philosophy and social thought were somewhat underrepresented in the debates of the early 1980s, and have come to be more influential in recent years. These include post-colonial theory, feminism, and now queer theory. All of these approaches emerge from ongoing political engagements, and continually remind us of the political character of the statements that we make about the past. In his article here, for instance, Thomas Dowson points to the ways in which contemporary archaeological writings bolster the claims to universality which are made on behalf of modern Western family values. But it is the strength of feminism and queer theory that as well as stressing the fundamental importance of a politicised archaeology they also enable us to see the world differently. In the ways that they address science, the body, materiality, gender, identity, space and social relations, queer theory and feminism dramatically expand the kinds of knowledge that we can create about the past.

It is their status as forms of political action (as well as philosophy) which explains why traditions like feminism, queer theory and post-colonial theory have produced such important insights. In each case a particular critique of Western society has been developed by those who are obliged to occupy cultural locations in which they are, to a greater or lesser extent, oppressed. These cultural and social positions necessitate a critical response, simply in the attempt to explain why one's life should be the way that it is. But at the same time they afford a critical distance on the mainstream, and for this reason if no other it is important for those of us who are male, white, middle-class and heterosexual to take these arguments very seriously indeed. An excellent example of the importance of these insights is provided by Moira Gatens' piece, which argues that Western scientific reason is not merely sexist in some superficial sense but constituted in and through the repudiation of a cluster of cultural categories which are associated with the female. As Joan Gero goes on to argue, this means that female scholars effectively have to struggle with systems of knowledge from which they have been excluded. Similarly, Gatens points to the legal and political institutions of the modern West, which implicitly assume a male subject, able to engage in civil society in a very specific set of ways. This in turn affects our expectations of the past, as Gero demonstrates in the case of Palaeoindian studies. Here it is the fluted stone point, and the male practices of big-game hunting with which it is associated which stand as the signatures of human presence.

In her article, Ruth Tringham presents the case that gender and the study of households have been neglected by archaeologists as a result of a series of deeply embedded prejudices. Gender is considered to be difficult to identify in the archaeological record, and consequentially it is commonly treated as if it were some metaphysical phenomenon whose very existence cannot be tested. Moreover, because gender relations operate at the interpersonal level, they are not seen as having any impact on the course of macro-scale social and political evolution. But as Alison Wylie (1992) has pointed out, archaeologists are frequently content to discuss entities that they have never actually 'seen', like settlement systems, subsistence economies, and social hierarchies. What makes them avoid any consideration of gender is a perception that it is 'unimportant'. The recognition that if we are to deal with gender relations in the past we will have to go beyond the kinds of statements which can be directly corroborated by the evidence has had a radicalising effect on archaeology, especially in the United States. As Tringham argues here, it forces a recognition that archaeologists have an active role to play in creating their interpretations. This in turn requires that they take responsibility for what they write.

While much gender archaeology has aspired to little more than the recognition that women existed and had social roles in the past, recent feminist theory has much more fundamental implications for the ways in which we think about past people. Moira Gatens makes the point that gender is not something which is added on top of some kind of human essence, which resides outside of time and history. Similarly, human biology does not provide a fixed substance which remains unchanging throughout the centuries. Archaeologists talk of 'anatomically modern humans', as if all that separated us from the Cro-Magnons was a bit of technological development. Human beings do not precede their gendering, and gender is one of the means through which we become recognisable as human. We should not expect gender identities to be held stable through time, and as Dowson adds there is nothing fixed and universal about homosexuality. The challenge to archaeologists inspired by feminism and queer theory is to imagine gender orders, sexualities and desires which are quite unlike our own.

Of course, if gender is not a fixed set of categories, and is not determined by a universal biological order, it must be created and performed in the material world. This compels us to think again about materiality: the materiality of the human body itself, as Judith Butler (1993) has argued, but also the materiality of our everyday world. In her paper, Henrietta Moore presents a striking analysis of the ways in which gender pervades the lived environment. In the process of growing up and living in a world of material things, people learn, perform and reproduce gender codes. The material traces which we investigate through archaeology are, among other things, technologies through which gender orders different from our own were produced and handed down.

16

HOMOSEXUALITY, QUEER THEORY AND ARCHAEOLOGY*

Thomas A. Dowson

In the final years of the twentieth century gay and lesbian people, their culture and politics are both enjoying and suffering considerable attention. Homosexuality is a topic that is widely discussed and hotly debated. People from all walks of life with wide-ranging positions of prominence and influence are increasingly finding it easier to 'come out'. Groups of political activists have united around the world to challenge homosexual discrimination. Despite these great steps forward the struggle to secure basic human rights remains a pitched battle against increased bigotry and intolerance. Homophobia is as rife now as it has ever been over the last hundred or so years. Archaeology is not detached from these debates and anxieties.

Classical scholars have been aware of same-sex relations between men in Ancient Greece and Rome since the last century. It was, however, largely ignored until the 1960s, since when it has become acceptable to mention and discuss 'homosexuality' in the context of Classical Greece and Rome. More recently, Matthews (1994) has used material from the Classical world to call for an archaeology of homosexuality. Despite this recent explicit interest in the construction of ancient homosexuality, archaeology has in fact always implicitly influenced the way in which we all think about homosexuality – past and present.

In this paper I explore that relationship between archaeology and homosexuality. More particularly, I suggest archaeology has been consistently underpinning a heterosexual artifice of human prehistory – archaeologists produce constructions that provide the origins for modern, Western family values. Consequently, archaeology has developed a strong (and conservative) tradition of establishing a norm that has influenced all archaeological method and practice. I begin my challenge of normative archaeology by outlining the way in which archaeology has informed contemporary homophobia, and how, more recently archaeology is used to sanction same-sex relations in the present and so construct an essentialist homosexuality. I then discuss the manner in which queer challenges the universality of homosexuality, and in so doing empowers a rethinking of desire, power and truth. I end by demonstrating

---

* First published in *Cota Zero* (1998), **14**, 81–7 (original in Catalan)

283

how queer theory disrupts the normativity of archaeological practice, truly enabling a radical rethinking of the past in ways that post-processualism has failed to accomplish.

Homosexuality and archaeology

Archaeology has always been implicated in discussions concerning homosexuality. Just as men were and to some extent still are assumed to be superior to women, heterosexuality definitely is considered the norm. The idea of heterosexual relations, based on male supremacy, has therefore influenced all archaeological constructions of the prehistoric family, community and society (cf. Rubin's discussion of 'obligatory heterosexuality' in anthropology, 1975). When re-constructing prehistoric living structures archaeologists impose modern, Western notions of a family unit; father, mother and children, and perhaps grandparents. Archaeology serves to provide the origins of modern family values. The possibility of other constructions of the family unit are not explored, despite considerable anthropological evidence. Yet in seeking the origins of the family some archaeologists excuse the present by suggesting the roots of homophobia lie in prehistory. For instance, Taylor (1996: 164–166) argues the development of permanent structures in the Neolithic allowed parents to monitor the reproductive lives of their sons and daughters. He explicitly states 'the Neolithic period saw the true birth of homophobia' (1996: 165). Such approaches are implicitly homophobic.

Other constructions are more explicitly homophobic in that the authors forcibly deny the existence of homosexuality in the past. For them homosexuality is an aberration of the present. An example of this can be seen in a recent book that attempts to construct the daily life of Egyptians in the age of the pyramids (Andreu 1997). Andreu, citing uncritically the writings of an ancient Egyptian sage, states that Ptahhotpe

> advises young men to found a household and watch over their wives [and] gives stern warning against the attractions of homosexuality and paedophilia: 'Do not copulate with an effeminate boy . . . do not allow him to spend the night doing what is forbidden; . . . thus he will be calm after staving off his desire'. In one literary tale, homosexuality is presented as ridiculous behaviour, the more so as it is attributed to a pharaoh suspected of maintaining a special friendship with the head of his army. This was a basic violation of Egyptian morality and of the code regulating the good conduct one had the right to expect of everyone and, *a fortiori*, of the highest personage in the state.
>
> (Andreu 1997: 84)

Such an ignorant dismissal of homosexuality is prevalent in many archaeological studies. This particular example, however, offers two interesting insights into archaeologically negotiated homophobia.

First, homosexuality is more often than not linked to paedophilia. Nowhere is this better seen than in the modern studies of homosexuality in Ancient Greece. Here writers concentrate on the erotic appeal of youths to older men. The relationship between an active, adult *erastes* and an effeminate, submissive, younger *eromenos* has been characterised by many scholars, starting with Dover (1978), as 'culturally sanctioned pederasty/paedophilia'. But as Sparkes (1998: 257) points out, such a view is 'too sanitized a version of a reality that was altogether more complex'. Sparkes' remark leads me to the second insight into the way in which archaeologists, in general, and Andreu's, in particular, constructions of the past are influenced by homophobic attitudes.

Modern homophobic attitudes are to blame for the sanitized and clinical discussions that so quickly link homosexuality with what is perceived to be unsocial behaviour. Pathologising homosexuality in this manner simply justifies the manner in which other evidence, that would allow for a more complex discussion, is ignored. For instance, in Athenian life same-sex unions did not only exist between men and younger boys; same-sex relations were also present in the army where both partners were older (Sparkes 1998: 257). Similarly, there exists evidence in Egypt that same-sex relations between men were in fact permissible in ancient times. At the necropolis of Saqqara there is a tomb that was purposefully built for two men, Niankhkhnum and Khnumhotep. Although both men were married to women, and had children, the manner in which these two men are depicted together in the bas-reliefs found in their joint tomb suggests they were in fact 'lovers' (Reeder n.d., see also Norton 1997).

Homophobic attitudes, then, heavily inform the way in which the past is produced today. At the same time, the presentation of the past also both informs and sanctions homophobic attitudes for consumers of that past. Homophobia is an obvious response to the way in which homosexuality in the past is interpreted and represented, and then consumed as deviant and pathological. Archaeology's complicity in Western society's institutionalised homophobia requires challenging. I briefly outline the way in which the past has been used by gay and lesbian writers to challenge our marginalisation.

While there is a long and powerful history of a number of groups in various places around the world challenging institutionalised homophobia (see, for example, Marcus 1992; Miller 1995) it is generally accepted that the Stonewall riots represent the birth of gay and lesbian liberation. Riots between gay men and police at the Stonewall Inn in New York on June 28, 1969, provided a powerful catalyst for gay and lesbian activists around the world (see Duberman 1993). Further, the outbreak of the AIDS epidemic in the 1980s provided a shocking reminder of the institutionalised homophobia that exists in our society. As a result of renewed political activism a very distinct gay and lesbian identity began to emerge. And, that identity, like all identities, requires a legitimising history.

From the 1980s on, there has been a proliferation of homosexual histories. These histories wrote of great men and women who were believed or known to be homosexual, and of turning points in homosexual history. Scholars began to explore further back in time. Boswell, for example, studied homosexuality in Western Europe from the beginning of the Christian Era to the fourteenth century (1980) and in the Greco-Roman word (1994). Archaeological studies from Classical Greece and Rome provided essential evidence for the origins of homosexuality in antiquity. Some writers explored even further back in time. Spencer (1995) traces homosexuality through mammalian sexuality, prehistory, early civilisation, the Roman Empire, the Celts, Medieval Europe, Renaissance England and Western Civilisation from then until the age of AIDS. The purpose of this grand sweep of human history is to show that 'homosexuality has been a constant theme in the sexuality of all societies' (1995: 11).

In other fields of discourse similar approaches are employed. For instance, by adopting the widest possible definition of what constitutes 'gay male literature', Woods

(1998) has identified a tradition that he argues is central to the world's major cultural traditions. That definition encompasses works from ancient Greece and Rome, the Middle Ages, the Orient; major writers such as Marlowe, Shakespeare and Proust; and such common themes as boyhood and masturbation. These grand sweeps through history and culture serve to remind the world, homosexual and homophobe alike, of the universality and importance of homosexuality and homo-eroticism.

These new gay and lesbian histories provide an interesting twist in the way in which the past is used and consumed. Whereas archaeology as it is professionally produced serves to sanction homophobia (with few exceptions), gay and lesbian writers use history and archaeology to challenge our cultural and historical marginalisation to expose contemporary homophobia. The archaeological past is thus becoming an integral part of a very powerful political ideology. An ideology that asserts both the internationalism of homosexual culture and a continuity of homoerotic traditions between prehistoric and ancient worlds and the present. By insisting on an ahistorical and asocial character this ideology legitimates a 'natural' gay and lesbian identity that is then mobilised and negotiated in contemporary politics for rights of equality. Modern gay and lesbian identity is thus grounded in a positive truth, and it is the task of gay and lesbian activists to reveal that truth to challenge modern institutionalised homophobia.

But, as Weeks (1989a: 207) and many others argue, 'Identity is not inborn, pregiven, or 'natural'. It is striven for, contested, regulated, and achieved, often in struggles of the subordinated against the dominant.' Today gay and lesbian identity hinges on their same-sex desires and behaviours. Sexuality in general and homosexuality in particular are in fact critical phenomena in the construction of the modern gay and lesbian identity. But as Foucault (1984) and Weeks (1977, 1989b) point out, such phenomena are historically and culturally situated. Thus both the assumption of the internationalism of homosexuality, and the idea of a continuity of homo-erotic traditions between past and present are flawed. Consequently, through the voices of many people, there has emerged in the 1990s a challenge to the assumed stability of sexual identities – homosexual and heterosexual alike. A challenge that has far-reaching implications, including for the practice of archaeology.

Queer theory

Queer theory derives from, and continues to be actively grounded in, political movements outside the academy. But it is also drawn into challenging the academic establishment, in that that establishment forms an integral and influential part of a wider set of hegemonic social and cultural formations. In contrast to gay and lesbian identity, queer identity is not based on a notion of a stable truth or reality. As Halperin (1995: 62) explains,

> 'queer' does not name some natural kind or refer to some determinate object; it acquires its meaning from its oppositional relation to the norm. Queer is by definition whatever is at odds with the normal, the legitimate, the dominant. *There is nothing in particular to which it necessarily refers.* (original emphases)

Consequently, queer theory is not about providing a positivity, rather 'a positionality vis-à-vis the normative' (Halperin 1995: 62).

To effect that positionality queer theory 'takes on various shapes, risks, ambitions and ambivalences in various contexts' (Berlant and Warner 1995: 343). In so doing, it allows for 'reordering the relations among sexual behaviours, erotic identities, constructions of gender, forms of knowledge, regimes of enunciation, logics of representation, modes of self-constitution, and practices of community – for restructuring, that is, the relations among power, truth, and desire' (Halperin 1995: 62; see also de Lauretis 1991). Queer theory is thus very definitely not restricted to homosexual men and women, but to any one who feels their position (sexual, intellectual or cultural) to be marginalised. The queer position then is no longer a marginal one considered deviant or pathological; but rather multiple positions within many more possible positions – all equally valid.

Queering archaeology

Recently Meskell (1998b) has suggested that a variety of constructions of Ancient Egypt, both popular and scholarly, are queer in terms of Halperin's definition of queer. According to Meskell the consumption of Ancient Egypt from early modern times until the present has centered around an eroticisation of the dead. Necrophilia explains the literal consumption of Egyptian bodies in Europe from the sixteenth century on. Since the nineteenth century Ancient Egyptian sex and death were captured in more visual and literary media – in paint, film and the novel. While I advocate strongly the queering of archaeology, I find the manner in which Meskell argues that our consumption and constructions of Egypt is queer to be misinformed.

As Halperin (1995: 62) explicitly states *queer* 'does not designate a class of already objectified pathologies or perversions' as in necrophilia. Nor is it about embracing 'all species of sexual outlaws' (Halperin 1995: 64). To identify and define the West's consumption of Ancient Egypt in terms of necrophilia in fact runs counter to the queering project in general, and the queering of archaeology in particular.

Meskell's misappropriation of *queer* highlights the misuse of the term. As Halperin warns:

> What makes 'queer' potentially so treacherous as a label is that its lack of definitional content renders it all too readily available for appropriation by those who do not experience the unique political disabilities and forms of social disqualification from which lesbians and gay men routinely suffer in virtue of our sexuality.

(See also Butler 1991.) By identifying necrophilia as *queer* Meskell's queer Egyptian legacy merely serves to support the contemporary, right-wing restigmatization of lesbians and gay men. Rather than representing a deep and meaningful encounter with *queer*, studies like Meskell's are nothing more than superficial attempts to be politically and academically fashionable.

Queering archaeology does not involve looking for homosexuals, or any other supposed sexual deviant for that matter, in the past. Nor is it concerned with the origins of homosexuality. Such is the agenda of an 'archaeology of homosexuality' (Matthews 1994) that proposes to use the experiences of gay men living in the twentieth century to provide a theoretical model of homosexual behaviour and material culture. Ethnographic evidence shows such an archaeological agenda to be futile.

The Berdache of Native American peoples and the Hijras of India, amongst others, are often seen as anthropological evidence for the universality of homosexuality. But if we examine carefully the constructions of these peoples' identities, it becomes clear that those identities are based on the modern construction of Western homosexuality (Whitehead 1981; Nanda 1993; Bleys 1996). The Berdache and the Hijras do not construct or define their identities on the basis of who they have sex with, as is true of a Western homosexual identity. Essentialist models of same-sex relations deny the diversity of sexual identities around the world, and the socio-historical contexts within which these identities emerge and transform.

Queering archaeology not only involves moving away from essentialist and normative constructions of presumed and compulsory heterosexuality (male: female – deviant third sex), but also the normative nature of archaeological discourse. A parallel to this can be seen in feminist archaeology. Feminists are at pains to point out that a feminist archaeology is more than simply looking for women in the past, and introducing women into constructions of the past. Feminist archaeology is about challenging the dominant masculist values that shape the nature of archaeological constructions. In this sense queer archaeologies are not at odds with feminist archaeologies. But queer archaeologies draw on the critiques of presumed and compulsory heterosexuality and its influence on masculist discourse from social and intellectual movements outside of feminism. Queer theory is thus uniquely situated to challenge masculist practice and the reverse discourse of archaeological feminism (cf. Butler 1990, 1997).

To demonstrate, very briefly, a queer archaeology I consider a restructuring of the forms of knowledge as constituted in the study of rock art in Sweden and South Africa. In spite of recent advances in the study of rock art, this imagery is still studied in a very traditional manner. That tradition involves describing and classifying rock art imagery and then producing a chronological sequence. It derives from thinking about rock art in terms of a post-industrial revolution definition of art, where a description of the formal qualities of a piece of art enables it to move in a dealer-critic system. This modern, Western definition of art provides the foundations of normativity inherent in much rock art research.

In a study of Swedish rock carvings, Yates (1993: 35) suggests that 'the way forward for rock art analysis, is not to address issues of chronology but to theorize the art – a theorization which must extend beyond the stale discussions of terminology – and study its appearance and meaning in local and regional terms.' Such a suggestion is not merely a subtle, albeit critical, shift, rather it is a radical, *queer* challenge that allows rock art scholars to break free of the debilitating normativity that permeates our research.

Yates's paper was published while I was writing a paper in which I was thinking about how to use rock paintings from the Drakensberg mountains of South Africa, for which we have no reliable dates, to write a new kind of history (Dowson 1994). In South Africa, because of the extensive ethnographic research, some researchers have been able to move beyond the empiricist methodology (see Dowson and Lewis-Williams 1994), but they have retained much of the normativity inherent in archaeological practice. I was trying to find something more in the art than representations of religious belief. Particularly as at the start of the 1990s new questions were being asked in and of South Africa. I was exploring a new way of theorizing the art to answer these new questions. In attempting to write a new kind of history I encountered considerable opposition, indeed open hostility, from archaeologists because I did not have a 'firm chronological framework' for the rock paintings. I was stepping away from accepted methodologies of both archaeological and historical practice. Like Yates, I was stepping away from the normative. Approaches such as these are not just critical of established methodologies in archaeology, but *queerly* critical. They explore what the establishment regards as deviant methodologies for archaeological practice.

Since 1994 discussions about dating in rock art have reached fever pitch. One only has to page through recent issues of academic journals to see how obsessed rock art researchers are becoming with their quest for dates and chronologies. I am not suggesting that knowing how old the images are is unimportant. Rather I am becoming increasingly concerned with the chronocentric character of rock art studies. There is a strong feeling that without dates we do not have much to go on. So researchers feel compelled to establish a chronological framework. This chrono-centrism I argue derives from the very core of masculist practice in archaeology. In fact, dating is a key component of most archaeological narratives, particularly those of origins – which are decidedly masculist in character (see Conkey and Williams 1991). Chronocentricism is the phallocentricism of archaeology – without a chronology your research is worthless. I do not believe, however, the path to methodological rigour is paved by normativity. Instead we should look more closely at what we do have, but without the masculist, hetrosexist values and assumptions that rule our society today.

Challenging the prominence afforded the direct and indirect dating of rock art imagery and the chronocentric nature of archaeology in general is decidedly *QUEER*. But, as Yates, myself and others have demonstrated, such an overt disruption is certainly not deviant, and no less methodologically rigorous. Being explicitly queer in one's approach provides a constant and necessary reminder of the need to challenge hegemonic social and cultural formations.

ACKNOWLEDGEMENTS

I thank Yvonne Marshall, Ben Alberti and Jayne Gidlow for commenting on drafts of this paper. Also, I have been fortunate to be able to discuss various issues raised here with other colleagues and students; in particular I thank Robert Wallis, Sally Titmus, Stephanie Moser, Mary Baker and Sue Pitt.

17

POWER, BODIES AND DIFFERENCE[*]

MOIRA GATENS

Over the last two decades the diversification of feminist theories has rendered the rather convenient tripartite division into Marxist feminism, liberal feminism and radical feminism virtually useless. These divisions no longer capture the salient features of the multiple ways in which current feminist theories interact with dominant socio-political theories.[1] Most noticeably, feminist theories today no longer feel compelled to carry their allegiances 'on their sleeves' (Marxist feminism, liberal feminism) in order to signal their authority to speak. In this sense, both Marxism and liberalism provided, and sometimes still provide, a legitimizing or patronymic function. Radical feminism distinguished itself from other forms of feminist theory by avowing its independence from so-called patriarchal theories. It alone claimed to be 'unmarked' by the name of the father.

The reluctance of contemporary feminisms to identify themselves with a theory-patronym may be seen as an indication of the profound suspicion and distrust which many feminists display towards dominant socio-political theories. Many contemporary feminist theorists no longer have faith in the utility of existing socio-political theories to explain or clarify the socio-political status of women. This 'loss of faith' in what has variously been named malestream, phallocentric or simply masculinist theories signals that many feminists no longer believe that these theories are marred by only a superficial sex-blindness, or sexism. The problem is now located at a much more fundamental level. It cannot be simply a matter of removing superficial biases from socio-political theories, since the bias is now understood as intrinsic to the structure of the theories in question (Gatens 1991a). For example, feminist philosophers have argued convincingly that reason is not something from which women have been simply excluded. Rather, rationality itself has been defined against the feminine and traditional female roles.[2] Likewise, it has been demonstrated that women's exclusion from the political body is not a contingent feature of their history but a consequence of the dominant conception of political society. Women have been

---

[*]First published in M. Barrett and A. Phillips (eds) (1992), *Destablising Theory: Contemporary Feminist Debates*, Cambridge: Polity Press, pp. 120–37.

constructed as 'naturally deficient in a specifically *political* capacity, the capacity to create and maintain political right' (Pateman 1989: 96). These studies have shown that the application of dominant theories of social and political life to the situation of women inevitably involves the devaluation of women and all that women have been associated with historically. The reason is that these theories harbour fundamental, not superficial, biases against women.

This analysis may be seen to imply that many contemporary feminist approaches to theory are themselves forms or varieties of radical feminism. This would be a rather simplistic description, since many recent developments in contemporary feminist theory explicitly stress the necessity to engage with dominant or 'malestream' theories of social and political life – an attitude not easily identified with radical feminism. Such engagement is active and critical. These feminist theorists do not go to Marxism or liberalism hoping for 'the answer'- or 'the solution' to 'the woman question' but, more probably, will approach dominant theories, and their implicit biases, as themselves part of the problem. For this reason it seems appropriate to name these contemporary feminist approaches to dominant socio-political theories 'deconstructive'.

For the purposes of this essay the term 'deconstructive' will not be used in the strict Derridean sense. Rather, it will be used to identify feminist approaches which eschew viewing theories such as Marxism, liberalism, existentialism, psychoanalysis and so on as essentially sex-neutral discourses through which an understanding of women's situation may be 'truly' grasped. Deconstructive feminism is concerned to investigate the elemental make-up of these theories and to expose their latent discursive commitments. For example, much political theory typically treats the family as a natural rather than a social phenomenon. A deconstructive approach highlights what is at stake in opposing the family, understood as natural, to the public sphere, understood as a social construct. It is this assumption which allows political theorists to mask the specifically political features of the relations between the sexes by treating these relations as natural.[3]

A feature common to most, if not all, dominant socio-political theories is a commitment to the dualisms central to western thought: nature and culture, body and mind, passion and reason. In the realm of social and political theory, these dualisms often translate as distinctions between reproduction and production, the family and the state, the individual and the social. As many feminists have argued, the left-hand side of these dualisms is more intimately connected with women and femininity and the right-hand side with men and masculinity. It is also important to note that it is only the right-hand side of these distinctions which is deemed to fall within the realm of history. Only culture, the mind and reason, social production, the state and society are understood as having a dynamic and developmental character. The body and its passions, reproduction, the family and the individual are often conceived as timeless and unvarying aspects of nature. This way of conceptualizing human existence is deeply complicit in claims such as 'women have no history'[4] and 'reproduction involves the mere repetition of life' (de Beauvoir 1975: 96).

It is this deep interrogation of the discursive commitments of socio-political theories that marks off current forms of feminist theory from their predecessors.

It distinguishes what has been termed deconstructive feminist theory from any feminist theory which theorizes women's existence by attempting to extend the terms of 'malestream' theories; for example, Marxist feminism, liberal feminism, existentialist feminism and so on. Yet deconstructive feminism is also distinct from radical feminism in that it does not take woman's essence or biology as somehow enabling her to produce, *ex nihilo*, pure or non-patriarchal theory. On the contrary, deconstructive feminisms view such claims with extreme scepticism. Michele le Doeuff, for example, claims that:

> [w]hether we like it or not, we are within philosophy, surrounded by masculine-feminine divisions that philosophy has helped to articulate and refine. The problem is to know whether we want to remain there and be dominated by them, or whether we can take up a critical position in relation to them, a position which will necessarily evolve through de-ciphering the basic philosophical assumptions latent in discourse about women. The worst metaphysical positions are those which one adopts unconsciously whilst believing or claiming that one is speaking from a position outside philosophy.
>
> (le Doeuff 1977: 2)

The last sentence of this passage may serve as a caution to those who believe that it is possible to create feminist theories which owe nothing to the culture from which they emanate. To acknowledge this is not, however, to take up a nihilistic or resigned attitude to the possibility of working towards alternatives to existing socio-political theories, where this might involve critically engaging with their 'latent assumptions'. Suppressed or marginalized philosophies – for example, those of Spinoza[5] or Nietzsche – also may be of use to feminist theorists in that they may emphasize features of existence which have been obscured or elided by traditional discourses.

It is obviously impossible to present a fair or extensive treatment of the great variety in contemporary feminist theories in the space of a single essay. Indeed, it is not possible even to present a fair outline of what have been named deconstructive feminisms. Rather, this chapter will attempt to offer an outline of what I take to be some of the most important conceptual shifts between feminist theories of the 1970s on the one hand, and contemporary deconstructive feminisms on the other. This contrast will be achieved by concentrating on shifts in the use of three key terms: power, the body and difference. These terms are used by both deconstructive and other feminist theorists; nevertheless it will be argued that they are used in quite different and incompatible ways. Inevitably, in an essay of this sort, there will be many generalizations. The aim is not to belittle feminisms of the 1970s but rather to show that deconstructive feminisms have developed in a historical context, where previous feminist research plays an integral and indispensable role in the articulation of contemporary feminist concerns. This is simply to say that if previous feminists had not attempted to use dominant theories to explicate women's socio-political status, the difficulties inherent in that project would not have come to light. Deconstructive feminisms assume and respond to these difficulties.

Power

Both liberal and Marxist political theories have tended to conceptualize power as something which an individual, or a group, either does or does not have. Power is conceived as something which is intimately connected with authority, domination or exploitation. In liberal political theory the role of the state is conceived in terms of the exercise of legitimate power over its subjects to ensure the peaceable and equitable opportunity of exchange. Power is thought to reside in, and radiate out from, sovereignty.

Marxist political theory, of course, takes a quite different view of the matter. Power is not thought to be the exercise of the legitimate authority of the sovereign. Rather, the state is conceived as being in the service of the ruling class and the exercise of power in society is the exercise of the power of one class over another. In this sense, power is held by one group which uses this power in order to dominate and exploit another group which lacks power. However, both philosophies assume that power is principally manifested in the regulation and control of politico-economic relations. It is in relation to these that power assumes material forms, although Marxists would also claim that power is exercised by ideological means. Louis Althusser formulated the difference between these two distinct forms of state power in terms of repressive state apparatuses, which include the police, judiciary, army and so on; and ideological state apparatuses, which include schools, religion, the family and so forth (Althusser 1977b: 121–73).

When feminist theorists seek to make use of these socio-political theories, the kinds of problem that they address tend to centre on the manner in which the power of the state operates in relation to women. Liberal feminists conceive the problem of women's confinement to the private sphere as central to their low socio-political status. Equality, wealth and opportunity are located in the public sphere. Hence the issue of providing women with access to power becomes the issue of providing them with equal access to the public sphere. The state is obliged to provide women with the same opportunities it provides for men. Thus, the struggle for liberal feminists tends to involve equality of opportunity in education and the workplace, equality under the law and so on. These demands inevitably spill over into related demands for child-care or maternity leave. However, since these demands must be put in terms that are sex-neutral, maternity leave must be matched by paternity leave and equal opportunity must be phrased in terms which include men.

The fundamental premise of liberal philosophy to provide equal access to power can be articulated only in terms that are sexually neutral. What this involves, for women, is the difficulty, if not impossibility, of occupying the public sphere on genuinely equal terms with men. Put simply, given that the public sphere has historically been an almost exclusively male sphere, it has developed in a manner which assumes that its occupants have a male body. Specifically, it is a sphere that does not concern itself with reproduction but with production. It does not concern itself with (private) domestic labour but with (social) wage-labour. This is to say that liberal society assumes that its citizens continue to be what they were historically, namely male heads of households who have at their disposal the services of an unpaid domestic worker/mother/wife.

In this sense, the (traditionally male) public sphere of liberal society can be understood as one which defines itself in opposition to the (traditionally female) private sphere. The status of women in liberal theory and society presents feminists with a series of paradoxes.[6] Equality in this context can involve only the abstract opportunity to become equal to men. It is the male body, and its historically and culturally determined powers and capacities, that is taken as the norm or the standard of the liberal 'individual'. Women can achieve this standard provided that they either elide their own corporeal specificity or are able to juggle both their traditional role in the private sphere and their new-found 'equality'. This situation fails to take account of the specific powers and capacities that women have developed in their historical and cultural context, a point which will be treated in the following section.

Marxism also tends to concentrate on a rather narrow use of power, one in which economic relations are taken to be the origin of all power relations. The effect of this, in the context of studying women's socio-political status, is that those forms of power which are specific to women's existence can only be perceived in their relation to the economic structure of society. It is tempting to suggest that women would first have to become genuine members of liberal society in order to lend credence to the relevance of the Marxist critique to their situation. This is particularly pertinent to those varieties of Marxism which take the structure of society to be determined by its economic base. It was the economism of much Marxist theory which placed the so-called domestic labour debate high on the agenda for Marxist feminists of the 1970s. This highlights the way in which theories can determine which questions are 'central', irrespective of the specificity of the object being studied. It is an example of how the deep biases in socio-political theories can obscure features of women's existence that may be crucial to an understanding of their situation, while emphasizing instead issues that appear prominent not because of women's situation but because of the underlying commitments of the theory in question (see di Stefano 1991).

The difficulties involved in offering a Marxist analysis of women under patriarchal capitalism are obviously tied to the fact that, in Marxist terms, women cannot be seen to constitute a class. Consequently, Marxist feminist theory found it difficult to offer an account of the operations of power in the lives of women. The theory, like the culture, could conceive women, *qua women*, only on the model of appendages to men. Capital extracts surplus-value from wage-labour, the price of which assumes the subsistence of not only the wage-labourer but also his household. Those women who do perform wage-labour were conceived as unsexed labour, while those women who do not perform wage-labour have only an indirect connection to capital and social relations. Power, as it operates in the lives of women, was largely conceived on the model of the power of ideology. Hence it is not surprising that many Marxist feminists welcomed the addition of psychoanalytic theory in order to explain the way in which the ideology of masculinity and femininity constructs men and women as appropriate patriarchal subjects in capitalist society. Moreover, in that many Marxist feminists took (traditional) women's work to involve the reproduction of labour-power, psychoanalysis offered a theoretical perspective from which to examine the way in which *appropriate* kinds of labourer are produced.

The most prominent exponent of the utility of psychoanalytic theory to Marxist feminism was Juliet Mitchell, in her extremely influential book *Psychoanalysis and Feminism* (Mitchell 1974). Mitchell claimed that Marxism offers an account of class and capital whereas psychoanalysis offers an account of sex and patriarchy. Significantly, these two theories were understood as concerned respectively with the economic infrastructure and the ideological superstructure. Men's exploitation centres on the state and class society whereas women's specific oppression centres on ideology and patriarchal society. Mitchell, following Althusser, thus managed to achieve the reduction of psychic life to the domain of ideology. This is an important consequence, primarily because it was often used to 'justify' the postponement of womens struggles or, more benignly, to tie the outcome of women's struggles to that of the class struggle.

This view of the operation of power and oppression in women's lives involved an unconvincing analysis of how gender operates in society, as well as of the way in which sexual difference intersects with power and domination. Kate Millett, for example, argued that '[s]ince patriarchy's biological foundations appear to be so very insecure, one has some cause to admire the strength of a 'socialisation' which can continue a universal condition 'on faith alone', as it were, or through an acquired value system exclusively' (Millett 1972: 31). This passage reveals the way in which Millett understood biology as referring to the sexed body (male or female) and ideology as referring to the masculine or feminine subject. Such an understanding fails to note the ways in which values are embedded in social practices that take the body as their target. The biology/ideology distinction treats 'value system[s]' in an idealist manner and so obscures the ways in which social values are embedded in bodies, not simply 'minds', a point to which I will return. Both the liberal and the Marxist analyses of society suffer from similar problems in relation to the study of women's socio-political status. The implicit theory of power held by both approaches is narrowly economic, which is inadequate in the context of women's historically tentative relation to the public sphere and wage-labour. This view of power is arguably suitable for an analysis of some aspects of men's socio-political lives, but inadequate when applied to women, or indeed in relation to other issues such as racial oppression.

Part of the problem here is the inability of both liberal and Marxist theory to address the issue of corporeal specificity in any terms other than those of biological 'facts' or ideology. Neither theory is able to think difference outside of the body/mind, fact/value or science/ideology distinctions. For example, these are precisely the terms in which the sex/gender distinction is couched. Sex concerns the body, facts and science (biology), whereas gender concerns the mind, values and ideology (conditioning).[7] Both theories are committed to a form of humanism which assumes a fundamental universality across history and across cultures in relation to the needs, capacities and 'nature' of the human being or the human body. This is, in part, an effect of assuming that bodies and their needs are a timeless part of nature. This puts the emphasis on the way in which the biologically given human being becomes a socially produced masculine or feminine subject. Since masculinity and femininity are conceived as psychological traits, their genesis and reproduction must be located at the level of the mind, values or ideology.

This approach to the issues of sexual difference, power and domination is not able to consider the ways in which power differentially *constitutes* particular kinds of body and empowers them to perform particular kinds of task, thus constructing specific kinds of subject. Put differently, one could argue that gender is a material effect of the way in which power takes hold of the body rather than an ideological effect of the way power 'conditions' the mind. To make this kind of claim would involve using quite a different notion of power and the body than that used in dominant socio-political theories.

Perhaps the most prominent exponent of this alternative account of power is Michel Foucault. He stresses that dominant accounts of power tend to conceive power on the model of repression, where power is reduced to that which says 'No' (Foucault 1978). Foucault's work has concentrated on the body–power relation and on the discourses and practices which he takes to involve productive operations of power. This is not to say that he disavows the existence, or indeed the importance, of state power or repressive state practices. Rather, it is to say that his work seeks to emphasize the less spectacular but more insidious forms of power. Moreover, these non-repressive forms of power cannot be adequately captured by the notion of ideology. He summarizes his reservations concerning the utility of the term ideology in three points:

> [first], like it or not, it always stands in virtual opposition to something else which is supposed to count as truth. Now I believe that the problem does not consist in drawing the line between that in a discourse which falls under the category of scientificity or truth, and that which comes under some other category, but in seeing historically how effects of truth are produced within discourses which in themselves are neither true nor false. The second drawback is that the concept of ideology refers, I think necessarily, to something of the order of a subject. Thirdly, ideology stands in a secondary position relative to something which functions as its infrastructure, as its material, economic determinant.
>
> (Foucault 1980a: 118)

Foucault's reservations about the concept of ideology overlap in an interesting way with the reservations which have been expressed here concerning the utility of Marxist and liberal socio-political theories to the situation of women. First, the science/ideology distinction has been relied upon in understanding women's oppression as linked to a patriarchal value-system which constructs gendered subjects, while the 'truth' of the sex of woman is to be determined by the scientific discourse of biology. Second, the notion that gender is a social addition to the human subject is coherent only on the condition that human subjects pre-exist their social contexts. Finally, the limitation in viewing patriarchy as operating primarily by ideological means is that it assumes that the determinant infrastructure of society is economic. For these reasons, the Foucauldian approach to the micro-politics of power is particularly appropriate to an investigation of the ways in which power and domination operate in relation to sexual difference.

One of the main benefits of Foucault's approach is that its emphasis on the body allows one to consider not simply how discourses and practices create ideologically appropriate subjects but also how these practices construct certain sorts of body with particular kinds of power and capacity; that is, how bodies are turned into individuals of various kinds (Foucault 1980a: 98). In short, it allows an analysis of the productiveness of power as well as its repressive functions. From this perspective one might also begin to appreciate how it may well make sense to speak of the body as having a history.

The body

There is probably no simple explanation for the recent proliferation of writings concerning the body. Clearly, Foucault's work has been influential in making the body a favoured subject for analysis in contemporary philosophy, sociology and anthropology. However, the impact of feminist theory on the social sciences has no less a claim to credit for bringing the body into the limelight. The difficulties encountered by primarily middle-class women, who have had the greatest access to 'equality' in the public sphere, may well have served as a catalyst for feminist reflections on the body.

One response to the differential powers and capacities of women and men in the context of public life is to claim that women just are biologically disadvantaged relative to men. From this perspective it seems crucial to call for the further erosion of the reproductive differences between the sexes by way of advances in medical science. On this view, social reform can only achieve so much, leaving the rectification of the remaining determinations of women's situation to the increase in control over nature; that is, biology. Simone de Beauvoir retains the doubtful privilege of being the clearest exponent of this view. In the 1970s, Shulamith Firestone's *The Dialectic of Sex* was influential in perpetuating the view that science could fulfil a liberatory role for women (Firestone 1970). Both theorists assumed that the specificity of the reproductive body must be overcome if sexual equality is to be realized.

An alternative response to questions of corporeal specificity is to claim that women should not aspire to be 'like men'. Interestingly, this response comes from both feminists and anti-feminists alike.[8] Recent feminist research suggests that the history of western thought shows a deep hatred and fear of the body (Spelman 1982). This somatophobia is understood by some feminists to be specifically masculine and intimately related to gynophobia and misogyny (Daly 1978: 109–12). In response to this negative attitude towards the body and women, some feminists advocate the affirmation and celebration of women's bodies and their capacity to recreate and nurture. In its strongest form this view argues that the specific capacities and powers of women's bodies imply an essential difference between men and women, where women may be presented as essentially peace-loving, 'biophilic' or caring, and men as essentially aggressive, 'necrophilic' or selfish (Daly 1978: 61–2). These theorists argue that there is an essential sexual difference which should be retained, not eroded by scientific intervention.

These two responses to women's corporeal specificity are often taken to exhaust what has been termed the 'sexual equality versus sexual difference debate'. Yet both responses are caught up within the same paradigm. Both understand the body as a given biological entity which either has or does not have certain ahistorical characteristics and capacities. To this extent, the sexual difference versus sexual equality debate is located within a framework which assumes a body/mind, nature/culture dualism. The different responses are both in answer to the question of which should be given priority: the mind or the body, nature or culture.

An alternative view of the body and power might refuse this dualistic manner of articulating the issue of sexual difference. Specifically, to claim a history for the body involves taking seriously the ways in which diet, environment and the typical activities of a body may vary historically and create its capacities, its desires and its actual material form (Foucault 1977). The body of a woman confined to the role of wife/mother/domestic worker, for example, is invested with particular desires, capacities and forms that have little in common with the body of a female Olympic athlete. In this case biological commonality fails to account for the specificity of these two bodies. Indeed, the female Olympic athlete may have more in common with a male Olympic athlete than with a wife/mother. This commonality is not simply at the level of interests or desires but at the level of the actual form and capacities of the body. By drawing attention to the context in which bodies move and recreate themselves, we also draw attention to the complex dialectic between bodies and their environments. If the body is granted a history then traditional associations between the female body and the domestic sphere and the male body and the public sphere can be acknowledged as historical realities, which have historical effects, without resorting to biological essentialism. The present capacities of female bodies are, by and large, very different to the present capacities of male bodies. It is important to create the means of articulating the historical realities of sexual difference without thereby reifying these differences. Rather, what is required is an account of the ways in which the typical spheres of movement of men and women and their respective activities construct and recreate particular kinds of body to perform particular kinds of task. This sort of analysis is necessary if the historical effects of the ways in which power constructs bodies are to be understood and challenged (see Gallagher and Laqueur 1987).

This would involve not simply a study of how men and women become masculine and feminine subjects but how bodies become marked as male and female. Again, Foucault made this point well, arguing that what is needed is:

an analysis in which the biological and the historical are not consecutive to one another, as in the evolutionism of the first sociologists, but are bound together in an increasingly complex fashion in accordance with the development of the modern technologies of power that take life as their objective. Hence, I do not envisage a 'history of mentalities' that would take account of bodies only through the manner in which they have been perceived and given meaning and value; but a 'history of bodies' and the manner in which what is most material and most vital in them has been invested.

(Foucault 1978: 152)

Foucault's studies tend to concentrate on the history of the construction of male bodies and are not forthcoming on the question of sexual difference.[9] However, a critical use of psychoanalytic theory, in particular the theory of the body image, in conjunction with Foucault's analysis of power can provide some very useful insights in this context.

The works of Jacques Lacan, Maurice Merleau-Ponty and Paul Schilder offer an account of the body image which posits that a body is not properly a human body, that is, a human subject or individual, unless it has an image of itself as a discrete entity, or as a *gestalt* (Lacan 1953; Lacan 1977a; Merleau-Ponty 1964; and Schilder 1978). It is this orientation of one's body in space, and in relation to other bodies, that provides a perspective on the world and that is assumed in the constitution of the signifying subject. Lacan, in particular, presents the emergence of this *gestalt* as, in some sense, genetic. His famous 'Mirror Stage' paper, for example, offers ethological evidence for the identificatory effect produced by images and movements of others of the same species and even images and movements which merely *simulate* those of the species in question.[10] Lacan takes this 'homeomorphic identification' to be at the origin of an organism's orientation toward its own species. It would seem that it is this genetic basis to his account of the mirror stage that allows him, even while stressing the cultural specificity of body images, to assert the 'natural' dominance of the penis in the shaping of the *gestalt* (Lacan 1953: 13).

Foucault's historically dynamic account of the manner in which the micro-political operations of power produce socially appropriate bodies offers an alternative to Lacan's ethological account. Using Foucault's approach, the imaginary body can be posited as an effect of socially and historically specific practices: an effect, that is, not of genetics but of relations of power. It would be beside the point to insist that, none the less, this imaginary body is in fact the anatomical body overlaid by culture, since the anatomical body is itself a theoretical object for the discourse of anatomy which is produced by human beings in culture. There is a regress involved in positing the anatomical body as the touchstone for cultural bodies since it is a particular culture which chooses to represent bodies anatomically. Another culture might take the clan totem as the essence or truth of particular bodies. The human body is always a signified body and as such cannot be understood as a 'neutral object' upon which science may construct 'true' discourses. The *human* body and its history presuppose each other.

This conception of the imaginary body may provide the framework in which we can give an account of how power, domination and sexual difference intersect in the lived experience of men and women. Gender itself may be understood on this model not as the effect of ideology or cultural values but as the way in which power takes hold of and constructs bodies in particular ways. Significantly, the sexed body can no longer be conceived as the unproblematic biological and factual base upon which gender is inscribed, but must itself be recognized as constructed by discourses and practices that take the body both as their target and as their vehicle of expression. Power is not then reducible to what is imposed, from above, on naturally differentiated male and female bodies, but is also constitutive of those bodies, in so far as they are constituted as male and female.

Shifting the analysis of the operations of power to this micro-level of bodies and their powers and capacities has an interesting effect when one turns to a consideration of the political body. If we understand the masculinity or maleness of the political body and the public sphere as an *arbitrary* historical fact about the genesis of states, then sexual equality should be achievable provided we ensure that women have equal access to the political body and the public sphere. However, the relation between the public sphere and male bodies is not an arbitrary one. The political body was conceived historically as the organization of many bodies into one body which would itself enhance and intensify the powers and capacities of specifically male bodies.[11]

Female embodiment as it is currently lived is itself a barrier to women's 'equal' participation in socio-political life. Suppose our body politic were one which was created for the enhancement and intensification of women's historical and present capacities. The primary aim of such a body politic might be to foster conditions for the healthy reproduction of its members. If this were the case, then presumably some men would now be demanding that medical science provide ways for them to overcome their 'natural' or biological disadvantages, by inventing, for example, means by which they could lactate. This may seem a far-fetched suggestion, but it nevertheless makes the point that a biological disadvantage can be posited as such only in a cultural context.

Difference

The crux of the issue of difference as it is understood here is that difference does not have to do with biological 'facts' so much as with the manner in which culture marks bodies and creates specific conditions in which they live and recreate themselves. It is beside the point to 'grant' equal access to women and others excluded from the traditional body politic, since this amounts to 'granting' access to the body politic and the public sphere in terms of an individual's ability to emulate those powers and capacities that have, in a context of male/masculine privilege, been deemed valuable by that sphere. The present and future enhancement of the powers and capacities of women must take account of the ways in which their bodies are presently constituted.

Clearly, the sketch of power and bodies that has been offered here is not one which would lend itself to an understanding of sexual difference in terms of essentialism or biologism. The female body cannot provide the ontological foundation required by those who assert an essential sexual difference. On the contrary, it is the construction of biological discourse as being able to provide this status that is in need of analysis. The cluster of terms 'the female body', 'femininity' and 'woman' need to be analysed in terms of their historical and discursive associations. If discourses cannot be deemed as 'outside', or apart from, power relations then their analysis becomes crucial to an analysis of power. This is why language, signifying practices and discourses have become central stakes in feminist struggles.

Writing itself is a political issue and a political practice for many contemporary feminists. For this reason it is inappropriate to reduce the project of *écriture féminine* to an essentialist strategy. The 'difference' which this form of writing seeks to promote is a difference rooted not in biology but rather in discourse – including biological discourses. It is unhelpful to quibble over whether this writing is an attempt to write the 'female body' or to 'write femininity', since it is no longer clear what this distinction amounts to.[12] What is clear is that discourses, such as Lacanian psychoanalysis, and social practices, such as marriage, construct female and male bodies in ways that constitute and validate the power relations between men and women.

The account of female sexuality offered by Lacanian psychoanalysis constructs female bodies as lacking or castrated and male bodies as full or phallic. This construction tells of a power relation where the actual understanding of sexual difference implies a passive/active reaction. Writing of a sexuality that is not simply the inverse or the complement of male sexuality presents a discursive challenge to the traditional psychoanalytic understanding of sexual difference, where difference is exhausted by phallic presence or absence. Irigaray's writing of the 'two lips' of feminine morphology is an active engagement with the construction of what here has been called the imaginary body. It is not an attempt to construct a true theory of sexual difference, starting from the foundation of female biology. Rather, it is a challenge to the traditional construction of feminine morphology where the bodies of women are seen as receptacles for masculine completeness. At the same time as Irigaray's writing offers a challenge to traditional conceptions of women, it introduces the possibility of *dialogue* between men and women in place of the monological pronouncements made by men over the mute body of the (female) hysteric.[13]

Legal practices and discourses surrounding marriage also assume this conception of sexual difference by allotting conjugal rights to the (active) male over the body of the (passive) female. Significantly, the act which is taken to consummate marriage is legally defined as an act performed by a man on a woman. Needless to say, these legal, psychoanalytic and social understandings of the female body have been articulated from the perspective of male writers, who take it upon themselves to represent women, femaleness and femininity. From this perspective, it is not surprising that women are represented as pale shadows and incomplete complements to the more excellent type: 'man'. The project of *écriture féminine* involves challenging the masculine monopoly on the construction of femininity, the female body and woman. It also involves a rejection of the notion that there can be a theory of woman, for this would be to accept that woman is some (*one*) thing.

The works of Luce Irigaray, Hélène Cixous and Adrienne Rich are each in their own ways involved in investigating the manner in which women's bodies are constructed and lived in culture (Irigaray 1985a and 1985b; Cixous 1981; and Rich 1987). Each could be seen to be writing from an embodied perspective about the female body, femininity and women. Yet none of these writers claims to represent (all) women or the multiplicity of women's experiences. This would be for them to take up a masculine attitude in relation to other women. Significantly, all three writers critically address the dualisms which have dominated western thought. Addressing constructions of the feminine in history necessarily involves addressing those terms which have been associated with femininity: the body, emotion and so on. When Irigaray, for example, writes of the 'repression of the feminine', she is also alluding to the repression of the body and passion in western thought. To attempt to 'write' the repressed side of these dualisms is not, necessarily, to be working for the reversal of the traditional values associated with each but rather to unbalance or disarrange the discourses in which these dualisms operate. It is to create new conditions for the articulation of difference.

To understand 'difference feminism' as the obverse of 'equality feminism' would be to miss entirely the point of this essay. Difference, as it has been presented here, is not concerned with privileging an essentially biological difference between the sexes. Rather, it is concerned with the mechanisms by which bodies are recognized as different only in so far as they are constructed as possessing or lacking some socially privileged quality or qualities. What is crucial in our current context is the thorough interrogation of the means by which bodies become invested with differences which are then taken to be fundamental ontological differences. Differences as well as commonality must be respected among those who have historically been excluded from speech/writing and are now struggling for expression. If bodies and their powers and capacities are invested in multiple ways, then accordingly their struggles will be multiple.

The conception of difference offered here is not one which seeks to construct a dualistic theory of an essential sexual difference. Rather, it entertains a multiplicity of differences. To insist on sexual difference as the fundamental and eternally immutable difference would be to take for granted the intricate and pervasive ways in which patriarchal culture has made that difference its insignia.

NOTES

1 An excellent collection of essays which offers an overview of feminist perspectives on political theory from Plato to Habermas is Shanley and Pateman 1991.

2 See Lloyd 1984, Grimshaw 1986, especially chapter 2, and Le Doeuff 1989.

3 S. Moller Okin's critique of John Rawls' influential *A Theory of Justice* provides a good example of this approach (Moller Okin 1991).

4 For example, Andrea Dworkin has stated 'I think that the situation of women is basically ahistorical' (Pateman 1989, 236).

5 I have used a Spinozistic approach in 'Towards a Feminist Philosophy of the Body' (Gatens 1988). More recently, G. Lloyd has used Spinoza's monist theory of existence to appraise the sex/gender distinction critically in 'Woman as Other: Sex, Gender and Subjectivity' (Lloyd 1989).

6 I have argued against the possibility of including women in liberal society, *on an equal footing with men*, in Gatens 1991a esp. ch. 2.

7 For a discussion of the difficulties involved in the sex/gender distinction see Gatens 1983.

8 For an example of the former, see Daly 1978, and for one of the latter, see McMillan 1982.

9 For a sympathetic feminist reading of Foucault's work, see Sawicki 1991.

10 Lacan writes:

it is a necessary condition for the maturation of the gonad of the female pigeon that it should see another member of its species, of either sex; so sufficient in itself is this condition that the desired effect may be obtained merely by placing the individual within reach of the field of reflection of a mirror. Similarly, in the case of the migratory locust, the transition within a generation from the solitary to the gregarious form can be obtained by exposing the individual at a certain stage, to the exclusively visual action of a similar image, provided it is animated by movements of a style sufficiently close to that characteristic of the species.

(Lacan 1977b: 3)

11 For a recent feminist account of the aims of the masculine political body, see Pateman 1989, ch. 4; and Gatens 1991b.

12 See, for example, Toril Moi's arguments in *Sexual/Textual Politics*
(Moi 1985: 102–26), which misunderstand the conception of difference being employed by Cixous.

13 See, for example, the writings of Freud and Breuer on hysteria and femininity in Freud 1974.

18

THE SOCIAL WORLD OF
PREHISTORIC FACTS[*]
Gender and Power in Paleoindian Research

JOAN M. GERO

At the very heart of feminist scholarship is the visionary argument that modern arrangements – in human relationships as well as in scientific understandings – might be radically otherwise. Feminist scholars in all scientific fields must contend not only with the systematic exclusion of women from systems of knowledge, but also with a myth of science as rational and transparent. As long as we consider that the making of an item of knowledge emerges directly out of natural reality, we stipulate the grounds for universal and irrevocable assent (Shapin and Schaffer 1985: 23). But if we can identify the role of human agency in the making of knowledge, we identify the possibility that we – as women – and we as scientists – today could know other things in new ways. This chapter explores the historic and contemporary boundaries that are in place in the organisation of scientific knowledge in general, and of archaeological knowledge in particular, to clarify the role that gender ideology has played in erecting taken-for-granted paradigms, and to show that at least some of the historical judgements that have accumulated to produce archaeological 'facts' are not truly self-evident or inevitable.

I take as my study case the North American Paleoindians, a set of widely known and firmly documented archaeological events (actually, among the best-known and most widely accepted archaeological events in North American prehistory), in order to account for their foundational assumptions and their organisational structure in gendered social terms. I shall want to demonstrate that the 'facts' about Paleoindians, the adequacy and objectivity of the knowledge claims we make about them, might be better seen as pragmatic decisions of a scholarly moment, as historical events unfolding in a series, as actors' judgements within a particular social and political context. Following Shapin and Schaffer (1985: 15), this will go a long way towards demonstrating how the solutions to these particular knowledge problems are embedded within solutions to the more general problems of social order . . . including gender.

---

[*]First published in H. Du Cros and L. J. Smith (eds) (1993), *Women in Archaeology: A Feminist Critique*, Canberra: Australian National University.

In order to look at the social – and engendered – world of prehistoric fact, then, this chapter will review the 'constructivist' model of how knowledge is produced. Following this, I draw out the historic implications of the constructivist position, arguing that, perhaps especially in archaeology, the strongly localised, craft-like aspects of scientific practice, coupled with the literary and social conventions that accompany scientific convergence, account for much of what is acknowledged as knowledge. Finally, I turn to the archaeological knowledge of Paleoindians in engendered, historised, constructivist terms.

A non-discovery model of knowledge, or knowledge as creative construction

Let me begin, then, by repeating Karin Knorr-Cetina's epilogue, quoting Dorothy Sayers: 'My lord, facts are like cows. If you look them in the face hard enough, they generally run away' (Knorr-Cetina 1981: 1):

> Dorothy Sayers' analogy between cows and facts [contains] both a philosophical and a methodological point . . . The philosophical point is that their nature is rather problematic – so much so that confrontation often scares them off. The methodological point is that the confrontation has to be long, hard and direct. Like cows, facts have become sufficiently domesticated to deal with run–of–the–mill events.
>
> (Knorr-Cetina 1981: 1)

Most models of how-science-is-done operate with an idea of scientists using various strategies and devices in order to pull back some sort of curtain on pregiven truths which had been previously concealed (Latour and Woolgar 1979: 129). Scientists themselves, in fact, employ language that conveys the misleading impression that the presence of objects, facts, sometimes even laws, are pregivens, and that such facts and laws merely await the timely revelation of their existence by scientists (Latour and Woolgar 1979: 128). Archaeology is particularly prone to an objectivist 'discovery' view of science because, quite apart from the relational facts and conceptual objects we produce, a large part of our *data* is often underground, literally covered up, and we must in fact UN-cover it up, or DIS-cover it up. Thus, archaeologists intuitively believe that they 'discover' knowledge even more directly than scientists in other fields.

In the constructivist view, however, science is not about discovery but about creativity and construction (Latour and Woolgar 1979: 129), about making order out of disorder, about finding the right statements that reduce noise in data, about chains of decisions and negotiations and selections that can only be made on the basis of previous selections (Knorr-Cetina 1981: 5). In this view, science is highly internally structured through the process of production, rather than being descriptive of a disarticulated, external reality.

In the words of Latour and Woolgar (1979: 170), 'having an idea represents a summary of a complicated material situation' and results from a particular historical sequence of events and interpersonal exchanges. Facts themselves are not simply recorded as they are observed; they are crafted out of a welter of confusing and conflicting observations, modified and reformulated out of knowledge of what other scientists are working on, and accepted more readily if their proponent is well credentialed. Once a 'fact' is arrived at, it is quickly freed from the circumstances of its production and loses all historical reference to the social and contextual conditions of its construction (Latour and Woolgar 1979: 106). Thus, the processes that account for and produce scientific facts or knowledge are always invisible since practitioners themselves use language and concepts as though the knowledge they produce had no history, no social-life, no culture . . . and no *gender*.

To view scientific investigation as constructive rather than descriptive, and to see scientific products – knowledge – as highly internally constructed in terms of the selectivity it incorporates (Knorr-Cetina 1981: 7) presents a serious challenge to an objectivist view of science. It has led to a research program that observes science close at hand, demystifying the 'facticity' of science and calling into question other scientific claims. For example, the constructivists' sociology of science gives grounds to doubt the purported independence of discovery and validation which is a prime feature of mature science. Observing science close at hand shows that the 'discovery' or fact production phase of research is actually inseparable from the validatior phase: in practice, scientists constantly relate their decisions and selections to the expected responses of specific members of the community of 'validators' (their colleagues), or to the dictates of the journals in which they wish to publish. That is, discoveries are made with a very explicit eye toward potential criticism or acceptance, as well as with respect to potential allies and enemies (Knorr-Cetina 1981: 7) and do not set out neutral propositions to be assessed independently by supposedly non-interested 'other' parties. In a similar vein, constructivist science questions the effectiveness of science to filter out bias and self-regulate truth claims, recognising that admission into, and on-going practice within, the scientific 'community' directly depends on adopting and embracing that same 'community's' starting assumptions, its research agenda, its accepted methodologies and its standards. Thus, the truth-testing system is at once closed, internally structured to insure compatibility, and self-serving.

The constructivist view of science, then, rejects the individualism and the spontaneity of discovery. It emphasises instead two different kinds of contingencies: first, historical contingency (or what Haraway [1988: 596] calls:

> the railroad industry of epistemology, where facts can only be made to run on the tracks laid down from [paradigmatic early work] out, and those who control the railroads control the surrounding territory).

Second, it emphasises social or relational contingency, where the self-serving, internally-related community of knowledge-makers forecloses the very universality and transparency that science is said to embody. To understand the archaeological community of knowledge-makers in constructivist terms offers us the possibility of insights into the profoundly androcentric boundaries of present-day prehistoric knowledge, the privileged position of specific research priorities and theoretical frameworks, and indeed the very 'facts' of prehistory. Let us look now to one very charged arena of prehistoric research, the Paleoindian construct, to see what it indicates about gender in the social world of prehistoric fact.

Introduction to Paleoindian studies
Paleoindian research, still widely known as 'Early Man' studies (for example, Lynch 1990) focuses on the aboriginal colonising and the earliest occupation of the

American continent, including routes and dates of the first migrations from Asia, environmental features to which these earliest colonisers adapted, and the technology and means of subsistence that characterised the earliest American lifeways. As a research niche, Paleoindian studies stand out as particularly circumscribed within a closely interactive group of scholars contained by boundaries of specialised journals dedicated solely to Paleoindian research (for example, *The Mammoth Trumpet*, or *Current Research in the Pleistocene*, or the short-lived *Megafauna Punchers' Review*). Paleoindian research is featured in high profile sessions at national conferences, frequent lead articles in prestigious archaeology journals, and a remarkable number of monographs and edited volumes devoted exclusively to this single chapter of 'Man's' past.[1] Not only is 'Early Man' highly contained and intensively pursued, but he is very well funded and enjoys perhaps the highest research status of any investigatory niche in North American prehistory.

Amazingly, or perhaps predictably, women are almost invisible in 'Early Man' research, both as subjects and as objects of research. Almost any measure reflects this systematic bias; for instance, 17 of the 18 major Paleoindian books that have appeared between 1965 and 1990 were written or edited by males . . . or pairs of males. Of the 140 articles contained in the nine edited volumes among these, only 14 (10%) are single-authored by women while 115 (or 89%) have male authors. *American Antiquity* articles that treat Pleistocene megafauna (elk, caribou, mammoth and mastodon) are exclusively written by males. Conference papers delivered in Paleoindian sessions over the past 13 years at the national meetings of the Society for American Archaeology, combined with papers from the regional Plains Anthropology meetings (known for a heavy focus on Paleoindian research) show a similar distribution: women delivered only 11 per cent of these[2] and are over-represented in the contributed sessions as opposed to the invited symposia.[3]

The Paleoindian literature thus presents a dramatic opportunity to understand the historical, theoretical and social relationships that function so centrally in determining the construction of archaeological knowledge in its androcentric form. It is here that we can start to unravel the technological, the literary and the social practices that are essential to success for research practitioners, the various arrangements and moral sensibilities that apply among these archaeologists, the historical events and contingent interpretations that manifest practical scientific solutions to larger economic and political problems (Shapin 1989: 562).

The establishment of an antiquity for 'man' in the New World that goes back at least 10,000 years (that is, back into the Pleistocene or Ice Ages) has an almost canonical character in the history of American archaeology (Wormington 1957; Wilmsen 1965, 1974; Mounier 1972; Meltzer 1983). Following a bitter controversy which lasted several see-sawing decades of professional dispute, a discovery was made in 1926 that 'was to have the most far-reaching effects on the course of American archaeology' (Wormington 1957: 23). Eight miles west of the little town of Folsom, New Mexico, on a small tributary of the Cimarron River, a party of palaeontologists from the Colorado Museum of Natural History recovered bones of a type of fossil bison believed to have been extinct for thousands of years (ibid.). Digging through 13 feet of clay and gravel, several pieces of worked flint artefacts were recovered in direct association with articulated bones, and two of these stone fragments could be fitted together to form the readily distinguishable part of a projectile point: leaf-shaped with a concave base and ear-like projections, evidence of grinding along the lower edges and base, pressure naked on the blade portion and, most significantly, characterised by the removal of the classic grooved or channel flake on both faces of the artefact. It required another two seasons of excavations, however, and the total recovery of 19 of the same distinctive artefact type from the undisturbed Pleistocene matrix, before the last hold-outs admitted that 'the men who had flaked the weapon points were contemporaries of the extinct bison' (Wormington 1957: 25; also Meltzer 1983: 35). The Folsom finds, credited to the director of excavation – J. D. Figgins, were considered unequivocable: 'For once in the long battle over the antiquity of man, the archaeological record had played fair, and the evidence was clear' says one modern commentary (Meltzer 1983: 38). And, in the hindsighted words of a senior practitioner, 'everybody breathed a sigh of relief that finally what had been supported was proven' (E. Haury, cited in Meltzer 1983: 38).

A deliberate effort to recover a larger sample of Folsom points spread quickly and was rapidly rewarded; the continued association of Folsom points with extinct bison stood up in every excavated occurrence, and they never occurred with a still existing faunal assemblage (Wormington 1957: 29). More ambitiously, the subsequent work in the late 1920s included a search for new classes of evidence: Folsom habitation areas that would yield a larger tool inventory than the bison-killing projectile points, and longer, deeper stratigraphic columns in which the relationship of Folsom materials to other types of tools could be established. Success on both counts was achieved in the 1934 excavations carried out at Lindenmeier (Roberts 1935); several thousand stone artefacts were recovered, including newly noted variations within the Folsom forms, a great many knives, scrapers of different forms and spokeshaves. 'All of these objects must have been useful in important activities such as shaping shafts for weapons, butchering animals, and preparing hides', says Wormington (1957: 35), still focusing exclusively on the meat and game of Paleo existence. But there is no comment on the function of the 'non-distinctive' artefact types; what do we make of the rubbing stones with red stains, ground cores of hematite, the bead and the carved bone disk? The question begins to form: might there have been more to Paleo life?

It was at Blackwater Draw, in 1933 and later in 1949–50, that a second distinctive fluted point type – the Clovis – was recovered below the now easily recognised Folsom varieties. Longer and more parallel-sided, these points exhibit less invasive channel flaking and lack the basal ears of the Folsom type. Subsequently, a variety of Folsom and Folsom-like, as well as other kinds of fluted points were reported throughout the high plains region and along both the eastern and western slopes of the Rocky Mountains, giving rise to a confusing nomenclature and classificatory arguments until a 1941 conference in Santa Fe resolved much of this debate by dropping the 'Folsom-like', 'Folsomoid' and 'Generalised Folsom' terms. All points showing fluting or grooving on one or more faces were referred to as 'Fluted' while 'Folsom' and 'Clovis' were retained only for the classic types. Although Folsom points have not proved to be the oldest of the Paleoindian artefact types,[4] because they were the first to be recognised as of Pleistocene age they emerged as a point of reference,

Figure 18.1 '*Men hunting game' is taken as the central fact of Paleoindian life.*
Courtesy of Canadian Museum of Civilization, Hull, Québec. Image no. S98–10743.

with other distinctive Paleoindian cultural materials described as younger than or older than Folsom, and noted geographically in relation to the Folsom area. Bison, together with mammoth, remained the dietary datum, and paleoman was fixed in time, space, occupation . . . and gender.

From these foundational beginnings, Paleoindian studies have converged with extraordinary single-mindedness on an uncontested (or perhaps only very recently questioned) research construct. In Gordon Willey's words:

> the big-game pursuit is the most characteristic and diagnostic feature of the culture shared by these particular early Americans. There can be no question that it was an activity of great and, probably, primary importance. Viewed in the perspective of all of pre-Columbian New World history, it imparted a design, a style to their lives
>
> (Willey 1966: 38)

Paleoindians, as specialised and vastly successful big-game hunters, expanded to fill the continent within a short period of economic bliss. Sites with fluted points or related paleo materials were identified from all the 50 United States as well as from southern Alberta, Saskatchewan, Manitoba, Ontario, Nova Scotia, and even the Northwest Territories. Although opinions vary still on the precise location of the origin of this technological hunting innovation, there is widespread consensus that the distinctive lanceolot fluted point, invented on the American continent, was responsible for – or at least intimately involved with – the success of Early Man, the Paleoindian Hunter. No wonder that these artefacts are centre-fold, pin-up displays in so many books on prehistory.

The Paleoindian period ends, then, when the fluted point and a few associated point types disappear from the archaeological record. Paleoindians 'evaporate' (in Marie Wormington's words) with a thoroughness that makes it hard to believe in even the biological, much less the cultural, continuity of humans in America. Without the fluted point there is no Paleoindian, and the construct falls off with a clarity of boundary. The historical contingency of the Paleoindian construction now begins to become clear: before the use of radiocarbon dating, the nature of evidence that might be used to demonstrate human presence in a Pleistocene America was limited. In fact, the identification of diagnostic Paleoindian markers could only be verified as 'early' by direct and incontestable association with extinct Pleistocene life forms. In its historic context, the equation of Early Man with hunting big game was integral, essential and convergent on proving 'man' early. Associated from the start with hunting big-game, Early MAN could only be a big-game hunter, with all the ideological loading that that entailed . . . and all that it left out: women!

Furthermore, the elegant simplicity of a widely distributed and distinctive tool leads easily to a conflation of variability into a single Fluted point tradition, one that was only occasionally and roughly sorted by time and space and that conflated the western high Plains materials with early materials everywhere. In one of the earliest reports on Paleoindian materials from eastern North America, for instance, William Ritchie (1953) reviewed a substantial amount of data from the Reagan Site in Vermont and concluded that all except one of his trait categories 'have parallels in sites attributable to the Paleo-Indian in various parts of the United States' (Ritchie 1953: 251). Indeed, types are described as having 'characteristically convex' edges as well as bases that are 'concave as usual' (Ritchie 1953: 253), underscoring the comparisons to materials from the Plains. A set of weak 'single shouldered knives' are made to correspond to two types of the well known 'Sandia' points, and Ritchie concludes that Reagan:

> is unequivocally linked to that large constituent of early man sites characterised by a fluted point tradition . . . it appears to represent another variation, in a new locality, on a basic theme which . . . suggests . . . widely disseminated parallel developments . . .
>
> (Ritchie 1953: 255)

Why this insistence on the 'likenesses outweigh[ing] the differences, both as respects typology and technology, in end and side scrapers, flake knives, gravers and combinations thereof'? Shouldn't we expect the differences to be seized upon as temporal and spatial markers, to increase the discriminations in paleo-dispersals and adaptations? And why dismiss the very intriguing engraved ground-stone pendants from Reagan, which clearly have no parallels in the Plains materials? The real question is, then: why has the Paleoindian construct been overlaid in eastern North America instead of viewing the at-least-partially distinct fluted materials as the earliest manifestations in a distinct regional sequence?

What has been created in this flattening process, significantly, has been a national paradigm. The constructed universality of the Paleo-phenomenon, despite the lack of a fine-grained chronology, provided the classic origin story for all American peoples that the almost exclusively male-archaeologists could study everywhere in the country.

Constructed not locally but nationally, Paleo-man is an earliest common denominator, a base-line of American technological prowess and ecological efficiency.

It is entirely logical, within this model, that Paleoindian research has concentrated and still concentrates on modes of dispatching Pleistocene fauna, as well as on the ecological, climatic and geomorphological reconstructions of the Paleo-environment: what was available to eat back then, and how was it taken? The point is well illustrated by reviewing the content categories of the recent Paleoindian journal *Current Research in the Pleistocene*, founded in 1983, which circumscribes research areas thus: appearing first in every issue is: 'Archaeology' (which reviews recent field results); then, 'Lithic Studies' (descriptions of distinctive industries, modes of tool manufacture – especially production and resharpening sequences, distinctive flint-knapping styles and hafting techniques, patterns of tool breakage upon impact, and sources of raw stone used for tool production, with implications for quarrying behaviour); 'Methods' (statistical as well as high-tech investigatory innovations); 'Taphonomy-Bone Modification' (these include counts of butchered individual animals, age distributions and the seasonality of killings, or differential distributions of animal parts at sites). Then there are 'Paleoenvironments: Plants'; 'Paleoenvironments: Invertebrates'; 'Paleoenvironments: Vertebrates'; and 'Paleoenvironments: Geosciences'. What we get is a natural environment and the taking of food from it; males studying what ancient men might have done – but even such narrowly empirical and accessible questions such as how this food was prepared are ignored. Continental expansion is never translated into frequently pregnant women carrying out productive and reproductive activities, and the social, engendered world of which eating megafauna meat must have been only a tiny part is utterly absent.

Gender as a factor in Paleoindian research

How, then, could Paleoindian studies be otherwise? And, most urgently, why are women archaeologists and women Paleoindians so depressingly and distortedly under-represented in this research? The persistence of Paleo-man, and persist he does!, throws us back to constructivist notions of science. How has the railroad industry of epistemology kept Paleoindian facts running on these same tracks for 60 years, up to and including two very prominent 1990 publications on the big-game hunting of Paleo-man? To understand this is to come to grips with the structure of the modern research community, with its divisions of labour, its hierarchies and its gendered social world. It is also to understand in what ways successful practitioners of research are forced to follow precedent and paradigm in specific technological, social and literary practices defined as central to the research endeavour. I take these, loosely, one by one: the technological, social and literary practices of research.

The technological practices demanded in paleo research involve producing, or gaining access to, previously unknown and unexamined Paleoindian material. Researchers need a data base, the 'means of production', and this presents an especially critical challenge in paleo-practice, where a central problem domain is defined by the challenges of fieldwork, marked by deeply buried components and complex stratigraphic displacements. It is here – in the field – that the most fundamental access to knowledge production is allowed, and, as my earlier research already showed, a division of labour in archaeology heavily biases fieldwork as a male domain (Gero

1983, 1985, 1988). Women are not supported in archaeology for directing fieldwork projects but are heavily concentrated in non-field oriented (analytic) projects. Indeed, women are systematically excluded at the level of field project funding (Yellen 1983, nd.), receiving both fewer and smaller grants for field projects than do their male counterparts. Males do fieldwork and in Paleoindian research, they do even more of it: 93 per cent of it during the late 1980s![5] Not surprisingly, male researchers have made the field male by elevating the field component, or data collection, to a position of greater value than the production of new understandings.

If we turn to the social practices of paleo research, the social relations of paleo research practice, we are tempted to pose the question another way. Do women archaeologists participate fully and equally in a broad spectrum of research events, or do women archaeologists construct a different kind of knowledge – or construct knowledge by a different process – than male archaeologists? Do women identify, construct and put forward different facts, and by different conventions of interaction and assertion, than men? And finding differences, what do such differences tell us about the version of paleo prehistory that we have gotten so used to hearing?

To pursue this, I need to step back from Paleoindians for a moment (since the number of women involved in paleo research is too limited), and see what women do in related archaeological research niches. Let me start with lithic analysis, an area central to paleo research and one in which a relatively large number of women archaeologists have built reputations and made significant contributions, but also one in which women evidently fail to make significant contributions in paleo circles. A careful inspection of what is done and who does it reveals that studies under-taken by women are not representative of the full range of interests in lithics, and entire areas of modern lithic studies include virtually no women investigators at all. Flint knapping, for instance, where archaeologists demonstrate ancient lithic production techniques, is exclusively an area in which males publish (see Gero 1991a), and we note that the tools replicated by modern (male) flint knappers concentrate exclusively on a narrow range of standardised tool forms dominated by the projectile point (and, most importantly, we note that the single most frequently replicated point in North American research is the fluted point!); beyond these, only a small suite of other elaborately retouched or heavily worked kinds of knives, core and blade technologies, polished celts and axes are reproduced by males.

It is also *exclusively* male archaeologists who experimentally *use* these replicated, standardised tools in modern, analogical activities, with an overwhelming emphasis on exaggeratedly 'male' activities: felling trees, making bows or arrows, hunting, spear throwing, butchering – and note particularly the research on throwing projectiles into, and carving up, modern analogs to big game – mostly elephants or rhinos – to translate male researchers directly into Pleistocene hunters. It is fascinating – or embarrassing – to observe the very fine line between male replicative science and macho-drama; shooting arrows into newly killed and (very importantly!) still warm boar strung up in wooden frames (Fischer *et al.* 1984), illustrates a particularly lurid kind of research design in which only males participate.

In contrast to the male-dominated areas of lithic studies, a very different line of investigation asks how tasks were carried out with stone tools. And it is female investigators who, in disproportionate and very over-representative numbers, have worked from a functional perspective to study expedient, non-standardised tools, at the level of micro-wear analysis, macro-wear analysis, or by means of studying the composition of assemblages (Gero 1991a). In fact, women represent a full 50 per cent of the research in micro-wear studies, although women account for only 20 per cent of the fully-employed research community in North America. Moreover, in contrast to males' experimental programs, women's replicative lithic studies focus on nutting (Spears 1975), leather-working (Adams 1988) and woodworking (Price-Beggerly 1976), all of which are done with modern analogs of unelaborated and non-standardised stone tools. 'Male' lithics focus on arrowheads and spearpoints, axes and adzes, while 'female' lithics are (non-diagnostic) flake tools and nutting stones. Since the assumption has been that fluted points *are* what is paleo, and since we 'know' what they're used for, and because, in fact, microwear analysis is not conveniently conducted on highly retouched tool edges, neither women's research concentration on micro-wear nor the emphasis of women's research on non-standardised tool forms is admitted as an area of interest in Paleoindian research, and women are again invisible here, as lithics analysts.

At the same time, the professional, colleaguial networks that are in place to share research interests and results operate to segregate males and females in their distinct arenas. This point is made clear by comparing general collected volumes on lithic studies edited by females (two volumes, edited by Robin Torrence [1989] and Susan Vehik [1985]) and by males (five volumes, edited by one or two males, from 1976–89). With women editors, an average of 39 per cent of the contributors are women, whereas in volumes edited by males, women overall average only 14 per cent of the contributors. Clearly, women's work is recognised and given venue when women edit volumes, and since they do not edit volumes of paleo research, their lithic studies have no support.

A similar pattern of exclusion is found in faunal analysis. We have already noted that women archaeologists are almost entirely invisible in the 'Big Bone Circle' of Pleistocene mammals: males entirely dominate studies of bison, mammoth, mastodon, caribou and elk. In contrast, women's contributions in faunal research lie in the identification of diversity among large numbers of species in assemblages, or in assessing MNI's. Like the concentration on flake tools, this work goes beyond the mere production of recognisable paleo-data, the bringing home of paleo-bacon, to involve the more painstaking study of large assemblages of minimally distinguishable elements. This division, too, ramifies into larger knowledge constructs: big-game hunting, considered among the 'great events of prehistory' is privileged as a central *all-male* activity. Reconstructions of Pleistocene hunting, with all the awe and reverence ascribed them, then create a high-prestige research niche for studying events from which women are excluded, prehistorically and in contemporary research. Women are reaffirmed as secondary citizens, in the past for not being hunters, and in the present, as archaeologists, for being outside the 'Big Bone Circle'. Women's exclusion from Pleistocene lithic and faunal analysis, then, is intrinsic to, and necessary for, the bison-mammoth knowledge construct. It is brought about by preselected, pre-erected, anticipatory, paradigmatic constructs that are supported by gender separations, by sociological gender-influenced networking in the formation of research groups, and finally by the manipulation and practice of power extensions in knowledge construction. The material symbols of Early Man, the fluted points and the big-bone recoveries, are socially made, socially maintained, and socially reproduced.

Finally, I want briefly to refer to the essential literary practices that also structure and keep Paleo-Man 'on track.' It is the reiteration of credibility in research that opens up fieldwork opportunities and offers technological and social access. In scientific knowledge-building, credibility is amassed by having work cited, and it will come as no surprise, here, that women in paleo studies, as part of a wider and more general pattern of citations in anthropology (Lutz 1990), are cited much less frequently than their male counterparts.

Consider that we have very few women paleo researchers to follow up on here. Our almost lone heroine for North American paleo field research, Eileen Johnson, has been cited only two and three times respectively for her singly authored pieces in the 1978 and 1980 volumes of the *Plains Anthropologist*. In contrast, comparable site data reported in the same journal by Dennis Stanford in 1978 and by Joe Ben Wheat in 1979, are cited eight and nine times respectively. Note too that Eileen Johnson's two co-authored pieces, with [male] Vance Holliday (in the same journal), dated 1980 and 1981, are cited eleven times and seven times. Finally, note too that Eileen Johnson's non-Paleoindian publications, on taphonomy and faunal analysis techniques, are frequently cited.

Literary practices, of course, go much deeper in the knowledge production process. The text of Paleoindian archaeological reports is expected to conform, not only to the basic narrative style demanded of all archaeological writing: (project goals, background research, project area, methodology, analysis, conclusions), but also to the specific vocabulary associated with this research paradigm. It is not just fad or fashion to use the right 'buzzwords'; this vocabulary provides strong demonstration that authors accept and will maintain the categorical boundaries that these terms set out, as well as the pre-selected knowledge constructions that underlie them. In many cases, the real significance of using the 'right word' is as what is called 'a speech act'; it provides a point of entry for disciplinary members into a domain of discourse that corresponds with practical requirements of their work: Paleoindian stone tool edges, for instance, are 'loaded' as in 'a sudden loading of weight from impact onto tool edges . . .' (Shea 1988), not because this is a better, more precise or more concise word for forceful exertions of pressure, but because 'loading' implicitly refers back to the mechanical robots that are often used in experimental designs to standardise force sustained by a replicated tool edge. We can, of course, follow out the gender implications of such speech acts in authorising and legitimating one's text; women may be less comfortable with this distancing or with this experimentation and select a more immediate and descriptive phrase, although I have yet to test this against a strong textual analysis of paleo writing.

Assertive arguments are made unequivocally, with active verbs and power-laden vocabularies. They are amply illustrated with symbols of the authors' technological power in archaeological production: the photographs, or, more often, drawings of fluted points with their significant channel scars deliberately forefronted. We might well question why the preponderance of the paleo literature is illustrated by always another fluted point: what purpose is served beyond symbolic testimony to The Boys' Club? Again and again, these literary, semantic and symbolic features characterise the paleo literature, written by males in a male syntax with male words.

Conclusion

So, what can we say by way of a conclusion here? It is evident in Paleoindian research, and indeed probably in many scientific areas of knowledge construction, that the research is carried forward by an agreed upon set of practices recommended to practitioners as important constitutive elements in the making of matters of fact, and in protecting such facts from discord and conflict. In paleo research, the technological, social and literary practices all function to reiterate and reproduce a gender/sex system that represents a complex mix of gender ideology, gender sociology and gender politics, and that represents a political solution to a knowledge problem.

The process of knowledge production as an engendered activity is, of course, amenable to analysis at different levels of organisational scale. At the extremely 'close-up' level, we might observe how the fine-grained, localised, deeply contextualised, heterogeneous and idiosyncratic constraints experienced by individual researchers, the particular encouragements and offers of research aid, the disapprovingly raised eyebrow at an interpretative solution, all play themselves out daily as part of the scientific and engendered conditioning of practice. At the same time and at the other end of the organisational range, much larger patterns are visible: note, for example, that the virtual exclusion of women in deep prehistory is matched by a full 50 per cent inclusion of women in historic archaeology in North America. Why are women allowed to play in the shallow pits of the past but not to penetrate the more limited resources of early time?

The intolerable part of this scenario is not that the sexual division of labour in research produces a sexual division of knowledge. Rather, what is intolerable is the recognition that a sexual division of labour is actually a hierarchy of labour, part of a shift toward a new scientific mode of commodity production where the products of women's analysis can never accumulate into power-laden constructs such as paleo-MAN. Female and male 'facts' are unequal in status, and the facts that have mattered in archaeology, in science, originate with men because, as Marx and Engels wrote, 'the ideas of the ruling class are in every epoch the ruling ideas'.

The perplexing part of this scenario is whether and how it can continue to operate. How long can men researchers insist on the centrality of bison and Pleistocene mammals in paleo life, to the exclusion of virtually all other social and cultural experiences? Or on defining the category of 'tools' on the basis of the small fraction of lithic remains that exhibit extensive retouch? Strathern's (1987) 'awkward relationship' of feminism to traditional disciplinary methods and goals is relevant here: women's research has the potential to challenge fundamentally the categories, divisions, assumptions and meanings attached to knowledge. Perhaps the knowledge, the sets of facts that archaeology has already put in place, have so internally structured and pre-ordained our inquiry that archaeology will continue to contain women's scholarship in a low-status, low technology, theoretically irrelevant position. But the 'competitive premises' (Strathern 1979: 284) that characterise women's and men's scholarship suggest that a massive reorganisation of archaeological knowledge in general, and Paleoindian knowledge more specifically, may be necessary and inevitable.

Finally, the exhilarating part of this scenario is the recognition and reclaiming of a social and engendered life for Paleoindians, reinforced and negotiated through

315

interactions with a material world that includes a fuller range of animal species than merely megafauna, and a broader range of material remains than only fluted projectile points. It will be the fascinating playing out of new social and gender roles that eclipses hunting and tool production and mammoths and bisons; this is the work that women researchers can contribute to.

ACKNOWLEDGEMENTS

I would like to thank Laurajane Smith and Hilary du Cros for providing the very stimulating forum in which this work was presented, and Sarah Colley, Dena Dincauze, Ruthann Knudson and Rita Wright for detailed comments on the text. Where their points are not addressed in this version, I have myself to blame. Stephen's mega-help deserves mega-applause.

NOTES

1   For four years, the *Archaeology of Eastern North America* was devoted exclusively to paleo research at the discretion of its editor, and no protest was voiced about this popularly supported bias.

2   My appreciative thanks to Melanie Cabak for her earnest research in assembling these data.

3   While men present only 29 per cent of their papers in general sessions, women present 36 per cent of their work as uninvited speakers.

4   The extremely lively controversy that dominates the current Paleoindian literature and provides a focus for the larger discipline's penchant for diatribe still relates to chronological matters, attempting to push back the date for the first human entrance into the New World earlier than the Clovis horizon. This debate is not taken up here although it clearly provides another fascinating case for examining constructionist versus objectivist claims. that matches the boundedness of the research community.

5   As reported in the years that *Current Research in the Pleistocene* has appeared.

19

BODIES ON THE MOVE: GENDER, POWER AND MATERIAL CULTURE*
Gender Difference and the Material World

HENRIETTA MOORE

Bodies take metaphors seriously. The phrase is Bourdieu's (1990c: 71–2), and its suggestive power has much to do with the immediate recognition that we all live our lives through actions performed in structured space and time. The material world that surrounds us is one in which we use our living bodies to give substance to the social distinctions and differences that underpin social relations, symbolic systems, forms of labour and quotidian intimacies. Theories of gender difference – and indeed other forms of difference – frequently give insufficient attention both to bodily praxis as a mode of knowledge and to the material context in which that practice takes place.[1]

The contemporary social sciences now take it as axiomatic that gender is a cultural construct, that, far from being natural objects, women and men are fundamentally cultural constructions. The obvious fact of biological differences between women and men tells us nothing about the general social significance of those differences; and although human societies all over the world recognize biological differences between women and men, what they make of those differences is extraordinarily variable. We cannot deal, therefore, with the observable variability in the cultural constructions of gender across the world or through historical time simply by appealing to the indisputable fact of sexual difference.

This argument is an uncontentious one for many people, but it is none the less easy to lose sight of the analytical consequences of this position because of the way gender ideologies work to appear natural, pre-given and eternal. For example, it is in the natural order of things that men head households; that women are responsible for child care; and that women do not wage war. We find these naturalizations of gender relations made explicit in the material world. The apparently evidential nature of the sexual division of labour is almost everywhere concretized through material objects. The earliest theorizations of the sexual division of labour, like many of those which have followed since, naturalized the differences between women and men through appeal to the material world.

---

*First published in H. Moore (1994), *A Passion for Difference*, Cambridge: Polity Press, pp. 71–85.

Division of labour was a pure and simple outgrowth of nature: it existed only between the sexes. The men went to war, hunted, fished, provided the raw material for food and the tools necessary for these pursuits. The women cared for the house, and prepared food and clothing, they cooked, weaved and sewed. Each was master in his or her own field of activity; the men in the forest, the women in the house. Each owned the tools he or she made and used; the men, the weapons and the hunting and fishing tackle, the women the household goods and utensils.

(Engels [1884] 1972: 149)

Thus, the world is divided into gender-specific domains and spaces, and into gender-specific tasks, and both domains and tasks are associated with particular material items. An established relationship between particular material items and persons of a specific gender seems to be common to societies all over the world, though more elaborated in some as compared to others. This makes it easy to fall into the trap of suggesting that gender-specific tasks and domains, with their associated material items, simply reflect the obvious division of the world into women and men. The relationship between gender and material culture remains unproblematic because the material world somehow reflects the appropriate cultural ideas about gender, and also demonstrates in a concrete and practical way the nature of relations between the sexes.

There is something to be said in favour of this 'reflectionist' type of argument, and there was a time when it was very popular in the social sciences and humanities. An anthropological example drawn from Caroline Humphrey's work on the organization of space inside a Mongolian tent makes the point:

In practice . . . the floor area of the tent was divided into four sections, each of which was valued differently. The area from the door, which faced south, to the fireplace in the centre, was the junior or low-status half, called by the Mongols the 'lower' half. The area at the back of the tent behind the fire was the honorific 'upper' part, named the *xoimor*. The division was intersected by that of the male or ritually pure half, which was to the left of the door as you entered, and the female impure, or dirty section to the right of the door, up to the *xoimor* . . . A woman's object was considered to pollute the men's area and a special ceremony might have to be performed to erase this.

(1974: 26)

Encoded in this passage, and made explicit in the rest of Humphrey's article, is a series of ideas about how the organization of space reflects the hierarchical nature of relations between women and men. Women are polluting and any object associated with them is also polluting, and the position of such objects within the tent must be controlled and monitored in order to make sure that they do not pass into the ritually pure, male part of the tent. Just as women themselves must be monitored and controlled by men. The divisions discussed by Humphrey also make appeal to a fairly common set of symbolic oppositions which are associated with the female and the male. So that women, or rather 'woman', as a symbolic category is associated with the left, the impure and the lower, while 'man' is associated with the right, the pure and the higher. Symbolic oppositions such as these, which may stand as transformations of or metaphors for each other, are by now the routine products of semiotic or structuralist analyses in the social sciences. The value of working out the inner logic and structural relations between cultural symbols, whilst emphasizing the contextual nature of symbolic meaning, is clear. Structuralist analysis has its place, as both Bourdieu (1977, 1990c) and Ricoeur (see Moore 1990a) argue, as long as it is recognized that the decoding of symbolic structures does not constitute an interpretation of those structures.

In the traditional social anthropological view cultural beliefs, attitudes and symbols were seen as reflecting primary sets of social relations, and for this reason Humphrey links the hierarchy which apparently exists between the symbolic categories 'woman' and 'man' to the existence of relations of dominance or to particular sets of social relations between women and men. She is not incorrect in doing this, but the complexity of the relationship between cultural symbols or ideologies and specific sets of social relations – that is, between cultural representations and what people really do in their day-to-day lives – defeats any attempt to specify such a relationship as being merely one of reflection. Marxist scholars in a number of disciplines, including social anthropology, tackled this problem by reversing the relationship and arguing that cultural ideologies, far from reflecting social relations, actually serve to distort and mystify them, in order to maintain the status quo through a misrecognition of the sources of power and oppression. Recent critiques, however, have pointed out that what is missing in both the structuralist/semiotic and Marxist type of analysis is the social actor. Meaning does not inhere in symbols, but must be invested in and interpreted from symbols by acting social beings. Interpretation is the product of a series of associations, convergences and condensations established through praxis, and not the result of an act of decoding by an observer. This privileging of the interpretations of social actors inevitably results in a series of questions about how to connect individual interpretations with collective discourses or ideologies. How is it that actors construct an understanding of their world, an understanding of themselves as gendered individuals and an understanding of social relations through the dominant cultural ideologies or dominant cultural discourses about gender, whilst at the same time apparently dissenting from those cultural discourses to a significant degree? It is clear that people in a variety of contexts do this, as discussed in the previous chapter [of the original volume]. If we take contemporary British society as an example, it is evident that many women construct themselves as women in ways which do not subscribe to the dominant cultural definitions of womanhood.[2] This point has particular pertinence when we come to consider the relationship between gender and material culture.

If we look at Caroline Humphrey's analysis, we can see that it is assumed that all persons are equally affected by dominant cultural ideologies and symbol systems, and that people's behaviour and/or their social relations will in some sense conform to these dominant representations of gender relations. This assumption has to be there to some extent in structuralist and semiotic analysis in anthropology because the link between cultural ideologies and social relations is supposed to be one of reflection. But I want to return to the problem raised in the previous chapter [of the original volume], and use the medium of material culture to pose again the question of how we theorize the relationship between dominant representations or cultural discourses about gender and what people actually think and do. How is it possible for people both to consent to and dissent from the dominant representations of gender when they are encoded in the material world all around them?

Space, place and interpretation

Pierre Bourdieu was one of the first analysts to try to integrate a structural analysis with what people do, and to try to integrate the self-images or self-representations people build up of themselves with dominant cultural ideologies or world-images, as Bourdieu would term them. He describes the interior of the Kabyle house:

> The interior of the Kabyle house, rectangular in shape, is divided into two parts by a low wall: the larger of these two parts, slightly higher than the other, is reserved for human use; the other side, occupied by the animals, has a loft above it. A door with two wings gives access to both rooms. In the upper part is the hearth and facing the door, the weaving loom. The lower, dark, nocturnal part of the house, the place of damp, green or raw objects – water jars set on the benches on either side of the entrance to the stable or against 'the wall of darkness', wood, green fodder – the place too of natural beings – sleep, sex, birth – and also of death, is opposed to the high, light-filled, noble place of humans and in particular of the guest, fire and fire-made objects, the lamp, kitchen utensils, the rifle – the attribute of the manly point of honour (*nif*) which protects female honour (*hurma*) – the loom, the symbol of all protection, the place also of the two specifically cultural activities performed within the house, cooking and weaving. The meaning objectified in things or places is fully revealed only in the practices structured according to the same schemes which are organised in relation to them (and vice versa).
>
> The guest to be honoured is invited to sit in front of the loom. The opposite wall is called the wall of darkness . . . a sick person's bed is placed next to it. The washing of the dead takes place at the entrance to the stable. The low dark part is opposed to the upper part as the female to the male.
>
> (Bourdieu 1977: 90)

Bourdieu is making a very familiar argument here, because he explicitly says that the Kabyle house is organized according to a set of oppositions – fire: water, cooked: raw, high: low, light: shade, day: night, male: female – and that these oppositions are all metaphors of each other. However, he goes beyond a standard structuralist analysis, and argues that these symbolic meanings are not inherent in the organization of space, but have to be invoked through the activities of social actors. It is only when you actually place a sick person against the wall of darkness or place an honoured guest in front of the loom that meanings are invoked. And, of course, failure to do such things also has significance, and may serve to confound the expectations of others, and thus potentially revoke or bring into question sedimented cultural meanings and values. Actors are continually involved, therefore, in the strategic interpretation and reinterpretation of the cultural meanings that inform the organization of their world as a consequence of their day-to-day activities in that world.

Bourdieu suggests that for an actor to strategically invoke or revoke certain meanings, it is not necessary for the actor to be involved in conscious, intellectual reasoning about alternative interpretations and strategies, though there will be occasions when this is the case. The ability to pursue alternative strategies within symbolically structured space requires no more than the practical knowledge of how to proceed within that space, of what you should and should not do.

> Adapting a phrase of Proust's, one might say that arms and legs are full of numb imperatives. One could endlessly enumerate the values given body, made body, by the hidden persuasion of an implicit pedagogy which can instil a whole cosmology, through injunctions as insignificant as 'sit up straight' or 'don't hold your knife in your left hand', and inscribe the most fundamental principles of the arbitrary content of a culture in seemingly innocuous details of bearing or physical and verbal manners, so putting them beyond the reach of conscious and implicit statement.
>
> (Bourdieu 1990c: 69)

This process of learning through practical enactment does not mean that actors can never bring these principles to discourse, nor does it mean that they are unable to manipulate meanings and outcomes – they can and do through day-to-day activities.[3] Not all these instances of manipulation will be conscious in the sense of thought out strategies that can be expressed in language. Bourdieu is frequently charged with having developed a theory that allows little room for agency and/or social change.[4] This is perhaps because his emphasis on the intersection of social location with sets of structuring principles that are embodied through repetition and enactment (habitus) implies that social reproduction and conformity are paramount. In fact, Bourdieu stresses, without providing many concrete examples, that because praxis is itself a moment of interpretation, if not actual manipulation, the role of the actor is crucial to his theory.[5] There is room here both for creativity and for social change because actions themselves can be a type of critical reflection that does not necessarily have to involve conscious, discursive strategizing. When it comes to the question of the body and its enactment of cultural principles, Bourdieu emphasizes that embodiment is a process, and that the body is never finished, never perfectly socialized.

Bourdieu's focus on the relationship between social location and embodiment means that a notion of position and positionality runs through his work. Bourdieu's analysis of power is closely linked to this notion of positionality through a consideration of distinctions based on gender and on class. Bourdieu makes it clear that actors' interpretations of the material world, and the kinds of activities they perform in socially structured space, are governed by their particular position within social relations and dominant cultural discourses. In the case of the Kabyle Bourdieu describes the different positions of women and men with regard to dominant discourses and social relations by concretizing them as a difference in physical perspective:

> One or other of the two systems of oppositions which define the house . . . is brought to the foreground, depending on whether the house is considered from the male point of view or the female point of view: whereas for the man, the house is not so much a place he enters as a place he comes out of, movement inward properly befits the woman.
>
> (1977: 91)

Bourdieu's grounding of perspective in the body makes his notion of position rather more physically specific than the feminist notion of a standpoint. Standpoint theory stresses that the positionalities arising from structured inequalities are much more than a perspective because they are institutionalized and collective. However, the two theories are simply using the term perspective in different ways. Bourdieu does recognize structural inequalities and he argues that they give rise to social divisions which produce what he terms the '*habitus*', that set of structuring principles and common schemes of perception and conception that generate practices and representations (1990c: 53). In fact, Bourdieu, like feminist standpoint theorists, tends to treat women as a class, thus obscuring differences within the category. But he does recognize that there is a link between the different positions of women and men with regard to dominant cultural values and their self-understandings and self-representations as gendered individuals (1990a).

> The opposition between the centrifugal, male orientation and the centripetal, female orientation, which as we have seen, is the true principle of the organisation of domestic space, is doubtless also the basis of the relationship of each of the sexes to their 'psyche', that is, to their bodies and more precisely to their sexuality.
>
> (Bourdieu 1977: 92)

This is no doubt Bourdieu's concession to a phenomenological view of the body, but its more powerful persuasiveness lies in the link he attempts to establish between the body and knowledge. Praxis is not simply about learning cultural rules by rote, it is about coming to an understanding of social distinctions through your body, and recognizing that your orientation in the world, your intellectual rationalizations, will always be based on that incorporated knowledge. Bourdieu's work contains a method for understanding the pervasive power of symbols and of the social distinctions on which they are based because he reminds us that whether we are actors or analysts we know that symbols are powerful because they do something to our bodies.

Bourdieu appears to hold psychoanalysis in some contempt, and he does not develop a theory of the body that could incorporate a notion of the distinction between conscious and unconscious motivations and actions.[6] Consequently, he does not focus on what happens when these different sets of motivations are in conflict. His strongly socialized and collective view of the body in its relationship to *habitus* means that he does not adequately theorize individual experiences and motivations. He does acknowledge that social actors have individual trajectories within social locations (fields), and this allows him to incorporate a certain conception of lived personal history, but one that is rather abstract. Bourdieu argues that the singular *habitus* of members of the same class is united through a series of homologies, and that each is a structural variant of the others. There is, therefore, room for something that Bourdieu terms 'personal style'. He acknowledges also that each individual has a singular trajectory based on a 'series of chronologically ordered determinations that are mutually irreducible to one another' (1990c: 60). He maintains that history is crucial since new experiences are always overdetermined by past ones, but, rather than seeing this as giving rise to distinct experiences for the individual subject, he chooses to emphasize instead that new experiences will be 'dominated by the earliest experiences, of the experiences statistically common to members of the same class' (1990c: 60).[7]

Bourdieu is keen to transcend what he sees as the sterile antinomies of the social sciences, including those between the individual and the collective (1977). His theory of the body is part of this attempt. In his discussion of the sexed body he is particularly concerned to emphasize the relationship between knowledge and recognition that provides the grounds for the apprehension of difference through bodily praxis (1990a: 12). Both emotions and knowledge are embodied forms that can never be brought entirely into discourse. However, his tendency to treat groups as classes makes it extremely difficult for him to specify the consequences of the intersections of sets of different social distinctions for individuals in specific contexts. Like feminist standpoint theory, once questions are raised about differences within the identified categories as opposed to between them – for example, differences between women – then the theory provides little guidance as to how to handle difference. One consequence for Bourdieu is that his concept of positionality is devoid of any notion of a multiple subjectivity constituted through multiple positions.

Bourdieu does raise the question of subjectivity, but he does not develop it theoretically in great detail.[8] The strength of his approach is its insistence on the materiality of subjectivity. This stems, in part, from certain strands of Marxist thinking in his work. He explicitly says that the schemes of perception and conception that form the *habitus* are derived from the conditions of existence, and particularly from the social divisions of labour.[9] Bourdieu's analysis of cognition and symbolism is not one that floats free from the conditions under which people actually live. This emphasis on the materiality of subjectivity allows Bourdieu to transcend, to a degree, the antinomy between the subjective and the objective, between the individual and the world. His subject is one born of a world of objects, where schemes of perception and thought are inculcated through the activities performed in symbolically structured space and time (1990c: 76). The subject is never separated from the material conditions of its existence, and the world is never free of the representations that construct it:

> the acts of cognition that are implied in misrecognition and recognition are part
> of social reality and . . . the socially constituted subjectivity that produces them
> belongs to objective reality.
>
> (Bourdieu 1990c: 122)

Bourdieu sees social structures and cognitive structures as recursively linked, and it is the correspondence between them that provides the foundation for social domination. He discusses these points at length in his work with regard to gender and class, but he gives little space to other forms of difference.[10] His relative inattention to questions of race is surprising given his theory of the body and of bodily praxis.

bell hooks has provided several powerful descriptions of the relationship between space, place and black identity in the United States (1991: chs 5,10,15). The differences of race are inscribed in such things as the physical process of leaving the community, crossing the tracks and going to work in white homes. hooks gives several examples of the gendered nature of physical space, emphasizing that houses belonged to women, and that they were sites of identification and resistance (1991: 41–3). These homes provided an alternative space for community and self-valorization removed from the topography of racial oppression and discrimination. Such spaces have to be constructed both imaginatively and physically, but through the way that they are lived bodily practices of incorporated knowledge bind the material and the symbolic indissolubly. hooks gives an account of working as a professional academic in a context where physical space is part of the unmarked category 'white', and where this fact dictates forms of comportment and forms of speech. She describes clear joy at returning to a space constructed in terms of understandings that form part of her sense of self, as when coming home to rest from the rigours of a lecture schedule.

hooks's descriptions of what it means to be a black intellectual are based on clear accounts of the intersections of race, class and gender. The reality of this experience is a series of complex crossings and re-crossings. To leave certain spaces and pass into others is to know in your body what the differences of race involve; it is to know oppression and discrimination intimately in a way which does not allow for the separation of the physical from the mental. The powerful symbolism of notions of place, location and positionality in contemporary feminist theory demonstrates just how much we come to know through our bodies, and how much our theorizing is dependent on that knowledge. The multiple nature of subjectivity is experienced physically, through practices which can be simultaneously physical and discursive. Current theories of multiple positionalities and multiple subjectivities are resonant for social analysts who live these contradictory, conflicting and compelling differences.[11]

Language and behaviour: the politics of domination

The most compelling question in any discussion of social domination is one about the possibilities for resistance. If embodied knowledge simply provides a physical form of interpellation as neat and tidy as that proposed by Althusser, then how can we account for resistance, contradiction and change? It seems implausible to suggest that the fit between physical practices and discursive interpretation will always be perfect. Language and behaviour are frequently at odds with one another, as psychoanalysis so amply demonstrates. What can no longer be spoken is repeated in behaviour. It seems clear, then, that body knowledge can both refuse us and traduce us. It can insist on things that we would like to leave behind and it can continue to guide us when we have lost all sense of strategy and purpose.

What emerges from this is that resistance does not need to be discursive, coherent or conscious.[12] The organization of the material world, however conventional and well established, is never complete or finished. The appearance of finality and completeness is a function both of the totalizing view of the analyst and of the nature of dominant value systems and discourses. Bourdieu's insistence on strategies of invocation and revocation, discussed earlier, reminds us that meanings are not static and that they do not inhere in the material world itself. Behaviour, sets of activities conducted in structured space, can be used to 'read against the grain' of dominant discourses, to expose the arbitrary nature of their construction. If one cannot resist by placing oneself outside dominant structures and discourses, one can none the less displace oneself within them. Individuals can refuse the construction of gender as it is presented, they can approach this construction deviously or ironically, they can refer to it endlessly, but do so against its purpose, against the grain.

Much of the difficulty in analysing social domination, power and resistance comes from an uncertainty about key terms. Resistance, for example, normally implies a conscious, coherent strategy. It is possible to extend the term to cover forms of inertia, but analysts usually assume that foot-dragging, go-slows and petty pilfering from employers are conscious strategies. 'When is resistance resistance?' 'When you realize you are doing it.' Much hinges, then, on whether an action is conscious or unconscious. The problem is a routine one and concerns the borderline. A great many actions are unthought and unthought out, unformulated and inchoate, half apprehended and concrete only after their effects are known. They do not come into discourse before their execution, and often not afterwards. But such actions are deliberate, calculated and calculating. They require no more, in those familiar words, than a knowledge of how to proceed. Are such actions really unconscious?

The problem is compounded because certain actions, particularly those involving resistance or possible resistance, can be of an indeterminate nature. It can be very difficult to tell whether someone is just making a mistake or deliberately doing something differently, being careful or going slow.

The issue of interpretation is an important one because it highlights the fact that dominant structures and discourses involve a high degree of indeterminacy.[13] Their very power comes from their generality, from the way in which the broad outlines of the principles of division they encode act as a backdrop against which conflict and contradiction can take place. Dominant discourses of gender, for example, may seem removed from the experiences of individual women, but that very distance means that they are rarely directly challenged by the vagaries of lived experience. 'Just like a woman' is a commonplace phrase in British society which says everything and tells us nothing. As an instance of the dominant discourse on gender, it will never be contradicted by the complexities of individual women's lives.

However, we know that dominant discourses are not impervious to change, and that one of the major ways in which change comes about is through processes of interpretation and reinterpretation (Bourdieu 1990c: ch. 3). Shifts in meaning can result from a reordering of practical activities. If meaning is given to the organization of space through practice, it follows that small changes in procedure can provide new interpretations of spatial layouts. Such layouts provide potential commentaries on established ways of doing things and divisions of privilege. Shifting the grounds of meaning, reading against the grain, is often something done through practice, that is, through the day-to-day activities that take place within symbolically structured space. This can involve small things, such as putting something in the wrong place or placing it in relation to something else from which it is normally kept separate. It can include using space in a different way or commandeering space for new uses or invading the space of others.

The importance of restructuring the physical relations of the material world in order to resist or combat and then change the conceptual and social relations of gender was clearly recognized by nineteenth-century feminist reformers. These women, who were engaged in campaigns to change relations between women and men, to change women's position within the home and to promote the economic autonomy of women, were convinced that domestic space must be altered in such a way as to make these reforms possible.[14]

Catherine Beecher was a reformer who accepted a conventional definition of the domestic world as women's sphere, but she argued that women should rule the home in their capacity as skilled professionals, and she designed a number of houses during the second half of the nineteenth century which made the kitchen area the central focus of the house.

Melusina Fay Pierce was one of the first women in the United States to make a detailed critique of domestic labour. She demanded pay for housework, she organized the women of her town to get it and she was a great proponent of what she called co-operative housekeeping. Co-operative housekeeping would consist of groups of fifteen to twenty-three women who would organize co-operative associations to perform all their domestic work collectively and then charge their husbands for these services. The association would have a headquarters equipped with the appropriate mechanical devices for cooking, laundry and so on. It would employ former servants who were skilled in particular tasks, and these women would be paid wages equivalent to those of skilled male workers. The association would charge retail prices for cooked food, laundry, clothing and provisions – cash on delivery! Pierce believed that when co-operating women had established their domestic industries in a central building, women architects should design houses without kitchens.

In her book *Women and Economics* Charlotte Perkins Gilman described a world where women worked for wages outside the home, where they had economic independence and where they lived with their families in private kitchenless houses or in apartments connected to central kitchens, dining rooms and day centres. Gilman believed that new domestic environments would promote the evolution of socialism, a view which has also been held to varying degrees by socialist governments in our own time.

Nineteenth-century science fiction novels, like those of the twentieth century, also linked the refiguration of social and sexual relations to changes in spatial relations and domestic environments (Moore 1990b). Novelists and reformers alike recognized the way in which the organization of the material world encodes dominant cultural meanings and discourses. The social practices and activities carried out in symbolically constructed space act as a mnemonic for dominant sets of conceptual and social relations. One example of this is that if a Carmelite nun spends sixty years in a Carmelite convent – all her life, in other words – she will kneel in the same place, at the same time, 42,800 times (D. Williams 1975). This reveals the crucial point about the relationship between gender and material culture. It is not that the material world, as a form of cultural discourse, reflects the natural division of the world into women and men, but rather that cultural discourses, including the organization of the material world, actually produce gender difference in and through their workings. It is not that our bodies naturally evince gender differences, or any other form of difference, it is rather that these differences are produced as an effect upon them. Teresa de Lauretis describes the process rather well in another context:

> Most of us – those of us who are women; to those who are men this will not apply – probably check the F box rather than the M box when filling out an application form. It would hardly occur to us to mark M. It would be like cheating, or, worse, not existing, like erasing ourselves from the world . . . For since the very first time we put a check mark on the little square next to the F on the form, we have officially entered the sex-gender system, the social relations of gender, and have become engendered as women; that is to say,

not only do other people consider us females, but from that moment on we have been representing ourselves as women. Now I ask, isn't that the same as saying that . . . while we thought that we were marking the F on the form, in fact the F was marking itself on us?

(1987: 11–12)

The moral of the story is, be careful how you tick the box.

NOTES

1 In anthropology this has much to do with the downgrading of the study of material culture, although it is now enjoying something of a renaissance (see Moore 1986). Architects, geographers and archaeologists have not been so neglectful of these matters. See for example, (Soja 1989; Gregory and Urry 1985; Pred 1990; Hodder 1991b; and Tilley 1990).

2 Denise Riley (1988) discusses the difficult relationship women *qua* women have to the category 'woman', and how that relationship has changed over time.

3 I believe that actors can bring such principles to discourse precisely because praxis can act as a moment of critical reflection. The situations and circumstances under which this becomes possible would have to be specified analytically and descriptively. Bourdieu, however, normally emphasizes that such principles are rarely brought to discourse, though he believes it is possible through an external process of clarification – a kind of consciousness raising. He also emphasizes, of course, and most notably with regard to gender, that the heritage of Descartes in the social sciences has meant that analysts are happy to discuss the agent's self-reflexive abilities, their reflections on action, but less willing to see action itself as a type of critical reflection (1990a: 12).

4 See Bourdieu and Wacquant (1992: 79–83), for a list of these critics and for a response from Bourdieu.

5 Bourdieu has produced a mass of empirical sociology, and as such his work is full of examples, but few of them can be used to demonstrate processes of social change.

6 One of Bourdieu's chief criticisms is that psychoanalysis reduces the relation to the body to the sexual (1990c: 77). However, Bourdieu does acknowledge the importance of fantasy, desire and self-image in his discussion of gender differences and masculine domination (1990a). Bourdieu is critical of psychoanalysis in this paper, but he also approaches it more positively than elsewhere, partly because he is concerned to link the body and the body praxis to notions of identity and, in particular, to sexed identities.

7 This produces a strange and unresolved tension where Bourdieu gives undue weight to childhood experiences, and indeed family interactions, but does not wish to integrate a psychoanalytic approach into his work.

8 Bourdieu has said he wants to escape from the philosophy of the subject without doing away with the agent (1985). This seems to be connected with Bourdieu's estrangement from French psychoanalysis, and he has certainly not attempted to develop a theory of subjectivity, but, once again, it is significant that he comes closest to having to treat this problem in his discussion of gender differences and masculine domination (1990a).

9 Bourdieu does make a number of very important assertions about female subjectivity, without actually using the tem 'subjectivity', in his essay on masculine domination (1990a: 26–9). One is that women are not able to be subjects in the same way as men, since subjectivity is defined in the male mode, so to speak. However, Bourdieu links this difference not only to women's position within relations of production and reproduction, but to their relationship to the acquisition of symbolic capital (1990a: 28).

10 Bourdieu is well aware that other forms of difference are important as well as those of gender and class (1990b: ch.8 1990a). However, he has made little attempt to theorize these axes of

differentiation terms of the concept of *habitus*. What Bourdieu's theory lacks is a notion of the multiplicity and simultaneity of difference.

11 The work of Chicana scholars has been notable in this regard, especially their treatment of narrative and personal history, see, for example Anzaldúa (1987), and articles by Sommer (1988), and Alarcon (1990), for a discussion of these issues.

12 This is exactly the point made by James Scott (1985) in his analyses of forms of peasant resistance, but from a rather different perspective. Bourdieu also emphasizes that actions can supply moments of reinterpretation and reformulation that have the potential to provide the conditions for resistance. However, he stresses in the case of women and masculine domination, all forms of resistance take place within the symbolic categories of the dominant male world view, and that symbolic revolution would have to be a collective act (1990a: 15, 30). Bourdieu certainly thinks resistance is possible (see his analysis of resistance by Algerian peasants to the imposition of colonialism, 1979b), but he sees it as being the product of collective rather than individual action, and he is critical of what he calls spontaneous populism because of his view that the dominated rarely escape the power relations of the dominated/dominant divide (1991: 90–102).

13 Bourdieu makes this point also about the habitus, and this is why he believes that his theory incorporates the potential for social change (1990a: 15, 1990c).

14 I draw all my examples in this section from the work of Dolores Hayden (1981) and I base my discussion of these issues on her material and on the work of Barbara Taylor (1983). The gender politics of the nineteenth-century feminist reformers were notably radical, but their race and class politics generally not.

20

ENGENDERED PLACES
IN PREHISTORY[*]

RUTH TRINGHAM

If you are interested in the history of place-making and the continuity of place, if you are interested in the history of the built environment, if you are interested in the context of the early struggles for power and tensions between women and men, children and elders, then the archaeological record has to be your starting point – if, that is, you believe that history includes the many thousands of years of prehistory. The archaeological record of the built environment is reported in hundreds of research reports. Yet, except for monumental architecture, the archaeological record of the built environment is ignored by writers outside of archaeological practice, who perceive it to be visually uninspiring and fraught with ambiguities (Lawrence and Low 1990: 454). Prehistoric non-monumental architecture has been used to write about the origins of building technology or the origins and diffusion of certain archetypal floor plans (Kostof 1985; Cataldi 1986). But writing about the prehistoric built environment tends to be arid, uncreative and dehumanized in comparison to the recent rich creative literature relating the built environment to space, place, gender and culture in the analysis of historic and modern traditional architecture (Tringham 1991a).

It is true that the poor preservation of most archaeological architecture is a severe limiting factor, especially that from the prehistoric period in which the architectural remains are bereft of any supporting written records. The ground plan and foundation works and, possibly, also the lower part of the superstructure are all that usually remain of a building on an archaeological site. The real limitations on the use of the archaeological record of the built environment have been created by the archaeologists themselves, the nature of their studies, and the presentation of their research to their prospective audience.

Archaeological reports have traditionally been presented as unambiguous 'facts' in which the detail of the process of making inferences is hidden (if it is presented at all) in obscure journals and monographs. It is a temptation for archaeologists and for researchers from other disciplines, as well as writers of popular literature, to use the 'facts' presented in the simplified synthesized version rather than to question

[*]First published in *Gender, Place and Culture* (1994), **1** (2), 169–203.

the inferences and to dig into the primary literature. For example, James Mellaart's popular book on the Neolithic settlement of Çatal Hüyük in Turkey has had a huge impact on current thought, as it is cited in almost every book on the history of architecture since the 1970s (Mellaart 1967). Even though his interpretation of the symbolic meaning of the wall-paintings and embellishments has been subject to re-analysis, his interpretations of house form, sequence and function have been accepted completely and uncritically (Todd 1976; Stea and Turan 1986; Hodder 1987a; Gadon 1989; Gimbutas 1991).

Such uncritical 'receiving' of the 'facts' of archaeology, however, can only entrench the uncreative understanding of the relationship of space, place and gender in the past. I shall show in this paper that this restricted use of the archaeological record of the built environment is not an inevitable fate to which we who use prehistoric data must resign ourselves. The restrictions are a construct of the archaeologists themselves and their framework of question-asking which traditionally ignores both gender and the application of feminist theory to space and place. The prehistoric archaeological record is ambiguous. This characteristic provides room for alternative perspectives and means that the 'archaeological facts' can be challenged by anyone either inside or outside archaeological practice (Tringham 1991a and b).

Traditional views of archaeological architecture

The 'New (modern) Archaeology', which is often termed by its opponents as 'processualist archaeology', emerged as an explicit participant in archaeological discourse in the late 1960s. The New Archaeologists separated themselves from what had gone before by focusing on explicit research design, quantification, and a search for predictability and generalizations in the explanation of the processes of prehistoric behavior, rather than concentrating on the description of culture history. The New Archaeology currently comprises the mainstream of archaeological practice in North American anthropology.

There is no doubt that the New Archaeology has added several dimensions to archaeological practice that enhance its incorporation into the social sciences and its acceptance within mainstream scientific disciplines. There are certain characteristics, however, that the New Archaeology and the more traditional (culture historical and functionalist) archaeologies of Europe and the Americas have in common.[1] These characteristics have guided the retrieval, analysis and interpretation of prehistoric architectural remains. For example, it has always been characteristic of traditional archaeological discourse to assume that the archaeological record be attributed to past behavior. With the New Archaeology, however, this assumption was emphasized as a required research step that enables hypotheses about behavior in the past to be empirically testable, according to the methodology of logical positivist science. This belief is underlain and enabled by another traditional premise, that is, that material culture – in the case of this paper, architecture – is a passive reflection of behavior. Any action that modified the material world can potentially be reconstructed and is, therefore, awarded primacy in archaeological investigations. For example, mechanical aspects of house construction can be inferred with a high degree of plausibility and consensus, since they involve the properties and manipulations of materials that are subject to principles of the 'exact sciences'.

The other side of this coin is that any action that cannot be identified as having modified materials preserved in the archaeological record cannot be reconstructed and is not testable. For example, it is extremely difficult, if not impossible, to demonstrate with 'scientific validity' *who* constructed a house in prehistory. Thus many aspects of the use and significance of space that are considered vital by anthropologists, geographers and architects, especially those involving gender, age, and the intentional action of individuals, have been consistently ignored or minimized in the treatments of architectural remains in archaeology. It is assumed that they are reflected so indirectly in the material culture and with such an unbearable degree of ambiguity, that the archaeological data cannot be attributed to these actions, categories or relationships (Tringham 1991b).

The end product of this assumption is that any behavior that is not testable or demonstrable and is subject to ambiguity is not valuable for investigation, and is probably not a valid object of knowledge. This leads us to the third characteristic of traditional archaeology, which states that macro-scale questions formulated from long-term and world-scale interests of technological development, social evolution and ecological adaptation continue to be the most valid and valued objects of knowledge. It is not surprising that, within this context, archaeologists in their treatment of the prehistoric built environment focus on such topics as construction, function and pattern recognition of the variability in ground plans (Tringham 1991a: 10). Conversely, topics that focus on prehistoric people and their variability at a *macro-scale* – the family, the household, men, women and children, housework, individual intentional action – have traditionally been regarded as marginal objects of knowledge. The rationale for this is not only that these categories are untestable archaeologically, but also that this scale of interpretation is thought to make no difference in the big picture of cultural evolution, being a constant rather than a variable in human social behavior.

These characteristics of mainstream archaeology bring us to the final point which declares that the general aim of traditional archaeological studies – New Archaeology and not-so-New (whether they are concerned with architecture or not) – is to normalize behavior in order to extrapolate from a well-studied but restricted sample, to a whole population (a culture, a stage of social evolution, an adaptation, a region). In the process of asking macro-scale questions, it is understandable and a legitimate part of the archaeological endeavor, that individual houses from specific sites become normalized to be 'typical of' and to 'stand for' the cultural whole.

Most archaeologists would also acknowledge the value of cross-cultural generalizations in making correlations between behavior and materials (the archaeological record). These generalizations are based on a comparative analysis of worldwide and time-wide ethnographic samples that are often coupled with more detailed work with a small ethnoarchaeological sample. In the archaeological investigation of the built environment, general principles that, for example, link the degree of complexity in segmenting space with the degree of social segmentation, have an inherent popularity in the quest to answer macro-scale questions that relate to the evolution of architectural styles and social complexity (Rapoport 1976, 1990; Kent 1990, 1991). Such generalizations prevail in spite of the demonstration by ethnoarchaeology of examples of exceptions to the rule (David 1971; Watson 1979; Horne 1982; Kramer 1982).

331

The use of such generalizations as reality rather than heuristic devices has been heavily criticized in anthropology in that they essentialize social units, such as the 'family' or 'household' or 'male' or 'female' role divisions whose rich variability is significant (Yanagisako 1979; Moore 1988). Likewise, in the process of normalizing and generalizing about the prehistoric built environment, individual variability – house histories, causes of individual house fires, and the lives, intentions and actions of individual men, women and children – are characterized as exceptionalist and irrelevant for archaeological enquiry (Tringham 1991b).

The form of finished houses: traditional models of the prehistoric built environment

Contrary to common belief, the archaeological record does not represent a single or fixed reality, rather it is a kind of spatial text that varies from reader to reader (Patrik 1985). I shall demonstrate with examples of the interpretation of the archaeological record of the built environment from the South-east European Neolithic/Eneolithic period how the archaeological record can be 'read' differently depending on different theoretical viewpoints. I will argue that an archaeological record can actually be changed or even expanded. Firstly, this is accomplished with re-interpretations of excavated materials that draw attention to aspects of the record that were overlooked by traditional interpretations, thereby turning into objects of investigation that which had previously been unquestioned, that is, taken for granted. Secondly, the archaeological record becomes an expandable text when the new ways of interpreting the data lead to a change in excavation methods in which details of the record that were previously ignored as irrelevant are now retrieved from the ground. Some of these examples are drawn from sites whose excavation I have directed (Opovo, Selevac), others where I have been merely an observer (Divostin, Ovcharovo). All are characterized by well-preserved remains of architecture, but they date firmly to the prehistoric period, that is, they are separated by many thousands of years from any written sources.

Opovo is at present a small town in the recently drained marshlands north of the Danube in what is left of Yugoslavia. In prehistoric times, there was a small hamlet (now called Ugar Bajbuk) located 2 kilometers from the modern town that was occupied for perhaps a 200-year period. The archaeological remains of the hamlet have been attributed to the Late Neolithic/Early Eneolithic Vinča culture (*ca.* 4400–4000 BC). The location of Opovo-Ugar Bajbuk in the inhospitable (for early farmers) marshlands contrasts with the location of the majority of settlements attributed to this culture, which are situated in the fertile wooded hilly area south of the Danube river (Tringham 1990, 1991a and b; Tringham *et al.* 1985, 1992).

Archaeologists in North America and Europe have traditionally treated artifacts – including buildings – as finished artifacts, whose variability in form, style and association is to be analyzed. Their reconstructions of Neolithic/Eneolithic period houses of Central and South-east Europe focus on house construction, form and subdivisions, and what artifacts and furnishings were found inside them (Stalio 1968; Benac 1973; Todorova 1982; Coudart 1987; Bogdanovic 1990; Brukner 1990). These archaeologists would have no quarrel with this description of the house remains from Opovo (taken from my own report):

Figure 20.1 Clay rubble of the burnt floor and superstructure of House 2 at Opovo, Yugoslavia (building horizon 1). Note the impressions of timber frame (photograph by M.Trninić)

The prehistoric settlement of Opovo, like all those of the Late Neolithic/ Early Eneolithic of Southeast Europe, is characterized by the . . . remains of dwellings that were traditionally built on a framework of upright wooden posts dug into the ground with walls of planks, logs or wattling covered on one or both surfaces by a thick layer of clay daub . . . On the archaeological site the structures appear as a bright orange or red mass of burned collapsed clay rubble in which is impressed the shadows of the wooden framework [Figure 20.1] . . . One to three rows of internal post(holes) indicate a gabled roof. The floorplan indicates a rectangular detached house, *c.* 6 meters wide . . . The houses at Opovo are at the low end of the length range of the Vinča culture houses, which varies from 6 to 20 meters [Figure 20.2]. Our overall impression of the houses at Opovo is that they were less well prepared and less long-lived than the majority of Vinča culture houses.

(Tringham 1991a: 14, 16)

During the Late Neolithic/Early Eneolithic period, the settlements of South-east Europe . . . are characterized by burned remains of houses which surpass in terms of their volume and their universality on the settlements those preceding and succeeding this period and those found anywhere else in Europe . . .

(Tringham 1991b: 122)

The characteristic end of the use-life of the Neolithic houses by intense conflagration has traditionally not been an object of investigation. It was assumed that no explanation was needed beyond an intuitive common-sense reasoning that the fires were village-wide, and that they were either accidental, resulting from the increased use of fire within houses and denser crowding of houses within the villages, or, for those looking for more dramatic explanations, fires that were started deliberately by invaders or raiders (Todorova 1978; Gimbutas 1991).

In the traditional excavation of prehistoric settlements in South-east Europe (and elsewhere), the 'fact' of house replacement, like house destruction, has not been thought to be something that required questioning. Thus such questions as: when a house dies, is it replaced; are its materials or foundations used in the construction of a new house; is there some kind of continuity demonstrable; where is a new house placed in relation to its predecessor? – have traditionally been ignored.

In addition, the village has commonly been seen to be the unit of social and economic action, thereby assuming primacy in excavation efforts and interpretation. Thus the ideal excavation of a village has traditionally exposed the maximum possible area within a single time horizon (hopefully the whole village). Excavations have also attempted to elucidate the 'sequence of building or occupation horizons or levels' (as it is referred to in archetypal archaeological jargon) and hence the cultural sequence of the village. At Çatal Hüyük, for example, 12 'occupation levels' were identified in which continuity of houses between levels was clearly present but the process of house replacement was never presented explicitly by the excavator (Mellaart 1967; Todd, 1976). In a sequence worked out at the 'tell' settlement of Ovcharovo in Bulgaria it was assumed that all the houses in a given 'building horizon' were occupied and then abandoned at the same time, and that they were then replaced at the same

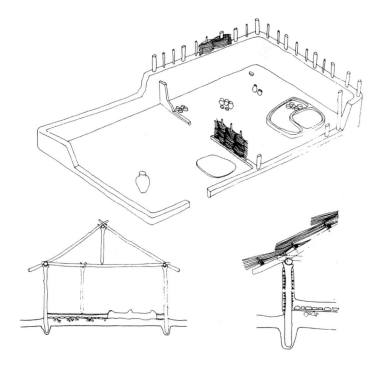

Figure 20.2 *Plan and reconstruction of Vinča culture house, from Obre, Bosnia (former Yugoslavia) (after Benac, 1973)*

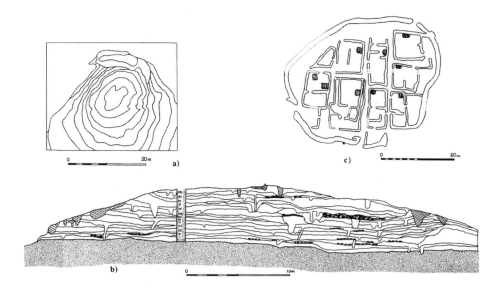

Figure 20.3 *The Eneolithic 'tell' settlement of Ovcharovo, Bulgaria. An archaeologist's traditional presentation: (a) contour plan of the mound; (b) cross-section drawn through the excavated mound; (c) the houses excavated in one occupation horizon of the mound (after Todorova 1982)*

335

time, forming a 'new building horizon' (Todorova 1982; Todorova, *et al.* 1983) (Figure 20.3).

The basis of this traditional lack of interest in the replacement history of individual houses has been the premise that there are no real inequalities in the Neolithic/ Eneolithic villages, and that any differentiation between households (or for that matter between individuals within a household) is irrelevant to the basic picture of 'egalitarian' society. Such a concept has been given its most eloquent expression in the Utopian scheme of peaceful co-existing matrilocal societies of Old Europe, an example of which is the passage below written by the archaeologist who coined the term 'Old Europe' (Gimbutas 1991; Tringham 1993; Conkey and Tringham, 1995).

> The Old European social structure was in direct contrast with the Indo-European system that replaced it. As archaeological, historical, linguistic, and religious evidence shows, Old European society was organized around a theocratic, communal temple community, guided by a queen-priestess, her brother and uncle, and a council of women as the governing body. In spite of the revered status of women in religious life, the cemetery evidence throughout the 5th and most of the 4th millennia BC does not suggest any imbalance between the sexes or a subservience of one sex to the other. It suggests, instead, a condition of mutual respect . . .
>
> (Gimbutas 1991: xi)

The use-lives of houses: processualist models of the prehistoric built environment in mainstream archaeological practice

These 'traditional' reconstructions and interpretations were enhanced by the New (processualist) Archaeology style research that my colleagues and I carried out as part of the Opovo Archaeological Project during 1983–89 (Tringham *et al.* 1985, 1992; Tringham and Stevanovic 1990; Tringham 1991b). The New Archaeology with its focus on the explanation of the process of cultural and behavioral change, rather than the more traditional explication of variability of cultural forms, treats the manipulation of materials – including the built environment – as a process. Thus artifacts and buildings are said to have use-lives, during which their form and utilization can be modified (Binford 1982c, 1983a; Schiffer 1987). The variable nature of these changes will affect the eventual appearance of the building as part of the archaeological record (McGuire and Schiffer 1983).

The ultimate aim of the study of the built environment in the New (processualist) Archaeology is to link the occupants of the building to the process of the evolution of social complexity. Towards this end the reconstructed use-life of a building – the container and reflector of social behavior – is used as a monitor of more generalized trends and patterns of social behavior.[2]

In our study, expectations of a building during its use-life, from planning, construction, occupation, maintenance, to its decay, abandonment, destruction and eventual replacement were proposed (using as sources ethnoarchaeological observations and experimentation with 'traditional' building materials) and tested with the available empirical archaeological data in the Opovo project (Tringham 1978, 1991a: 13–16). The aim of this enterprise was to be able to design 'middle range research' that would provide a rigorous framework for attributing the archaeological record to behavior (Raab and Goodyear 1984; Tringham and Krstic 1990). During the excavation part of the research at Opovo we were attempting to attribute certain architectural features and spatial patterns of associated materials to units of economic and social co-operation. This would provide a first – and scientifically (within the conditions of logical positivist 'science') legitimate – step in identifying and, eventually, reconstructing the prehistoric households at Opovo. Our hypothesis was that Opovo-Ugar Bajbuk was a typical village that had been established on agriculturally marginal land during the socioeconomic transformations of the Eneolithic period of South-east Europe, an important aspect of which involved changes in the degree of permanence of settlement (sedentism) (Tringham 1990).

The New (processualist) Archaeology view that the built environment has a use-life is based on the research carried out by traditional archaeologists, as described in the previous section. It takes the study of archaeological architecture much further, however, by opening up for questioning many aspects of archaeological architecture that traditionally had been taken for granted as common sense: what happens to a building after construction (production), how long it lasted, how and why it reached the end of its use-life, and what happened after its abandonment. Such aspects had previously been considered to have no need of investigation. The analysis of the use-life of artifacts, including architectural features, is now part of mainstream archaeological practice in North America. But these questions are by no means common in European prehistoric archaeology, and it was a question of debate with our Yugoslav colleagues in the Opovo archaeological project whether or not we should include them in the project, since their study increases the degree of detail (and therefore time and money) needed for excavation. The rewards for such increased effort were not obvious to them.

For example, they could see no reason to question the causes of the house fires of the Eneolithic villages. For those of us participating in the Opovo project who were interested in the use-lives of houses and villages, however, the causes and context of the fires were priority objects of investigation (Tringham et al. 1985, 1992). My interest in the explanation of the ubiquity of the Eneolithic house fires, and that of my colleague Mirjana Stevanovic, began in the earlier excavation (1976–78) of Selevac and (1980–82) of Gomolava. The research at Selevac:

> . . . although not pinpointing the immediate causes of the fires, helped considerably to define the context of socio-cultural transformation which may have contributed ultimately to the widespread burning of houses in southeast Europe at this time. We see that the burning of houses is associated with a period of intensification of economic production, . . . with the increased use of fires in closed ovens . . . inside the houses, . . . with the increased use of clay in the construction of the houses, using . . . solid and long-lasting wattle-and-daub construction. It is associated with increased population density and with increased complexity in the use of space in villages and density of houses, . . . with the increased longevity of settlements, . . . with a change in storage method, possibly comprising storage inside the houses of such flammable materials as grains, and with an increase in the accumulation and storage of surplus goods and

Figure 20.4
Photographs
showing the
process of detailed
excavation of
the floor and
superstructure of
houses at Opovo,
Yugoslavia

prestige items. Finally . . . it is also associated hypothetically with increased differentiation within a village in access to resources and the production process and with complex organization of production and social relations (including transmission of property) by households . . .

Any or all of these conditions could have led either to an increase in the occurrence of accidental fires during the occupation of houses or to an increase in the occurrence of deliberate fires during their construction, maintenance, and abandonment . . . On the basis of preliminary information from . . . sites such as Gomolava and Opovo, we would say intuitively that, contrary to the modern local folklore of Selevac which tells of how the settlement perished in a great conflagration, the fires did not all occur at once, nor did they have a single cause, nor did they all happen at the same stage in the use-life of a building. Our model of the transformation of the social relations of production leads us to favor intuitively the idea that the houses . . . were burned deliberately at the end of the household cycle.

(Tringham 1990: 609–610)

In order to investigate these questions, we developed a technology to excavate and record carefully the collapsed debris of the burned house superstructure and floors layer by layer (Figure 20.4). This was in high contrast to the strategy of excavation practised by those with a traditional interest in the *construction* of the house who focused on revealing the house plan, any standing architecture (wall bases) and foundations (postholes and trenches) with a relatively quick removal and undetailed record of the 'messy' 'debris' which lay above it (for example Todorova *et al.* 1983). At Opovo, details of the use-lives of the artifacts and their fragments on the floors and in the superstructural rubble were recorded, in addition to the more traditional recording of superficial form (Schiffer 1987). We searched in the area excavated for traces of houses that did not burn and found none. We looked carefully in the collapsed debris for data reflecting the path and nature of the fires.

The lack of burned materials in the areas between houses indicates that the houses burned in separate fires. The houses burned at temperatures that in some parts of each house reached over 1000°C. Such temperatures are regarded as very high for accidental fires of wattle-and-daub houses and indicate that the fires are likely to have been 'helped' by deliberate fueling and tending (Kirk 1969). Plausible explanations of deliberate burning of a single house include arson to eradicate property, pests, insects, disease, ghosts, or to signify the death of the household head as a symbolic end of the household cycle.

We also challenged the assumption that the village in its entirety is the best or more representative unit of analysis – a challenge begun previously by a number of other archaeologists (Kaiser and Voytek 1983; Bogucki 1988; Chapman 1990a and b; Tringham 1990, 1991a). Thus a basic premise of the Opovo project was that individual households within a village, rather than the village as a whole, were the units of social and economic action. Moreover, we looked for and expected short-term but very real inequalities in terms of dominance and access to human and material resources between households, and between genders (Lawrence and Low 1990: 461).

The idea of inequality between and within the households encouraged a much more detailed comparison of household units within villages. One set of data that we expected to reflect such differentiation was the process of the household cycle, through which each household and its house has its own 'biography' reflecting demographic and life changes at different rates and times. Although we were aware of the dangers of equating 'household' with house, we used this assumption as a starting point in our studies of the detached houses of prehistoric Europe. Thus the details of the modification, abandonment and replacement history of *each* house became important, as did the spatial and temporal relationships of houses with one another, and with other features of the built environment, such as garbage pits and wells.

This means that each building was excavated as though it were going to provide different evidence on construction, occupation and destruction, and that these different stages in life-history would occur at different times. This led to a highly non-traditional excavation strategy which entailed careful microstratigraphic observation of house relationships and the detailed examination of the superstructural and foundation data of each house (Tringham *et al.* 1985, 1992).

The pattern of modified vertical superimposition of house replacement at Opovo conforms to the pattern of house replacement in places where the area for residence was restricted, similarly to settlement mounds or 'tells'. The formation of 'tells' are the result of a restricted settlement area in combination with intensive, yet not necessarily continuous occupation and intensive accumulation of domestic debris caused, for example, by the burning of large amounts of clay daub (Davidson 1976; Rosen 1986). Many have assumed that 'tells' are an adaptive response of long-term occupants to particular topographic restrictions on settlement, such as river or (in Opovo's case) marshland and the availability of cultivable soils and water. Others have suggested other kinds of restrictive factors, such as defence against flood (Sherratt 1972: 522), defence against marauders (Todorova 1978), or unequal social access to land for residence through inheritance and ownership (Tringham 1990). There is often an implied, although not critically examined assumption, that these settlements reflect greater social complexity and continuity of tradition and place than in more 'open' settlements. The contrast may, however, have more to do with social control (Chapman 1989) or what is defined by the occupants as a significant 'place' (Bailey 1990).

Both the traditional and New (processualist) Archaeologists offer authoritative and optimistically-worded statements about what they have found. They interpret the built environment according to a very specific set of questions that they deem both relevant and answerable. These questions are based on a number of very specific premises (usually unexpressed) about how people behave and have behaved in the past. These mainstream studies provide statements on the archaeologists' 'facts' which in turn become reiterated and reconfirmed in secondary studies that incorporate the prehistoric built environment and all the archaeologists' limitations into their own works on space and place.

My task in the following part of this paper is to show that archaeological practice itself is being transformed, not so much by any new techniques of retrieval and analysis, but by thinking *beyond* the boundaries of both traditional and New (processualist) Archaeology.

The Post-processualist transformation of archaeology

Just as New Archaeologists thought that they had squeezed the 'true' prehistory out of the archaeological record, the very premises on which their work was based were themselves challenged by what has often been referred to collectively as 'post-processualist' archaeology, that emerged in Europe and to a certain extent in North America in the early 1980s, but has yet to be accepted as mainstream in archaeological practice (Hodder 1985; Patrik 1985; Patterson 1987; Shanks and Tilley 1987a). Amongst those challenging processualist thinking were archaeologists whose work, though varied in the details of its approaches, may collectively be termed 'feminist archaeology' (Conkey 1989; Gero and Conkey 1991). Margaret Conkey, Joan Gero, Alison Wylie and others have described how archaeology did not participate in the feminist challenges to social anthropology in the 1970s, how archaeologists before the mid–1980s may have included gender in their models, but they were by no means feminist archaeologists. They did not challenge the androcentrist bias of prehistory, they did not challenge the essentialist view of the sexual division of labor, nor did they challenge the dominant macro-scale at which prehistory was written, whether it concerned the evolution of social complexity or the origins of plant-gathering or the origins of urban civilization (Conkey and Spector 1984; Gero 1990; Conkey and Gero 1991; Wylie 1991b, 1992; Conkey 1992).

Much of what I describe below as characteristic of a feminist archaeology coincides with post-processualist archaeology. First, the epistemological basis for the construction of knowledge about the past is re-evaluated (Leone 1982b; Wylie 1982, 1991b; Keller 1985; Hodder 1986; Harding 1987; Longino 1990a). Post-processualist archaeology is essentially interpretive in nature by contrast with the positivist empiricist characteristic of New (processualist) Archaeology (Hodder 1991b). Thus a researcher is not required to demonstrate gender or 'domestic unit' in the archaeological record in order to think about the prehistoric construction and practice of gender ideologies and dominance relations within the household (Conkey and Gero 1991: 11–14). It seems to have been this challenge to logical positivism in archaeological research that paved the way for the acceptance of more feminist ways of thinking in archaeology (Stacey and Thorne 1985). Thus, to consider gender in prehistory (i.e. to *engender archaeology*) as Gero and Conkey have coined the term [Gero and Conkey 1991]) does not mean to search for the material correlates of gender roles (e.g. women's spaces, women's tasks) in the archaeological record (Conkey and Gero 1991: 11–14). The aim must be rather to produce a visibiliy of gender when visualizing the human social actors in and around the built environment of the past (Moore 1986; Tringham 1991b).

Secondly, the feminist critique of archaeology encourages us to be self-reflexive of the sociopolitical context of archaeological practice and to scrutinize critically the processes whereby knowledge is produced. It reminds us to be aware that all researchers hold biases and make assumptions (often implicitly) as to what need not be questioned. The New Archaeology's claim to be an objective science that reconstructs a prehistoric reality has been challenged by post-processualist archaeologists, including feminists, who claim that the past is a fiction that is constructed according to the subjective biases of the writer (Hodder 1985; Shanks and Tilley 1987a). The degree of subjectivity in this challenge varies from extreme to moderate. Within this challenge, however, lies an attempt to make explicit the basis of the ambiguities of archaeological interpretation and the writing of prehistory.

Ambiguities are inherent in the interpretation of archaeological architecture from its very retrieval to its visualized reconstruction (Tringham 1991a and b). As the 'reading' of the archaeological record expands, especially to include questions of the construction of gender and other ideologies, the ambiguities and lack of consensus in its interpretation increase. A plurality of interpretations, according to a feminist critique of science, does not indicate a weakness of will or ambivalence (Wylie 1989a). Rather, the same empirical data can and should be subject to a critical interplay of a variety of interpretations and 'readings' by different archaeologists holding different perspectives and philosophies about the past and the nature of archaeology (Conkey and Gero 1991). Rather than feeling that our interpretations are in competition and persuading each other that one is more accurate than the other, feminist archaeologists encourage a recognition and acceptance of the ambiguity of archaeological data.

Alison Wylie reminds us, however, that archaeological data are not 'infinitely plastic' (Wylie 1989b, 1992). The free flow of the imagination in interpretation is constrained on the one hand by consideration of the material parameters of architectural variability provided in the archaeological record. On the other hand ethnoarchaeological studies and ethnographic observations about the built environment may be used for more than cautionary tales and cross-cultural generalizations. They also constrain and at the same time broaden our *plausible* expectations in terms of variability in architectural remains that express and reflect changes in the role, relations and actions of men and women in the household in prehistory (Hodder 1987c).[3] Together these two sources of information lead to certain constructions of the past which are more plausible than others.

While maintaining high standards of empirical investigation, it is also crucial, according to the feminist critique of science, that the ambiguity of interpretation and plurality of plausible views is maintained during the *presentation* of the interpretations. It is this target that lies behind the visual and textual challenge to conventional (academic) methods of reporting and presenting archaeological research of the kind provided in this paper and elsewhere through the media of narratives, creative visual images, and non-linear texts (Hodder 1989a; Handsman 1990; Shanks 1992a; Spector 1991; Tringham 1991a and b, 1992).

Archaeologists have always been mediators between the data and its interpretation, structuring their reader's and their own experience through selection of what to re-present and how to represent it: by text or by image. Post-processualist archaeology and the last part of this paper is about the critical awareness of the archaeologist as active mediator limiting and encouraging the reader to view, visualize, imagine and participate in the interpretation of the built environment of the past (Bourdier 1989; Tringham 1991a). The traditional passive reflective role of material culture, including the past built environment, as expressed in the New Archaeology and its predecessors, is thereby turned on its head into an 'active' role in structuring social action and a symbolic expression of, for example, the tensions of gender relations and dominance structures. This perspective is not mutually exclusive of the more traditional view, but, together with it, definitely offers a richer view of material culture. The built environment can thus be both a passive container and reflection of social action *and* in a dialectical relationship – an 'active' arena: a medium for and symbolic expression of the social actions, practices, negotiations and dominance structures of the inhabitants and visitors, that constrains and materially channels cultural practices (Bourdieu 1977; Cosgrove 1984; Giddens 1984; Pred 1984, 1990; Hodder 1986, 1987b, 1990a; Moore 1986; Bourdier 1989; Harvey 1989; Soja 1989; Donley-Reid 1990; Lawrence and Low 1990; Stea and Turan 1990; Rodman 1992).

These transformations in the construction of knowledge and the treatment of archaeological data have enabled and encouraged an enormous expansion in the range of legitimate objects of knowledge considered by post-processualist (including feminist) archaeologists. These include themes that have been marginalized by mainstream New (processualist) Archaeologists (and their predecessors) as not only untestable, but irrelevant to or as constant variables within the main course of human evolution. Such themes are individual intentionality and social action, the cultural construction of gender and other ideologies, the meaningfulness as well as the meaning of material culture in the playing out of these ideologies in social practice, and the dominance struggles and tensions within and between households, and the histories of small social groups.

Most of the above-mentioned themes incorporate what we might call multiscalar theorizing within the realm of social relations. Thus they focus not only on the conventional macro-scale supra-domestic world of public buildings that was the arena of political action, but they articulate this world in a dialectical sense with the micro-scale world of what women and men do in relation to domestic space, their negotiations for power, their negotiations about housework and where to put the garbage.

From space to place, and from evolution to history: the practice of post-processualist archaeology of the built environment

I came late to 'engendered' (see the definition of this term above) post-processualist and feminist archaeology (Tringham 1991b: 93). I had embraced the themes and methodology of the New (processualist) Archaeology during my field research in South-east Europe. My own transformation had an effect not so much on the retrieval of data at Opovo, as on its subsequent interpretation. The burned houses at prehistoric Opovo were excavated and analyzed according to the philosophy and values of New (processualist) Archaeology (Tringham *et al.* 1985). With my own broadening of horizons of imagination, experience and question-asking, their interpretation is very different in terms of presentation, the envisaging of the social context, and their meaningfulness (Tringham 1991a and b).

In a feminist interpretation of the archaeological record at Opovo, I have assumed that every aspect of material culture is endowed with some kind of significance for the original occupants, and that we have to be ready to use our imaginations and anthropological experience to envisage what that significance might have been. Even domestic garbage – a material that was assumed to need no questioning – cannot be presumed to be without symbolic significance along gendered lines (Moore 1986; Hodder 1987d). The disposal of rubble from burned houses in garbage pits can be more meaningful than the 'rational' function of getting rid of unwanted mess or of filling-in pits. At Opovo the remains of a feasting roast are deposited in special pits;

ash is separated out from other kitchen debris; the rubble from burned houses was, on one occasion, thrown immediately into a well, but in other cases was placed on top of a garbage pit perhaps several years after the fire. Now it is up to us to think through plausible meaningfulness within the context provided by the archaeological record and our interpretive powers.

Feminist archaeology means writing the prehistory of *people*. This means social actors who have gender, personalities, biographies. To envisage the drama of a house-burning means to imagine that event as one which was created by those social actors, and one that had a significant but different impact on each of their lives. Houses, events and places have multiple meanings and these meanings can be considered at multiple scales of social practice (Rodman 1992: 643). Moreover, a place will be perceived differently through the eyes of the different prehistoric actors, whose differences are marked by age, gender, power and life-history. It is up to archaeologists to enrich our interpretations by imagining and presenting these multiple perceptions – meanings at different scales – rather than choose the most obvious, or the most demonstrable, or the most functional explanation.

Archaeology, I believe, can make a real contribution to such *multiscalar* explorations of history. Archaeology has traditionally given priority to the evolutionary long-term comparative view and to the regional and generational scale of analysis. At this scale of analysis it is possible (although this is rarely done) to consider the cultural construction of gender and other ideologies and ideal structures through the patterns and trends of expression in the built environment. Post-processualist and feminist archaeology adds a focus on the micro-scale of the lives and intentional actions of individuals as they practice, negotiate and change those structures.

I find that Allan Pred's theory of the production of place is an appropriate method of implementing the multiscalar view of history/prehistory by archaeologists. Pred recognizes, among universally present components of history, the *life-histories of made objects* such as the built environment (the transformation of nature) in addition to other elements such as an unbroken flow of local events and 'projects' (the reproduction of social and cultural forms), and the formation of biographies of social actors (men and women) (Pred 1984, 1990). These universal components are not subject to universal laws and general principles, but are interwoven differently with each local historical circumstance in the formation and transformation of actual historically contingent places (Pred 1984: 284, 291). Local 'places' are interwoven dialectically to larger 'places,' and daily paths and practices are interwoven to life paths and generational and long-term paths in the formation of 'historical geographies' (Pred 1990).

The broadening and enriching of interpretation that post-processualist and feminist archaeology bring to the understanding of concepts such as place and gender in prehistory can be demonstrated by the changes in the treatment of the built environment at prehistoric Opovo, during and after the excavation of the houses. As a New (processualist) Archaeologist excavating the prehistoric village of Opovo in 1983–89, I was able to retrieve important data on the final stages in the use-life of houses. The following passages are extracts from one of the project's preliminary reports published in an academic journal. They describe observations made on the process of house replacement at prehistoric Opovo (Figure 20.5):

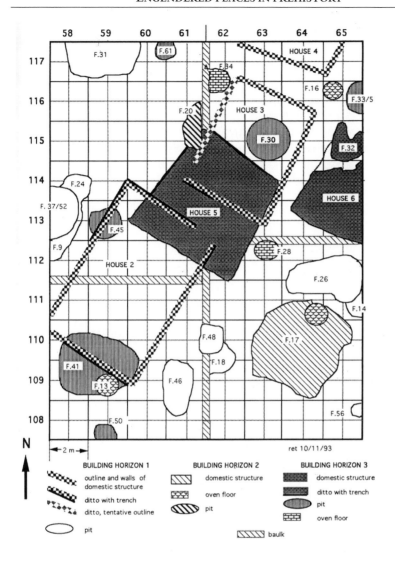

Figure 20.5 Schematized plan of the houses whose histories comprise the occupation of the excavated part of the Eneolithic village at Opovo, Yugoslavia

At Opovo, the deposits of different building horizons piled up to form a low mound over what was already a natural island in the marshes. The two well-preserved building horizons (BH I [later] and BH 3 [earlier]) at Opovo are not chronologically contiguous, being separated perhaps by one or two generations. Efforts were made, sometimes immediately after the burning events, to flatten the burned remains of the houses and deposit them in pits, in one case filling a probable well. In many other cases the rubble was used – long after it had lain on the surface and had weathered – to top off garbage pits just before new building was started.

(Tringham et al. 1992: 382)

Thus the builders of the BH I structures were probably well aware of the remains of earlier building horizons, either through tradition or direct observation on or near their occupation surface. But the new houses display a certain amount of (but not complete) horizontal displacement in that their locations are not exactly above that of the old ones, I suspect because the exact location of the previous house was not known. This impression is made more plausible when we see that the corner of one of the new houses was placed directly over a previous well that had been filled in immediately after the fire of the old house.

(Tringham et al. 1992: 365)

As I became involved in the practice of post-processualist and feminist archaeology (from 1989 onwards) I began to interpret the houses at Opovo as having *life-histories* rather than *use-lives*. The prehistoric houses and their surrounding landscape become the tangible expression of the continuity of place, which the social actors use and to which the inhabitants give meaning in their own biographies. The burning of the houses and the placing of a new house in relation to the old become meaningful within the context of social action in the village and beyond. The deposition of their rubble in garbage pits and a well are perhaps part of the 'burial rites' of the dead house to ensure continuity of place. The ultimate aim of archaeology in post-processualist and feminist archaeology may thus be expressed as the (re)construction of the interweaving (pre)histories of places.

Constructing a prehistory of engendered places

To write the prehistory of intertwining biographies of places is one way to construct a prehistory of Europe but it demands a more detailed retrieval and interpretation of the archaeological record, since the biography of every village, house, garbage pit and well – of every place – is unique within its historical context. Thus, in extrapolating from a sample of houses to all houses in a village, or from one site to other (unexcavated) villages we lose the point of the prehistory of places. The prehistory that we can write in this genre may be about only one village, but it involves socioeconomic transformations that have been recognized over a whole continent and that span a historical trajectory of many thousands of years, in which the occupation of Opovo lies in a small fraction of time somewhere in the middle (Figure 20.6).

The general theoretical framework of the prehistory of Europe, and more specifically that of the Neolithic/Eneolithic phase of Balkan prehistory, provides us with a general context of social and economic transformations in which the prehistory of Opovo can be written. A suite of significant changes in the archaeological record has been observed in South-east and Central Europe and identified as the transition from Eneolithic to Early Bronze Age. These include a change from aggregated to a dispersed pattern of settlements and a ceasing of the custom of burning houses. There is consensus amongst archaeologists that these changes *do* represent significant transformations in the structures of social reproduction, but there are very different characterizations of the nature of these transformations, and their causes.

Traditionally these changes in the material record have been interpreted as reflecting a population replacement as the result of invasion of Indo-European pastoralists from the North Pontic area (Tasic 1989; Gimbutas, 1991: 352–401). In this model it is

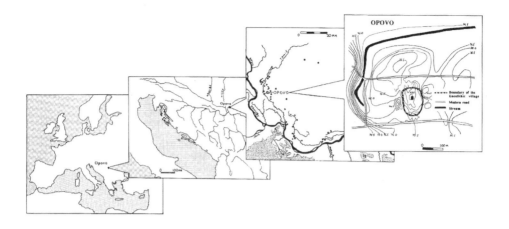

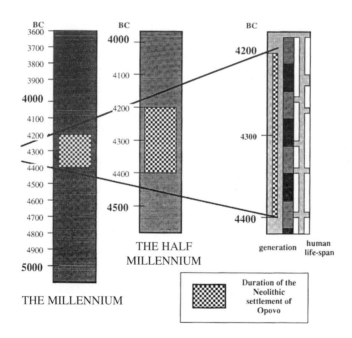

Figure 20.6 *Chart showing the place of Opovo in multi-scalar time and space*

347

believed that an Indo-European invasion nipped in the bud Old (Neolithic-Eneolithic) Europe's progress towards state formation and urban settlements. While there is general consensus that continental temperate Europe lacks the occurrence of urban settlements, centralized authority and state formation until the end of the first millennium BC, not everyone agrees that Indo-European invasion is the explanation! By contrast, other archaeologists have suggested that the record reflects the internal social transformations of an existing population unaffected by population replacement or supplement (Sherratt 1984; Anthony 1986; Tringham 1990).

Some of these archaeologists have explained the hypothesized internal transformation from Eneolithic to Early Bronze Age by ecological conditions and population growth in combination with adaptive technological responses and concomitant changes in labour organization and social relations (Chapman 1982; Sherratt 1984; Chapman 1990a). Although I have been drawn towards these functionalist explanations, I have preferred to explain the internal transformation predominantly as a transformation in the social relations of production.

In what was explicitly a New (processualist) Archaeology-style model (if of a traditional Marxist nature), I suggested that, in the domestic mode of production, in which there is a flexible and temporary basis both of power and inequality, there are real limits to the number of members who may belong to a household and to the number of households that can interact together in an aggregated settlement (Johnson 1982; Fletcher 1986; Tringham 1990). I proposed that at many times during the Neolithic and Eneolithic periods in Europe (4000–3300 BC), these organizational limits were reached. Thus, for example, the trajectory of intensification of production and growth of population that we see in the Late Neolithic/Early Eneolithic settlements of South-east Europe could be continued only by changing to a system of organization and power structure which comprised a more centralized and more permanently hierarchical social organization. In Balkan and temperate European prehistory, however, this latter option was resisted until the late first millennium BC, preferring to maintain the household as the main unit of social and economic co-operation.

In such a model the dispersal of the large aggregated villages and the establishment of a small hamlet like Opovo represent a development away from any growth of centralized organization *toward* the maintenance of the smaller, co-resident, kin-based domestic groups as units of social and economic organization. This model for the local Balkan transformation can be expanded to explain the apparent resistance in European prehistory to any trends towards centralization of settlement, of labor control, of distribution, or of production, or the emergence of a class system, by the strategy of fissioning and dispersal of settlement along household lines (Rowlands 1980; Demoule, n.d.). In this view, the social formation based on household organization as the dominant social unit of economic and social action remained throughout the prehistory of Europe, until the Romanization of Europe.

The prehistoric hamlet of Opovo is placed in the center of these transformations. It was established as a new village in the later part of the Vinča culture in a marshy location that was contrary to the ideal (prescribed) location of late Neolithic or Eneolithic settlements which was in close proximity to large areas of easily cultivated land. Opovo represents the fissioning of a larger village that was situated somewhere in a more ideal location, part of whose population dispersed to the agriculturally marginal marshlands north of the Danube. Opovo seems to have been established right from the beginning as a village to be occupied all the year round, with an emphasis on hunting red deer and procuring lithic resources. It lasted at this place for 5–7 generations (200 years?) and probably was never occupied at any one time by more than 10 households, in contrast to the possibly hundred households suggested for some of the larger late Neolithic and Eneolithic villages (Chapman 1989, 1990a).

Coming from a processualist examination of Opovo, I would argue that the establishment of Opovo lies at the beginning of a process that was to be seen more and more frequently in this part of Europe in the late Eneolithic period, culminating in the much changed archaeological record that is typically seen in the Early Bronze Age of South-east Europe. I would argue also that, at Opovo, much of the social and economic structure of the Vinča culture, as seen in large villages of the fertile valleys south of the Danube, which includes the styles of elaborating material culture, remained intact, that the changes that we see, for example an importance given to red deer hunting and the dispersed settlement pattern, represent an attempt to resist and to change the traditional dominance pattern. I would argue, however, that in the big picture of cultural evolution, Opovo had a very small marginal part to play, that it reflects a very small step in the long-term transformations of European society.

A feminist standpoint, however, says; that no hamlet, nor any man or woman, is 'marginal to the big picture'. Thus in a post-processualist and feminist interpretation, the prehistory of Opovo becomes a significant object of investigation. It is obvious that the establishment of such a small hamlet in this place where agriculture was difficult – where killing wild animals became a common occupation, where the ground was constantly waterlogged, where the plant and animal life was different from south of the Danube, where the network of communication and exchange was so different (flint was nearer, obsidian was more accessible, copper was very far away) – would have had considerable implications for the division of labor and access to resources for the occupants. An interest in gender relations and social action at a micro-scale enables me to broaden these implications to suggest that in this small settlement, there would have been a rapid decrease in the pooling of labor between households and extra-kin support especially for the female members of the households. Each household would have a different history in terms of how relations were still maintained with the large villages further south, and how they became self-sustaining and different from those large villages during the course of the 200 years of prehistory in the place called Opovo.

In writing the feminist prehistory of this place called Opovo, I interpret the archaeological record in terms of the interweaving of house biographies, the biographies of the imagined actors who lived in the houses (the dialectic between their life path and daily path, and between their individual and institutional roles), and the social action itself that took place in the houses and outside them and in the fields, marshes and woods that made up this place (production and distribution projects as social forms, the dominance structure of social practice [using the terminology of Pred (1984, 1990)]). This interpretation comprises an interplay between the different levels of analysis of the archaeological record (continental, regional, archaeological culture, archaeological site, millennia, archaeological phase, generation, lifetime, event). Different levels of consensus and ambiguity are presented in the interpretation, in which 'scientific demonstration' is interwoven with a more interpretive strategy, the use of creative imagination and alternative forms of textual and visual expression.

Here I can only present some fragments of what such a prehistory looks like. It focuses on the interpretation of the archaeological record of architecture. These fragments are *en route* to a fuller account which would be embraced in the final excavation report of Opovo. On the other hand, if the academic world protests too much, I may revert to a more conventional report.

Much of the data from which the house biographies will be written and through which the continuity of place will be considered – for example on the micro-stratigraphic relations between house floors, house foundations and method of destruction – can be (and have been) reported with consensus in conventional 'scientific' format (Tringham *et al.* 1985, 1992). As I have described earlier in this paper, we have already emphasized the careful collection of these data within our original New (processualist) Archaeology theoretical framework of the Opovo project. Even though my theoretical preference has shifted towards a post-processualist and especially feminist interpretation of the archaeological record, I certainly would not advocate a rejection of the collection of data through the New Archaeology's 'middle range research' methodology. These data provide us with some basic material parameters of architectural variability in terms of how the houses were built, furnished and destroyed. They form the starting point as well as the constraints on the free flow of our creative imagination as we visualize social action at a micro-scale and consider the range of plausible interpretations in writing the post-processualist and feminist prehistory of a place called Opovo (Wylie 1989a).

It takes a great deal of effort and imaginative power to consider humans in the past, who engaged in social acts for many years for many hours of each day with many other people, who each had a history, and whose acts were carried out within the context of this history, of their gender, and of their age (generation). But we cannot deny that these social actors were an essential aspect of the archaeological architecture that we excavate and reconstruct. Prehistoric places are created by girls and boys, young men and young women, old men and women as individuals and members of a social group; they are created differently throughout their lives through their experience, perception and memory of social practice (Tuan 1977; Boschetti 1986; Rybczynski 1986). The action of each has contributed to what we see as archaeologists.

This fragment is written as we look at the burned rubble of the house in Opovo in Figure 20.1. I have interpreted the rubble in terms of what seems to me a plausible scenario, that of deliberate burning of houses at the end of the household cycle.

How to end the use-life of a house

She watched the house burn.

He had died. He's strung up in the tree now, safe. Now it's time to kill the house.

Finally after all these years living in these godforsaken marshlands. Stuck in this place, with no one to turn to or to help, except him, or worse, her.

It was all right for him, he could escape *that* one by running off to the village. 'Time to take the deer timber down there' or 'my turn to tell the story to the new ones down there'. And off he'd go. Leaving me. And her. And the others, but they don't count.

It's burning nicely now. What a crummy house they built. Nothing but kindling for its bones. Only an outer skin. I'm surprised the loft didn't fall down on our heads, with all his pots and her rugs up there. Well it doesn't take long to collapse and kill it. They wouldn't think much of this house down in the village. You can't kill a house by yourself down there. But then you can't do anything by yourself down there.

Here it goes! Watch the flame! Look at it burn! Yellow, purple, sunlight, moonlight, orange, marshlight. Ugh! What's that smell? Must be her clothes! Or maybe he was hiding something else up there. Ooops, step back a little. My hair's scorching. It makes my eyes water. I'm crying! I haven't done that for a long time.

What a roaring! It sounds like those dreadful other men – the deer – when they come looking for us – the women. Why do they always have to fight? There go his pots. All killed. Finally! They seem to be throbbing in the middle there. Mustn't let the fire die, or he'll come back. More wood. Pile it up a bit more here. Let in some more air! A house must breathe to die. Push the air into its cavity. That's better. Flaming again!

Burn his pots! Kill his stuff! Now I'm in charge. The circle is complete. I can go back to the village. Away from the heat, away from the creatures that torture and bite. Back to village noise, complaints, shrieks, laughter, gossip, friends, life.

(Tringham 1991b: 124)

Prehistoric places are also created by archaeologists: people who are acting within socially created ideologies about gender, history, and work. The archaeologist's interpretation of these ancient places depends very much on his/her own outlook on and experience of the same phenomena, as well the breadth of his/her imagination and reading from ethnography and history. It depends also on the archaeologist's experience of participating in the revealing of these long-distant events through excavation. This does not give to the excavator personal and exclusive access or rights to interpret the Opovo data, but it does make a difference to the interpretation. The following passages are extracted from my own unpublished day-books or diaries that were written during the 1985–89 field seasons of the Opovo archaeological project:

Excavation as drama: events from the excavation of Feature 30 'The Well' (Figure 20.7)

June 10–July 17, 1985: Excavation of house floor called Feature 4 (a BHI house). We noticed a circular area in the NE corner of this feature where there was no burned clay daub rubble – mystery! . . . a later tree? . . . or a later pit?

July 19–26, 1986: Under the 'mystery hole' is a lense of yellow: Feature 30. Underneath this lense is a compact mass of burned clay rubble pieces: what a surprise! Meanwhile to the south of Feature 30, two BH3 houses are now being excavated (House 5 and 6). Some of the rubble is vitrified (result of high temperature burning). What is going on? Bogdan thinks it's another house below BH3. I don't believe it!

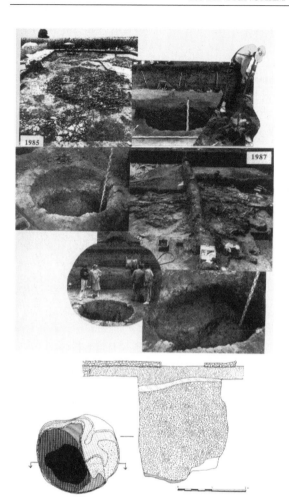

Figure 20.7

Photograph/drawing collage of the history of the well (Feature 30) excavated in the Eneolithic village of Opovo, Yugoslavia

July 1987: Feature 30 not excavated this season, we have burned houses (5 and 6) to excavate.

July 13–26, 1988: We go down 10 cm more and suddenly after last night's rain, the pit edge becomes very clear. It is a perfectly circular *c.* 2-meter diameter damp stain filled with burned clay rubble. It's finally contrasting with the surrounding area that is dry light brown earth. This is certainly no house floor but a pit. How high up did it start? How much of it have we missed? What house does it go with? It must be dug from the BH3 house level. Yes, that's it. We remove the southern half of Feature 30 and retain a cross-section. The fill comprises almost entirely loose crumbly rubble, which is now at least 1 metre deep – extraordinary! I never saw anything like this! The large lumps of waterlogged rubble look as fresh as though they were burned and dumped in the pit before any weathering was able to affect them i.e. immediately after the fire. We have to stop now, too much water, need to pump. Fill clearly keeps going on down. Decide to wait for later in summer after excavation season. Ljuba will come out here.

July 11–24, 1989: Take out north side of this well; it down to same level as that finished in 1988 on south side. Sides of the pit are virtually vertical. A well? Water level is much lower this year so we can go down deeper.

July 25 1989: Underneath rubble well-fill is a lense of grey clay that probably represents primary deposition of well muck. Excavate this to the sterile loess bottom of pit/well. *Now* I can understand what's going on! In originally digging the pit (6000 years ago), the underlying loess was left as a spiral ramp winding from its lowest point at the southern edge of the pit, up and around the eastern side of the pit, to its highest point at the northern edge of the pit. Into this ramp there appear to be steps cut, which are mostly now worn down and smoothed but are nevertheless discernible even after 6000 years of being under water, mud, soil and rubble. The ramp lifts the floor of the pit/well up to about 1 meter above the bottom. It is possible that the top of the ramp was then the base for a ladder and from there you would climb down with your bucket to the water of the well which (varying year by year and season by season) lay in the bottom 1 meter of this 3-meter deep pit. While excavating this year, for example, we had no problem with the water table, in contrast to 1988. We used the top of the ramp as the base for a peasant ladder in order to climb up and down into this pit to draw it and excavate it.

For me personally gender and age are such powerful dimensions to social life that it seems essential to consider them in any prehistoric narrative. This fragment takes another perception of the house-fire, through the eyes of the one referred to as 'she' and 'her' in the first narrative:

But the place goes on

She's killed the house, as though she killed us all. But she can't kill this place!

Now she's run off, back to her mother's house. So soon does she forget this place. It's always a problem bringing them here from so far away. They aren't the same as us. So many people live there. They talk so loudly. So much noise. I couldn't stand it down there in the big village. The young ones are wild and bossy.

She wanted to be in charge. She was always trying to get me to help her bring up the water from the well. Said everyone did it in her village. What cheek! She had no respect for my place.

Well, now I have to put things in order by myself. She left the job half done as usual. There's still work to do. I'll try to finish it today. Maybe I'll get the boy to help finish the job when I go over there. At least he does what I tell him. Now I'll have to get used to that one in his house. Moving. Moving. Why can't we ever stay in one place?

Finally it's quiet here. The fire's died down. It's cool enough now I think. What a roaring it made; I suppose it was hard for it to die. There's a rat that died with it. There goes one, it must have been eating the remains. That looks like a piece of my cloth in its mouth . . . So much ash . . .

Dump it all in the well. Its burned skin, dump it down there, its ribs – no, better save that one. That's a safe place for it. It'll all rest peacefully there. So much ash! . . . It's choking me. How it swirls around. It stings my eyes. How much is sticking to my wet face? If they could see me now. They'd laugh. I wouldn't. I used to be happy down at the bottom of this well! So quiet, so cool. That was my place!

a

Figure 20.8 a *above,* b *opposite,* c *opposite: People negotiating with people in the reconstruction of House 14 of the Eneolithic village of Divostin, Yugoslavia (drawings by C. Chang)*

Figure 20.9
below: People
negotiating with
the material
world in a
traditional
archaeological
reconstruction
(from Petrequin
and Petrequin,
1988)

In the interpretation of the destruction and replacement of houses at Opovo, I have introduced through the media of narratives and visual imagery the actors themselves, some of the women and men who lived in those houses through the many generations (Figure 20.8) (Tringham 1991a and b, 1992). Through these narratives and images I present several different moments of engendered prehistory, moments of social action, in which the women and men, girls and boys are all actors in social negotiations and dominance relations between spouses, between siblings, between neighbors, between age-groups as they move within and between the space that we call the built environment. These are not the personalities of conventional prehistoric reconstructions who are for the most part presented negotiating with their material world (Figure 20.9).

Each of these moments of social action is linked to what we call 'moments of archaeological deposition,' that is, actual observation of the archaeological record – in this paper, the house that was burned to its foundations and the well that was filled immediately after the burning event with the probably still warm rubble (Harris 1979; Schiffer 1987). This is actually the scale at which archaeological excavation is conducted. Most of what we excavate is the result of a 'domestic' social act.

After the excavation of the 'depositional events', an archaeologist always has a choice of scale in which to consider the archaeological record. I have shown in this paper that, in the New (processualist) Archaeology and its predecessors, archaeologists have chosen to consider it essentially at a macro-scale in which social acts and the perceptions and intentions of the actors have been normalized into a conglomerate that stands for many different 'places'. Post-processualist and feminist archaeology argues that, while social transformation at such a macro-scale is essential to consider, it is also essential to consider the scale of the social action of individual actors at particular moments of their history in particular places.

When historians, geographers, and ethnographers consider social action and places, they have a wealth of information on individual life-histories to which archaeologists just have no access. Archaeologists, however, need not throw up their hands in despair of being able to theorize at a micro-scale and contribute a prehistory of engendered social action and places. This kind of interpretive dialectical interplay between material remains, comparative historical or ethnographic observation, and imagined actors, acts and places is designed to encourage researchers from outside of archaeological practice to participate in the interpretive historical construction of prehistoric places, rather than be passive receptors – or, more commonly, ignorers – of the authoritative wisdom of mainstream archaeology's analysis of the archaeological architecture to reconstruct the general trends, structures and patterns of the prehistoric built environment.

NOTES

1 See the following studies that have usefully summarized the recent developments in archaeological theory and practice (Klejn 1977; Wylie 1982; Lamberg-Karlovsky 1989; Trigger 1989b; Hodder 1991a).

2 Such an aim is more in line with Stea and Turan's 'Production of Places' (Stea and Turan 1990), they also use formal cross-cultural observation of ethnographic and archaeological data to come up with a generally applicable theory that correlates mode of production with the production of places.

3 The various ways in which ethnographic and ethnoarchaeological data have been used by prehistoric archaeologists and the biases that are inherent in their selection of these sources are the subject of a long-standing and much publicized debate in archaeology (Gould and Watson 1982; Wylie 1985a). In this debate, some have argued for finding the best 'fit' for their archaeological data among ethnographic societies at the same 'level' of social complexity; or among those societies living in the same environmental conditions; or among those societies in which some continuity from the historic to the prehistoric periods may be observed. Many seek analogies in ethnography for prehistoric material culture in terms of function and technology, or in terms of behavioral correlates and significance in social relations. Many ethnoarchaeologists seek to create short cuts to the dilemma of the gap between the dead static archaeological record and living dynamic social action by making cross-cultural generations about material culture–behavior correlates. There is no correct answer as to how ethnographic sources should be used. But there is a growing self-awareness amongst archaeologists as to the implications of using these data (as well as ethnohistorical and Western historical data), that include, for example, the dangers of taking the data out or their own historical context.

For example, in writing the narratives at the end of this paper, my consideration of a particular situation – the effect of disintegration of extra-kin support for the female population at Opovo – was inspired by Henrietta Moore's discussion of ethnographic examples (Moore 1988), by the Annales school accounts of Renaissance France (Ladurie 1978), and by sociological discussions of twentieth-century housework (Hartmann 1981). The envisaging of this situation in combination with architectural and other spatial conditions has been inspired by a large number of sources (see the bibliography of Tringham [1991a]). I personally feel that all of human experience can and should be used to inspire archaeologists' writing, that they should be aware of what has inspired them, and that they should be using these sources within the constraints discussed in the body of this paper.

PART V

MATERIAL CULTURE

INTRODUCTION

As much as anything, it has been the reconceptualisation of material culture which has been the defining element in changes in archaeological thought over the past two decades. For the culture-historic archaeology of the early twentieth century, material things were the mute products of internalised traditions, 'ways of doing things' which were passed down from generation to generation unchanged. Changes in the form and appearance of artefacts were the product of contact between communities, or of the actual displacement of population. Pots equated almost directly with people. During the 1960s this 'normative' view was challenged by the New Archaeology's vision of material culture as an 'extrasomatic means of adaptation' (Binford 1965, 205). Under this conception, artefacts were not the product of a traditional mental template but existed at the interface between people and their environment. Should ecological circumstances change, people could change their material culture in order to accommodate to new conditions. However, even this framework has proved too limited and reductionist. Christopher Tilley's paper in this section presents a condensed account of the impact of structuralist and post-structuralist ideas on archaeology, and concentrates on the more subtle conceptions of the object world that have resulted. For Tilley, material culture provides the context for human interaction, and a means of creating and encoding meanings, and a medium for social action. It is the issue of meaning which has proved most contentious in recent debates. Tilley notes that meaning is not a latent quality which is encapsulated within an artefact; it is produced in the object's 'reading' or use. Consequentially, it is difficult to produce a definitive reading of an artefact. What an object means depends upon the context in which we encounter it, and also upon the social conditions attending the reader. In his contribution, Victor Buchli points to the way in which this productivity of things can lead to a plethora of multiple interpretations.

Already, in outlining these points, I have had to resort to the metaphor of the written text in order to address the meanings of material things. It is unquestionable that the comparison between artefacts and texts has yielded considerable insights into the ways in which human beings inhabit a world of significance (e.g. Moore 1986). Buchli, however, asks whether there are ways in which material culture operates that are distinct from all forms of verbal and written communication. Perhaps it is as well to remember that a metaphor is a means of suggesting similarities between dissimilar things, which has the effect of revealing them to us in new ways. Artefacts are like texts in some ways, but they also possess specific qualities through their very materiality. One of the most important senses in which objects are more than containers of meaning lies in the way in which they can articulate social relationships. In non-Western societies the giving of gifts can establish alliances, create indebtedness, build prestige and engender memory. In his paper, Igor Kopytoff explores the similarities between artefacts and human beings. As he points out, the notion that people are unique individuals with intrinsically separate identities while objects are interchangeable is a curiosity of the modern West. It is more helpful to think of both persons and things gradually gathering their own identities or histories through their relationships. The classic example of this process is found in the Kula valuables of Melanesia, which acquire greater significance as they pass from hand to hand in exchange transactions (Cambell 1983). This way of thinking has encouraged archaeologists to discuss the 'biographies' of artefacts: manufactured, circulated, consumed and discarded. At each point in its life history an artefact is engaged in human social relationships: human beings live through the material things that surround them.

Artefacts support, contextualise and facilitate social action. In this respect the meanings of things are crucial, and it is unhelpful to think of meaning as a quality which 'added on' to the physical existence of a thing. Indeed, it often makes no sense to prize apart the 'symbolic significance' of an artefact and the more prosaic ways in which it can be understood. Keith Ray's study of the Igbo Ukwu assemblage from Nigeria discusses the way in which artefacts can bring metaphorical associations and connections with them, linking different contexts of action and 'presencing' absent persons and abstract qualities within social interaction. In such circumstances meaning and materiality are not opposed, but implicated in one another.

21

INTERPRETING MATERIAL CULTURE*
The Trouble With Text

VICTOR A. BUCHLI

A very brief history of text

Discussions of text have dominated the interpretation of material culture in post-processual archaeology for over ten years now since the emergent disenchantment with the New Archaeology in the early 1980s. At that time there was a shift from systems-orientated functionalist approaches which minimised the role of symbolic systems and ideology towards postprocessual approaches which placed primary emphasis on systems of meaning and interpretation. This new direction was further propelled by the inheritance of ethnoarchaeology from the New Archaeology and the resultant increased engagement of archaeologists with developments in ethnography, particularly the ethnographic applications of critical theory and literary criticism.

The comparison of material culture with text, however, has been around many years in one veiled form or another as Parker Pearson noted in 1982 (Parker Pearson 1982: 100) when he referred to Gordon Childe's insistence that material culture be treated 'always and exclusively as concrete expressions and embodiments of human thoughts and ideas' (Childe 1956a: 1). The notion that material culture could express or contain ideas as language does lends itself to the application of structuralist and semiotic analysis. However, a purely structuralist approach as evidenced in the work of Leroi-Gourhan (1965, 1982) did not really take off. Ian Hodder writing in 1986 saw this as a tendency for structuralist approaches to be subsumed rather flirtatiously within the New Archaeology for its innate systemness in that both approaches emphasised the role of general systems to explain all aspects of human behaviour. It was then later rejected for its inability to conform to the New Archaeology's positivist requirements of hypothesis testing and falsifiability (Hodder 1986: 35). However, as Hodder noted, the attraction survived in one form or another in the works of a variety of authors throughout the seventies and early eighties (1986: 34).

It was not really until the early eighties that the comparison with text resurged with increased force. In the preceding years with the publication of Bourdieu's

---

*First published in I. Hodder, M. Shanks, A. Alessandri, V. Buchli, J. Carman, J. Last and G. Lucas (eds) (1995), *Interpreting Archaeology: Finding Meanings in the Past*, London: Routledge, pp. 181–93.

Outline of a Theory of Practice (1977) and Anthony Giddens' *New Rules of Sociological Method* (1976) and *Central Problems in Social Theory* (1979) a more satisfactory critique of structuralism arose in the pursuit of understanding systems of meaning, shifting the emphasis from static structures of meaning subordinating all individual actions to the dictates of underlying structures, to actively manipulated generative principles (i.e., rules for making structures) exploited by individuals pursuing various independent social goals – actively manipulating structures of meaning rather than being manipulated by them. This approach inspired those archaeologists dissatisfied with the New Archaeology's treatment of meaning to pursue their interests with renewed vigour and establish a generation of practitioners critical of the New Archaeology more forcefully than ever before. The works of individuals such as Henrietta Moore (1986), Daniel Miller (1982a, c, 1985a), Michael Parker Pearson (1982, 1984 a, b), Shanks and Tilley (1987a, b), Mark Leone (1982b), Leone, Potter and Shackel (1987), Ian Hodder (1982d, b, 1986) and others attempted to reassess comparisons with text with the infusion of the poststructuralist critiques of structuralism by Bourdieu and Giddens as well as the critiques of structuralism by Roland Barthes, Jacques Derrida, Michel Foucault, Paul Ricoeur and the Marxist tradition of Critical Theory.

Thomas Patterson (1989: 556) sorts out this unruly variety of responses and influences into three reasonably distinct but inevitably forced strains of thought that manage more or less to capture the dominant tone of the works involved. The first, which is essentially 'Hodderian', draws on the work of the historian/theoretician Robin Collingwood and is articulated through the diverse works of Pierre Bourdieu, Clifford Geertz, Anthony Giddens and Paul Ricoeur. Most notable in this tradition are the works, of course, of Ian Hodder himself and Henrietta Moore. They approach the archaeological record as most directly analogous to a text or narrative to be decoded and manipulated by various historical agents and accessible to the archaeologist, 'privileging the cryptographic skill and eloquence of the archaeologist as interpreter' (Patterson 1989: 556). The second strain, filtered through the works of Michel Foucault and Marxian critiques, focuses more on relations of power and domination in social practice and the creation of knowledge, particularly emphasising the implications of archaeology to late capitalism and the roles that it plays in reproducing society and how that might be changed. The work of Shanks and Tilley (1987a, b and Shanks 1992a) and Tilley 1989a, b), Daniel Miller (1987), and Miller and Tilley (1984b) can be used to characterise this strain. Text here is still understood as a narrative to be decoded but the importance of social conditions under which material culture and other narratives are produced and interpreted to reinforce and reproduce dominant social structures are accorded greater significance. The third strain, very closely related to the second, is more emphatically concerned with the role and implication of communication and ideology in the constitution of archaeological discourse in the present day. The primary influences are the works of Jürgen Habermas, Louis Althusser and the tradition of Critical Theory. From this strain Mark Leone (1982b), Potter and Shackel (1987), Leone and Potter (1992), and Alison Wylie (1985b, 1987) are notable in providing a critique of how archaeological texts themselves and the archaeological record, which constitutes these texts, are produced and disseminated – in short, a more overtly political critique of the production of archaeological texts, their uses, and how the raw material, the constituted physical archaeological record, is used to generate these texts and the audiences they serve.

More recently in the past three years there has emerged a certain uncertainty and wavering brought on in part by the expansion and interaction between these arguments. Hodder has reappraised his contextual approach in the light of H. G. Gadamer's hermeneutics (Hodder 1991a). This reassessment came at about the same time his critics claimed that his contextual approach was essentialist, presuming a unified narrative text 'out there' to be read as well as the competence of the archaeologist would permit, denying the historically contingent nature of interpretation (Johnsen and Olsen 1992) and the multiplicity of interpretations in the past and the present (Barrett 1987b).

Similarly, more Marxist interpretations of the second and third strain have come under increasing scrutiny for their tendencies to create holistic, totalising representations of interpretive and historic processes – another form of alternative 'systemness' akin to the functionalist systems theorising of the New Archaeologists (Barrett 1992; Bauman 1992). Hence a certain uncertainty has developed, particularly amongst more strident Marxists, and a waning of the confidence and vigour of the mid-eighties when postprocessualism and discussions of text broke on the scene. Concurrently there has been an increasing awareness of the unique qualities attributed to material culture distinguishing it from some established definitions of text (Hodder 1989b).

Despite these waverings, text is still discussed quite vigorously. The papers presented in *Interpreting Archaeology: Finding Meaning in the Past* (Hodder *et al.* 1995) point towards, in a rather unexpected way, a certain consensus concerning the viability of the comparison for material culture. Individuals otherwise quite diverse in their approaches stand together to defend the direction. Perhaps the 'death knell' for the undertaking to be is quite premature – 'not all texts after all are literary texts', 'the analogy needs to be stretched' (H. Moore, pers. comm.). Others somewhat impatient with the highly abstracted discussion on the issue might demand that we finally just implement the comparison 'and put it to use and see how it works' (C. Renfrew, pers. comm.).

There is a danger of a 'false consensus', however. One of the things that has emerged in the volume is that we still are not quite sure what exactly we mean by a 'text' and on what data we can appropriately apply the comparison. Resolving this issue, however, is fraught with many difficulties. Considering Moore's earlier statement, there is a great deal of disagreement as to the meaning of the terms involved. When we say 'text' do we mean a semiotic system (de Saussure) or structuralist system (Lévi-Strauss), a hermeneutic interpretive system based on structuralism (Gadamer and Ricoeur) or something entirely different? Up to now I have intentionally avoided using the words 'metaphor' or 'analogy' to describe this comparison. However, despite their tendency to be used interchangeably, the two words are not identical and their distinctions are highly problematic. Is material culture analogous to texts structurally and functionally? Or is material culture like a text, a metaphor without structural similarities but imaginatively linked? If it is an analogy, then how do we make the analogy to the things we study, and for what categories of material culture is the analogy appropriate or inappropriate? For the most part, these issues have not been problematised and the distinction is rarely made, with the resulting confusion that the term is often used inconsistently as analogy, metaphor, or just as the thing itself in ways that might contradict the overt intention of the author under consideration.

The trouble with text

Much of the confusion concerning text is related to how one falls along a continuum of belief, from whether one believes a retrievable 'Past' (unified, monolithic and directly retrievable) to many little 'pasts' (multiple, contradictory and oftentimes inferred) or to the opposite belief that there is no past at all that can be meaningfully grasped. This is a question of faith ridden with intense anxiety for the archaeologist concerned with 'The Past' or 'pasts' and for whom an analogic approach to text and material culture can yield useful correspondences with which to 'recover' meaning. Conversely, those archaeologists leaning towards the position that there is no such thing as a retrievable past might find an analogic approach has little value and text is more usefully understood in metaphoric terms in attempting to use the material record to address contemporary concerns and not futilely retrieve past ones.

Commentary
Colin Richards

Such anxieties can be felt in Colin Richards' paper (Richards 1995) despite his statement that 'there are no past truths, no single meanings any more than there are contemporary truths'. He proposes to view the highly empirical practice of excavation less as the neutral and objective extraction of data, and more as a process of culture contact, drawing on analogies with ethnographic fieldwork. He compares the gradual observation, selection and piecing together of data from an archaeological field site to the process by which an ethnographer comes in contact with an alien culture, by observing, selecting data, and performing an analysis.

This analogy, however, is rather problematic if Richards takes the view that 'there are no past truths'. Ethnographic culture contact is a dialogue whereby two agents, the ethnographer and the informant, are involved in a mutually reconstitutive account of social phenomena. Cultural concepts in a sense are literally being created at the point of contact between the ethnographer and the informant in the form of the ethnographer's description and the 'native' theorising of the informant who attempts to engage the ethnographer's queries thereby re-creating or even articulating cultural concepts, previously left unobjectified. 'Contact' as such in the strict ethnographic sense is clearly not possible in the course of excavation since the numerous individuals responsible for the artefacts excavated, as the artefacts themselves, are not capable of talking back, 'speaking' as it were, engaging themselves with their interlocutors during the course of excavation. 'Contact' never occurs and neither does the mutual reconstitution of cultural practices. Excavation in this sense is profoundly monologic – monologue with a pile of debris, incapable of ever responding on its own to the questions put towards it. Yet Richards claims that 'the past' (as signified by the material record) does indeed speak – 'but only through a dialectical relationship between subject and object, the present and recognised past'. This, however, is not the same sort of dialogue characterising ethnographic cultural contact, but a dialogue with oneself, with a 'recognised past' constituted in the present; a monologue and nothing ever more. 'Contact' as such can be nothing more than contact with oneself mediated through the meaningful constitution of material remains into the material culture and artefacts of the present. This is not to deny the constitution and recognition of patterning in material remains or the constraints such patterning would have to our interpretive endeavours; anything does not go. Our interpretive requirements will always prevail and be meaningful to us but not to 'them', whoever they might be. The 'contact' metaphor is potentially misleading, imputing the sense that a 'past' must exist because one could then retrieve it (take it down from the shelf) and read it, or 'interrogate' it during the course of a mutually constitutive conversation of culture 'contact' with the meaningfully constituted remains of a past people. If one could not engage the archaeological record in this way, it would simply be 'gibberish' and all our endeavours presumably meaningless; without the authority to guide us in our present-day endeavours. If it is 'out there', then it can 'speak', be 'read', or 'coaxed to speak' through dialogue, and amenable to interpretation through its analogy to text.

However, Richards' understanding of 'contact', despite problems with the use of this metaphor, entails a provocative understanding of the interpretation of material culture that suggests better ways of coping with the contingent multiplicities of its interpretation. He questions prevailing excavation techniques that restrictively constitute material culture, forcing it into alien geometries of order; reducing it from three to two dimensions and forcing a loss of complexity of understanding in the excavation process that denies the multiplicity of potential voices used in the production of the monolithic, single-authored, 'objectivising' enterprise we normally call a site report. Rather, Richards calls for alternatives to our excavation practices that might break up the Procrustean hold these techniques have had on our ability to further constitute and elaborate our interpretations of material culture.

Felipe Criado

For Felipe Criado (1995) the idea of the archaeological record and material culture as meaningless 'gibberish' is less anxiety provoking and the utility of a textual analogy consequently is limited. Criado proposes an alternative approach to interpreting material culture, replacing the textual metaphor with a visual metaphor of visibility strategies. Criado identifies four visibility strategies: to inhibit, to hide, to exhibit and to monumentalise, and suggests an opposite strategy of a 'will-to-unvisibilising' – to not engage in any visual strategy at all. To do nothing in fact, thereby focusing on the significance of meaninglessness in understanding.

This typology of visibility strategies is proposed as an alternative to existing periodisations which, Criado feels, are implicitly teleological and of questionable use. A periodisation based on visibility strategies therefore has as one of its advantages its obviously stated, consciously assumed strict formal cognitive criteria which serve to recontextualise information into new contexts towards presumably more immediate contemporary 'socio-cultural discourses'. It would not pretend to reveal any pre-existing meanings 'out there' in the 'Past'. Similarly the designation of a particular visual strategy or 'will-to-visibility' does not imply a specific meaning; rather, it intuits the existence of a meaning or intentions towards the articulation of something inherently indeterminable.

However, as Criado points out, the temptation to characterise socio-economic formations in terms of specific strategies towards visuality can become problematic. In his scheme one senses the presence of lingering deterministic ideas of evolutionary stages of society. One could imagine passing through stages of complexity from unvisibility, inhibition (prehistory), hiding (Palaeolithic), exhibition (Neolithic) and monumentalisation (Late Neolithic and early states); reproducing established periodisations of history. Rather than describing an aspect of material culture in a particular society with the very likely possibility that several of these strategies might be pursued simultaneously, these stages are presented as discrete representations of a dominant and determining social quality (hierarchical, within nature, without nature, nature and culture opposed) at the expense of other competing strategies. In keeping with this it follows that any combination of strategies represents some social instability involving the competition between two or more tendencies for domination in the next stage of social development, rather than the coexistence and interdependence of multiple strategies.

Criado, in his system of visibility strategies, recognises no 'pre-existing meaning' to be revealed in the course of analysis, but, rather, the 'reading' of his system 'would involve the recombinations of relations into new contexts involving codes from other social-cultural discourses'. In short, the material remains of past behaviour become the raw material of which new contexts – that is, present concerns and discourses – are constituted. The exploitation and engendering of meaning of otherwise meaningless material remains are not some empty intellectual exercise, but integral to the constitution of our being.

Julian Thomas

'The "Past" has "to be" for us to structure existence' (J. Thomas, conference comments). Humans can only think in narratives or totalities; 'totalities don't exist but we need to create them' (ibid.) otherwise how would we cope as individuals, as societies and as a species with the meaningless chaos surrounding us? In producing these necessary fictions Thomas sees significant problems relating to the use of the textual analogy leading to a dichotomy between symbolism and materiality. Central to this dilemma is the role of time in interpreting material culture, particularly as time and time-depth are considered one of the unique insights archaeology provides within anthropology. Thomas (1995) notes that discussions of time are frequently separated from the often structuralist and synchronic discussions of material culture, creating a changeless and fossilised representation of material culture that belies its constantly changing significance.

By reintroducing the element of time and time-depth to the interpretation of material culture, Thomas proposes to overcome this false dichotomy between symbolism and materiality and break free from the ossifying effects inherited from structuralism. Rather than seeing material culture as embodying anything in particular, Thomas suggests that material culture be viewed as the raw material for the creation of narratives, recontextualised and redeployed as agents continuously change their use of material culture in the creation of narrative expressions of identity. More significantly, he proposes to shift from the artefact of material culture itself to the agent herself and her manipulation of material objects in the world as a way of locating herself in that world. The object itself loses primacy and is viewed merely as the vehicle of multiple, mutating interpretations, uses and fetishisations. These manipulations, though constantly changing and shifting, are organised by certain pre-understandings or hermeneutic perspectives that are the standpoints from which the world is perceived, interpreted and acted upon. As Thomas writes, we hear soundwaves as motorcycles or as birds and debate understanding material culture as texts. These are all pre-understandings which establish a specific vanishing-point about which the field of our discursive perspective is delineated and structured. Consequently, Thomas's suggestion places the agent and her actions as the fulcrum about which material culture is to be understood as Parker Pearson and others have sought to do. Material culture does not function 'as text' in Thomas's scheme but, rather, it is the stuff of which texts or narratives are made to help us cope with the contingencies of our existence.

Michael Parker Pearson

Parker Pearson, like others, found the textual analogy strictly problematic (Parker Pearson, conference presentation). He suggested an understanding of text more as the object of semiotic analysis and less the hermeneutic interpretive process. Material culture should not conform strictly to semiotic analyses of text; material culture's uses are often far more utilitarian than communicative. Rather, texts should be seen as just another category of material culture. The analogy to Parker Pearson (1995) seemed overstretched and even downright misleading since it denied the opportunity to adequately incorporate notions of agency and structure in understanding material culture because of the rather fixed communicative nature of literary texts.

Parker Pearson's use of the word 'text' implied that it was static, sealed off, and unidirectional in that it had the specific function of communicating written information. It was not as polysemous as an item of material culture such as the crown that he mentioned, which could be interpreted and used in a variety of ways such as headgear, a symbol of rank, or as a gloss for the state. Such a definition of text assumed there was in fact something explicit and essential to be grasped, uncovered, deconstructed towards, which with discipline, good hard work and critical vigilance would yield through the investigator's labours that which was true, intended, and explicitly communicated. However, much poststructuralist understanding of literary texts, notably the work of Jacques Derrida, would not accept such a fixed definition of literary texts and would see it as similarly fluid if not more so than material culture.

In referring to how much texts and material culture were not alike, Parker Pearson observed several significant contrasting characteristics. Material culture was more use-bound, less abstract and more practical; it was more directed towards the physical exploitation of the environment rather than being explicitly communicative. It therefore did not primarily function to represent directly, though it could and often did as in the crown metonym mentioned above. It was more likely to be taken for granted, since once constituted it no longer required constant reiteration. One simply picks up a hammer and uses it, once its function and the rules for its use have been established without second thoughts or reinterpretations. Literary texts require reiteration and reinterpretation, in short reinvention, in order to function. In this respect the banality of much of material culture's use is much like the rules of grammar, not conscious, taken for granted until a rule has been misapplied and one uses a wrench to chop down a tree. The last and probably most salient distinction Parker Pearson observed was the durability of non-textual items of material culture. Their ability to exist mutely, survive physical degradation and remain visible makes them qualitatively distinct in most respects from ordinary literary texts. There were dangers, however, in attributing specific qualities to this durability. The primacy of material culture in contemporary consumerist post-industrial societies was not to be assumed in past societies. There was the risk of fetishising such material goods and inappropriately attributing meaning. The sheer physicality of material cultural data, pregnant with expectant meaning, could exert a very seductive and transfixing force within the dearth of contextual data, obscuring pressing questions of agency and context.

Parker Pearson, however, pointed towards something far more provocative to our interpretive practices as archaeologists. We transform one type of material culture, the material record, into another: a literary text, site report or academic publication. What were the advantages of this transformation of something so rich into something so two-dimensional as a site report contained within a three-dimensional object we call a 'text'? The once rich environment of three-dimensional objects situated meaningfully within the context of three-dimensional space was lost for ever through the course of our controlled destruction of a site. This environment is resurrected again as a literary text, illustrated and supported only by objects that have now become artefacts pulled out of their contexts, forever dependent on that text and the structure of the process of destruction which brought those objects into the world. What are the advantages of such transformations to our endeavours when they might involve considerable gain or loss to our experience? Parker Pearson suggests that maybe we could consider other ways of transforming the archaeological record. If we as archaeologist are to be considered the legitimate specialists charged with transforming and interpreting the archaeological record, maybe our consumption and experience of the archaeological record and the experience of other publics consuming and experiencing the fruits of our labours might be meaningfully expanded by not just creating one form of material culture such as archaeological texts but others as well.

Underlying several of the papers in *Interpreting Archaeology* (Hodder *et al.* 1995) is the old issue of theory and practice: how to relate our theories of material culture to the actual interpretation of material culture in our work. Parker Pearson's paper (1995) attempts to alleviate this problem with an actual case-study. This paper challenges the accepted wisdom that the Sutton Hoo burial is associated with the Kingdom of East Anglia. Armed with better chronologies, a revaluation of previous 'culture historical' approaches and a broader sensitivity to the symbolic and idiosyncratic associations of certain items of material culture at the burial, Parker Pearson suggests an alternative association that is East Saxon, and very persuasively argues for a specific identification of the burial as that of the East Saxon king, Saebert. The argument is presented as an example of the utility of the use of multiple interpretive or theoretical approaches in gaining a better understanding of material culture. Parker Pearson here proposes an understanding of multiple interpretations, less as the simultaneity and management of multiple views in the pursuit of various immediate goals (political, academic, or social) as some others have suggested. Rather, the dynamics of multiple interpretations are seen more as the competition of various viewpoints to interpret the data most persuasively where the best interpretive fit prevails until a better one challenges the existing order.

Maurice Bloch

Maurice Bloch (1995) offers an example of how the analogy to text, especially when understood in semiotic or structuralist terms as something to be 'read' or decoded, can be entirely inappropriate. To illustrate the difficulties of analogy, he discusses the problems entailed in dealing with carvings on Malagasy house-posts. The carvings on these posts, Bloch suggests, do not in fact mean anything, even though they might be evocative or representative of specific things such as the rain or the moon. The figures do not in fact mean those things; they simply have some superficial resemblances to these things so they can be more easily named and referred to. In short, they do not signify. That is, they do not function as signifiers revealing something signified – the way a literary text would signify constituted by arbitrary signifiers. Signifying nothing, the best Bloch can do in light of our disciplinary requirements to ascribe meaning and significance to these figures is to say they 'magnify' something. They are expletives, exclamation points, crescendo marks of several generations in the 'magnificat' of a lineage's founders who erected these posts.

The lesson of Bloch's cautionary tale is that we should use our analytical tools where appropriate and not make everything have to behave as text and signify, however compelling the objects at hand may be. This naturally creates a problem as to when to use this analogy and when not to. The preoccupation of ethnographers and archaeologists alike with ascribing significance to all manner of observed phenomena can result, as Bloch's cautionary tale so clearly points out, in demanding answers to entirely irrelevant questions, as witnessed by the frustration experienced by Bloch and other researchers. To insist on the equation that elaborately incised patterns of circles must represent some thing, be a signifier with a corresponding signified, is one of the fundamental operations associated with the textual analogy. It insists, rather tautologously, that the observable universe is constituted by signifiers, much like Foucault's medieval episteme: everything means, signifies something and is waiting for someone to read it (Foucault 1970). The possibility of non-significance or, more specifically, some thing that does not follow the equation of signifier/signified becomes lost.

Bloch's Malagasy carvings, however, illustrate in many ways what Thomas was theorising: that objects participate in a greater associated context of shifting meanings, rather than having any specific designative sense. In the case of the carvings, they participate in a larger cultural sensibility that is more connotative than denotative, where a larger narrative of family history and growth are played out against commonly shared Malagasy sensibilities and aesthetics. Ironically, 'fossilisation' actually does occur here but in a somewhat playful and metaphoric sense of 'hardening': that is, making more 'physical' and 'enduring' the meditation of a lineage on its origins and its maintenance or, rather, the 'magnification' of this expression within in a common cultural practice. In short, a metaphoric exploitation of the physical properties of a material, to fix and magnify a certain idea, in this case the longevity of a founding couple. This is not unlike the 'fossilisation' of archaeological data or any other 'hard' data – that is, the process of making it 'bony', structuring it (not to mention actually hardening it and preserving it from physical decay), fixing it in time and space, as in a field report or collection and having it *'vouloir dire'* and constituted to designate a very specific something. The irony here is that the archaeologist when queried might not respond like the Malagasy carver that he is just making some thing or other, making it beautiful or honouring it. The archaeologist might actually believe that he is designating something like the 'moon', 'social contradiction' or 'incipient state formation' rather than performing a *'magnificat'* elaborating the very serious myths of his own origins.

Material culture and physicality

In discussing the appropriateness or inappropriateness of 'text' towards the understanding of material culture, a common distinctive feature of material culture has been continuously invoked either distinguishing it at times from literary 'texts', subsuming literary 'texts' to it, or alternately functioning alongside with literary 'texts' in the creation of narratives – namely the fact that material culture is a thing, hard, durable and physical. This might seem banal and horribly obvious at first, but the constituted physicality of material culture is what distinguishes it most specifically from other data. It is the cornerstone of Criado's 'will-to-visibility' scheme, essential to the poetry of Malagasy carving in Bloch's discussion, the point of 'culture contact' in Richards' presentation, and the fulcrum about which narratives are spun out in Thomas's paper. It is the one thing that distinguishes most saliently the data of the archaeologist from any other anthropologist (see the extensive discussions of materiality by Shanks 1992a, 1992b, 1993).

The attribution of physicality – the constitution of otherwise inchoate matter with physical attributes, beyond being a statement that that which is under consideration assumes three dimensions, implies an intention towards imbuing a particular expression with durability to sustain physicality over time for some specified or indefinite period. The constitution of physicality and durability is almost without question one of the central preoccupations of archaeologists (the generation and elaboration of artefacts) and others who attempt meaningfully to constitute and appropriate physical properties in the material world. In short, the constitution of physicality implies a desire for some form of sustained expression or utility, be it a literary text to be circulated indefinitely, a house to be built for a generation or several, or a cup to be used once or for an entire lifetime. The produced durability of an object often has everything to do with how long one wants the expressive quality of the object of material culture to be sustained – built for eternity in stone, or out of paper to last just the day. Or conversely, as in the case with rubbish, something to be forgotten becomes an artefact through incidental preservation and subsequent reconstitution as artefact. The critical quality of durability associated with material culture by Richards often falls out of the conscious discursive realm precisely because it is so familiar and taken for granted. Similarly, overlooking the relation of physicality to expressive significance is one of the central dichotomies Thomas refers to affecting archaeology. And lastly the production of durability predicates all of Criado's visibility strategies.

Of course, the production of physical attributes in the generation of material culture is what we constitute and document so obsessively – the size, material composition, position, weight and number of discrete objects. Empiricism as such is nothing more than this obsession with the production and documentation of physical attributes of the material world. This predilection of our highly empirical discipline has been pointed out as having its pitfalls. Over-enthusiastic documentation without explanation is decried as 'facticism' (Moore 1995), 'fetishism' (Parker Pearson 1995) or 'obsessive systematisation' (Richards 1995). The prevailing belief has been the more we constitute and document physical attributes of the material world, the more we can become 'objective' and get a better 'picture' of what actually 'is there' and understand its essence. The poststructuralist disenchantment with the enterprise of establishing 'totalities' and 'essences' can only call into question the tools of objectivising enterprises that try to document something – to know what it really and truly 'is'. To continue incessantly to constitute and document the physicality of the material world and know that 'there is no there there' to document (apologies to Gertrude Stein) is only to come up with an increasingly 'harder', 'two-dimensional image' (Moore 1995) of the material world that resists interpretation of its obsessive, speedy and somewhat ecstatic documentation. Such a process can potentially disempower disfranchised groups and individuals trying to establish control over interpretations and representations that oppress them by consistently denying any form of 'authentic' interpretation. Abject obsession with the physicality of data can be seen as just as potentially harmful to the disfranchised as any claims to objectivity that silence others.

But the physicality we have produced is all we really are left with after we have purged ourselves, as most poststructuralists would have us do, of most of our essentialist yearnings. Physicality as such is probably the last bastion of such essentialism – a banal vice, however, I would argue, and for purely pragmatic reasons very necessary for the production and sustainment of our narratives. We know the objects we have created cannot 'really' denote 'incipient state formation' or 'clouds', but we can safely collect any references made about the object, photograph it, X-ray it, thin-slice it, irradiate it, conserve it, digitise it and put it in a database on disc or CD and relay it within split seconds on computer networks to all our colleagues around the world. Such obsessiveness with the production of objectivity in the pursuit of the objectification of the myriad refractions of the physical world is generally met with the accusation of 'fetishisation'. Clearly if such exercises are not fixed, denotative, explanatory, 'anchored in an adequate social theory', they are simply highly indulgent, irresponsible practices whose only aim is simply to continue endlessly in this self-reproducing and self-referencing process – producing objectifications without a subject, signifiers without a signified, hollow, empty and two-dimensional – fetishes of bourgeois scholarship.

The derogatory associations related to fetishisation seem to stem from a lingering Marxian contempt of excrescences beyond use-value (Marx 1983) – the persistence of the idea that a commodity or object has inherent use-value true to the amount of physical labour exerted to produce it, its physical nature and its utility. This is contrasted with exchange-value which attaches increasing value to the commodity and its culturally (not naturally inherent) determined value as ever-increasing superfluous non-utilitarian embellishments or 'fetishisations' of the commodity. This characterisation of exchange-value betrays a contempt for contingent, culturally determined superfluity of associative meaning in deference to a utilitarian, directed and fundamentally essentialist use-value. In this scheme some 'thing' must be doing something other than just being itself for its own sake, fetishised, with no 'thing' to designate, refer to or have use-value for. To claim innocence while signifying without signification at best is highly superficial and fetishistic, even silly, while highly suspect and pernicious at worst.

However, it is material culture's apparent ability to subvert and resist the metaphysics of use-value through various commodifications and fetishisations that makes it so dynamic, particularly in comparison with its kindred objects, literary texts, which are often attributed (arguably so) with rather stable fixed values and referents. The ambiguous and polysemic attributes of material culture so frequently referred to in the course of this conference attest to material culture's stubborn resistance to meaning in terms of functionalist use-value. Rather, it is precisely these associated qualities of ambiguity that are critical to understanding material culture and the role it plays in human affairs (Thomas 1995). In short, it is all the various permutations, fetishisations and recontextualisations which make material culture important. Its constituted physicality, ironically, is precisely what enables it to pass so freely from one context to another. You can pick it up and move it from a grave-site to a museum vitrine or buy it and use it as a flower-vase rather than a funeral urn. Precisely because it is rendered durable it can accommodate a great degree of ambiguity regarding its associative meanings in various recontextualisations, repeatedly moved or seen many different times and ways in many different contexts (Thomas 1995).

Obviously, since any attempt to fix a single referent to any material object in light of its continuously shifting recontextualisations and reconstitutions with the concomitant loss of any single meaning leaves us with just material culture itself, the object, in all its produced, dazzling and compelling physicality infinitely pregnant with potential meanings. Since it is considered by most of us now distasteful if not immoral to fix a single meaning, how are we to negotiate the plurality of associative meanings let forth? Once we have relinquished our authority we cannot say that only certain kinds of associative meaning sanctioned by our professional institutions are legitimate and others (say, the claims of New Agers, historical theme parks, Druids, or my next-door neighbour) are not. How, then, is this cacophony to be managed and, more important, how can it be maintained and preserved against attempts to silence it?

The raw material used to generate this cacophony is material culture itself in all its constituted and evocative physicality. Managing physicality involves the establishment of parameters for access to the objects themselves (the establishment of Criado's visibility strategies) and for the constitution and expression of that physicality (that is, the representation of the object in varying contexts, its physical reconstitution as coded data, exhibit, video, public database, or theme park) in tune with deliberately chosen visibility strategies. As professionals, one of the things we most certainly do best is create the data, constituting it and giving it form. John Fritz has asked why it is that the data of older, less theoretically sophisticated archaeologists are so much richer than the data produced by problem-orientated 'one-shot' investigations of more recent, theoretically sophisticated archaeologists (John Fritz, conference comments). Christopher Tilley's multiple interpretations of rock carvings at Näomforsen (Tilley 1991) attest to the richness of the data set provided by his highly empirical and non-theoretical predecessor G. Hallström, who compiled the data used by Tilley. Hallström's otherwise fetishistic constitution and recording of the objects at hand in all their various aspects elaborated a physicality of the carvings in such a way as to create an even greater trove of material in more readily accessible and visible form for the further elaboration of new and different associative meanings. The interpretations otherwise reached by Hallström might have little but purely historical value at the present time in light of pre-existing disciplinary concerns, but the data so richly constituted are invaluable.

Hallström in his desire for creating the conditions by which his conclusions could be reproducible and his authority confirmed, ironically created the conditions whereby his authority could be challenged – not in terms of whether he did the job properly or not, but in terms of the constitution and maximisation of visibility and physicality and creating the conditions of multiple authority as evidenced in the text by Tilley. Parker Pearson criticised highly theoreticised postprocessual texts as inaccessible and consequently stifling of meaning and called for 'developing new media of experience' (Parker Pearson 1995) to break the hold of these rather constrictive texts on interpretation. Similarly, Richards (1995), challenges the authority of the site report or final text as the culmination of the interpretive process. He proposes to break it up, expose the various localised authorities and interpretations in the course of excavation, refracting and documenting the interpretive process at as many points as possible of interpretive 'encounters' in archaeological procedure, thereby breaking up the authority of the fictive single author of the site report into an elaboration of archaeological procedure producing many authorities and interpretations.

Elaborating on and constituting the material culture of archaeological work in so many media, expanding upon all the intricacies of the interpretive process cannot but be susceptible to the accusation of 'fetishisation' and 'commodification' of questionably commodifiable objects. Such materialist concerns, however, are unavoidable and integral to the sort of society we find ourselves in. As Thomas points out, the objects and things we produce are the touchstone from which we weave narratives about ourselves, others and the past, probably something we as a species have been doing for quite some time, emphasising certain things, intentionally forgetting some and simply disregarding others. What becomes critical and problematic is managing this process. It is probably unquestionable that we want to constitute and consolidate material culture in the production of our pasts and presents. This production is vital for the creation and maintenance of our narratives in the present. This might be a violation of the attributed intentions of past authors associated with the artefacts we have produced and preserved who may have intended their productions to decay and be forgotten. But, then, archaeology has always been particularly aggressive and violent against notions of origins and intent through its destructive excavation practices and interpretive contortions whether in the name of 'Science' or creating the necessary physical conditions for creating our and other pasts. To mourn this violence is to believe in loss – a loss of something 'true' and 'original', a rather false sentimentality in light of much that is discussed in this volume. Our material concerns and 'fetishisations' are very much non-issues in this respect. It is difficult to see how the inclusion of day-to-day reports of excavation observations and multiple conclusions in site reports is very different in degree of fetishisation from the techno-empirico-fantasies of some hardline New Archaeologists. They both, however, elaborate and constitute data, making it more accessible for other authors to use and weave further narratives.

This all brings us back to the problem of how to manage all these voices, all these 'authorities' and archaeologies regarding material culture. A general feeling is that no one should be prohibited access to the material cultural data produced and denied legitimacy in interpreting it outside the profession. But John Fritz did bring up the question of whether other groups ought to be actually allowed to constitute the data and dig up sites as pot-hunters in North America often do (John Fritz, conference comments). A possible criterion for deciding these issues and the exertion of professional authority might be to ask what acts inhibit the constitution of potential data least. Pot-hunters often lose much detail regarding the deposition of artefacts in their work, constituting the data poorly in its detail and inhibiting the circulation of these artefacts by maintaining them in virtually inaccessible collections. The physicality and visibility of these objects are obviously hindered, severely inhibiting the richer constitution and use of these artefacts of material culture by others. One of the goals of the profession ought to be to ensure maximal access while maximising the constitution of the artefacts of material culture. Such a goal is largely curatorial and preservational and dominated by the questions of what gets preserved, why, by whom, for whom, and how to allocate resources towards these goals.

Peter Fowler noticed an interesting shift from theory to money in the discussions above (Peter Fowler, conference comments). Mark Leone spoke of his concerns of how to tie all our 'high falutin' theory to the actual management of resources in producing the archaeological record (Mark Leone, conference comments; see Leone and Potter 1992 for an in-depth discussion). How do we decide to spend the money we have and what are the bases of these decisions? Fowler himself called for archaeologists to be more bold about demanding money for archaeological work. What started out as esoteric discussions of 'text' ended up on how to get more money and how to use it. So how did we get from text to money? Was it disillusion with theoretical meanderings, even a rejection of the enterprise in light of the overwhelming pragmatics of getting things done in an environment where such meanderings leave the discipline distracted and unable to deal with the realities of competing interest groups? The reburial of Native American human remains, the archaeologies competing for recognition of under-represented groups (racial, ethnic and sexual), government intervention, funding, commercialisation, and threats by rapid development to the archaeological record all force themselves upon us in the course of our interpretive labours. Much of the discipline's previous efforts to establish 'origins', 'scientific objectivity', or 'anchoring in an adequate social theory' have more or less failed to provide us with the tools to contend with this increasingly cacophonous environment. After all the theoretical fervour of the past ten years we are finally left with the constituted objects themselves and the seemingly banal but vital question of their management. This preoccupation with physicality, in our discussions of 'text', focuses our attention on the issues surrounding our notions of durability, interpretation, and contextualisation that favours increasingly new constitutions of material culture. Consequently, this current in our theoretical debates on 'text' demands a new concern with management, pragmatics, access and presentation to ensure the fundamental and equitable conditions of interpretation.

22

THE CULTURAL BIOGRAPHY OF THINGS*
Commoditization as Process

IGOR KOPYTOFF

For the economist, commodities simply are. That is, certain things and rights to things are produced, exist, and can be seen to circulate through the economic system as they are being exchanged for other things, usually in exchange for money. This view, of course, frames the commonsensical definition of a commodity: an item with use value that also has exchange value. I shall, for the moment, accept this definition, which should suffice for raising certain preliminary issues, and I shall expand on it as the argument warrants.

From a cultural perspective, the production of commodities is also a cultural and cognitive process: commodities must be not only produced materially as things, but also culturally marked as being a certain kind of thing. Out of the total range of things available in a society, only some of them are considered appropriate for marking as commodities. Moreover, the same thing may be treated as a commodity at one time and not at another. And finally, the same thing may, at the same time, be seen as a commodity by one person and as something else by another. Such shifts and differences in whether and when a thing is a commodity reveal a moral economy that stands behind the objective economy of visible transactions.

Of persons and things
In contemporary Western thought, we take it more or less for granted that things – physical objects and rights to them – represent the natural universe of commodities. At the opposite pole we place people, who represent the natural universe of individuation and singularization. This conceptual polarity of individualized persons and commoditized things is recent and, culturally speaking, exceptional. People can be and have been commoditized again and again, in innumerable societies throughout history, by way of those widespread institutions known under the blanket term 'slavery'. Hence, it may be suggestive to approach the notion of commodity by first looking at it in the context of slavery.

---

*First published in A. Appadurai (ed.) (1986), *The Social Life of Things*, Cambridge: Cambridge University Press, pp. 64–91.

Slavery has often been defined, in the past, as the treatment of persons as property or, in some kindred definitions, as objects. More recently, there has been a shift away from this all-or-none view toward a processual perspective, in which marginality and ambiguity of status are at the core of the slave's social identity (see Meillassoux 1975; Vaughan 1977; Kopytoff and Miers 1977; Kopytoff 1982; Patterson 1982). From this perspective slavery is seen not as a fixed and unitary status, but as a process of social transformation that involves a succession of phases and changes in status, some of which merge with other statuses (for example, that of adoptee) that we in the West consider far removed from slavery.

Slavery begins with capture or sale, when the individual is stripped of his previous social identity and becomes a non-person, indeed an object and an actual or potential commodity. But the process continues. The slave is acquired by a person or group and is reinserted into the host group, within which he is resocialized and rehumanized by being given a new social identity. The commodity-slave becomes in effect reindividualized by acquiring new statuses (by no means always lowly ones) and a unique configuration of personal relationships. In brief, the process has moved the slave away from the simple status of exchangeable commodity and toward that of a singular individual occupying a particular social and personal niche. But the slave usually remains a potential commodity: he or she continues to have a potential exchange value that may be realized by resale. In many societies, this was also true of the 'free', who were subject to sale under certain defined circumstances. To the extent that in such societies all persons possessed an exchange value and were commoditizable, commoditization in them was clearly not culturally confined to the world of things.

What we see in the career of a slave is a process of initial withdrawal from a given original social setting, his or her commoditization, followed by increasing singularization (that is, decommoditization) in the new setting, with the possibility of later recommoditization. As in most processes, the successive phases merge one into another. Effectively, the slave was unambiguously a commodity only during the relatively short period between capture or first sale and the acquisition of the new social identity; and the slave becomes less of a commodity and more of a singular individual in the process of gradual incorporation into the host society. This biographical consideration of enslavement as a process suggests that the commoditization of other things may usefully be seen in a similar light, namely, as part of the cultural shaping of biographies.

The biographical approach

Biographies have been approached in various ways in anthropology (for a survey, see Langness 1965). One may present an actual biography, or one may construct a typical biographical model from randomly assembled biographical data, as one does in the standard Life Cycle chapter in a general ethnography. A more theoretically aware biographical model is rather more demanding. It is based on a reasonable number of actual life histories. It presents the range of biographical possibilities that the society in question offers and examines the manner in which these possibilities are realized in the life stories of various categories of people. And it examines idealized biographies that are considered to be desirable models in the society and the way real-life departures from the models are perceived. As Margaret Mead remarked, one way to understand a culture is to see what sort of biography it regards as embodying a successful social career. Clearly, what is seen as a well-lived life in an African society is different in outline from what would be pronounced as a well-lived life along the Ganges, or in Brittany, or among the Eskimos.

It seems to me that we can profitably ask the same range and kinds of cultural questions to arrive at biographies of things. Early in this century, in an article entitled 'The genealogical method of anthropological inquiry' (1910), W. H. R. Rivers offered what has since become a standard tool in ethnographic fieldwork. The thrust of the article – the aspect for which it is now mainly remembered – is to show how kinship terminology and relationships may be superimposed on a genealogical diagram and traced through the social-structure-in-time that the diagram mirrors. But Rivers also suggested something else: that, for example, when the anthropologist is in search of inheritance rules, he may compare the ideal statement of the rules with the actual movement of a particular object, such as a plot of land, through the genealogical diagram, noting concretely how it passes from hand to hand. What Rivers proposed was a kind of biography of things in terms of ownership. But a biography may concentrate on innumerable other matters and events.

In doing the biography of a thing, one would ask questions similar to those one asks about people: What, sociologically, are the biographical possibilities inherent in its 'status' and in the period and culture, and how are these possibilities realized? Where does the thing come from and who made it? What has been its career so far, and what do people consider to be an ideal career for such things? What are the recognized 'ages' or periods in the things 'life', and what are the cultural markers for them? How does the thing's use change with its age, and what happens to it when it reaches the end of its usefulness?

For example, among the Suku of Zaire, among whom I worked, the life expectancy of a hut is about ten years. The typical biography of a hut begins with its housing a couple or, in a polygynous household, a wife with her children. As the hut ages, it is successively turned into a guest house or a house for a widow, a teenagers' hangout, kitchen, and, finally, goat or chicken house – until at last the termites win and the structure collapses. The physical state of the hut at each given age corresponds to a particular use. For a hut to be out of phase in its use makes a Suku uncomfortable, and it conveys a message. Thus, to house a visitor in a hut that should be a kitchen says something about the visitor's status; and if there is no visitors' hut available in a compound, it says something about the compound-head's character – he must be lazy, inhospitable, or poor. We have similar biographical expectations of things. To us, a biography of a painting by Renoir that ends up in an incinerator is as tragic, in its way, as the biography of a person who ends up murdered. That is obvious. But there are other events in the biography of objects that convey more subtle meanings. What of a Renoir ending up in a private and inaccessible collection? Of one lying neglected in a museum basement? How should we feel about yet another Renoir leaving France for the United States? Or for Nigeria? The cultural responses to such biographical details reveal a tangled mass of aesthetic, historical, and even political judgments, and of convictions and values that shape our attitudes to objects labeled 'art'.

Biographies of things can make salient what might otherwise remain obscure. For example, in situations of culture contact, they can show what anthropologists have so often stressed: that what is significant about the adoption of alien objects – as of alien ideas – is not the fact that they are adopted, but the way they are culturally redefined and put to use. The biography of a car in Africa would reveal a wealth of cultural data: the way it was acquired, how and from whom the money was assembled to pay for it, the relationship of the seller to the buyer, the uses to which the car is regularly put, the identity of its most frequent passengers and of those who borrow it, the frequency of borrowing, the garages to which it is taken and the owner's relation to the mechanics, the movement of the car from hand to hand over the years, and in the end, when the car collapses, the final disposition of its remains. All of these details would reveal an entirely different biography from that of a middle-class American, or Navajo, or French peasant car.

One brings to every biography some prior conception of what is to be its focus. We accept that every person has many biographies – psychological, professional, political, familial, economic and so forth – each of which selects some aspects of the life history and discards others. Biographies of things cannot but be similarly partial. Obviously, the sheer physical biography of a car is quite different from its technical biography, known in the trade as its repair record. The car can also furnish an economic biography – its initial worth, its sale and resale price, the rate of decline in its value, its response to the recession, the patterning over several years of its maintenance costs. The car also offers several possible social biographies: one biography may concentrate on its place in the owner-family's economy, another may relate the history of its ownership to the society's class structure, and a third may focus on its role in the sociology of the family's kin relations, such as loosening family ties in America or strengthening them in Africa.

But all such biographies – economic, technical, social – may or may not be culturally informed. What would make a biography cultural is not what it deals with, but how and from what perspective. A culturally informed economic biography of an object would look at it as a culturally constructed entity, endowed with culturally specific meanings, and classified and reclassified into culturally constituted categories. It is from this point of view that I should like to propose a framework for looking at commodities – or rather, speaking processually, at commoditization. But first, what is a commodity?

The singular and the common

I assume commodities to be a universal cultural phenomenon. Their existence is a concomitant of the existence of transactions that involve the exchange of things (objects and services), exchange being a universal feature of human social life and, according to some theorists, at the very core of it (see for example Homans 1961; Ekeh 1974; and Kapferer 1976). Where societies differ is in the ways commoditization as a special expression of exchange is structured and related to the social system, in the factors that encourage or contain it, in the long-term tendencies for it to expand or stabilize, and in the cultural and ideological premises that suffuse its workings.

What, then, makes a thing a commodity? A commodity is a thing that has use value and that can be exchanged in a discrete transaction for a counterpart, the very fact of exchange indicating that the counterpart has, in the immediate context, an equivalent value. The counterpart is by the same token also a commodity at the time of exchange. The exchange can be direct or it can be achieved indirectly by way of money, one of whose functions is as a means of exchange. Hence anything that can be bought for money is at that point a commodity, whatever the fate that is reserved for it after the transaction has been made (it may, thereafter, be decommoditized). Hence, in the West, as a matter of cultural shorthand, we usually take saleability to be the unmistakable indicator of commodity status, while non-saleability imparts to a thing a special aura of apartness from the mundane and the common. In fact, of course, saleability for money is not a necessary feature of commodity status, given the existence of commodity exchange in non-monetary economies.

I refer to the transaction involving commodities as discrete in order to stress that the primary and immediate purpose of the transaction is to obtain the counterpart value (and that, for the economist, is also its economic function). The purpose of the transaction is not, for example, to open the way for some other kind of transaction, as in the case of gifts given to initiate marriage negotiations or to secure patronage; each of these cases is a partial transaction that should be considered in the context of the entire transaction. While exchanges of things usually involve commodities, a notable exception is the exchanges that mark relations of reciprocity, as these have been classically defined in anthropology. Here, gifts are given in order to evoke an obligation to give back a gift, which in turn will evoke a similar obligation – a never-ending chain of gifts and obligations. The gifts themselves may be things that are normally used as commodities (food, feasts, luxury goods, services), but each transaction is not discrete and none, in principle, is terminal.

To be saleable for money or to be exchangeable for a wide array of other things is to have something in common with a large number of exchangeable things that, taken together, partake of a single universe of comparable values. To use an appropriately loaded even if archaic term, to be saleable or widely exchangeable is to be 'common' – the opposite of being uncommon, incomparable, unique, singular, and therefore not exchangeable for anything else. The perfect commodity would be one that is exchangeable with anything and everything else, as the perfectly commoditized world would be one in which everything is exchangeable or for sale. By the same token, the perfectly decommoditized world would be one in which everything is singular, unique, and unexchangeable.

The two situations are ideal polar types, and no real economic system could conform to either. In no system is everything so singular as to preclude even the hint of exchange. And in no system, except in some extravagant Marxian image of an utterly commoditized capitalism, is everything a commodity and exchangeable for everything else within a unitary sphere of exchange. Such a construction of the world – in the first case as totally heterogeneous in terms of valuation and, in the second, as totally homogeneous – would be humanly and culturally impossible. But they are two extremes between which every real economy occupies its own peculiar place.

We can accept, with most philosophers, linguists, and psychologists, that the human mind has an inherent tendency to impose order upon the chaos of its environment by classifying its contents, and without this classification knowledge of the world and adjustment to it would not be possible. Culture serves the mind by imposing a collectively shared cognitive order upon the world which, objectively, is totally heterogeneous and presents an endless array of singular things. Culture achieves order by carving out, through discrimination and classification, distinct areas of homogeneity within the overall heterogeneity. Yet, if the homogenizing process is carried too far and the perceived world begins to approach too closely the other pole in the case of goods, that of utter commoditization – culture's function of cognitive discrimination is undermined. Both individuals and cultural collectivities must navigate somewhere between the polar extremes by classifying things into categories that are simultaneously neither too many nor too embracing. In brief, what we usually refer to as 'structure' lies between the heterogeneity of too much splitting and the homogeneity of too much lumping.

In the realm of exchange values, this means that the natural world of singular things must be arranged into several manageable value classes – that is, different things must be selected and made cognitively similar when put together within each category and dissimilar when put into different categories. This is the basis for a well-known economic phenomenon – that of several spheres of exchange values, which operate more or less independently of one another. The phenomenon is found in every society, though Westerners are most apt to perceive it in uncommercialized and unmonetized economies. The nature and structure of these spheres of exchange varies among societies because, as we can expect with Durkheim and Mauss (1963, original publication 1903), the cultural systems of classification reflect the structure and the cultural resources of the societies in question. And beyond that, as we may expect with Dumont (1972), there's also some tendency to impose a hierarchy upon the categories.

Spheres of exchange

A concrete example of an economy with clearly distinct spheres of exchange will help the discussion. In what is a classic analysis of a 'multi-centric economy', Bohannan (1959) describes three such spheres of exchange as they operated before the colonial period among the Tiv of central Nigeria: (a) the sphere of subsistence items – yams, cereals, condiments, chickens, goats, utensils, tools, and the like; (b) the sphere of prestige items – mainly cattle, slaves, ritual offices, special cloth, medicines, and brass rods; and (c) the sphere of rights-in-people, which included rights in wives, wards, and offspring.

The three spheres represent three separate universes of exchange values, that is, three commodity spheres. Items within each were exchangeable, and each was ruled by its own kind of morality. Moreover, there was a moral hierarchy among the spheres: the subsistence sphere, with its untrammelled market morality, was the lowest, and the rights-in-people sphere, related to the world of kin and kin-group relations, was the highest. In the Tiv case (in contrast to that of many other similar systems), it was possible to move – even if in a rather cumbersome manner – between the spheres. Brass rods provided the link. In exceptional circumstances, people relinquished, unwillingly, rods for subsistence items; and, at the other end, one could also initiate with rods some transactions in the rights-in-people sphere. The Tiv considered it satisfying and morally appropriate to convert 'upward', from subsistence to prestige and from prestige to rights-in-people, whereas converting 'downward' was shameful and done only under extreme duress.

The problem of value and value equivalence has always been a philosophical conundrum in economics. It involves the mysterious process by which things that are patently unlike are somehow made to be alike with respect to value, making yams, for example, somehow comparable to and exchangeable with a mortar or a pot. In the terms we have been using here, this involves taking the patently singular and inserting it into a uniform category of value with other patently singular things. For all the difficulties that the labor theory of value presents, it at least suggests that while yams and pots can conceivably be compared by the labor required to produce them (even while allowing for the different investment in training that the labor represents in each case), no such common standard is available in comparing yams to ritual offices or pots to wives and offspring. Hence, the immense difficulty, indeed impossibility, of lumping all such disparate items into a single commodity sphere. This difficulty provides the natural basis for the cultural construction of separate spheres of exchange. The culture takes on the less sweeping task of making value-equivalence by creating several discrete commodity spheres – in the Tiv case, palpable items of subsistence created by physical labor, as opposed to the prestige items of social maneuvering, as opposed to the more intimate domain of the rights and obligations of kinship.

The drive to commoditization

From this perspective, a multi-centric economy such as that of the Tiv is not an exotically complicated rendering of a straightforward exchange system. It is rather the opposite – a feat of simplification of what is naturally an unmanageable mass of singular items. But why only three spheres and not, say, a dozen? The commoditization seems to be pushed to the limits permitted by the Tiv exchange technology, which lacked a common denominator of value more convenient than brass rods. One perceives in this a drive inherent in every exchange system toward optimum commoditization – the drive to extend the fundamentally seductive idea of exchange to as many items as the existing exchange technology will comfortably allow. Hence the universal acceptance of money whenever it has been introduced into non-monetized societies and its inexorable conquest of the internal economy of these societies, regardless of initial rejection and of individual unhappiness about it – an unhappiness well illustrated by the modern Tiv. Hence also the uniform results of the introduction of money in a wide range of otherwise different societies: more extensive commoditization and the merger of the separate spheres of exchange. It is as if the internal logic of exchange itself pre-adapts all economies to seize upon the new opportunities that wide commoditization so obviously brings with it.

One may interpret Braudel's recent work (1983) in this light – as showing how the development in early modern Europe of a range of new institutions shaped what might be called a new exchange technology and how this, in turn, led to the explosion of commoditization that was at the root of capitalism. The extensive commoditization we associate with capitalism is thus not a feature of capitalism *per se*, but of the exchange technology that, historically, was associated with it and that set dramatically wider limits to maximum feasible commoditization. Modern state-ordered, noncapitalist economies certainly show no signs of being systematically exempt from this tendency, even though they may try to control it by political means. Indeed, given their endemic shortages and ubiquitous black markets, commoditization in them expands into novel areas, in which the consumer, in order to purchase goods and services, must first purchase access to the transaction.

Commoditization, then, is best looked upon as a process of becoming rather than as an all-or-none state of being. Its expansion takes place in two ways: (a) with respect to each thing, by making it exchangeable for more and more other things, and (b) with respect to the system as a whole, by making more and more different things more widely exchangeable.

Singularization: cultural and individual

The counterdrive to this potential onrush of commoditization is culture. In the sense that commoditization homogenizes value, while the essence of culture is discrimination, excessive commoditization is anti-cultural – as indeed so many have perceived it or sensed it to be. And if, as Durkheim (1915; original publication 1912) saw it, societies need to set apart a certain portion of their environment, marking it as 'sacred', singularization is one means to this end. Culture ensures that some things remain unambiguously singular, it resists the commoditization of others; and it sometimes resingularizes what has been commoditized.

In every society, there are things that are publicly precluded from being commoditized. Some of the prohibitions are cultural and upheld collectively. In state societies, many of these prohibitions are the hand-work of the state, with the usual intertwining between what serves the society at large, what serves the state, and what serves the specific groups in control. This applies to much of what one thinks of as the symbolic inventory of a society; public lands, monuments, state art collections, the paraphernalia of political power, royal residences, chiefly insignia, ritual objects, and so on. Power often asserts itself symbolically precisely by insisting on its right to singularize an object, or a set or class of objects. African chiefs and kings reserve to themselves the right to certain animals and animal products, such as the skins and teeth of spotted wild cats. The kings of Siam monopolized albino elephants. And British monarchs have kept their right to dead whales washed ashore. There may be some practical side to these royal pretensions, which ecological and cultural materialists will no doubt diligently discover. What these monopolies clearly do, however, is to expand the visible reach of sacred power by projecting it onto additional sacralized objects.

Such singularization is sometimes extended to things that are normally commodities – in effect, commodities are singularized by being pulled out of their usual commodity sphere. Thus, in the ritual paraphernalia of the British monarchy, we find a Star of India that, contrary to what would normally have happened, was prevented from becoming a commodity and eventually singularized into a 'crown jewel'. Similarly, the ritual paraphernalia of the kings of the Suku of Zaire included standard trade items from the past, such as eighteenth-century European ceramic drinking mugs brought by the Portuguese, carried by the Suku to their present area, and sacralized in the process.

Another way to singularize objects is through restricted commoditization, in which some things are confined to a very narrow sphere of exchange. The Tiv system illustrates the principle. The few items in the prestige sphere (slaves, cattle, ritual offices, a special cloth, and brass rods), though commodities by virtue of being exchangeable one for the other, were less commoditized than the far more numerous items of the subsistence sphere, ranging widely from yams to pots. A sphere consisting of but two kinds of items – as in the classic model of the Trobriand kula exchange sphere of arm bands and bracelets – represents an even greater degree of singularization. The Tiv exchange sphere of rights-in-person achieved a singular integrity by a different though related principle, that of the homogeneity of its components. The two upper Tiv spheres, it may be noted, were more singular, more special, and hence more sacred than the lowest sphere, containing the many objects of mundane subsistence. Thus the moral hierarchy of the Tiv exchange spheres corresponded to a gradient of singularity.

If sacralization can be achieved by singularity, singularity does not guarantee sacralization. Being a non-commodity does not by itself assure high regard, and many singular things (that is, non-exchangeable things) may be worth very little. Among the Aghem of western Cameroon, with exchange spheres not unlike those of the Tiv, one could detect yet another and lower sphere, one below that of marketable subsistence items. Once, when trying to find out the precolonial exchange value of various items, I asked about the barter value of *manioc*. The response was indignant scoffing at the very idea that such a lowly thing as *manioc* should have been exchangeable for anything: 'One eats it, that's all. Or one gives it away if one wants to. Women may help out one another with it and other such food. But one doesn't *trade* it.' Lest the outburst be misunderstood and sentimentalized, let me stress that the indignation was not about a suggested commercial corruption of a symbolically supercharged staple, on the order, say, of bread among Eastern European peasants. The Aghem are and were a commercially minded people, with no disdain for trade. The scoffing was rather like what an Aghem would get from a Westerner whom he asked about the exchange value of a match he proffers to light a stranger's cigarette. *Manioc* was part of a class of singular things of so little worth as to have no publicly recognized exchange value. To be a non-commodity is to be 'priceless' in the full possible sense of the term, ranging from the uniquely valuable to the uniquely worthless.

In addition to things being classified as more or less singular, there is also what might be called terminal commoditization, in which further exchange is precluded by fiat. In many societies, medicines are so treated: the medicine man makes and sells a medicine that is utterly singular since it is efficacious only for the intended patient. Terminal commoditization also marked the sale of indulgences in the Roman Catholic Church of half a millennium ago: the sinner could buy them but not resell them. In modern Western medicine, such terminal commoditization is achieved legally; it rests on the prohibition against reselling a prescribed drug and against selling any medicine without proper licensing. There are other examples of legal attempts to restrict recommoditization: paperbound books published in Great Britain often carry a bewildering note forbidding the buyer to resell it in any but the original covers; and in America, an equally mystifying label is attached to mattresses and cushions, forbidding their resale.

Other factors besides legal or cultural fiat may create terminal commodities. Most consumer goods are, after all, destined to be terminal – or so, at least, it is hoped by the manufacturer. The expectation is easily enough fulfilled with such things as canned peas, though even here external circumstances can intrude; in times of war shortages, all sorts of normally consumable goods begin to serve as a store of wealth and, instead of being consumed, circulate endlessly in the market. With durable goods, a second-hand market normally develops, and the idea that it does may be fostered by the sellers. There is an area of our economy in which the selling strategy rests on stressing that the commoditization of goods bought for consumption need not be terminal: thus, the promise that oriental carpets, though bought for use, are a 'good investment', or that certain expensive cars have a 'high resale value'.

The existence of terminal commoditization raises a point that is central to the analysis of slavery, where the fact that a person has been bought does not in itself tell us anything about the uses to which the person may then be put (Kopytoff 1982: 223ff.). Some purchased people ended up in the mines, on plantations, or on galleys; others became Grand Viziers or Imperial Roman Admirals. In the same way, the fact that an object is bought or exchanged says nothing about its subsequent status and whether it will remain a commodity or not. But unless formally decommoditized, commoditized things remain potential commodities – they continue to have an exchange value, even if they have been effectively withdrawn from their exchange sphere and deactivated, so to speak, as commodities. This deactivation leaves them open not only to the various kinds of singularization I have mentioned so far, but also to individual, as opposed to collective, redefinitions.

In the Bamenda area of western Cameroon, people prized large decorated calabashes that came over the border from Nigeria. The conduit for them was the Aku, a pastoral group whose women used them extensively and normally were willing to sell them. I had acquired several in this way. Yet one day I failed completely to convince an Aku woman to sell me a standard *calabash* to which she had added some minor decorations of her own. Her friends told her that she was being silly, arguing that for the money she could get a far better and prettier calabash. But she would not budge, no more than does that ever-newsworthy man in our society – part hero, part fool – who refuses to sell his house for a million dollars and forces the skyscraper to be built around it. And there is also the opposite phenomenon: the ideological commoditizer, advocating, say, the sale of public lands as a way of balancing the budget, or, as I have seen in Africa, calling for the sale of some piece of chiefly paraphernalia in order to provide a tin roof for the schoolhouse.

What these mundane examples show is that, in any society, the individual is often caught between the cultural structure of commoditization and his own personal attempts to bring a value order to the universe of things. Some of this clash between culture and individual is inevitable, at least at the cognitive level. The world of things lends itself to an endless number of classifications, rooted in natural features and cultural and idiosyncratic perceptions. The individual mind can play with them all, constructing innumerable classes, different universes of common value, and changing spheres of exchange. Culture, by contrast, cannot be so exuberant, least so in the economy, where its classifications must provide unambiguous guidance to pragmatic and coordinated action. But if the clash is inevitable, the social structures within which it takes place vary, giving it different intensities. In a society like the precolonial Tiv or Aghem, the culture and the economy were in relative harmony; the economy followed the cultural classifications, and these catered successfully to the individual cognitive need for discrimination. By contrast, in a commercialized, monetized, and highly commoditized society, the value-homogenizing drive of the exchange system has an enormous momentum, producing results that both culture and individual cognition often oppose, but in inconsistent and even contradictory ways.

Complex societies

I said above that the exchange spheres are, to us, more visible in non-commercial, non-monetized societies like the Tiv than in commercial, monetized ones like our own. Partly this is a matter of noticing the exotic and taking the familiar for granted. But it is more than that.

Certainly, in our society, some discrete spheres of exchange exist and are nearly unanimously accepted and approved. Thus, we are adamant about keeping separate the spheres of material objects and persons (a matter I shall elaborate on later). We also exchange dinners and keep that sphere discrete. We blandly accept the existence of an exchange sphere of political or academic favors, but would be as shocked at the idea of monetizing this sphere as the Tiv were at first at the idea of monetizing their marriage transactions. Like the Tiv, who carefully moved from the sphere of mundane pots to that of prestigeful titles by using the mediation of brass rods, so do our financiers cautiously navigate between exchange spheres in such matters as gift-giving to universities. A straight money donation in general funds, if it is of any size, is suspect because it looks too much like purchasing influence, and such donations, when made, are normally anonymous or posthumous. A money donation in instalments would be particularly suspect, implying the donor's power to withhold the next check. But converting a large donation into a building moves the money into a nearly decommoditized sphere, freezes the gift into visible irrevocability, and shields the donor from suspicion of continuous undue influence on the university. Putting the donor's name on the building thus honors not simply the donor but also the university, which declares in doing so that it is free of any lingering obligations to the specific donor. The values underlying such transactions are, on the whole, society wide, or at least are held by the groups who wield cultural hegemony in our society and define much of what we are apt to call our public culture. 'Everyone' is against commoditizing what has been publicly marked as singular and made sacred: public parks, national landmarks, the Lincoln Memorial, George Washington's false teeth at Mount Vernon.

Other singularizing values are held by more restricted groups. We have explicit exchange spheres recognized only by segments of society, such as professional and occupational groups, which subscribe to a common cultural code and a specially focused morality. Such groups constitute the networks of mechanical solidarity that tie together the parts of the organic structure of the wider society, the latter being ruled in most of its activities by commodity principles. Let me lead into my discussion by looking at an activity in one such group: the collection of African art among American Africanists.

In the simpler days of thirty or more years ago, African art picked up randomly in the course of fieldwork was placed entirely in a closed sphere with a sacred cast. The objects collected were greatly singularized; they were held to have for their collector a personal sentimental value, or a purely aesthetic one, or a scientific one, the last supported by the collector's supposed knowledge of the object's cultural context. It was not considered entirely proper to acquire an art object from African market traders or, worse, from European traders in Africa, or worse still, from dealers in Europe or America. Such an object, acquired at second hand, had little scientific value, and it was vaguely contaminated by having circulated in a monetized commodity-sphere – a contamination that was not entirely removed by keeping it thereafter in the same category as the objects 'legitimately' acquired in the field. The exchange sphere to which African art objects belonged was extremely homogeneous in content. It was permissible to exchange them for other African (or other 'primitive art') objects. One could also give them as gifts. Students returning from the field usually brought one or two as gifts to their supervisors, thus inserting them into another circumscribed sphere, that of academic patron–client relationships. The morality governing the sphere did not allow for them to be sold, except at cost to a museum. Nevertheless, as among the Tiv, for whom it was permissible though shameful to sell a brass rod for food, so here extreme need justified 'liquidation' on the commercial art market, but it had to be done with appropriate discretion and it was certainly seen as converting 'downward'.

As Douglas and Isherwood (1980) show, the public culture in complex societies does provide broadly discriminating value markings of goods and services. That is, the public culture offers discriminating classifications here no less than it does in small-scale societies. But these must constantly compete with classifications by individuals and by small networks, whose members also belong to other networks expounding yet other value systems. The discriminating criteria that each individual or network can bring to the task of classification are extremely varied. Not only is every individual's or network's version of exchange spheres idiosyncratic and different from those of others, but it also shifts contextually and biographically as the originators' perspectives, affiliations and interests shift. The result is a debate not only between people and groups, but within each person as well. To be sure, the seeds for such debates also exist in societies like the precolonial Tiv, but there the culture and the economy joined hands to provide an approved model of classification. In a commercialized, heterogeneous, and liberal society, the public culture defers most of the time to pluralism and relativism and provides no firm guidance, while the only lesson the economy can teach is that of the freedom and dynamism that ever-wider commoditization clearly brings with it.

The results can be partly glimpsed in what has happened to African art collecting over the past quarter century. The rules have been loosened in some of the same ways that monetization, according to Bohannan, loosened the rules among the Tiv – namely, by merging the previously distinct exchange spheres. There are, for example, no strictures now on buying an African art object at an auction in America, let alone from an African trader in Africa. Monetization in itself has become less contaminating as it has become more seductive, for no one can remain unaware that these objects are what every newspaper and magazine calls 'collectibles'. But the most noticeable change has been, quite simply, to make the rules less clear and more open to individual interpretations and to idiosyncratic systems of values. Where before the professional culture decreed that the value of these objects was sentimental when it was not scientific, now sentimental value is conferred as a matter of individual choice, perhaps more sincerely but also less widely. At the same time, puritans have arisen, thundering about the immorality of any kind of circulation of these objects and calling for their complete singularization and sacralization within the closed boundaries of the society that produced them. In brief, the rules of the professional culture have become less tight and the rules of propriety have become more idiosyncratic. The widespread rejection, since the 1960s, of the very idea of cultural restraints has, here as elsewhere, opened the door to a great variety of definitions by individuals and small groups.

What I am arguing here is that the crucial difference between complex and small-scale societies does not lie simply in the extensive commoditization in the former. There have been, we must not forget, small-scale societies in which commoditization (helped by indigenous money) was very extensive, such as the Yurok of northern California (Kroeber 1925) or the Kapauku of western New Guinea (Pospisil 1963). The peculiarity of complex societies is that their publicly recognized commoditization operates side by side with innumerable schemes of valuation and singularization devised by individuals, social categories, and groups, and these schemes stand in unresolvable conflict with public commoditization as well as with one another.

The dynamics of informal singularization in complex societies

There is clearly a yearning for singularization in complex societies. Much of it is satisfied individually, by private singularization, often on principles as mundane as the one that governs the fate of heirlooms and old slippers alike – the longevity of the relation assimilates them in some sense to the person and makes parting from them unthinkable.

Sometimes the yearning assumes the proportions of a collective hunger, apparent in the widespread response to ever-new kinds of singularizations. Old beer cans, matchbooks, and comic books suddenly become worthy of being collected, moved from the sphere of the singularly worthless to that of the expensive singular. And there is a continuing appeal in stamp collecting – where, one may note, the stamps are preferably cancelled ones so there is no doubt about their worthlessness in the circle of commodities for which they were originally intended. As among individuals, much of the collective singularization is achieved by reference to the passage of time. Cars as commodities lose value as they age, but at about the age of thirty they begin to move into the category of antiques and rise in value with every receding year. Old furniture, of course, does the same at a more sedate pace – the period that begins to usher in sacralization is approximately equal to the span of time separating one from one's grandparents' generation (in the past, with less mobility and more stylistic continuity, more time was required). There is also the modern and appropriately unhistorical adaptation of the antiquing process so perceptively analyzed by Thompson (1979) – the instant singularization of objects in the trash-pile-to-living-room decor of the upwardly mobile young professionals, bored with the homogeneous Scandinavian aridity preferred by the previous generation of their class.

As with African art, however, these are all processes within small groups and social networks. What to me is an heirloom is, of course, a commodity to the jeweler, and the fact that I am not divorced from the jeweler's culture is apparent in my willingness to price my priceless heirloom (and invariably overestimate its commodity value). To the jeweler, I am confusing two different systems of values: that of the marketplace and that of the closed sphere of personally singularized things, both of which happen to converge on the object at hand. Many of the new 'collectibles' of the beer can variety are similarly caught in this paradox: as one makes them more singular and worthy of being collected, one makes them valuable; and if they are valuable, they acquire a price and become a commodity and their singularity is to that extent undermined. This interpenetration within the same object of commodity principles and singularization principles is played upon by firms specializing in manufacturing what might be called 'future collectibles', such as leather-bound editions of Emerson, bas-relief renditions of Norman Rockwell's paintings on sculptured plates, or silver medals commemorating unmemorable events. The appeal to greed in their advertising is complex: buy this plate now while it is still a commodity, because later it will become a singular 'collectible' whose very singularity will make it into a higher-priced commodity. I can think of no analogy to such possibilities among the Tiv exchange spheres.

Singularization of objects by groups within the society poses a special problem. Because it is done by groups, it bears the stamp of collective approval, channels the individual drive for singularization, and takes on the weight of cultural sacredness. Thus, a community of a few city blocks can suddenly be mobilized by a common outrage at the proposed removal and sale of scrap metal of the rusting Victorian fountain in the neighborhood. Such public conflicts are often more than mere matters of style. Behind the extraordinarily vehement assertions of aesthetic values may stand conflicts of culture, class, and ethnic identity, and the struggle over the power of what one might label the 'public institutions of singularization'.[1] In liberal societies, these institutions are higher nongovernmental agencies or only quasi-governmental ones – historical commissions, panels deciding on public monuments, neighborhood organizations concerned with 'beautification,' and so on; who controls them and how says much about who controls the society's presentation of itself to itself.

A few years ago, there was a public controversy in Philadelphia about a proposal to install a statue of the cinematic boxing hero Rocky on the Parkway in front of the Art Museum – an institution that happens simultaneously to serve as a public monument to the local social establishment and to satisfy the artistic needs of the professional intelligentsia. The statue came directly from the movie set of *Rocky*, the success story of an Italian-American boxing champion from South Philadelphia. To the 'ethnic' working-class sector of the Philadelphia population, the statue was a singular object of ethnic, class, and regional pride – in brief, a worthy public monument. To the groups whose social identities were vested in the museum, it was a piece of junk, deserving instant recommoditization as scrap metal. Here, the issues of singularization and commoditization were directly linked into disparate and morally charged systems. But the opponents of the statue were in a position to clothe their argument in the garb of public aesthetics, a field in which they held cultural hegemony. The statue was installed not at the Art Museum but in South Philadelphia, next to a stadium.

Most of the conflict, however, between commoditization and singularization in complex societies takes place within individuals, leading to what appear to be anomalies in cognition, inconsistencies in values, and uncertainties in action. People in these societies all maintain some private vision of a hierarchy of exchange spheres, but the justification for this hierarchy is not, as it was among the Tiv, integrally tied to the exchange structure itself; rather, the justification must be imported from outside the system of exchange, from such autonomous and usually parochial systems as that of aesthetics, or morality, or religion, or specialized professional concerns. When we feel that selling a Rembrandt or an heirloom is trading downward, the explanation for our attitude is that things called 'art' or 'historical objects' are superior to the world of commerce. This is the reason why the high value of the singular in complex societies becomes so easily embroiled in snobbery. The high value does not visibly reside in the exchange system itself – as it traditionally did among the Tiv, when, for example, the superiority in prestige (rather than mere exchange) of brass rods over pots was palpably confirmed by the ability of the brass rods to bring in ritual cloth or slaves. In a complex society, the absence of such visible confirmation of prestige, of what exactly is an 'upward' conversion, makes it necessary to attribute high but non-monetary value to aesthetic, stylistic, ethnic, class, or genealogical esoterica.

When things participate simultaneously in cognitively distinct yet effectively intermeshed exchange spheres, one is constantly confronted with seeming paradoxes of value. A Picasso, though possessing a monetary value, is priceless in another, higher scheme. Hence, we feel uneasy, even offended, when a newspaper declares the Picasso to be worth $690,000, for one should not be pricing the priceless. But in a pluralistic society, the 'objective' pricelessness of the Picasso can only be unambiguously confirmed to us by its immense market price. Yet, the pricelessness still makes the Picasso in some sense more valuable than the pile of dollars it can fetch – as will be duly pointed out by the newspapers if the Picasso is stolen. Singularity, in brief, is confirmed not by the object's structural position in an exchange system, but by intermittent forays into the commodity sphere, quickly followed by re-entries into the closed sphere of singular 'art'. But the two worlds cannot be kept separate for very long; for one thing, museums must insure their holdings. So museums and art dealers will name prices, be accused of the sin of transforming art into a commodity, and, in response, defend themselves by blaming each other for creating and maintaining a commodity market. It would, however, be missing the point of this analysis to conclude that the talk about singular art is merely an ideological camouflage for an interest in merchandising. What is culturally significant here is precisely that there is an inner compulsion to defend oneself, to others and to oneself, against the charge of 'merchandising' art.

The only time when the commodity status of a thing is beyond question is the moment of actual exchange. Most of the time, when the commodity is effectively out of the commodity sphere, its status is inevitably ambiguous and open to the push and pull of events and desires, as it is shuffled about in the flux of social life. This is the time when it is exposed to the well nigh-infinite variety of attempts to singularize it. Thus, singularizations of various kinds, many of them fleeting, are a constant accompaniment of commoditization, all the more so when it becomes excessive. There is a kind of singularizing black market here that is the mirror-image of, and as inevitable as, the more familiar commoditizing black market that accompanies regulated singularizing economies. Thus, even things that unambiguously carry an exchange value – formally speaking, therefore, commodities – do absorb the other kind of worth, one that is non-monetary and goes beyond exchange worth. We may take this to be the missing non-economic side of what Marx called commodity fetishism. For Marx, the worth of commodities is determined by the social relations of their production; but the existence of the exchange system makes the production process remote and misperceived, and it 'masks' the commodity's true worth (as, say, in the case of diamonds). This allows the commodity to be socially endowed with a fetishlike 'power' that is unrelated to its true worth. Our analysis suggests, however, that some of that power is attributed to commodities after they are produced, and this by way of an autonomous cognitive and cultural process of singularization.

Two Western exchange spheres: people vs objects

I have so far emphasized the sweeping nature of commoditization in Western society as representative of an ideal type of highly commercialized and monetized society. But the West is also a unique cultural entity, with a historically conditioned set of predispositions to see the world in certain ways.

One of these predispositions I have referred to before: that of conceptually separating people from things, and of seeing people as the natural preserve for individuation (that is singularization) and things as the natural preserve for commoditization. The separation, though intellectually rooted in classical antiquity and Christianity, becomes culturally salient with the onset of European modernity. Its most glaring denial lay, of course, in the practice of slavery. Yet its cultural significance can be gauged precisely by the fact that slavery did present an intellectual and moral problem in the West (see Davis 1966, 1975), but almost nowhere else. Whatever the complex reasons, the conceptual distinction between the universe of people and the universe of objects had become culturally axiomatic in the West by the mid-twentieth century. It is therefore not surprising that the cultural clash over abortion should be more fierce in the twentieth century than it ever was in the nineteenth, and that this clash should be phrased by both sides in terms of the precise location of the line that divides persons from things and the point at which 'personhood' begins. For both anti-abortion and pro-abortion forces agree on one point: that 'things' but not 'persons' can be aborted. Hence the occasional court battles when pro-abortionists seek court injunctions against anti-abortionists' attempts to ritualize the disposal of aborted fetuses, since ritual disposal presumes personhood. In terms of underlying conceptions, both sides here stand together in striking cultural contrast to the Japanese. The latter have few misgivings about abortion but acknowledge the personhood of aborted children, giving them the special status of *misogo*, lost souls, and commemorating them by special shrines (see Miura 1984).

There is, therefore, a perennial moral concern in Western thought, whatever the ideological position of the thinker, about the commoditization of human attributes such as labor, intellect, or creativity, or, more recently, human organs, female reproductive capacity, and ova. The moral load in these matters comes partly from the long debates on slavery and the victory of abolition. Hence the tendency to resort to slavery as the readiest metaphor when commoditization threatens to invade the human sphere, slavery being the extreme case in which the totality of a person is seen as having been commoditized. The moral indictments of capitalism by both Marx and Pope Leo XIII derived their force from the notion that human labor should not be a mere commodity – hence the rhetorical power of such terms as 'wage slavery'. The conceptual unease of conjoining person and commodity renders, in most modern Western liberal societies, the adoption of a baby illegal if it involves monetary compensation to the natural parent – something that most societies have seen as satisfying the obvious demands of equity. In the modern West, however, adoption through compensation is viewed as child-selling and therefore akin to slavery because of the implicit commoditization of the child, regardless of how loving the adoptive parents may be. Thus, the law specifically punishes such compensation in Britain, in most Canadian provinces, and in almost all states in the United States.

The hallmark of commoditization is exchange. But exchange opens the way to trafficking, and trafficking in human attributes carries with it a special opprobrium. For example, we do not – we cannot at this point – object to the commoditization and sale of labor (by its nature, a terminal commodity). But we do object to the trafficking in labor that a complete commoditization of labor would imply. We have abolished indentured labor, and the courts have struck down the commoditization of the contracts of athletes and actors. The cultural argument against a team's or a film studio's 'selling' a ballplayer or an actor to another employer is cast in the idiom of slavery. The transfer of a contract forces the worker to work for someone whom he had not chosen himself, hence forces him to work involuntarily. We see here a significant cultural detail in the Western commoditization of labor – the commoditization must be controlled by the laborer himself. By contrast, contractual obligations to pay, as in promissory notes or instalment buying, and rent contracts are legally negotiable; they can be and are regularly sold and resold. By the same cultural logic, the idea of nearly confiscatory taxation is far less shocking to us than even a modest amount of *corvée* labor. As with trafficking in labor, we find the direct commoditization of sexual services (also a terminal commodity) by the immediate supplier less objectionable than the trafficking in them by pimps. And so also we find the imminent possibility of terminal sales of human ova somewhat more morally acceptable than the idea of a commercial traffic in them.

The question remains, however: how secure are the Western cultural ramparts that defend the human sphere against commoditization, especially in a secularized society that finds it increasingly difficult to appeal to any transcendental sanctions for cultural discrimination and classification? I have suggested that economies are inherently responsive to the pressures of commoditization and that they tend to commoditize as widely as the exchange technology allows. What then, we may ask, are the effects, on the divide between the human and the commodity spheres, of the developing technology of transfer of human attributes? I am speaking here of recent medical advances in the transfer of organs and ova and the development of surrogate motherhood. The realm of human reproduction is one in which the difference between persons and things is particularly difficult to define, defying all attempts at drawing a simple line where there is a natural continuum.

The idea of direct surrogate motherhood – in which a woman simply bears a child for the future legal mother – required, of course, a legal more than a technical innovation. The idea had taken hold at the same time that technical advances in coping with female infertility had begun to raise the hopes of childless couples but without, in fact, helping many of them. It also came in response to the shrinkage in the supply of babies for adoption that occurred in the 1960s with the pill and the 1970s with the wider legalization of abortions. More recently, the picture has been complicated by the development of technical means for the actual transplantation of ova, opening the possibility of trading in the physical means of reproduction. The popular objections to surrogate motherhood are usually phrased in the idiom of the impropriety of commoditization. In the words of a Canadian provincial minister of social services, expressing his opposition: 'You can't buy a baby in Ontario.' It is, however, more acceptable, at least to some, when the surrogate mother announces that she receives not 'payment' but 'compensation' of ten thousand dollars 'because of the inconvenience to my family and the risk involved'. And the agency arranging for surrogate child production makes a point of declaring 'We are not in the rent-a-womb business.' In the meantime, while ethicists and theologians argue, the cost of securing a surrogate mother has now risen to around twenty-five thousand dollars (Scott 1984).

There is, of course, a precedent for the commoditization of physical human attributes: the supply of blood in American medical practice depends overwhelmingly on a straightforward commodity market in blood – in contrast, for example, to most European countries, which have deliberately rejected the commodity approach (Cooper and Culyer 1968). At present, advances in organ transplants and the inadequate supply of organs raises the same question of public policy that was confronted in the past in the case of blood: what are the best ways of ensuring an adequate supply? In the meantime, advertisements have begun to appear offering to buy kidneys for transplantation.

How to deal with ova is only beginning to be discussed. Culturally, the situation is perceived as being more complex than in the case of sperm, which has been commoditized for some time without a great deal of discussion. Is this because the ovum is seen as the basic core of the future human being? Or because women are expected to feel maternal toward the ova as potential babies and should not sell them whereas men are not expected to have paternal feelings about their sperm?[2] (Many societies describe the generation of life as the union of two elements; Westerners, however, choose the scientific metaphor in which one speaks of the fertilization of the ovum by the sperm, so that the ovum becomes a homunculus being activated into life.) The inevitable development into routine procedures of the transplantation of ova and the freezing of ova for storage will represent an expansion of the possibilities of the exchange technology for human attributes, including the possibility of trafficking in them. The question is whether this will increase the permeability of the boundary between the world of things and that of people, or whether the boundary will be displaced by recourse to new definitions but itself remain as rigid as before.

Conclusion: kinds of biographies
Although the singular and the commodity are opposites, no thing ever quite reaches the ultimate commodity end of the continuum between them. There are no perfect commodities. On the other hand, the exchange function of every economy appears to have a built-in force that drives the exchange system toward the greatest degree of commoditization that the exchange technology permits. The counterforces are culture and the individual, with their drive to discriminate, classify, compare, and sacralize. This means a two-front battle for culture as for the individual – one against commoditization as a homogenizer of exchange values, the other against the utter singularization of things as they are in nature.

In small-scale uncommercialized societies, the drive to commoditization was usually contained by the inadequacies of the technology of exchange, notably, the absence of a well-developed monetary system. This left room for a cultural categorization of the exchange value of things, usually in the form of closed exchange spheres, and it satisfied individual cognitive needs for classification. The collective cultural classification thus constrained the innate exuberance to which purely idiosyncratic and private classifications are prone.

In large-scale, commercialized, and monetized societies, the existence of a sophisticated exchange technology fully opens the economy to swamping by commoditization. In all contemporary industrial societies, whatever their ideologies, commoditization and monetization tend to invade almost every aspect of existence, be it openly or by way of a black market. New technological advances (for example, in medicine) also open previously closed areas to the possibilities of exchange and these areas tend to become quickly commoditized. The flattening of values that follows commoditization and the inability of the collective culture of a modern society to cope with this flatness frustrate the individual on the one hand, and, on the other, leave ample room for a multitude of classifications by individuals and small groups. These classifications, however, remain private and, except in the case of culturally hegemonic groups, without public support.

Thus, the economies of complex and highly monetized societies exhibit a two-sided valuating system: on one side is the homogenous area of commodities, on the other, the extremely variegated area of private valuation. Further complications arise from the constant referring of private valuation to the only reliable public valuation that exists – which is in the commodity area. It is inevitable that if worth is given a price, the going market price will become the measure of worth. The result is a complex intertwining of the commodity exchange sphere with the plethora of private classifications, leading to anomalies and contradictions and to conflicts both in the cognition of individuals and in the interaction of individuals and groups. By contrast, the structure of the economies of small-scale societies in the past resulted in a relative consonance of economic, cultural, and private valuations. These differences lead to quite different biographical profiles of things.

A caveat is required at this point. While in this discussion I have dwelt on the gross contrast between two ideal and polar types of economies, the most interesting empirical cases to be studied, with ultimately the highest theoretical returns, are the cases in between. It is from these cases that we can learn how the forces of commoditization and singularization are intertwined in ways far more subtle than our ideal model can show, how one breaks the rules by moving between spheres that are supposed to be insulated from each other, how one converts what is formally unconvertible, how one masks these actions and with whose connivance, and, not least, how the spheres are reorganized and things reshuffled between them in the course of a society's history. Equally interesting would be the cases where the different systems of commoditization of different societies interact. For example, Curtin (1984) has shown the importance, for the history of world trade, of trade diasporas; in these, traders, constituting a distinct *quasi*-cultural group, provided the channels for the movement of goods between disparate societies. The usefulness of such trading groups in mediating between the different exchange systems is manifest. By cushioning the direct impact of world trade, this mediation spares the societies involved from seeing their particular ideas of commoditization challenged, sheltering their baroque exchange systems in the comfort of their cultural parochialism. This, perhaps, would explain the striking viability, historically, of parochial economic systems in the midst of worldwide networks of trade. And it might also explain what has long been a puzzle in economic anthropology – namely, the limited spread, until the twentieth century, of 'all- purpose' currency, a spread far more limited than diffusion theory or commonsense utilitarianism would have suggested. Having said all this, let me nevertheless return to the gross contrast between the 'complex, commercialized' and the 'small-scale' societies, the implications of which I have pursued throughout this paper.

One can draw an analogy between the way societies construct individuals and the way they construct things. In small-scale societies, a person's social identities are relatively stable and changes in them are normally conditioned more by cultural rules than by biographical idiosyncrasies. The drama in an ordinary person's biography stems from what happens within the given status. It lies in the conflicts between the egoistic self and the unambiguous demands of given social identities, or in conflicts arising from interaction between actors with defined roles within a clearly structured social system. The excitement in the biographies is of the picaresque variety. At the same time, the individual who does not fit the given niches is either singularized into a special identity – which is sacred or dangerous, and often both – or is simply cast out. Things in these small-scale societies are similarly modeled. Their status in the clearly structured system of exchange values and exchange spheres is unambiguous. An eventful biography of a thing is for the most part one of events within the given sphere. Any thing that does not fit the categories is clearly anomalous and it is taken out of normal circulation, to be either sacralized or isolated or cast out. What one glimpses through the biographies of both people and things in these societies is, above all, the social system and the collective understandings on which it rests.

In complex societies, by contrast, a person's social identities are not only numerous but often conflicting, and there is no clear hierarchy of loyalties that makes one identity dominant over the others. Here, the drama of personal biographies has become more and more the drama of identities – of their clashes, of the impossibility of choosing between them, of the absence of signals from the culture and the society at large to help in the choice. The drama, in brief, lies in the uncertainty of identity – a theme increasingly dominant in modern Western literature where it is pushing aside dramas of social structure (even in the eminently structural cases dealt with in writings on women and 'minorities'). The biography of things in complex societies reveals a similar pattern. In the homogenized world of commodities, an eventful biography of a thing becomes the story of the various singularizations of it, of classifications and reclassifications in an uncertain world of categories whose importance shifts with every minor change in context. As with persons, the drama here lies in the uncertainties of valuation and of identity.

All this suggests an emendation to the profound Durkheimian notion that a society orders the world of things on the pattern of the structure that prevails in the social world of its people. What also happens, I would suggest, is that societies constrain both these worlds simultaneously and in the same way, constructing objects as they construct people.

ACKNOWLEDGEMENTS

I owe thanks to Arjun Appadurai and Barbara Klamon Kopytoff for discussions that led to the writing of this paper, and to Jean Adelman, Sandra Barnes, Muriel Bell, Gyan Prakash, Colin Renfrew, and Barbara Herrnstein Smith for comments and suggestions that helped shape its final version.

NOTES

1 I wish to thank Barbara Herrnstein Smith for drawing my attention to the importance of such institutions in the processes I am describing.

2 I am grateful to Muriel Bell for this suggestion.

23

MATERIAL METAPHOR, SOCIAL INTERACTION AND HISTORICAL RECONSTRUCTIONS*

Exploring Patterns of Association and Symbolism in the Igbo-Ukwu Corpus

KEITH RAY

Introduction

The Igbo-Ukwu corpus is a set of interrelated assemblages, mostly of copper, lead-bronze and ceramic artefacts from a number of different contexts across three sites excavated twenty-five years ago near Awka in south-eastern Nigeria, together with a group of metal objects recovered accidentally at one of these sites nearly fifty years ago. This material is important in Nigerian archaeology for several reasons, four of which are outlined here.[1] Firstly, in contrast to many traces in archaeological sites in this part of the world, the materials were found for the most part in clearly defined disposal contexts, two of which allowed fairly precise reconstruction. Thus in addition to sealed groups of materials from disposal pits and from filled-in water cisterns dug deep into the natural Awka sands, a coherent group of objects was found to have been laid out on the floor of an apparently rectangular building at one site, while a ritual burial complex was discovered at another (Shaw 1970: 58–80).

Secondly, the assemblages themselves display considerable technical elaboration and represent a concentration of wealth apparently at odds with an orthodox view of Igbo society as stateless and virtually acephalous. Thus in addition to simple domestic wares, the pottery from the sites includes some of the most elaborate ancient pottery known from anywhere in Africa (see Figure 23.1). Other assemblages, such as of copper and of bronze artefacts, not only include over a hundred complex and highly elaborate pieces of metalwork (some containing up to 3 kg of metal), but these pieces are chased or cast with an almost baroque profusion of intricate surface detail. Such complexity was carried over into the decoration of textiles and calabashes, of which, however, only fragments were preserved. Wealth is also attested by finds of ivory elephant tusks and of tens of thousands of beads, but interestingly there were no items in gold at all.

Thirdly, the available dating evidence suggests that at least some of the deposits were created, and the associated artefacts produced, as early as the eleventh century AD (Shaw 1970 and forthcoming). This makes it the earliest site in Nigeria where such elaborate metalwork is known, and suggests that it considerably antedates the better-known traditions of Ife and Benin. And fourthly, the representational diversity

*First published in I. R. Hodder (ed.) (1987), *The Archaeology of Contextual Meanings*, Cambridge: Cambridge University Press, pp. 66–77.

and complexity of particularly the copper and bronze objects allow a rare opportunity to examine not only individual associations but also patterns of association of both animate and inanimate portrayals across the various items and contexts.

The excavations responsible for elucidating these contexts and for recovering the bulk of the finds were conducted by Thurstan Shaw between 1960 and 1964. The detail in which the fieldwork and the finds were described in a major two-volume report (Shaw 1970) also serves to make the Igbo-Ukwu corpus important, since such comprehensive and rapid publication is itself somewhat rare. Despite the descriptive detail, however, an admitted shortcoming of this report was the dearth of extensive interpretation. This latter was limited to a few pages of comparisons between the Igbo-Ukwu finds and similar materials known from elsewhere, and to inferences about aspects of the technical, economic and social context of a pristine 'Igbo-Ukwu Culture'. This was presented as temporally remote from recent Igbo society in the area, although Shaw was in fact aware of the kinds of links to the present embodied in the Igbo-Ukwu material symbols (1970: 281). A popular publication was subsequently produced (Shaw, 1977) which included more information concerning the possible cultural and historical context of the finds following researches by an Igbo anthropologist, Michael Onwuejeogwu.

Material metaphor, social interaction, historical reconstruction

The popular publication also included an attempt to elucidate patterning in the motifs used on the Igbo-Ukwu metalwork. Basically, a list of motifs was drawn up, and their occurrences on different classes of object tabulated. No significant patterns of association were revealed by this analysis (Shaw 1977: 77). The structure of association of the various motifs and embodiments is in fact readily apparent if attention is focused upon their coincidence on individual objects rather than on their correspondence as classes on items grouped as classes. The other main reason why no clear associations were revealed was that the pattern only has significance within a culturally and historically determined structure of meaning which can be reconstructed with reference to the ethnography and iconography of the recent historical inheritors of the Igbo-Ukwu tradition.

Such reconstruction is predicated upon the identification of the form and content of various kinds of material statement of social codes embodied within the corpus of items. One of the most effective ways in which such social statements are communicated is through the use of what I would term 'material metaphor'. Here, a representation or association of representations encapsulates in material form certain kinds of moral or social or ritual relationships, or certain kinds of interaction, by means of either a simple metaphorical or complex proverbial portrayal of objects or creatures. Such a portrayal thus produces a material counterpart to articulations of such interactions or relationships in various categories of verbal discourse, such as sayings, stories, metaphors and proverbs. I propose that the direction of meaning can be suggested with reference to the conjunction of oral evidence, recent historical material practices, and a cumulative structuring of associational instances within a past material assemblage. However, it should be added that this will be more convincingly achieved where we can securely relate the material concerned to a definite, and local, historical and cultural trajectory.

Figure 23.1 *Decorated pot from Igbo Jonah, with detail*

Thus within this theoretical framework, material metaphor is used actively, helping to articulate social relationships and interaction. However, it is not the only means of doing so. Some objects which are not obviously metaphorical in that they do not involve embodiments or representations of clear symbolic import nevertheless make the kind of communicative statement alluded to above. They may do so by the power of connotation in a practice I would term 'presencing'. This is the remote introduction of individuals or categories of person into contexts and interactions they are not directly involved in. The means of such remote introduction is the inclusion in such contexts or interactions of objects which connote attributes of persons who habitually use them.

I have developed the concept of 'presencing' from that of time–space 'distanciation' formulated by Giddens in his 'theory of structuration', wherein devices such as writing are perceived as means of increasing the power of dominant over subordinate groups in society (Giddens 1981: 38–9, 94–5). This extension of power is achieved through an ability to record activity which happens at a distance from the point of information storage, and through the extension of memory by the relative permanency and immutability of these records. It follows that the dissemination of writing through inscriptions can serve to 'presence' the generators and users of such surveillance. Although on a global historical plane aspects of Giddens' notion of distanciation help to explain the way in which elites have gained control over subordinates, I believe that he underestimates the role of mnemonics in oral tradition, and ignores the role of focal material symbols in non-literate contexts. Items of material culture are in my view habitually used to 'presence' people even in literate contexts: in non-literate eras it is likely that their place was still more important, and that they were used actively in strategies of social control.

Most archaeological contexts are the outcome of long-term processes, but some, such as burials, often encapsulate the outcomes of specific practices enacted within a limited period of time. Such contexts thereby represent pinpointed instances within the working out of long-term processes. To this extent they can be said to be examples of the instantiation of practices which were responsible not only for the actions leading to the production of the residues, but also for determining the form of the objects included. In this way, such practices are situated historically not only within a determinate physical context on the one hand, and within abstract cumulative processes on the other, but also in terms of the intentions behind and the consequences arising from interactions occurring at the point of instance (Giddens 1979: 56). In such circumstances, any historical reconstruction must itself situate interpretation of material remains contextually within a historical trajectory which is expressed in terms of both immediate interactions and the longer-term processes they assist in working out.

Interpretative baselines: site contexts and the Nri ritual system

The above theoretical formulations are considered further in relation to specific observations of patterns of association and symbolism in the Igbo-Ukwu corpus in later sections of this chapter, and the general discussion of the nature of historical reconstructions is returned to in the concluding section. As further preface to the observations alluded to, the present section outlines the direction of immediate synthetic interpretation of the three Igbo-Ukwu sites, as well as aspects of the recent historical context.

At Igbo Isaiah (see Figure 23.2), the principal context comprised a group of objects placed on an almost level surface 60–70 cm below modern ground level, grouped in such a way as to suggest to the excavator the existence of a defining edge to the north and west. Four possible post-holes were seen as candidates for support-poles for some form of roofing over the area on which these objects were set (Shaw 1970: 263). Two principal concentrations of the objects were recorded, and a few associations were recoverable, although the removal of the eastern part of the deposit in 1938 during cistern digging has meant that about half of the previously extant associations are not recoverable.

Among the notable features of the assemblage from this deposit at Igbo Isaiah was the large number of metal staff-heads and staff-ornaments. Another was the fact that traces of fabric were found adhering to the surfaces of a number of the metal objects, which hinted at their being stored rather than displayed within the putative structure. On analogy with contemporary practice in this part of Igboland, the structure was therefore interpreted as an *obu*, or lineage temple, where present-day elders and title-holders meet to discuss any problems or decisions affecting the lineage. Here they also venerate the ancestors and tutelary gods of the lineage, and store its collective wealth and prestige items. It therefore normally contains a number of shrines, and serves as both temple and council chamber.

Fifty metres away to the west at the site named Igbo Richard, a modern cistern and an ancient cistern were located, and at 30 cm below ground level a pile of broken pots together with pottery pegs shaped from sherds was unearthed and was interpreted as a former shrine. This shrine had apparently served to mark the site of an important burial. Just below and to one side of the pile of pots were uncovered the bone remains

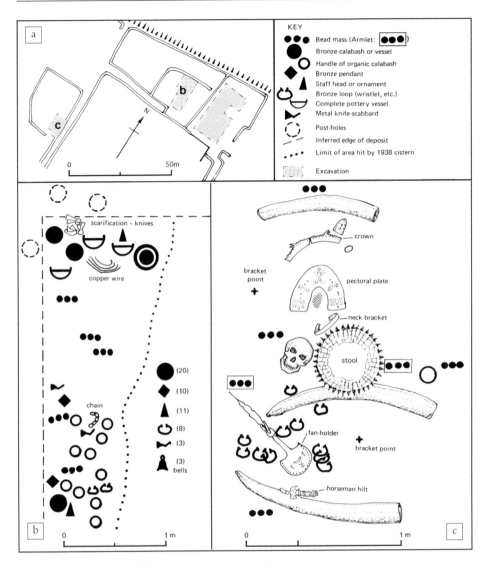

Figure 23.2 *Igbo Isiah* b *and Igbo Richard,* c

of at least five individuals together with over 300 beads and two thick copper wristlets (or 'manillas'). At a lower level were traces of decayed wood defining a burial chamber inside which were located the remains of a single burial accompanied by elaborate grave goods (see Figure 23.2). This burial was interpreted (Shaw 1970: 264) as that of an *eze Nri*, or priest-king of the Umunri, a group of people linked by a belief in a common origin and by their possession of a complex ritual system (see below, and Onwuejeogwu 1981). The interpretation was suggested by the form of the burial in a wood-lined chamber, and by the presence of a composite copper crown among the items that the corpse had apparently been dressed in for burial. These items also included a beaded headdress of at least 30 000 beads, lower-arm coverings of

Figure 23.3 Staff ornament [a] and bronze pendant [b] with snake motifs

0   5 cm

0   5 cm

more thousands of beads strung on a copper wire matrix, a decorated copper pectoral plate, and simple copper wristlets and armlets. Further accompaniments were a complex copper 'fan-holder', the bronze hilt of what may have been a fly-stick, three elephant tusks, copper calabash fittings, a copper staff surmounted by a cast bronze leopard skull, copper fittings for a wooden stool, and two copper rods surmounted by Y-shaped brackets. These last-mentioned were located on either side of the corpse, and along with a simpler bracket are most likely to have been used to fix the corpse in an upright seated position (Shaw 1970: 265).

Despite Onwuejeogwu's apparent reservations about the identification of this burial as that of an *eze Nri* on the grounds of its lavish accompaniments which he considers more appropriate for a lower-grade title personage (Shaw 1977: 98–9), the available ethnohistorical data allows precise confirmation. Thus among the injunctions for the 'correct' burial of an *eze Nri* recounted by priests of one of the royal lineages in the early 1930s were those that the dead king must be sat upright in the corner of a wood-lined burial chamber (in part to distinguish the burial from that of commoners, in part to facilitate spirit conversations with former *eze Nri*), must have his arms covered with beads, and must be wearing his full coronation regalia (Jeffreys 1936: 27–9).

A number of ancient filled-in pits and cisterns were the principal features discovered at the third site excavated, Igbo Jonah. One of these pits seemed to have been dug purposefully (Shaw 1970: 89, 226) to receive deposits of a mixed group of objects

403

including knotted copper bars, fifteen copper wristlets, links from a copper chain, fragments of bronze bells, bronze staff ornaments, and an elaborate handled pot.

It should be reiterated at this point that the potential meaning of the forms, associations, and iconography of these items can only be elucidated with reference to a culturally and historically definite structure of symbolism and practice. It has further been claimed above that this process of elucidation is best facilitated where local cultural continuity can be shown to exist. From the available linguistic, oral historical, and iconographical evidence (Afigbo 1981; Jeffreys 1936, Ch. II; Onwuejeogwu 1977) there seems no reason to suppose that (besides the infiltration of small Aro Igbo groups from the south-east in historically recent times) any significant dislocations of peoples or cultural traditions have taken place in the area east of Onitsha over many centuries. We can therefore feel confident in using ethnohistorical information concerning the central institutions of the Umunri (now reasonably full, thanks to Jeffreys and others) as an analogical framework for our interpretations.

The Umunri (people of the Nri maximal lineage) are a sub-group of the Igbo interspersed often in the same village-groups with non-Nri peoples across a low dissected plateau southeast of Onitsha in the present-day Anambra State of Nigeria. All lineages which claim Nri identity also express allegiance to the *eze Nri* either of Agukwu or of Oreri. The parallel existence of two priest-kings is widely explained in terms of the Oreri group having broken away from Agukwu and having set up its own dynasty some time in the distant past. Since the early years of this century the Agukwu community has styled itself simply 'Nri'. This version is, however, disputed in some places and although some sections even of Oreri agree with the Agukwu primacy model, others claim that Oreri was senior in the *eze*-ship to Agukwu. All Nri groups are, nevertheless, united in their belief in an ultimate common origin as descendants of the mythical ancestors Eri and his son Nri, and in their view of themselves as being at the centre of a ritual system which formerly had considerable religious and political influence over a wide area of Igboland, on both sides of the river Niger.

The Nri ritual system articulated in concrete terms a series of widely-held views concerning the nature of impurity, abomination, prestige and the moral order. For communities holding these beliefs a number of occurrences in human affairs, such as the bearing of twins, were abominations against the earth-deity, *Ala*, who ultimately controlled fertility and community fortune. The pollution caused by such abominations could be removed by Nri agents, priests and traders from the Nri communities, who were seen as representatives of the *eze Nri*, and through him of the folk hero Nri who, it was believed, brought food to all Igbo peoples (see below). Nri agents therefore travelled widely within Igboland, rendering ritual services, the most important of which was the removal of pollution, but which also involved the validation of prestige-seekers through affirming the passage of wealthy aspirants through the grades of the title system, the arbitration of major disputes in the name of the *eze Nri* and assisting in the enactment of new codes of ritual behaviour formulated in the Agukwu/Oreri Nri centres (Onwuejeogwu 1981: 16).

The Nri agents were immediately recognisable by their distinctive parallel-groove facial markings called *ichi*, and by their carriage of club-like staffs of authority, *ofo*, and spear-like staffs of peace, *otonsi*. As such, they were immune from violence and were assured safe passage wherever they went. Nri people also allegedly established colonies from among their own lineages throughout the area of their ritual influence, a factor which would have helped to consolidate the system and sustain both spiritual and secular dimensions of its power.

At the centre, a hierarchy of officials probably surrounded the reigning *eze Nri*. Among these was a kind of chief priest, at Oreri called the *Okpala*. He officiated at major rites concerning the ritual functions of the *eze Nri* and he alone could assist the king bodily (as in dressing for rituals), although at Agukwu any member of the Amada or priestly lineage could so render assistance. The rituals in which such priests assisted the *eze Nri* were those associated with his investiture and coronation, and those within diurnal and seasonal cycles concerned with assuring the continuing fertility of crops and animals (Jeffreys 1936).

As the pivot of the whole system, the *eze Nri* had to observe the strictest safeguards of his ritual purity. Thus in addition to a demanding schedule of personal and often private rituals and sacrifices, he had to observe literally dozens of personal taboos (Onwuejeogwu 1981: 52–3). Among other ritual injunctions was one that he should take all meals alone and in silence. He was expected to read omens and make prophecies, and among his other powers he was believed to be capable of directing the forces of nature for man's benefit. Thus as well as generating the fecundity of domestic animals he could control the activities of creatures such as grasshoppers, locusts, flies, soldier ants, birds, and yam-beetles to the advantage or to the discomfort of his people.

Informants in this century have often expressed the belief that the power of the Nri ritual system has waned significantly from an earlier apogee. The degree of impoverishment registered in recent kingly regalia would seem to support such a contention: both Agukwu and Oreri *eze Nri* have in recent times used necklaces of leopard's teeth, and headdresses including eagle feathers, but other items have been simple in form and base in metal content. Staffs may thus have simple copper bindings but the major metal components are of iron. Copper crowns (at Agukwu) have been simple rings of metal fitted onto a cap, and pectorals have been Benin-style brass face-masks which although claimed to be obtained for each successive king and buried with him at death, were believed by Jeffreys to be inherited.

Other prestige accoutrements such as beads, ivory wristlets, elephant-tusk horns, and iron gongs are common to all the higher title grades, but their use is not necessarily the same. For instance, one means by which the *eze Nri*, invisible to his people much of the time, is 'presenced' daily is by the banging of one of his large iron gongs in the marketplace to announce his mealtime. For the duration of the meal, it is forbidden for anyone present to utter a word (Jeffreys 1936: 9).

Pervasive metaphor: snakes and their messages

The studies presented in the next three sections of this chapter are intended as a preliminary exploration of the interpretive possibilities arising out of an explicitly contextual approach to patterns of association and symbolism among the Igbo-Ukwu sites and materials. The first of these studies focuses upon one kind of figural embellishment which occurs widely on both metal and ceramic items. Embellishments on the Igbo-Ukwu metalwork often take the form of naturalistic or stylised representations of a variety of creatures including elephants, leopards, rams, monkeys, human beings, birds, fish, pangolins, frogs, chameleons, grasshoppers, locusts, beetles, spiders and flies. Such representations occur simultaneously on many objects in different combinations, and in some cases they are even superimposed on one another. It is this practice of deliberate and complex juxtapositioning of creatures which gives rise to my proposition that such associations can be deciphered in terms of metaphorical statements embodying reference to aspects of Nri morality, belief, power relations and history. Of all the forms of animate representation mentioned, however, those of snakes are by far the most varied and pervasive.

While leopards, elephants, rams and snakes are used to symbolise power in a general way in West African societies, where the symbol is combined with other culturally specific symbols, a connotation of specific powers such as those associated with kingly authority can be more convincingly argued for. A case in point within the Igbo-Ukwu corpus is the complex pot already mentioned which was found in pit IV at Igbo Jonah. This vessel has five moulded figures between and below ribbed handles on the lower part of its shoulder (Figure 23.1). These figures manifest a four-fold symbolism which recalled attributes of Onitsha kingly powers to one commentator (Henderson 1972). Thus a representation of a ram's head with curving horns was seen as a possible reference to the king as warrior epitomising *ikenga* the force of personal destiny and the strength of the right hand itself usually represented in the form of carved wooden figures featuring upthrusting horned projections. A humped rectangle decorated with cross-ridged patterning suggested a cloth body-covering, a metaphor for the king's protection of the vulnerabilities of his people. A chameleon in such a context was proposed as a means of indicating the inscrutable nature of kingly wisdom. And fourthly, two poised coiled snakes were interpreted as standing for the self-control and judgement of 'the snake who waits for his prey' (Henderson 1972: 44).

Coiled snakes do in fact occur very often among the Igbo-Ukwu finds, both on metalwork and on pottery. The poised stance with the head and neck emerging from a coil is complemented by embodiments which determine the entire shape of the object concerned, as with the coiled and intertwined snakes forming staff-ornaments, and by simple, flat, and sometimes quite abstract embellishments and motifs. And the coiled snake motif and representations also occur widely within local contemporary contexts, on sculpted mud walls, carved wooden doors and panels, on wooden *ikoro* or war-drums, in wall-paintings and on shrine furniture (cf. Cole and Aniakor 1984). That such representations are moreover widespread in Igboland may be due to the almost universal taboo against killing and eating pythons, and informants will on occasion specifically identify the portrayals as constituting representations of *eke* (the python), as in the case of paintings on a major community shrine in Agukwu itself which I observed early in 1984. The pervasiveness of the specifically coiled form may refer similarly to the widespread Igbo proverb *Okilikili bu ije agwo* ('circular, circular is the snake's path!'), which put more figuratively means that events occur in cycles (Cole and Aniakor 1984: 18). The Igbo-Ukwu snakes by no means always appear as coiled representations, however. A form which often occurs jointly with the coiled variety is the wavy-portrayal of the forward-slithering snake featured most often on pottery pedestals and rims. In contemporary communities this form figures most prominently on doorways.

In contrast to these widespread forms, the occurrence of representations of snakes so closely intertwined that they form a knotted tangle is restricted within the Igbo-Ukwu corpus to just two examples, both of which are so highly structured as to demand more specific interpretation. Once again I believe that this is going to be possible within the terms of reference of the symbolic structures of the Nri ritual system. Beginning with observations of the examples themselves, one is an example of full-figure embodiment in the form of a staff-ornament, while the other is a complex miniature figure within a circular bronze loop fitted for suspension as a pendant. In the first case, the common portrayal of a spiralling body terminating at each end in a single head is complicated by the deliberate presentation of two interlooped bodies (carefully distinguished from one another by the use of contrasting patterns of surface embellishment) each of which terminates in a head either end, I believe deliberately evoking the knotting together of four snakes (Figure 23.3a). In the second case two snake bodies are inter-looped across a flat openwork surface within an outer metal circlet. Each body again terminates in a conventionalised snake head, giving another total of four snakes represented (Figure 23.3b). A further feature which characterises both pieces is the additional depiction of minute animate representations, which although hitherto described in detail (Shaw 1970: 145 and 176) appear to have been regarded as incidental or inexplicable. If we accept the principle that the association of these figures with the figures on which they appear is not only non-random but actually highly structured, then these figures too need to be fitted into a coherent framework of meaning.

We have already described the key ritual offices at Agukwu and Oreri, such as the *eze Nri* themselves, and the chief priest or *Okpala*. In the ethnohistorical record we have the testimonies from the 1930s not only of the relevant incumbents of these offices, but also of candidates for them, parts of which testimonies refer to the omens which contributed to an indication that the individuals concerned were being chosen for office by super-human forces and beings; and I believe that the Igbo-Ukwu items above can be interpreted in reference to these accounts. The *Okpala* of Oreri at that time was one Okaka, whose story included the following account of the incidence of such omens:

> Then I began to receive indications of a divine message from the ancestors and spirits, that I was to take up my sacred post. Firstly, in the dry season and for no apparent reason the high mud walls of my compound fell down, and when rain fell the surface water flooded the enclosure and even entered the house. Soon afterwards, other omens occurred: four snakes all knotted together appeared mysteriously in my compound: a matchet suddenly broke and cut my hand: although apparently healthy my first wife suddenly died.
>
> (Paraphrased from Jeffreys 1940)

The significance of the collapse of the compound walls as integral to the omen is that alone among the compounds of titled men, those of Nri officials are unenclosed. In the case of the staff-ornament example, an association of such a knotted-snake omen with a focal Nri office might be adduced with reference to the six miniature figural embellishments which portray human heads, all of which bear characteristic Nri parallel-groove *ichi* facial scarification marks, and each of which is individualised by the choice of deliberately differently designed headgear. If further confirmation of the association of these objects with the Nri chieftaincy is required it lies in the fact that the staff-ornament also carries representations of beetles, and that the focal point of the pendant is a depiction of a grasshopper/locust. Both locusts and yam-beetles are closely linked with the *eze Nri* (as noted above). This ethnohistorical information thus enables us to situate the two material items we have been focussing on here within certain key cosmographic structures organising and articulating central elements of the Nri cultural system. In this light the pieces are revealed to us as complex and moreover compound metaphorical statements in material form. As such they bind together the concept of the snake as a divine messenger with that of the *eze Nri* as a divine representative.

Other observable patterns of association can be cited which serve to express the kinds of linkages between snakes, gods and the *eze Nri* which have been inferred as operating in the example of the knotted-snake pieces. One such pattern of association is the frequency with which snakes are depicted swallowing frogs and at least holding but possibly also swallowing eggs. Of these, the frog depictions occur on the widest range of objects, from the 'altar stand' and one of the skeuomorphic seashells, through staff-heads to the elaborate knife-scabbards, with a grading from highly stylised to closely naturalistic representation in the same direction. Now, the python (*eke*) is in several areas of Igboland both conceived of and represented as the messenger and living agent of the Earth goddess, *Ala*. One example of deliberate articulation of this role of *eke* with reference to a visible symbol is the focal representation of pythons among the moulded mud sculptures within the large cult shrines or *Mbari* houses of Owerri and adjacent areas. In those areas where the python is so venerated as *Ala*'s agent, when someone dies from an actual or suspected snake-bite it is widely believed to have been *Ala*'s judgement on that person for having stolen something or for having sworn falsely in a dispute. Such a belief may be encapsulated in the saying '*Ala* kills, and eats, always swallowing people.' I have not so far been able to trace a contemporary case of the expression of this metaphor transposed to the material manifestation of the python enacting *Ala*'s practice as her agent, but it seems to me to be entirely plausible that the Igbo-Ukwu representations just mentioned are expressing the metaphor in just such a way as this.

Along with the fact that the python is widely regarded as taboo and often as otherwise sacred throughout Igboland, it has also already been noted that only Nri people are regarded as endowed with the spiritual power to cleanse communities of abominations against the Earth, and *Ala*, goddess of the Earth. People go to great lengths to protect individual pythons from harm because prominent among such abominations is that arising out of the accidental killing of a python. Thus conceptually and ritually there is a close link within and beyond the Nri communities between *Ala*, the python, *eke*, and the *eze Nri* (in his role as focus of the ritual system). One way of viewing the interrelationship would be to see both *eke* and the *eze Nri* as beings 'between worlds' mediating relations between gods and men. (This, for instance, is how recent informants in Benin have expressed the relationship between the *Oba*, both snakes and fish, and *Olokun*, Lord of the Great Waters: see Ben-Amos 1980).

Given the possibility that the *eze Nri* may together with *eke* have occupied such a mediatory position it is perhaps surprising to note that there appears to be no direct

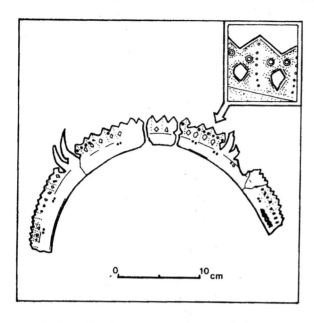

0 _____ 10 cm

Figure 23.4 Copper crown
from Igbo Richard

association of snake representations with the person of the *eze Nri* among the Igbo–
Ukwu materials and sites, especially in view of our assertion of the accuracy with
which we can identify the burial in the wood-lined chamber at Igbo Richard with
a former *eze Nri*. It was the apparent absence of snake depictions upon the objects
buried with the Igbo Richard corpse which led me to a closer scrutiny of these
objects, and in particular, a focus upon the copper crown. Shaw (1970: 156–7)
describes this composite artefact in careful detail in terms of its production from
thin copper sheeting, the close association of the pieces making up the semicircular
band with two roundels and a curved-ended rectangular plate, and the curious
decoration of the band which features a serrated outer circumference and below
this a band of lozenges punched out through the metal. Even closer attention to these
latter decorative features, however, transfers the focus from the outer indentations
and the holes in the metal, to the larger conjoined lozenges of metal which these
indentations and holes define. After an immersion in the multifarious stylisation's
of snake-heads among the Igbo Isaiah representations, it is apparent that each
projection carries simple circular portrayal of two eyes and an axial line of punched
dots representing the line of a snout. Thus the outer line of the mouth is formed
by the serration in each case, and the neck is outlined in respect of the lateral apex
of adjacent lozenges (Figure 23.4).

In total, forty-six snake-heads are depicted on the central band of the crown in
this way, fifteen small ones on each side below double long curving projections (?stylised
feathers), and sixteen larger ones over its apex, between these projections. I think
that the fact that these snakes are thus represented on the crown is of considerable
significance not only because they are thereby as closely as imaginable associated
with the *eze Nri* and focussed exclusively there, but also because the apparent mode
of wearing of the headpiece would have had the effect of making the snakes appear
to directly issue out of the king's head in a manner extremely closely analogous with

the way in which snakes are frequently depicted issuing from the brows and nostrils of kings in court art from Benin, Yorubaland, and the lower Niger area from the fifteenth century onwards (cf. Williams 1974; Eyo 1977; Ben-Amos 1980). The historical implications of this observation are considered in the concluding section of this chapter, but it is surely possible that the expressive meaning of these more recent depictions (cf. Ben-Amos 1983; Gallagher 1983) and that of the Igbo Richard one are also closely analogous, namely as expressions of the power of kings as semi-divine beings to call up and despatch agents of the gods to inflict punishments on transgressors of the divine and kingly order.

Social interaction at Igbo Isaiah: elders, women, youth

Thus the snake, and in particular the python, appears to have been used symbolically to make a number of metaphorical statements concerning beliefs, morals, and authority at early Igbo-Ukwu. Now I want to shift the focus from a specific category of material embodiment, to the practice of 'presencing' groups of people by the inclusion in a focal context of objects which connote actions which themselves characterise these groups. The focal context concerned here is again the deposit at Igbo Isaiah which has been interpreted as a lineage temple, or *obu*.

Inevitably, the group best represented in this context is going to be the section of the community which wields most power, which in Nri society was the collectivity of elders and titleholders. This is more especially so since it was this section which was charged with the responsibility of ancestral veneration by practices conducted within the *obu*, and since this section alone was entitled to use the building habitually for 'policy' meetings for the lineage, and for more casual daily gatherings. I think that the most appropriate starting point for a conceptualisation of the 'presencing power' represented by the Igbo Isaiah objects is to regard them initially simply as a more diverse and complex set of items connoting lineage authority than those to be found in present-day *obu*. Thus staffs are by far the commonest item to have been found on the floor of this early structure, and they account for some of the most profusely decorated items present. In recent times iron staffs have been concentrated in the same way in lineage temples, some curated in honour of deceased title-holders, but the majority being stored for use on ceremonial occasions, along with elephant tusks and bells. Thus although concentrated together and concealed from public view in a storage context, these symbols of lineage authority are diffused outwards through the community (in the grasp of the title-holders themselves) and are openly displayed and clearly visible during events where prestige is overtly expressed.

Much of the powerful effect of such deployment inheres in the community's knowledge that these insignia are ever-present but relatively infrequently openly displayed, in much the same way that the masks used in secret-society spirit embodiment are concealed and only rarely displayed (cf. Ottenberg 1975). Among the other items that fit into this category at Igbo Isaiah are the strings of beads (mostly presumably sewn onto articles of ceremonial dress), simple copper bracelets, the various pendant ornaments, and the miniature bronze plaques interpreted as probably having formed a composite belt.

Many of the other items from this ancient context attest the wealth of this section of society, and serve as indicators of status, but within the scope of our concern with their active symbolic role they are yet more important as means of connoting activities characterising the focal ritual and political position occupied by these elders and titled persons. Thus the individual bells and the groups of crotal 'bells' present embody reference to the travels of such people as Nri agents and traders. The wearing of bells on such journeys was important since the ringing of the bells announced their presence, ensuring their personal safety, and warning ritually impure individuals to avoid them (Onwuejeogwu 1981). In another direction, the presence of bronze drinking vessels, bronze and organic calabashes, and spherical ceramic palm-wine jars denotes the festivities which titled elders are the focus of during title-taking ceremonies and during funeral celebrations termed 'second burial'.

One group of objects which has remained somewhat anomalous within the Igbo Isaiah *obu* assemblage can perhaps also be accounted for in terms of the evocation of activities of the lineage seniors. This is the group of two bronze scabbards and three copper scabbard supports. From the published descriptions it is possible to get the impression that the iron blades associated with these pieces are in fact those of swords, ceremonial or otherwise. I would argue that the miniature nature of these blades (*c.* 30 cm long) precludes such a possibility. In contrast it seems that unless these pieces are themselves merely metaphorical of larger-scale versions, they are likely to be in some way connected with the more specifically ritual activities of the elders and title-holders. One such activity is the performance of sacrifice at shrines both within the *obu* itself, and more publicly in the compound and in the community squares.

The complex evocation of the actions, powers and privileges of titled men in the community thus 'presences' them in the acts both of diffusion and concentration of these material embodiments within the community. The centrality of ritual acts connoted by classes of item which are used in them needs stressing here, since the location of the items within the *obu* provides a counterpoint to the display of some of the objects in 'open' community rituals. Thus 'presencing' occurs even if such items never leave the lineage temple: they provide enduring material markers of the position of their guardians in Nri society and cosmos in a context mediatory between gods, lineage ancestors, and the living community.

In counterpoint to this abundance of material acting to 'presence' senior males in the community, just a few of the Igbo Isaiah objects may have served recursively to evoke the involvement and activities of women. An example is the inclusion of the elaborate pottery vessels, as a class referred to as *mbo'oma* (Onwuejeogwu and Onwuejeogwu 1977). In each *obu* in recent times such vessels have been used as altar-like receptacles for ritual offerings to the ancestors: meat, chalk, kola nuts and chicken feathers. In a domestic context they were traditionally used as eating dishes by titled men. However, not only were they made by women potters and purchased by women in the market, but women also used to decorate the main reception room in their part of each compound by perforating such pots for suspension from the walls. Any such pot could subsequently be given as an offering at a shrine, and it may have been by such a route that the perforated pedestal pot from Igbo Isaiah reached that *obu*.

Various media of exchange were in use among the Nri communities long before the introduction of coinage. The degree of development of this monetary exchange system can be gauged from the observation in the early years of this century that all transactions involved conversions through currency (usually the smaller variety of cowry, or copper bars for more precious commodities) and no direct-exchange bartering was conducted (Basden 1921: 197). When such monetisation of marketing began is obviously difficult to ascertain. However, the presence of knotted copper bars, either with a small central knot and extended ends or of heavier more bunched form with terminals similar to European coastal trade 'manillas' (and in one instance the added presence of thin copper loops reminiscent of the chi of recent historical times) at all three of the Igbo-Ukwu sites may represent the first steps towards the use of currency for some transactions in this part of the world. Transferable wealth of this sort would always have been useful for making dowry payments, and could have been used for purchasing domestic slaves. In either of such cases, the possession of such readily convertible wealth would represent instrumental power of the dominant group over the destiny of subordinates. The placing of these classes of object in the *obu* could equally serve to 'presence' the subordinates within the sphere of the overtly symbolised power of the dominant group.

Such inclusion for the sake of control may also have carried over into the symbolisation of the presence of social groups subordinate by virtue of their youth. Such a perspective may assist us in the identification of further objects within the Igbo Isaiah *obu* corpus which have also escaped specific comment in previous accounts. One example is a mass of very fine coiled copper wire. In the early years of this century such coils were made of brass wire, and were worn encasing the legs of adolescent women during the period in which their puberty initiation rites were held. These *nza* were not only burdensome to their wearers, but required constant polishing in order not to become immediately tarnished (Basden 1921: 92). A second example are chains made up from coiled loops of copper, or from cast bronze loops embellished with representations of flies. Such chains were worn by the unmarried male youth or *okwolobia* when engaging in displays of acrobatics in the marketplaces, designed to show their prowess and feats of endurance. The chains themselves were produced as apprentices' trialpieces by the early twentieth century:

> An apprentice [blacksmith at Awka] . . . usually begins to practise by making small chains. For this, odd bits of brass can be used up; they are beaten out into fine wire and then fashioned into links. These chains are much in demand among the young bloods of some towns; they are bound tightly upon the leg, which must be harmful, and is certainly not ornamental.
>
> (Basden 1921: 172–3)

Such usage might explain why the links of the less elaborate of the two Igbo Isaiah chains 'show considerable evidence of wear' (Shaw 1970: 154). Finally, one other group of finds should be mentioned which denotes another aspect of the relationship between the elders and the youth, and that is a group of iron knives with curving or triangular blades found in a tight pile on the extreme northern edge of the deposit. The form of the triangular-bladed examples immediately facilitates their identification as scarification knives as recorded widely in the early years of this century (e.g. Basden 1921: 112). Such knives were kept by Nri men for use by Umodioka scarification specialists in making distinctive *ichi* markings on the faces of their children as they reached adulthood, the symbolic significance of which is brought out more fully in the following section.

Historical metaphor: children of Nri

Other kinds of metaphorical relationship are embodied in the Igbo-Ukwu artefact forms and representations, and in the third study of association and symbolism here I want to focus on what I would term 'historical metaphor'. In this example, the metaphorical relationship is between a people and their beliefs about their history. In the Igbo-Ukwu corpus, I believe that this relationship is embodied in portrayals of people, and in particular in their depiction as possessing *ichi* facial scarification. This form of scarification is either restricted to the forehead or is full-face, and is characterised by a pattern of closely set parallel grooves incised out of the facial skin. In some cases rings or semicircles are additionally incised above the upper boundary of the grooving. In the 1930s, two regional variants of the practice were

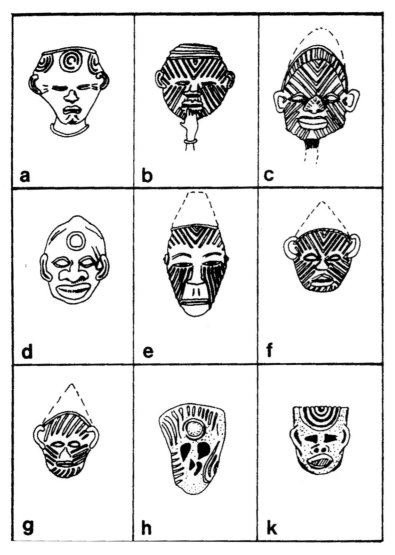

Figure 23.5 Examples of *ichi* face markings

413

defined, and termed the Nri and the Agbaja styles (Jeffreys 1951), the former distinguished by the addition of the circle and semicircle motifs, apparently to represent the sun (*anyanwu*) and the moon (*onwu*). *Ichi* are today only found on men and women over fifty. These people stress how painful the cutting operation was, but point out also the compensating prestige and immunity. The practice was mostly limited to elder sons and daughters, perhaps due to the great costs of the ceremony, but also perhaps because of its symbolic connotation in reference to the Nri origin legend.

According to this legend, the first people, Eri and his wife Namaku lived on *azu igwe* ('back of the sky': sky-substance), but when Eri died this food supply ceased and Nri (Eri's son) complained to the great spirit, Chukwu, that there was nothing to eat. Chukwu told Nri that he would send from the sky to earth one Dioka who would carve *ichi* marks on the faces of Nri's eldest son and daughter. Nri was then to cut their throats and bury them in separate graves. Nri reluctantly did so, and when shoots appeared he dug up yams from his son's grave and cocoyam from his daughter's grave (thus establishing the farming practice whereby men cultivate yam and women cocoyam). Accordingly, although a man taking up the post of *eze Nri* no longer has to kill his first-born son and daughter, both are still marked with *ichi* in remembrance of the time when the first *eze Nri* thereby brought food among men (Jeffreys 1956: 122–3). The practice is optional for other household heads, but the marking of first-born son and daughter by each king was obviously widely emulated.

That the marking is habitually associated with this origin story is shown by the words of a song sung by the *umu okpu* (a group of women known as 'the daughters of the lineage') when a young person is recovering from the risky operation: 'Nwa ichi nyem agwuabgunem, Ichi Eze nwa di Okpala', which means '*Ichi* child give me food that I may not die of hunger, the *Ichi* that belong to the first child of Eze [Nri]' (Onwuejeogwu 1981: 81). Furthermore, although there was some confusion about the exact meaning of each set of the marks among informants in Miss Yeatman's interviews in the 1930s, at least one of them said that the parallel grooves were called *ogba ubi* (farming furrows), hence making a direct connection between their form and their legendary origin (Jeffreys 1951: 100).

Thus the depiction of *ichi* on twelve out of the fourteen representations of human heads among the Igbo-Ukwu assemblages not only underlines the importance attached to the identification of these people as belonging to the Nri lineages, but may also make reference back to their mythical origins. Significantly, one of the most prominent of these instances comes from one of the two most securely dated contexts, the burial chamber at Igbo Richard, likely to have been constructed no later than the eleventh century AD. The portrayal is on the face of the miniature horserider surmounting the bronze hilt closely accompanying the burial. Three other instances take the form of bronze human head pendant ornaments from the Igbo Isaiah *obu*, while yet another is in a different medium, a pottery antefix from an infilled early water cistern at Igbo Richard (see Figure 23.5).

Perhaps a key occurrence is that already noted upon the six tiny heads which adorn the staff ornament depicting four knotted snakes, since a putative association of this piece with the office of *okpala* could be correlated with the literal meaning of the word 'okpala' as 'first son'. If the general line of connectivity can be upheld at all, however, the most explicit reference back to the origin myth may be considered to come from the two figures depicted on the 'altar stand'. On one side of this is a figure of a female with *ichi* marks which appear to include a formalised representation of the sun and moon marks. She is also shown wearing ankle cords which denote titled status (as indeed is the horse rider). On the opposite side of the stand is the figure of a male, again with ankle cords. He has a contrasting kind of facial marking, and body markings as well. Given the preponderance on carvings, wall-paintings and architectural mud sculpture of representations of the sun in the form of a circle, what I would suggest is being represented here is another form of the sun/moon markings. Since both *anyanwu* (the sun) and *igwe* (the sky) are widely associated with Chukwu in northern Igbo life and thought (cf. Henderson 1972: 114) I think that the whole piece can be regarded as a characterisation of one of the key elements of the Nri origin story, the two figures representing Nri's first-born son and daughter. Other elements of the decoration can be seen as potentially underlining such a link, the lozenges filled with parallel-groove decoration perhaps serving as an enlargement on the theme of the farming furrows, and the snakes eating frogs as we have seen drawing into focus both *Ala* and the *eze Nri*.

Meanwhile, another dual figure appears among the Igbo-Ukwu finds, this time on a miniature ornament formerly fixed to a larger artefact, again from the Igbo Isaiah *obu*. Although worn, there are again here traces of a circular scarification on the forehead this time of both faces in parallel. The pottery antefix already referred to is particularly interesting for its apparent combination of such a circle with the *ichi* marks in a distinctive way, and some support for the idea that such representations were common in ceramic or terracotta media comes from a recent find of the head of a baked clay figurine from the site of a shrine in a village group closely bordering on Igbo-Ukwu.

Conclusion

The theoretical starting point for this study was essentially that the obvious symbolic references of the Igbo-Ukwu artefacts were not only highly structured, they were also clearly amenable to meaningful interpretation. It has been the purpose of the foregoing sections to illustrate how this task of iconographical and associative interpretation has been initiated, and to outline its preliminary results. It remains now in conclusion to address the question of how recognition of the communicative uses of material culture at early Igbo Ukwu adds to our knowledge of the overall historical context of the corpus.

Firstly, I believe that the change in emphasis from previous concern with the significance of metal compositions and with the identification of objects which might indicate trade contacts, to a concentration instead on the context of symbolism and interaction enables us to appreciate more fully the determinative historical contribution of local actions for the form and disposition of the objects and traces concerned. This serves to emphasise that although in respect of sources of raw materials and of a limited number of stylistic motifs external contacts are important, social and historical reconstructions must account for the materials first and foremost in terms of local production and interaction.

Secondly, this study lends greater substance than hitherto established to the link between these eleventh-century materials and the institution of Nri sacred kingship, by demonstrating not only how overt leadership symbols but also how pervasive ritual symbols serve to project aspects of the pivotal role of the priest-king within Nri Igbo life and thought. Making this link with renewed emphasis on the ritual and cognitive bases of power in turn enables fresh light to be cast on the development of kingship in Nigeria in the late first and early second millennia AD. The Nri use of particular forms of snake symbolism such as on the burial chamber crown anticipates similar usages west of the Niger, and the implication that I would draw from this is that the Nri system must therefore have exerted at least some direct influence over the form that developing kingship systems took elsewhere.

Thirdly, the attention paid to human representations, and to *ichi* facial markings in particular, has emphasised the importance which the artists and presumably therefore commissioning title-holders also placed upon the expression of Nri identity, and upon the common links between the Nri communities articulated in their origin legend. Thus such specific material statements could have been part of an historical process of conscious creation of a separate identity for Nri people among other surrounding Igbo peoples. The overall aim would, I think, have been to secure for themselves access to a privileged ritual, political and economic position not only in respect of these immediate communities, but also in a wider regional setting. Part of this process seems also to have involved the inclusion in the origin story already recounted of allusions to an external origin for the Nri from north of the Igbo area, and the idea of a common ancestry before this with the Igala, a people now living further north up the river Niger. Such a device, a legend embodying reference to an external origin, is almost universal among West African societies with kingship systems as a means of legitimising the power exercised by dominant groups within those societies.

Finally, perhaps the most important new interpretative orientation that this study promotes for the determination of historical contexts for the Igbo-Ukwu materials is itself a focus upon the concept of power. Having established that most of the objects at Igbo Isaiah can be interpreted among other things as means of expressing the dominance of elders, we are left with the question of the motivation behind the considerable investment of skill and materials in the production of that assemblage. The key factor here might have been the manifestation of control not only over subordinates, and over the deployment of material resources (Giddens' allocative and authoritative resources), but also over the material expression of how the world is. In this light I would view the pervasive practice of metaphorical representation not simply as an example of the delight artists and craftsmen take in demonstrating an ability to adapt a theme to any medium, but over and above this the ability of powerful personages to control the manner of statement of basic moral attitudes and cultural traditions in this way. Additionally I believe that skeuomorphic representations may also have been demonstrating the power of the collective owners of the items concerned to transform the potential meaning and actual appearance of both everyday and prestige objects at will.

At the same time, the production of the symbols pertaining to power and ritual leadership in more durable form than in their original composition (as in the production of calabashes as bronze artefacts) also serves to make the power these objects connote more enduring. Recognition that such production may have been part of a deliberate power-seeking strategy leads us directly to conceptualise these contexts and their materials as a distant instantiation of an historical process. Thus it seems plausible that the process concerned was the formalisation of the social and political control exerted by the titled men who surrounded the office and person of the priest-king, and that this instantiation was the crucial point in time at which wealth was used to create relatively permanent and durable expressions of this power.

NOTE

1. Fred Anozie, Acting Head of the Department of Archaeology at the University of Nigeria, Nsukka, gave me vital encouragement in the work upon which this paper is based while I was on his teaching staff from 1982 to 1984. Ekpo Eyo and Bassey Duke of the Nigerian Federal Commission for Museums and Monuments helpfully gave me permission to study the Igbo-Ukwu items in their care. Both Ian Hodder and Thurstan Shaw kindly read and commented upon an earlier draft of the paper. A first version was presented at a seminar at the University of Glasgow in 1985, for which opportunity I wish to thank John Barrett. Finally, I owe the largest debt of thanks to Rosalind Shaw of the University of Aberdeen whose constructive criticism has sustained the project as a whole since its inception in 1983.

24

INTERPRETING MATERIAL CULTURE*

CHRISTOPHER TILLEY

If one wishes to talk about paradigms in archaeology, where the term 'paradigm shift' means a fundamental change in the way in which archaeologists actually see the world of material culture, the decisive break occurs not in 1962 with the substitution of one form of empiricism for another (Binford 1962), but in 1982 with the appearance of *Symbolic and Structural Archaeology* ([Hodder] 1982a). This break involves, primarily, the conception of material culture as a signifying system in which the external physical attributes of artefacts and their relationships are not regarded as exhausting their meaning. This chapter briefly looks back at some of the assumptions involved in the 'structuralist' encounter in archaeology, then charts a course leading from structuralism to the post-structuralism of Derrida, Barthes and Foucault.[1] The change now occurring in archaeology is a move away from attempts to establish what basically amounted to the search for a methodology for assigning meaning to artefact patterning to a more fully self-reflexive position involving consideration of what is involved in the act of *writing the past*.

Saussure and the diacritical sign

Saussure, the father of contemporary linguistics, drew a fundamental distinction between *langue* and *parole*. *Langue* constitutes the system of codes, rules and norms structuring any particular language, whereas *parole* refers to the situated act of utilization of this system by an individual speaker (Saussure 1966). The object of linguistics was, according to Saussure, the synchronic analysis of *langue* as opposed to the diachronic analysis of specific changes in elements of languages through time. The essential building-block of *langue* on which linguistic analysis was to work was the diacritical linguistic sign consisting of a union of two facets or components, the 'signifier' and the 'signified'. The signifier is an audible utterance or a sound 'image' referring to a particular concept, the signified:

SIGN: signifier   :   signified
               (acoustic image) :   (concept)

---

* First published in I. Hodder (ed.) (1989), *The Meanings of Things*, London: Unwin Hyman, pp. 185–94.

A number of points may be noted about this conception of the linguistic sign. It exists in no direct relationship with reality, because the relationship between the signifier and the signified is entirely arbitrary, a matter of convention. The arbitrariness involved here is directly analogous to that existing between words and things. In English we use the utterance 'dog' to refer to a class of creatures with four legs, whereas in other languages an equally arbitrary sound image (e.g. *chien*, *Hund*) may be used. The sign only gains meaning diacritically because the meaning is derived from the system in which it is constituted as different from other signs. In other words, 'dog' is only meaningful because it is *not* cat, rope or axe, and vice versa. Meaning therefore resides in a system of *relationships between signs* and not in the signs themselves. A sign considered in isolation would be meaningless. Furthermore, the meaning of a sign is not pre-determined, but is a matter of cultural and historical convention. Consequently, it does not matter how a signifier appears, so long as it preserves its difference from other signifiers.

Saussure was not interested in actual speech or the social utilization of signs in encounters between individuals or groups, or both, but with the objective structures making such parole possible. This position had a number of consequences:

(a) the study of linguistics moves from concrete manifestations of speech to unconscious rules and grammars;
(b) an emphasis on relations between signs rather than the signs themselves;
(c) a conception of signs forming part of an overarching system; and
(d) an aim of determining principles underlying different linguistic systems.

From language to culture

Saussure regarded the study of linguistic systems as eventually forming part of a general science of signs – semiology. Language might then be regarded as one sign system among many which would have relative degrees of autonomy from each other. By the 1960s semiology or semiotics had, indeed, developed as a major intellectual field. It is difficult, and perhaps undesirable, to draw any clear distinction between structuralism and semiology, other than to say that the former constitutes a general method of enquiry, whereas the latter forms a field of study of particular sign systems, e.g. advertising, fashion and facial gestures. What both have in common is to use, modify or build on aspects of the linguistic theory outlined above in order to study areas of human culture other than language.

Language becomes the paradigm for understanding all other aspects of social life. If language is an exchange of messages constituted in their difference, governed by an underlying system of codes and grammatical rules, then the move made by Lévi-Strauss is quite understandable. Marriage practices are analysed in terms of systems of underlying rules, such systems being variant realizations of a limited number of structured oppositions defined in their relational difference. Totemism is explained as a way of structuring the relationship between social groups (Lévi-Strauss 1969). If clan A traces descent from the iguana and clan B from the kangaroo, then this is merely a way of stating that the relation of clan A to clan B is analogous to that between the two species. So iguana and kangaroo are logical operators, concrete signs. Hence, one can deduce the canonical formula, archetypal of any structural analysis:

$$\text{iguana} : \text{kangaroo} \quad :: \quad \text{clan A}: \text{clan B}$$

To understand the meaning of 'iguana' and 'kangaroo' they must be situated within an overall structured system of signs. Lévi-Strauss' most ambitious project is the study of myth (1970, 1973), in which he aims to show that the seeming arbitrariness of myths is in fact only tenable in terms of a superficial surface reading of the narratives. Instead myths can be understood in terms of fundamental principles or laws operating at a deeper level. The consequence is that if the human mind can be shown to be determined even in its creation of myths, then *a fortiori* it will also be determined in other spheres. He isolates a number of fundamental oppositions such as male–female, culture–nature, day–night, raw–cooked, and others of a less obvious nature. In doing so Lévi-Strauss is analysing codes and the manner in which categories drawn from one area of experience can be related to those in other areas and used as logical tools for expressing relations. He does not ask so much what the codes are that account for the meaning that myths have in a particular culture, since he is interested in constructing a transcultural logic of myth. This means that myths are always, and primarily, signs of the logic of myth itself. Myths can be broken down into 'mythemes' which, like phonemes (the basic sound units of language), acquire meaning only when combined in particular ways. The rules governing the combinations constitute the true meaning of myth residing beneath the surface narrative, and ultimately to be related to universal mental operations. People do not so much make up myths, but rather myths think themselves through people.

Material culture and structure

Barthes, in *Mythologies* (1973), is not concerned with general structures, but with particular cultural practices. All such practices are endowed with signification, and this is a fundamental feature running throughout the entire gamut of social life from a wrestling match to eating steak and chips to hairstyles – the list is endless. There is no 'innocent' or transparent fact or event. All facts and events 'speak' to their culturally conditioned observers and participants. Culture is a kind of speech embodying messages coded in various forms and requiring decoding. Furthermore, the meaning of signification may be analogous for those who 'produce' and those who 'consume' the signs. At other times signs act asymmetrically, becoming ideological, linked to the maintenance of power. Given the intellectual force and power of the general perspectives outlined above, it seems, in retrospect, almost inevitable that archaeologists would come to reframe an understanding of their basic data – material culture – as constituting a meaningful significative system, the analysis of which should go far beyond a reductionist conception of it as merely constituting an extrasomatic means of adaptation, or as vaguely functioning in utilitarian or social terms. Such frameworks have no way of coping with variability or specific form. All that a functional argument can ever be expected to do is to rule on conditions of existence or non-existence. For example, ritual may exist because it performs the function of asserting social solidarity – but why any particular ritual? Such a question remains unanswered. Similarly, a consideration of economic practices must go far beyond simplistic accounts of how food resources might be obtained efficiently or inefficiently. The economy has a style, is part of a cultural and symbolic scheme. Of course, people eat to survive, but eating is a cultural practice. It involves a way of thinking and provides a medium for thought. This symbolic dimension is part of that which is to be explained. It might be said that the primary significance of material culture is not its pragmatic use-value, but its significative exchange value.

In archaeology the particular use of a structuralist or semiological perspective has not been concerned to analyse material culture in terms of the transcultural perspective of Lévi-Strauss. Rather, there has been a concern with historical and social specificity and context: particular rather than universal structures. Much of this work has been indelibly linked with Marxism, involving consideration, in particular, of ideology and power and dynamic processes of structuration or structural change. Here it is not the intention either to review or to analyse the strengths or shortcomings of this work, but rather to focus in a more abstract manner on archaeology as being a pursuit of sign systems.

If archaeology is anything, it is the study of material culture as a manifestation of structured symbolic practices meaningfully constituted and situated in relation to the social. This relationship is active, and not one of simple reflection. Material culture does not provide a mirror to society or a window through which we can see it. Rather, there are multiple transformations and relationships between different aspects of material culture and between material culture and society of, for example, parallelism, opposition, inversion, linearity and equivalence. In order to understand material culture we have to think in terms that go entirely beyond it, to go beneath the surface appearances to an underlying reality. This means that we are thinking in terms of relationships between things, rather than simply in terms of the things themselves. The meaning of the archaeological record is always irreducible to the elements which go to make up and compose that record, conceived as a system of points or units. Such a study involves a search for the structures, and the principles composing those structures, underlying the visible and the tangible. The principles governing the form, nature and content of material culture patterning are to be found at both the level of microrelations (e.g. a set of designs on a pot) and macrorelations (e.g. relations between settlement space and burial space). Such relations may be held to be irreducibly linked, each forming a part of the other. So each individual act of material culture production and use has to be regarded as a contextualized social act involving the relocation of signs along axes defining the relationship between signs and other signs which reach out beyond themselves and towards others becoming amplified or subdued in specific contexts.

Such an analysis is undeniably difficult, but it does at least have the merit of trying to capture the sheer complexity of what we are trying to understand. Several points require emphasis:

(a) Material culture is a framing and communicative medium involved in social practice. It can be used for transforming, storing or preserving social information. It also forms a symbolic medium for social practice, acting dialectically in relation to that practice. It can be regarded as a kind of text, a silent form of writing and discourse; quite literally, a channel of reified and objectified expression.

(b) Although material culture may be produced by individuals, it is always a social production. This is because it does not seem to be at all fruitful to pursue a view of the human subject as endowed with unique capacities and attributes, as the source of social relations, font of meaning, knowledge and action. As Foucault (1974) pointed out, this 'liberal' humanist view of humanity is largely an 18th century creation. In regarding material culture as socially produced, an emphasis is being placed on the constructedness of human meaning as a product of shared systems of signification. The individual does not so much construct material culture or language, but is rather constructed through them.

Structure and archaeological analysis

An underlying assumption of much structuralist work in archaeology has been that such studies either have discovered the real structures generating the observed variability in the archaeological record, or at the very least, are working painfully towards this end. The questions become: what are the signs at work? How can we recognize them? How do they differ? How did they operate in a past life-world? This involves a search for recurrent associated elements in relation to their contextual patterning. The meaning of the past is something that the archaeologist does not have but wants to work towards by means of an analysis going 'beneath' the materials to reveal the underlying principles at work, principles which may be held to be not only structuring the observed archaeological materials, but also implicated in the overall structuration of the social order.

The problem has always been the precise assignation of meaning. For example, a formal analysis of pottery decoration (e.g. Hodder 1982a; Tilley 1984) is not concerned with the actual perceived designs, whether a triangle or a zig-zag line, but with the differences between these designs, which may then be recoded in various ways – for example, in terms of horizontal and vertical distinctions, or alphabetically. How far does such an analysis take us? The structure so arrived at remains a simulacrum (almost Platonic!) of the design sequence, something previously invisible. A paradox is involved here. On the one hand, analysis becomes a form of repetition. We are not told anything about the pot design which is not already there in it. On the other hand, the implication of the analysis is that something new has indeed been produced. The archaeologist has discovered the inner essence residing in the object, in this case the pot design, but what is the meaning of this 'recovery'?

Several strategies may be utilized. Meaning may be established by linking the pot design structure to other structures in the overall material culture patterning, e.g. refuse disposal and burial practices, such that these different structural aspects of the material culture can be regarded as being transformations of each other. The same basic structure may then be held to 'generate' how people are buried, how they design their pots, organize their disposal of refuse and the use of space in settlements. Ultimately, general overarching structuring principles (principles which structure structures) may be recognized. In the case of Hodder's (1982b) study of the Nuba these are:

pure–impure: cattle–pig: male–female: clean–dirty: life–death

So pure is to impure as cattle is to pig, and so on – all very neat.

Another way of assigning meaning, this time in a 'purely' archaeological study, involves a more abstract double-edged conceptual strategy. First, again, different types of material culture are analysed in terms of structural oppositions (usually entirely abstract), e.g. left-right and bounded–unbounded, in different contexts such as settlement and burial. So pot designs may be analysed in terms of boundedness and the treatment of human body parts (Tilley 1984). Secondly, a conceptual link is then drawn between boundedness in body parts and boundedness in pot designs and, through time, the archaeological record can be examined to see whether such an 'expression' of boundedness intensifies or decreases. The abstracted reconceptualized 'data' may then have its assigned meaning further mobilized by the introduction of social concepts such as contradiction, power and ideology.

In both these and other studies, a notion of 'context' and 'wholeness' is invoked, into which the material culture fitted as meaningful code. This whole may, or may not, be conceived as a fissured or contradictory totality. The archaeologist stands outside this whole, his or her gaze directed towards its internal structuring. A commentary is then produced, bringing order to the superficial chaos of the external appearances and forms of the artefacts. What is happening is the enclosure of the enigmatic (interpreted) object within the interpretative theory's pre-existent system, which then further comments on it.

The metacritical sign and polysemy

More comments on these commentaries are now required. First, is the notion of the diacritical sign one which can be sustained? If the meaning of a sign is just a matter of difference from other signs, then this conception can be pressed further until it breaches Saussure's notion of language forming a closed and stable synchronic system. This is because if a sign is what it is by virtue of its differences from all other signs, then each sign must be made up of a vast and never-ending network of differences from other signs. The outcome of such a line of reasoning is that there can be no clear symmetrical unity between one signifier and one signified. Meaning is then to be related to a potentially endless play of signifiers, and signifiers keep on changing into signifieds, and vice versa. So, the signifier and the signified become conceptually split (Derrida 1976, 1978). We arrive at what might be termed the metacritical sign. The meaning of the metacritical sign is never transparently present in it, but is a matter of what the sign is not. So meaning is both present and absent – to state this more simply, meaning is dispersed along chains of signifiers. Another piece of willed and deliberate obfuscation? Perhaps, but no more so than to mention a minimax satisficer strategy, ringing a dulcet tone of clarity in the attuned economistic archaeological ear. The corollary to the position just taken is quite simple – the meaning of material culture can never be objectified or exactly pinned down. Its meaning always, to some extent, evades the analyst.

Considering the concept of polysemy may clarify this further. An object, any object, has no ultimate or unitary meaning that can be held to exhaust it. Rather, any object has multiple and sometimes contradictory meanings. The meanings depend on a whole host of factors. One appropriate example is the safety-pin in contemporary

Britain (Hodder 1985: 14) which, according to who wears it – an infant, a grand-mother or a 'punk', changes its meaning. However, this is only part of the story. The meaning also changes according to the context in which the interpretation takes place (a kitchen or an underground station), who is carrying out the interpretation (to various people the safety pin may mean aggression, pity, children or bondage); and why they are bothering to interpret it in the first place. This last point is an appropriate cue to draw the archaeologist into the text.

From reading the past to writing the past

The previous section left the intrepid archaeologist grappling with the notion of meaning not being so much present in the artefact but absent, and being faced with a situation in which the notion of any unitary meaning residing in the past to which our analyses might strive to reach – whether by producing a structural simulacrum or by any other means – as a dangerous chimera. Meaning therefore becomes indeterminate and problematic. What is to be done, if anything? On one point we can at least be certain, the archaeological pursuit of signs is no easy business.

One possible escape route might be to renounce linguistic imperialism and develop a theory of the meaning of material culture not based on linguistic analogies. We might strongly assert that what material culture communicates is totally different from language. For example, it would require a vast number of material objects to 'say', in a material form, even the simplest sentence. If someone makes a statement and you do not understand what they mean, there is the possibility that a Socratic dialogue may bring illumination. Such dialogue is not possible with a pot! On the other hand, a stress can be made on the fact that material culture acts in multidimensional channels as a non-verbal mode of communication. In this respect its meanings could be held to be more complicated than those conveyed in speech. We could say that material culture is a material language with its own meaning product tied to production and consumption. Endless permutations of such arguments could be produced, but none of them can escape language. Thinking about material culture inevitably involves its transformation into linguistic concepts. However much we might try to escape from language, we are trapped in its prison house. So, although it might appear a laudable aim to escape a linguistic frame, this is an impossibility. There can be no meaningfully constituted non-linguistic semiological system.

The detour of attempting to embrace a radically non-linguistic analogy for the interpretation of material culture has apparently failed, leading us back once more to the archaeologist. Undecidability then, ambivalence: a free play of meaning? The 'structuralist', 'contextualist' or 'dialectical-structuralist' encounter as it has appeared in archaeology seems to be too important to be abandoned. In favour of what? The fact that such an enterprise leads inexorably towards its own critique and extension may be a sign of its vitality. A notion of metacritical and polysemous signs leads us to the margins of such an approach and our better understanding of it as an active interpretative exercise creating a past in a present which must renounce either finality or the notion that in the future we will be producing better, truer or more precise accommodations to the truth of the past – whatever that might be.

The interpretation of the meaning and significance of material culture is a contemporary activity. The meaning of the past does not reside in the past, but belongs in the present. Similarly, the primary event of archaeology is the event of excavation or writing, not the event of the past. Consequently, the archaeologist is not so much reading the signs of the past as writing these signs into the present: constructing discourses which should be both meaningful to the present and playing an active role in shaping the present's future. Here an irony crops up. Archaeologists write, but many do not feel they should be writing! At best such textual production may be regarded as a transparent resource, a mere medium for expression. However, writing always transforms. The process of writing the past in the present needs to become part of that which is to be understood in archaeology. The ultimate aim of much contemporary archaeological discourse is to put an end to writing, to get the story right. Empiricism inexorably encourages such a futile goal. To the contrary, there will be no correct stories of the past that are not themselves a product of a politics of truth. There can only be better or worse re-presentations of history: his [*sic*] story.

What is important is the development of a truly self-reflexive archaeological discourse, aware of itself as discourse and systematically refusing the usual imperative of producing yet another methodology for grasping the past's meaning. Archaeological discourses are, by and large, framed in specific institutional settings and transmitted and disseminated through definite forms of media in which archaeological knowledge is located. Such discourses have their bases in forms of pedagogy imposing 'a will to truth'. As yet there is no true alternative discourse in archaeology. A crucial act in creating one will be the disruption of the discursive authority of the texts we have to hand at present. This will involve an awareness of the politics of discourse and the power structures in which it is embedded. This requires consideration of what kind of past we want in the present and why we produce the past in one manner rather than another.[2]

The general position being taken in this chapter suggests that material culture can be regarded as providing a multidimensional 'text' from which the archaeologist can construct his or her texts: not, therefore, an entirely free process. The text that the archaeologist writes will consist, in part, of a tissue of 'quotations' drawn from the material record and meaningfully activated in fresh constellations in relation to a particular argumentative frame of reference. The assignation of the meaning of the quotations drawn from the archaeological record requires a self-reflexive problematic.

We might set up a chain of signifiers to help us to understand the process of writing the past. First we might put interest. We are interested in interpreting some aspect of the archaeological record, making it meaningful for ourselves and others. However, this interest is at the outset dependent on our values (why we are carrying out this activity in the first place). These values are, in turn, dependent on our politics and our morality, which relate more generally to the sociopolitical context in which we find ourselves situated and positioned as agents. The chain we actually end up with is: positioned subject – politics, morality – values – interests – meanings – text.

The meaning of the past has to be inserted into the present through the medium of the text. So there is no meaning outside the text (conceived broadly to include film, etc.). This meaning has to be argued for and against. The act of writing always presupposes a politics of the present, and such writing is a form of power. It cannot escape power. Any kind of writing about the past is inevitably simultaneously a domestication of the difference of the past, an imposition of order. Writing the past is not an innocent and disinterested reading of an autonomous past produced as image. Writing the past is drawing it into the present, re-inscribing it into the face of the present.

This text is a pastiche or montage, a material production built on other texts, an extended footnote which, if anything interesting has been said, may become incorporated into another text. A formal conclusion is out of keeping with the spirit in which it is written. It will suffice to mention that in ending this contribution I wonder whether I should be saying what I have said. I would like to be looking over your shoulder and saying 'No, no – I didn't exactly mean it to be interpreted like *that!*'

NOTES

1 These authors are names for problems rather than formalized doctrines, and this is precisely their interest. Both Foucault and Barthes, in their early work, have been labelled structuralists. Both have renounced the structuralist enterprise. Post-structuralism is characteristically a term not amenable to any rigid definition. It is simply a term applied to work without any unitary core that is temporally removed from a structuralist position. Those interested might look at Barthes (1974, 1977b), Foucault (1972, 1984), Derrida (1976, 1981) and Sturrock (1979).

2 Aspects of post-structuralism, discourse, textuality, power, ideology and politics in relation to archaeology are discussed in detail in *Re-constructing Archaeology* and *Social Theory and Archaeology* (Shanks and Tilley 1987a, b).

PART VI

ARCHAEOLOGY, CRITIQUE AND THE CONSTRUCTION OF IDENTITY

INTRODUCTION

It has often been argued that once we admit that epistemology alone cannot provide us with a secure knowledge of the past, we must begin to see our interpretations as political (Shanks and Tilley 1987a, 65). The statements that we make about the past are not generated exclusively by the application of a methodology to a body of data, producing an unequivocal result. The reasons why we study particular phenomena in particular ways require consideration, and this is the objective of critical theory. Critical theory in its present form originated with the Frankfurt School, a group of western Marxists who were active in the middle years of the twentieth century (Jay 1973). The Frankfurt School were anxious to understand why capitalism continued to survive in the West, despite the conspicuous exploitation of working people. They came to focus on the role of ideology, which served to make people's own interests obscure to them. A critical archaeology might draw on the work of Horkheimer, Adorno, Benjamin and the other members of the Frankfurt School, but it might equally make use of ideas from feminism, post-structuralism or hermeneutics. Its principal task would be to evaluate the unacknowledged prejudices and motivations which underlie our accounts of the past. As Leone, Potter and Shackel argue here, one of the most important tasks for critical theory in archaeology is to demonstrate that certain taken-for-granted aspects of our everyday lives are transient, and have a history. In their study of historic Annapolis the timelessness of individuality, personal freedom and other aspects of the American way of life are called into question.

If we begin to undermine the universality of our own way of life, the past springs into relief as different and alien. We start to recognise people in the past as unlike ourselves, following rationalities and motivations that we can barely grasp. Archaeology becomes more like anthropology, in its attempt to comprehend a cultural order which lies outside of our own. This focus on difference is fundamental to a critical archaeology, for it de-legitimises the present. It denies us the arrogance of imagining that our own lives are the norm against which others can be judged. As J. D. Hill argues in his paper, many aspects of the prehistoric past are considered to be unproblematic simply because they are presumed to be unchanging and universal. In contesting these arguments, critical archaeology at once puts the present in question and makes the past more interesting.

One of the areas in which this kind of critical approach has been most effective has been in the investigation of past identities. In the earlier part of this century, culture historic archaeology operated on the basis that tribes and peoples had existed in prehistory, and that they should be directly reflected in the archaeological record. The stylistic variation of material culture was considered to be generated by norms of behaviour which were internalised by members of particular communities. Being born into a certain tribe, one would learn to make and decorate pots in a specific way. The New Archaeology was deeply critical of this 'normative' understanding of culture, preferring instead to see culture as a means of adaptation to environmental change. But it did little to address the relationship between material things and human identity, beyond suggesting that stylistic variation in artefacts might itself have an adaptive function in conveying survival information between people. Siân Jones argues in her paper that much of the legacy of culture history remains intact, in that we still assume that artefacts should form bounded distributions which correlate with the lifespace of discrete prehistoric communities. This conception of a people with a territory and a fixed cultural identity is perhaps anachronistic when applied to the deep past, since it approximates closely to the nation-state, the characteristic political entity of the modern era. As Jones suggests, it is more helpful to consider that human identities are constructed, through the use of material culture amongst other things.

Archaeology itself constructs identities, in the present. When we talk of 'tribes' and 'peoples' who existed in the past, we are creating entities which can potentially have a mythic or political significance, as in the case of the Aryans. This draws our attention to the writing of archaeology, and the influence which authoritative texts can exert. Anthony Sinclair's detailed analysis of the life histories of archaeological writings demonstrates the way in which books and papers can become parts of the disciplinary 'archive', a body of recognised knowledge which subsequent work must build upon or dispute. Sinclair points out that one of the side-effects of the use of the metaphor of the text as a means of discussing the signifying potential of material culture has been that we have come to take the practices of reading and writing more seriously. Texts do not simply convey information from person to person in a transparent way: they have material effects. One consequence of a critical approach to our writing of the past is a greater feeling of responsibility for the statements that we make. We might say that processual archaeology is at times *irresponsible*, in that it claims that our knowledge is an objective product of observation and testing. While many of those who could be described as 'post-processualists' would accept that we bear the responsibility for our own arguments, Sinclair suggests that it is often unclear to whom this responsibility is owed. His answer is that we are answerable to the present, to contemporary society, since past people are dead and gone. But it is also arguable that we have a responsibility to the dead. The ways in which we describe them, represent them and package them surely betray at attitude toward human beings in general. If we are willing to reduce past generations to figures in equations and dots on maps, we are that much more willing to see the living dehumanised as well.

25

CAN WE RECOGNISE A DIFFERENT EUROPEAN PAST?*

A Contrastive Archaeology of Later Prehistoric Settlements in Southern England

J. D. HILL

Introduction

> We have, with no little success, sought to keep the world off balance; pulling out rugs, upsetting tea tables, setting off firecrackers. It has been the office of others to reassure; ours to unsettle. Australopithicines, Tricksters, Clicks, Megaliths – we hawk the anomalous, peddle the strange. Merchants of astonishment.
>
> (Geertz 1986: 275)

At their heart, European archaeologies have always been discourses on our identity. The 'evidences' they have provided have helped shape ethnic, nationalist, and racist histories in the nineteenth and first half of the twentieth century. Such discussions still abound, but a new discourse can be seen to be emerging implicit in recent discussions of Indo-European origins, pan-Celtic connections across the continent, and, in the essentially proto-capitalistic interpretations of prehistoric exchange systems: a new discourse that stresses far more our common European heritage than individual ethnicities. Archaeology cannot avoid discussing such issues, but it can discuss them more critically. In particular, it can attempt to avoid writing the past as if it were the same as, or a pale reflection of, the present. This paper offers a contrastive archaeology to show that at least one society in later-prehistoric Europe was very different from what our premises expect, arguing the need to recognise a different Europe in prehistory.

Later-prehistoric settlement studies and their background

An important feature of later prehistory in northern and western Europe is the increasing dominance of settlement in the archaeological record. The number of excavated settlements increases through the later Bronze and Iron Ages, becoming longer-lived and increasingly visible through more substantial houses and boundary ditches. The wealth of evidence that settlement excavations provide for understanding

---

*First published in *Journal of European Archaeology* (1993), **1**, 57–75.

prehistoric societies has recently been emphasised in an extensive synthesis (Audouze and Buchenschutz 1989). But the purpose of the paper is to ask whether more can be asked of this data by posing a new range of questions to later-prehistoric settlements. Such new ways of looking at the past must be seen as part of the development of a wider, self-critical archaeology, ready to question the largely unchanged nineteenth-century assumptions upon which most later-prehistoric archaeology still rests; as an attempt to make the Iron Age, in particular, less boring (Hill 1989).

Current approaches to the study of later-prehistoric settlements are characterised by the narrow range of questions asked of the data and the assumption that these can be answered in a straightforward manner. Excavation is concerned with recovering plans, establishing chronologies, cataloguing finds, and, increasingly, reconstructing palaeo-economies from plant and animal remains. There have been very few attempts to study the organisation of space or to consider the symbolic and ritual aspects of settlements (exceptions Clarke 1972b; Therkorn 1987). Indeed, it seems a common assumption that everyday life in prehistory is simple to understand, essentially unchanging, and merely a backdrop against which the more important action was played out. Where everyday life is discussed or portrayed, it is usually in popular accounts, museum displays, and reconstruction drawings. The picture painted contains little which is not immediately familiar to our own lived experience, or at least to our recent rural forebears. Assumptions about the use of space, the motivations behind behaviour, family structure, and, especially, gender relations are those of our own culture. Although people might have used different styles of pottery, worn different clothes, lived in differing social forms, most archaeology implicitly assumes that people in the past were essentially the same.

The familiarity of later-prehistoric settlements rests firstly on the widespread assumption that settlement data can 'speak for themselves' (Champion 1987). Because of the secular: sacred, economic: symbolic oppositions within our thinking, settlement evidence is assumed to be the product of human behaviours motivated by rational and explicable considerations such as convenience, utility, and the need for shelter. We do not expect, nor do we look for situations where this might not be the case. However, this familiarity of settlement evidence must be set within deeper-rooted premises about the nature of European prehistory. In contrast to American archaeology, which has always been the study of other peoples' pasts, European archaeology is the study of our past. There is not space here to consider the socio-political background of European later-prehistoric archaeology, nor to offer a critique of the continued uncritical discussions of Celts, Germans, and Iberians. However, we must recognise that we have rarely questioned the nineteenth-century assumptions upon which European later-prehistoric archaeology is still largely grounded (Champion 1987; Hill 1989), and here I want to stress the consequences of an archaeology of our past, an archaeology as genealogy.

Later-prehistoric archaeology's original objectives were to trace the origins of the first peoples known in Europe back from written sources. Such continuity between past and present has been strongly stressed. In a nationalist and racist climate, which saw the origins of contemporary national and ethnic groups in the classical descriptions of Celts and Germans, archaeology played an important role exploring and creating their identities. Continuity, especially of essential characteristics, was important in arguments that saw peoples in the past as the same as contemporary Europeans, or an ideal version of what they should be (Merriman 1987). Similar Eurocentric and 'presentist' assumptions lie behind attempts to answer the question of the 'origins of Europe'. This question is at the heart of the recently invigorated debate about the origins of Indo-European languages in Europe (Renfrew 1987; Hodder 1990a; Mallory 1989), and also behind Childe's proto-capitalistic interpretation of the Bronze Age (Rowlands 1984, 1987b). The end result of such concerns is a European past written as Same. These narratives stress continuity with later history and the present; narratives that find it easy, natural to draw analogies, if not direct identifications, from our known later history, but not ethnographies. A past-as-same (Ricoeur 1984) is reinforced by processual archaeologies which explain the past through presumed universal laws of behaviour, based on the assumption that all homo sapiens behave essentially according to one vision of ideal modern westerners.

Writing a different past

Rowlands (1986) characterised those views which construct prehistories in the light of modern discourse as 'modernist fantasies in prehistory' and expressed the hope that archaeologists might become better at recognising and criticising the common-sense ideologies they project into the past. As archaeology is written in the present, invariably it will reflect current concerns. It is natural that archaeologists explain their data using analogies that are familiar to them: Hallstatt society is seen as organised along essentially feudal lines with princes in their castles because of the limited range of non-capitalist social forms we know from studying European history.

However, this need not mean archaeology inevitably must construct a past in the image of the present. Archaeological data are usually strong enough to resist the imposition of an interpretation, if given the chance, and can suggest new lines of inquiry. Equally, we can become critical of our own interpretations and, particularly, the assumptions on which they are grounded. It is this self-reflexivity that lies at the heart of the post-processual archaeologies that emerged in the 1980s (Hodder 1986; Shanks and Tilley 1987a). One essential feature of such approaches is the need to make explicit our assumptions about our subject matter. Another is the recognition of the difference of the past. Heterology, a discourse on difference, is central to the critique of processual archaeologies and the recognition that the past is other is essential for any interpretive archaeology (Hodder 1991a).

But where does the difference of the past lie? Traditional culture-historical or processual archaeologists would probably argue that they do see the past as different from the present, but such difference lies at the level of social organisation or interaction with the environment; that prehistoric societies were not modern nation states in a capitalist world economy but bands or proto-states, with lineage or household modes of production, forming cores or peripheries, practising slash and burn or in-field/out-field agricultures. The point I wish to make here is that the difference of the past resides at a far more fundamental level. Drawing on anthropology and social theory, we can say that the otherness of the past lay in the structures and practice of everyday life; in exactly those areas of life which previous archaeologies have felt to be unchanging, familiar, commonsensical, and readily understandable. A series of studies have questioned the universal and utilitarian explanations of the everyday. They show that attitudes to dirt; refuse-maintenance strategies; the construction and use of space; the procurement, production, and exchange of objects; the preparation and consumption of food; the classification and perception of the natural world; time; and the nature of gender relations are not universal constants. They differ considerably between historically- and culturally-specific contexts, and are all closely bound up with each other as part of the social construction of reality (e.g. Bourdieu 1977; Douglas 1966; Hodder 1982b; Hugh-Jones 1979; Moore 1986; Gregory and Urry 1985; Tambiah 1969).

Not even the human body nor subjectivity can be considered as fixed or universally the same for all peoples at all times (Bourdieu 1977; Blacking 1977; Carrithers *et al.* 1985; Foucault 1984). What it was to be human was considerably different in middle-Iron-Age Wessex from late-Neolithic South Jutland, and probably quite different from middle-Iron-Age Aisne valley. We should not see what it is to be human as eternally constant, just clothed in different material cultures in different times and places. Human subjectivities, which include emotions, perceptions, motivations, understanding of the body, world view etc., are intimately linked, moulded, and sustained through their participation with the material world. As such, we should question accounts in archaeology and history which imply that people remained the same even though pot shapes, house forms, dress styles, burial rites, and social forms changed.

The problem of the structure and practice of everyday life and the difference of the past need to be placed as central concerns in our studies of later-prehistoric settlement. This is a contrast to an archaeology that seeks out our origins, stressing the continuities in reconstructing the European family tree back into prehistory. Rather, Thomas (1990b, 1991), following Nietzsche and Foucault, has suggested the possibility of a different kind of genealogy. An archaeology that attempts to recover the difference of the past and so seeks to de-legitimise the present by criticising attempts to impose our 'presentist' common sense, categories, and premises (cf. Geertz 1986; Rowlands 1986, 1987a):

> Genealogy, a contrastive history, can be argued to provide a paradigm for effective archaeological research . . . .. Our efforts can be directed at those supposedly static and ahistorical spheres like the appropriation of landscape, the preparation and consumption of food, the disposal of household waste, the organisation of domestic space and the use of the human body in mortuary practice. Each of these has been conventionally looked on by archaeologists in universal terms.
>
> (Thomas 1990b)

The rest of this paper will briefly sketch a contrastive archaeology of later-prehistoric settlement. Summarising some of the results of recent work on Iron-Age settlement in southern England, it does not suggest that all later-prehistoric settlements in temperate Europe share the same peculiarities found in Britain. But if the British material reveals structures and practices of everyday life very different to the common sense expectations with which we have always approached such data, then it is to be expected that settlements in Denmark, Holland, or France will be equally different.

A different Southern-English Iron Age

British Iron-Age studies are currently in a state of flux and revision. Recent papers, mostly within the pages of the journal *Scottish Archaeological Review*, have begun to question traditional assumptions and interpretations of the period, seeking to apply similar theoretical perspectives to those that have transformed the study of the British Neolithic and early Bronze Age (e.g. Barrett, Bradley, and Green 1991; Bowden and McOmish 1989; Foster 1989; Hill 1989; 1996; Hingley 1990a, 1990b; Parker Pearson forthcoming; Sharples 1991; Stopford 1987). The later Bronze (*c.* 1200 to 700 BC) and Iron Ages (*c.* 700 BC to AD 50) in southern Britain are characterised by an apparently secular archaeological record dominated by settlements and field systems. This is in marked contrast to the Neolithic and early Bronze Age (4000 BC to 1200 BC) where communal and funerary monuments abound, but evidence for settlement and subsistence is sparse (Bradley 1991). The transition between these manifestations of two very different types of social discourses is a central issue in British prehistory (Barrett, Bradley, and Green 1991). How it is to be understood rests crucially on our understanding of the apparently secular, familiar world of later-prehistoric settlements.

For the Iron Age in southern Britain we must envisage a heavily-utilised, densely packed landscape with settlements 1 or 2 km apart (Cunliffe 1991). Traditionally the hillfort has been seen as the archetypal monument of this period, central to the operation of society. But it is now recognised that large areas of the country had few hill-forts, including those areas which witnessed the most dramatic transformations in the late Iron Age. Essentially, the whole period should be characterised as one of small, agrarian settlements. Hunting and other wild resources contributed very little to the overall diet. Most settlements appear to be self-sufficient, with little evidence for specialised production or long-distance exchange (Hill forthcoming; Stopford 1987). Burials are essentially absent. Unlike the continent, there are no cemeteries for most of this period, except in eastern Yorkshire. A tiny proportion of the population is represented by whole corpses and other remains in pits and ditches in settlements. It is assumed the rest were excavated and the bones disposed of in unrecoverable ways (Wait 1985). The nature of social organisation for most of the period has become controversial. Some have proposed a model of a classic 'Celtic' hierarchical society, with hillforts acting as economic and political central places (e.g. Cunliffe 1984). This view has been challenged, and the existence of a more egalitarian society centred on independent households has been suggested (Hill 1996; Stopford 1987). The late Iron Age (*c.* 150 BC to AD 50) witnessed dramatic changes, particularly in the south-east, with the appearance of 'oppida', coinage, shrines, and cremation cemeteries, the resumption of metalwork deposition in watery places, and an increase in importance of long-distance exchange (Haselgrove 1989).

Iron-Age settlements

A variety of non-hillfort settlements is known for the period (Cunliffe 1991; McOmish 1989). Conglomerations of unenclosed settlements and villages were particularly common in lowland regions such as the Thames valley and East Anglia. However, enclosed small settlements, essentially similar to Little Woodbury (Bersu 1940; Evans 1989), represent the commonest form of southern British settlement.

These consist of a few round houses, storage pits, and ancillary structures within a banked and ditched enclosure which may vary considerably in size and shape. Settlement form and organisation clearly changed through time. For example, during the Early/Middle Iron Age, the long-established modular pattern of a large porched round house, associated with predominantly-male activities, and a smaller ancillary house associated with food storage and preparation, female activities (Ellison 1981), was replaced by single, small round houses. Due to poor preservation, such sites are usually only represented by sub-soil features such as pits, ditches, and post-holes, whose fills produce considerable quantities of ecofacts and artefacts. These enclosed settlements are well known through major excavation reports (e.g. Bersu 1940; Wainwright 1979; Fasham 1985), general accounts, and the almost obligatory pictures of reconstructions such as at Butser (Reynolds 1984).

The study of such settlements is typified by the assumptions of a familiar, similar past; settlement evidence is considered to be unproblematic to use and interpret. The functions of the different excavated features is felt to be self-explanatory; a ditch is to keep animals out or in, houses are houses, and pits store grain, even if stylistic convention requires some discussion of their function and its experimental proof. Large numbers of finds recovered from sites give analyses an air of statistical security: for example 10,193 bone fragments and 108.135 kg of pottery from the Iron-Age phases at Winnall Down (Fasham 1985). These are simply regarded as refuse; their distribution felt to reflect the original location of the activities that produced the rubbish. As such, this material is felt to more or less directly represent the nature and scale of agricultural and craft activities on sites. Usually people are absent from discussions of Iron-Age settlements. Indeed, eliminating the human factor appears to be at the heart of the experimental archaeology, such as Butser, which has strongly influenced understandings of later-prehistoric settlement (Reynolds 1984). Beliefs, customs, and traditions, even people, are seen as secondary phenomena simply grafted on to an economically-functioning unit. Such discussions imply that the inhabitants structured their settlements and lives along functional, rational lines similar to the way in which modern Europeans are supposed to behave. That this might not have been the case is not considered and the fact that ethnographic parallels or analogies have not been felt necessary, if not violently rejected, is telling (Reynolds 1985). Yet, can such functionalist, Eurocentric assumptions explain the archaeology found on such sites? Has anyone looked for a different Iron Age?

Ritual and rubbish
Arguably one of the most important features of British prehistoric archaeology during the 1980s has been the recognition of 'structured deposition' (Richards and Thomas 1984). An increasing concern has been to understand the processes through which material entered the archaeological record as an essential prerequisite for interpreting the role that material culture played within social discourses. The social and cultural implications of the careful arrangement and selection of certain categories of objects and human remains in the obviously ritual contexts of Neolithic and Bronze-Age tombs (e.g. Shanks and Tilley 1982; Thomas 1991) have been extended to hoards (Bradley 1990) and communal monuments and pit groups (Thomas 1991; Hodder 1990a). The deposition of pottery, stone tools, bones, etc., on Neolithic sites was not

the random disposal of 'rubbish', but represented deliberate and occasional social practices in which the location of deposition and the types of the materials involved were clearly structured according to cultural 'rules'. As such the original deposition of the majority of all material from the Neolithic and early Bronze Age cannot be explained through behavioural terms, and falls outside the archaeological formation processes described by Schiffer (1976) (Bradley 1990; Thomas 1991).

It is becoming apparent that structured deposition also occurred on later-prehistoric settlement sites (Barrett, Bradley, and Green 1991). It has been stressed that the large quantities of all classes of finds recovered from Iron-Age settlements have simply been regarded as 'rubbish', more or less directly reflecting the status and activities that took place at a site. The representativity of this material must be questioned; simple calculations of the average quantities annually incorporated into sub-soil

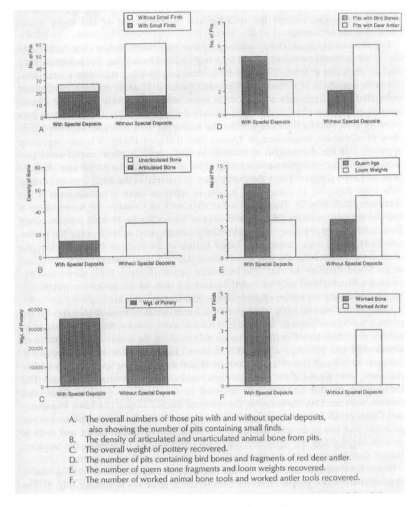

A. The overall numbers of those pits with and without special deposits, also showing the number of pits containing small finds.
B. The density of articulated and unarticulated animal bone from pits.
C. The overall weight of pottery recovered.
D. The number of pits containing bird bones and fragments of red deer antler.
E. The number of quern stone fragments and loom weights recovered.
F. The number of worked animal bone tools and worked antler tools recovered.

Figure 25.1 Structured, ritual deposits not random rubbish. These groups illustrate some of the relationships between the presence of 'special deposits' of human remains and/or articulated animal remains in pits and the other contents of such pits at Winnall Down

features suggest that only a tiny fraction of the objects used and the waste produced on a site entered the record. Calculations for the early-Iron-Age settlement at Winnall Down suggest as little as an average of eleven animal bone fragments, not whole bones, and less than half a rim sherd entered the archaeological record each year (Hill forthcoming). This is not surprising as approximately 80 per cent of such material is excavated from the fills of disused storage pits and the infilling of a pit was probably a rare event, perhaps only once a decade on most settlements. It could be that such pits received a random selection of the refuse discarded or lying about a site at the short time of its filling. However, a study of over 1500 pits from twelve sites in Wessex suggests otherwise (Hill forthcoming).

The initial impetus to study such pits was to consider the range of human deposits (complete and partial skeletons, skulls, articulated limbs, individual bone fragments) and 'animal special deposits' (complete and partial skeletons, placed skulls, articulated limbs) found in Iron-Age pits and ditches (Wait 1985). These occur in approximately a quarter of all pits, but the consequences for the other contents of these features given the presence of such ritual deposits has not been considered. The contents are simply regarded as rubbish, a key element in the interpretation of the human burials in 'domestic refuse' as those of non-persons, social outsiders (Walker 1984).

It is becoming clear that contents of pits with such ritual deposits differ from other pits and are not simply 'rubbish'. A series of relationships can be identified between the presence of human remains, animal special deposits, small finds, and large concentrations of animal bone and pottery. The pits containing such structured, intentional deposits can constitute up to 33 per cent of the pits excavated on settlements. Not all of these need contain human or articulated animal remains; some have concentrations of small finds or large dumps of inarticulated, but freshly-deposited animal bone (Maltby 1985). They represent an infrequent and distinctive social practice, which, if it took place at regular intervals, would have occurred only once or twice in an Iron-Age individual's life-time. This 'pit ritual tradition' (Hill 1996) involved the deposition of offerings and refuse from feasting; the manipulation of human remains as part of a complex minority mortuary rite, if not some human sacrifice; the deposition of complete and freshly, perhaps deliberately, broken pottery and other small finds (Figure 25.1). It is not the intention here to discuss the detailed nature and social implications of this tradition, except to argue that it involved the manipulation of symbols of human and agricultural fertility and abundance (Barrett 1989a; Bradley 1990).

Within this social discourse around the essentially-undifferentiated reproduction of humans and domesticated nature, the position of the wild is important. Wild mammal and bird bones make up less than 1 per cent of the total bone recovered from Iron-Age settlements, but on several sites the deposition of wild animal especially bird bones, is significantly associated with those pits with deposits of human remains (Hill forthcoming). Although perhaps not of great calorific significance, wild resources had considerable symbolic importance, and one might suggest that the unusual occasion of their being brought into settlements was carefully controlled and ritually prescribed (cf. Bulmer 1967; Tambiah 1969).

Here it is important to stress that the contents of pits are not simple undifferentiated rubbish. The majority of finds come from apparently ritual deposits, or are at least structured by cultural classifications very different from our own. As such we must question whether the material recovered from settlement sites directly reflects past activities and question the uncritical interpretations of all finds, be it for dating, palaeo-economic reconstruction, or exchange studies. It is also apparent that only certain types of artefact were considered proper to deposit within settlements, or more specifically pits. Weaponry and other 'prestige' metalwork are largely absent from later-prehistoric settlements, not because such objects were not used by their inhabitants, but because the production and use of a particular category of object seems also to determine a particular context in which that object might be deposited (Barrett 1991; Bradley 1990).

Symbolic spaces: boundaries and houses

The 'pit ritual tradition' served to presence and renegotiate a cluster of symbolic resources within the settlement, through which the implicit meanings of everyday life were articulated and enhanced. These deposits, also found in boundary ditches, acted as ways of introducing and renegotiating guidelines into the Iron-Age universe. They sketched out a cosmology and the topography needed before space could be given meaning. The boundaries of these settlements are increasingly recognised as being as much symbolic as practical. Considerable recent attention has been paid to these large boundary ditches and banks (Bowden and McOmish 1989; Hill 1996; Hingley 1984, 1990b). Defence is not generally felt to have been a major consideration, and their size would appear to exceed the basic requirements of keeping animals in their places and simple demarcation. These could have been achieved with slighter earthworks, fences, or hedges. It is increasingly accepted that such boundaries represent significant discontinuities in social/symbolic space, and not simply ecological/economic space. Hingley (1984) argues that the significance of the enclosure was that in certain circumstances it symbolically defined the social group. The enclosure resulted from and created the isolation and independence of the social group occupying the settlement.

Bowden and McOmish (1989) have argued that many such ditches were deliberately backfilled soon after excavation, and long sequences of backfilling and re-cutting may explain ditch fills at Winnall Down (Hill forthcoming). Ditch fills often contain considerable quantities of deliberately-deposited material. Human remains, particularly individual bone fragments often occur in some numbers in ditch fills, while human remains in pits are often in those pits close to the settlement limits (Wait 1985). Iron currency bars, standardised units of iron for exchange, were also only deposited in or close to settlement boundaries on Wessex sites (Hingley 1990c). It is also becoming apparent that the distribution of material in ditch deposits show considerable patterning, in many ways comparable to that at the shrine of Gourney (Brunaux 1988). At Winnall Down (Fasham 1985), the distribution of material in the ditch does not simply reflect the dumping of refuse from houses or activities close to certain parts of the enclosure ditch (Figure 25.2). These, and other sites such as Gussage All Saints, show a marked contrast between the back and front of the enclosure. Human remains, small finds, and fine-ware pottery were deliberately concentrated in the front of the enclosure ditch, coarse-ware pottery and infant burials at the rear. At Winnall Down, the ditch at the front of the site was more substantial, and recut several times, compared to the slight ditch at the rear. The excavation report (Fasham 1985) shows that the internal

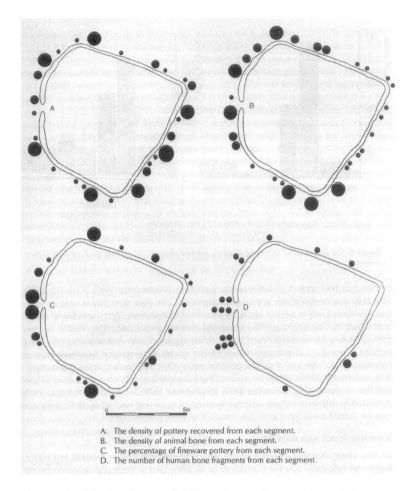

A. The density of pottery recovered from each segment.
B. The density of animal bone from each segment.
C. The percentage of fineware pottery from each segment.
D. The number of human bone fragments from each segment.

Figure 25.2 The distribution of different classes of material around the enclosure ditch of the early Iron-Age phrase at Winnall Down

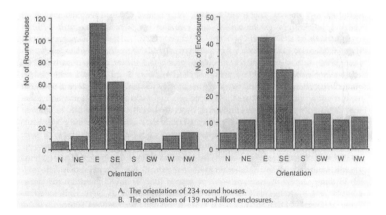

A. The orientation of 234 round houses.
B. The orientation of 139 non-hillfort enclosures.

Figure 25.3 The orientation of house and enclosure entrances in Iron-Age southern England

palisade/bank only extended around the front of the enclosure, creating an impressive facade but not an effective barrier (Hill forthcoming).

Much of this concern with facades and the frontal areas of these settlements served to mark the 'rite of passage' in crossing the settlement entrance. Deposits of fine-ware pottery are concentrated in the ditches on either side of the entrances at several later-Bronze-Age and Iron-Age sites, which in some cases also show a clear north–south contrast. At Winnall Down large quantities of pottery, including much freshly-broken fine ware, were placed in the northern ditch terminal, but almost no animal bone (Hill forthcoming); this situation was reversed in the southern terminal. Given this concern with marking the entrance, the antennae ditches at sites like Little Woodbury and Gussage All Saints, and long, flanked approaches to the banjo-type enclosures, probably had less to do with managing the movement of animal herds, and more to do with highlighting the important rite of passage involved in crossing the 'required barrier' that demarcated and helped define the settlement and its occupants.

Given this marked emphasis on the entrance, it may not be surprising that it appears there was a proper direction from which to enter the settlement (Figure 25.3). The majority of such settlements had entrances that faced east, although this rule could be modified to take into account other concerns (Hill 1996). At Winnall Down, the entrance faced due west, reversing the standard pattern. The doorways of round houses show a similar, but more marked, easterly orientation (Boast and Evans 1986; Hill 1996; Parker Pearson 1996). This has previously been explained as a functional adaption, either to avoid prevailing westerly winds or to maximise the amount of sunlight entering the house. Recent work has questioned these explanations, showing that even in more extreme climates, functional requirements rarely determine the orientation of doorways. Indeed, if they did in later-prehistoric Britain, then we should expect a southerly, not an easterly, orientation (Oswald 1991). This rigid easterly orientation, towards the rising sun, was rarely compromised and often led to a striking lack of integration between different houses and communal spaces, even in larger, unenclosed villages. As such, Clarke's (1972b) provisional model of Iron-Age society based on modules of facing houses is not applicable to the majority of southern-British Iron-Age settlements, including Glastonbury itself (Oswald 1991). This brief discussion of the spatial organisation of Iron-Age settlements again stresses that functional explanations cannot account for the archaeological evidence, which was clearly produced by actions organised according to a rationality that is not our own. The easterly orientation of thresholds suggests the importance of embodying time and cosmological principles into lived-in spaces. Ethnography has demonstrated how the layout and use of domestic space plays a key role in the physical manifestation and renegotiation of major structuring principles, drawn on in the daily reproduction of society (e.g. Bourdieu 1977; Hugh-Jones 1979; Moore 1986; Roben 1989; Yates 1989). It is in this light, not simply as convenient and neutral spatial containers, that we should investigate later-prehistoric European settlements.

Iron-Age bodies and subjects
Studies show that the category of the person is not universally constant but historically and culturally specific (Carrithers et al. 1985; Geertz 1983c) and demonstrate the ontological importance of childhood experiences within the home and its environs

in forming the subject (Bourdieu 1977). Demonstrating the very different ways of conceiving and constructing domestic spaces in later prehistory should lead us to expect that what it was to be a person then would have been very different from our experience. Therefore, we should question the assumption that people in the past were essentially the same as us. But is it possible to go further than arguing that people in the past were different because the demonstrably different organisations of space must have had ontological implications? The human body is often an important social metaphor and how it is classified, treated, or divided up is closely related to, although not the same as, the notion of the subject (Blacking 1977; Bourdieu 1977; Thomas 1989). Studying the treatment of the human body can allow archaeology to come to a fuller understanding of the culturally- and historically-specific subjectivities in prehistory. Recent work with Scandinavian rock art provides one example of such approaches (Yates 1990b). But it is the approach to the sorting and use of different parts of the skeleton in Neolithic chamber tombs and other contexts that may be useful for the southern-British Iron Age (Shanks and Tilley 1982; Thomas 1991; Hodder 1990a). The treatment of human remains in pit and other deposits on settlement sites demonstrates the existence of systems of classifications. Here I want only to discuss the similarities between the treatment of human and domestic-animal carcasses. In the past, these similarities in treatment have not elicited comment. This stems largely from our assumptions which have treated human remains as obviously ritual, but animal remains as economic evidence, assumptions that have helped prevent the recognition of ritual animal deposits until comparatively recently. Human and animal carcasses are not simply found in the same contexts but are often deposited in similar manners, and according to similar classifications of how bodies were butchered and divided up. Thus, both humans and animals exist as (Hill forthcoming):

> Complete skeletons, sometimes with the skull displaced;
> Partial skeletons with head and/or some limbs missing;
> Complete skulls;
> Articulated limbs.

Although there are differences in the treatment of humans and animals, as there are between different animal species, it would appear that there was no radical distinction in the way humans and animals were treated and conceived in these deposits. Rather we may discern a continuum in which certain species were more like humans than others, and certain animals more appropriate replacements for humans in deposits. Whatever the exact details, that humans and domestic animals could have been conceived of as essentially similar within this ritual discourse suggests a powerful metaphor through which human subjects and society were reproduced simultaneously. It suggests one way in which we may begin to appreciate that not all Europeans in the past necessarily were the same as our contemporary Europeans.

Conclusions

Traditional approaches to Iron-Age settlements in southern England expected the existence of a familiar past in which our common sense and taken-for-granted assumptions about everyday life were felt to apply. The contrastive archaeology briefly outlined here has sought to demonstrate a different past in which the sacred and profane, symbolic and practical were intimately interwoven in early- and middle-Iron-Age settlements. Recognising the difference of this past has wide implications for how we study later-prehistoric settlements, not least in that it dramatically increases the range and types of questions we must ask of our data. Meanwhile, the traditional questions we ask and uncritical uses of the evidence recovered from settlement excavations must be questioned. The demonstration that only a tiny proportion of the material used and discarded on a prehistoric settlement ever entered archaeologically-recoverable deposits poses a question mark over all the interpretations we have previously made of pottery, bones, and small finds. It forces us to consider how that limited and distorted sample entered the archaeological record as a prerequisite for any further consideration. As Maltby (1985) has shown, the overall proportions of the different domestic-animal species recovered in the bone assemblage from an excavation bear no direct relation to the original proportions in the live herds kept or consumed by the occupants of a settlement. When it is also clear that many of the finds recovered from southern-English Iron-Age sites were deposited as part of highly-structured, if not ritual activities then simple, uncritical, economic reconstructions of settlement evidence are questioned further.

Most importantly we must recognise that in studying the European past we need to understand the specific character of the difference of this past and avoid interpreting the ways past societies were organised through those only characteristic of the present. This means we should neither rely on later European historical analogies, nor on the Celts, Germans, or Iberians. Nor does it mean we should reduce the self-evident diversity in European prehistory through applying generalised anthropological models. Rather the past took place in the context of historically-specific material conditions which we recover as fragmentary remains today. It follows that we must think in more detail about our understanding of those historically- and culturally-specific material contexts and of the ways in which humans acted in relation to their material world.

This is not to imply a radical break between historical and prehistoric Europe. Clearly there are connections and continuities. But the stress on the continuities, on the search for similarities and identifications between prehistory and later 'known' history, cannot allow for the richness, diversity, and difference of historically-specific cultures in the past. Such a stress on unchanging continuities is particularly strong in studies of Celtic religion, which take diverse written sources to create a timeless image of Celtic religion (Fitzpatrick 1991), for which evidence is sought in prehistory by plucking individual fragments out of their own contexts. This approach fails to recognise that archaeology can only work forwards in time to cope with the ever-shifting and variable ways cultural traditions constantly remake themselves (Barth 1987). As such, in Hodder's (1990a) account of the developments and variations on the theme of the domus in the European Neolithic, none of the specific regional sequences he outlines developed in a predictable way. Nor would it be possible to infer backwards from any one stage to any of the precedents. History is contingent, not predictable and does not move in a straight line but in a curve whose direction is constantly changing.

In the contextual archaeology of later-prehistoric settlements, a contrastive archaeology is only a first step, not a goal in itself. It is not enough simply to demonstrate a strange, alien, and presumably unintelligible past. We need to interpret that difference, to tell a story (Thomas 1990b). For later-prehistoric settlements this means going beyond the stagnation and sterility of structuralism. There is a danger in simply stopping at demonstrating the existence of the symbolic settlement and constructing series of binary oppositions (e.g. Hingley 1990b; Parker Pearson 1996). This approach only deals with the structures, not the practices, of everyday life. These are deterministic interpretations in which human agents are largely absent. They fail to connect the daily lives and routines of the inhabitants of these settlements to the wider reproduction of society. Nor do such approaches consider how power relations, exchange, and ways of organising societies are embedded in everyday life. To go beyond this stage is to recognise that the study of the structure and practice of everyday life must be an understanding of the structuration of past societies (Barrett 1987a; Giddens 1984).

Final remarks

> The historian has only become the ethnologist of days gone by.
> (Ricoeur 1984)

This paper has argued that we need to become far more critical of the assumptions through which we do later-prehistoric European archaeology. A contrastive archaeology of Iron-Age settlements in southern England has shown that the motivations for depositing material, attitudes to the wild, the organisation and perception of space, the classification of the human body, and, possibly, notions of human subjectivity, were very different to our own or those we assume to have been held by the Celts. Because it is the study of our past, we have seen the peoples of prehistoric Europe as essentially the same as ourselves, inhabiting past worlds organised along lines familiar to those in our own worlds, or at least known in European history. However, we must learn to recognise that past worlds, including those in history, could have been otherwise. This is not to argue for any archaeological objectivity, that we can freely encounter the otherness of the past. But we can become far more reflexive of our own assumptions and their grounding in current discourses, and become more open to the otherness in the past. 'Criticising our common-sense understanding of past lifeworlds can help turn European prehistorians into critics of the categories of thought whose origins we are attempting to understand' (Rowlands 1986: 746). This is to bring us back to the fundamental question of identity, that images of the European past and present have always been inexorably intertwined. As such, be it the Europe of the distant past, or the immediate future, we must learn to conceive of a Europe that is not our Europe (Hill 1989).

ACKNOWLEDGEMENTS

Much of this chapter is based on work for my forthcoming PhD thesis, and I would particularly like to thank Dave Allen, Frank Green, Andrew Fitzpatrick, Eliane Morris, and, especially, Mark Maltby for their help in giving me access to unpublished data in site archives. I would also like to thank Julian Thomas, Mark Edmonds, Brian Boyd, Koji Mizoguchi for their comments on this chapter, but particularly Samantha Lucy and Ian Hodder for their efforts in making my English more readable.

26

DISCOURSES OF IDENTITY IN THE INTERPRETATION OF THE PAST*

SIÂN JONES

The uniqueness and unity of European history must be dismantled . . . If our cultural consciousness has become objectified in a particular historical, genre (cf., Sahlins 1985: 52) that is *linearised and continuous,* analysis reveals the *non-synchronicity and discontinuity* of social experience.

(Hastrup 1992: 2; my emphasis)

The mode of European cultural consciousness explored by Hastrup is integral to dominant discourses of cultural identity in Europe, whether they be European, national or ethnic. Typically group identities are represented as unified, monolithic wholes, with linear and continuous histories which in turn are used in the legitimation of claims to political autonomy and territory within the prevailing ideological climate of ethnic nationalism (see Chapman *et al.* 1989; Danforth 1993; Just 1989; Shore 1993). Thus, whilst competing interpretations of the past arise in the context of political disputes, they tend to share a common mode of representation; a mode which is not restricted to ethnic and national groups, but also extends to supra-national entities. For instance, despite the emphasis on the co-existence of supra-national, national and regional cultural identities, the symbolic terrain on which the New Europe is being actively produced, 'is precisely that upon which the nation-state has traditionally been constructed' (Shore 1993: 791). That is the 'New Europe' is being constructed as a unified entity with a unilinear continuous history (see Shore, chapter 6 [in the original volume]).

   Archaeology has undoubtedly played a central role in the construction of such identities, and the details of particular liaisons between archaeology and nationalism have been the subject of a number of recent studies (e.g., Kristiansen 1993; Kohl 1993; Olsen 1986; Ucko 1995). In this essay I take a more abstract approach and examine the common discourses of identity[1] which have characterised myths of origin and historical continuity during the nineteenth and twentieth centuries. There is always a tension between past and present in archaeological interpretation; between

---

*First published in P. Graves-Brown, S. Jones and C. Gamble (eds) (1996), *Cultural Identity and Archaeology: The Construction of European Communities,* London: Routledge, pp. 1–24.

the past meanings and processes which we wish to reconstruct from the material remains, and the meanings which we wish these remains to reveal to us in the present. This tension is nowhere greater than in accounts of past cultural groups. The critical role of the past in the assertion and legitimation of group identities often leads to a problematic slippage between contemporary concepts of group identity and the mapping of past groups in archaeology. Here, I explore the way in which contemporary, historically-contingent concepts of culture and identity shape our understanding of the past (see also Diaz-Andreu, chapter 3; Hides, chapter 2 [both in the original volume]), and I suggest that we need to adopt a radically different theoretical framework for the analysis of cultural identity in the past. Such a theoretical framework must accommodate the fluid and contextual nature of cultural identity and facilitate the exploration of alternative associations of identity, history and place.

Peoples and cultures

Archaeology, like anthropology, has tended to deal with 'wholes'; a concern epitomised in the identification of past peoples and cultures, which continues to provide a basic conceptual framework for archaeological analysis today. Throughout the history of archaeology, from its antiquarian origins onwards, the material record has been attributed to particular past peoples (see Daniel 1978 [1950]; Trigger 1989b). However, it was with the development of the culture history paradigm in the late nineteenth and early twentieth centuries that a systematic framework for the classification of cultures in space and time was established. Despite the diverse histories of archaeology in different regions and countries, culture history has provided the dominant framework for archaeological analysis throughout most of the world during the twentieth century (see contributions in Ucko 1995). Processual and post-processual archaeologies have rejected culture historical interpretation as an end product in itself. Yet even these archaeological 'schools' are still largely dependent upon material evidence which has been described and classified on the basis of an essentially culture historical epistemology (see Jones 1994: 19–20 and 1996).

One of the main assumptions underlying the culture-historical approach is that bounded uniform cultural entities correlate with particular peoples, ethnic groups, tribes and/or races. Thus, Kossinna, one of the pioneers of culture history, asserted that 'in all periods, sharply delineated archaeological culture areas coincide with clearly recognisable peoples or tribes' (cited in Malina and Vasicek 1990: 63).[2] This assumption is based on a normative conceptualisation of culture: that within a given group cultural practices and beliefs tend to conform to prescriptive ideational norms or rules of behaviour. It is assumed that culture is made up of a set of shared ideas or beliefs, which are maintained by regular interaction within the group, and the transmission of shared cultural norms to subsequent generations through the process of socialisation, which, it is assumed, results in a continuous cultural tradition. Childe was explicit about this process, arguing that 'Generation after generation has followed society's prescription and produced and reproduced in thousands of instances the socially approved standard type. An archaeological type is just that' (Childe 1956a: 8).

Within such a theoretical framework the transmission of cultural traits/ideas is generally assumed to be a function of the degree of interaction between individuals or groups. A high degree of homogeneity in material culture is regarded as the product of regular contact and interaction (e.g. Gifford 1960: 341–2), whereas discontinuities in the distribution of material culture are assumed to be the result of social and/or physical distance. Gradual change is attributed to internal drift in the prescribed cultural norms of a particular group, whereas more rapid change is explained in terms of external influences, such as diffusion resulting from culture contact, or 'the succession of one cultural group by another as a result of migration and conquest. Distributional changes [in diagnostic types] should reflect displacements of population, the expansions, migrations, colonisations or conquests with which literary history is familiar' (Childe 1956a: 135).

It has been argued (Trigger 1978: 86) that the widespread adoption of the culture-historical approach in archaeology was a product of the need to establish a system for classifying the spatial and temporal variation in material culture which became evident in the nineteenth century. However, such an argument implies that discrete monolithic cultures constitute a natural and universal mode of socio-cultural differentiation waiting to be discovered by the discipline of archaeology. Certainly spatial and temporal variation in human ways of life is an unequivocal fact which is manifested in the archaeological record, but it can be argued that the particular classificatory framework developed in archaeology in order to describe and explain such variation was based on historically contingent assumptions about the nature of cultural diversity. That rather than '*discovering* a general form of universal difference' archaeologists, along with other social scientists, invented it (Fardon 1987: 176, my emphasis).

The expectations of boundedness, homogeneity and continuity which have been built into ideas concerning culture since the nineteenth century are related to nationalism and the emergence of the nation-state (see Diaz-Andreu, chapter 3 [in the original volume]; Handler 1988: 7–8; Spencer 1990: 283; Wolf 1982: 397). As Handler points out:

> nationalist ideologies and social scientific inquiry [including that of archaeology] developed in the same historical context that of the post-Renaissance European world – and . . . the two have reacted upon one another from their beginnings.
>
> (Handler 1988: 8)

Nations are considered, in the words of Handler, to be 'individuated beings'; endowed with the reality of natural things, they are assumed to be bounded, continuous, and precisely distinguishable from other analogous entities (Handler 1988: 6, 15). The idea of culture is intricately enmeshed with nationalist discourse; it is culture which distinguishes between nations and which constitutes the content of national identity. Moreover, 'culture symbolises individuated existence: the assertion of cultural particularity is another way of proclaiming the existence of a unique collectivity' (Handler 1988: 39). The representation of culture in nationalist discourses is strikingly mirrored in the pre-suppositions which have dominated traditional concepts of 'culture' and 'society' in academic theory and practice. Such categories have been traditionally seen as well integrated, bounded, continuous entities, which occupy exclusive spatio-temporal positions and which are assumed to be the normal and healthy units of social life (see Clifford 1988; Handler 1988).

The concept of an archaeological culture represents a particular variant of this formula. As discussed above, bounded material culture complexes are assumed to be the material manifestation of past peoples, who shared a set of prescriptive learned norms of behaviour. Archaeological cultures came to be regarded as organic individuated entities, the prehistorian's substitute for the individual agents which make up the historian's repertoire: 'prehistory can recognise peoples and marshal them on the stage to take the place of the personal actors who form the historian's troupe' (Childe 1940: 2; see also Piggott 1965: 7). Moreover, as in the case of contemporary claims concerning the relationship between nations and cultures, the relationship between archaeological cultures and past peoples is based on teleological reasoning in that culture is both representative of, and constitutive of, the nation or people concerned. As Handler points out:

> The almost *a priori* belief in the existence of the culture follows inevitably
> from the belief that a particular human group . . . exists. The existence
> of the group is in turn predicated on the existence of a particular culture.
> (Handler 1988: 39)

Through the concept of an archaeological culture the past is reconstructed in terms of the distribution of homogeneous cultures whose history unfolds in a coherent linear narrative measured in terms of objectified events, such as contacts, migrations and conquests, with intervals of homogeneous, empty time in between them.[3] Furthermore, the understanding of culture which is embodied by the notion of an archaeological culture enables history, place and people to be tied together in the exclusive and monolithic fashion common to contemporary representations of ethnic, national and European identity. Yet recent anthropological research (see Fardon 1987: 176; Handler 1988: 291) suggests that the relationship between culture and peoplehood is not so straightforward, and that the idea that ethnic and national groups are fixed, homogeneous, bounded entities extending deep into the past is a modern classificatory invention.[4] On the contrary it has been shown that ethnic and national identities are fluid, dynamic and contested.

Ethnicity and culture

During the 1960s and early 1970s there was a shift in the analysis of cultural differentiation in the context of critiques of existing social scientific concepts.[5] This shift was marked by the proliferation of research into ethnicity, and the use of 'ethnic group' in place of 'tribe' and 'race'. However, it was not merely a terminological sleight of hand, it also represented important changes in the orientation of research and theories of cultural differentiation (see Cohen 1978; Jones 1994). Increasing emphasis was placed on the self-identifications of the social actors concerned, the processes involved in the construction of group boundaries, and the inter-relationships between socio-cultural groups. Such approaches contrast sharply with the traditional holistic analysis of supposedly discrete, organic entities.

As early as 1947 Francis had argued that the ethnic group constitutes a community based primarily on a shared subjective 'we-feeling' and that 'we cannot define the ethnic group as a plurality pattern which is characterised by a distinct language, culture, territory, religion and so on' (1947: 397). A number of other authors adopted a similar argument (e.g., Moerman 1965; Shibutani and Kwan 1965: 40; Wallerstein 1960: 131). Yet the real turning point in the definition of ethnic groups seems to have followed Barth's (1969) reiteration of the subjective aspects of ethnic identity within a programmatic theoretical framework (Cohen 1978). He argued that ethnic groups cannot be defined by the cultural similarities and differences enumerated by the analyst, but rather on the basis of 'categories of ascription and identification by the actors themselves' (Barth 1969: 10). In many instances ethnic groups may possess social and cultural commonalities across boundaries and exhibit considerable variation within the group. Yet in the process of social interaction both real and assumed cultural differences are articulated in the maintenance of ethnic boundaries (Barth 1969). Ethnographic research has confirmed that ethnicity involves subjective processes of classification, and in much of the recent literature it has been regarded as a consciousness of real or assumed cultural difference *vis à vis* others; a 'we'–'they' opposition (e.g., Chapman *et al.* 1989; Cohen 1978; Ringer and Lawless 1989; Shennan 1989).

This emphasis on the formation and persistence of subjective ethnic categories in the context of embracing social systems also contributed to a concern with the economic and political dimensions of ethnicity. Ethnic identity, it is argued, is 'instrumental' in that it provides a group with the boundary maintenance and organisational dimensions necessary in order to maintain, and compete for, a particular socio-economic niche (e.g., Barth 1969; Cohen 1974). In this sense ethnic groups are a product of differential socio-structural and/or environmental conditions. Moreover, it is argued that ethnicity is manipulated and mobilised, on an individual and group level, in the pursuit of economic and political interests (e.g., Barth 1969; Patterson 1975). For instance, some of the hoe-agricultural Fur of the Sudan have adopted the lifestyle and identity of the nomadic cattle Arabs, the Baggara (see Barth 1969: 25–6; Haaland 1969); a shift in identity which can be explained by the limited opportunities for capital investment in the village economy of the Fur, in contrast to the opportunities presented by the Baggara economy.

Broadly speaking, instrumentalist approaches dominated research on ethnicity in the 1970s and 1980s. The recent literature on ethnicity has further illustrated the dynamic nature of ethnicity, not only historically (see contributions in Tonkin *et al.* 1989), but also in different social contexts according to the interests and positions of the actors (e.g. Cohen 1978; Wallman 1977).

The recognition that ethnic groups are fluid self-defining systems which are embedded in economic and political relations, represents an important contribution to our understanding of the maintenance and transformation of ethnicity. Most significantly in terms of this discussion, such an approach to ethnicity reveals a critical break between culture and ethnicity. Whilst it is still assumed that there is some relation between ethnicity and culture, it is generally accepted that there is rarely a straightforward correlation between cultural similarities and differences and ethnic boundaries. Hence, recent theories of ethnicity mark a significant departure from the notion of ethnic groups as culture-bearing units; a notion which, as discussed above, is central to nationalist discourses as well as traditional social scientific theory. However, whilst ethnographic research supports a distinction between culture and ethnicity, the precise nature of the relationship between ethnicity and culture has been a neglected area of research. Instrumentalists tend to focus on the organisational aspects of ethnicity and take the cultural differences on which ethnicity is based for granted. Culture is reduced to an epiphenomenal and arbitrary set of symbols (Eriksen 1992: 30) manipulated in the pursuit of changing individual and/or group interests (Bentley 1987: 26, 48; Eriksen 1992: 44).

Towards a practice theory of ethnicity

One important problem which subjective instrumental approaches to ethnicity fail to resolve is the relationship between agents' perceptions of ethnicity, and the cultural contexts and social relations in which they are embedded. Such a question can be addressed by drawing on theories of practice that are concerned with the general relationship between the conditions of social life and agents' subjective constructions of social reality. For instance, Bourdieu (1977) argues that social actors possess durable, often subliminal, dispositions towards certain perceptions and practices (such as those relating to the sexual division of labour, morality, tastes and so on) which he calls '*habitus*'. Such dispositions, which are inculcated into an individual's sense of self at an early age (Bourdieu 1977: 78–93), are generated by the conditions constituting a particular social environment, such as, modes of production or access to certain resources (Bourdieu 1977: 77–8). However, the practices engendered by such conditions are not constituted by the mechanistic enactment of a system of normative rules which exist outside of individual history (Bourdieu 1977: 72). Rather, structural orientations exist in the form of the embodied knowledge and dispositions of social actors, but these structures depend for their existence on the practices and representations of social actors, which lead to their reproduction or transformation. As Postone *et al.* (1993: 4) point out, the orientations of the *habitus*, 'are at once "structuring structures" and "structured structures"; they shape and are shaped by social practice'.

The concept of the *habitus* can be used to articulate the way in which subjective ethnic classifications are grounded in the social conditions and cultural practices characterising particular social domains. Ethnicity is not a passive reflection of the cultural similarities and differences in which people are socialised, as traditional normative approaches assume. Nor is ethnicity, as some instrumental approaches imply, produced entirely in the process of social interaction, whereby epiphenomenal cultural symbols are manipulated in the pursuit of economic and political interests. Rather, drawing on Bourdieu's theory of practice, it can be argued that the subjective construction of ethnic identity in the context of social interaction is grounded in the shared subliminal dispositions of the *habitus* which shape, and are shaped, by commonalities of practice. As Bentley puts it: '[a] shared *habitus* engenders feelings of identification among people similarly endowed. Those feelings are consciously appropriated and given form through existing symbolic resources' (Bentley 1987: 173).

Moreover, these 'symbolic resources' are not essentially arbitrary. The cultural practices and beliefs which become objectified as symbols of ethnicity are derived from, and resonate with, the habitual practices and experiences of the agents involved, as well as reflect the instrumental contingencies of a particular situation. As Eriksen argues, symbols of ethnicity:

> are intrinsically linked with experienced, practical worlds containing specific, relevant meanings which on the one hand contribute to shaping interaction,

and on the other hand limit the number of options in the production of ethnic signs.

(Eriksen 1992: 45)

Yet within this theoretical approach the *habitus* and ethnicity are not directly congruent, thereby constituting a similar position to the traditional equation of culture and ethnicity. There is a break between the structured dispositions constituting the *habitus* as a whole, and the objectified representation of cultural *difference* involved in the production and reproduction of ethnicity. Shared habitual dispositions provide the basis for the recognition of commonalities of sentiment and interest, and the basis for the perception and communication of cultural affinities and differences which ethnicity entails. However, social interaction between actors of differing cultural traditions engenders a reflexive mode of perception contributing to a break with forms of knowledge which, in other contexts, constitute subliminal, taken for granted modes of behaviour. Such exposure of the arbitrariness of cultural practices, which had hitherto been taken as self-evident and natural, permits and requires a change 'in the level of discourse, so as to rationalise and systematise' the representation of those cultural practices, and, more generally, the representation of the cultural tradition itself (Bourdieu 1977: 233). It is at such a discursive level that ethnic categories are produced, reproduced and transformed through the systematic communication of cultural difference with relation to the cultural practices of particular 'ethnic others'.[6]

This process can be further elaborated by reference to a specific example, that of the construction of Tswana ethnicity in the context of European colonialism (see Comaroff and Comaroff 1992: 235–63). In the process of interaction and communication between the Tswana and evangelist missionaries, both groups began to recognise distinctions between them; 'to objectify their world in relation to a novel other, thereby inventing for themselves a self-conscious coherence and distinctness – even while they accommodated to the new relationship which enclosed them' (Comaroff and Comaroff 1992: 245). This objectification is not a fabrication; an entirely instrumental construction. Tswana ethnicity is based on the perception of commonalities of practice and experience in *Setswana* (Tswana ways) in opposition to *Sekgoa* (European ways). Yet the form which Tswana self-consciousness takes in this context is different from the cultural identities which prevailed in pre-colonial times when they were divided into political communities based on totemic affiliations. In both pre- and post-colonial times the construction of identity involves the marking of contrast – the opposition of selves and others – but colonialism provided a new context in which Tswana tradition was objectified as a coherent body of knowledge and practice uniting the Tswana people.

Thus, the objectification of cultural difference involves the dialectical opposition of different cultural traditions. The particular forms which such oppositions take is a product of the intersection of people's *habitus* with the social conditions constituting any particular context. These conditions include the prevailing power relations, and the relative distribution of the material and symbolic means necessary for the imposition of dominant regimes of ethnic categorisation. For instance, in many colonial contexts ethnic or 'tribal' categories were imposed by colonial regimes (see Colson 1968; Fried 1968), or were a product of large-scale urban migration and associated social and cultural dislocation (see Comaroff and Comaroff 1992). Hence, the extent to which ethnicity is embedded in pre-existing cultural realities represented by a shared *habitus* is highly variable. The extent of contiguity depends upon the cultural transformations brought about by the processes of interaction and the nature of the power relations between the interacting 'groups' (Comaroff and Comaroff 1992: 56). In some instances, for example as in colonial situations, minority ethnic groups may be composed of people of diverse origins, and 'the substance of their identities, as contrived from both within and outside, is inevitably a *bricolage* fashioned in the very historical processes which underwrite their subordination' (Comaroff and Comaroff 1992: 57). However, even when ethnicity is as much a product of the historical relations of inequality between 'groups' as it is a reflection of pre-existing cultural realities, the reproduction of these emergent forms of cultural difference will, over time, lead to their internalisation as part of the structured dispositions of the *habitus*.

Thus, manifestations of ethnicity are the product of an ongoing process involving multiple objectifications of cultural difference and the internalisation of those differences within the shared dispositions of the *habitus*. Such processes will lead to fluctuations in the correspondence between constructions of a particular ethnic identity, in terms of objectified cultural difference, and the overall cultural practices and historical experience of the people involved. Furthermore, the expression of cultural difference depends upon the particular cultural practices and historical experience activated in any given social context, as well as broader idioms of cultural difference. Consequently the cultural content of ethnicity may vary substantively and qualitatively in different contexts, as may the importance of ethnicity in general (see Eriksen 1991 and 1992).

On the basis of this theoretical approach it can be argued that there is unlikely to be a one-to-one relationship between expressions of a particular ethnic identity and the entire range of cultural practices and social conditions associated with that particular 'group'. Yet this is not because culture is an epiphenomenal resource which is consciously and deliberately manipulated in the pursuit of individual and group interests. Whilst ethnicity always involves active processes of performance and interpretation in the objectification of cultural difference, it is still constituted in the context of specific cultural practices and historical experiences which provide the basis for the perception of similarity and difference.

From a 'bird's eye view' the construction of ethnicity is likely to be manifested as multiple overlapping boundaries constituted by representations of cultural difference, which are at once transient, but also subject to reproduction and transformation in the ongoing processes of social life. Such a view of ethnicity undermines conventional methodological approaches which telescope various spatially and temporally distinct representations of ethnicity onto a single plane for the purposes of analysis and attempt to force the resulting incongruities and contradictions into an abstract conceptualisation of the ethnic group as a discrete, internally homogeneous entity characterised by continuity of tradition. The theoretical approach developed here suggests that such a methodological and conceptual framework obliterates the reality of the dynamic and creative processes involved in the reproduction and transformation of ethnicity.

A reconsideration of archaeological approaches to ethnicity

The traditional assumption that a one-to-one relationship exists between the sum of the cultural similarities and differences and the ethnic group has recently been criticised in archaeology (e.g., Hodder 1982b; Shennan 1989), as in other disciplines. It has also been argued that ethnic groups are not the product of social and physical isolation, but rather a consciousness of difference reproduced in the context of ongoing social interaction. Consequently archaeologists cannot continue to regard variation in the archaeological record as a passive measure of physical/social distance between groups (see Hodder 1982b). Nor can they assume that close contact between groups or the incorporation of one group by another will lead to gradual and uniform acculturation. However, it is necessary to make more wide-reaching changes to our analytical frameworks in order to analyse the construction of ethnicity in the past. In particular, there is a need to discard classificatory and interpretive frameworks based upon the presumed existence of bounded socio-cultural units; frameworks which are still fundamental to much archaeological theory and practice (and see Conkey 1990: 12).

Ethnicity must be distinguished from mere spatial continuity and discontinuity in that it refers to self-conscious identification with a particular group of people (Shennan 1989: 19). I have argued that ethnicity involves the objectification of cultural difference *vis à vis* others in the context of social interaction. Such objectifications are based upon the perception of commonalities of practice and experience, as well as the conditions prevailing in particular social and historical contexts. A variety of scenarios may arise. At one extreme there may be a high degree of homology between the structuring principles of the *habitus* and the signification of ethnicity in both material and non-material culture (as in Hodder's (1982b) study of the Baringo District). Whereas at the other end of the spectrum there may be a dislocation of such homologous relationships to the extent that the generation and expression of a common ethnic identity incorporates a bricolage of different cultural traditions characterised by heterogeneous structuring principles in many social domains (see Rowlands 1982: 164 for a similar argument).

Yet whatever the degree of homology between the *habitus* and ethnicity, it must be emphasised that archaeologists may not be able to find a reflection of past 'ethnic entities' in the material record (see also Miller 1985a: 202 with relation to caste). It is possible to question the very existence of bounded, homogeneous ethnic entities except at an abstract conceptual level. As Bourdieu (1977) has pointed out, such conceptual categories are based on the methodological reification or objectification of transient cultural practices taking place in different spatial and temporal contexts, and the 'group' exists only in the context of interpretation where it justifies and explains past practices and modes of interaction, and structures future practices.

In contrast, the praxis of ethnicity results in multiple transient realisations of ethnic difference in particular contexts. These realisations of ethnicity are both structured and structuring, involving, in many instances, the repeated production and consumption of distinctive styles of material culture. Yet they are a product of the intersection of the perceptual and practical dispositions of social agents and the interests and oppositions engendered in a particular social context, rather than abstract categories of difference.

Hence, configurations of ethnicity, and consequently the styles of material culture involved in the signification and structuring of ethnic relations, may vary in different social contexts and with relation to different forms and scales of social interaction. From an archaeological point of view the likely result is a complex pattern of overlapping material culture distributions relating to the repeated realisation and transformation of ethnicity in different social contexts, rather than discrete monolithic cultural entities. Patterns in the production and consumption of material culture involved in the communication of the 'same' ethnic identity may vary qualitatively as well as quantitatively in different contexts. Furthermore, items of material culture which are widely distributed and used in a variety of social and historical contexts may be curated and consumed in different ways and become implicated in the generation and signification of a variety of expressions of ethnicity.

The analysis of these contextual realisations of ethnicity, and ultimately the manifestation of ethnicity in the past, is not beyond the possibilities of archaeological interpretation. The systematisation and rationalisation of distinctive cultural styles in the process of the recognition, expression, and negotiation of ethnic identity are likely to result in discontinuous, non-random distributions of material culture of the type suggested by Hodder (1982b) and Wiessner (1983). However, in order to analyse such patterns in archaeological material it will be necessary to adopt a radically different framework for both classification and interpretation.

Most archaeological classification is ultimately based on the assumption that stylistic groupings are co-extensive with normative historical entities. Two particular principles are central: (i) that change in material culture is a gradual, regular process which occurs in a uniform manner throughout a spatially homogeneous area; (ii) that the prime cause of variation in design is the date of manufacture. Such an approach to classification presupposes a normative view of culture and produces what is essentially an illusion of bounded uniform cultural entities. Artefacts are extrapolated from their contexts of deposition, grouped together into predetermined classes of material and classified, spatially and temporally, according to the principles noted above. Such an approach obscures the kind of information which is of interest in the analysis of ethnicity (and arguably past cultural processes in general).

Ethnicity, amongst other factors, may disrupt regular spatio-temporal stylistic groupings, resulting in boundaries which are discontinuous in place and time. Yet in order to analyse such patterns it is necessary to consider artefact assemblages within a contextual framework, and to date assemblages, where possible, on the basis of independent methods and stratigraphy. Such an approach to the basic classification of material culture will enable the analysis of variation in the deposition and use of material culture in different social domains. Any distinctive non-random distributions of particular styles and forms of material culture in different contexts which emerge from such an analysis may plausibly relate to the expression of ethnicity. Yet a variety of factors may be involved in producing such variation, and it will be necessary to employ independent contextual evidence in the interpretation of ethnicity, as the significance of material culture in terms of ethnicity is culturally and historically specific (Hodder 1982d; Shennan 1989: 21; Wiessner 1989: 58).

Thus, a broad understanding of past cultural contexts derived from a variety of sources and classes of data is a necessary part of any analysis of ethnicity in archaeology. As ethnicity is a product of the intersection of the *habitus* with the conditions prevailing in any particular social and historical context, it will be important to have a broad understanding of such conditions, including the distribution of material and symbolic power. An adequate knowledge of past social organisation will also be important, as ethnicity is both a transient construct of repeated acts of interaction and communication, and an aspect of social organisation which becomes institutionalised to different degrees, and in different forms, in different societies.

Moreover, an historical approach will be particularly important given the role of historical context in the generation and expression of ethnicity. A diachronic framework may enable archaeologists to pick up shifts in the expression of ethnicity, and those dimensions of material culture which signify it, over time. Such shifts may involve greater or lesser fixity and institutionalisation of expressions of ethnic difference, and changes in the use of particular aspects of material culture in the signification of ethnicity. In short, the use of a diachronic contextual framework may reveal something about the contexts in which ethnicity is generated, reproduced and transformed; to examine 'the mobilisation of group as process' (Conkey 1990: 13).

Conclusions: discourses of history and place in the construction of ethnicity

> Ultimately, in the state-its conception of the nation, state and nation become one, an 'imagined community' that ignores the various nations/identities/histories it may include. To maintain this conception of the nation-state it is necessary constantly to stress the existence of only one possible cultural model, one history, one language, one social project.
>
> (Devalle 1992: 20)

In this essay I have argued that the very concepts used in the archaeological identification of past peoples are historically contingent (see also Diaz-Andreu, chapter 3; Hides, chapter 2 [both in original volume]). The concept of 'a culture' which has been embraced in archaeological epistemology, and its conflation with ethnicity, is the product of a particular ideology of cultural differentiation which emerged in the context of post-Enlightenment European nationalism. Cultures are considered to be bounded, continuous, unified entities, that bear witness to the existence of the nations which are their bearers. This conceptualisation of culture contributes to the assertion of a congruency between territorial contiguity and ethnic unity across an historical stage – a mosaic of discrete spatially and temporally bounded, monolithic entities. Such a conflation of social scientific and political ideological concepts serves to hinder the analysis of the real nature of the processes involved in the construction of ethnic and national identity (Llobera 1989: 248). Instead, the unfortunate implication is that social scientists (including anthropologists and archaeologists) may have developed paradigms 'to explain that which they have themselves created' (Bond and Gilliam 1994: 13; see also Handler 1988).

In some spheres of archaeology, culture history, and its equation of cultures with peoples, has been rejected (for a review see Jones 1994; Shennan 1989). However, a normative concept of culture still underlies much of archaeological description and classification (see Jones 1994), and ethnic groups are still considered to be bounded continuous, if dynamic, entities. The presupposition that an exclusive congruence exists between ethnic unity, territory and history remains intact, although more elastic (e.g., see Blackmore *et al.* 1979; Kimes *et al.* 1982). Drawing upon recent research, I have argued that ethnicity is a dynamic, contested phenomenon, which is manifested in different ways in different contexts, with relation to different forms and scales of interaction. Moreover, the representations of cultural difference involved in the articulation of ethnicity are transient, although subject to reproduction and transformation in the ongoing processes of social life. Such an approach to ethnicity challenges the assumption that bounded, homogeneous ethnic or cultural entities constitute the natural units of socio-cultural differentiation. Furthermore, it explodes the exclusive association of ethnic entities with a single, discrete, territory and history. From an archaeological perspective the material manifestation of ethnicity, amongst other factors, may disrupt regular spatio-temporal stylistic patterning, resulting in an untidy and overlapping web of stylistic boundaries in different classes of material culture and in different contexts; boundaries which may be discontinuous in space and time.

My aim has been to suggest alternative ways of conceptualising the relationship between history, place, and identity in archaeological theory and practice. Returning to the representation of European identities the argument presented here inevitably represents a threat to certain understandings of European, national and ethnic identity. As Boyarin points out in his analysis of Israeli nationhood:

> It seems almost gratuitous to state that my point is not to dismantle the state of Israel. But if the Israeli state, once established, is implicitly understood by its own elites as a static reality dependent on functional equilibrium, then a threat to any of its parts (including its self-generated history) is a threat to its very existence. Related to the equilibrium model is the image of the nation as an integral collective.
>
> (Boyarin 1992: 118)

It is necessary to challenge such static functional conceptions of cultural groups (whether they be ethnic, national or Europe-wide), and their self-generated histories, in order to explore the possibility of a plurality of histories and identities.

Ethnicity is not constituted by the historical legacy of a primordial, essentialist identity; rather, the formation and transformation of ethnicity is contingent upon particular historical structures which impinge themselves on human experience and condition social action. As Devalle (1992: 18) points out, ethnicity is an historical process, as 'time provides the necessary ground on which ethnic styles are maintained (recreated) and collective identities formulated' providing such identities with substance and legitimation. However,

> Being firmly grounded in the concrete history of a particular social reality, an ethnic style cannot be simply understood as the immutable and intangible 'essence' of a given people, or as a fixed sociological idealised type.
>
> (Devalle 1992: 19)

Archaeologists have tended to utilise such immutable 'essentialised' (Conkey 1990: 113) categories of ethnicity, leading to the projection of a modern classificatory framework onto all of human history. Instead, we need to develop theoretical frameworks that allow us to explore the ways in which ethnicity is manifested in particular historical contexts, and to explore multiple associations between kinds of identity and notions of time and place. Frameworks which will facilitate analysis of the multiple, twisted and discontinuous histories of the 'New Europe', rather than attempt to impose a linear, continuous and homogeneous past.

ACKNOWLEDGEMENTS

Many thanks to Andrew Crosby, Clive Gamble, Paul Graves-Brown, Claire Jowitt, Tony Kushner, Yvonne Marshall, Stephan Shennan, Cris Shore, Julian Thomas and Peter Ucko for their helpful comments on earlier drafts of this chapter. Of course any errors or deficiencies remain my own.

NOTES

1 The term discourse is being used here to refer to a clustering of ideas, an ideological configuration, which structures knowledge and experience in a particular domain, in this case in the construction of group identity.

2 Further expressions of this basic principle can be found in Childe (1929: v–vi and 1956a: 2), Hawkes (1940: 1) and Piggott (1958: 88).

3 This kind of temporal framework is what Fabian (1983: 23) identifies as 'typological time'.

4 The argument, that the representation of human groups as the bearers of bounded, monolithic cultures is a product of post-Enlightenment discourses of identity (in particular those associated with nationalism), is clearly supported by studies of cultural identity in the context of European colonialism (e.g., see Comaroff and Comaroff 1992; Fardon 1987). However, I do not support the related theory that ethnicity is an entirely modern phenomena. Instead I suggest that different forms of ethnicity are produced in different socio-historical contexts, and the nationalist conflation of political and cultural units (and the associated concept of culture as homogeneous, bounded and spatially contiguous) cannot be assumed to be a universal form of socio-cultural organisation. In fact, there are many examples to the contrary today (see Eriksen 1993), as there are in Medieval Europe (see Greengrass 1991) and other areas of the world prior to European colonisation (see Comaroff and Comaroff 1992).

5 Throughout the first half of the twentieth century a number of anthropologists expressed concern about both abstract and pragmatic definitions of the 'cultural' or 'tribal' entities which constituted the objects of their research (for example, see Fortes 1969). By the 1950s and 1960s critiques of the concept of tribe had emerged challenging the traditional assumption that social, cultural and political boundaries are commensurate with the boundaries of the tribe (for example, Leach 1954). Others indicated the pejorative connotations of the concept of tribe and suggested that the category, as well as its socio-cultural referents, were constructs of colonial regimes (for example, Colson 1968, Fried 1968). Sociologists also became increasingly aware of problems with the conceptual frameworks which dominated their discipline. In particular the presupposition that continuous cultural contact would lead to acculturation and homogenisation was challenged by the persistence of cultural difference and ethnic self-consciousness amongst minority groups. It is important to note that these critiques were connected in a plurality of ways with processes of colonisation and decolonisation in the 'third' world, as well as the increasing political salience of minority voices in 'western' countries.

6 If this argument is extended to national identity it contradicts Foster's suggestion that national culture and identity is 'doxic' in nature (1991: 240). In fact, Foster's own discussion of the contested and negotiated nature of many national identities and culture suggests that his use of Bourdieu's concept of 'doxa' is inappropriate, as does Eriksen's (1992: 3) analysis of Mauritian and Trinidadian nationhood, in which he states that in these two cases nationhood belongs to 'the sphere of opinion, not to that of doxa'.

27

TOWARD A CRITICAL ARCHAEOLOGY[1*]

MARK P. LEONE, PARKER B. POTTER, JR. AND PAUL A. SHACKEL

Critical theory is a set of varied attempts to adapt ideas from Marx to the understanding of events and circumstances of 20th-century life that Marx did not know. It began with the Frankfurt school of philosophy in the 1920s and was in large part an effort to explore and add to Marx's insights into the nature of knowledge of human society. Members of the Frankfurt group include Adorno, Horkheimer, Benjamin, and Marcuse; Lukács and Gramsci, although not representatives of the school, are also important. Critical theory has been applied to a variety of human sciences and humanistic disciplines and is now having an impact on archaeology in Britain and the United States. An important issue in critical theory is epistemology. As Geuss (1981: 1) argues:

> Marx's theory of society, if properly construed, does clearly give us knowledge of society, but does not easily fit into any of the accepted categories of 'knowledge.' It obviously isn't a formal science like logic or mathematics or a practical skill . . . yet neither would it seem to be correctly interpreted as a strictly empirical theory like those in natural science . . . Rather Marxism is a radically new kind of theory; to give a proper philosophic account of its salient features requires drastic revisions in traditional views about the nature of knowledge.

> Critical theory aims at 'producing enlightenment . . . enabling those who hold [it] to determine what their true interests are'. Its goal is emancipation from coercion, including coercion that is self-imposed. To this end, it is 'reflective'.
>
> (Geuss 1981: 2)

Critical theory has had substantial impact in law (Unger 1976); it has been applied in history (Eagleton 1985–86; Lowenthal 1985; Wallace 1981, 1984), the decorative arts (St. George 1985; Sweeney 1984), literature (Carravetta 1984), geography (Peet 1975, 1977; Peet and Lyons 1981), and museum studies (Baranik *et al.* 1977) and, of course, has been a part of the history and philosophy of science (Brannigan 1981;

*First published in *Current Anthropology* (1987), **28**(1), 283–302.

Feyerabend 1970; Latour and Woolgar 1979). Almost invariably, one of the reasons given for employing critical theory is to describe and deal with factors – social, economic, political, and psychological – that have been observed to influence conclusions and their social uses but that, under many ordinary rules of scholarship, should not be present.

Archaeologists are invited to consider critical theory by, for one thing, the fact that archaeological interpretations presented to the public may acquire a meaning unintended by the archaeologist and not to be found in the data. Leone's (1981a, b) analysis of the use of archaeology and history at Colonial Williamsburg and at Shakertown is part of a body of work (Clarke 1973b; Gero *et al.* 1983; Handsman 1981; Handsman and Leone n.d.; Kehoe 1984; Landau 1984; Lowenthal 1985; Meltzer 1981; Perper and Schrire 1977; Wylie 1985b) showing that, in contrast to the general perception among American archaeologists, archaeology in some environments in the United States is used to serve political aims. A further encouragement to explore a reflexive epistemology is the growing controversy in archaeology over ownership and control of remains and interpretations of the past. The reburial of human remains and 'repatriation' of some artifacts to native groups may be a political issue as well as a scientific one, as may be the use of preservation, including archaeology, to change the value of property in towns and cities in connection with changing the locales of different wealth and ethnic groups. Beyond these, and both less visible and more complex, is the effort by archaeologists in federal and state agencies in the United States to control the use and preservation of archaeological remains in ever greater areas, including private land. Ostensibly a neutral effort to protect a resource uncritically regarded as valuable, this inevitably raises concerns about monopolizing access to data and interpretations. It is clear, then, that the practice of archaeology is affected by political, economic, and social decisions. The claim of a critical archaeology is that seeing the interrelationship between archaeology and politics will allow archaeologists to achieve less contingent knowledge.

A central concept for addressing the relationship between knowledge of the past and the social and political context of its production is ideology. Critical theory uses 'ideology' in many senses (see Geuss 1981). We use it as it has been employed by Althusser (1971a) and introduced into anthropology by Barnett and Silverman (1979). Ideology in this sense comprises the givens of everyday life, unnoticed, taken for granted, and activated and reproduced in use. It is the means by which inequality, bondage, frustration, etc., are made acceptable, rationalized, or hidden. Ideology serves to reproduce society intact; knowledge, or consciousness of ideology, may lead to illumination or emancipation.

The concept of ideology has been employed in archaeology by Tilley (1982), Miller (1982a, b), Shanks and Tilley (1982), Shennan (1982), Miller and Tilley (1984a), Shanks and Tilley (1987a), and others in describing inequality. Inequality implies the alienation of labor – the use of goods or services without a full return of value to their producers. One word for this asymmetrical relationship is exploitation. Ideology hides and masks exploitation or rationalizes by naturalizing or supernaturalizing it. Ideology acts within a stratified or class society to reproduce inequality without serious resistance, violence, or revolution. In various senses, the term 'ideology' has been applied to the Bronze Age of northwestern Europe by Shanks and Tilley (1982) and Thorpe (1981), to the

Inca by Patterson (1984), to 18th- and 19th-century western Connecticut by Handsman (1980, 1981, 1982), to the Harappan civilization by Miller (1985b), and to 19th- and 20th-century industrial communities in Binghamton, New York, by McGuire (1988). All these examples are stratified societies with changing relations of wealth holding. In all cases, the resulting analyses order the data in a novel way and account for aspects that have sometimes been overlooked or considered puzzling.

Ideology, presupposing as it does contradiction, potential conflict, or periodic violence in society, is part of a set of assumptions that may be strongly at odds with the finished products of functionalism, systems theory, and much of ecological theory. The concern is not smooth functioning *per se* but how conflict and contradiction are masked or naturalized. The reconstruction of ideology in prehistoric, protoliterate, or extinct societies is possible, and it is valuable for addressing some archaeological data heretofore unexplained. Ideology is relevant to class stratification, wealth holding, and power relations, and, in general, its study may illuminate what is already known of past societies. We argue that this is an extension into archaeology of critical theory.

Critical theory asks of any set of conclusions from what point of view they are constructed. The question is intended to help establish their degree of validity. To require that studies of the past provide knowledge of current circumstances or illuminate obscure relationships today would risk the subordination of the past, but Lukács (1971) does provide useful instruction on bridging the gap between historical knowledge, often disembodied, and his vision of the historian's obligation within the framework of critical theory. As he sees it, the task of the historian is to illuminate the roots of modern ideology – to identify the mystified relations between classes and agents, to show how that mystification is maintained through ideology, and to give a history to the ideas used in its maintenance. These ideas include, for example, the idea of an objectively separate past and the idea of the person as an individual or as possessing personal freedom. Ideas like these have active power. Once they are seen as ideological, notions of the past, of the individual, or of personal freedom can no longer be taken as timeless givens. They can be given a history, placed in context, and shown to be politically active, and this procedure may produce illumination. We feel that this logic can be worked out in a convincing way for some of historical archaeology; whether it can be done for prehistory is an open question.

A critical archaeology retains and reaffirms the discipline's commitment to understanding the past, but what past to construct becomes a matter of conscious choice that inevitably involves an understanding of context and meaning. These terms, now so much used in symbolic anthropology and by Hodder (1982a, 1984b, 1985), do not mean the same thing to everyone. For the critical theorist, ideology provides much of the meaning in a society, although not all meaning is necessarily ideology. Because it is not epiphenomenal, a mere reflection of other realities, but central to maintaining the status quo in stratified societies, it is considered active or recursive, analogous to language in its formative qualities. This may add an important dimension to the New Archaeology's definition of material culture. Critical theory is materialist, but our use of it rejects the ranked order of causal relationships of White, Harris, and Vayda. The philosophers who initiated critical theory sought to integrate the notion of consciousness into epistemology and thus to create both a convincing and an active link between material reality and an awareness of it.

Our exploration of a critical approach takes place in the context of a broader understanding of the role of positivism in the discipline. Positivism, an approach that seeks more reliable knowledge of the past by stressing the relationship between scientific statements and their testing, has come under criticism for frequently producing knowledge so narrow as to seem irrelevant (see, e.g., Hodder 1984b, 1985; Wylie 1985a). For Wylie, whose lead we tend to follow, positivism is not therefore to be abandoned but rather to be adjusted to the realities of archaeological data. We acknowledge that positivism and critical theory in archaeology have not yet been synthesized, and we do not attempt a synthesis here. We do suggest that a critical archaeology may produce more reliable knowledge of the past by exploring the social and political contexts of its production.

The way in which critical theory can be applied to archaeology may be illustrated by an analysis of 18th-, 19th-, and 20th-century data from a citywide project conducted in Annapolis, Maryland. From its inception, this project, called 'Archaeology in Annapolis', aimed at demystifying archaeology, teaching about how a past is constructed, and discovering how the past was used locally so as to understand local ideology and identify the aspects of it that need illuminating.

Critical theory and the ethnography of Annapolis

When 'Archaeology in Annapolis' began in 1981, as a collaboration between the University of Maryland and Historic Annapolis, Inc. (a private, state-chartered research-oriented preservation organization founded in 1952), it was recognized that Annapolis was not just an old and well-preserved city but also a historic one. Because Annapolis had considered itself historic since at least the 1880s it was possible to do an anthropological analysis of its histories, and this effort has shown how political factors have been embedded in the city's presentation of itself over the last 100 years. Given this, we assumed that archaeological findings would not exist in a vacuum but would be assimilated into the community's understanding of its own past. For this reason, and because of our critical approach, the research program and the associated museum program[2] had to be rooted in the interests and conflicts of the community in which they were to take place. Consequently, the project has had an ethnographic component from the outset.

The ethnographic research, conducted by Potter, flowed from the assumption that, for as long as it has considered itself historic, Annapolis has structured a past for itself that aids and legitimizes its contemporary activities. Potter's first step was an examination of a wide variety of presentations of the past in Annapolis.[3] Particular attention was paid to the separations (Barnett and Silverman 1979) imposed on the past that were treated not as constructs contemporary with the composition of a history but as given or quasi-natural categories. Many of these separations play strategic roles in underpinning the balance of power in Annapolis today.

Annapolis is a small (pop. *ca.* 32,000) but complex city. It has a municipal government, is the seat of Anne Arundel County, is the capital of Maryland, and is the location of the United States Naval Academy, a federal institution. Its economy revolves around state government, the Naval Academy, tourism, and yachting, categories that are not mutually exclusive.

The city was founded around 1650; Maryland itself was founded in 1634. The capital of Maryland was removed from St. Mary's City, in the southern part of the colony, to Annapolis in 1695, and the city was chartered in 1708. It experienced what it calls a 'golden age' of wealth and fame from about 1760 until the end of the American Revolution. During this period it was the social, political, and economic center of the Chesapeake Bay. The end of its 'golden age' coincided with two events that took place in the Maryland State House at Annapolis: on December 23, 1783, George Washington resigned his command of the Continental Army (a move designed to subordinate military to civil authority), and on January 14, 1784, the Treaty of Paris with Britain was ratified, officially ending the American Revolution. After the Revolution, Annapolis remained the capital but became a regional market town as many of its wealthiest residents moved to Baltimore and invested in that city's rapid expansion into an international commercial and industrial port.

In 1845 the United States Naval Academy was founded in Annapolis, but for the most part throughout the 19th century the city was in what one writer termed 'gentle eclipse' (Norris 1925). The 1950s saw the beginning of a commercial revival based on yachting, tourism, and new highways that made Annapolis an attractive suburb for Washington, D.C., less than 30 miles away. Historic preservation has played a major role in Annapolis's commercial renaissance. It is this basic outline, or part of it, that is conveyed to the public by tour guides, guidebooks, and historic-house museums as the history of Annapolis.

Potter's initial lead was his sense that the history of Annapolis as presented to tourists in the city today is a series of fragments. History is recounted by a wide range of groups and institutions, some overlapping, some in competition, some in cooperation. More important, there is no history of Annapolis that demonstrates how all the different parts of the city fit together. The city is presented as a collection of unconnected units (time periods and institutions). Left unconnected are the black and the white populations, on the one hand, and the city and the United States Naval Academy, on the other.

In Annapolis, black history is presented separately from white history. By segregating the races temporally (white history is 18th-century history and black history is 19th-century history), history in Annapolis, written almost exclusively by whites, imposes a frame of reference that ignores the principal historical relationship between blacks and whites in Maryland and the rest of the southern United States: slavery. This in turn makes it difficult for slavery to be seen as antecedent to relations between the groups today. It also prevents blacks from using slavery as a reference point in comparing their present with their past.

The same kind of logic works with the relationship between the city and the United States Naval Academy. There is ample basis for presenting the city and the academy either as historically connected or as historically separate. The choice of the city's historians is made clear by the title of one influential history: *Annapolis: Its Colonial and Naval Story* (Norris 1925). The mixing of categories in the title is instructive. Norris's subtitle could have been *Its 18th- and 19th-Century History* or *The History of the City and the Naval Academy*. By mixing temporal and institutional terms, he reinforces the identity between city and 18th century, academy and 19th century. Detailed analysis shows a consistent presentation of the city as 18th-century (or, as its residents say, 'ancient'), brick, small, slow, evocative, and associated with white residents and the academy as 19th- and 20th-century, granite, fast, scientific, and associated with the white transients who are its students and the black residents it employs. Against these separations are the extensive historical and contemporary connections between the city and the academy, among them the city's economic dependence on the academy and the academy's numerous expansions into the city.

Separations represented as accurate historical interpretations of the past are presented to residents and visitors as data about the past, but they conceal politically live conflicts between institutions and groups in the contemporary city. It is our hypothesis that these conflicts, should they be discovered in the historical presentations and used as a basis for action, would pose threats to competing political forces: city government, Naval Academy, preservationists, and minorities. These forces and the separations that hide their real relationships are important and meaningful to contemporary Annapolis.

To summarize, the major separations in Annapolis are 18th-century: 19th-century, white:black, Historic District:Naval Academy, residents:visitors. An overarching separation which unifies the rest is insiders:outsiders.[4] This separation, too, is grounded in history. The history of the city's relationship to the outside world is one of self-imposed subservience. Annapolis worked hard to have itself made the capital of Maryland (Riley 1976 [1887]: 57). It tried and failed to become the permanent capital of the United States just after the Revolution (Riley 1976 [1887]: 198–200). The Naval Academy was founded there after the city had carried on a 20-year courtship to get it (Riley 1976 [1887]: 264). In the late 19th century the city mounted a largely unsuccessful campaign to lure business and industry to Annapolis (Riley 1976 [1887]: 323–4; 1897; 1901; 1906). Finally, Annapolis in the 1980s works to promote itself as a yachting and tourist centre, a part being played in this by the historic preservation movement. In each of these cases, Annapolis has invited outsiders in and profited by doing so while presenting itself as a stable, historically significant resource not especially dependent on outsiders.

While the analysis of the white:black and city:academy separations is based primarily on *how* history is presented in Annapolis, the analysis of the resident:visitor separation depends more on *what* is presented. Much has been made of George Washington's 20-some visits (Baldridge 1928; Historic Annapolis, Inc. n.d.; Norris 1925: 191–224; Riley 1976 [1887]: 200–207, 218–20; Thomas 1952), and in presentations of his connections to the city Washington the Father of His Country is overshadowed by Washington the horse fancier, patron of the arts, and partygoer, in short, Washington the tourist. Potter's hunch is that from the example of Washington visitors learn how Annapolis wishes them to conduct themselves during their stay in the city. They should be wealthy, fashionable, considerate, and social, and they should return home leaving just enough of their 'aura' to attract others like themselves. Washington is a model of the perfect outsider.

The ethnography just summarized serves as a guide to what an archaeological program based on critical theory should teach the 5,000–10,000 people a year who visit the open archaeological sites in Annapolis. Since 1982, 'Archaeology in Annapolis' has addressed two of the separations identified through archaeological excavations open to the public.

In the spring of 1985, archaeologists conducted a tour of the State House Inn site.[5] The purpose of the excavation was to gather fine-grained information about the city's 290-year-old street pattern, called the Nicholson plan, and the history of changes in it. Participants in the tour were told, to begin with, that there are two ways of looking at the city's baroque street plan of two circles and radiating streets laid out by Governor Francis Nicholson in 1695: as a work of art, an unchanged relic of the 1600s, or as continually altered and adjusted to meet the needs of people living and working in Annapolis over the centuries. The reason for digging at the State House Inn, it was explained, was that comparisons between the earliest known map of Annapolis (the Stoddert survey of 1718) and modern maps showed that State Circle, on which the inn was situated, had been reduced by 30–60 feet without any record of the changes. The archaeological evidence for the shrinkage of State Circle was then pointed out: two cuts into the natural subsoil that may represent edges of earlier, larger circle diameters and a row of postholes near one of the cuts that may have been the line of a fence serving as a boundary between a larger State Circle and a yard (Hopkins 1986). It was suggested that data from the State House Inn site would be combined with information from other sites around the circle, such as the Calvert House site (Yentsch 1983), to produce a more complete and cumulative picture of all the small alterations that have added up to a wholesale difference between the 18th-century State Circle and the State Circle of today. From small-scale alterations to the Nicholson plan such as this one, the presentation went on to a description of the largest alteration to the 18th-century street pattern, which was made by the United States Naval Academy in 1906 when it walled itself off from the rest of the city and created its own street plan. It was pointed out that roads and town plans carry information intended to direct the behavior and thought of people who use them. The academy's replacement of the 18th-century elements of the city with a plan of its own was part of a larger attempt to make the academy appear separate from the rest of the city while in fact there were many powerful connections between the two. The tour showed how one may see the streets of Annapolis as ideology, as masking a significant and potent reality.

To illuminate the separation between residents and visitors and at the same time to process archaeological data in a way that revealed the details of 18th-century life, materials from the Victualling Warehouse site, the Hammond-Harwood House site, and the Thomas Hyde House site (193 Main Street) have been analyzed[6] and incorporated into the presentation at the last, an 18th-century work and domestic locale. We hypothesized that the increasing variation found in the ceramic assemblages at the 18th- and early 19th-century sites in Annapolis is a reflection of increasing participation in the culture associated with mercantile capitalism. A colonial city characterized by importing, exporting, merchants, planters, manufacturing, and consumption of a wide range of mass-produced goods should be characterized by increasing segmentation and standardization of many aspects of daily activity (Braudel 1979a: 207; 1979b: 377-78; Deetz 1977, 1983; Detweiler 1982: 24–25; Smith 1937[1776]: 3–13). We postulate that the growth of mercantile capitalism that we know characterized Annapolis in the 18th century (Carr and Walsh 1977; Papenfuse 1975; Middleton 1953) is associated with the standardization of life's domains, on the one hand, and the increasing interchangeability of things, acts, and persons, on the other. We argue that segmentation and standardization in ceramic use in Annapolis accompany an etiquette associated with the accumulation of profit. Both segmentation and standardization will be reflected in the material culture used in many aspects of daily life, including the table and its setting, as people are incorporated into the life of capitalism (Braudel 1979a: 203–9).

Deetz (1977) and Carr and Walsh (n.d.; Walsh 1983) have argued that during the 17th-century people in Anglo-America lived a less differentiated way of life, one characterized by mechanical solidarity in Durkheim's sense. Eating, sleeping, and other activities tended to occur in a single room. Members of a family would eat sitting on beds, chests, or benches drawn up to a table. One trencher or one mug was used by several persons. Table forks, spices, and imported ceramics were luxury items seen only in wealthier households. In the 18th century the parts of everyday life became more differentiated from each other, with performance being defined by place, rules, tools and audience. New rules for behaviour that separated people developed and were written down (Braudel 1979a; Deetz 1977, 1983; Glassie 1975). Braudel (1979a: 203–9) cites *Les délices de la campagne* (*The Pleasures of the Countryside*) by Nicholas de Bonnefons, published in 1654, as one example. It recommends that places at the table be spaced at a distance of a chair's width and specifies the number of courses to be served, the changing of plates at the end of each course, and the replacement of napkins after every two courses. This trend is observed in probate inventories of 18th-century Annapolis (Shackel 1986a). Items of dining defined by rules that segmented the dinner table into many parts (salad dishes, tureens, dish covers, plate warmers, pudding and custard cups, bottles or cruets for serving condiments, butter boats, and wineglasses)[7] occurred exclusively among the wealthy until the third quarter of the 18th century. At this point, consumption patterns changed drastically (Carr and Walsh 1977: 32–33; Walsh 1983), and many segmenting items began to be used on all wealth levels except for the lowest.[8]

Segmentation of tasks, standardization of products through mass production, and standardization of productive behavior through rules came to permeate everyday life in Annapolis in the course of the 18th century. Archaeologically, we know that work was first separated from domestic activities in the home space, then moved to a different building or area, then transferred to an entirely different part of Annapolis by the early 19th century. Braudel (1979b: 377-78) suggests that such segmentation accompanies a profit-making order. We argue that greater variety in sizes and types of dishes, which measures both segmentation of people while eating and segmentation of food in courses and by type, is also a measure of the larger process at work in mercantile society.

The three sites we examined varied in socioeconomic characteristics. The Victualling Warehouse site was a middle-wealth-group commercial-residential structure, the Hammond-Harwood House site an upper-wealth-group home, and the Thomas Hyde House site a merchant's business and home, owned by a man who had climbed from the lowest wealth group in the 1740s to the upper wealth group by the third quarter of the 18th century.[9] To determine whether a new order of behavior was visible archaeologically, we examined the variety of recovered ceramic types and plate diameters over time.[10] The formula (type-sizes/types) (sizes) = index value was developed to quantify the variation in each ceramic assemblage. 'Types' is the number of standard ceramic types (e.g., porcelain, pearlware, creamware), 'sizes' the number of different plate diameters (rounded to the nearest half-inch), and 'type-sizes' the number of type-and-size combinations represented. Therefore, in the hypothetical assemblage of Table 27.1, with a 7-inch and a 9-inch pearlware plate, a 4-inch and a 9-inch whiteware plate, and an 8-inch porcelain plate, there are three types, four sizes, and five type-sizes. According to our formula, $(5/3)(4) = 20/3$ or 6.67 as a measure of variation. Values of this kind from different sites or different strata at the same site can be compared to measure changes over time and differences between wealth groups. A value close to 1.0 indicates low variation, greater values increasing variation. The data from the three sites were divided into early–18th-century, mid-to-late–18th-century, late–18th-to-early–19th-century, and mid–19th-century, and the indices of variation calculated for each set suggest that the residents of all three sites were participating increasingly in a standardized and segmented way of life (Table 27.2). The greater variety of dish sizes and wares in the archaeological record reflects a new etiquette, an increasing segmentation at the table that served both as a training ground for the new order and as reinforcement for it.

Table 27.1 Variation in a hypothetical ceramic assemblage

	Plate diameter (inches)					
Ceramic type	4	5	6	7	8	9
Porcelain	–	–	–	-	×	–
Pearlware	–	–	–	×	–	×
Whiteware	×	–	–	–	–	×

Table 27.2 Variation in ceramic assemblages from three Annapolis sites, early 18th to mid-19th century

	Period			
Site	Early 18th	Mid– late 18th	Late 18th– early 19th	Mid 19th
Victualling warehouse	n.a.	3.6(n=572)	12.0 (n=1,698)	n.a.
Hammond-Harwood house	n.a.	2.0 (n=122)	27.0 (n=926)	n.a.
Thomas Hyde house	1.0 (n=22)	2.0 (n=37)	24.5 (n=76)	73.1 (n=368)

An archaeological site tour informed by critical theory

Visitors to Annapolis interact directly with archaeologists involved in excavating materials related to the past. Not all of the sites being excavated in Annapolis (about 70 since 1981) are open to visitors, but those in the heart of the tourist area (6 since 1982) have been. Tours of some sites are given on demand, with as many as 40 per day on a busy day at a busy site, and the average number of visitors per tour is about five. The tours are intended to teach participants how to question and challenge their guides and others who create, interpret, and present the past. Each open site has its own presentation. In consultation with a media expert,[11] the following basic structure has been developed: (1) welcome, (2) introduction of the archaeologist-guide, (3) introduction of the archaeological team, (4) introduction of the project, including sources of funding, (5) introduction of the specific site, (6) discussion of archaeological techniques, (7) anthropological content or argument, (8) conclusion, and (9) question period (see Leone 1983; Potter and Leone 1986, 1988).

During the summer of 1986, excavations were conducted in a parking lot on Main Street[12] that until the 1930s had contained the two-and-a-half-story house of Thomas Hyde. The argument at the site was as follows:

Now that I've told you about who we are and how we dig, I'd like to tell you about why we're digging here.

As I mentioned a few minutes ago, one important class of archaeological finds is ceramics. Most ceramic tableware used in this country through the first half of the 19th century was made in England, and since we know when these items were made, we can use fragments of them to help us date archaeological sites.

But ceramics are useful for more than dating. There was a revolution in the manufacture and marketing of English earthenware ceramics led by Josiah Wedgwood in the middle of the 1700s. Wedgwood and others developed materials and techniques that allowed the mass manufacture of relatively inexpensive tableware in matched sets. Before the middle of the 1700s ceramic items usually didn't come in sets and were generally used communally, several people eating from one vessel and sharing another for drinking. The Wedgwood revolution changed all that. Wedgwood introduced plates that allowed each diner to have his or her own plate identical to those of the other diners. He also created sets of dishes which included many different sizes and shapes of vessels for different courses. A proper set of dishes had soup plates and breakfast plates and dessert plates and butter plates, in addition to regular dinner plates. And so on.

We feel that the use of a fully elaborated set of dishes, then as now, was not simply a matter of manners, unconnected to the rest of life. In the elaboration of sizes and shapes of dishes is a dual process of both segmentation and standardization. Separate plates separate the diners at a table from each other along with the use of proper manners – using the 'right fork' and so on. Manners and dishes provided clear rules and divisions which told and showed individuals how to relate to each other. The meal became segmented here by 1750, and the rules for eating segmented society by separating people.

Meanwhile, the process of segmented labor and mass production which standardized dishes standardized many other kinds of manufactured goods as well. The plates whose sherds we are digging up here served to regularize the eating behavior of those who used them, and at the same time the regularity was the product of both a regulated manufacturing process and a regulated life for the workers who made them. Much of material culture was being standardized, and much of human behavior. These ideas are worth our attention because, while they were new in the middle of the 1700s, many of them are still with us today and are taken for granted as ways we assume the world has always operated. And if we take these things as givens, we forfeit the opportunity to understand their impact on us or to change them. This is how we think about the ceramics we dig up.

These ideas about segmentation don't just have to do with dishes. Just as individual plates and specialized serving dishes separated foods and diners, houses came to have more and more rooms, with different activities being performed apart from each other in separate rooms. Before 1700 many work-related and domestic activities took place in the same room of the house. By 1750 people were building houses with separate rooms for eating, sleeping, cooking, and working. And the richer folks, like those in the Paca and Brice Houses, carried this even further with music, card, and ballrooms. Dishes and eating were segmented; houses and domestic life were segmented; so too were lives segmented into work life, social life, and family life. In the early 1700s work and domestic activities usually all went on in the same place. By 1800 in Annapolis people divided work from home life by preferring shops, taverns, and offices in separate buildings from their homes. Houses like this one we are excavating were used only for domestic life by 1800. By the time large-scale manufacturing began in Baltimore in 1850, work was located far from home, and the distance got greater and greater.

We think that people learned how to divide their lives and accept the divisions and the rules for division at home at the table and at all the other tasks which were also becoming separate.

So far I've talked about several different separations beginning to enter American life in the 1700s. I would like to turn to one final separation, that between work time and leisure time. This segmentation of time creates the possibility of something that many of you may be involved with right now, a vacation. Bear in mind for the next few minutes, if you would, that this particular cultural invention, the idea of a vacation, only entered American life about 100 years ago, about 100 years after Thomas Hyde built his house on this site.

Vacations and tourism are a major industry and a big issue in Annapolis, as in many other small historic towns. Each year over 1,000,000 people visit Annapolis, a city of only about 32,000 people, so it is easy to understand the city's interest in paying close attention to tourism here; the city works hard to protect the things about it that attract visitors. As I said, the need to control a large influx of visitors is not at all unique to Annapolis. What is unique is one part of Annapolis's solution to this potential problem.

In some very subtle ways, Annapolis attempts to use George Washington to guide visitor behavior. For as long as the town has considered itself historic, local guidebooks and histories have included many references to George Washington and his 20 or so visits to the city. In many of these accounts there is a strong emphasis on the social and domestic aspects of Washington's visits to the city: his trips to the race-track, the balls he attended, the plays he saw, and the family members and friends he visited. The picture of Washington that emerges is very similar to the profile of the kind of visitor Annapolis has very publicly said it wants to attract, the 'quality tourist'. As defined during a local election campaign and since then in the local papers, a 'quality tourist' is one who spends some money in town without disrupting anyone or anything or leaving a mess behind. The effect of presentations of Washington that make him look like the kind of visitor that Annapolis tries to attract today is that Washington ends up as a model tourist or a model for tourist behavior. What makes this subtle and unaware portrayal of Washington as a model tourist so interesting is that tourism and vacations were not even invented until 80 years or more after Washington died. George Washington could never have been a tourist because tourism as we know it, apart from the Grand Tour, did not exist during his lifetime.

In the last 15 minutes I've tried to do two things. By discussing the origins of some taken-for-granted aspects of contemporary life, separations and segmentation, I have tried to show that our way of life is not inevitable; it has its origins and its reasons, and it is open to question and challenge as a result. The second thing that I've tried to do, through the George Washington example, is to show ways in which history is often made and presented for contemporary purposes. The next time you see a presentation of history, visit a museum, take a tour, watch a television show about the past, or whatever, you can ask yourself what that version of history is trying to get you to do.[13]

This is the kind of presentation given at each of the six open archaeological sites in Annapolis.[14] Each presentation ends with a statement about the relevance of the past to the present by addressing one of the separations, such as insider:outsider, that was uncovered by the ethnography of uses of the past in Annapolis. Each presentation also includes a statement of our hope that the tour has helped people become more critical of presentations of the past. This fulfils one requirement of a critical archaeology: illuminating elements of daily life that are normally concealed. Whether illumination should lead to social action to address the contradiction masked by ideology is an open question.

The final step in making the project one of critical archaeology is assessment of the impact of the tours on participants. There are many informal measures, mostly adapted from museum evaluation procedures, of the degree to which messages are understood. One of these is the number of questions asked by visitors at the end of a tour. We record visitors' questions and comments, thus treating the open archaeological site as an ethnographic context. It is not at all uncommon for visitors to return to sites a second, third, or fourth time, demonstrating their understanding of the sites as continually changing educational environments. Visitors sometimes return to a site with friends for whom they act as guides; such visitors have certainly been enfranchised.

Since 1982, a one-page evaluative questionnaire has been distributed to visitors at the end of a tour. Respondents are self-selected, and the sample is about 10% of the visitors to any one site, a large sample compared with those used in most museum evaluations (Zannieri 1980: 7). In addition to questions that visitors answered simply by selecting responses from a list, we have asked questions requiring short written answers. One such question, used in our evaluation form at the Shiplap House site,[15] that generated many informative responses was 'What did you learn about archaeology that you did not know before you visited the site?' Responses to this question fall into three broad categories:

1   Responses that show visitors realizing that archaeologists dig to answer questions, implying an understanding that archaeological data, like any historical or scientific data, are collected from a particular point of view – one of the most important and most accessible insights of critical theory.

2   Responses that show visitors recognizing that archaeology is about more than excavation, discovery, and artifacts. Someone who claims to have learned about the 'connection of archaeology to behavior' may well have learned how to challenge the traditional popular perception that archaeology is about objects. The ability to challenge a taken-for-granted understanding is the very ability we hope to cultivate in visitors and have them apply to other aspects of their lives.

3   Responses that show visitors understanding archaeology as relevant to today. At one level, such responses are like those previously discussed in suggesting an ability to challenge the idea that archaeologists dig up old things unconnected to today by anything other than their curio value. However, in the context of our tour of the Shiplap House site, which deals with the origins of some typically unexamined aspects of contemporary life, acknowledgement of archaeology's relevance to today may indicate a willingness to challenge the inevitability of some of the foundations of contemporary life.

These characterizations of visitor responses to our tours are extracted from over 1,000 evaluations we have collected in five seasons. Several broad conclusions may be drawn from this body of data. First, we do not have to talk down to visitors; we can discuss ideas rather than trowels, stratigraphy, potsherds, or holes in the ground. In addition, that a surprising number of visitors are willing to write long and detailed responses to questions on the evaluation form means that people see the site as an educational setting and are willing to let us teach them rather than simply entertain them. Moving from the practical to the theoretical, it seems clear that visitors see historical archaeology as able to teach them about the roots of contemporary life. However, when visitors say that archaeology is relevant to today because it shows 'the continuity of evolution into our own day' they demonstrate, in addition to the dawning of critical awareness, the strength and embeddedness of the concept of evolution as a cultural metaphor for long-term change. Because the concept of evolution makes change seem inevitable and its direction beyond human agency, providing histories for separations may not be enough to make local ideology challengeable. To bring about the kind of enlightenment aimed at by critical theory, we need to pay attention to how people think and not just what they think. From visitor evaluations we have learned both about the possibility of imparting to visitors a critical perspective and about the obstacles to their embracing it. We have not yet solved all the problems of mounting a public program based on critical theory, but the demonstrated willingness of visitors to let us teach them and their ability to learn constitute an invitation to keep on trying.

NOTES

1   This paper is based on the results of excavations and/or interpretive programs at five archaeological sites in Annapolis. All have been conducted by 'Archaeology in Annapolis', which is co-directed by Richard J. Dent (University of Maryland College Park), Mark P. Leone and Anne E. Yentsch (Historic Annapolis Inc.). The project is a 10-year, citywide research program sponsored jointly by the University of Maryland and Historic Annapolis Inc., a 35-year-old private non-profit preservation organisation for Annapolis and Anne Arundel County. In addition to their support and funds from the city of Annapolis, 'Archaeology in Annapolis' received grants from many sources for the excavation and interpretation of these sites. The Victualling Warehouse site is owned by the state of Maryland and managed by Historic Annapolis Inc.; funds for its excavation and interpretation came from the Maryland Humanities Council (Grants 546, 601-E, 738-F) . Work at the Hammond-Harwood House was conducted by Historic Annapolis Inc., under contract to the Hammond-Harwood House Association, owner of the property. The State House Inn is owned by Paul Pearson and Historic Inns of Annapolis, and work there was funded in part by the National Geographic Society (Grant 3116–85). The Shiplap House is owned by Donald O. Jackson and work there was supported by the Maryland Humanities Council (Grant 780-G). The Main Street site is owned by a partnership headed by Paul Pearson and this partnership and the Maryland Humanities Council (Grant 842-G) supported the work there. Other interpretive work, which has led to the perspectives developed in this paper, has been supported by the Maryland Heritage Committee and the National Endowment for the Humanities (Grant GM–21645–83). Although Historic Annapolis Inc., a non-profit educational and preservation organization founded in 1952 to preserve the National Historic Landmark District of Annapolis and its history, has provided funding for and shared its research findings with 'Archaeology in Annapolis', the opinions and theories of the authors do not necessarily reflect the views of Historic Annapolis Inc.

2   'Archaeology in Public', the program of public interpretation for 'Archaeology in Annapolis', consists of four elements, in four media, which may be experienced in any order: (i) 'Annapolis: Reflections from the Age of Reason', a 20-minute, 12-projector computer-synchronized audiovisual production, (ii) *Archaeological Annapolis: A Guide to Seeing and Understanding Three Centuries of Change* (Leone and Potter 1984b), a 24-page guidebook to one part of the Historic District of Annapolis, (iii) a 15-minute tour of a working archaeological site given by an archaeologist and (iv) three small archaeological exhibits located in museum buildings around the district. The audiovisual presentation is about ways of understanding the increasing segmentation and standardization of material culture in 18th-century Annapolis as these are related to profit making. The guidebook leads the reader to eight spots and at each shows how historical interpretations in Annapolis have changed – and continue to change – with changing political concerns. The site tour, discussed in detail below (and see Leone 1983- Potter and Leone 1986), focuses on archaeological logic or method and on the connections between the aims of the archaeological work and political issues in Annapolis today. The artifact exhibits (see n. 13) display our understanding of material culture as recursive.

3   Potter's ethnographic database includes 4 book-length histories of Annapolis, 20 historical guidebooks and picture books, a half-dozen major historical re-enactments and special tours, two dozen historical talks, tours, and minor events, a half-dozen formal interviews, the products of participant observation in the downtown Historic District for over three years, and several hundred hours of informal but intensive and engaged interaction in the local historical preservation community.

4   The classification of people associated with the academy as 'visitors' is obvious; some teachers, most administrators, and all students pass through the academy on tours of duty lasting about four years. Further, in the description of contemporary Annapolis that begins his influential history of the city, Stevens (1937) says that the best time to visit Annapolis is during Naval Academy

Commissioning Week, the academy's graduation, because then the old town comes to life. He says it is at its best when it is filled up with the families and girlfriends of graduating midshipmen. The transformation of black residents into 'visitors' is less obvious, but Stevens points the way. In the course of only about 30 pages, he refers to a black neighborhood as 'Ethiopia' and a black taxi driver as 'an ancient Senegambian'. The effect, if not the intent, of linking blacks to African countries is to make them 'visitors', or at least not original residents of Annapolis. By making groups associated with the academy and blacks into 'visitors', those who wrote and used history in the city attempted to define themselves as 'residents', thus strengthening their claim to local political power to have itself made the capital of Maryland (Riley 1976 [1887]: 57). It tried and failed to become the permanent capital of the United States just after the Revolution (Riley 1976 [1887]: 198–200). The Naval Academy was founded there after the city had carried on a 20-year courtship to get it (Riley 1976 [1887]: 264). In the late 19th century the city mounted a largely unsuccessful campaign to lure business and industry to Annapolis (Riley 1976[1887]: 323–24; 1897; 1901; 1906). Finally, Annapolis in the 1980s works to promote itself as a yachting and tourist center, a part being played in this by the historic preservation movement. In each of these cases, Annapolis has invited outsiders in and profited by doing so while presenting itself as a stable, historically significant resource not especially dependent on outsiders.

5 Excavations at the State House Inn site were supervised by Joseph W. Hopkins, III (University of Maryland, College Park), assisted by Donald K. Creveling (University of Maryland, College Park) and Paul A. Shackel. The site tour was conducted by Pamela Henderson and Kristen Peters for more than 4,300 visitors between April 22 and June 1, 1985.

6 The Victualling Warehouse site was excavated under the direction of Constance A. Crosby (University of California, Berkeley) during the summers of 1982 and 1983. The excavations at the Hammond-Harwood House site were supervised by Richard J. Dent (University of Maryland, College Park) during the spring of 1983 and the spring of 1984, assisted in the second season by Robert C. Sonderman. Excavations of the Thomas Hyde House site in the winter of 1985–86 and in the summer of 1986 were directed by Paul A. Shackel, assisted by Dorothy Humpf (Pennsylvania State University) and Lynn Clark (State University of New York at Binghamton) during the summer of 1986. The measurement of ceramic sherds on which the analysis was based was done by Raymond Tubby, Diana Kehne, and Theresa Churchill (University of Maryland, College Park).

7 This inventory of elements of leisurely dining was compiled by Lorena Walsh of the Colonial Williamsburg Foundation. Its use in Shackel's analysis was suggested by Lois Green Carr of the St. Mary's City Commission.

8 These changing consumption patterns were products of improved transportation, marketing, and technology (Carr and Walsh 1977; Walsh 1983: 113) as well as a new, routinized type of labor.

9 The Victualling Warehouse site lies within the commercial district of Annapolis close to the harbor. From the middle of the 18th century until 1790, the site contained two structures used for commercial and residential purposes. Both structures burned on January 21, 1790. One was rebuilt shortly thereafter, while the other was demolished at about the same time (Crosby 1982: 1–3). The fire provided a firm chronological control for our analysis.

The Hammond-Harwood House is a five-part Georgian mansion designed and built by William Buckland between 1774 and 1775 for Mathias Hammond. This site was excavated in stratigraphic layers (Dent 1985) that provided the basis for chronological control.

The Thomas Hyde House was a Georgian-style brick structure built in the 1760s in the heart of the social and political center of the city. The site contained numerous outbuildings including a summer kitchen, a milk house, and privies. The house had been constructed upon an earlier structure dating to the first quarter of the 18th century. This site was also excavated in stratigraphic layers (Shackel 1986b), allowing for chronological control and facilitating comparison with other sites.

10 Our analysis is both experimental and preliminary. Because minimum vessel counts have not yet been done for these sites, the data are in terms of sherds only. Ezra Zubrow (State University of New York at Buffalo) helped write the formula that measures variation.

11 The media consultant is Philip Arnoult, director of the Theatre Project in Baltimore.

12 The public program at the Thomas Hyde House was directed by Patricia A. Secreto (University of Maryland, College Park) and Christine Hoepfner (University of Pennsylvania). Along with Samuel T. Brainerd, Lynn Clark, Teri Harris, Bill Helton, and Anne A. Tschirgi, they conducted the tour there from July 10 through August 16, presenting it to over 3,800 visitors.

13 In addition to the tour at the Thomas Hyde House, visitors in 1986 were invited to visit three archaeological exhibits, to which they were directed by a flier. Archaeologically recovered toothbrushes were on display in the Historic Annapolis, Inc., tour office in an exhibit designed and written by Paul A. Shackel. The exhibit was intended to demonstrate the increasing standardization of the manufacture of toothbrushes during the 19th century while at the same time explaining that increasing use of toothbrushes and other items of personal hygiene signaled an increasing self-regulation and adherence to rules for behavior on the part of Annapolitans. (In addition to toothbrushes excavated in Annapolis, this exhibit contained three toothbrushes on loan from the Baltimore Center for Urban Archaeology.) A second exhibit, designed and written by Christine Hoepfner, focused on tea wares excavated from Annapolis sites. A third exhibit, also mounted by Christine Hoepfner, contained ceramics from the Thomas Hyde House site and was a demonstration of the ceramic analysis just described. Visitors were directed from any one exhibit to the others by a series of fliers designed and written by Christine Hoepfner. Each of these fliers also served to reinforce the message of the exhibit at which it was available, rephrasing it and presenting quantitative data that could be examined later.

14 For the purposes of this essay, the site interpretation is presented as if archaeologist-guides were the only source of information; in fact, it was split between an oral presentation and four 400-word placards posted on the site.

15 Excavations at the Shiplap House site were supervised by Donald K. Creveling, assisted by Paul A. Shackel. The site tour was directed by Nancy J. Chabot (State University of New York at Binghamton), assisted by Kristen Peters. They, along with Simon Coleman, Matthew Johnson, Barbara Lichock, Barbara Ray, Ellen Saintonge, Patricia A. Secreto, Helen Sydavar, Raymond Tubby, and Patricia Walker, gave tours to over 5,800 visitors. Along with the tour, an eight-page brochure, designed and edited by Nancy J. Chabot and Parker B. Potter, Jr., was used to present the interpretation of the site.

28

THIS IS AN ARTICLE ABOUT ARCHAEOLOGY AS WRITING*

ANTHONY SINCLAIR

The text has become a metaphor by which we might understand the role of interpretation in individual action and the relationship of individual action to the larger structures in which it occurs. More recently this concern with the creation of meaning has moved to one of understanding the texts which we ourselves write. Anthropologists, in particular, have examined the way in which fieldwork accounts are written, exploring how their textual structures do not simply translate the other world but actively create an understanding of it in the mind of the reader. Fieldwork accounts exist within genres, structures of (written) expression related to specific historical conditions, both within the discipline and the wider arena of the Western capitalist system itself.

In this paper I shall consider a number of themes. I begin with a rapid look at nature of interpretation in anthropology and the relationship which has been drawn between interpretation and the status of the text. This draws largely on recent work by anthropologists. Following this I shall attempt to consider what this offers for archaeology. I shall argue that although much of this work is undoubtedly of relevance (and, thus, in some senses analogous) to archaeological writing, it is very much tied into particular problems and concerns of anthropology, which are not, *de facto*, those of archaeology. Archaeology is a tremendously varied discipline both in its subject matter and in the ways in which it produces its knowledge. As a result it is often significantly different from anthropology. This variation, though, is something which archaeologists could exploit and through which they could explore a number of different approaches to writing which do not simply echo those of social anthropology. As an example of this I look at writing from the perspective of structured learning and argue that it can be considered as a form of perception, with a number of concomitant effects. Such an approach takes us beyond an obviously genre-centred work and urges us to consider some of the more unconscious effects of our production of knowledge which like the examination of particular genres can be an important part of the search for 'critical self-consciousness' so important to archaeology since the time of Clarke (1973a).

*First published in *Archaeological Review from Cambridge* (1989), **8**, 212–33.

The thick and the thin; producing descriptions

Interpretive anthropology has argued that culture should be conceived of as a 'web of significance which people spin' (Geertz, quoted in Scholte 1986). People act in a certain way because of the association between meanings and actions. Anthropological fieldwork, therefore, does not just involve the recording of physical actions but attempts to understand the reasons that people have for acting as they do. 'The trick is not to achieve some inner correspondence with your informants . . . [it] is to figure what the devil they think they are up to' (Scholte 1986: 6).

This process is made most clear in the distinction which Geertz has drawn (following the philosopher Ryle) between 'thick' and 'thin' description (Geertz 1973c). As an observer we might notice that an individual has closed one eye. We might record as a 'twitch', a physical action. This would be *thin* description. On the other hand, we might consider that this is not simply a physical action; it is an act of communication, designed to achieve an effect. As such it is an element within a system of communication, where such elements take/are given their meaning through their relationship to other elements within that system. We could, therefore, record this movement not as a closing of the eye but as a 'wink'. This would be *thick* description. To describe thickly is not just to describe physical actions in great detail; it is to uncover the conceptual structures on which people draw and on which actions are based. It is to look at their symbolic content, and, thus, to plunge deeply into people's lives.

So far so good. Such interpretive approaches portray subjects as acting rationally (thoughtfully and consistently on the basis of some previous structure of ideals), and yet at the same time manage to account for action that might appear to us, as 'outside' observers, incomprehensible. From here, though, the problem changes. It now becomes a matter of attempting to convey this understanding of 'otherness' to a 'foreign' audience. This is done through the ethnographic fieldwork account; a monograph in which the participant observer, the anthropologist, writes up these thick descriptions and in so doing translates their 'otherness' to an audience.

All just a matter of difference?

The situation changes immediately once writing is involved. We pass from the interpretation of observed communication to one where communication is indirect, through the medium of the written text. It is written text which causes problems. It is here that we need to understand the difference between text, textuality and the matter of distance between reader and writer (see Hanks 1989). For 'text' we may understand 'any configuration of signs that is coherently interpretable by some community of users' (ibid.: 95). 'Textuality', on the other hand, is 'the quality of coherence and connectivity that characterises a text' (ibid.: 96). Between speech and writing there is a difference in the relationship between text and textuality.

The work of de Saussure has emphasised the way in which meaning within language is conveyed not through the referential quality of words themselves, but rather through the differences between words. Moreover, each word (signifier) has no necessary relationship to that to which it refers (the signified). The relationship between the signifier and the signified is, thus, arbitrary. Adequate meaning is conveyed through an understanding of the choice of a word in relation to other possible words (the context).

During speech, the boundaries and the structure of this difference can be made clear by the speaker. Meaning is continually reinforced through non-verbal means of communication (Miller 1989) whether it be a shrug to convey ignorance, or the lifting of an arm to indicate direction. It is also immediately possible to clarify meaning (to supply context and coherence) when it is felt by the speaker that the intended meaning has been misunderstood. This is not to allege that misunderstanding is impossible; but rather that the close nature of the physical contact is such that spoken communication is in many ways saturated with meaning. This situation no longer exists when communication takes place indirectly through writing.

When communication takes place through writing, the nature of language (the differential basis of meaning) takes its toll on the clarity of the intended meaning. When reading (interpreting) a written text there is not the degree of direct communication that takes place during speech. Ambiguities, for example, cannot be immediately clarified. Moreover, if one follows Derrida (1988a), problems lie not just at the level of interpreting the coherence between words, but even at the level of the word itself. For Derrida, there can be no necessary tie between a signifier and its signified. Language is, therefore, made up solely of signifiers and meaning is in reality forever absent, dispersed in the never ending stream of signifiers. Such a point of view suggests that the text can have a new meaning at every reading.[1]

Despite its logical consistency, practice suggests that this is an overstatement. The very fact that Derrida would appear to be able to communicate his views seems to undermine his position.[2] This leaves a problem; how is it that meaning would also seem to be conveyed? Here we must look more deeply at the structure of the text. Through the structure employed, the limitless dispersion of meaning is managed. Difference itself is contained and context is supplied. In the employment of a particular form of textuality, authors play a game; they develop a strategy such that they encourage/constrain the reader to understand the text as they do. The structure of the text is this strategy. Although it is clear that a full context can never be supplied within the text (and therefore, the reader draws upon personal knowledge/context to complete it), the text is likewise never completely open.

We might appear to have wandered some distance from the matter of interpretation, with which I started. However, it is precisely the effects of textual strategies which have recently preoccupied anthropologists when looking at their own written work. Although anthropology had obviously been concerned with the way in which individuals and groups interpreted events and actions, it had overlooked the manner by which this understanding had been conveyed. It was assumed that fieldwork accounts told it 'as it was', once the anthropologist had understood what was going on. The fieldwork account itself, was simply a matter of 'translation'[3] (Asad 1986). However, when the textual strategy employed is examined, this notion of translation seems very misleading.

Textually-aware anthropologists have set themselves the task of exploring strategies used in the representation of the anthropological fieldwork encounter. One of the aspects of this work has been to show that there are genres of anthropological writing. For instance, one particular genre, used by Anglo–American anthropologists writing in the middle of the twentieth century, they have termed 'ethnographic realism' (Marcus and Cushman 1982). I shall look at two (of many) areas where it has been suggested that fieldwork accounts written within this genre are misleading, as an example of the problems identified by anthropologists using this manner of representation. These concern the practical nature of fieldwork and the subject matter of anthropological research.

Since the work of Malinowski, anthropological understanding has been achieved through 'participant observation', by which the observer learns the ways of a society through direct observation and participation. This term, 'participant observation' suggests that anthropologists understand societies on the basis of their *own* observations and understandings. In other words, access to the cultural 'web of significance' is open to the observing anthropologist. For example, when describing the Balinese cockfight, Geertz notes how the anthropologist is left to 'read the text [by which he means the way in which individuals interpret the pre-given structures of their own society – a metaphor for reading a text] over the shoulders' (1973c: 449) of the people taking part.

According to Clifford (1980), however, this is not the case. Anthropologists figure out 'what the devil they [the members of a society] think they are up to' with the help of informants. Such knowledge is properly thought of as data, 'things given' (Clifford 1980: 528). Therefore, anthropological knowledge is not purely anthropologists' knowledge. It is, amongst other things, the product of a complex relationship between anthropologists and their informants. Of crucial importance here is that informants, themselves, are a part of a society, and thus the knowledge which they convey can only be that which they themselves have access to.[4] Their information is clearly partial, as they are particularly placed members within that society.

It is argued, though, that this relationship is rarely mentioned in anthropological texts.[5] In his classic work on the Nuer, Evans-Pritchard (1940) fails to represent the diversity of Nuer society, through his textual strategy, by ignoring the relationship between himself and his informants. They appear (all of them) the same (Spencer 1989: 153). When anthropological informants are given some textual recognition, it is often at the very beginning of the work and in a manner which reinforces the apparent validity and objectivity of the observers' remarks (see Rosaldo 1986). The body of the text can then occupy itself with presenting the society (the whole society). Recent anthropological writings have attempted to recognise this aspect of knowledge production and portray it more accurately within the body of the text, making clear their informants and their relationship with them (see Rabinow (1977) for an example). Others have apparently gone further and structured the text in the form of a dialogue, so that the information *given* is made clear (see the works by Crapanzano (1980) and Shostak (1983) for examples of this technique).

Turning to the subject matter of anthropological research, the genre of the fieldwork account presents a society, 'as it is'. The time and place of its production (in relation to other anthropological texts or changes within the discipline itself) are unimportant/marginal. However, anthropology is a developing discipline where the foci of interest are always changing. As data and theory are inextricably inter-related, so the information learned during one piece of fieldwork is always different – even when conducted within the same society and by the same person (see Caplan (1988) for a discussion of this). Likewise, the information sought is often that thought by the anthropologist to be most relevant to the society from which s/he comes. This is not simply a problem of ethnographic realism. For example, the work of Margaret Mead on life in Samoa (1949) emphasising the greater equality of sexual relations can be read as an allegorical critique of contemporary American society. The same can be seen in the work of Shostak on Nisa, a !Kung woman, who in telling the story of her life (the book is presented in the form of dialogue), reveals the communality of the shared female experience (Clifford 1986b: 109). This link between theory and data through the medium of the anthropologist is passed over in the genre of the ethnographic text. By examining the allegories that structure many anthropological texts, anthropologists have recognised the political and ethical dimensions that lie behind their work (ibid.: 111).

'Ethnographic Realism', as a genre of anthropological writing and, therefore, of anthropological representation is misleading. Amongst other things, it misrepresents important aspects of anthropological fieldwork. In attempting to simply convey the meanings, for Western readers, through which a society 'works', to present a picture of how a society 'really is', it has denied and masked its very own social and political context of production. What can be learned from this is not simply that ethnographic realism is wrong. Much more important is the way this work reveals that textual representations are also productions. In their representation of the 'other' they also create other meanings. This has important consequences for the validity of any representation, observed through anthropological fieldwork.

Textual criticism in anthropology has been primarily directed towards the representation of the anthropological encounter. The encounter acts as a fulcrum on which other issues can be made to revolve. Epistemologically, critique has focussed on the transient and subjective status of knowledge when considered as the product of participant observation. Whilst, from an empirical point of view, anthropologists have stressed the ways in which particular reports and their associated genres have structured a view of anthropological understanding which can be considered misleading.

Despite the possibility that much of this work has lapsed into a (self-)obsession with writing *per se* (Scholte 1987; Spencer 1989) and is itself a strategy for gaining/maintaining power within the discipline (Scholte 1987),[6] it is clearly tied into a particular problematic faced by anthropologists concerning the way in which the discipline should develop, given that anthropologists can no longer consider themselves separate from the people whom they study. Their writings represent people who are still alive. Anthropologists affect these people through their work and, thus have a responsibility towards them. This has become clear through the relationship between anthropology and colonialism (see papers in Asad 1973). Textual criticism, therefore, has been used to study the power relations behind the encounter and the production of the written representation of this (see Asad 1986; Rosaldo 1986 and Spencer 1989). Much experimental writing has been framed so that it tries to allow normally 'observed' people to, in fact, speak through anthropologists for themselves. This should be the real role of anthropology according to some (Spencer 1989: 161).

Anthropological writings and archaeological practice
While archaeologists have not, as yet, produced such a developed literary/textual critique of their own works, similar problems of misrepresentation have already been

noted (Burtt 1987). It is argued that archaeological works have been written from an apparently objective (and detached) point of view when, in fact, they represent particular theoretical political positions. Given the current polarity between processual and post-processual approaches, it is understandable that post-processual criticism has likened and described many genres as cases of 'positivist/empiricist discourse' (Shanks and Tilley 1987a: 23).

Not surprisingly, aspects of this critique have been much influenced by contemporary anthropological discussion. For example, the archaeological site report, as currently written, has been criticised for the way in which it misrepresents the nature of archaeological practice (Hodder 1989c; Tilley 1989a).[7] The report follows a genre that is designed to convey an impression of archival status and detached objectivity (Shanks and Tilley 1987a: 15–19) presenting the data just as it 'comes from the ground', ready (and willing) for any later interpretation that may use it. What it ignores is the way in which a site is actually understood, the dialogue and the categorisation that takes place between all those involved in excavation and interpretation. The modern site report, therefore, appears to misrepresent the archaeological fieldwork 'encounter' as much as 'ethnographic realism' masks that of anthropology. It is, similarly, the product of personal opinion and judgement; it comprises 'data given', in the sense used by Clifford (1980), even though this 'giving' might not be between subject and object of analysis. These criticisms give the impression that the use of a narrative structure, taking the form of (reported?) dialogue, would convey this aspect of archaeological work (it could represent it more accurately.[8]) This has even been suggested (Hodder 1989c).

By appealing so closely to previous anthropological work, archaeologists would seem to be not only using it as inspiration but suggesting that archaeology shares exactly the same problematic. There are, indeed, situations which are clearly analogous and which could be examined in the same way. The most obvious is the attention which (Western) academic archaeology needs to pay when representing the (pre-)history of indigenous peoples. In the matter of aborigine land-rights in Australia, the reburial issue in general and the representation of the American Indians (see Trigger 1980b), archaeological practice and representation clearly have a direct effect on the people represented and still living. The indiscriminate use of ethnographic analogy within an evolutionary context is another such area. Paralleling the !Kung to the early African hominids denies their own history. But much archaeology is clearly not so directly analogous.

The people of the past whom archaeologists represent are not affected by their representation. Their current non-existence makes such effects impossible. As a result there can be no necessary responsibility to the observed (of the past) as there is in anthropology to their observed (in the present). Our responsibility can only be a present affair, whether this be formed as a striving for academic objectivity or the desire to recognise the political nature of most academic archaeological communication. This is certainly the case for archaeological work which has concerned itself with the problems of textual representation. This work has concentrated upon the links between archaeological representations and aspects of the contemporary world, particularly as seen through the power relations which structure the production of archaeological texts.

The genre as a tool of criticism is both appropriate and problematic. Like many aspects of structuralism, it works by setting up a synchronic structure (a timelessness) in which the various elements within it can be seen as related to some more internal (archetypal?) structure. This approach, however, encourages us to ignore history (somewhat surprisingly for a discipline whose main advantage is often seen as its historical time frame). The categories that are employed in our present genres of writing, whether problematic or not, have a history. They have been developed previously. In this way the past directs the present, unconsciously or consciously, because the categories which we use in the present bring with them meanings and emphases which they have accrued in the past. In this way we never write as though for the first time, but always within an historically placed time. If we are to understand fully the complexity that lies behind our genres we need to give consideration not only to the relationship between the genre and present-day activity, but we also need to consider closely the way in which genres have been determined by ones previous.

In this vein I would suggest that we need to consider written texts through a more historical perspective than our current genre-based approach allows. We need to understand the history behind the categories which are the building blocks of any genre. One way of doing this is to consider our representations of the archaeological past not just in their own synchronic time frame, but all together *diachronically*. In so doing, we should concentrate on how categories which are the basis of our own representations and understandings change (these give some clue to changes in our perception/understanding of an other and construction of meaning). There is a need to explore the way in which we amplify certain aspects and in so doing pass over others. In exploring this idea I draw heavily on ideas presented by Don Ihde.

Instrumentality and the construction of knowledge

In *Technics and Praxis*, Ihde focuses upon the 'hermeneutics of perception' (Ihde 1979). He is particularly interested by the way in which we get to know an other when knowledge of that other is provided by means of an instrument. The key problematic for Ihde concerns the question of the transparency between the instrument, the observer and the world observed, which can be examined by looking at the nature of the relationship between the observer and the world as mediated by the instrument. There are two basic types of relationship of perception according to Ihde; the 'embodiment' relationship and the 'hermeneutic' relationship (ibid.: 13).

In the first relationship, the instrument is effectively transparent. We might imagine in the place of such an instrument a magnifying glass. It is a part of the observer and not of the 'world'. It may magnify the world, but that world is unmistakable the same world that would be perceived without the aid of the magnifying glass. Indeed, around the edges of the glass the world is still very much the same. This relationship, the 'embodiment relationship' can be described thus;

$$(\text{Observer} + \text{instrument}) \longleftrightarrow \text{World}$$

At first sight it might appear that such a relationship encompasses the manner of perception of all instruments; but this is not the case. According to Ihde, instrumental perception spans a continuum of observer–world relationships. At one end are instruments which involve 'embodiment relationships'. At the other end of this continuum are those instruments which radically transform the world. When we use instruments of this type we observe not the same world as we would without their aid, but a new world, a world that has been created by the instrument. This relationship he calls an 'hermeneutic relationship' and can be described thus;

Observer ⟵⟶ (instrument + World)

There are two particular effects created by the hermeneutic relationship that Ihde draws special attention to. These are the effects of 'amplification' and 'reduction'. Amplification occurs when particular features of the observed world are enhanced beyond 'normal'. This may extend to the point where they become so important that they are almost the whole new world in itself. An equal corollary of this effect of amplification is the effect of reduction. As aspects of the world are enhanced and structure the new world, so other features are reduced and become invisible in the newly observed world. This hermeneutic relationship is therefore, significantly different to the embodiment relationship of other instruments.

An example of an instrument which creates this kind of relationship is that of the scanning electron microscope, or particular forms of colour biased photography. Although, in principle, through these instruments one is seeing the world as it is, the actual world that is observed is completely different. The new observed world is structured along a new axis of observations which transform it. This situation is even more dramatic when one thinks of the observed world created by radio–astronomy and in practical archaeological work, the same effects are created by the methods of magnetometer and resistivity survey methods.

In some senses, the split between the embodiment and the hermeneutic relationship is unreal. They both stand at either ends of a continuum of relationships of perception. Despite this continuum, though, the difference between the two ends is such that it is worth considering them as separate.

Ihde's work concerns itself with the immediate effects of technical equipment when used as a means of perception. I wish to use it as inspiration for a more diachronic approach. Instrumentality might appear to bear no relevance, and thus validity, to the study of written texts. Indeed, it does not provide a tremendously useful model for exploring the nature of the genre, for example. But if we move aside from the genre and consider writing within the context of learning, with which texts are intimately involved, then it is, perhaps, relevant. We perceive the archaeological record through previous work which gives it structure. When analysing archaeological texts, we can explore the changes in the categories used as though they were a means of perception which is developing. They are evidence of the way in which the outside world has been structured. Through time changes in this structure have cumulative effects and these transform the perceived world. As time passes, our means of perception (continually learned through exposure to texts), becomes less like a magnifying glass and more like the electron microscope, giving particular emphasis to one feature out of a previously greater number. We, thus, perceive the archaeological record in a manner which resembles Ihde's hermeneutic relationship, amplifying certain aspects and reducing others.

To illustrate this I shall use a body of writings which I currently know best. These writings concern the Palaeolithic period, and in particular the Palaeolithic in France.

I have divided these works into four ideal episodes of writing; those of the de Mortillets, Breuil, Bordes and Binford. They can be looked at together where one period of writing sets up a series of observations which structures that of later writings. Over the longer term a particular world is created/amplified through this self-reinforcing pattern of observation. Although each period of writing can be considered within the framework of a genre, over the longer period an hermeneutic relationship develops.

The first episode is that of the writing of the brothers de Mortillet. Their work begins with a classification of the materials within the museum at St. Germain in Paris in 1867. It represents one of the first pieces of 'archaeological' work, along with the work of Thomsen and others. It is, however, clearly inspired by palaeontological and geological ideas and methods. Fossils are identified, in palaeontological fashion, which can be used to give identity to epochs. For such a method to work it is important to concentrate upon forms that change and their manner of change. For the Palaeolithic, these fossils take the form of 'tools', and the epochs and the tools take on the same name. This research method, therefore, combines both palaeontological methods with archaeological materials. It is given material embodiment in the form of the museum. The work of the de Mortillets clearly parallels that of other early 'archaeological' workers.

In its textual form, the work of the de Mortillets (1903) is a straightforward translation of the museum to the format of the book. *Le Musée Préhistorique* is intended to fulfil the role of a portable museum (1903: 5). In so doing it is a combination of text and illustration on facing pages; both of which are equally important. Stone tools are 'displayed' in illustrations much as were the artefacts themselves in the cabinets of the museum. Likewise the artefacts chosen to be illustrated are those considered to be the best and most typical (1903: 6). The text is minimal, closely aligned to the illustration opposite and acting as though it were a kind of museum label describing the object. The book itself is layered like time. As the numbers progress on the pages so the march of time, represented in the changes of the fossils, passes by.

Looking at the work of Breuil (1912), typical of the work before the Second World War, we can see differences and developments. Textually the work is significantly different. It is much more modern in feel, like a product of current academic discourse. Names and bibliographic references abound. Most strikingly different is the relationship between the text and the illustrations. The illustrations now play a secondary role to the text enhancing the importance of the text and thus the importance/authority of the author, who no longer reveals the obvious but has to interpret it. This is given further weight by the fact that the illustrations are not referenced within the body of the text. They are not, however, totally without importance. They are constructed in such a way that they illustrate the inherent development ('evolution') of the forms of artefacts between earlier and later variants. Artefacts, thus, appear to follow an inherent logic in their transformation (suggested previously by the 19th-century, German art historians Semper and Golle (Podro 1982, Chapter 5)), something which does not appear in the work of the de Mortillets at first. Most clearly the illustrations of Breuil parallel those of Pitt-Rivers in his work on *The Evolution of Culture* (Pitt-Rivers 1875; reprinted in Thompson 1977, Appendix II).

If we now turn to the work of Bordes, the situation is yet again different. François Bordes is famous, amongst other things, for inventing 'La Méthode Bordes' and encouraging its widespread use in the study of stone tool assemblages. It is the relationship between this method and the perceived object of analysis on which I shall concentrate.

'La Méthode Bordes' (Bordes 1950, 1953; Bordes and Bourgon 1951) is avowedly scientific. Judgements are made on the basis of an accurate and statistically based assessment of the evidence. Description is formal, standardised and explicit. All the tools within an assemblage are named on the basis of an explicit, illustrated type-list (Bordes 1961).[9] Tools are perceived both as individual types and also the members of larger groups of tools with aspects in common (for example scrapers or burins). On the basis of this information, it is possible to examine how many examples of specific types are present, as well as the numbers of tools within each group. Such information can be plotted graphically in the form of the cumulative percentage graph (for the individual tool types) and the bar chart (for the larger families of tools). The same method was applied to both the tools of the Middle and the Upper Palaeolithic.

Textually the work of Bordes reflects this concern with formality and the truth of the statistical method, that his method attempts to engender. Tables detail accurately the actual pieces found within a site, set out according to the order of the type list. Discussion centres upon the evidence itself and remains impersonal. More importantly the illustrations reveal that the 'truth' about tool assemblages is to be found not in their appearance but in their relations as revealed by the cumulative percentage graph. Assemblages of tools can be compared without ever looking at a tool itself. The type profiles of these assemblages have in effect become the assemblages themselves, along with the indices that put numbers to the specific genera of tools.[10]

With the arrival of Binford, and the New Archaeology, the pattern of writing changes. His initial work (Binford and Binford 1969) is similar to that of Bordes in style, if not in content. Collections of tool types are statistically manipulated. Illustrations are graphic in form and the manner of writing is impersonal. The then overt concern with hypotheses and testing is to some extent paralleled in the text where the theory and its associated hypotheses are set out at the beginning and then followed up with empirical examination later on.

The real differences, though, appear when he criticises this manner of working on the basis of his own experience gained during a period of ethnographic fieldwork among the Nunamiut of Alaska. Following this study, his work is expressed in a curious manner akin to a mixture between ethnographic realism and general scientific statement. Binford's authority in this work is gained not through statistical rigour, as previously, but from the fact that he was 'there', living with a group of hunter-gatherers (see the introductory chapter to *Nunamiut Ethnoarchaeology* 1978a). Yet this personal knowledge (ethnographic data in Clifford's sense, 1983) is rendered impersonal and timeless as generalised statements (printed in italics) that utter 'truths' about hunter-gatherer life which are then illustrated/proven with personally observed detail. Particular examples of this approach concern the preparation of tool kits (Binford 1977b) and the role of mental templates in the making of 'men's knives' among the Alyawara of Australia (Binford 1985).

I have passed over the work of these authors all too rapidly. The work is more varied than it has been made to appear and I have selected but a few (hopefully typical) examples within this repertoire. Each of these periods of writing is worthy of examination as a genre, in the sense used by literary critics and anthropologists. As such, each deserves a greater depth in its analysis than I have found the space to give.[11] Textual criticism of these genres, though, is not my purpose in this section. Although these episodes of writing can be profitably considered as genres, worthy in their own right of investigation, they can also be considered diachronically/historically using the ideas of Ihde.

For the sake of brevity, I shall concentrate upon just one example; the way in which the profound variability (and hence ambiguity in an interpretive sense) present in all lithic collections is gradually controlled. Meaning is given and formalised to the extent that the stone tools themselves are no longer what is observed but rather the profiles of assemblages on graphs and the indices of particular families of stone tools types.

The work of de Mortillet, evidences the first aspect of this fixedness. The palaeontological method used requires fossils which can demarcate periods. This directs attention to visible pieces which change through time (to the fossil directors, which still provide the foundations of contemporary study of the Palaeolithic succession). The structure of the work by the de Mortillets then makes sense; the emphasis upon particular forms and the use of the best examples of pieces to play the role of archetypes. The ordering of this work also results from the manner of perception. The different periods are linked to each other through the natural likeness of one group of fossils to another. In this way the de Mortillets saw a natural progression from the Mousterian industries as exemplified by the Mousterian point (a bifacial point-shaped implement) to the Solutrean (with fine bifacial leaf-shaped points) to the Neolithic industries (as represented by the fine bifacial flintwork of the later dagger imitations). It did not seem to matter that stratigraphically this succession was incorrect.

In the work of the Abbé Breuil the single period-related fossil directors recognised by de Mortillet are developed, through extension to other elements within the industries, to become a sort of 'group fossil director', an element which we would recognise as the archaeological culture. In this work we see a steady process of amplification of the concerns set out by de Mortillet. The elements of Breuil's work and his approach directly stem from de Mortillet. The emphasis is once again on stability, punctuated by moments of evolutionary change. Moreover he works on the units already created by the previous work. In so doing Breuil also emphasises formal design over manner of production, all of which contributes to the loss of utility of stone tools. The Palaeolithic group fossil becomes the unit itself. It is easy to understand in this context the development of the textual approach of Burkitt (1933), accounting for the history of the Upper Palaeolithic in terms that would not be out of place in a history of the great barbarian invasions of the beginning of the 1st millennium AD (Burkitt 1933). The invasion text is a direct product of the developing characterisation of units of archaeological analysis.

With the work of Bordes, the process of amplification increases still further. Ironically we know that Bordes himself was well aware of the variability in lithic assemblages and their manner of production as a result of his personal experience of stone tool manufacture. He acknowledged that there can be different levels and scales of variation.

Yet his method and its textual representation deny this, especially when practised by others. The standardisation of names within the format of a typology continues the denial of variation at an individual level. Tools are still examples of some more basic changeless pattern. Whilst the use of the method of the cumulative percentage graph restricts observation to a strict area of difference within the assemblage; the percentage presence of tool types. At another level it also takes perception further away from the assemblage in its original form. Attention can now be directed not to the stone artefacts themselves but to their traces on a paper graph. This directs a whole genre of articles which discuss lithic assemblages at the level of their differences as traces on cumulative percentage graphs. Following the emphasis upon consistency, there are also naturally, of course, archetypal cumulative graph profiles.

This, then, is the actual process of amplification in Ihde's terms. The original emphasis upon markers of periods (itself determined by the prevailing palaeontological approach to understanding a material record through time) is steadily amplified so that all elements are seen in this light. There is also a move away from considering the assemblage in its entirety. Another aspect which is amplified is the desire to study tools in terms of their formal design and dimensions as opposed to their manner of production.[12] It is only more recently with an emphasis upon technical systems that this bias in perception (this reduction) has been tackled.

It is interesting to go beyond this discussion and look at some of the 'side-effects'. For instance, it can be argued that directing our attention to the tools which change, in fact, has had the effect of emphasising the importance of a particular aspect of lithic assemblages and through this a particular view of Palaeolithic prehistory. For the Upper Palaeolithic the elements which change most are projectile points. Aspects of the 'Perigordian', the 'Solutrean' and the 'Magdalenian' of the French Upper Palaeolithic, not to mention the Mesolithic, are all defined on such points. Projectile points are always associated with men, the mighty hunters. (The title of the *Man the Hunter* symposium volume (Lee and DeVore 1968) has been noted for a long time as evidence of this.) The humble scraper, that never seems to change is associated with women, whose role, therefore, remains the same through time. Moreover, the study of the Palaeolithic subsistence economy, which is so often used as a means of defining the important moments of change in Stone Age prehistory more often than not refers to the study of *hunting* techniques. For example the change from the early to the Later Upper Palaeolithic is defined on the basis of the appearance of specialised hunting techniques and the use of upland areas for resource acquisition. It is easy to draw a parallel to the denial of time to the American Indian (Trigger 1980b; Wolf 1982) and the consequences which this has had for their prehistory. From here it is but a small step to the unforeseen side of Marx's statement that 'Men make their own history' (Marx 1950). They certainly appear to do so in the Palaeolithic.

Such an analysis of writing is clearly not textual in the sense employed by anthropologists. It does not pay specific attention to word order and textual structure, and the power relations involved in the production of the text are not the key problematic. What I have tried to show is that writing cannot only be treated in such a manner. When it is approached through other perspectives, in this case that of the diachronic effects of perception, other not necessarily conscious features become clear. For writings about the Palaeolithic, each successive genre has inherited and amplified a particular perception of its material. It is these perceptions which are then embodied within genres of representation. A genre is essentially a created synchronic structure, a particular form abstracted from a continuous process. The categories used within any genre, however, have a history. Treating the text as evidence of patterns of changing perception helps to identify the continuous thread of history that passes through and beyond the individual genre. To focus upon the text simply in terms of the immediate conditions of its production is to engage in a dramatic process of amplification (and reduction), just as outlined above. It is a particular perception of the text.

Blurring the genres?

In a somewhat prophetic essay, Clifford Geertz argued that the boundaries between many of the disciplines in the social sciences were beginning to break down, as the rigid distinction between subject and object in analysis eroded and recognition arose of the role of subjectivity in analysis (Geertz 1973a). The current concern with writing and the status of the text is one such area where practitioners of the disciplines are finding common ground.

There seems little doubt that the attention recently given to the text is beneficial. It broadens the types of explanation that we offer and enables us to develop more coherent accounts of social action than previously possible within the frameworks of explanation of the positivist/empiricist approaches (such as New Archaeology in archaeology) and even their immediate structuralist 'descendants'. It is also a clear area where the social sciences have begun to blur. Textual criticism is just one facet of this blurring. It represents perhaps the most powerful means that is available to explore the links between theory and data, and the political/epistemological consequences of this relationship (the inherent subjectivity that resides in the act of explanation and interpretation).

A matter which needs further consideration though, is whether the genre as a tool of analysis should be the only means by which archaeologists explore their writings. (Is discussion of the effects of genres of writing common to 'textually-aware' criticism itself about to be encrusted into a genre?) The genre as a means of analysis is quite appropriate to the problematic within which anthropologists find themselves. There is a very real emphasis upon the present time brought about by the concurrent existence of both anthropologists, the people they observe and the people who read the representations which anthropologists write. The study of the power relations behind the production of the text are highly relevant to considering the role of anthropology in the anthropological encounter. Whilst aspects of archaeological practice face problems which are clearly analogous to those encountered by anthropologists, there is no overriding reason why we should restrict ourselves to just that perspective, other than the feeling, derived from our observation of what is happening in anthropology, that textual criticism is simply the identification and criticism of genres. The blurring of disciplinary genres should not render them indivisible.

One of the ways by which we can and need to broaden our approach is to examine our writings from a more historical point of view, using a more hermeneutic understanding of perception and its associated effects as a means of understanding the development of categories which comprise the building blocks of our genres. We need to look carefully at the ways in which these categories have developed through time examining the particular aspects that get amplified and those that are reduced. Such an approach would enable us to grasp more clearly the latent assumptions that lie behind our words, the unconscious structuring, which we inherit. Clearly it cannot replace an examination of the power relations that lie behind the text in the present, but it adds the greater and needed depth that is lacking at the moment.

Part of the importance of the recent focus upon writing and textual structure has been the attention it has drawn to our own role in producing an image of the past. It clearly represents a central part of what Clarke called 'critical self-consciousness' (1973b). Without a sense of history, though, there is a danger that what will be emphasised is the self. Genres are as much a product of their past as of the relations of power involved in their present production. We need to consider just as much their history if we are going to be critical as well.

ACKNOWLEDGEMENTS

I would like to thank Simon Coleman for useful criticism concerning my all too limited understanding of the nature of social anthropology and for inspiration concerning the title of this paper, as well as John Carman and Mark Edmonds for useful comments on earlier drafts. I am indebted to Christopher Evans for drawing to my attention the neglect of illustrations in current writings on textuality.

NOTES

1 The title of this paper provides an example of this. This is an article about archaeology as writing is true and complete statement and can be read as such. On the other hand, some might also observe that it bears a certain resemblance to the title of an article by Ian Hodder (1989c), *This is not an article about material culture as text* (even though it clearly is). Going further, it could also be inferred that both of these papers make reference to work by Foucault and surrealist art (for example the picture of a pipe by Magritte, entitled *This is not a pipe*). Different readers would interpret different meanings for the text on the basis of the extra context they bring to the moment of interpretation.

2 It ought to be mentioned that Derrida is, himself, not unaware of this apparent contradiction and does have arguments to reinforce his case. (He is using a means of apparent communication to undermine it from within.)

   It also needs to be pointed out that *his position* will vary to some extent according to the reader. The problem is not one of total consistency in interpretation but whether there is any consistency whatsoever.

3 It has long been recognised that translation is not simply a matter of replacing one word with another. More important is the conveyance of meaning, which requires the close attention to context. It is in the sense of conveying meaning that anthropological writings parallel translation. The anthropologist has to try and translate other people's meanings, their rationale for action to an outside observer.

4 Given that cultures are no longer considered to be homogeneous but in fact heterogeneous, replete with different understandings of that society, then the understanding of one informant must of necessity be considered as limited.

5 There are exceptions to this and they include the work of Victor Turner (1968), and Audrey Richards (1956).

6 It is also clearly an unequal strategy, in that only certain members of the discipline (those with some degree of established position) can actually engage in experimental/radical writing (Rabinow 1986).

7 Other genres that have received attention are those of the 'synthesis of data' and the 'grand synopsis of archaeological material' (such as *Prehistoric Europe* Champion *et al.* 1984), and the 'introduction to archaeology' text (Shanks and Tilley 1987a: 15–23). Moreover, a very good case could also be made for examining the 'history of archaeology' genre, wherein the 'discipline' (it is always considered as such, even for work that took place in the middle of the 19th century) is portrayed as heading to greater truth, with different theoretical perspectives complementing each other. Whilst this may have been initially excusable, such histories now appear as merely Whiggish in their focus upon the past as precursor of the present and their inattention to the circumstances that lie behind the writing of particular texts (Yates 1988; but see McVicar(1983)and other articles in ARC 3:1 for different approaches). They clearly also embody a politics of knowledge in which the radical nature of new approaches is neutralised by stressing its similarity to previous work, no matter how superficial, rather than any difference.

8 One is immediately reminded of the work of Flannery (1976) and the debates that take place between the 'Skeptical Graduate Student', the 'Synthesiser' and the 'Old Mesoamericanist'. Although, of course, here the technique of reported dialogue is a means used by Flannery to come to terms with the different sides/interest of his own self.

9 The type list that accompanies the development of 'a Méthode Bordes' is very similar textually to La Musée Préhistorique of the de Mortillets. The emphasis is upon the illustrations, with the text as just detailing.

10 It is curious to note that in Bordes' more popular works such academicism is hard to find. *The Old Stone Age* (1968), a popular academic work, for instance harks back to the method of the museum. The book is arranged chronologically and geographically. The cultures that make up the Palaeolithic are set out and illustrated by figures showing their ideal tool. *A Tale of Two Caves* takes the form of an intellectual autobiography, where the development of Bordes' own ideas are put into the context of his excavation of two caves, *Pech de L'Aze* and *Combe Grenal*. Here the text is obviously more personal and the illustrations more varied than the line drawings of tools and section drawings and the cumulative percentage graphs present in his academic texts.

11 For example, it would be very worthwhile to study the genre of writing of the earliest archaeological texts (1860–1900), a time when archaeology was not a unique academic discipline but one of a number of the natural sciences including anthropology, and was closely allied to developments within the museum world. In such a work, the form and content of illustrations would clearly be important for the key role that the physical artefact, as opposed to immaterial behaviour, played at this time in archaeology.

12 Bordes, himself, was clearly aware of the manner of production of stone tools. Indeed this figures prominently in some of his earlier works (Bordes 1950; Bordes and Bourgon 1951). What is interesting, though, is how little use is made of this in La Méthode Bordes, and how the orientation of the approach to stone tools (looking for consistency) remained the same.

PART VII

SPACE AND LANDSCAPE

INTRODUCTION

One consistent theme in archaeological writings over the past two decades has been an interest in space, whether as place, landscape or architecture. Indeed, each theoretical approach which has been pursued within archaeology over the years has addressed the issue of spatiality in quite different ways. Bruce Trigger (1989, 99) has drawn attention to the relative lack of concern with spatial information in nineteenth-century evolutionary archaeology, which emphasised temporal and stratigraphic sequence. Yet with the emergence of diffusionism and culture history distribution maps of artefact types came to be a major disciplinary preoccupation: a means of identifying prehistoric peoples. In the processual era, spatial analysis took on a more complex and precise character. On the large scale, patterns of exchange and redistribution were investigated through the fall-off of artefacts from their sources (Renfrew 1976), while site catchments were seen as a key to understanding prehistoric subsistence economies (Higgs and Vita-Finzi 1972). Within sites, distributions of artefacts were used as a means of identifying activity areas (Whallon 1973), in tune with the notion of archaeological evidence as a record of past behaviour. However, all of these approaches assume what we might call a Cartesian conception of spatiality: space as homogeneous, measurable, an inert stage or setting for human actions. Within human geography, this perspective had increasingly come under critical scrutiny from the 1970s onwards (Gregory 1978). The combination of critical theory, phenomenology and structuralism advocated by Derek Gregory is one which prefigured developments in archaeology, so it was perhaps to be predicted that a critical spatial archaeology would eventually emerge.

A hallmark of post-processual approaches to landscape and architecture has been the recognition that spaces are differentiated according to their significance. Places are not equivalent if they are experienced and understood in different ways. One piece of work which inspired many archaeologists to consider the meanings of spaces was Pierre Bourdieu's classic paper on the Berber house, reprinted here. Bourdieu describes the way in which a constellation of meanings structure the interior of the house, providing a microcosm of the social world. The conceptual categories which differentiate the internal space of the dwelling are the same as those that divide up the outside world. And yet Bourdieu's account does not degenerate into a static structuralism. The meanings of the hearth, the loom and the byre are not fixed, but learned and carried forward in the practice of everyday life conducted within the house.

This emphasis on practice is also found in Paul Lane's study of the life histories of two Bronze Age barrows in south Wales. Lane rejects the way in which sites are pigeon-holed as 'ritual' or 'domestic', as if these categories were attributes which differentiate places. Particular locations will have had complex histories of practice played out in and through them. However, Lane demonstrates that the evidence at the Mount Pleasant Farm site has had to be read in a selective way for the sequence to constitute a straightforward change from domestic to ritual. A related argument is pursued by Tim Ingold in evaluating the concept of landscape. For Ingold, landscape is not land, bare space, or nature, but a lived context which is experienced from the position of the human being. Landscape gains its structure from the human projects which are carried out through it, which means that landscape is as much a process as an entity. Discussing the prehistoric landscapes of Orkney, Colin Richards shows how particular symbolic elements are shared by sites which might be defined as being of different 'types'. Separate and remote locations appear to refer to one another through their spatial configuration and deployment of symbolic resources. Yet it is through practice, physical movement and bodily inhabitation that these different spaces are drawn together. It is the human presence which makes them parts of a landscape.

One of Ingold's most striking and important assertions is that archaeology is itself a form of dwelling within a landscape. Survey, excavation, or simply walking the land in search of traces of the past are a form of inhabitation which builds upon the history of past actions. Much of the more recent archaeology of landscape (e.g. Tilley 1994) has used present-day observations and experiences of places and monuments as a way into their significance. However, it is important to stress that this is not a way of recovering past people's thoughts or emotions. On the contrary, the use of one's own body as a medium for exploring ancient spaces creates a modern-day experience which at best stands as an allegory for past experience. In so doing, we are bringing past landscapes back to life, but only to the extent that we create an interpretation of them which is situated in the present.

29

THE BERBER HOUSE
OR THE WORLD REVERSED*

PIERRE BOURDIEU

The interior of the Kabyle house is rectangular in shape and is divided into two parts at a point one third of the way along its length by a small lattice-work wall half as high as the house. Of these two parts, the larger is approximately 50 centimeters higher than the other and is covered over by a layer of black clay and cow dung which the women polish with a stone; this part is reserved for human use. The smaller part is paved with flagstones and is occupied by the animals. A door with two wings provides entrance to both rooms. Upon the dividing wall are kept, at one end, the small clay jars or esparto-grass baskets in which provisions awaiting immediate consumption, such as figs, flour and leguminous plants, are conserved, at the other end, near the door, the waterjars. Above the stable there is a loft where, next to all kinds of tools and implements, quantities of straw and hay to be used as animal-fodder are piled up; it is here that the women and children usually sleep, particularly in winter.[1] Against the gable wall, known as the wall (or, more exactly, the 'side') of the upper part or of the *kanun*, there is set a brick-work construction in the recesses and holes of which are kept the kitchen utensils (ladle, cooking-pot, dish used to cook the bannock, and other earthenware objects blackened by the fire) and at each end of which are placed large jars filled with grain. In front of this construction is to be found the fireplace; this consists of a circular hollow, two or three centimeters deep at its centre, around which are arranged in a triangle three large stones upon which the cooking is done.[2]

In front of the wall opposite the door stands the weaving loom. This wall is usually called by the same name as the outside front wall giving onto the courtyard (*tasga*),[3] or else wall of the weaving-loom or opposite wall, since one is opposite it when one enters. The wall opposite to this, where the door is, is called wall of darkness, or of sleep, or of the maiden, or of the tomb;[4] a bench wide enough for a mat to be spread out over it is set against this wall; the bench is used to shelter the young calf or the sheep for feast-days and sometimes the wood or the water-pitcher. Clothes, mats and blankets are hung, during the day, on a peg or on a wooden cross-bar against

*First published in *Social Science Information* (1970), **9**, 151–70.

the wall of darkness or else they are put under the dividing bench. Clearly, therefore, the wall of the *kanun* is opposed to the stable as the top is to the bottom (*adaynin*, stable, comes from the root ada, meaning the bottom) and the wall of the weaving-loom is opposed to the wall of the door as the light is to the darkness. One might be tempted to give a strictly technical explanation to these oppositions since the wall of the weaving-loom, placed opposite the door, which is itself turned towards the east, receives the most light and the stable is, in fact, situated at a lower level than the rest; the reason for this latter is that the house is most often built perpendicularly with contour lines in order to facilitate the flow of liquid manure and dirty water. A number of signs suggest, however, that these oppositions are the centre of a whole cluster of parallel oppositions, the necessity of which is never completely due to technical imperatives or functional requirements.[5]

The dark and nocturnal, lower part of the house, place of objects that are moist, green or raw — jars of water placed on benches in various parts of the entrance to the stable or against the wall of darkness, wood and green fodder — natural place also of beings — oxen and cows, donkeys and mules — and place of natural activities — sleep, the sexual act, giving birth — and the place also of death, is opposed, as nature is to culture, to the light-filled, noble, upper part of the house: this is the place of human beings and, in particular, of the guest; it is the place of fire and of objects created by fire — lamp, kitchen utensils, rifle — the symbol of the male point of honour (*ennif*) and the protector of female honour (*horma*) — and it is the place of the weaving-loom — the symbol of all protection; and it is also the place of the two specifically cultural activities that are carried out in the space of the house: cooking and weaving. These relationships of opposition are expressed through a whole set of convergent signs which establish the relationships at the same time as receiving their meaning from them. Whenever there is a guest to be honoured (the verb, *qabel*, 'to honour' also means to face and to face the east),[6] he is made to sit in front of the weaving-loom. When a person has been badly received, it is customary for him to say: 'He made me sit before his wall of darkness as in a grave', or: 'His wall of darkness is as dark as a grave'. The wall of darkness is also called wall of the invalid and the expression 'to keep to the wall' means to be ill and, by extension, to be idle: the bed of the sick person is, in fact, placed next to this wall, particularly in winter. The link between the dark part of the house and death is also shown in the fact that the washing of the dead takes place at the entrance to the stable.[7] It is customary to say that the loft, which is entirely made of wood, is carried by the stable as the corpse is by the bearers, and the word *tha'richth* refers to both the loft and to the stretcher which is used to transport the dead. It is therefore obvious that one cannot, without causing offence, invite a guest to sleep in the loft which is opposed to the wall of the weaving-loom like the wall of the tomb.

In front of the wall of the weaving-loom, opposite the door, in the light, is also seated or rather, shown off, like the decorated plates which are hung there, the young bride on her wedding-day. When one knows that the umbilical cord of the girl is buried behind the weaving-loom and that, in order to protect the virginity of the maiden, she is made to pass through the warp, going from the door towards the weaving-loom, then the magic protection attributed to the weaving-loom becomes evident.[8] In fact, from the point of view of the male members of her family, all of the girl's life is, as it were, summed up in the successive positions that she symbolically occupies in relation to the weaving-loom which is the symbol of male protection:[9] before marriage she is placed behind the weaving-loom, in its shadow, under its protection, as she is placed under the protection of her father and her brothers; on her wedding-day she is seated in front of the weaving-loom with her back to it, with the light upon her, and finally she will sit weaving with her back to the wall of light, behind the loom. 'Shame, it is said, is the maiden', and the son-in-law is called 'the veil of shames' since man's point of honour is the protective 'barrier' of female honour (Bourdieu 1966: 191–241).

The low and dark part of the house is also opposed to the high part as the feminine is to the masculine: besides the fact that the division of work between the sexes, which is based upon the same principle of division as the organization of space, entrusts to the woman the responsibility of most objects which belong to the dark part of the house – water-transport, and the carrying of wood and manure, for instance.[10] The opposition between the upper part and the lower part reproduces within the space of the house the opposition set up between the inside and the outside. This is the opposition between female space and male space, between the house and its garden, the place *par excellence* of the *haram*, i.e., of all which is sacred and forbidden, and a closed and secret space, well-protected and sheltered from intrusions and the gaze of others, and the place of assembly (*thajma'th*), the mosque, the café, the fields or the market: on the one hand, the privacy of all that is intimate, on the other, the open space of social relations; on the one hand, the life of the senses and of the feelings, on the other, the life of relations between man and man, the life of dialogue and exchange. The lower part of the house is the place of the most intimate privacy within the very world of intimacy, that is to say, it is the place of all that pertains to sexuality and procreation. More or less empty during the day, when all activity which is, of course, exclusively feminine – is based around the fireplace, the dark part is full at night, full of human beings but also full of animals since, unlike the mules and the donkeys, the oxen and the cows never spend the night out of doors; and it is never quite so full as it is during the damp season when the men sleep inside and the oxen and the cows are fed in the stable. It is possible here to establish more directly the relationship which links the fertility of men and of the field to the dark part of the house and which is a particular instance of the relationship of equivalence between fertility and that which is dark, full (or swollen) or damp, vouched for by the whole mythico-ritual system: whilst the grain meant for consumption is, as we have seen, stored in large earthenware jars next to the wall of the upper part, on either side of the fireplace, the grain which is intended for sowing is placed in the dark part of the house, either in sheep-skins or in chests placed at the foot of the wall of darkness; or sometimes under the conjugal bed, or in wooden chests placed under the bench which is set against the dividing wall where the wife, who normally sleeps at a lower level, beside the entrance to the stable, rejoins her husband. Once we are aware that birth is always rebirth of the ancestor, since the life circle (which should be called the *cycle of generation*) turns upon itself every third generation (a proposition which cannot be demonstrated here), it becomes obvious that the dark part of the house may be at the same time and without any contradiction the place of death and of procreation, or of birth as resurrection.[11]

In addition to all this, at the centre of the dividing wall, between 'the house of the human beings' and 'the house of the animals' stands the main pillar, supporting the governing beam and all the framework of the house. Now this governing beam which connects the gables and spreads the protection of the male part of the house to the female part (*asalas alemmas*, a masculine term) is identified explicitly with the master of the house, whilst the main pillar upon which it rests, which is the trunk of a forked tree (*thigejdith*, a feminine term), is identified with the wife (the Beni Khellili call it 'Mas'uda', a feminine first name which means 'the happy woman'), and their interlocking represents the act of physical union (shown in mural paintings in the form of the union of the beam and the pillar by two superimposed forked trees) (Dewulder 1954: 14-15). The main beam, which supports the roof, is identified with the protector of family honour; sacrifices are often made to it, and it is around this beam that, on a level with the fire-place, is coiled the snake who is the 'guardian' of the house. As the symbol of the fertilizing power of man and the symbol also of death followed by resurrection, the snake is sometimes shown (in the Collo region for example) upon earthen jars made by the women and which contain the seed for sowing. The snake is also said to descend sometimes into the house, into the lap of the sterile woman, calling her mother, or to coil itself around the central pillar, growing longer by the length of one coil of its body after each time that it takes suck.[12] In Darna, according to René Maunier, the sterile woman ties her belt to the central beam which is where the foreskin is hung and the reed which has been used for circumcision; when the beam is heard to crack the Berbers hastily say 'may it turn out well', because this presages the death of the chief of the family. At the birth of a boy, the wish is made that 'he be the governing beam of the house', and when he carries out his ritual fast for the first time, he takes his first meal on the roof, that is to say, on the central beam (in order, so it is said, that he may be able to transport beams).

A number of riddles and sayings explicitly identify the woman with the central pillar: 'My father's father's wife carries my father's father who carries his daughters'; 'The slave strangles his master'; 'The woman supports the man'; 'The woman is the central pillar'. To the young bride one says: 'May God make of you the pillar firmly planted in the middle of the house'. Another riddle says: 'She stands but she has no feet'; a forked tree open at the top and not set upon her feet, she is female nature and as such, she is fertile or, rather, able to be fertilized.[13] Against the central pillar are piled the leather bottles full of *hij* seeds, and it is here that the marriage is consummated.[14] Thus, as a symbolic summing up of the house, the union of *asalas* and *thigejdith*, which spreads its fertilizing protection over all human marriage, is in a certain way primordial marriage, the marriage of the ancestors which is also, like tillage, the marriage of heaven and earth. 'Woman is the foundations, man is the governing beam', says another proverb. *Asalas*, which a riddle defines as 'born in the earth and buried in the sky', fertilizes *thigejdith*, which is planted in the earth, the place of the ancestors who are the masters of all fecundity, and open towards the sky.[15]

Thus, the house is organized according to a set of homologous oppositions: fire: water :: cooked: raw :: high: low :: light: shadow :: day: night :: male: female :: *nif: horma* :: fertilizing: able to be fertilized :: culture: nature. But in fact the same oppositions exist between the house as a whole and the rest of the universe. Considered in its relationship with the external world, which is a specifically masculine world of public life and agricultural work, the house, which is the universe of women and the world of intimacy and privacy, is *haram*, that is to say, at once sacred and illicit for every man who does not form part of it (hence the expression used when taking an oath: 'May my wife – or my house – become illicit – *haram* – to me if . . . '). As the place of the sacred or the left-hand side, appertaining to the *horma* to which are linked all those properties which are associated with the dark part of the house, the house is placed under the safeguard of the masculine point of honour (*nif*) as the dark part of the house is placed under the protection of the main beam. Any violation of the sacred space takes on therefore the social significance of a sacrilege: thus, theft in an inhabited house is treated in everyday usage as a very serious fault inasmuch as it is offence to the *nif* of the head of the family and an outrage upon the *horma* of the house and consequently of all the community. Moreover, when a guest who is not a member of the family is introduced to the women, he gives the mistress of the house a sum of money which is called 'the view'.[16]

One is not justified in saying that the woman is locked up in the house unless one also observes that the man is kept out of it, at least during the day.[17] As soon as the sun has risen he must, during the summer, be in the fields or at the assembly house; in the winter, if he is not in the field, he has to be at the place of assembly or upon the benches set in the shelter of the pent-roof over the entrance door to the courtyard. Even at night, at least during the dry season, the men and the boys, as soon as they have been circumcised, sleep outside the house, either near the haystacks upon the threshing-floor, beside the donkey and the shackled mule, or upon the fig-dryer, or in the open field, or else, more rarely, in the *thajma'th*.[18] The man who stays too long in the house during the day is either suspect or ridiculous: he is 'the man of the home', as one says of the importunate man who stays amongst the women and who 'broods at home like a hen in the henhouse'. A man who has respect for himself should let himself be seen, should continuously place himself under the gaze of others and face them (*qabel*). He is a man amongst men (*argaz yer irgazen*).[19] Hence the importance accorded to the games of honour which are a kind of dramatic action, performed in front of others who are knowing spectators, familiar with the text and all the stage business and capable of appreciating the slightest variations. It is not difficult to understand why all biological activities such as eating, sleeping and procreating are excluded from the specifically cultural universe and relegated to the sanctuary of intimacy and the refuge for the secrets of nature which is the house,[20] the woman's world. In opposition to man's work which is performed outside, it is the nature of woman's work to remain hidden ('God conceals it'): 'Inside the house, woman is always on the move, she flounders like a fly in whey; outside the house, nothing of her work is seen.' Two very similar sayings define woman's condition as being that of one who cannot know any other sojourn than that tomb above the earth which is the house and that subterranean house which is the tomb: 'Your house is your tomb'; 'Woman has only two dwellings, the house and the tomb'.

Thus, the opposition between the house and the assembly of men, between the fields and the market, between private life and public life, or, if one prefers, between the full light of the day and the secrecy of the night, overlaps very exactly with the opposition between the dark and nocturnal, lower part of the house and the noble and brightly-lit, upper part.[21] The opposition which is set up between the external world and the house only takes on its full meaning therefore if one of the terms of this relation, that is to say, the house, is itself seen as being divided according to the same principles which oppose it to the other term. It is therefore both true and false to say that the external world is opposed to the house as male is to female, or day to night, or fire to water, etc., since the second term of these oppositions divides up each time into itself and its opposite.[22]

In short, the most apparent opposition: male (or day, fire, etc.)/female (or night, water, etc.) may well mask the opposition: male/ [female-male/ female-female], and in the same way, the homology: male/female: female-male/female-female. It is obvious from this that the first opposition is but a transformation of the second, which presupposes a change in the field of reference at the end of which the female-female is no longer opposed to the female-male and instead, the group which they form is opposed to a third term: female-male/female-female -› female (= female-male + female-female)/male.

As a microcosm organized according to the same oppositions which govern all the universe, the house maintains a relation with the rest of the universe which is that of a homology: but from another point of view, the world of the house taken as a whole is in a relation with the rest of the world which is one of opposition, and the principles of which are none other than those which govern the organization of the internal space of the house as much as they do the rest of the world and, more generally, all the areas of existence. Thus, the opposition between the world of female life and the world of the city of men is based upon the same principles as the two systems of oppositions that it opposes. It follows from this that the application to opposed areas of the same *principium divisionis*, which in fact forms their very opposition, provides, at the least cost, a surplus of consistency and does not, in return, result in any confusion between these areas. The structure of the type a: b:: b₁: b₂ is doubtless one of the simplest and most powerful that may be employed by a mythico-ritual system since it cannot oppose without simultaneously uniting (and inversely), while all the time being capable of integrating in a set order an infinite number of data, by the simple application of the same principle of division indefinitely repeated.[23]

It also follows from this that each of the two parts of the house (and, by the same token, all of the objects which are put there and all of the activities which take place there) is in a certain way qualified to two degrees, namely, firstly as female (nocturnal, dark, etc.) inasmuch as it participates in the universe of the house, and secondly as male or female inasmuch as it participates in one or the other of the divisions of this universe. Thus, for example, when the proverb says: 'Man is the lamp of the outside and woman the lamp of the inside', it is to be understood that man is the true light, that of the day, and woman the light of the darkness, the dark light; moreover, she is, of course, to the moon what man is to the sun. In the same way, when she works with wool, woman produces the beneficent protection of weaving, the whiteness of which symbolizes happiness;[24] the weaving-loom, which is the instrument *par excellence* of female activity and which faces the east like the plough, its homologue, is at the same time the east of the internal space of the house with the result that, within the system of the house, it has a male value as a symbol of protection. Likewise, the fireplace, which is the navel of the house (itself identified with the womb of the mother), where smoulder the embers, which is a secret, hidden and female fire, is the domain of woman who is invested with total authority in all matters concerning the kitchen and the management of the food-stores;[25] she takes her meals at the fireside whilst man, turned towards the outside, eats in the middle of the room or in the courtyard. Nevertheless, in all the rites where they play a part, the fire-place and the stones which surround it derive their potent magic from their participation in the order of fire, of that which is dry and of the solar heat, whether it is a question of providing protection against the evil eye or against illness or to summon up fine weather.[26] The house is also endowed with a double significance: if it is true that it is opposed to the public world as nature is to culture, it is also, in another respect, culture; is it not said of the jackal, the incarnation of all that is savage in nature, that it does not have a home?

The house and, by extension, the village[27] which is the full country (*la'mmara* or *thamurth i'amran*), the precincts peopled by men, are opposed in a certain respect to the fields empty of men which are called *lakhla*, the space that is empty and sterile. Thus, according to Maunier, the inhabitants of Taddert-el-Djeddid believed that those who build outside the village precincts lay themselves open to the extinction of their family; the same belief is found elsewhere and exception is only made for the garden, even if it is far from the house (*thabhirth*), for the orchard (*thamazirth*) or the fig-dryer (*tarha*), all of which are places which participate in the village and in its fertility. But the opposition does not exclude the homology between the fertility of men and the fertility of the field, both of which are the product of the union of the male principle and the female principle, of the solar fire and the dampness of the earth. This homology is in fact responsible for bringing together most of the rites whose purpose is to ensure the fertility of human beings and of the earth, whether it is a question of cooking, which comes under the strict control of the oppositions which govern the agrarian year and hence is dependent upon the rhythms of the agricultural calendar, whether it is a question of the renewal rites for the fireplace and the stones (*iniyen*), marking the passage from the dry season to the wet season or the beginning of the year or, more generally, of all the rites performed within the house, which is a small-scale image of the topocosm; whenever women take a part in specifically agrarian rites, the homology between agrarian fertility and human fertility, which is the form *par excellence* of all fertility, is still at the base of their ritual acts and it imparts to them their magic potency. There is a limitless number of rites performed within the house which appear to be domestic rites but which in fact aim at ensuring at one and the same time the fertility of the field and the fertility of the house, neither of which can be dissociated from the other. In order for the field to be full, the house must be full and woman contributes to the prosperity of the field by dedicating herself, amongst other things, to accumulating, to saving and to conserving all the goods produced by man and to keeping within the house all the riches that may enter into it. It is said that: 'Man is like the furrow and woman like the basin: the one supplies and the other holds'. Man is 'the hook on which the baskets are hung'; like the beetle, the spider and the bee, he is the provider. That which is provided by man is protected, put away and saved by woman. It is also said that: 'A thrifty woman is worth more than a pair of plough-oxen'. As 'the full country' is opposed to the 'empty space' (*lakhla*), 'the full one of the house' (*la'mmara ukham*), who is usually 'the old woman' who saves and stores, is opposed to the 'empty one of the house' (*lakhla ukham*), who is usually the daughter-in-law.[28] During the summer the door of the house must remain open all day long so that the fertilizing light of the sun may enter, and with it prosperity. A closed door means penury and sterility: to sit down upon the threshold means, by obstructing it, to close the passage to happiness and plenitude. When one wishes prosperity to someone one says: 'May your door remain open', or: 'May your house be open like a mosque'. The rich and generous man is he of whom it is said: 'His house is a mosque, it is open to all, poor and rich alike, it is made of bannock and cous-cous, it is full' (*tha'mmar*); generosity is a manifestation of that prosperity which ensures prosperity.[29] Most technical and ritual acts which are the business of woman are guided by the objective intention of making of the house, like *thigejdith* opening its fork to *asalas alemmas*, the receptacle of prosperity which comes to it from outside, or the womb which, like the earth, receives the seed which the male has caused to enter into it; and inversely, the purpose of the rites is to thwart the action of all centrifugal forces that might dispossess the house of all that has been entrusted it and placed within it. Thus, for example, it is forbidden to give anyone a light.

On the day that a child or a calf is born or at the beginning of the tillage[30] when all the grain has been threshed nothing must go out of the house and the woman gets back all the objects which have been loaned out; the milk produced during the three days which follow calving must not go out of the house; the bride cannot cross the threshold before the seventh day after her marriage; the woman who has given birth must not leave the house before the fortieth day; the baby must not go out before the *Aïd Seghir*; the hand-mill must never be loaned out, and to leave it empty is to bring famine upon the house; the weaving must not be taken off the loom before it is finished: like giving a light, sweeping, which is an act of expulsion, is forbidden during the first four days of tillage; the exit of a dead person is 'facilitated' so that he does not carry off any prosperity with him;[31] the 'first exits', that of the cow, for instance, the fourth day after calving, or that of the calf, are marked by sacrifices.[32] 'Emptiness' may result from an act of expulsion; it may also accompany certain objects like the plough which may not be brought into the house between two days of ploughing, or the shoes of the ploughman (*arkassen*) which are associated with *lakhla*, and with empty space, or it may accompany certain people, like old women because they carry sterility (*lakhla*) with them and because numerous are the houses that they have caused to be sold or where they have brought thieves. On the other hand, a number of ritual acts aim at bringing about the 'filling-up' of the house, such as those which consist in throwing the remains of a marriage lamp (the form of which is a representation of sexual union and which plays a role in most fertility rites) into the foundations, upon the first stone, after having spilt an animal's blood, or in making the bride sit upon a leather bottle full of seeds. Every time something comes into the house for the first time, this constitutes a danger to the plenitude of the internal world. The rites of the threshold, which are both propitiatory and prophylactic, must ward off this danger: the new pair of oxen is received by the mistress of the house – *thamgharth ukham* – which means, as we have seen, 'the plenitude of the house', *la'mmara ukham* – , who places upon the threshold the sheepskin in which the hand-mill is kept and in which the flour is put (*alamsir*, also called 'the door of provisions', *bab errazq*). Most rites which seek to bring fertility to the stable and, thus, to the house (a house without a cow is said to be 'an empty house'), have a tendency to reinforce magically the structural relation which unites the milk, the green-blue (*azegzaw* which is also that which is raw, *thizegzawth*), the grass, the spring, the infancy of the natural world and of man: at the spring equinox, at the time that the *azal* returns, the young shepherd whose participation in the increase of his field and of his cattle is twofold on account of his age and his function, gathers a bouquet in order to hang it from the lintel of the door; this bouquet comprises 'all that flutters in the wind in the country' (with the exception of the oleander, which is most often used for prophylactic ends and in rites of expulsion, and scilla which marks the division between fields); a bag of seasoning herbs is also buried at the threshold of the stable, containing cumin, benjamin and indigo at the same time one says 'O green blue (*azegzaw*), let not the butter go on the wane!' Freshly-picked plants are hung on the butter-churn and the utensils in which the milk will be put are rubbed with them.[33] The entrance of the young bride is, above all things, pregnant with consequences for the fertility and the plenitude of the house: while she is still seated on the mule which has carried her from her father's house, she is presented with water, with grains of wheat, with figs, nuts, baked eggs or fritters, all of which are things (whatever variation there might be according to the area) associated with the fertility of woman and the earth, and she throws them in the direction of the house, thus causing herself to be preceded by the fertility and plenitude which she must bring to the house.[34] She is carried across the threshold upon the back of a relation of the groom or sometimes, according to Maunier, on the back of a negro (but never, in any case, on the bridegroom's back) who, by interposing himself, intercepts the evil forces which might affect her fertility and of which the threshold, which is the meeting-point between opposed worlds, is the seat: a woman must never sit near the threshold holding her child: the young child and the young wife should not tread on it too often. Thus, woman, through whom fertility comes to the house, makes her own contribution to the fertility of the agrarian world: dedicated to the world of the inside, she also acts upon the outside by ensuring the plenitude of the inside world and by controlling, as guardian of the threshold, those unreciprocated exchanges that only the logic of magic can conceive and through which each part of the universe expects to receive from the other nothing but the whole, whilst offering to it nothing but emptiness.[35]

But one or the other of the two systems of oppositions which define the house, either in its internal organization or in its relationship with the outside world, will take prime importance according to whether the house is considered from the male point of view or the female point of view: whereas, for the man, the house is less a place one goes into than a place from which one goes out, the woman can only confer upon these two movements and the different definitions of the house which form an integral part with them, an inverse importance and meaning, since movement towards the outside consists above all for her of acts of expulsion and it is her specific role to be responsible for all movement towards the inside, that is to say, from the threshold towards the fireplace. The significance of the movement towards the outside is never quite so apparent as in the rite performed by the mother, on the seventh day after a birth, 'in order that her son be courageous': striding across the threshold, she sets her right foot upon the carding comb and simulates a fight with the first boy she meets. The sallying forth is a specifically male movement which leads towards other men and also towards dangers and trials which it is important to *confront* like a man, a man as spiky, when it is a question of honour, as the points of the comb.[36] Going out, or more exactly, opening (*fatah*), is the equivalent of 'being in the morning' (*sebah*). A man who has respect for himself should leave the house at daybreak, morning being the day of the daytime, and the sallying forth from the house, in the morning, being a birth: whence the importance of things encountered which are a portent for the whole day, with the result that, in the case of bad encounters (blacksmith, woman carrying an empty leather bottle, shouts or a quarrel, a deformed being), it is best to 'remake one's morning' or 'one's going out'.

Bearing this in mind, it is not difficult to understand the importance accorded to the direction which the house faces: the front of the main house, the one which shelters the head of the family and which contains a stable, is almost always turned towards the east, and the main door - in opposition to the low and narrow door, reserved for the women, which opens in the direction of the garden, at the back of the house – is commonly called the door of the east (*thabburth thacherqith*) or else the door of the sheet, the door of the upper part or the great door.[37] Considering the way in which the villages present themselves and the lower position of the stable, the upper part of the house, with the fireplace, is situated in the north, the stable is in the south and the wall of the weaving-loom is in the west. If follows from this that the movement one makes when going towards the house in order to enter it is directed from the east to the west, in opposition to the movement made to come out which, in accordance with the supreme direction, is towards the east, that is to say, towards the height, the light and the good: the ploughman turns his oxen towards the east when he harnesses them and also when he unharnesses them, and he starts ploughing from west to east; likewise, the sacrificial ox facing the east. Limitless are the acts which are performed in accordance with this principal direction, for these are all the acts of importance involving the fertility and the prosperity of the group.[38] It will suffice to note that the verb *qabel* means not only to face, to affront with honour and to receive in a worthy manner, but also to face the east (*lqibla*) and the future (*qabel*).

If we refer back now to the internal organization of the house we will see that its orientation is exactly the inverse of that of the external space, as if it had been obtained by a semi-rotation around the front wall or the threshold taken as an axis. The wall of the weaving-loom, which one faces as soon as one crosses the threshold, and which is lit up directly by the morning sun, is the light of the inside (as woman is the lamp of the inside), that is to say, the east of the inside, symmetrical to the external east, whence it derives its borrowed light.[39] The interior and dark side of the front wall represents the west of the house and is the place of sleep which is left behind when one goes from the door towards the *kanun*; the door corresponds symbolically to the 'door of the year', which is the beginning of the wet season and the agrarian year. Likewise, the two gable walls, the wall of the stable and the wall of the fireplace, take on two opposed meanings depending on which of their sides is being considered: to the external north corresponds the south (and the summer) of the inside, that is to say, the side of the house which is in front of one and on one's right when one goes in facing the weaving loom; to the external south corresponds the inside north (and the winter that is to say, the stable, which is situated

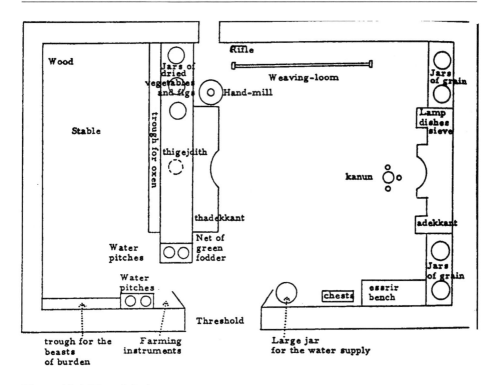

Figure 29.1 *Plan of the house*

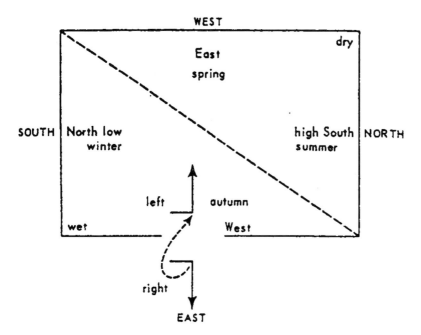

Figure 29.2 *The double space orientation of the house (The right-angle arrows indicate the person's positions)*

behind and on the left when one goes from the door towards the fireplace).[40] The division of the house into a dark part (the west and north sides) and a light part (the east and south sides) corresponds to the division of the year into a wet season and a dry season. In short, to each exterior side of the wall (*essur*) there corresponds a region of interior space (which the Kabyles refer to as *tharkunt*, which means roughly, the side) which has a symmetrical and inverse sense signification in the system of internal oppositions; each of the two spaces can therefore be defined as the set of movements made to effect the same change of position that is to say a semi-rotation, in relation to the other,[41] the threshold acting as the axis of rotation.[42]

It is not possible completely to understand the importance and symbolic value attached to the threshold in the system, unless one is aware that it owes its function as a magic frontier to the fact that it is the place of a logical inversion and that, as the obligatory place of passage and of meeting between the two spaces, which are defined in relation to socially qualified movements of the body and crossings from one place to another, it is logically the place where the world is reversed.[43]

Thus, each of the universes has its own east and the two movements that are most pregnant with meaning and magical consequences, the movement from the threshold to the fireplace, which should bring plenitude and whose performance or ritual control is the responsibility of woman, and the movement from the threshold towards the exterior world which, by its inaugural value, contains all that the future holds and especially the future of agrarian work, may be carried out in accordance with the beneficent direction, that is to say from west to east.[44] The twofold orientation in the space of the house means that it is possible both to go in and to go out starting from the right foot, both in the literal and the figurative sense, with all the magical benefit attached to this observance, without there ever being a break in the relation which unites the right to the upper part, to the light and to the good. The semi-rotation of the space around the threshold ensures then, if one may use the expression, the maximization of the magical benefit since both centripetal and centrifugal movement are performed in a space which is organized in such a way that one comes into it facing the light and one goes out of it facing the light.[45]

The two symmetrical and inverse spaces are not interchangeable but hierarchized, the internal space being nothing but the inverted image or the mirror-reflection of the male space.[46] It is not by chance that only the direction which the door faces is explicitly prescribed whereas the interior organization of space is never consciously perceived and is even less desired to be so organized by the inhabitants.[47] The orientation of the house is fundamentally defined from the outside, from the point of view of men and, if one may say so, by men and for men, as the place from which men come out. The house is an empire within an empire, but one which always remains subordinate because, even though it presents all the properties and all the relations which define the archetypal world, it remains a reversed world, an inverted reflection.[48] 'Man is the lamp of the outside and woman the lamp of the inside'. One must not be misled by the appearance of symmetry: the lamp of the day is only apparently defined in relation to the lamp of the night; in fact, the nocturnal light, male/female, remains under and subordinate to the diurnal light, the lamp of the day, that is to say, to the day of the daytime. 'Woman, so it is also said, is twisted like a sickle'; thus, even the most right-hand sided of these left-hand sided natures is never more than simply straightened up. The married woman also has her east, within the man's house, but her east is only the inversion of a west: is it not said that 'the maiden is the Occident'? The special favour accorded to the movement towards the outside, by which man affirms himself as man, turning his back upon the house in order to go and face men and choosing the way of the Orient of the world, is but a form of categorical refusal of nature, which is the inevitable origin of the movement away from it.

NOTES

1 The place of sleep and sexual relations seems to vary, but only within the 'dark part' of the house: the whole family may sleep in the loft, especially in winter, or merely the women without husbands (widows, divorced women, etc.) and the children, or else they may sleep next to the wall of darkness; or else the man may sleep on the upper part of the dividing wall and the woman on the lower part, next to the door, and the woman will then go and rejoin her husband in the darkness.

2 All the descriptions of the Berber house, even the most exact and methodical ones (such as Maunier's, 1930: 120–177), or those that are most rich in detail concerning the interior organization of space (such as those made by Laoust, 1920: 50–53, 1912: 12–15, or Genevois 1955: 46) contain, in their extreme meticulousness, regular omissions, particularly when it is a question of precisely situating things and activities. The reason for this is that these descriptions never consider objects and actions as part of a symbolic system. The postulate that each of the observed phenomena derives its necessity and its meaning from its relation with all the others was the only way of proceeding to a systematic observation and examination capable of bringing out facts which escape any unsystematic observation and which the observers are incapable of yielding since they appear self-evident to them. This postulate is rendered valid by the very results of the research-programme which it establishes: the particular position of the house within the system of magical representations and ritual practices justifies the initial abstraction by means of which the house is taken out of the context of this larger system in order to treat it as a system itself.

3 With only this exception, the walls are designated by two different names, according to whether they are considered from the outside or from the inside. The outside is plastered over with a trowel by the men whilst the inside is made white and hand-decorated by the women. This opposition between the two points of view is, as will be seen, a fundamental one.

4 Concerning a father who has many daughters one says: 'He is setting up evil days for himself', and, in the same way, one says: 'The maiden is the dusk', or: 'The maiden is the wall of darkness'.

5 The situating of the house in geographical and social space, and also its internal organization, form one of the 'places' in which are joined together symbolic or social necessity and technical necessity. The symbolic system only perhaps reveals its ability to re-interpret, in terms of its own logic, data proposed to it by other systems in cases where, as here, the principles of the symbolic organization of the world cannot be freely applied and have, as it were to adjust to external constraints, such as the constraints of technique, for example, which necessitate the construction of a house perpendicularly with contour lines and facing the rising sun (or, in other cases, the constraints imposed by social structure which demand that every new house be built in a particular area defined by genealogy). Without wishing to become further involved in an extremely difficult debate, it might be suggested that the dependence of the mythico-ritual system in relation to other systems does not always have the same force and the same form in every society.

6 The opposition between the part reserved for receiving guests and the more intimate part (an opposition which is also found in the nomad's tent which is separated by a piece of material

into two parts, one part open to guests and the other reserved for women) is expressed in ritual forecasts such as the following: whenever a cat, an animal that is beneficent, comes into the house with a feather in its fur or a thread of white wool and it goes towards the fireplace, this is a portent of the arrival of guests who will be offered a meal with meat; if the cat goes towards the stable, this means that a cow will be bought, if it is the season of spring, or an ox if it is the season of tillage.

7 The homology of sleep and death is explicitly expressed in the precept according to which one should first lie for a moment upon the right side and then on the left, because the first position is that of the dead in the tomb. The funeral chants represent the grave – 'the house beneath the earth' – as an inverted house (white/dark, high/low, adorned with paintings/clumsily scooped out); they do this by referring to homonymies such as the following which are bound up with the analogy of form: 'I found people digging a grave/With their pickaxe they were carving out the walls,/They were making benches (*thiddukanin*) there,/With a mortar below the mud' – so runs a chant sung at a vigil over the newly-buried (Genevois 1955: 27). *Thaddukant* (plural *thiddukanin*) designates the bench set against the dividing wall, opposite the one which leans against the gable wall (*addukan*), and it also signifies the bench of earth upon which rests the head of the man in the tomb (the slight hollow in which is lain the head of the woman is called *thakwath*, like the small recesses scooped out in the walls of the house, in which little objects are kept).

8 Amongst the Arabs, in order to carry out the magic rite of iron-binding whose purpose is to make women unfit for sexual relations, the betrothed one is made to pass through the slackened warp of the weaving-loom, from the outside towards the inside, that is to say, from the centre of the room towards the wall next to which work the weavers; the same operation, carried out in the opposite direction, destroys the iron-binding (Marcais and Guiga 1925: 395).

9 E. Laoust links up with the root *zett* (to weave) the word *tazettat* which, amongst the Berbers of Morocco, designates the protection granted to every person travelling in foreign territory or the payment received by the protector in exchange for his protection (Laoust 1920: 126).

10 When they first come into the stable the new pair of oxen is received and led in by the mistress of the house.

11 The building of the house which always takes place on the occasion of the marriage of a son and which symbolizes the birth of a new family is forbidden in May, as is marriage. The transport of the beams which are identified, as will be seen, with the master of the house, is called *tha'richth*, like the loft and like the stretcher used to transport the dead or a wounded animal that has to be slain far from the house, and it occasions a social ceremony whose significance is quite similar to that of burial. On account of its lofty nature and the ceremonial form which it assumes, and also the number of people that it mobilizes, this collective task (*thiwizi*) has no equivalent other than burial: the men go to the place where the wood has been felled after having been called from the top of the mosque as for a burial. People are expected to participate in the transport of the beams as this is considered as a pious act which is always carried out without obtaining anything in return: there is as much *hassana* (merit) to be derived from it as from participation in collective activities connected with a funeral (digging the grave, removing flagstones or transporting them, helping to carry the coffin or witnessing a burial).

12 On the day of the *thanurith wazal* (8th April in the Julian calendar) which is a decisive turning-point in the agrarian year and which comes between the wet season and the dry season, the shepherd goes very early in the morning to draw water and sprinkles the central beam with it; at the time of the harvest, the last sheaf, cut according to a special ritual (or a double ear of corn) is suspended from the central beam and remains there all the year.

13 Concerning the young bride who adapts well to the house one says 'tha'mmar', that is to say, among other things (cf. 161, n. 29), 'she is full' and 'she fills'.

14 Amongst the Berbers of the Aurès, the consummation of the marriage takes place on a Monday, a Thursday or a Saturday, which are *dies fasti*. The day before, the maidens of the husband's family

pile up against the central pillar *hiji*, made up of six leather bottles dyed red, green, yellow and violet (representing the bride) and a seventh which is white (the bridegroom), all of which are full of seeds. At the base of the *hiji* an old woman throws salt in order to chase away the evil spirits, plants a needle in the ground to give more virility to the bridegroom and lays down a mat turned towards the east which will act as the bed of the newly-weds for a week. The women of the bridegroom's family perfume the *hiji* whilst his mother throws, in the same way as during tillage, a shower of dates into the air which the children fight for. The following day the bride is carried by a close relation of the bridegroom to the foot of the *hiji* where the mother throws once again flowers, dates, ripened wheat, sugar and honey.

15 In certain regions the share of the plough is placed in the fork of the central pillar with its point turned towards the door.

16 Such is the case not only when one is invited for the first time into a house, but also when, on the third day of a marriage, a visit is paid to the bride's family.

17 In order to hint at how much the men are ignorant of what happens in the house, the women say: 'O man, poor unfortunate, all day in the field like a mule at pasture'.

18 On account of the difference in rhythm connected to the division between the dry season and the wet season being revealed, among other things, in the running of the home, the opposition between the lower part of the house and the upper takes on, during the summer, the form of the opposition between the house itself, where the women and the children retire to bed and where the stores are kept, and the courtyard where the fireplace and the hand-mill are set up, where meals are taken and where gatherings take place on the occasion of feast-days and ceremonies.

19 Relationships between men must be established outside: 'Friends are friends of the outside and not of the *kanun*'.

20 'The hen, so it is said, does not lay eggs at the market'.

21 The opposition between the house and the *thajma'th* may clearly be seen in the difference between the designs of the two buildings: whilst the house is opened by the door in the front, the assembly house takes the form of a long covered passage, completely open at the two gables, and which is crossed from one side to the other.

22 This structure is also to be found in other areas of the mythico-ritual system: thus, the day is divided into night and day, but the day itself is divided into a diurnal-nocturnal part (the morning and the evening); the year is divided into a dry season and a wet season, and the dry season is comprised of a dry-dry part and a dry-wet part. There should also be an examination of the relation between this structure and the structure which governs the political order and which is expressed in the saying: 'My brother is my enemy, my brother's enemy is my enemy'.

23 There should perhaps be seen in the extreme pregnance of this structure one of the foundations of the preponderance accorded, in the case of Kabyle society, to the mythico-ritual system amongst other systems.

24 'White days' refer to happy days. One of the functions of marriage is to make the woman 'white' (sprinkling of milk, etc.)

25 The smith is the man who, like woman, spends all his time indoors, near the fire.

26 The hearth is the place of a certain number of rites and is subject to interdicts which oppose it to the dark part of the house. For example, it is forbidden to touch the ashes during the night, to spit into the fireplace or to weep tears there (Maunier). Likewise, those rites whose object is to effect a change in the weather and which are based upon a reversal utilize the opposition between the dry and damp parts of the house: for example, in order to pass from damp weather to dry weather, a comb used for packing wool (an object which is created by fire and which is associated with weaving) and a burning coal are placed upon the threshold during the night; inversely, in order to pass from dry weather to damp weather, the combs used for packing and carding wool are sprinkled with water upon the threshold during the night.

27 The village also has its *horma* which every visitor must respect. Just as one must take off one's shoes before going into a house or a mosque or onto a threshing-floor, so one must set one's feet upon the earth when going into a village.

28 The word *'ammar* used about a woman means to be thrifty and a good housewife; it also means to establish a home and to be full. To *'ammar* is opposed *ikhla*, which refers to a person who is a spendthrift, but also to a man who is sterile and isolated, or *enger*, a sterile bachelor which means, in a sense, wild and, like the jackal, incapable of founding a home.

29 Here again it can be seen that the system of moral values takes its basic principles from the mythico-ritual system (Bourdieu 1966: 191–241).

30 Inversely, the introduction into the house of new stones for the fireplace, on dates of inauguration is a filling-up, the introduction of the good and of prosperity; and so the forecasts made in these circumstances are directed towards prosperity and fertility: if a white worm is found under one of the stones, there will be a birth during the year; if there is some green grass, there will be a good harvest; if there are ants, the flock will be increased; if there is a woodlouse there will be new heads of cattle.

31 When one wants to console someone, one says: 'He will leave you the *baraka*' if it is an adult who has died, or: 'The *baraka* has not gone out of the house' if it is a baby. The dead person is placed next to the door with his head turned towards the door; the water is heated beside the stable and the washing is performed at the entrance to the stable; the embers and the ashes of the fire are scattered outside the house; the board which has been used in the washing of the dead person remains in front of the door for three days, after the burial, from the Friday to the following Saturday, three nails are planted in the door.

32 The cow has to pass over a knife and broad beans that have been placed on the threshold; drops of milk are poured on the fireplace and on the threshold.

33 Into the milk vase is also sometimes put a stone which the young shepherd will have gathered up when he heard the cuckoo for the first time and which he will have placed upon his head. It also sometimes happens that the milk is drawn through the ring of the pickaxe and a pinch of earth is thrown into the vase.

34 She may also be sprinkled with water or made to drink water and milk.

35 From the door are hung different objects whose common purpose reveals the twofold function of the threshold which, as a selective barrier, responsible for stopping emptiness and evil, allows fullness and all that is good to enter and predisposes towards fertility and prosperity all that crosses the threshold towards the outside world.

36 Whereas at her birth a girl is wrapped in the softness of a silk scarf, a boy is swathed in the dry and rough bindings which are used to tie the sheaves that have been reaped.

37 It is self-evident that an inverse arrangement (as in the mirror-image of the diagram shown) is possible, although rare. It is explicitly said that all that comes from the west brings bad luck and that a door facing this direction can only receive darkness and sterility. In fact, if the inverse plan of the 'ideal' plan is rare, it is primarily because the secondary houses, when they are arranged at a right-angle around the courtyard, are often simply rooms in which people may stay, without kitchen or stable, and because the courtyard is often closed off, on the side opposite the front of the main house, by the back of the house which is next to it and which is itself turned towards the east.

38 It is known that the two *çuff-s*, which were political leagues of warriors who became mobilized immediately when an incident occurred (and who maintained varying relationships with the social units based upon kinship, ranging from exact overlapping to complete dissociation) were named *çuff* of the higher part (*ufella*) and *çuff* of the lower part (*buadda*) or *çuff* of the right-hand side (*ayafus*), and *çuff* of the left-hand side (*azelmach*), or *çuff* of the east (*achergi*) and *çuff* of the west (*aghurbi*), this last name, which was less usual, being conserved to designate rival camps in the ritual games (whence the traditional fights between the *çuff* derived their logic) and surviving today in the vocabulary of children's games.

39 It is to be remembered that the master of the house receives (*qabel*) his guest on the side of the weaving-loom which is the noble part of the house.

40 The four cardinal points and the four seasons must therefore be added to the series of oppositions and homologies presented above (the fact that these significations both belong to and fit in with the mythico-ritual system taken as a whole can, moreover, be demonstrated): . . . culture: nature :: east: west :: south: north :: spring: autumn :: summer: winter.

41 An attempt will be made elsewhere to draw out the theoretical implications from the fact that the rules of transformation which make it possible to pass from one space to the other may be reduced to movements of the body.

42 It is therefore understandable that the threshold be associated, directly or indirectly with rites whose function is to bring about an inversion in the course of things by carrying out an inversion of the basic oppositions: the rites to obtain rain or fine weather, for instance or those that are practised at the thresholds between different periods of time (the night before En-nayer, for example, which is the first day of the solar year, when charms are buried at the threshold of the door).

43 In certain regions of Kabylia, the young bride and a young circumcised boy (on the occasion of the same celebration) must cross paths over the threshold.

44 The correspondence between the four corners of the house and the four cardinal points is clearly expressed in certain propitiatory rites that are observed in the Aurès: when the fireplace is renewed, on new year's day, the Chaouïa woman cooks some fritters, divides up into four pieces the first one that is cooked and throws the pieces in the direction of the four corners of the house. She does the same with the ritual dish on the first day of spring (Gaudry 1928: 58–59).

45 We shall attempt to show elsewhere that the same structure is to be found in the order of time. But in order to show that this is doubtless a very general form of magical thought, one more, very similar, example will suffice: the Arabs of Maghreb considered it to be a good sign, reports Ben Cheneb, for a horse to have its right front foot and its left back foot white in colour; the master of such a horse cannot fail to be happy since he mounts towards white and also dismounts towards white (Arabic horsemen, as is known, always mount on the right and dismount on the left) (Cheneb 1905–1907: 312).

46 The mirror plays a great role in inversion rites and particularly in rites to obtain fine weather.

47 This explains why it has always escaped the notice of observers, even the most attentive.

48 In the interior space also the two opposed parts are hierarchized. Here, beside all the other indications quoted, is one more saying: 'It is better to have a house full of men than full of goods (*el mal*)', that is to say, of cattle.

30

THE TEMPORALITY
OF THE LANDSCAPE*

Tim Ingold

Prologue

I adhere to that school of thought which holds that social or cultural anthropology, biological anthropology and archaeology form a necessary unity – that they are all part of the same intellectual enterprise (Ingold 1992a: 694). I am not concerned here with the link with biological or 'physical' anthropology, but what I have to say does bear centrally on the unifying themes of archaeology and social-cultural anthropology. I want to stress two such themes, and they are closely related. First, human life is a process that involves the passage of time. Second, this life-process is also the process of formation of the landscapes in which people have lived. Time and landscape, then, are to my mind the essential points of topical contact between archaeology and anthropology. My purpose, in this article, is to bring the perspectives of archaeology and anthropology into unison through a focus on the temporality of the landscape. In particular, I believe that such a focus might enable us to move beyond the sterile opposition between the naturalistic view of the landscape as a neutral, external backdrop to human activities, and the culturalistic view that every landscape is a particular cognitive or symbolic ordering of space. I argue that we should adopt, in place of both these views, what I call a 'dwelling perspective', according to which the landscape is constituted as an enduring record of – and testimony to – the lives and works of past generations who have dwelt within it, and in so doing, have left there something of themselves.

For anthropologists, to adopt a perspective of this kind means bringing to bear the knowledge born of immediate experience, by privileging the understandings that people derive from their lived, everyday involvement in the world. Yet it will surely be objected that this avenue is not open to archaeologists concerned with human activities in the distant past. 'The people', it is said 'they're dead' (Sahlins 1972: 81); only the material record remains for their successors of our own time to interpret as best they can. But this objection misses the point, which is that the *practice of archaeology is itself a form of dwelling*. The knowledge born of this practice is thus on a par with that

*First published in *World Archaeology* (1993), **25**, 152–74.

which comes from the practical activity of the native dweller and which the anthropologist, through participation, seeks to learn and understand. For both the archaeologist and the native dweller, the landscape tells – or rather is – a story. It enfolds the lives and times of predecessors who, over the generations, have moved around in it and played their part in its formation. To perceive the landscape is therefore to carry out an act of remembrance, and remembering is not so much a matter of calling up an internal image, stored in the mind, as of engaging perceptually with an environment that is itself pregnant with the past. To be sure, the rules and methods of engagement employed respectively by the native dweller and the archaeologist will differ, as will the stories they tell, nevertheless – in so far as both seek the past in the landscape – they are engaged in projects of fundamentally the same kind.

It is of course part of an archaeological training to learn to attend to those clues which the rest of us might pass over (literally, when they are below the surface), and which make it possible to tell a fuller or a richer story. Likewise, native dwellers (and their anthropological companions) learn through an education of attention. The novice hunter, for example, travels through the country with his mentors, and as he goes, specific features are pointed out to him. Other things he discovers for himself, in the course of further forays, by watching, listening and feeling. Thus the experienced hunter is the knowledgeable hunter. He can tell things from subtle indications that you or I, unskilled in the hunter's art, might not even notice. Called upon to explicate this knowledge, he may do so in a form that reappears in the work of the non-native ethnographer as a corpus of myths or stories, whereas the archaeologist's knowledge – drawn from the practices of excavation rather than hunting – may appear in the seemingly authoritative form of the site report. But we should resist the temptation to assume that since stories are stories they are, in some sense, unreal or untrue, for this is to suppose that the only real reality, or true truth, is one in which we, as living, experiencing beings, can have no part at all. Telling a story is not like weaving a tapestry to cover up the world, it is rather a way of guiding the attention of listeners or readers into it. A person who can 'tell' is one who is perceptually attuned to picking up information in the environment that others, less skilled in the tasks of perception, might miss, and the teller, in rendering his knowledge explicit, conducts the attention of his audience along the same paths as his own.

Following that preamble, I shall now go on to lay out the burden of my argument. This is presented in four principal sections. In the first two, I attempt to specify more precisely what I mean by my key terms – landscape and temporality. I argue that temporality inheres in the pattern of dwelling activities that I call the taskscape. In the third section I consider how taskscape relates to landscape and, ultimately by dissolving the distinction between them, I proceed to recover the temporality of the landscape itself. Finally, I draw some concrete illustrations of my arguments from a well-known painting by Bruegel, *The Harvesters*.

Landscape

Let me begin by explaining what the landscape is not. It is not 'land', it is not 'nature', and it is not 'space' . Consider, first of all, the distinction between land and landscape. Land is not something you can see, any more than you can see the weight of physical objects. All objects of the most diverse kinds have weight, and it is possible to express how much anything weighs relative to any other thing. Likewise, land is a kind of lowest common denominator of the phenomenal world, inherent in every portion of the earth's surface yet directly visible in none, and in terms of which any portion may be rendered quantitatively equivalent to any other (Ingold 1986a: 153–4). You can ask of land, as of weight, how much there is, but not what it is like. But where land is thus quantitative and homogeneous, the landscape is qualitative and heterogeneous. Supposing that you are standing outdoors, it is what you see all around: a contoured and textured surface replete with diverse objects – living and non-living, natural and artificial (these distinctions are both problematic, as we shall see, but they will serve for the time being). Thus at any particular moment, you can ask of a landscape what it is like, but not how much of it there is. For the landscape is a plenum, there are no holes in it that remain to be filled in, so that every infill is in reality a reworking. As Meinig observes, one should not overlook 'the powerful fact that life must be lived amidst that which was made before' (1979a: 44).

The landscape is not 'nature'. Of course, nature can mean many things, and this is not the place for a discourse on the history of the concept. Suffice it to say that I have in mind the rather specific sense whose ontological foundation is an imagined separation between the human perceiver and the world, such that the perceiver has to reconstruct the world, in consciousness, prior to any meaningful engagement with it. The world of nature, it is often said, is what lies 'out there'. All kinds of entities are supposed to exist out there, but not you and I. We live 'in here', in the intersubjective space marked out by our mental representations. Application of this logic forces an insistent dualism, between object and subject, the material and the ideal, operational and cognized, 'etic' and 'emic'. Some writers distinguish between nature and the landscape in just these terms – the former is said to stand to the latter as physical reality to its cultural or symbolic construction. For example, Daniels and Cosgrove introduce a collection of essays on *The Iconography of Landscape* with the following definition: 'A landscape is a cultural image, a pictorial way of representing or symbolising surroundings' (1988: 1).

I do not share this view. To the contrary, I reject the division between inner and outer worlds – respectively of mind and matter, meaning and substance – upon which such distinction rests. The landscape, I hold, is not a picture in the imagination, surveyed by the mind's eye; nor, however, is it an alien and formless substrate awaiting the imposition of human order. 'The idea of landscape', as Meinig writes, 'runs counter to recognition of any simple binary relationship between man and nature' (Meinig 1979b: 2). Thus, neither is the landscape identical to nature, nor is it on the side of humanity against nature. As the familiar domain of our dwelling, it is with us, not against us, but it is no less real for that. And through living in it, the landscape becomes a part of us, just as we are a part of it. Moreover, what goes for its human component goes for other components as well. In a world construed as nature, every object is a self-contained entity, interacting with others through some kind of external contact. But in a landscape, each component enfolds within its essence the totality of its relations with each and every other. In short, whereas the order of nature is explicate, the order of the landscape is implicate (Bohm 1980: 172).

The landscape is not 'space'. To appreciate the contrast, we could compare the everyday project of dwelling in the world with the rather peculiar and specialized project of the surveyor or cartographer whose objective is to *represent* it. No doubt the surveyor, as he goes about his practical tasks, experiences the landscape much as does everyone else whose business of life lies there. Like other people, he is mobile, yet unable to be in more than one place at a time. In the landscape, the distance between two places, A and B, is experienced as a journey made, a bodily movement from one place to the other, and the gradually changing vistas along the route. The surveyor's job, however, is to take instrumental measurements from a considerable number of places, and to combine these data to produce a single picture which is independent of any point of observation. This picture is of the world as it could be directly apprehended only by a consciousness capable of being everywhere at once and nowhere in particular (the nearest we can get to this in practice is by taking an aerial or 'bird's-eye' view). To such a consciousness, at once immobile and omnipresent, the distance between A and B would be the length of a line plotted between two points that are simultaneously in view, that line marking one of any number of journeys that could potentially be made (cf. Bourdieu 1977: 2). It is as though, from an imaginary position above the world, I could direct the movements of my body within it, like a counter on a board, so that to say 'I am here' is not to point from somewhere to my surroundings, but to point from nowhere to the position on the board where my body happens to be. And whereas actual journeys are made through a landscape, the board on which all potential journeys may be plotted is equivalent to space.

There is a tradition of geographical research (e.g. Gould and White 1974) which sets out from the premise that we are all cartographers in our daily lives, and that we use our bodies as the surveyor uses his instruments, to register a sensory input from multiple points of observation, which is then processed by our intelligence into an image which we carry around with us, like a map in our heads, wherever we go. The mind, rather than reaching into its surroundings from its dwelling place within the world, may be likened in this view to a film spread out upon its exterior surface. To understand the sense of space that is implicated in this cartographic view of environmental perception, it is helpful to draw an analogy from the linguistics of Ferdinand de Saussure. To grasp the essence of language, Saussure invites us to picture thought and sound as two continuous and undifferentiated planes, of mental and phonic substance respectively, like two sides of a sheet of paper. By cutting the sheet into pieces (words) we create, on one side, a system of discrete concepts, and on the other, a system of discrete sounds; and since one side cannot be cut without at the same time cutting the other, the two systems of division are necessarily homologous so that to each concept there corresponds a sound (Saussure 1959: 112–13). Now when geographers and anthropologists write about space, what is generally implied is something closely akin to Saussure's sheet of paper, only in this case the counter-side to thought is the continuum not of phonic substance but of the surface of the earth. And so it appears that the division of the world into a mosaic of externally bounded segments is entailed in the very production of spatial meanings. Just as the word, for Saussure, is the union of a concept with a delimited 'chunk' of sound, so the place is the union of a symbolic meaning with a delimited block of the earth's surface. Spatial differentiation implies spatial segmentation.

This is not so of the landscape, however. For a place in the landscape is not 'cut out' from the whole, either on the plane of ideas or on that of material substance. Rather, each place embodies the whole at a particular nexus within it, and in this respect is different from every other. A place owes its character to the experiences it affords to those who spend time there – to the sights, sounds and indeed smells that constitute its specific ambience. And these, in turn, depend on the kinds of activities in which its inhabitants engage. It is from this relational context of people's engagement with the world, in the business of dwelling, that each place draws its unique significance. Thus whereas with space, meanings are attached to the world, with the landscape they are *gathered from* it. Moreover, while places have centres – indeed it would be more appropriate to say that they *are* centres they have no boundaries. In journeying from place A to place B it makes no sense to ask, along the way, whether one is 'still' in A or has 'crossed over' to B (Ingold 1986a: 155). Of course, boundaries of various kinds may be drawn in the landscape, and identified either with natural features such as the course of a river or an escarpment, or with built structures such as walls and fences. But such boundaries are not a condition for the constitution of the places on either side of them; nor do they segment the landscape, for the features with which they are identified are themselves an integral part of it. Finally, it is important to note that no feature of the landscape is, of itself, a boundary. It can only become a boundary, or the indicator of a boundary, in relation to the activities of the people (or animals) for whom it is recognized or experienced as such.

In the course of explaining what the landscape is not, I have already moved some way towards a positive characterization. In short, the landscape is the world as it is known to those who dwell therein, who inhabit its places and journey along the paths connecting them. Is it not, then, identical to what we might otherwise call the environment? Certainly the distinction between landscape and environment is not easy to draw, and for many purposes they may be treated as practically synonymous. It will already be apparent that I cannot accept the distinction offered by Tuan, who argues that an environment is 'a given, a piece of reality that is simply there', as opposed to the landscape, which is a product of human cognition, 'an achievement of the mature mind' (Tuan 1979: 90, 100). For that is merely to reproduce the dichotomy between nature and humanity. The environment is no more 'nature' than is the landscape a symbolic construct. Elsewhere, I have contrasted nature and environment by way of a distinction between reality of – 'the physical world of neutral objects apparent only to the detached, indifferent observer', and reality for – 'the world constituted in relation to the organism or person whose environment it is' (Ingold 1992b: 44). But to think of environment in this sense is to regard it primarily in terms of *function*, of what it affords to creatures – whether human or non-human – with certain capabilities and projects of action. Reciprocally, to regard these creatures as organisms is to view them in terms of their principles of dynamic functioning, that is as organized systems (Pittendrigh 1958: 394). As Lewontin succinctly puts it (1982: 160), the environment is 'nature organised by an organism'.

The concept of landscape, by contrast, puts the emphasis on form, in just the same way that the concept of the body emphasizes the form rather than the function of a living creature. Like organism and environment, body and landscape are complementary terms: each implies the other, alternately as figure and ground. The forms of the landscape are not, however, prepared in advance for creatures to occupy, nor are the bodily forms of those creatures independently specified in their genetic makeup. Both sets of forms are generated and sustained in and through the processual unfolding of a total field of relations that cuts across the emergent interface between organism and environment (Goodwin 1988). Having regard to its formative properties, we may refer to this process as one of embodiment. Though the notion of embodiment has recently come much into fashion, there has been a tendency – following an ancient inclination in Western thought to prioritize form over process (Oyama 1985: 13) – to conceive of it as a movement of inscription, whereby some pre-existing pattern, template or programme, whether genetic or cultural, is 'realized' in a substantive medium. This is not what I have in mind, however. To the contrary, and adopting a helpful distinction from Connerton (1989: 72–3), I regard embodiment as a movement of incorporation rather than inscription, not a transcribing of form onto material but a movement wherein forms themselves are generated (Ingold 1990: 215). Taking the organism as our focus of reference, this movement is what is commonly known as the life-cycle. Thus organisms may be said to incorporate, in their bodily forms, the life-cycle processes that give rise to them. Could not the same, then, be said of the environment? Is it possible to identify a corresponding cycle, or rather a series of interlocking cycles, which build themselves into the forms of the landscape, and of which the landscape may accordingly be regarded as an embodiment? Before answering this question, we need to turn to the second of my key terms, namely 'temporality'.

Temporality

Let me begin, once again, by stating what temporality is not. It is not chronology (as opposed to history), and it is not history (as opposed to chronology). By chronology, I mean any regular system of dated time intervals, in which events are said to have taken place. By history, I mean any series of events which may be dated in time according to their occurrence in one or another chronological interval. Thus the Battle of Hastings was an historical event, 1066 was a date (marking the interval of a year), and records tell us that the former occurred in the latter. In the mere succession of dates there are no events, because everything repeats; in the mere succession of events there is no time, as nothing does. The relation between chronology and history, in this conception, has been well expressed by Kubler: 'Without change there is no history; without regularity there is no time. Time and history are related as rule and variation: time is the regular setting for the vagaries of history' (1962: 72).

Now in introducing the concept of temporality, I do not intend that it should stand as a third term, alongside the concepts of chronology and history. For in the sense in which I shall use the term here, temporality entails a perspective that contrasts radically with the one, outlined above, that sets up history and chronology in a relation of complementary opposition. The contrast is essentially equivalent to that drawn by Gell (1992: 149–55) between what he calls (following McTaggart) the A-series, in which time is immanent in the passage of events, and the B-series, in which events are strung out in time like beads on a thread. Whereas in the B-series, events are treated as isolated happenings, succeeding one another frame by frame, each event in the A-series is seen to encompass a pattern of retensions from the past and protentions for the future. Thus from the A-series point of view, temporality and historicity are not opposed but rather merge in the experience of those who, in their

515

activities, carry forward the process of social life. Taken together, these activities make up what I shall call the 'taskscape', and it is with the intrinsic temporality of the taskscape that I shall be principally concerned in this section.

We can make a start by returning for a moment to the distinction between land and landscape. As a common denominator in terms of which constituents of the environment of diverse kinds may be rendered quantitatively comparable, I compared land with weight. But I could equally have drawn the comparison with *value* or with *labour*. Value is the denominator of commodities that enables us to say how much any one thing is worth by comparison with another, even though these two things may be quite unlike in terms of their physical qualities and potential uses. In this sense, the concept of value (in general) is classically distinguished from that of *use*-value, which refers to the specific properties or 'affordances' of any particular object, that commend it to the project of a user (Ingold 1992b: 48-9, cf. Gibson 1979: 127; Marx 1930: 169). Clearly, this distinction, between value and use-value, is precisely homologous to that between land and landscape. But if we turn to consider the work that goes into the making of useful things, then again we can recognize that whilst the operations of making are indeed as unlike as the objects produced – involving different raw materials, different tools, different procedures and different skills – they can nevertheless be compared in that they call for variable amounts of what may simply be called 'labour': the common denominator of productive activities. Like land and value, labour is quantitative and homogeneous, human work shorn of its particularities. It is of course the founding premise of the labour theory of value that the amount of value in a thing is determined by the amount of labour that went into producing it.

How, then, should we describe the practices of work in their concrete particulars? For this purpose I shall adopt the term 'task', defined as any practical operation, carried out by a skilled agent in an environment, as part of his or her normal business of life. In other words, tasks are the constitutive acts of dwelling. No more than features of the landscape, however, are tasks suspended in a vacuum. Every task takes its meaning from its position within an ensemble of tasks, performed in series or in parallel, and usually by many people working together. One of the great mistakes of recent anthropology – what Reynolds (1993: 410) calls 'the great tool-use fallacy' – has been to insist upon a separation between the domains of technical and social activity, a separation that has blinded us to the fact that one of the outstanding features of human technical practices lies in their embeddedness in the current of sociality. It is to the entire ensemble of tasks, in their mutual interlocking, that I refer by the concept of *taskscape*. Just as the landscape is an array of related features, so – by analogy – the taskscape is an array of related activities. And as with the landscape, it is qualitative and heterogeneous: we can ask of a taskscape, as of a landscape, what it is like, but not how much of it there is. In short, the taskscape is to labour what the landscape is to land, and indeed what an ensemble of use-values is to value in general.

Now if value is measured out in units of money, and land in units of space, what is the currency of labour? The answer, of course, is time – but it is time of a very peculiar sort, one that must be wholly indifferent to the modulations of human experience. To most of us it appears in the familiar guise of clock-time: thus an hour is an hour, regardless of what one is doing in it, or of how one feels. But this kind of chronological time does not depend upon the existence of artificial clocks.

It may be based on any perfectly repetitive, mechanical system including that (putatively) constituted by the earth in its axial rotations and in its revolutions around the sun. Sorokin and Merton (1937), in a classic paper, call it 'astronomical' time: it is, they write, 'uniform, homogeneous; . . . purely quantitative, shorn of qualitative variations'. And they distinguish it from 'social time', which they see as fundamentally qualitative, something to which we can affix moral judgements such as good or bad, grounded in the 'rhythms, pulsations and beats of the societies in which they are found', and for that reason tied to the particular circumstances of place and people (1937: 621–3). Adopting Sorokin and Merton's distinction, we could perhaps conclude that whereas labour is measured out in units of astronomical time, or in clock-time calibrated to an astronomical standard, the temporality of the taskscape is essentially social. Before we can accept this conclusion, however, the idea of social time must be examined a little more closely.

In my earlier discussion of the significance of space, I showed that in the cartographic imagination, the mind is supposed to be laid out upon the surface of the earth. Likewise in the chronological perspective, time appears as the interface between mind and 'duration' – by which is meant an undifferentiated stream of bodily activity and experience. Taking time in this sense, Durkheim famously likened it to 'an endless chart, where all duration is spread out before the mind, and upon which all possible events can be located in relation to fixed and determinate guidelines' (1976 [1915]: 10). Rather like Saussure's sheet of paper, it could be compared to a strip of infinite length, with thought on one side and duration on the other. By cutting the strip into segments we establish a division, on the one hand, into calendrical intervals or dates, and on the other hand, into discrete 'chunks' of lived experience, such that to every chunk there corresponds a date in a uniform sequence of before and after. And as every chunk succeeds the next, like frames on a reel of film, we imagine ourselves to be looking on 'as time goes by', as though we could take up a point of view detached from the temporal process of our life in the world and watch ourselves engaged now in this task, now in that, in an unending series of present instants. Whence, then, come the divisions which give chronological form to the substance of experience? Durkheim's answer, as is well known, was that these divisions – 'indispensable guidelines' for the temporal ordering of events – come from *society*, corresponding to the 'periodical recurrence of rites, feasts, and public ceremonies' (ibid.). Thus for Durkheim, time is at once chronological *and* social, for society itself is a kind of clock, whose moving parts are individual human beings (Ingold 1986b: 341).

This is not, however, the way we perceive the temporality of the taskscape. For we do so not as spectators but as participants, in the very performance of our tasks. As Merleau-Ponty put it, in reckoning with an environment, I am 'at my task rather than confronting it' (1962: 416). The notion that we can stand aside and observe the passage of time is founded upon an illusion of disembodiment. This passage is, indeed, none other than our own journey through the taskscape in the business of dwelling. Once again we can take our cue from Merleau-Ponty: 'the passage of one present to the next is not a thing which I conceive, nor do I see it as an onlooker, I *effect it*' (1962: 421, my emphasis). Reaching out into the taskscape, I perceive, at this moment, a particular vista of past and future; but it is a vista that is available from this moment and no other (see Gell 1992: 269). As such, it *constitutes* my present, conferring upon it a unique character. Thus the present is not *marked off* from a past that it has replaced or a future that will, in turn, replace it; it rather gathers the past and future into itself, like refractions in a crystal ball. And just as in the landscape, we can move from place to place without crossing any boundary, since the vista that constitutes the identity of a place changes even as we move, so likewise can we move from one present to another without having to break through any chronological barrier that might be supposed to separate each present from the next in line. Indeed the features that Durkheim identified as serving this segmenting function – rites, feasts and ceremonies – are themselves as integral to the taskscape as are boundary markers such as walls or fences to the landscape.

The temporality of the taskscape is social, then, not because society provides an external frame against which particular tasks find independent measure, but because people, in the performance of their tasks, *also attend to one another*. Looking back, we can see that Durkheim's error was to divorce the sphere of people's mutual involvement from that of their everyday practical activity in the world, leaving the latter to be carried out by individuals in hermetic isolation. In real life, this is not how we go about our business. By watching, listening, perhaps even touching, we continually feel each other's presence in the social environment, at every moment adjusting our movements in response to this ongoing perceptual monitoring (Ingold 1993: 456) . For the orchestral musician, playing an instrument, watching the conductor and listening to one's fellow players are all inseparable aspects of the same process of action: for this reason, the gestures of the performers may be said to *resonate* with each other. In orchestral music, the achievement of resonance is an absolute precondition for successful performance. But the same is true, more generally, of social life (Richards 1991; Wikan 1992). Indeed it could be argued that in the resonance of movement and feeling stemming from people's mutually attentive engagement, in shared contexts of practical activity, lies the very foundation of sociality.

Let me pursue the analogy between orchestral performance and social life a little further since, more than any other artistic genre, music mirrors the temporal form of the taskscape. I want, by means of this analogy, to make three points. First, whilst there are cycles and repetitions in music as in social life, these are essentially rhythmic rather than metronomic (on this distinction, see Young (1988: 19)). It is for precisely this reason that social time, *pace* Durkheim, is not chronological. A metronome, like a clock, inscribes an artificial division into equal segments upon an otherwise undifferentiated movement; rhythm, by contrast, is intrinsic to the movement itself. Langer has argued that the essence of rhythm lies in the successive building up and resolution of tension, on the principle that every resolution is itself a preparation for the next building-up (1953: 126–7). There may of course be rests or sustained notes within a piece, but far from breaking it up into segments, such moments are generally ones of high tension, whose resolution becomes ever more urgent the longer they are held. Only our last exhalation of breath is not a preparation for the next inhalation – with that, we die; similarly with the last beat the music comes to an end. Social life, however, is never finished, and there are no breaks in it that are not integral to its tensile structure, to the 'ebb and flow of activity' by which society itself seems to breathe (Young 1988: 53).

My second point is that in music as in social life, there is not just one rhythmic cycle, but a complex interweaving of very many concurrent cycles (for an exemplary analysis of 'the rhythmic structures of economic life', see Guyer (1988)). Whilst it reflects the temporal form of social life, music in fact represents a very considerable simplification, since it involves only one sensory register (the auditory), and its rhythms are fewer and more tightly controlled. In both cases, however, since any rhythm may be taken as the tempo for any of the others, there is no single, one-dimensional strand of time. As Langer puts it: 'life is always a dense fabric of concurrent tensions, and as each of them is a measure of time, the measurements themselves do not coincide' (1953: 113). Thus the temporality of the taskscape, while it is intrinsic rather than externally imposed (metronomic), lies not in any particular rhythm, but in the network of interrelationships between the multiple rhythms of which the taskscape is itself constituted. To cite a celebrated anthropological example: among the Nuer of southern Sudan, according to Evans-Pritchard, the passage of time is 'primarily the succession of [pastoral] tasks *and their relations to one another*' (1940: 101–2; my emphasis). Each of these relations is, of course, a specific resonance. And so, just as social life consists in the unfolding of a field of relationships among persons who attend to one another in what they do, its temporality consists in the unfolding of the resultant pattern of resonances.

Third, the forms of the taskscape, like those of music, come into being through movement. Music exists only when it is being performed (it does not pre-exist, as is sometimes thought, in the score, any more than a cake pre-exists in the recipe for making it). Similarly, the taskscape exists only so long as people are actually engaged in the activities of dwelling, despite the attempts of anthropologists to translate it into something rather equivalent to a score – a kind of ideal design for dwelling – that generally goes by the name of 'culture', and that people are supposed to bring with them into their encounter with the world. This parallel, however, brings me to a critical question. Up to now, my discussion of temporality has concentrated exclusively on the taskscape, allowing the landscape to slip from view. It is now high time to bring it back into focus. I argued in the previous section that the landscape is not nature; here I claim that the taskscape is not culture. Landscape and taskscape, then, are not to be opposed as nature to culture. So how are we to understand the relation between them? Where does one end and the other begin? Can they even be distinguished at all? If music best reflects the forms of the taskscape, it might be thought that painting is the most natural medium for representing the forms of the landscape. And this suggests that an examination of the difference, in the field of art, between music and painting might offer some clues as to how a distinction might possibly be drawn between taskscape and landscape as facets of the real world. I begin by following up this suggestion.

Temporalizing the landscape

At first glance the difference seems obvious: paintings do not have to be performed, they are presented to us as works that are complete in themselves. But on closer inspection, this contrast appears more as an artefact of a systematic bias in Western thought, to which I have already alluded, that leads us to privilege form over process. Thus the actual work of painting is subordinated to the final product; the former is hidden from view so that the latter alone becomes an object of contemplation. In many non-western societies, by contrast, the order of priority is reversed: what is essential is the act of painting itself, of which the products may be relatively short-lived – barely perceived before being erased or covered up. This is so, for example, among the Yolngu, an Aboriginal people of northern Australia, whose experience of finished paintings, according to their ethnographer, is limited to 'images fleetingly glimpsed through the corner of their eyes' (Morphy 1989: 26). The emphasis, here, is on painting as *performance*. Far from being the preparation of objects for future contemplation, it is an act of contemplation in itself. So, too, is performing or listening to music. Thus all at once, the contrast between painting and music seems less secure. It becomes a matter of degree, in the extent to which forms endure beyond the immediate contexts of their production. Musical sound, of course, is subject to the property of rapid fading: speeding outwards from its point of emission, and dissipating as it goes, it is present only momentarily to our senses. But where, as in painting, gestures leave their traces in solid substance, the resulting forms may last much longer, albeit never indefinitely.

Returning now from the contrast between music and painting to that between taskscape and landscape, the first point to note is that no more than a painting is the landscape given ready-made. One cannot, as Inglis points out, 'treat landscape as an object it is to be understood. It is a living process; it makes men; it is made by them' (1977: 489). Just as with music, the forms of the landscape are generated in movement: these forms, however, are congealed in a solid medium – indeed, to borrow Inglis's words again, 'a landscape is the most solid appearance in which a history can declare itself' (ibid.). Thanks to their solidity, features of the landscape remain available for inspection long after the movement that gave rise to them has ceased. If, as Mead argued (1977 [1938]: 97), every object is to be regarded as a 'collapsed act', then *the landscape as a whole must likewise be understood as the taskscape in its embodied form*: a pattern of activities 'collapsed' into an array of features. But to reiterate a point made earlier, the landscape takes on its forms through a process of incorporation, not of inscription. That is to say, the process is not one whereby cultural design is imposed upon a naturally given substrate, as though the movement issued from the form and was completed in its concrete realization in the material. For the forms of the landscape arise alongside those of the taskscape, within the same current of activity. If we recognize a man's gait in the pattern of his footprints, it is not because the gait preceded the footprints and was 'inscribed' in them, but because both the gait and the prints arose within the movement of the man's walking.

Since, moreover, the activities that comprise the taskscape are unending, the landscape is never complete: neither 'built' nor 'unbuilt', it is perpetually under construction. This is why the conventional dichotomy between natural and artificial (or 'man-made') components of the landscape is so problematic. Virtually by definition, an artefact is an object shaped to a pre-conceived image that motivated its construction, and it is 'finished' at the point when it is brought into conformity with this image. What happens to it beyond that point is supposed to belong to the phase of use rather than manufacture, to dwelling rather than building. But the forms of the landscape are not pre-prepared for people to live in – not by nature nor by human hands – for it is in the very process of dwelling that these forms are constituted. 'To build', as Heidegger insisted, 'is itself already to dwell' (1971: 146). Thus the landscape is always in the nature of 'work in progress'.

My conclusion that the landscape is the congealed form of the taskscape does enable us to explain why, intuitively, the landscape seems to be what we *see* around us, whereas the taskscape is what we *hear*. To be seen, an object need do nothing itself, for the optic array that specifies its form to a viewer consists of light reflected off its outer surfaces. To be heard, on the other hand, an object must actively emit sounds or, through its movement, cause sound to be emitted by other objects with which it comes into contact. Thus, outside my window I see a landscape of houses, trees, gardens, a street and pavement. I do not hear any of these things, but I can hear people talking on the pavement, a car passing by, birds singing in the trees, a dog barking somewhere in the distance, and the sound of hammering as a neighbour repairs his garden shed. In short, what I hear is *activity*, even when its source cannot be seen. And since the forms of the taskscape, suspended as they are in movement, are present *only* as activity, the limits of the taskscape are also the limits of the auditory world. (Whilst I deal here only with visual and aural perception, we should not underestimate the significance of touch, which is important to all of us but above all to blind people, for whom it opens up the possibility of access to the landscape – if only through proximate bodily contact.)

This argument carries an important corollary. Whilst both the landscape and the taskscape presuppose the presence of an agent who watches and listens, the taskscape must be populated with beings who are themselves agents, and who reciprocally 'act back' in the process of their own dwelling. In other words, the taskscape exists not just as activity but as *interactivity*. Indeed this conclusion was already foreshadowed when I introduced the concept of resonance as the rhythmic harmonization of mutual attention. Having said that, however, there is no reason why the domain of interactivity should be confined to the movement of human beings. We hear animals as well as people, such as the birds and the dog in my example above. Hunters, to take another example, are alert to every sight, sound or smell that reveals the presence of animals, and we can be sure that the animals are likewise alert to the presence of humans, as they are also to that of one another. On a larger scale, the hunters' journeys through the landscape, or their oscillations between the procurement of different animal species, resonate with the migratory movements of terrestrial mammals, birds and fish. Perhaps then, as Reed argues, there is a fundamental difference between our perception of animate beings and inanimate objects, since the former- by virtue of their capacity for autonomous movement – 'are *aware* of their surroundings (including us) and because they act on those surroundings (including us)' (Reed 1988: 116). In other words, they afford the possibility not only of action but also of interaction (Gibson 1979: 135). Should we, then, draw the boundaries of the taskscape around the limits of the animate'?

Though the argument is a compelling one, I find that it is ultimately unsatisfactory, for two reasons in particular. First, as Langer observes, 'rhythm is the basis of life, but not limited to life' (1953: 128). The rhythms of human activities resonate not only with those of other living things but also with a whole host of other rhythmic phenomena – the cycles of day and night and of the seasons, the winds, the tides, and so on. Citing a petition of 1800 from the seaside town of Sunderland, in which it is explained that 'people are obliged to be up at all hours of the night to attend the tides and their affairs upon the river', Thompson (1967: 59–60) notes that 'the operative phrase is "attend the tides": the patterning of social time in the seaport follows *upon* the rhythms of the sea'. In many cases these natural rhythmic phenomena find their ultimate cause in the mechanics of planetary motion, but it is not of course to these that we resonate. Thus we resonate to the cycles of light and darkness, not to the rotation of the earth, even though the diurnal cycle is caused by the earth's axial rotation. And we resonate to the cycles of vegetative growth and decay, not to the earth's revolutions around the sun, even though the latter cause the cycle of the seasons. Moreover these resonances are embodied, in the sense that they are not only historically incorporated into the enduring features of the landscape but also developmentally incorporated into our very constitution as biological organisms. Thus Young describes the body as 'an array of interlocking (or interflowing) cycles, with their own spheres of partial independence within the solar cycle' (1988: 41). We do not consult these cycles, as we might consult a wrist-watch, in order to time our own activities, for the cycles are inherent in the rhythmic structure of the activities themselves. It would seem, then, that the pattern of resonances that comprises the temporality of the taskscape must be expanded to embrace the totality of rhythmic phenomena, whether animate or inanimate.

The second reason why I would be reluctant to restrict the taskscape to the realm of living things has to do with the very notion of animacy. I do not think we can regard this as a property that can be ascribed to objects in isolation, such that some (animate) have it and others (inanimate) do not. For life is not a principle that is separately installed inside individual organisms, and which sets them in motion upon the stage of the inanimate. To the contrary, as I have argued elsewhere, life is 'a name for *what is going on* in the generative field within which organic forms are located and "held in place"' (Ingold 1990: 215). That generative field is constituted by the totality of organism-environment relations, and the activities of organisms are moments of its unfolding. Indeed once we think of the world in this way, as a total movement of becoming which builds itself into the forms we see, and in which each form takes shape in continuous relation to those around it, then the distinction between the animate and the inanimate seems to dissolve. The world itself takes on the character of an organism, and the movements of animals – including those of us human beings – are parts or aspects of its life-process (Lovelock 1979). This means that in dwelling in the world, we do not act *upon* it, or do things *to* it; rather we move along *with* it. Our actions do not transform the world, they are part and parcel of the world's transforming itself. And that is just another way of saying that they belong to time.

For in the final analysis, everything is suspended in movement. As Whitehead once remarked, 'there is no holding nature still and looking at it' (cited in Ho 1989: 19–20). What appear to us as the fixed forms of the landscape, passive and unchanging unless acted upon from outside, are themselves in motion, albeit on a scale immeasurably slower and more majestic than that on which our own activities are conducted. Imagine a film of the landscape, shot over years, centuries, even millennia. Slightly speeded up, plants appear to engage in very animal-like movements, trees flex their limbs without any prompting from the winds. Speeded up rather more, glaciers flow like rivers and even the earth begins to move. At yet greater speeds solid rock bends, buckles and flows like molten metal. The world itself begins to breathe. Thus the rhythmic pattern of human activities nests within the wider pattern of activity for all animal life, which in turn nests within the pattern of activity for all so-called living things, which nests within the life-process of the world. At each of these levels, coherence is founded upon resonance (Ho 1989: 18). Ultimately, then, by replacing the tasks of human dwelling in their proper context within the process of becoming of the world as a whole, we can do away with the dichotomy between taskscape and landscape – only, however, by recognizing the fundamental temporality of the landscape itself.

The Harvesters

In order to provide some illustration of the ideas developed in the preceding sections, I reproduce here a painting which, more than any other I know, vividly captures a sense of the temporality of the landscape. This is *The Harvesters*, painted by Pieter Bruegel the Elder in 1565 (see Figure 30.1). I am not an art historian or critic, and my purpose is not to analyse the painting in terms of style, composition or aesthetic effect. Nor am I concerned with the historical context of its production. Suffice it to say that the picture is believed to be one of a series of twelve, each depicting a month of the year, out of which only five have survived (W. Gibson 1977: 147). Each panel portrays a landscape, in the colours and apparel appropriate to the month, and shows people engaged in the tasks of the agricultural cycle that are usual at that time of year. *The Harvesters* depicts the month of August, and shows field hands at work reaping

Figure 30.1 The Harvesters *(1565) by Pieter Bruegel the Elder. Courtesy of The Metropolitan Museum of Art, Rogers Fund. 1919 (19.164). All rights reserved. The Metropolitan Museum of Art.*

and sheafing a luxuriant crop of wheat, whilst others pause for a midday meal and some for a well-earned rest. The sense of rustic harmony conveyed in this scene may, perhaps, represent something of an idealization on Bruegel's part. As Walter Gibson points out, Bruegel was inclined to 'depict peasants very much as a wealthy landowner would have viewed them, as the anonymous tenders of his fields and flocks' (1977: 157–8). Any landowner would have had cause for satisfaction in such a fine crop, whereas the hands who sweated to bring it in may have had a rather different experience. Nevertheless, Bruegel painted during a period of great material prosperity in the Netherlands, in which all shared to some degree. These were fortunate times.

Rather than viewing the painting as a work of art, I would like to invite you – the reader – to imagine yourself set down in the very landscape depicted, on a sultry August day in 1565. Standing a little way off to the right of the group beneath the tree, you are a witness to the scene unfolding about you. And of course you hear it too, for the scene does not unfold in silence. So accustomed are we to thinking of the landscape as a picture that we can look *at* like a plate in a book or an image on a screen, that it is perhaps necessary to remind you that exchanging the painting for 'real life' is not simply a matter of increasing the scale. What is involved is a fundamental difference of orientation. In the landscape of our dwelling, we *look around* (Gibson 1979: 203). In what follows I shall focus on six components of what you see around you, and comment on each in so far as they illustrate aspects of what I have had to say about landscape and temporality. They are: the hills and valley, the paths and tracks, the tree, the corn, the church, and the people.

The hills and valley

The terrain is a gently undulating one of low hills and valleys, grading off to a shoreline that can just be made out through the summer haze. You are standing near the summit of a hill, from where you can look out across the intervening valley to the next. How, then, do you differentiate between the hills and the valley as components of this landscape? Are they alternating blocks or strips into which it may be divided up? Any attempt at such division plunges us immediately into absurdity. For where can we draw the boundaries of a hill except along the valley bottoms that separate it from the hills on either side? And where can we draw the boundaries of a valley except along the summits of the hills that mark its watershed? One way, we would have a landscape consisting only of hills, the other way it would consist only of valleys. Of course, 'hill' and 'valley' are opposed terms, but the opposition is not spatial or altitudinal but kinaesthetic. It is the movements of falling away from, and rising up towards, that specify the form of the hill; and the movements of falling away towards, and rising up from, that specify the form of the valley. Through the exercises of descending and climbing, and their different muscular entailments, the contours of the landscape are not so much measured as *felt* – they are directly incorporated into our bodily experience. But even if you remain rooted to one spot, the same principle applies. As you look across the valley to the hill on the horizon, your eyes do not remain fixed: swivelling in their sockets, or as you tilt your head, their motions accord with the movement of your attention as it follows its course through the landscape. You 'cast your eyes' first downwards into the valley, and then upwards towards the distant hill. Indeed in this vernacular phrase, to 'cast one's eyes', commonsense has once again grasped intuitively what the psychology of vision, with its metaphors of retinal imagery, has found so hard to accept: that movement is the very essence of perception. It is *because*, in scanning the terrain from nearby into the distance, your downward glance is followed by an upward one, that you perceive the valley.

Moreover someone standing where you are now would perceive the same topographic panorama, regardless of the time of year, the weather conditions and the activities in which people may be engaged . We may reasonably suppose that over the centuries, perhaps even millennia, this basic topography has changed but little. Set against the duration of human memory and experience, it may therefore be taken to establish a baseline of permanence. Yet permanence, as Gibson has stressed, is always relative; thus 'it is better to speak of persistence under change' (Gibson 1979: 13). Although the topography is invariant relative to the human life-cycle, it is not itself immune to change. Sea-levels rise and fall with global climatic cycles, and the present contours of the country are the cumulative outcome of a slow and long drawn out process of erosion and deposition. This process, moreover, was not confined to earlier geological epochs during which the landscape assumed its present topographic form. For it is still going on, and will continue so long as the stream, just visible in the valley bottom, flows on towards the sea. The stream does not flow between pre-cut banks, but cuts its banks even as it flows. Likewise, as we have seen, people shape the landscape even as they dwell. And human activities, as well as the action of rivers and the sea, contribute significantly to the process of erosion. As you watch, the stream flows, folk are at work, a landscape is being formed, and time passes.

The paths and tracks

I remarked above that we experience the contours of the landscape by moving through it, so that it enters – as Bachelard would say – into our 'muscular consciousness'. Reliving the experience in our imagination, we are inclined to recall the road we took as 'climbing' the hill, or as 'descending' into the valley, as though 'the road itself had muscles, or rather, counter-muscles' (Bachelard 1964: 11). And this, too, is probably how you recall the paths and tracks that are visible to you now: after all, you must have travelled along at least some of them to reach the spot where you are currently standing. Nearest at hand, a path has been cut through the wheat-field, allowing sheaves to be carried down, and water and provisions to be carried up. Further off, a cart-track runs along the valley bottom, and another winds up the hill behind. In the distance, paths criss-cross the village green. Taken together, these paths and tracks 'impose a habitual pattern on the movement of people' (Jackson 1989: 146). And yet they also arise out of that movement, for every path or track shows up as the accumulated imprint of countless journeys that people have made – with or without their vehicles or domestic animals – as they have gone about their everyday business. Thus the same movement is embodied, on the side of the people, in their 'muscular consciousness', and on the side of the landscape, in its network of paths and tracks. In this network is sedimented the activity of an entire community, over many generations. It is the taskscape made visible.

In their journeys along paths and tracks, however, people also move from place to place. To reach a place, you need cross no boundary, but you must follow some kind of path. Thus there can be no places without paths, along which people arrive and depart; and no paths without places, that constitute their destinations and points of departure. And for the harvesters, the place to which they arrive, and whence they will leave at the end of the day, is marked by the next feature of the landscape to occupy your attention . . .

The tree

Rising from the spot where people are gathered for their repast is an old and gnarled pear-tree, which provides them with both shade from the sun, a back-rest and a prop for utensils. Being the month of August, the tree is in full leaf, and fruit is ripening on the branches. But this is not just *any* tree. For one thing, it draws the entire landscape around it into a unique focus: in other words, by its presence it constitutes a particular place. The place was not there before the tree, but came into being with it. And for those who are gathered there, the prospect it affords, which is to be had nowhere else, is what gives it its particular character and identity. For another thing, no other tree has quite the same configuration of branches, diverging, bending and twisting in exactly the same way. In its present form, the tree embodies the entire history of its development from the moment it first took root. And that history consists in the unfolding of its relations with manifold components of its environment, including the people who have nurtured it, tilled the soil around it, pruned its branches, picked its fruit, and – as at present – use it as something to lean against. The people, in other words, are as much bound up in the life of the tree as is the tree in the lives of the people. Moreover, unlike the hills and the valley, the tree has manifestly grown within living memory. Thus its temporality is more consonant with that of human dwelling. Yet in its branching structure, the tree combines an entire hierarchy of temporal rhythms, ranging from the long cycle of its own germination, growth and eventual decay to the short, annual cycle of flowering, fruiting and foliation. At one extreme, represented by the solid trunk, it presides immobile over the passage of human generations; at the other, represented by the frondescent shoots, it resonates with the life-cycles of insects, the seasonal migrations of birds, and the regular round of human agricultural activities (cf. Davies 1988). In a sense, then, the tree bridges the gap between the apparently fixed and invariant forms of the landscape and the mobile and transient forms of animal life, visible proof that all of these forms, from the most permanent to the most ephemeral, are dynamically linked under transformation within the movement of becoming of the world as a whole.

The corn

Turning from the pear-tree to the wheat-field, it is no longer a place in the landscape but the surrounding surface that occupies your attention. And perhaps what is most striking about this surface is its uniformity of colour, a golden sheen that cloaks the more elevated parts of the country for as far as the eye can see. As you know, wheat takes on this colour at the particular time of year when it is ripe for harvesting. More than any other feature of the landscape, the golden corn gathers the lives of its inhabitants, wherever they may be, into temporal unison, founded upon a communion of visual experience. Thus whereas the tree binds past, present and future in a single place, the corn binds every place in the landscape within a single horizon of the present. The tree, we could say, establishes a vivid sense of duration, the corn an equally vivid sense of what Fabian (1983: 31) calls *coevalness*. It is this distinction that Bachelard has in mind when he contrasts the 'before-me, before-us' of the forest with the 'with-me, with-us' of fields and meadows, wherein 'my dreams and recollections accompany all the different phases of tilling and harvesting' (Bachelard 1964: 188). You may suppose that the sleeper beneath the tree is dreaming of corn, but if so, you may be sure that the people and the activities that figure in his dream are coeval with those of the present and do not take him back into an encounter with the past. (Note that the distinction between coevalness and duration, represented by the corn and the tree, is not at all the same as the classic Saussurian dichotomy between synchrony and diachrony: the former belongs to the perspective of the A-series rather than the B-series, to the temporality of the landscape, not to its chronology [Ingold 1986b: 151]).

Where the corn has been freshly cut, it presents a sheer vertical front, not far short of a man's height. But this is not a boundary feature, like a hedge or fence. It is an interface, whose outline is progressively transformed as the harvesters proceed with their work. Here is a fine example of the way in which form emerges through movement. Another example can be seen further off, where a man is engaged in the task of binding the wheat into a sheaf. Each completed sheaf has a regular form, which arises out of the co-ordinated movement of binding. But the completion of a sheaf is only one moment in the labour process. The sheaves will later be carried down the path through the field, to the haycart in the valley. Indeed at this very moment, one woman is stooped almost double in the act of picking up a sheaf, and two others can be seen on their way down, sheaves on their shoulders. Many more operations will follow before the wheat is eventually transformed into bread. In the scene before you, one of the harvesters under the tree, seated on a sheaf, is cutting a loaf. Here the cycle of production and consumption ends where it began, with the producers. For production is tantamount to dwelling: it does not begin here (with a preconceived image) and end there (with a finished artefact), but is *continuously going on*.

The church

Not far off, nestled in a grove of trees near the top of the hill, is a stone church. It is instructive to ask: how does the church differ from the tree? They have more in common, perhaps, than meets the eye. Both possess the attributes of what Bakhtin (1981: 84) calls a 'chronotope' – that is, a place charged with temporality, one in which temporality takes on palpable form. Like the tree, the church by its very presence constitutes a place, which owes its character to the unique way in which it draws in the surrounding landscape. Again like the tree, the church spans human generations, yet its temporality is not inconsonant with that of human dwelling. As the tree buries its roots in the ground, so also people's ancestors are buried in the graveyard beside the church, and both sets of roots may reach to approximately the same temporal depth. Moreover the church, too, resonates to the cycles of human life and subsistence. Among the inhabitants of the neighbourhood, it is not only seen but also heard, as its bells ring out the seasons, the months, births, marriages and deaths. In short, as features of the landscape, both the church and the tree appear as veritable monuments to the passage of time.

Yet despite these similarities, the difference may seem obvious. The church, after all, is a *building*. The tree by contrast, is not built, it grows. We may agree to reserve the term 'building' for any durable structure in the landscape whose form arises and is sustained within the current of human activity. It would be wrong to conclude, however, that the distinction between buildings and non-buildings is an absolute one. Where an absolute distinction is made, it is generally premised upon the separation of mind and nature, such that built form, rather than having its source within nature, is said to be superimposed by the mind upon it. But from the perspective of dwelling, we can see that the forms of buildings, as much as of any other features of the landscape, are neither given in the world nor placed upon it, but emerge within the self-transforming processes of the world itself. With respect to any feature, the scope of human involvement in these processes will vary from negligible to considerable, though it is never total (even the most 'engineered' of environments is home to other species). What is or is not a 'building' is therefore a relative matter; moreover as human involvement may vary in the 'life history' of a feature, it may be *more or less* of a building in different periods.

Returning to the tree and the church it is, evidently too simple to suppose that the form of the tree is naturally given in its genetic makeup, whereas the form of the church pre-exists, in the minds of the builders, as a plan which is then 'realized' in stone. In the case of the tree, we have already observed that its growth consists in the unfolding of a total system of relations constituted by the fact of its presence in an environment, from the point of germination onwards, and that people, as components of the tree's environment, play a not insignificant role in this process. Likewise, the 'biography' of the church consists in the unfolding of relations with its human builders, as well as with other components of its environment, from the moment when the first stone was laid. The 'final' form of the church may indeed have been prefigured in the human imagination, but it no more issued from the image than did the form of the tree issue from its genes. In both cases, the form is the embodiment of a developmental or historical process, and is rooted in the context of human dwelling in the world.

In the case of the church, moreover, that process did not stop when its form came to match the conceptual model. For as long as the building remains standing in the landscape it will continue – as it does now – to figure within the environment not just of human beings but of a myriad of other living kinds, plant and animal, which will incorporate it into their own life-activities and modify it in the process. And it is subject, too, to the same forces of weathering and decomposition, both organic and meteorological, that affect everything else in the landscape. The preservation of the church in its existing, 'finished' form in the face of these forces, however substantial it may be in its materials and construction, requires a regular input of effort in maintenance and repair. Once this human input lapses, leaving it at the mercy of other forms of life and of the weather, it will soon cease to be a building and become a ruin.

The people
So far I have described the scene only as you behold it with your eyes. Yet you do not only look, you listen as well, for the air is full of sounds of one kind and another.

Though the folk beneath the tree are too busy eating to talk, you hear the clatter of wooden spoons on bowls, the slurp of the drinker, and the loud snores of the member of the party who is outstretched in sleep. Further off, you hear the swish of scythes against the cornstalks and the calls of the birds as they swoop low over the field in search of prey. Far off in the distance, wafted on the light wind, can be heard the sounds of people conversing and playing on a green, behind which, on the other side of the stream, lies a cluster of cottages. What you hear is a taskscape.

In the performance of their particular tasks, people are responsive not only to the cycle of maturation of the crop, which draws them together in the overall project of harvesting, but also to each other's activities as these are apportioned by the division of labour. Even within the same task, individuals do not carry on in mutual isolation. Technically, it takes only one man to wield a scythe, but the reapers nevertheless work in unison, achieving a dance-like harmony in their rhythmic movements. Similarly the two women carrying sheaves down into the valley adjust their pace, each in relation to the other, so that the distance between them remains more or less invariant. Perhaps there is less co-ordination between the respective movements of the eaters, however they eye each other intently as they set about their repast, and the meal is a joint activity on which all have embarked together, and which they will finish together. Only the sleeper, oblivious to the world, is out of joint – his snores jar the senses precisely because they are not in any kind of rhythmic relation to what is going on around. Without wakeful attention, there can be no resonance.

But in attending to one another, do the people inhabit a world of their own, an exclusively *human* world of meanings and intentions, of beliefs and values, detached from the one in which their bodies are put to work in their several activities? Do they, from within such a domain of intersubjectivity, look at the world outside through the window of their senses? Surely not. For the hills and valley, the tree, the corn and the birds are as palpably present to them (as indeed to you too) as are the people to each other (and to you). The reapers, as they wield their scythes, are *with* the corn, just as the eaters are with their fellows. The landscape, in short, is not a totality that you or anyone else can look *at*, it is rather the world *in* which we stand in taking up a point of view on our surroundings. And it is within the context of this attentive involvement in the landscape that the human imagination gets to work in fashioning ideas about it. For the landscape, to borrow a phrase from Merleau-Ponty (1962: 24), is not so much the object as 'the homeland of our thoughts'.

Epilogue
Concluding an essay on the ways in which the Western Apache of Arizona discover meaning, value and moral guidance in the landscape around them, Basso abhors the tendency in ecological anthropology to relegate such matters to an 'epiphenomenal' level, which is seen to have little or no bearing on the dynamics of adaptation of human populations to the conditions of their environments. An ecology that is fully cultural, Basso argues, is one that would attend as much to the semiotic as to the material dimensions of people's relations with their surroundings, by bringing into focus 'the layers of significance with which human beings blanket the environment' (Basso 1984: 49). In rather similar vein, Cosgrove regrets the tendency in human geography to regard the landscape in narrowly utilitarian and functional

terms, as 'an impersonal expression of demographic and economic forces', and thus to ignore the multiple layers of symbolic meaning or cultural representation that are deposited upon it. The task of decoding the 'many-layered meanings of symbolic landscapes', Cosgrove argues, will require a geography that is not just human but properly *humanistic* (Cosgrove 1989: 120–7).

Though I have some sympathy with the views expressed by these writers, I believe that the metaphors of cultural construction which they adopt have an effect quite opposite to that intended. For the very idea that meaning *covers over* the world, layer upon layer, carries the implication that the way to uncover the most basic level of human beings' practical involvement with their environments is by stripping these layers away. In other words, such blanketing metaphors actually serve to create and perpetuate an intellectual space in which human ecology or human geography can flourish, untroubled by any concerns about what the world means to the people who live in it. We can surely learn from the Western Apache, who insist that the stories they tell, far from putting meanings upon the landscape, are intended to allow listeners to place themselves in *relation* to specific features of the landscape, in such a way that their meanings may be revealed or disclosed. Stories help to open up the world, not to cloak it.

And such opening up, too, must be the objective of archaeology. Like the Western Apache – and for that matter any other group of people who are truly 'at home' in the world – archaeologists study the meaning of the landscape, not by interpreting the many layers of its representation (adding further layers in the process) but by probing ever more deeply into it. Meaning is there to be *discovered* in the landscape, if only we know how to attend to it. Every feature, then, is a potential clue, a key to meaning rather than a vehicle for carrying it. This discovery procedure, wherein objects in the landscape become clues to meaning, is what distinguishes the perspective of dwelling. And since, as I have shown, the process of dwelling is fundamentally temporal, the apprehension of the landscape in the dwelling perspective must begin from a recognition of its temporality. Only through such recognition, by temporalizing the landscape, can we move beyond the division that has afflicted most inquiries up to now, between the 'scientific' study of an atemporalized nature, and the 'humanistic' study of a dematerialized history. And no discipline is better placed to take this step than archaeology. I have not been concerned here with either the methods or the results of archaeological inquiry. However, to the question, 'what is archaeology the study *of*?', I believe there is no better answer than 'the temporality of the landscape'. I hope, in this article, to have gone some way towards elucidating what this means.

31

PAST PRACTICES IN THE RITUAL PRESENT*

Examples from the Welsh Bronze Age

PAUL LANE

Introduction

The aim of this paper is to question the common archaeological conception of space and time as passive environments *for* action, by proposing instead that time and space are constituents *of* action, which take an active role in the reproduction and transformation of society. The perceived advantage of this perspective is that it redirects attention away from the search for material correlates of behaviour of a universal nature, towards the explication of the specificity of individual contexts.

More specifically, this paper will discuss problems of inference with social reference to the use of the terms 'ritual' and 'domestic' to describe various categories of archaeological entity. It will be argued that while both terms are a useful short-hand for defining the dominant characteristics of particular entities, their use introduces a set of largely ethnocentric, and frequently androcentric, assumptions, which serve to reinforce and reproduce an appearance of mutual exclusiveness and opposition between these two aspects of human action. That is, without wishing to deny the empirical existence of activities that can be described as ritual or domestic, I shall question the validity of the assumptions which underpin the *division* of social practice alone such lines, and point to problems of inference that such a division introduces into the interpretation of archaeological deposits.

Archaeological inference: defining domestic and ritual contexts

At the heart of the ritual/domestic dichotomy lie particular conceptualisations of human action and of the relationships which pertain between action and the representation of notional phenomena, especially through the medium of material culture. However, there are initial definitional problems with the terms 'domestic' and 'ritual'. Within archaeology the term 'ritual' is conventionally used to refer to archaeological entities which cannot be adequately accommodated by technological or economic processes, and, in this sense, is employed to explain the unexplainable. This idea can be seen in Hawkes' 'ladder of inference', which ranks inferences into

*First published in *Archaeological Review from Cambridge* (1986), **5**, 181–92.

a scale of ascending difficulty, from fairly straightforward ones about technology and economic subsistence through those concerning socio-political organisation to those relating to religious and spiritual life (Hawkes 1954: 161–2). These divisions are based on the assumption that the respective classes of activity are inherently different, and can be arranged alone a continuum 'leading up (*sic*) from the generically animal in man to the more specifically human' (Hawkes l954: 162).

Hawkes may have been right to postulate that the natural laws governing physical, chemical and biological processes impinge as constraints more acutely on technical and economic activities. However, this is very different from arguing that all possible technological and economic explanations must be exhausted before recourse is made to either socio-political or ritual explanations, which appears to have been the way in which the scheme has been applied.

It might be that a liberty is being taken here in treating ritual as synonymous with what Hawkes had in mind when he used the phrase 'religious and spiritual life'. Nevertheless, the implication of his scheme is clear, namely that the meaning of some types of activity is more self-evident than it is for other types. This should be stressed, for it has an important consequence on the manner in which the nature of the relationship between action and meaning is perceived, and probably accounts for a common assumption that the symbolic is exclusive to ritual. Let me try to elaborate on this: if the meanings of ritual actions are characterised as obscure, in some way 'hidden' and not revealed directly by the actions themselves, then in this sense they can be called 'symbolic'. But, since ritual acts are defined in contradistinction to the more self-evident technical and economic activities, this necessarily precludes the possibility of more characteristically pragmatic acts of ever having a symbolic connotation. A logical outcome of this dichotomy, although not invariably followed, is the extension of the principle so that domestic contexts are interpreted in an utilitarian manner, by virtue of being perceived, principally, as a locale for the performance of routine, *pragmatic* activities. This in turn helps to reinforce a set of assumptions about the universal nature of domestic activities, a point further discussed below.

How can one escape this basic problem? One possibility which suggests itself might be to differentiate the two types of activity according to their formal properties rather than their normative content, moving on to identify the observable characteristics and material correlates of the two categories of action. Since within such a theoretical framework, direct behavioural links are held to exist between society and material culture, and because behaviour is lacking from the archaeological record, an apparent need is created for actualistic, ethnoarchaeological studies. Despite differences in specific research concerns, the latter have been construed, by the majority of ethnoarchaeologists, as the search for the 'signature patterns' of various forms of behaviour. Yet, after almost twenty years of research, most ethnoarchaeologists have steadfastly avoided making an effort to identify the material correlates of ritual.

A major reason for this reluctance to consider 'ritual' must lie in the conceptualisation of human action employed by these researchers. Action, normally referred to as behaviour, is thought to be reducible to the purely mechanical properties of bodily movement. This is for two reasons, firstly, an assumption that notional phenomena, things held in the mind, are less real than behavioural phenomena. Secondly, the relative status of knowledge, value, and belief across cultures. If these are thought not to pose too great a problem within an ethnographic context, it is argued that they do so with regard to archaeology, by virtue of the fact that human behaviour of interest to archaeologists is past and therefore non–observable. In order to make inferences about past behaviour from contemporary observations, therefore, it is proposed that unambiguous relationships between the two sets of phenomena must be established (Binford 1981a: 21–5).

What this amounts to is an assumption that all actions have in common the mechanical properties of bodily movement. The goals of ethnoarchaeology are therefore seen as identifying relationships between formally different behaviours and their physical and material consequences, even though the precise construal of this relationship might vary from researcher to researcher. I believe this search for material correlates to be one of the most fundamental shortcomings current in ethnoarchaeology and archaeology today, and I shall argue that the concept of behaviour be replaced by that of human agency. Before this case is developed, however, I want to review, briefly, how anthropologists have viewed ritual. For it could be held that the lack of success at identifying material correlates derives from an inadequate understanding of the nature of ritual, rather than a negation of the principle that material culture passively reflects society.

In a recent review of anthropological definitions of ritual, Lewis has suggested that the majority portray ritual as a kind of performance in which the actions of participants are largely prescribed and stylized (Lewis 1980: 10–11). Although so defined this suggests that ritual is something practical; and guides action, there is still no way of distinguishing it from behaviour governed by custom and tradition. In fact, Lewis suggests that definitions of both ritual and tradition are based on an assumption that the relationship which exists between the form and intent of such behaviour is essentially non–intrinsic, that is either irrational or non–rational (Lewis 1980: 13). As such, both can be contrasted with craft and skill, and other categories of pragmatic activity, for which a clear means–end relationship is thought to exist. However, this dichotomy cannot be sustained, in that aspects of ritual may have a practical intent just as elements of pragmatic activity can have a symbolic connotation. Thus, rather than assuming that ritual is a particular *kind* of action, it seems more reasonable to treat it, as Lewis suggested, as an *aspect* of action.

It was intimated, also, that an analogous dichotomy reinforces the assumption that domestic functions are somehow universal. Although it would take another paper to elaborate this fully, a few general points can be made. The main point at issue is whether the functions of domestic units, of households, are universal. Part of the problem is definitional, for, although the term household minimally refers to individuals who share a common residence, in current usage more than this is implied by the term. Specifically, it is assumed that those who share a common living space share some set of activities, generally those connected with food production and consumption (Yanagisako 1979: 165). Added to this is the assumption that household units coincide with families, and thereby represent the nexus of both biological and social reproduction, as well as the day-to-day servicing of human beings (Harris 1981: 61). As commentators have pointed out, we find this range of activities glossed under the term 'domestic functions', which ultimately results in a tautology where families and households are defined as domestic groups.

Furthermore, it is often held that domestic functions link individuals within a household to each other into a cohesive entity. The net effect of this is to create an artificial image of the household as a separate and private sphere, which can be contrasted with a public sphere typified by political and religious activities. This can effectively ask any relations of inequality which might exist within residential units thus reinforcing the false dichotomy between domestic domains and the wider social collective in which such groupings are situated. Critics of this kind of conceptualisation of the domestic, have argued that such gross assumptions should be abandoned in favour of the explication of the exact nature of each social unit, and that the empirical existence of private and public spheres, domestic and ritual contexts must not be taken as self-evident. In other words, we should not separate the '*practices* which distinguish the private and the public from the establishment, negotiation and confirmation of the *concepts* "private" and "public" in everyday social life' (Sayer 1982: 498).

The crucial point about action, then, which distinguishes it from mechanical acts that are outwardly similar, is that actions have a semantic content which the latter lack. That is, they are indissoluble from meaning and intention. Thus, to treat material culture merely as the material correlates of behaviour, or extrasomatic adaptive appendages, actually *precludes* the possibility of ever recognising that its meaning is both concept-dependent and intersubjectively constituted. That is, the meanings of the acts of material production use, exchange, consumption and discard exist in their realisation through action, and are mediated by and through socially available forms, such as language and material culture. Both have a recursive effect on action, but material culture, because of its durability, can often have a more lasting influence. Meanings may thus come to be sedimented in its material form.

Past practices in mortuary ritual

Keeping these points in mind, this argument will be illustrated with regard to specific archaeological data. The principal aim is to contrast the kinds of inferences about the past reached from the theoretical stance I have forwarded, with those made by the more conventional methods I have criticised. I do not intend to offer a complete re-working of the Welsh Bronze Age, merely to establish the initial building blocks.

The main reason for choosing the site discussed below was that its phases of use exhibit an apparent change from a domestic context to one of ritual, specifically mortuary, activity. The example provides, therefore, a good opportunity to contrast the processes of inference employed by the excavator, whose work can be taken to be fairly representative of much of archaeology.

Located in Glamorgan, the site of Mount Pleasant Farm, Nottage (N.G.R. SS 833796) was initially selected for excavation as a probable Bronze Age cairn, in advance of its imminent destruction. Excavated in 1952, it overlooks a small coombe on the edge of a plateau above Porthcawl. It comprised of a ring cairn, enclosed by an irregular quarry ditch with a burial pit to the west of the apparent centre, containing a small Hilversum urn (Savory 1980) and another deposit near the southern edge of the cairn containing part of an adult cremation and an inverted collared-rim cinerary urn of Earlier Bronze Age type. Beneath the centre of the cairn, and partially covered by a buff-coloured layer of earth, were the remnants of dry-stone walling, outlining three sides of a small rectangle, six metres by three metres, and several post holes. Sherds of several different forms and fabrics, all of probable Neolithic date, were found in the buff-coloured layer and in some of the post-hole fills (Figure 31.1: Savory 1952: 76–80).

The excavator interpreted the underlying structure as a dwelling, and the associated artefactual and botanical remains distributed through the layer of darker coloured earth as occupation debris, on the basis of the particular associations of several elements. Specifically, these were the form and material of the structure, and the condition and composition of the associated artefactual assemblage. The surviving

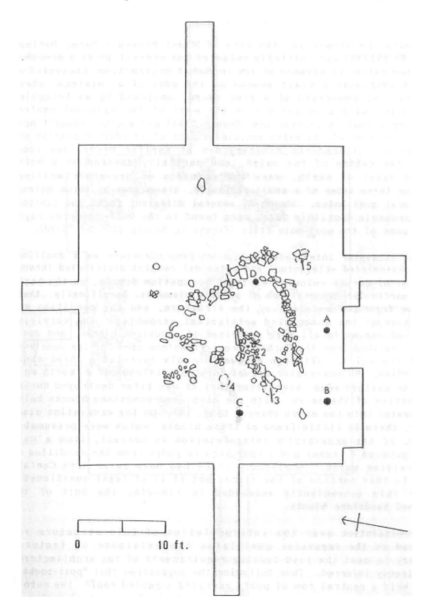

Figure 31.1 *Mount Pleasant Farm, Nottage, Neolithic phase (after Savory 1952)*

courses of the walls were all comprised of sandstone blocks, and could be distinguished from the Carboniferous limestone used for the construction of the cairn. Although excavation only revealed a three-sided construction, the excavator argued for the existence of a fourth wall alone the western edge, suggesting that it was later destroyed during the erection of the cairn, with the displaced sandstone blocks being incorporated into the cairn (Savory 1952: 78). On the excavation plan, however, there is little trace of these blocks, which were presumably removed. If the excavator's interpretation is correct, from a wall course between 9 inches and 1 foot high to judge from the condition of the surviving walls. Admittedly there had been later 19th century damage to this portion of the cairn, but it is at least questionable whether this conveniently succeeded in removing the bulk of the disturbed sandstone blocks.

Uncertainties over the interpretation of this structure are increased as the excavator postulates the existence of features necessary to meet the load-bearing requirements of the architectural form already inferred. Thus following the suggestion that 'post-sockets 1 to 3 held a central row of posts carrying a gabled roof' the author assumes that 'there was a fourth socket about six feet west of number 3', furthermore, the large hollows marked 4 and 5 on the plan are linked, on architectural grounds, with post holes 'C' and, 'A' and 'B' respectively despite being of a different size, having different profiles, possibly different fillings, although this is unclear from the text, and that the few diagnostic sherds from these different forms are possibly of different date, earlier Neolithic in feature 5, and a later, Peterborough derivative form in post-hole 'C'.

The composition and condition of the pottery assemblage, as outlined above, is used to support the conclusion that the earliest levels of the site represent a domestic context. The majority of sherds recovered were small, although in a few instances larger pieces were recovered (Savory 1952: 82). Distinct, localised distributions of sherds could be defined, and no pottery was found along the southern edge. As the excavator noted, the assemblage was 'far from uniform in character' (Savory 1952: 82), containing diagnostic sherds of both early and later Neolithic forms. Moreover, the earlier material could be distinguished from that recovered from other sites 'by its abundant furrowed, fluted, stamped or stabbed decoration and the association with it of sherds of "Peterborough" in attribution' (Savory 1952: 85), that is, as an atypical assemblage. Thus, it is on the basis of sherd size, mixed assemblage and contrasts in decorative motifs, that the material was judged to represent an occupation deposit.

These points have been rather laboured to make the simple observation that, when viewed critically, the evidence does not support, unequivocally, the favoured interpretation. My reason for doing this is not that I prefer a 'ritual' interpretation of the earlier context, but to suggest that in terms of understanding the mortuary practices at the site, it is both inappropriate to impose our own categories 'ritual' and 'domestic' on to the archaeological contexts, and that such a distinction is largely unnecessary.

In view of the attention given to identifying the formal properties of each functional context, it is surprising, to say the least, that the excavator made very little of the observed stratigraphic relationships with respect to the interpretation of Early Bronze Age mortuary rituals. Indeed, the evidence from the cairn is dismissed as less important than the house-foundation found beneath it (Savory 1952: 87). The archaeological

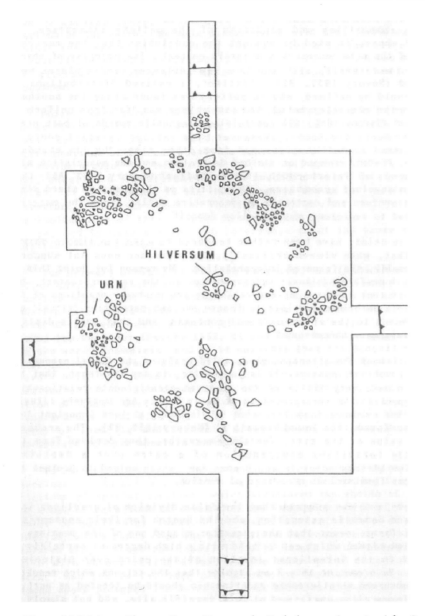

Figure 31.2 *Mount Pleasant Farm, Nottage, the Early bronze Age cairn (after Savory 1952)*

value of the site, for the excavator, thus derived from the apparently fortuitous construction of a cairn over a Neolithic habitation at some point in the Bronze Age, which helped to protect the settlement from various processes of erosion.

Again, one can suggest that the false division of practices into ritual and domestic categories, and the search for their appropriate material forms, meant that the excavator missed one of the meanings of the burial ritual which can be held with a high degree of certainty as embodied in the intentional location of the cairn over historical remains. By proposing this I am arguing that the actions which resulted in the observed stratigraphic relationship should be treated as part of the mortuary rites performed at this specific site, and not simply as the outcome of functional expediency.

That the association was intentional is clearly supported by the archaeological evidence. For, although it is conceivable that the observed relationships came about purely by chance, this is not an opinion that the excavator held. Instead, he argues that traces of the earlier site would have been visible as a field monument and concentration of exposed stone, which were in any case disturbed during the erection of the cairn. My main disagreement with him, therefore, is whether the reason for selecting the site for a burial was entirely because it presented a ready supply of stone, and it is on the evidence for alternative, or even complementary reasons that it will now be discussed.

While I have suggested that it might be inappropriate to categorise the earlier structure as a dwelling, on the available evidence we can at least say that it was not used for burial. Hence, by virtue of the superimposition of the cairn and the deposition of an urn cremation on its southern edge, the mortuary ritual, as well as identifying with the past, entailed a transformation of a specific locale into a place of burial. It is important to see this change in use as the realisation of intentions, which were neither immutable nor trivial. Before pursuing the implications of this, I want to reconsider the nature of the burial *per se*, and to make a number of inferences about the sense of these specific acts of burial.

The primary burial, it will be recalled, was found in a shallow hollow on the southern edge of the cairn, covered by loosely-packed limestone blocks. It was composed of the cremated bones of an adult, of indeterminate age and sex, covered by an inverted urn, of early collared-rim type, with a herring bone design of 'maggot' impressions around the shoulder (Savory 1952: 81 and 86). Both the cremation and the urn were incomplete, and it is possible that the deposit had been reburied in its final context after the construction of the cairn (Savory 1952: 81). Despite this indeterminacy regarding the original location of the burial deposit, we can infer that, not only did the notion of human burial, in this instance, entail a heat-mediated transformation, but also that the context and practices, that is the choice of locality and the acts of cremation and enurnment, were appropriate to this specific individual.

To put it another way, the observed configuration of material forms described as 'the primary burial', was generated according to specific relations of spatial location, which structured the choice of context, and a set of relations of exclusion and inclusion which affected the choice of particular forms. There are several levels of spatial location, which range from the association between cremated bones and collared urn, through the deposition of this urn in or beneath a stone cairn with an encircling ditch, to the topological location of the cairn. Had the burial been placed outside the cairn, or the cairn placed above ploughed fields rather than above an historical monument, the significance of the burial, its external reference may have been different. In much the same vein, the relations of exclusion and inclusion govern the selection of specific forms from the entire corpus of a particular artefact type (see also Miller 1985). By this I mean, for instance, the use of a decorated urn, rather than an undecorated one, the herringbone motif rather than a chevron design, and a ring-cairn rather than a kerb-circle. These reflections effectively determine which forms are interchangeable, without altering the sense of the act, and which forms would be inappropriate.

Without further comparison with other contemporary burials in the region, at this juncture it is only possible to say that an inverted collared urn with a specific decorative motif, situated within a stone cairn, conveyed a meaning appropriate to the age, gender and standing of the deceased, even though we cannot specify these latter dimensions of personality. This might appear a somewhat trivial observation, but it is important to introduce these concepts, for they underlie my points about the contextual specificity of meaning, and raise to the fore the 'could-have-been-otherwise' feature of action. The latter, as Giddens has indicated, links action to power and domination (1979: 88; 1981: 58) in that the realisation of the specific acts of burial and cairn construction required a certain autonomy of purpose and legitimacy of intention. It is this capacity to act, such that a particular interpretative reading of the natural and social worlds finds expression, which is of importance here.

As I have said, what was realised through the mortuary rituals was the conceptual link between a particular category of the dead and the visible remains of a past order. In addition, I wish to argue that because this link was objectified through practice, the rituals had as their outcome the transformation of 'the past' into a legitimating resource. To elaborate, I have suggested that immediately prior to the construction of the cairn, the locality existed, for the local population, as an historical monument. By virtue of being used for burial, the locale was subsequently *appropriated* in the dual sense of being taken out of a pre-existing topological order and integrated into another, *and*, of being intentionally selected as 'appropriate' to the context of the specific ritual (Thornton 1980: 16–20). If prior to the acts of burial and cairn construction the place had significance as a 'monument', the rituals, simultaneously added a dimension, of an ancestral or spiritual kind, which it had previously lacked, and reintegrated the space into the domain of contemporary practice. Thus not only was the meaning of space transformed, but also that of time, in that the conceptual boundary of 'the past' was extended to incorporate aspects of the social as embodied in the deceased's identity.

This re-introduction of the past into the present, in a specific guise, raises a fresh set of questions about the relations of power. Specifically, the possession of a capacity to transform an allocative resource, potentially available to the community, into an authoritative one. By the latter is meant the particular symbolic constructs of the legitimate post-mortem statuses of the deceased individuals and their relationships with the living. Without precise knowledge of their age or sex, and the chronological relationship between the primary and secondary burials, it would be inappropriate to speculate on the specificity of either of these. What I think we do have evidence for, in a more general sense, is the use of history to give contemporary practices the appearance of emanating from the past, and, as a consequence of this, a shift in the boundaries of a tradition (cf. Shils 1979: 262–3).

Wider contextual evidence would be needed to support this, and the provisional nature of these remarks is intentional. Even so, the preceding discussion has opened up a set of questions for future research, and to this end a number of general and concluding remarks can be made. Firstly, the contextual associations of a cairn and burial over the remains of an earlier structure are not unique to Nottage. Certainly two other comparable sites are known elsewhere in Glamorgan, namely Sant-y-Nyll, to the west of Cardiff (N.G.R, ST 101783), and the Mumbles, or Newton site, near Swansea (N.G.R. SS 606887).

At the former, excavation of a denuded cairn revealed a deposit of cremated bones in a shallow, circular pit, cut through another putative occupation deposit, containing quantities of bone and fragmentary pottery, and associated with a complex of shallow post-holes, thought to represent three huts (Savory 1959–60). Like the so-called secondary cremation at Nottage, the cremation pit was covered by a sandstone block and a heap of stones loosely bonded with earth. Although no grave objects were found, it was possible, in this case, to identify some of the bones as belonging to at least one adult, probably female, and a child aged between 15 and 24 months (Irvine 1959–60: 26–7). The Newton site also comprised of a cremation pit beneath a denuded cairn, with 'the bones of two adults (one female) and a child scattered throughout' its fill (Savory 1972: 126). Close by, to the north west of the pit, lay part of a crushed Food Vessel. A semi-circular arrangement of post-holes was found beneath this layer in association with fragments of Beaker pottery of a Long Necked variety,

The second, general, point emerges out of these resemblances, in that comparison between these three sites and with other burial and non-burial sites should indicate how different organising principles were structured and related. Only through contextual studies will it be possible to establish how, for instance, the nature of spatial boundaries within and between sites, other heat-mediated transformations, such as cooking and metal working, or the decorative motifs on pottery, stood in relation to the divine and the dead, and the age and gender categories of the former. Again, our interests in these similarities and contrasts should be less with the fact that they are symbolic representations, and more with why such a conceptual ordering of the physical and social worlds was appropriate, and how that order was sustained.

Finally, it has been indicated that the search for 'material correlates' is not a necessary prerequisite for archaeological inference, and that it is possible to make sense of the lived experience of past actors from archaeological remains. This task is helped by the fact that in order to make sense of their lives, these same actors represented their experience, and interpretations of that experience, to others in a structured and communicable way. Various media are available to the human species to communicate with others, some of the most durable being physical artefacts and architectural forms. It is precisely because of this durability that material culture is so amenable to the task of conveying meaning across generations, and yet, as a vehicle for meaning, it is also subject to both constraints and multivalency introduced by the context of use and intentions of users. It is this discursive element and the changing emphases of the more dominant modes, that archaeologists should endeavour to understand.

ACKNOWLEDGEMENT

I would like to thank Colin Shell for helping to clarify aspects of contemporary Bronze Age pottery typologies.

32

MONUMENTAL CHOREOGRAPHY*

Architecture and Spatial Representation in Late Neolithic Orkney

COLIN RICHARDS

For anyone who has visited the late Neolithic henge monuments of Avebury or Durrington Walls, the passage graves of New Grange or Gavrinis, or the stone circles of Callanish or Brodgar, there can be little doubt of the feelings of awe and excitement which these spectacular monuments inspire. To see and move around the monuments invokes a brief encounter with a totally different culture which inevitably generates both intrigue and wonder. On a personal level it is a combination of these experiences which has guided my research into what I regard as the most exciting period of European prehistory. Of course, these impressions are not mine alone nor restricted to other archaeologists, but are experienced by the majority of people who visit the monuments. Neither is this a contemporary phenomenon as the numerous historical accounts so vividly demonstrate, and the survival of many late Neolithic monuments for over 4000 years aptly testifies.

Given the lavish scale of architecture encountered within the monuments it is not unreasonable to wonder at their original meanings and enquire into the purpose behind their construction, 'what do we know about the role of monuments in their own right? Why were they built in the first place and what roles did they play afterwards?' asks Bradley (1984: 62). In pursuing these questions some of the monuments appear easier to interpret than others. For instance, there is no controversy or debate in the designation of Knowth or West Kennet as megalithic chambered tombs, built to house the dead. In contrast, such a direct interpretation of henge monuments or stone circles is apparently fraught with danger and generally avoided, with discussion being reduced to problems of definition and classification (e.g. Clare 1986; Harding with Lee 1987). This notable discrepancy in ability to interpret different monuments does not lie within a problem of their 'enigmatic nature' but resides in the range and level of our experience and understanding and demonstrates most clearly the frequently unacknowledged degree of subjectivity inherent within all our interpretations of archaeological material.

---

*First published in C. Tilley (ed.) (1993), *Interpretive Archaeology*, London: Berg, pp. 143–78.

In the following account I aim to pursue Bradley's questions concerning the monuments, and to offer my interpretation of a group of well-known late Neolithic sites situated on the Stenness promontory, Mainland, Orkney. This account is not intended as a general model for all monuments of similar appearance nor for other groups of similar monuments situated in different regions of Britain, it is simply an interpretation based on my understanding and knowledge of a particular body of archaeological material which is the product of Neolithic people's understanding and knowledge of their own world.

The Late Neolithic monuments of Stenness, Orkney

In western Mainland, Orkney, lies a large natural bowl containing the lochs of Stenness and Harray. These lochs are divided by two promontories; the Ness of Brodgar and the Stenness peninsular. A number of monuments are situated on both the projecting land masses, including henge monuments with internal stone circles, chambered tombs and numerous single standing stones (Figure 32.1). Although separated by a narrow stretch of water the two groups of monuments tend to be viewed as a single unit; either a ritual pairing or clustering (Harding with Lee 1987: 45), complex (Renfrew 1979: 254) or centre (Mackie 1977). As concentrations of Neolithic monuments in other areas of Britain have been discussed in terms of 'ritual landscapes' (see papers in Bradley and Gardiner 1984), it has been just a simple step to extend this idea to Orkney.

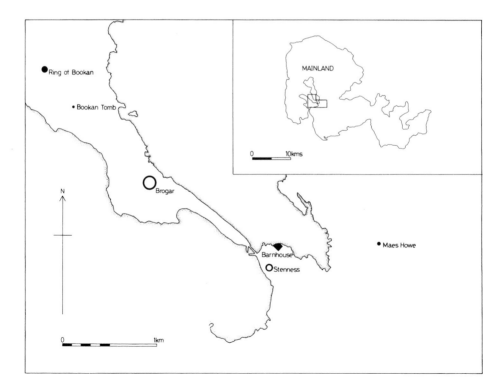

Figure 32.1 The Stenness promontory

The recent discovery of the late Neolithic Barnhouse settlement (Richards in press) on the tip of the Stenness promontory serves to alter the proposed scheme. On the one hand, the presence of a settlement within an area deemed to be a 'ritual landscape' causes certain conceptual and definitional problems; on the other, when Barnhouse is considered in conjunction with a likely second large settlement, closely situated on the Brodgar promontory at Bookan (Callander 1931), the possibility is raised of the two areas constituting discrete groups of monuments. Although today the narrow stretch of water dividing the two promontories is forded by a road bridge it still constitutes a natural boundary between the Stenness and Sandwick parishes. Unfortunately, the monuments of the Brodgar promontory are either ruinous or unexcavated and do not provide the quality of evidence presently available in the Stenness area. Given these limitations this contribution will concentrate on the monuments of the Stenness promontory.

At a brief glance these famous monuments, Maes Howe passage grave, the Stones of Stenness henge monument, and a number of isolated standing stones, and the monumental House 2 and Structure 8 at Barnhouse, appear to be of an apparently different nature. Under these circumstances it is quite unnecessary to attempt to explain the formation of this group in a purely evolutionary framework as has been suggested for a similar group of monuments elsewhere (Thorpe and Richards 1984). Instead, questions of composition should be directed towards understanding why the monuments maintain spatial integrity in assuming different locations within a small geographic area as opposed to superimposition or a sequence of remodelling and reconstruction as occurs with many chambered tombs (cf. Kinnes 1981).

When each of the buildings is architecturally distinct, as with the Stenness monuments, there is a tendency to divide and classify. For instance, Maes Howe stands at the head of a whole class of passage graves bearing its name (Davidson and Henshall 1989: 37–51), while the Stones of Stenness is a class 1 henge monument (Ritchie 1985: 119), being recognized as a classic type (Harding with Lee 1987). Due to their position within the Barnhouse settlement, House 2 and Structure 8 would under normal procedure be placed and discussed within a general typology of house designs (e.g. Clarke 1976: Figure 4). Hence, although physically situated in close proximity to one another each of these monuments remain typologically distant. Interestingly, within the confines of typological classification minute architectural detail is introduced into arguments concerning the evolutionary position and definition of different sites. Apart from classification, the architectural differences of the Orkney monuments tend to be virtually ignored (see however, Hodder 1982b: 218–28), except in the calculation of labour investment in monumental construction (Renfrew 1979: 214–18; Fraser 1983: 360).

Clearly, both monumentality and architecture are important, but it is noticeable that these ideas are highly reductionist, being restricted to the actual phenomenon of construction. Consequently, no concern is given to the intended use of the building, the activities undertaken within it, the paths of people moving through it or the principles of order and ideas of cosmology embodied within its form.

Monumental architecture
It is all too easy for archaeologists to represent sites and monuments as two-dimensional plans. The sites are always drawn as plans and are subsequently analysed

as plans, normally in the guise of phases and artefact distributions. Consequently, they are visualized and interpreted as plans. The unfortunate corollary of this traditional procedure is that the people who originally inhabited the sites which the archaeologist excavates become difficult to accommodate and are quickly consumed in the search for interesting two-dimensional patterns. Furthermore, better preserved sites which have standing remains tend to be treated in a similar manner to the more frequently encountered plough-damaged sites. In either situation a false view of the world is being projected onto the material remains. For instance, how many archaeologists think of their homes or workplaces (apart from excavations) in terms of a two-dimensional plan? Presumably, very few. Like other human beings, archaeologists make sense of the world through interpretive practice. Neolithic people did exactly the same, which is why architecture, and its reconstruction, are so vitally important.

Although obvious, the planning and raising of a monumental building, or for that matter any form of construction which delineates space, require a clear idea of the spatial representation which is to be achieved. This will obviously be dependent on the use for which the building is envisaged. To produce a recognizable and appropriate form the construction will necessarily draw on established social, and therefore, cosmological principles of order. Monumental architecture may consequently be 'defined not only by what is built but also by the interpretations – and therefore the intentions – of those who build and use it' (Guidino 1975: 9). Hence, the organization of the world as effected through the creation of architecture may only be fully understood in terms of those people who lived and acted within its influence. There is no intrinsic meaning in constructed space (Moore 1986: 107–20), the invocation and interpretation of spatial symbolism are therefore totally contingent on social practices. Thus, the physical presence of people moving through areas, negotiating boundaries and undertaking particular activities at appropriate places allows spatial meanings to be continually invoked. These actions both draw on and recreate meaning through a recursive relationship between the material world and the subject (Hodder 1982b). This process allows spatial definition to be frequently altered within various social situations (Richards 1990).

If spatiality and temporality are the essence of human action, and therefore existence, then it follows that the creation of spatial order within the world, through architecture, is also a temporal manifestation. This recalls the belief of Hall (1966: 163), that the way in which a society structures space is dependent on their conception of time. Since architecture effects a coincidence of space and time, it must also embody a conjunction of cosmology and social practices. Now we can fully understand the suggestion that within pre-literate societies time is frequently conceived in terms of particular events and the place at which they occur. Thus, it is the presence of people at specific 'places' or 'locales' which constitute the routines and cycles of everyday life (Giddens 1981: 40).

Architecture, therefore, fuses space and time in the creation of places which structure the routines of life by representing fixed points in the fluidity of existence. In assuming this role, architecture is obviously a potent medium for controlling people: where they go, and what they see and do. Such a manipulation of social space enables an element of control to exist in the everyday transactions of life since the restriction of people from certain areas allows a partial monopoly over knowledge and emphasises 'the historical role of architecture, in all its particulars, as a fundamental instrument of power' (Guidino 1975: 10).

If architecture creates spatial representations in the form of interpretive practice then it cannot be meaningfully considered independent of social practices. The movement of people through constructed space creates a fluidity which is temporal in nature. Space and time are no longer seen as backdrops to human action but rather an embodiment of it.

In reconsidering the idea of 'place', as a fusion of space and time transcending everyday social practices, the monumentality expressed within the construction of Maes Howe, the Barnhouse monuments, Stones of Stenness and the numerous standing stones becomes clearer to understand. In the creation of such highly visible 'places' at appropriate positions within the landscape a spatial and temporal order of some magnitude was being committed to the world.

Maes Howe: a place apart

Described as 'the most accomplished and sophisticated chambered tomb in the British Isles' (Megaw and Simpson 1979: 136), Maes Howe stands in splendid isolation. Lying within a highly visible position it is set approximately 1 kilometre to the south-east of the Barnhouse settlement and the Stones of Stenness. Although recognizable as a passage grave, 'the beautiful dressing of the stones and the spaciousness of the main chamber' (Renfrew 1979: 203) combine to create an architectural image which is significantly different from any of the other Orcadian passage graves (ibid.: 201). This variation has been responsible for many ups and downs on the typological ladder; sometimes it is presented as the earliest of its type (e.g. Piggott 1954: 234, Figure 64), at other times it is the glorious final product (Davidson and Henshall 1989: 90), occasionally it is even excluded from its type altogether (Renfrew 1979: 201). Fraser, after undertaking numerous analyses, concedes that 'as happens so frequently, Maes Howe emerges as an exception' (1983: 94), and eventually ends up sitting uncomfortably, with Quanterness, in a separate class (ibid.: 132). It is these very difficulties of fit which serve to express the ambiguity of Maes Howe and reveal the simple fact that it is different.

Although different, Maes Howe is inescapably a representation of a passage grave and would consequently have been imbued with all the associations of a place of the dead. In this respect it is important to examine its architecture within a historical context. The adoption of passage grave architecture in Orkney is clearly significant since it depicts an altered conception of the relationship between the living and the dead (Sharples 1985: 71). However, within its spatial organization lie the ingredients of separation and restriction. The long, low entrance passage linking the outside world to the high vaulted inner chamber is more than an extended division creating the necessary precautionary partition between the living and dead. The small dimensions of the passage physically restrict bodily movement into and out of the central chamber; it is, in fact, very difficult to move along the passageway except upon hands and knees. The presence of a long passage also effectively removes any visual access to the activities occurring within the central area. Indeed, people observing the proceedings from the outside would lose sight of those entering the chamber after they had travelled no more than a metre or so along the passage.

Hence, on the assumption that very few people were physically able, or had the social position, to witness or participate in the ritual events occurring within the central chamber, the only medium by which people situated externally would have obtained any knowledge of the internal happenings was through sound. It is in respect to these restrictions that the enhanced acoustic properties of the Orcadian passage graves take on greater significance. Loud noise tends to be absorbed and dampened within the size and height of the central chamber, however, the long passage acts as a megaphone projecting sound outwards. This creates the disconcerting effect of increasing the volume as the subject exits back along the passage and provides enhanced clarity of sound outside the entrance.

Passage grave architecture should, therefore, be viewed in relation to secretive and restrictive practices which were inevitably linked to the control of ritual knowledge by certain people in society. It is in this context that Maes Howe should be examined, for despite its magnificence of construction it retains the essential characteristics of a passage grave.

Architecturally, Maes Howe is the same and yet different from other Orcadian passage graves, and it is these features which are crucial in its interpretation. The actual building is situated on a clay platform which is bounded by a circular ditch separating the monument from the outside world. Access into the central chamber involves passing along a passage of approximately 10 metres in length, 90 cm in width and 1.36 metres high. The overall scale of the passage is greater than any other Orcadian passage grave, allowing comparatively easier entry and exit while maintaining minimal visual access.

The journey to the centre of Maes Howe initially involves negotiating the boundary ditch and crossing the open platform area where the subject remains in full view of observers positioned outside the monument, beyond the ditch. Admission into the building is gained by and crouching into the low passage (Figure 32.2). Entering the monument the subject is presented with a darkened, apparently undifferentiated corridor (Figure 32.3). This space has no visible demarcation in the form of divisional uprights or threshold slabs, or megalithic art (Richards 1991). In fact, the opposite occurs with an impression of uniformity and stretched space being enhanced by the use of long single slabs for the walls, floor and ceiling of the badly lit passageway. On moving forwards along this constructed path a feeling of rising towards a goal is experienced by virtue of the almost 'imperceptible' incline of the passage towards the central chamber (Henshall 1963: 220). That this was an intentional feature of design is beyond doubt, given the precise and sophisticated method of construction. Thus, in proceeding along a lengthy undifferentiated passage towards the darkness, the subject experiences the ascendant position of their ultimate destination; the central chamber and its contents both physical and metaphysical.

After moving almost 10 metres in a crouched position, entry into the central chamber is marked by two slightly taller upright stones 'resembling door jambs' (ibid.), which project in from the passage walls, reducing the width to 70 cm (Figure 32.3). On passing between these divisional slabs the transitional stage of the journey is completed, and entry into the central chamber initiated. It is now possible to stand upright and look around. If some form of illumination is available the sophisticated nature of the

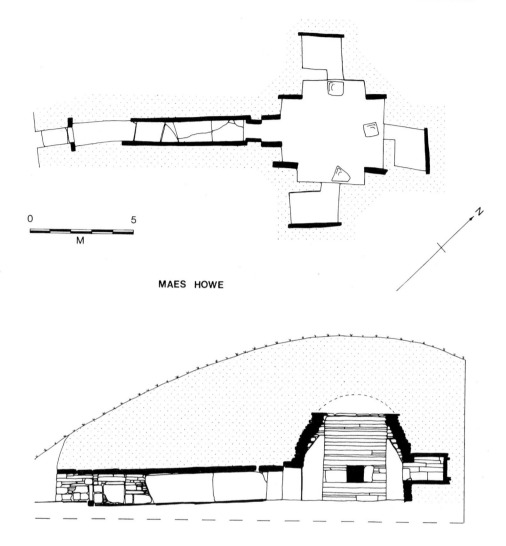

0 5

M

MAES HOWE

N

Figure 32.2 *Plan and elevation of Maes Howe*

masonry becomes visible as the roof height begins to rise from this point reaching a spectacular 5 metres directly ahead at the centre of the chamber. The vaulted ceiling is certainly the highest known example within Neolithic buildings and was quite probably the highest enclosed space ever experienced by Neolithic Orcadians.

As the restrictive space of the passage abruptly opened out into the central chamber with its lofty corbelled roof, there could have been little doubt in the mind of the subject as to the awe and importance of the inner sanctum. Four large monoliths externally facing each corner buttress emphasize the impression of height. The presence of corner buttresses creates four recesses in the central chamber. The entrance passage is centrally placed in the front recess and in each of the remaining, at approximately one metre above the floor, is the entrance to a cell

Figure 32.3 *Moving into the passage at Maes Howe*

or small chamber. This arrangement recreates that of the house with the notable absence of the central hearth.

Superfluous to structural necessity (J. Hill pers. comm.), the incorporation of four monoliths in the architecture of Maes Howe reproduces a feature present in other monuments of the Stenness promontory. In each case it is their height which consistently dwarfs and overwhelms the subject. Their inclusion within Maes Howe is of interest since they are enclosed within the chamber and out of sight. However, due to the large dimensions of the stone holes and the required space for manoeuvre, the erection of the stones would have been a primary operation in the construction of Maes Howe which would almost certainly have been surrounded by a series of rituals involving demarcation and sanctification. Consequently, for a period of time, early in the construction, the four menhirs would have stood proud, in full view of everyone.

In gaining entry to the central chamber the subject has taken a path which through its spatial representation conveys certain impressions which are duly interpreted. The undifferentiated passage which appears as a single space linking the inside and outside is a single prolonged period of liminality which effects an impression of moving upwards, towards a special goal. After passing through the semblance of a doorway the towering inner chamber is reached, the journey is complete and the subject halts. The use of contrasting ceiling heights to convey impressions of neutrality and importance is a simple architectural technique, however, its effects are extremely dramatic in the context of Maes Howe.

On leaving the chamber more than a reversal occurs, since the subject is now heading back towards the light of the living and the outside world and leaving the darkness, damp and cold of the interior (Figure 32.4). Maes Howe is a place of the

Figure 32.4 *Leaving the main chamber at Maes Howe*

dead and its entry and brief visitation must have involved a high degree of risk and concern on the part of the subject.

Visibility and therefore illumination are obviously crucial to the interpretation of space. The interior of Maes Howe is dark, there is no life-giving hearth to provide heat and light. Hence, when people ventured into the passageway they either stumbled through the darkness or relied on fire or sunlight to illuminate their path. In other Orcadian passage graves there is extensive evidence of internal burning, for instance, the central chamber at Quanterness contained large quantities of burnt and charred material (Renfrew 1979: 52). No such evidence is known from Maes Howe (Davidson and Henshall 1989: 145), although it is unlikely that simple burning torches would leave extensive traces. The choice between fire and sunlight involves far more than the practicality of illumination, since neither light sources are culturally neutral, but are highly potent symbols which may be deemed appropriate to particular places at particular times.

The question of the illumination of the monument by the sun (see Bradley 1989), introduces the most significant aspect of Maes Howe architecture; its orientation. Unlike other passage graves whose passages tend to face south-east (Fraser 1983: 371; Davidson and Henshall 1989: 85), the passageway into Maes Howe is built on a south-west–north-east axis facing the setting sun at the winter solstice, thereby allowing the passage and part of the inner chamber, areas normally in perpetual darkness, to be fully illuminated at precisely the height of winter darkness which in Orkney accounts for up to eighteen hours of the day. Whether illumination and a path created by the suns rays were related to the time and path of movement within the monument is difficult to establish (Rapoport 1969: 75), however, the marking of the end of the shortest day of the year is an annual event of great significance and celebration since it marks the beginning of a new agricultural cycle and a period of regeneration.

Clearly, Maes Howe is an anomaly in chambered tomb classification, but this is because it is different. As a spatial representation of a passage grave; a place of the dead, the architecture links death with darkness, cold and importantly temporal and spatial qualities: midwinter and the south-west. However, in embodying a fusion of time and space the monumental proportions of Maes Howe create a 'place' of special significance which is a constantly visible part of the landscape at all times of the year.

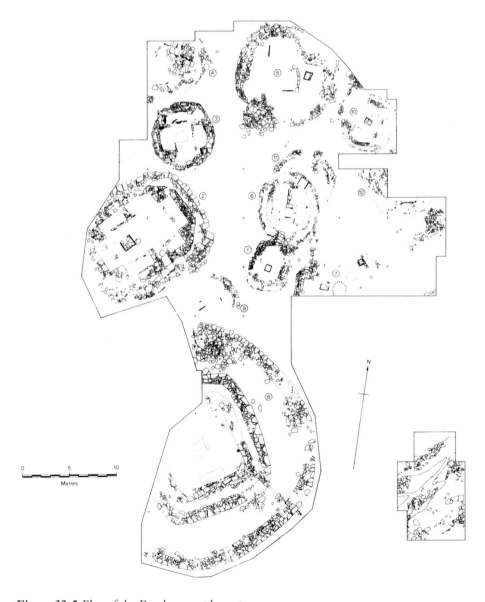

Figure 32.5 *Plan of the Barnhouse settlement*

The public presentation of such themes of meaning is nevertheless contrary to passage grave architecture which pertains to exclusion and restriction. In the spatial order of Maes Howe, however, the constructed building within the mound does not constitute the division between the inside of the monument and the outside world, that is effected by the enclosure ditch. By expanding the external boundary the highly visible clay platform becomes part of the interior of the monument. This allows visual access to events occurring 'within' the monument on the platform. It is clear that the spatial arrangement of Maes Howe, while maintaining the category of passage grave, successfully reverses the restrictive logic of passage grave architecture. In this respect the symbolism of death, and associated concepts, is brought into the public domain at an appropriate place and time.

Barnhouse: home is where the hearth is

On the northern tip of the Stenness promontory lies the contemporary village of Barnhouse (Figure 32.5). Initially, the focal point of the settlement is the large monumental building House 2. In contrast to Maes Howe, a place of the dead, House 2 lies in a central position within the realms of the living. In outward prospect it appears as a large rectangular structure with rounded corners. The entrance is low and narrow being oriented to the south-east. As with Maes Howe, to understand the architecture of this building it is necessary to fall under its influence, therefore, it will be examined as if it were a standing construct.

To gain access involves passing through the entrance and stepping down into an immense interior which rises up before the subject. Since the left half of the building is entirely obscured by a buttress wall projecting inwards to the left of the entrance, and a massive stone upright assumes a similar position to the right, it is only by moving forward into a more central position that the whole of the interior becomes visible (Figure 32.6).

Directly ahead, set in the floor, lies a large triangular shaped flagstone cover of a cist which is thought to contain human remains. This is flanked on either side by two wooden posts. To the right of the cist is a large square stone fireplace with low upright stone slabs positioned to the front and rear. Even within the smoke-filled interior there is enough illumination from the doorway and fire to see the sophisticated masonry which is only paralleled within Maes Howe. The flush straight-sided walls and corner buttresses reaching up to the roof creating recesses present an identical image to that seen within Maes Howe (Figure 32.7). The left-hand side of the building remains in a gloomy half light being barely visible for inspection, creating a similar situation to that encountered within the smaller houses of the settlement.

Movement around the inside of House 2 is carefully controlled through the presence of the central hearth and cist, and the divisional stone uprights bounding off the six recesses. The internal area is divided into two halves by a line of stone uprights, approximately 1 metre in height, running between the two central buttress walls. This arrangement ensures that access into the left side of the house involves walking over the visible stone cist cover and between the two wooden posts and only then turning to the left through a gap in the stone partitioning. On entering the left half an identical spatial arrangement is once again presented to the subject.

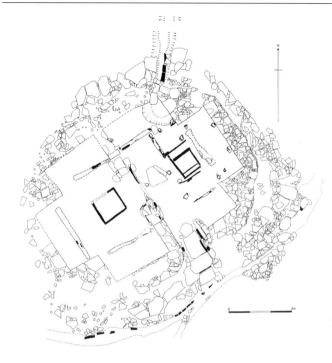

Figure 32.6
House 2 at
Barnhouse
settlement (drawing
by Jane Downes)

Figure 32.7
Moving into the
interior of House 2
(drawing by Paul
Birbeck)

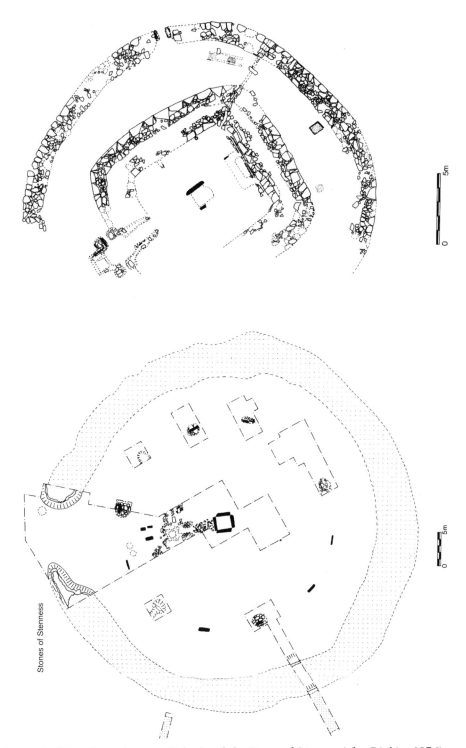

Figure 32.8 *Barnhouse Structure 8 (top) and the Stones of Stenness (after Ritchie, 1976)*

At a later date in the history of the settlement the inside of House 2 is remodelled. The stone divisional uprights are removed and the whole of the central area is refloored in clay, completely covering the stone cist cover and adjacent fireplace in the eastern area. Now the large hearth in the western or left-hand side of the house comes into full operation. These alterations, although lifting the physical restrictions on movement within the house, effectively remove the focal point of activities to the most inaccessible portion of the inside area. Thus, on entering House 2 the subject has no immediate visual contact with any of the activities centred on the hearth. It is only after moving into the heart of the interior that these activities become visible. In this remodelling we are again seeing the removal of particular practices away from public scrutiny, into the depths of the house.

This trend of exclusion through architecture is continued when House 2 is finally replaced by a building of much greater proportions: Structure 8 (Figure 32.8). Although the main building is effectively a large 'house' it assumes monumental status. It also features an identical spatial organization to Maes Howe in having a central building being surrounded by a laid clay platform. In this case the platform is enclosed by a substantial wall prohibiting physical or visual access. However, of greatest significance is the orientation of the entrance passage of the main building towards the north-west and the setting sun of the summer solstice.

These striking similarities and contrasts between Maes Howe, House 2 and Structure 8 may be linked to the wider categorical difference of the house and tomb. Although Structure 8 is far larger and more elaborate than the typical late Neolithic house, it retains the essential architecture of the house (see Richards 1990), and consequently assumes a certain correspondence.

While only the lowest course of masonry remain intact it is possible partially to reconstruct Structure 8. The central building is a massive and lavishly constructed 'house' of sophisticated design. The entrance passage, much shorter than Maes Howe, but constructed in a similar manner with long single stone slabs facing either wall, leads directly through a 3 metre thick wall into the interior. Externally, the entrance projects from the house wall in a porch-like arrangement and positioned on the threshold is the remains of a hearth.

Inside the house a massive fireplace is centrally positioned, behind which, adjacent to the rear wall, lie the slots for a stone 'dresser'. A stone-lined drain runs along the inside of the base of the rear wall and out through the rear left corner. Slots for large stone boxes, equivalent to the right and left box beds within the smaller houses, are located either side of the central hearth. Immediately behind the left-hand box a grooved ware vessel is set into the clay floor.

Outside the building, on the surrounding clay platform, a number of hearths, stone boxes and pits are located in its south-eastern section, to the rear of the central building. Since a quantity of broken pottery and stone and flint tools was recovered from around these features, it appears they saw frequent use. Significantly, this area of activity coincides with the small entrance through the outer wall which is over 1 metre in thickness and would have acted as an extremely effective barrier to the outside world besides restricting views of any of the activities occurring on the platform.

The path of people entering this monument is of particular importance in understanding the architecture of Structure 8. The outer wall was penetrated by the single entrance passage to the east. Being less than 1 metre in width and probably no more than 1 metre in height, the doorway would have been no larger than that to a normal dwelling. Squeezing through this small aperture, the subject steps out into an open platform area, to the left and right are a number of square stone fireplaces and pits holding grooved ware pots. Moving to the right around the perimeter of the platform in between the large outer wall and the towering inner building finally brings the impressive 'monumental' porched entrance of the inner building into view. Since the activities being undertaken on the platform are now out of sight, behind the main building, this seems to introduce Goffman's front-back distinction of social performance (1959: 114). Moving towards the porched entrance, the subject is finally ready to undertake the journey into the inner building.

This involves entering a wide passage and walking over the fireplace marking the threshold, which may have been covered by paving slabs. Crouching through the outer entrance, past two door jambs, the passage shrinks to a restrictive 90 cm width for its 3 metre length, the subject finally emerges into an interior lit and heated by the central fire, and perhaps other forms of lighting, such as small stone lamps.

This illumination would have revealed an enormous internal area of over 7 metres square. Just as the central chamber of Maes Howe may have been the highest enclosed space, Structure 8 would almost certainly have been the largest covered and enclosed space experienced by Neolithic people in Orkney. Also visible behind the fire would be the stone 'dresser', the role of which is impossible to determine. Nevertheless, in being positioned at the rear of the building, it occupies the 'deepest' space which may have been imbued with supernatural properties (Collett 1987).

If movement into the interior of this building was by way of the right-hand side of the hearth, as appears to be the case within the ordinary dwelling (see Richards 1990), then the left-hand side becomes the deepest and most inaccessible space. It is clear that the presence of a central hearth not only introduces the symbolic associations of the dwelling house, but also constitutes a central reference point for all people and all things; an axis mundi.

Structure 8 is a representation of a house in just the same way that Maes Howe is a representation of a tomb although neither appears to fulfil its function; there is little evidence of habitation in the former and there is no convincing evidence for human burial in the latter. Instead, they are tied into wider classifications of the world, involving life and death, decay and regeneration; social and cosmological categories which are expressed through the construction of particular 'places' which fuse time and space within their architecture and situation. One is oriented towards the summer solstice and the other to the winter solstice. Maes Howe is a place of the dead and situated away from the habitation of the living, while House 2 and Structure 8 lie within the confines of the Barnhouse settlement. Although Structure 8 and Maes Howe have an identical internal spatial organization, a lavishly spacious inner building, a surrounding clay platform and an external boundary, there is a substantial difference between them. Activities occurring within Maes Howe, on the platform, are open to view, as opposed to Structure 8 which remains visually inaccessible and therefore restrictive in nature.

Stones of Stenness: removing the barriers

The Stones of Stenness is situated a mere 150 metres south of the main Barnhouse settlement, and recent excavation has revealed even closer occupation deposits situated within 50 metres of the entrance (Richards in press). It is beyond doubt the most immediately striking of the Stenness monuments, originally having twelve tall angle-topped stones laid out in a large circle. The stone circle was enclosed within a massive 2-metre deep, rock-cut ditch surrounded by an outer bank or wall (Figure 32.9). Either boundary form would have been of sufficient stature to prevent visual access into the interior except across the wide single causeway which is oriented north–north west. This entrance appears not to be aligned on any solar movement but rather towards the stone of Odin monolith (Challands in press) and the Barnhouse settlement.

The excavation of the Stones of Stenness was undertaken in 1973–4 by Graham Ritchie (Ritchie 1976). Besides three cuttings across the ditch and investigations of the stone circle, an internal area was examined extending north from the centre of the site to the single causeway entrance. In this area a number of features were discovered (Figure 32.9), including a central stone setting with four large slabs laid to form a 2-metre square. To the north of the central feature lay an area of flat

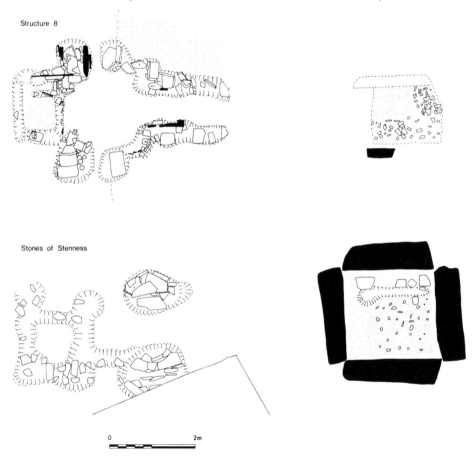

Structure 8

Stones of Stenness

0   2m

Figure 32.9 *The central features at Barnhouse Structure 8 and the Stones of Stenness*

slabs extending to two adjacent stone holes, set 70 cm apart. Directly beyond the stone holes, in exact alignment with the entrance causeway, was located the 'remains of an almost square structure 2 metres in overall measurement' (ibid.: 13). Each corner of the square slots had circular depressions and although the feature appeared badly eroded 'possibly from ploughing' (ibid.: 14) it was interpreted as the remains of a 2-metre square wooden structure.

An interpretation of the apparently nebulous features encountered by Ritchie within the Stones of Stenness becomes clearer when considered in respect to Barnhouse Structure 8. Hodder (1982b: 222) drew attention to the similarity between the central hearth of the house and the central square stone setting at the Stones of Stenness. A closer examination of this massive hearth reveals it to have been reconstructed on at least three occasions. Of particular interest is the similarity between the early construction and reconstruction at both the Stones of Stenness and Barnhouse Structure 8, where the central hearths begin life as identically proportioned 'L'-shaped slots dug into the natural. Both are modified through time, however, at the Stones of Stenness the hearth undergoes further remodelling and is truly monumentalized by the laying of four enormous stone slabs (Figure 32.10).

Furthermore, the features situated towards the entrance of the Stones of Stenness are also paralleled on the platform of Barnhouse Structure 8. Entrance to the inner

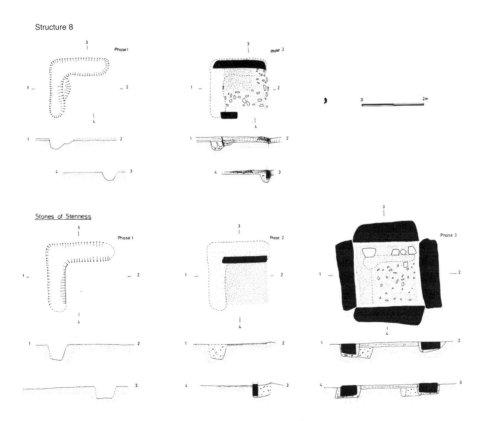

Figure 32.10 *Remodelling of the central hearth at Structure 8 and the Stones of Stenness*

'house' at the latter is defined by a characteristic square hearth set at the threshold of the porch (Figure 32.9). At the Stones of Stenness the 'remains of an almost square structure' (Ritchie 1976: 13) may be reinterpreted as the negative impression of a hearth, 'the east and west sides of this little structure were approximately in line with the position of the upright stones in the two holes, and it seems likely that these two stones would have formed a porch or monumental entrance' (ibid.: 14). This interpretation may now be inverted, the hearth becomes part of the monumental porch or entrance into the inner area of the henge monument.

In the absence of any evidence to the contrary it must be assumed that the central precinct of the Stones of Stenness, was open and not, as at Barnhouse Structure 8, enclosed by a building. Nevertheless, as Hodder (1982b: 222) recognized, the Stones of Stenness draws once again on the architecture of the house to create a similar spatial structure to that confronted by Neolithic people on a daily basis within the home.

Whether approaching the Stones of Stenness along a prescribed path, perhaps involving a route governed by the surrounding menhirs, or in a less formalized manner, the large bank or wall running around its perimeter would do little to obscure the higher internal ring of pointed monoliths, some of which rise to over 5 metres in height (Figure 32.11). The break in the outer barrier provides the only means of admittance to the monument and as this entrance is approached so the central stones and hearth, together with those already present, fall into view. Gaining entry to the interior involves passing through and over two successive boundaries; one rising above the ground the other cut into its depths. The subject moves through a breach in the outer bank or wall and then proceeds over a causeway dividing the substantial rock cut ditch which is over 4 metres wide and almost 3 metres deep. At the base of the ditch lie the remains

Figure 32.11 Approaching the Stones of Stenness

of earlier activities within the monument, including the ash from past fires, and the animal bones and grooved ware vessels from feasts.

On entering the enclosure, its monumental proportions become dramatically apparent with the circle of huge monoliths towering above. This architecture serves to invoke sensations, both of wonder at the achievement and awe inspired by the height – impressions which tend to embrace the whole of the internal area.

Once inside the monument the eye is inevitably drawn to the central area with its massive hearth and the two monoliths standing 5 metres away on a direct line with the entrance. Significantly, this is the same distance as that between the monumental porch and the central hearth within Structure 8 (Figure 32.10), and there can be little doubt that the pair of free standing uprights within the Stones of Stenness constituted a symbolic entrance into the central area with its monumental hearth.

The relationship between the two monuments becomes clearer if the Stones of Stenness is considered as simply a larger version of Structure 8. Indeed, if the wall of the inner 'house' within Structure 8 is removed and the circular outer wall expanded, then it effectively mirrors the spatial organisation of the Stones of Stenness. Of course, the notable absentee is the surrounding circle of monoliths. However, it would have represented an impossible feat to roof the vast area within the Stones of Stenness, therefore, the inclusion of a towering circle of monoliths symbolizes and creates a forcible and overwhelming impression of height. This is the importance of the Stones of Stenness, it is a monument which allows people to see what is occurring inside.

Monumental choreography

In attempting to understand the monuments of the Stenness promontory it has become clear that they operate upon several planes of meaning. A recognizable cosmologically-based sense of order is manifest in the architecture of all the monuments. This facilitates the necessary metaphorical links between everyday contexts of life and the contexts of ritual and religion. The potency of the architecture and the rituals which took place within the monuments lies in the reconstitution of broader categories of such knowledge which is apparently cosmologically-based and derived from elsewhere – beyond the everyday world of the living (cf. Barrett 1991).

In the use of the monuments certain people will have gone through elaborate routines of ritual performance while the majority looked on. However, by virtue of moving into the confines or proximity of the monument the subject becomes involved and presenced within the proceedings. Through interpretive practice different meanings and levels of understanding will be derived from the experience; an experience which transcends daily life, but is inextricably linked through metaphorical association. Hence, it is in the arena of daily living that such metaphorical knowledge comes into play, in the guise of analogy and social classification.

This is what makes the Stenness monuments so important. Not only do they contain a clarity of statement previously unseen (or unrecognized) through rituals confined to particular times of the year, but they also directly impinge on everyday life, all of the time. If the naturalization of power resides in the religious experiences and cosmological beliefs of Neolithic people then the monumental architecture of the Stenness promontory is truly an emblem of that power.

Scale of construction and high visibility, however, should not be confused with greater social awareness. Nevertheless, within the architecture of both Maes Howe and the Stones of Stenness, the two larger and more prominent members of the group, an emphasis is apparently placed on greater public access to the events occurring within their confines. In fact, both monuments allow that which was previously enclosed and restricted to be revealed. This facility is, however, only realized by people travelling to the monument at a particular time and participating through their very presence. In this fusion of space and time we see the monuments as representing 'places' effecting a conceptual and physical order on the fluidity of existence and the natural world.

In conclusion, by offering an interpretation of a discrete group of late Neolithic monuments in Orkney, it is to be hoped that an alternative line of enquiry to the typological and evolutionary models which still influence prehistoric studies has been provided. For instance, it is no longer necessary to invoke cloaked arguments of social evolution to suggest that henge monuments followed chambered tombs or that the two need be somehow incompatible (e.g. Sharples 1985). Still worse is to see the monuments as 'things' having a life of their own (e.g. Fraser 1983). I would suggest that to do so is to lose sight of the people who intentionally built and used them and perhaps having done so never escaped their influence.

ACKNOWLEDGEMENTS

This paper certainly benefited from discussions with Patrick Ashmore, John Barrett, Jane Downes, Joffy Hill, Ian Kinnes, Mike Parker Pearson and Graham Ritchie. Richard Bradley and Ian Hodder kindly read earlier drafts. I also wish to thank Paul Birkbeck for drawing House 2 at very short notice.

BIBLIOGRAPHY

Unless otherwise stated, works by Freud are listed according to the date of their original publication and references are to the translations in the respective volumes of the Pelican Freud Library (PFL) (London: Penguin Books, 15 volumes, 1973–85).

Where the text in the original volume was forthcoming, the date of publication has since been added, if known.

Abercrombie, N., Hill, S. and Turner, B. (1980) *The Dominant Ideology Thesis* (London: Allen and Unwin).

Adams, J. L. (1988) Use-wear analysis on manos and hide processing stones, *Journal of Field Archaeology* 15: 307–15.

Afigbo, A. E. (1981) *Ropes of Sand: Studies in Igbo History and Culture* (Ibadan: Enugu University Press Ltd in assoc. with Oxford University Press).

Aglietta, M. (1980) *A Theory of Capitalist Regulation: The US Experience* (London: New Left Books).

Alarcon, N. (1990) The theoretical subject(s) of *This Bridge Called My Back* and Anglo-American feminism, in Gloria Anzaldúa (ed.) *Making Face, Making Soul: Haciendo Caras* (San Francisco: Aunt Lute) 356–69.

Alcock, J. (1975) *Animal Behavior: an Evolutionary Approach* (Sunderland, MA: Sinauer).

Allen, F. L. (1952) *The Big Change* (New York: Harper Brothers).

Allen, W. L. and Richardson, J. B. (1971) The reconstruction of kinship from archaeological data: the concepts, the method, and the feasibility, *American Antiquity* 36: 41–53.

Almgren, B. (1975) Hällristningarnas tro: till tolkningen av de Svenska hällristningarna från bronsåldern', *Kungl. Gustav Adolfs Akademien Årsbok* (Stockholm: Historiska Museum) 69–108.

Almgren, O. (1927) *Hällristningar och Kultbruk: Bidrag till Belysning av de Nordiska Bronsåldersristningarnas* (Stockholm: Innebors, Kungl. Vitterhets Historie och Antikvitets Akademiens Handlingar 35).

Althusser, L. (1969) *For Marx* (New York: Vintage).

Althusser, L. (1971a) *Lenin and Philosophy* (New York: Monthly Review Press).

Althusser, L. (1971b) Ideology and ideological state apparatuses, in *Lenin and Philosophy*, translated from the French by Ben Brewster (New York: Monthly Review Press).

561

Althusser, L. (1976) *Essays in Self-Criticism* (London: New Left Books).

Althusser, L. (1977a) *For Marx* (London: New Left Books).

Althusser, L. (1977b) Ideology and Ideological State Apparatuses, in *Lenin and Philosophy and Other Essays* (London: New Left Books), pp. 121–73.

Althusser, L. and Balibar, E. (1970) *Reading Capital* (London: Verso).

Altmann. J. (1980) *Baboon Mothers and Infants* (Cambridge, MA: Harvard University Press).

Altmann, S. and Altmann, J. (1971) *Baboon Ecology* (Chicago: Chicago University Press).

Amsden, J. (1979) Introduction, in Daniel Guerin (ed.) *100 Years of Labor in the USA* (London: Ink Links Ltd), pp. 1–30.

Andreu, G. (1997) *Egypt in the Age of the Pyramids* (London: John Murray).

Anon. (1961) Funerals, *Which?* 43–5.

Anon. (1975) *The History of Modern Cremation in Great Britain – from 1874* (London: Cremation Society Pamphlet).

Anthony, D. W. (1986) The Kurgan culture: Indo-European origins and the domestication of the horse: a reconsideration, *Current Anthropology* 27: 291–313.

Anzaldúa, G. (1987) *Borderlands/La Frontera* (San Francisco: Spinsters/Aunt Lute).

Apel, K. O. (1986) Scientists, hermeneutics, critique of ideology: an outline of a theory of science from an epistemological-anthropological point of view, in K. Mueller-Vollmer (ed.) *The Hermeneutics Reader* (Oxford: Blackwell), pp. 321–45.

Ardener, E. (1978) Some outstanding problems in the analysis of events, in E. Schwimmer (ed.) *Yearbook of Symbolic Anthropology* 1 (London: Hurst). Reprinted in M. L. Foster and S. Brandes (eds) *Symbol as Sense* (New York: Academic Press), pp. 301–21.

Asad, T. (1973) (ed.) *Anthropology and the Colonial Encounter* (London: Ithaca).

Asad, T. (1979) Anthropology and the analysis of ideology, *Man* (N.S.) 14: 607–27.

Asad, T. (1986) *The Concept of Cultural Translation in British Social Anthropology*, in J. Clifford and G. Marcus (eds) *Writing Culture* (Berkeley, CA: University of California Press).

Athens, J. S. (1993) Cultural resource management and academic responsibility in archaeology: a further comment, *SAA Bulletin* 11 (2): 6–7.

Audouze, F. and Buchenschutz, O. (1989) *Villes, Villages et Campagnes de l'Europe Celtique* (Paris: Hachette).

Bachelard, G. (1964) *The Poetics of Space* (Boston: Beacon Press).

Bahn, P. (1982) Inter-site and inter-regional links during the Upper Palaeolithic: the Pyrenean evidence, *Oxford Journal of Archaeology* 1 (3): 247–68.

Bailey, D. (1990) The living house: signifying continuity, in R. Samson (ed.) *The Social Archaeology of Houses* (Edinburgh: Edinburgh University Press), pp. 19–48.

Bailey, G. N. (1983) Concepts of time in quaternary prehistory, *Annual Review of Anthropology* 12: 165–92.

Bailey, G. N. (1987) Breaking the time barrier, *Archaeological Review from Cambridge* 6: 5–20.

Baker, F., and Hill, J. D. (eds) (1988) Archaeology and the heritage industry, Theme Issue *Archaeological Review From Cambridge* 7(2).

Bakhtin, M. M. (1981) *The Dialogic Imagination: Four Essays*, trans. C. Emerson and M. Holquist, in M. Holquist (ed.) (Austin, TX: University of Texas Press).

Baldridge, H. A. (1928) Washington's visits to colonial Annapolis, *Naval Institute Proceedings*, February.

Baltzer, L. (1881) *Glyphes des Rochers du Bohuslan (Suède)* (Göteborg: Göteborg Handelstidnings Aktiebolaget).

Baltzer, L. (1911) *Några af de Viktigaste hällristningarna samt en del af defasta fornminnena i Bohuslän* (Göteborg: Göteborg Handelstidnings Aktiebolaget).

Bapty, I. and Yates, T. (eds) (1990) *Archaeology After Structuralism* (London: Routledge).

Baranik, R., Bromberg, S., Charlesworth, S., Cohen, S., Duncan C., *et al.* (1977) *An Anti-Catalog* (New York: Catalog Committee, Artists Meeting for Cultural Change).

Barnett, S. and Silverman, M. G. (1979) *Ideology and Everyday Life* (Ann Arbor, MI: University of Michigan Press).

Barrett, J. (1991) Review of Richard Bradley (1990), *The Passage of Arms: an Archaeological Analysis of Prehistoric Hoards and Votive Deposits, Antiquity* 65: 743–4.

Barrett, J. (1987a) Fields of discourse, *Critique of Anthropology* 7: 5–16. And this volume.

Barrett, J. (1987b) Contextual archaeology, *Antiquity* 61: 468–73.

Barrett, J. (1989a) Food, gender and metal: questions of social reproduction, in M.-L. Stig-Sorensen and R. Thomas (eds) *The Transition from Bronze to Iron* (Oxford: British Archaeological Reports).

Barrett, J. (1989b) Time and tradition: the rituals of everyday life, in H.-A. Nordstrom and A. Knape (eds) *Bronze Age Studies* (Stockholm: Statens).

Barrett, J. (1991) Toward an archaeology of ritual, in P. Garwood, D. Jennings, R. Skeates and J. Toms (eds) *Sacred and Profane* (Oxford: Oxford University Committee for Archaeology Monograph) 32: 1–9.

Barrett, J. (1992) Comment, *Archaeological Review from Cambridge* 11 (1): 157–62.

Barrett, J., Bradley, R. and Green, M. (1991) *Landscape, Monuments and Society: The Prehistory of Cranbourne Chase* (Cambridge: Cambridge University Press).

Barrett, J. (1994) *Fragment from Antiquity: An Archaeology of Social Life in Britain, 2900–1200 BC* (Oxford: Blackwell).

Barth, F. (1969) Introduction, in F. Barth (ed.) *Ethnic Groups and Boundaries* (Boston: Little Brown), pp. 9–38.

Barth, F. (1975) *Ritual and Knowledge among the Baktaman of New Guinea* (Oslo: Universitetsforlaget).

Barth, F. (1987) *Cosmologies in the Making: A Generative Approach to Cultural Variation in Inner New Guinea* (Cambridge: Cambridge University Press).

Barthes, R. (1968) *Elements of Semiology*, trans. A. Lavers and C. Smith (New York: Hill & Wang).

Barthes, R. (1973) *Mythologies* (London: Paladin).

Barthes, R. (1974) *S/Z* (New York: Hill & Wang).

Barthes, R. (1977a) The death of the author, *Image–Music–Text*, trans. S. Heath (London: Collins).

Barthes, R. (1977b) *Image, Music, Text* (New York: Hill & Wang).

Barthes, R. (1979) *Mythologies*, trans. A. Lavers (New York: Hill & Wang).

Basden, G. (1921) *Among the Igbos of Nigeria* (London: Cass).

Basso, K. (1984) 'Stalking with stories': names, places, and moral narratives among the Western Apache, in E. M. Bruner (ed.) *Text, Play and Story: The Construction and Reconstruction of Self and Society* (Washington, DC: American Ethnological Society), pp. 19–55.

Baudrillard, J. (1978) *Système des objets* (Paris: Gallimard).

Baudrillard, J. (1988) Simulacra and simulations, in M. Poster (ed.) *Jean Baudrillard: Selected Writings,* (Cambridge: Polity Press), pp 166–84.

Bauman, Z. (1971) Semiotics and the Function of Culture, in T. A. Sebeoh (ed.) *Approaches to Semiotics* (The Hague: Mouton), 15: 279–91.

Bauman, Z. (1992) *Intimations of Postmodernity* (London: Routledge).

Bauman, Z. (1993) *Postmodern Ethics* (Oxford: Blackwell).

Behrensmeyer, A. K. (1978) Taphonomic and ecologic information from bone weathering, *Paleobiology* 4: 150–62.

Behrensmeyer, A. K. and Hill A. P. (eds) (1980) *Fossils in the Making: Vertebrate Taphonomy and Paleoecology* (Chicago: University of Chicago Press).

Bell, D. (1974) *The Coming Of the Post-Industrial Society* (London: Heinemann).

Bell, J. (1987) Rationality versus relativism: a review of 'Reading the Past', *Archaeological Review from Cambridge* 6: 75–86.

Benac, A. (1973) *Obre II, a Neolithic settlement of the Butmir Group at Gornje Polje*, Wissenschaftliche Mitteilungen des Bosnisch-Herzegowinischen Landesmuseums, III (A).

Ben-Amos, P. (1980) *The Art of Benin* (London: Thames and Hudson).

Ben-Amos, P. (1983) *The Art of Power: The Power of Art: Studies in Benin Iconography* Monograph Series 19. (Los Angeles: Los Angeles Museum of Cultural History, University of California).

Bender, B. (1978) Gatherer-hunter to farmer: a social perspective, *World Archaeology* 10: 204–22.

Bender, B. (1985) Emergent tribal formations in the American midcontinent, *American Antiquity* 50: 52–62.

Bender, B. (1989) Comments on archaeology into the 1990s, *Norwegian Archaeological Review* 22 (1): 12–14.

Bennett, A. (1987) Texts in history: the determination of readings and their texts, in D. Atridge, G. Bennington and R. Young (eds) *Poststructuralism and the Question of History* (Cambridge: Cambridge University Press), pp. 63–81.

Bentley, G. (1987) Ethnicity and practice, *Comparative Studies in Society and History* 29: 24–55.

Berlant, L. and Warner, M. (1995) What does queer theory teach us about X? *PMLA* 110 (3): 343–9.

Bernstein, I. and Ehardt. C. (1985) Agonistic aiding: kinship, rank age, and sex influences, *American Journal of Primatology* 8: 37–52.

Bernstein, R. J. (1983) *Beyond Objectivism and Relativism* (Philadelphia: University of Pennsylvania Press).

Bersu, G. (1940) Excavations at Little Woodbury, Wiltshire. Part 1, *Proceedings of the Prehistoric Society* 6: 30–111.

Binford, L. (1962) Archaeology as anthropology, *American Antiquity* 28: 217–25.

Binford, L. (1964) A consideration of archaeological research design, *American Antiquity* 9: 425–41.

Binford, L. (1965) Archaeological systematics and the study of cultural process, *American Antiquity* 31: 203–10.

Binford, L. (1968) Archaeological perspectives, in S. R. Binford and L. R. Binford (eds) *New Perspectives in Archaeology* (Chicago, Aldine), pp. 5–32.

Binford, L. R. (1971) Mortuary practices: their study and potential, in J. A. Brown (ed.) *Approaches to the Social Dimensions of Mortuary Practices* (New York: Memoirs of the Society for American Archaeology) 25: 6–29.

Binford, L. (1972a) *An Archaeological Perspective* (New York: Seminar Press).

Binford, L. (1972b) Mortuary practices: their study and their potential, in L. Binford (ed.) *An Archaeological Perspective* (New York: Seminar Press).

Binford, L. (1972c) Evolution and horizon as revealed in ceramic analysis in historical archaeology – a step toward the development of archaeological science, in *The Conference on Historic Site Archaeology Papers 1971*, 6: 117–25.

Binford, L. (1977a) *For Theory Building in Archaeology* (London: Academic Press).

Binford, L. (1977b) Forty-seven trips: a case study in the character of archaeological formation processes, in R. V. S. Wright (ed.) *Stone Tools as Cultural Markers* (Canberra: Australian Institute of Aboriginal Studies), pp. 24–36.

Binford, L. (1978a) *Nunamiut Ethnoarchaeology* (New York: Academic Press).

Binford, L. (1978b) Dimensional analysis of behaviour and site structure: learning from an Eskimo hunting stand, *American Antiquity* 43: 330–61.

Binford, L. (1981a) *Bones – Ancient Men and Modern Myths* (London: Academic Press).

Binford, L. (1981b) Behavioral archaeology and the 'Pompeii Premise', *Journal of Anthropological Research* 7: 195–208.

Binford, L. (1982a) Objectivity – explanation – archaeology 1981, in C. Renfrew, M. J. Rowlands, and B. A. Segraves (eds) *Theory and Explanation in Archaeology: The Southampton Conference* (New York: Academic Press), pp. 125–38.

Binford, L. (1982b) Comment on R. White's paper: Rethinking the Middle/Upper Palaeolithic transition, *Current Anthropology* 23 (2): 177–81.

Binford, L. (1982c) The archaeology of place, *Journal of Anthropological Archaeology*, 1: 5–31.

Binford, L. (1982d) Meaning, inference and the material record, in C. Renfrew and S. Shennan (eds) *Ranking Resource and Exchange* (Cambridge: Cambridge University Press).

Binford, L. (1983a) *In Pursuit of the Past: Decoding the Archaeological Record* (London: Thames and Hudson).

Binford, L. (1983b) *Working at Archaeology* (New York: Academic Press).

Binford, L. (1985) An Alyawara day: making men's knives, *American Antiquity* 51: 257–84.

Binford, L. (1987) Data, relativism and archaeological science, *Man* 22: 391–404.

Binford, L. (1989) *Debating Archaeology* (London: Academic Press).

Binford, L. and Binford, S. (1969) Stone tools and human behaviour, *Scientific American* 220: 70–84.

Binford, L. and Sabloff, J. A. (1982) Paradigms, systematics, and archaeology, *Journal of Anthropological Research* 38: 137–53.

Bintliff, J. (ed.) (1990) *Extracting Meaning from the Past* (Oxford: Oxbow Books).

Bintliff, J. (1991) Post-modernism, rhetoric and scholasticism at TAG: the current state of British archaeological theory, *Antiquity* 65: 274–8.

Bintliff, J. (1993) Why Indiana Jones is smarter than the postprocessualists, *Norwegian Archaeological Review* 26: 91–100.

Black, M. (1962) *Models and Metaphors* (Ithaca, NY: Cornell University Press).

Blackham, I. J. (1952) *Six Existentialist Thinkers* (London: Routledge and Kegan Paul).

Blacking, J. (ed.) (1977) *The Anthropology of the Body* (London: Academic Press).

Blackmore, C., Braithwaite, M. and Hodder I. (1979) Social and cultural patterning in the Late Iron Age in southern Britain, in B. C. Burnham and J. Kingsbury (eds) *Space, Hierarchy and Society: Interdisciplinary Studies in Social Area Analysis* (Oxford: BAR), pp. 93–112.

Blakey, M. L. (1983) Socio-political bias and ideological production in historical archaeology, in J. M. Gero, D. M. Lacy and M. L. Blakey (eds) *The Socio-Politics of Archaeology* Department of Anthropology, Amherst, MA: University of Massachusetts, Research Report 23.

Blakey, M. L. (1986) American nationality and ethnicity in the depicted past. Paper presented at the World Archaeological Congress, Southampton and London.

Bleys, R. C. (1996) *The Geography of Perversion: Male-to-Male Sexual Behaviour Outside the West and the Ethnographic Imagination* 1750–1918 (London: Cassell).

Bloch, M. (1971) *Placing the Dead* (London: Seminar Press).

Bloch, M. (1974) Symbols, song, dance and features of articulation, *Archives of European Sociology* 15: 55–81.

Bloch, M. (1977) The past and the present in the present, *Man* 12: 278–92.

Bloch, M. (1995) Questions not to ask of Malagasy carvings, in I. Hodder, M. Shanks, A. Alexandri, V. Buchli, J. Carman, J. Last and G. Lucas (eds) *Interpreting Archaeology: Finding Meaning in the Past* (London: Routledge), pp. 212–15.

Bloom, A. (1987) *The Closing of the American Mind* (New York: Simon and Schuster).

Blurton-Jones, N. G. (1987) Tolerated theft, suggestions about the ecology and evolution of sharing, hoarding and scrounging, *Social Science Information* 26.

Boast, R. and Evans, C. (1986) The transformation of space: two examples from British prehistory, *Archaeological Review from Cambridge* 5: 193–205.

Boese, G. (1975) Social behavior and ecological considerations of West African baboons, in R. Tuttle (ed.) *Socioecology and Psychology of Primates* (The Hague: Mouton).

Bogdanovic, M. (1990) Die spätneolithischen Siedlungen in Divostin, in D. Srejovic and N. Tasic (eds), *Vinča and its World* (Belgrade: Serbian Academy of Sciences and Arts), pp. 99–106.

Bogucki, P. (1987) The establishment of agrarian communities on the north European plain, *Current Anthropology* 28: 1–24.

Bogucki, P. (1988) *Forest Farmers and Stockherders: Early Agriculture and its Consequences in North-Central Europe* (Cambridge: Cambridge University Press).

Bogue, R. (1989) *Deleuze and Guattari* (London: Routledge).

Bohannan, P. (1959) The Impact of Money on an African subsistence economy, *Journal of Economic History* 19: 491–503.

Bohm, D. (1980) *Wholeness and the Implicate Order* (London: Routledge & Kegan Paul).

Bond, G. C. and Gilliam, A. (1994) Introduction in G. C. Bond and A. Gilliam (eds) *Social Construction of the Past: Representation as Power* (London: Routledge), pp. 1–22.

Bordes, F. (1950) Principes d'une méthode d'étude des techniques et de la typologie du Paléolithique ancien et moyen, *L'Anthropologie* 54: 19–34.

Bordes, F. (1953) Essai de classification des industries 'moustériennes'. *Bulletin de la Société Préhistorique Française* 50: 457–66.

Bordes, F. (1961) *Typologie du Palaéolithique ancien et moyen* (Bordeaux: Delmas).

Bordes, F. (1968) *The Old Stone Age* (London: Weidenfeld and Nicolson).

Bordes, F. (1972) *A Tale of Two Caves* (London: Harper and Row).

Bordes, F. and Bourgon, M. (1951) Le complexe moustérien: Moustérien, Levalloisien et Tayacien, *L'Anthropologie* 55: 1–23.

Bosanquet, B. (1898) *Rich and Poor* (London: Macmillan).

Boschetti, M. (1986) Emotional attachment to homes past and present: continuity of experience and integrity of self in old age, in D. Saile (ed.) *Architecture in Cultural Change: Essays in Built Form and Culture Research* (Kansas: School of Architecture and Urban Design, University of Kansas), pp. 31–44.

Boswell, J. (1980) *Christianity, Social Intolerance, and Homosexuality* (Chicago: The University of Chicago Press).

Boswell, J. (1994) *Same-Sex Unions in Premodern Europe* (New York: Villard Books).

Bothwell, L. (1983) *Broome County Heritage* (Woodland Hills, NY: Windsor Publications).

Bourdier, J.-P. (1989) Reading tradition, in J.-P. Bourdier and N. AlSayyad (eds) *Dwellings, Settlements and Traditions: cross-cultural perspectives* (Lanham, MD: University Press of America), pp. 35–51.

Bourdieu, P. (1966) The sentiment of honour in Kabyle society, in J. G. Peristiany (ed.) *Honour and Shame* (Chicago/London: Weidenfeld and Nicolson).

Bourdieu, P. (1977) *Outline of a Theory of Practice* (Cambridge: Cambridge University Press).

Bourdieu, P. (1979a) Symbolic power, *Critique of Anthropology*, 4 13/14: 77–85.

Bourdieu, P. (1979b) *Algeria 1960* (Cambridge: Cambridge University Press).

Bourdieu, P. (1985) The genesis of the concepts of 'habitus' and 'field', *Sociocriticism* 2 (2): 11–24.

Bourdieu, P. (1990a) La domination masculine, *Actes de la recherche en sciences sociales* 84: 2–31.

Bourdieu, P. (1990b) *In Other Words* (Cambridge: Polity Press).

Bourdieu, P. (1990c) *The Logic of Practice* (Cambridge: Polity Press).

Bourdieu, P. (1991) *Language and Symbolic Power* (Cambridge: Polity Press).

Bourdieu, P. and Wacquant, L. (1992) *An Invitation to Reflexive Sociology* (Cambridge: Polity Press).

Bowden, M. and McOmish, D. (1989) Little boxes: more about hillforts, *Scottish Archaeological Review* 6: 12–16.

Boyarin, J. (1992) *Storm from Paradise: The Politics of Jewish Memory* (Minneapolis, MN: University of Minnesota Press).

Boyer, P. and Nissenbaum, S. (1974) *Salem Possessed: The Social Origins of Witchcraft* (Cambridge, MA: Harvard University Press).

Bradley, R. (1984) Studying monuments, in R. Bradley and J. Gardiner (eds) *Neolithic Studies: A Review of Some Current Research* BAR Brit. Series 133, Oxford.

Bradley, R. (1989) Darkness and light in the design of Megalithic tombs, *Oxford Journal of Archaeology*, 8, pt 3: 251–8.

Bradley, R. (1990) *The Passage of Arms: An Archaeological Analysis of Prehistoric Hoards and Votive Deposits* (Cambridge: Cambridge University Press).

Bradley, R. (1991) The patterns of change in British prehistory, in Timothy Earle (ed.) *Chiefdoms: Power, Economy, and Ideology* (Cambridge: Cambridge University Press), pp. 44–70.

Bradley, R. and Gardiner, J. (1984) *Neolithic Studies: A Review of Some Current Research* BAR Brit. Series 133, Oxford.

Braithwaite, R. B. (1963) *Scientific Explanation* (Cambridge: Cambridge University Press).

Braithwaite, M. (1982) Decoration as ritual symbol: a theoretical proposal and an ethnographic study in Southern Sudan, in I. Hodder (ed.) *Symbolic and Structural Archaeology* (Cambridge: Cambridge University Press), pp. 80–8.

Braithwaite, M. (1984) Ritual and prestige in the prehistory of Wessex *c.*2,000–1,400 BC: a new dimension to the archaeological evidence, in D. Miller and C. Tilley (eds) *Ideology, Power and Prehistory* (Cambridge: Cambridge University Press), pp. 93–110.

Brandes, S. (1981) Like wounded stags: male sexual ideology in an Andalusian town, in S. B. Ortner and H. Whitehead (eds) *Sexual Meanings: The Cultural Construction of Gender and Sexuality* (Cambridge: Cambridge University Press), pp. 21–39.

Brannigan, A. (1981) *The Social Basis of Scientific Discoveries* (Cambridge: Cambridge University Press).

Braudel, F. (1958) Histoire des sciences sociales, la longue durée, *Annales, Economies* 13:725–53.

Braudel, F. (1979a) *The Structure of Everyday Life: Civilization and Capitalism, 15th–18th Century* (New York: Harper and Row).

Braudel, F. (1979b) *The Wheels of Commerce: Civilization and Capitalism, 15th–18th Century* (New York: Harper and Row).

Braudel, F. (1983) *The Roots of Modern Capitalism* (New York: Harper and Row).

Braverman, H. (1974) *Labor and Monopoly Capital: The Degradation of Work in the Twentieth Century* (London: Monthly Review Press).

Breuil, H. (1912) *Les subdivisions du paléolithique supérieur et leur signification,* Cong. Internationale d'Anthropologie et d'Archaeologie Préhistorique, Geneva.

Brigden, S. (1984) Youth and the English Reformation, in *Rebellion, Popular Protest and the Social Order in Early Modern England*, edited by P. Slack, (Cambridge: Cambridge University Press), pp. 77–107.

Brodhead, F. (1981) Social control, *Radical America* 15(6): 69–78.

Brown, J. (1971) The dimensions of status in the burials at Spiro, in J. Brown (ed.) *Social Dimensions of Mortuary Practices*, Memoir No. 25 Society for American Archaeology, *American Antiquity* 36: 92–112.

Brukner, B. (1990) Typen und Siedlunge Modellen und Wohnobjekte der Vinča-Gruppe in der Panonisehen Tierebene in D. Srejovic and N. Tasic (eds) *Vinča and its World*: (Belgrade: Serbian Academy of Sciences and Arts), pp. 79–83.

Brunaux, J. L. (1988) *The Celtic Gauls: Gods, Rites and Sanctuaries* (London: Seaby).

Bulmer, R. (1967) Why is the Cassowary not a bird? *Man* 2: 5–25.

Burenhult, G. (1978) *Hällristningar: Hällbilder från sten-och bronsålder i Norden* (Malmö: Malmö Museum).

Burkitt, M. C. (1933) *The Old Stone Age* (Cambridge: Cambridge University Press).

Burrell, A. (trans.) (1931) *Piers Plowman: The Vision of a People's Christ* (New York: Everyman).

Burtt, F. (1987) 'Man the Hunter': male bias in children's archaeology books, *Archaeological Review from Cambridge* 6(2): 157–74.

Busse, D. and Hamilton, W., III (1981) Infant carrying by male chacma baboons, *Science* 212: 1281–3.

Butler, J. (1990) *Gender Trouble: Feminism and the Subversion of Identity* (London: Routledge).

Butler, J. (1991) Imitation and gender insubordination, in D. Fuss (ed.) *Inside/out: Lesbian Theories, Gay Theories* (London: Routledge).

Butler, J. (1993) *Bodies That Matter: On the Discursive Limits of 'Sex'* (London: Routledge).

Butler, J. (1997) Against proper objects, in E. Weed and N. Schor (eds) *Feminism Meets Queer Theory* (Bloomington, IND: Indiana University Press).

Callander, J. G. (1931) Notes on (1) certain prehistoric relics from Orkney and (2) Skara Brae: its culture and its period. *Proceedings of the Society of Antiquaries of Scotland* 65: 78–111.

Callinicos, A. (1983) *Marxism and Philosophy* (Oxford: Oxford University Press).

Callon, M. and Latour, B. (1981) Unscrewing the big Leviathans: how do actors macrostructure reality and how sociologists help them, in K. Knorr and A. Cicourel (eds) *Advances in Social Theory and Methodology* (London: Routledge & Kegan Paul), pp. 277–303.

Cambell, S. F. (1983) Attaining rank: a classification of shell valuables, in J. Leach and E. Leach (eds) *The Kula: New Perspectives on Massim Exchange* (Cambridge: Cambridge University Press), pp. 229–48.

Caplan, P. (1988) Engendering knowledge: the politics of ethnography (Parts 1 and 2) *Anthropology Today* 4 (5): 8–12, 4(6): 14–17.

Carneiro, R. (1968) Cultural adaption, in D. Sells (ed.) *International Encyclopaedia of the Social Sciences* 3: 551–4.

Carr, L. G. and Walsh, L. S. (1977) Inventories and the analysis of wealth and consumption patterns in St. Mary's County, Maryland, 1658–1777. Paper presented at the Newberry Library Conference on Quantitative and Social Science Approaches in Early American History, 6–8 October.

Carr, L. G. and Walsh, L. S. (n.d.) Changing lifestyles and consumer behavior in the colonial Chesapeake. MS, Maryland Hall of Records.

Carravetta, P. (1984) An interview with William Spanos, *Critical Texts* 3(1): 10–27.

Carrithers, M., Collins, S. and Lukes, S. (1985) *The Category of the Person: Anthropology, Philosophy, History* (Cambridge: Cambridge University Press).

Carroll, J. (1993) *Humanism: The Wreck of Western Culture* (London: Collins).

Carver, T. N. (1926) *The Present Economic Revolution in the United States* (London: Allen and Unwin).

Cataldi, G. (1986) *All' Origine dell'Abitare* (Florence: Museo Nazionale di Antropologia e Etnologia).

Chadwick, E. (1843) *A Special Enquiry into the Practice of Internment in Towns* (London: HMSO).

Challands, A. (in press) The Stone of Odin, in C. Richards (ed.) *The Late Neolithic Settlement Complex at Barnhouse Farm, Stenness, Orkney.*

Champion, T., Gamble, C., Shennan, S. and Whittle, A. (1984) *Prehistoric Europe* (London: Academic Press).

Champion, T. C. (1987) The European Iron Age: assessing the state of the art, *Scottish Archaeological Review* 4: 98–107.

Chandler, A. D. (1967) *Giant Enterprise, Ford, General Motors and the Automobile Industry* (New York: Random House).

Chapais, B. and Schulman, S. (1980) An evolutionary model of female dominance relations in primates, *Journal of Theoretical Biology* 82: 47–89.

Chapman, J. (1982) 'The secondary products revolution' and the limitations of the Neolithic, *Bulletin of the Institute of Archaeology*, University of London 19: 107.

Chapman, J. (1989) The early Balkan village, *Varia Archaeologica*, 2: 33–55, Budapest.

Chapman, J. (1990a) Regional study of the North Sumadija region, in R. Tringham and D. Kristic (eds) *Selevac: A Neolithic Village in Yugoslavia* (Los Angeles, CA: UCLA Institute of Archaeology Press).

Chapman, J. (1990b) Social inequality on Bulgarian tells and the Varna problem, in R. Samson (ed.) *The Social Archaeology of Houses* (Edinburgh, Edinburgh University Press), pp. 49–92.

Chapman, M., McDonald, M. and Tonkin, E. (1989) Introduction, in E. Tonkin *et al.* (eds) *History and Ethnicity* (London: Routledge), pp. 1–33.

Cheneb, B. (1905–1907) *Proverbes arabes d'Alger et du Maghreb* vol. 3: 312 (Paris, E. Leroux).

Cheney, D. (1977) The acquistion of rank and the development of reciprocal alliances among free-ranging immature baboons, *Behavior, Ecology and Sociobiology* 2: 303–18.

Chepko-Sade, B. (1974) Division of Group F at Cayo Santiago, *American Journal of Physical Anthropology* 41: 472.

Chepko-Sade, B. and Olivier, T. (1979) Coefficient of genetic relationship and the probability of intrageneological fission in Macaca mulatta, *Behavior, Ecology and Sociobiology* 5: 263–78.

Chepko-Sade, B. and Sade, D. (1979) Patterns of group splitting within matrilineal kinship groups, *Behavior, Ecology and Sociobiology* 5: 67–86.

Cherry, J. F., Gamble, C. and Shennan, S. (eds) (1978) *Sampling in Contemporary British Archaeology*. BAR British Series 50. Oxford.

Childe, V. G. (1929) *The Danube in Prehistory* (Oxford: Clarendon Press).

Childe, V. G. (1935) Changing aims and methods in prehistory, *Proceedings of the Prehistoric Society* 1: 1–15.

Childe, V. G. (1936) *Man Makes Himself* (London: Collins).

Childe, V. G. (1940) *Prehistoric Communities of the British Isles* (London: W. and R. Chambers).

Childe, V. G. (1942) *What Happened in History* (London: Penguin).

Childe, V. G. (1945) Directional changes in funerary practices during 50,000 years. *Man* 4: 13–19.

Childe, V. G. (1949) *Social Worlds of Knowledge* (Oxford: Oxford University Press).

Childe, V. G. (1956a) *Piecing Together the Past* (London: Routledge and Kegan Paul).

Childe, V. G. (1956b) *Society and Knowledge: the Growth of Human Traditions* (New York: Harper).

Chippindale, C. (1983) *Stonehenge Complete* (London: Thames and Hudson).

Chippindale, C. (1986) Stoned Henge: events and issues at the Summer Solstice, 1985, *World Archaeology* 18(1): 38–58.

Chippindale, C., Devereux, P. F., Jones, P. R. and Sebastian, T. (1990) *Who Owns Stonehenge?* (London: Batsford).

Chomsky, N. (1959) A review of B. F. Skinner's *Verbal behavior*, *Language* 35 (1): 26–58.

Cixous, H. (1981) Castration or decapitation? *Signs* 7: 41–55.

Clare, T. (1986) Towards a reappraisal of henge monuments, *Proc. Prehist. Soc* 52: 281–316.

Clark, J. G. D. (1939) *Archaeology and Society* (London: Methuen).

Clark, J. G. D. (1975) *The Earlier Stone Age Settlement of Scandinavia* (Cambridge: Cambridge University Press).

Clarke, D. L. (1968) *Analytical Archaeology* (London: Methuen).

Clarke, D. L. (1972a) (ed.) *Models in Archaeology* (London: Methuen).

Clarke, D. L. (1972b) A provisional model of an Iron Age society and its settlement system, in D. L. Clarke (ed.) *Models in Archaeology* (London: Methuen), pp. 801–69.

Clarke, D. L. (1973a) Archaeology: the loss of innocence, *Antiquity* 47: 6–15.

Clarke, D. L. (1973b) The past and the present in the present, *American Antiquity* 50: 52–62.

Clarke, D. V. (1976) *The Neolithic Village at Skara Brae, Orkney, 1972–3 Excavations: An Interim Report* (Edinburgh, HMSO).

Clarke, G. (1975) Popular movements and Late Roman Cemeteries, *World Archaeology* 7: 46–56.

Clifford, J. (1980) Fieldwork, reciprocity and the making of ethnographic texts: the example of Maurice Leenhardt, *Man* 15: 518–32.

Clifford, J. (1986a) Introduction: partial truths, in J. Clifford and G. Marcus (eds) *Writing Culture* (Berkeley, CA: University of California Press).

Clifford, J. (1986b) On ethnographic allegory, in J. Clifford and G. Marcus (eds) *Writing Culture* (Berkeley, CA: University of California Press).

Clifford, J. (1988) *The Predicament of Culture* (Cambridge, MA: Harvard University Press).

Clifford, J. and Marcus, G. (eds) (1986) *Writing Culture: the Politics and Poetics of Ethnography* (Berkeley, CA: University of California Press).

Cohen, A. (1974) Introduction: the lesson of ethnicity, in A. Cohen (ed.) *Urban Ethnicity* (London: Tavistock Publications), pp. ix–xxiv.

Cohen, I. (1986) The status of structuration theory: a reply to McLennan, *Theory, Culture and Society* 3: 123–34.

Cohen, P. (1968) *Modern Social Theory* (London: Heinemann).

Cohen, R. (1978) Ethnicity: problem and focus in anthropology, *Annual Review of Anthropology* 7: 379–403.

Cole, H. and Aniakor, C. (1984) *Igbor Arts: Community and Cosmos* (Los Angeles, CA: Museum of Cultural History, University of California).

Collcutt, S. (1993) The archaeologist as consultant, in J. Hunter and I. Ralston (eds) *Archaeological Resource Management in the UK: An Introduction* (Dover: Alan Sutton), pp. 158–68.

Collett, D. (1987) A contribution to the study of migrations in the archaeological record: the Ngoni and Kololo migrations as a case study, in I. Hodder (ed.) *Archaeology as Long-Term History* (Cambridge: Cambridge University Press), pp. 105–16.

Collier, J. F. and Rosaldo, M. Z. (1981) Politics and gender in simple societies, in S. B. Ortner and H. Whitehead (eds) *Sexual Meanings: The Cultural Construction of Gender and Sexuality* (Cambridge: Cambridge University Press), pp. 275–329.

Collingwood, R. G. (1946) *The Idea of History* (London: Oxford University Press).

Colsen, E. (1968) Contemporary tribes and the development of nationalism, in J. Helm (ed.) *Essays on the Problem of Tribe* (Seattle: University of Washington Press), pp. 201–6.

Comaroff, J. and Comaroff, J. (1992) *Ethnography and the Historical Imagination* (Boulder, COL: Westview Press).

Conkey, M. (1977) Context, structure and efficacy in Palaeolithic art and design, paper presented at the Burg Wartenstein Symposium, 74.

Conkey, M. (1978) Style and information in cultural evolution: towards a predictive model for the Palaeolithic, in C. Redman, M. Berman, E. Curtin, W. Langhorne, N. Versaggi and J. Wanser (eds) *Social archaeology: Beyond Subsistence and Dating* (New York: Academic Press), pp. 61–85.

Conkey, M. (1980) Context, structure, and efficacy in Paleolithic art and design, in M. L. Foster and S. Brandes (eds) *Symbol as Sense* (New York: Academic Press), pp. 225–48.

Conkey, M. (1982) Boundedness in art and society, in I. Hodder (ed.) *Symbolic and Structural Archaeology* (Cambridge: Cambridge University Press), pp. 115–28.

Conkey, M. (1985) Ritual communication, social elaboration, and the variable trajectories of Palaeolithic material culture, in T. Price and J. Brown (eds) *Prehistoric Hunters and Gatherers: The Emergence of Cultural Complexity* (New York: Academic Press).

Conkey, M. (1989) A report from the year 2050, *Archeology* January/February: 35–82.

Conkey, M. (1990) Experimenting with style in archaeology: some historical and theoretical issues, in M. W. Conkey and C. A. Hastorf (eds) *The Uses of Style in Archaeology* (Cambridge: Cambridge University Press), pp. 5–17.

Conkey, M. (1992) Does it make a difference? Feminist thinking and archaeologies of gender, in *The Archaeology of Gender* (Calgary, Alberta: Chacmool Archaeological Association), pp. 24–34.

Conkey, M. W. and Gero, J. (1991) Tensions, pluralities, and engendering archaeology: an introduction to *Women and Prehistory*, in J. Gero and M. W. Conkey (eds) *Engendering Archaeology: Women and Prehistory* (Oxford: Blackwell), pp. 3–30.

Conkey, M. W. and Spector, J. (1984) Archaeology and the study of gender, in M. Schiffer (ed.) *Advances in Archaeological Method and Theory* (New York: Academic Press), pp. 1–38.

Conkey, M. W. and Tringham, R. E. (1995) Archaeology and The Goddess: exploring the contours of feminist archaeology, in A. Stewart and D. Stanton (eds) *Feminisms in the Academy: rethinking the disciplines* (Ann Arbor, MI: University of Michigan Press).

Conkey, M. W. and Williams, S. H. (1991) Original narratives: the political economy of gender in archaeology, in M. di Leonardo (ed.) *Gender at the Crossroads of Knowledge: Feminist Anthropology in the Postmodern Era* (Berkeley, CA: University of California Press).

Connerton, P. (1989) *How Societies Remember* (Cambridge: Cambridge University Press).

Conwell, R. H. (1905) *Acres of Diamonds* (New York: Random House).

Cooper, M. H. and Culyer, A. J. (1968) *The Price of Blood: An Economic Study of the Charitable and Commercial Principles* (London: Institute of Economic Affairs).

Cosgrove, D. (1984) *Social Formation and Symbolic landscape* (London: Croom Helm).

Cosgrove, D. (1989) Geography is everywhere: culture and symbolism in human landscapes, in D. Gregory and R. Walford (eds) *Horizons in Human Geography* (Basingstoke: Macmillan), pp. 11–35.

Coudart, A. (1987) Tradition, uniformity and variability of the architecture in the Danubian Neolithic, in *Proceedings of the International Seminar of the Neolithic Site of Bylany*, Prague, AUCSAV.

Crapanzano, V. (1980) *Tuhami: Portrait of a Moroccan* (Chicago: Chicago University Press).

Criado, F. (1995) The visibility of the archaeological record and the interpretation of social reality, in I. Hodder, M. Shanks, A. Alexandri, V. Buchli, J. Carman, J. Last and G. Lucas (eds) *Interpreting Archaeology: Finding Meaning in the Past* (London: Routledge), pp. 194–204.

Crook, J. (1970) Social organization and the environment, aspects of contemporary social ethology, *Animal Behavior* 18: 197–209.

Crook, J. and Gartlan, J. (1966) On the evolution of primate societies, *Nature* 210: 1200–3.

Crosby, C. (1982) Excavations at the victualling warehouse site, AN 14, 1982: Preliminary report. MS, Historic Annapolis, Inc.

Culler, J. (1976) *Saussure* (London: Collins).

Cunliffe, B. (1982) *The Report of a Joint Working Party for the Council for British Archaeology and the Department of the Environment* (London: Department of the Environment and Her Majesty's Stationery Office).

Cunliffe, B. (1984) Iron Age Wessex: continuity and change, in B. Cunliffe and D. Miles (eds) *Aspects of the Iron Age in Central Southern Britain* (Oxford: Oxford University Committee for Archaeology Monograph 2), pp. 12–45.

Cunliffe, B. (1990) Publishing in the City, *Antiquity* 64: 667–71.

Cunliffe, B. (1991) *Iron Age Communities in Britain*, 3rd edition (London: Routledge).

Cunningham, R. D. (1979) Why and how to improve archaeology's business work, *American Antiquity* 44: 572–74.

Cunnington, P. and Lucas, C. (1972) *Costume for Births, Marriages and Death* (London: Black).

Curl, J. S. (1972) *The Victorian Celebration of Death* (Newton Abbot: David and Charles).

Curtin, P. D. (1984) *Cross-Cultural Trade in World History* (Cambridge: Cambridge University Press).

Dahlberg, F. (ed.) (1981) *Woman the Gatherer* (New Haven, CT: Yale University Press).

Daly, M. (1978) *Gyn/Ecology: The Metaethics of Radical Feminism* (Boston, MA: Beacon Press).

Danforth, I. (1993) Competing claims to Macedonia identity: the Macedonian question and the break up of Yugoslavia, *Anthropology Today* 9 (4): 3–10.

Daniel, G. (1978) [1950] *One Hundred and Fifty Years of Archaeology* (London: Duckworth).

Daniel, G. E. (1962) *The Idea of Prehistory* (Harmondsworth: Penguin).

Daniels, S. and Cosgrove, D. (1988) Introduction: iconography and landscape, in D. Cosgrove and S. Daniels (eds) *The Iconography of Landscape* (Cambridge: Cambridge University Press), pp. 1–10.

Darwin, C. (1977) *The Collected Papers of Charles Darwin* (ed.) P. Barett (Chicago: University of Chicago Press).

David, N. (1971) The Fulani compound, *World Archaeology*, 3(2): 111–31.

Davidson, D. A. (1976) Processes or tell formation and erosion, in D. A. Davidson and M. Shackley (eds) *Geoarchaeology: Earth Sciences and the Past* (London: Duckworth), pp. 255–66.

Davidson, J. L. and Henshall, A. S. (1989) *The Chambered Cairns of Orkney* (Edinburgh: Edinburgh University Press).

Davies, D. (1988) The evocative symbolism of trees, in D. Cosgrove and S. Daniels (eds) *The Iconography of Landscape* (Cambridge: Cambridge University Press), pp. 32–42.

Davis, D. (1966) *The Problem of Slavery in Western Culture* (Ithaca, NY: Cornell University Press).

Davis, D. (1975) *The Problem of Slavery in the Age of Revolution: 1770–1823* (Ithaca, NY: Cornell University Press).

de Beauvoir, S. (1975) *The Second Sex* (Harmondsworth: Penguin).

Deagan, K. (1982) Avenues of inquiry in historical archaeology, in M. B. Schiffer (ed.) *Advances in Archaeological Method and Theory* Vol. 5: (New York: Academic Press), pp. 151–77.

DeCicco, G. (1988) A public relations primer, *American Antiquity* 53: 840–56.

Deetz, J. (1967) *Invitation to Archaeology* (New York: Natural History Press).

Deetz, J. (1968) The inference of residence and descent rules from archaeological data, in S. R. Binford and L. Binford (eds) *New Perspectives in Archaeology* (Chicago: Aldine).

Deetz, J. (1977) *In Small Things Forgotten: The Archaeology of Early American Life* (New York: Anchor Press).

Deetz, J. (1983) Scientific humanism and humanistic science: a plea for paradigmatic pluralism in historical archaeology, *Geoscience and Man* 23 (April 29): 27–34.

de Laet, S. (1957) *Archaeology and its Problems* trans. R. Daniel (London: Phoenix House Ltd).

de Lauretis, T. (1987) *Technologies of Gender: Essays on Theory, Film and Fiction* (London: Macmillan).

de Lauretis, T. (1991) Queer theory: lesbian and gay sexualities, an introduction, *Differences* 3 (2): iii–xviii.

Deleuze, G. (1986) *Foucault* (Paris: Editions de Minuit).

Deleuze, G. and Guattari, F. (1984) *Anti-Oedipus: Capitalism and Schizophrenia* (London: Athlone).

Deleuze, G. and Guattari, F. (1988) *A Thousand Plateaus: Capitalism and Schizophrenia* (London: Athlone).

de Mortillet, G. and de Mortillet, G. (1903) *Le Musée Prehistorique* (2nd edition; Paris: Schleicher Frères and Co.).

Demoule, J.-P. (n.d.) L'Archéologie du Pouvoir: oscillations et résistances dans l'Europe protohistorique, in A. Daubigney (ed.) *Actes du colloque: fonctionnement social de l'Age du Fer: opérateurs et hypothèses pour la France* (Besançon: Université de Besançon).

Dent, R. T. (1985) Archaeological excavations at the Hammond-Harwood House, Annapolis, Maryland. *Report prepared by Historic Annapolis, Inc., for the Hammond-Harwood House Association.* MS, Historic Annapolis, Inc.

Department of the Environment (1975) *Principles of Publication in Rescue Archaeology. Report by a Working Party of the Ancient Monuments Board for England. Committee for Rescue Archaeology* (The Frere Report) (London: Her Majesty's Stationery Office).

Department of the Environment (1990) *Planning Policy Guidance Note 16: Archaeology and Planning* (London: Her Majesty's Stationery Office).

Derrida, J. (1973) *Speech and Phenomena and Other Essays on Husserl's Theory of Signs*, trans. D. B. Allison (Evanston, IL: North-Western University Press).

Derrida, J. (1976) *Of Grammatology*, trans. G. C. Spivak (Baltimore: Johns Hopkins University Press).

Derrida, J. (1977) Limited Inc. abc. . ., *Glyph* 2: 162–254.

Derrida, J. (1978) *Writing and Difference*, trans. A. Bass (London: Routledge and Kegan Paul).

Derrida, J. (1979) Living on border lines, in H. Bloom *et al.*, *Deconstruction and Criticism* (New York: Seabury).

Derrida, J. (1981) *Dissemination*, trans. B. Johnson (London: Athlone).

Derrida, J. (1986) *Memoires for Paul de Man*, trans. C. Lindsay, J. Culler and E. Cadava (New York: Columbia University Press).

Derrida, J. (1987a) *The Archaeology of the Frivolous: Reading Condillac*, trans. J. P. Leavey (Lincoln and London: University of Nebraska Press).

Derrida, J. (1987b) *The Truth in Painting*, trans. G. Bennington and I. Mcleod (Chicago: Chicago University Press).

Derrida, J. (1988a [1966]) Structure, sign and play in the discourse of the human sciences, in D. Ledge (ed.) *Modern Criticism and Theory* (London: Longman).

Derrida, J. (1988b) *The Post Card*, trans. A. Bass (Chicago: Chicago University Press).

Detweiler, S. G. (1982) *George Washington's Chinaware* (New York: Harry N. Abrams).

Devalle, S. B. C. (1992) *Discourses on Ethnicity: Culture and Protest in Jharkland* (London: Sage Publications).

DeVore, I. (1965) Male dominance and mating behavior in baboons, in F. Beach (ed.) *Sex and Behavior* (New York: John Wiley).

DeVore, I. and Hall, K. R. L. (1965) Baboon ecology, in I. DeVore (ed.) *Primate Behavior* (New York: Holt, Rinehart and Winston).

DeWaal, F. (1982) *Chimpanzee Politics* (London: Jonathan Cape).

Dewulder, M. (1954) Peintures murales et pratiques magiques dans la tribu des Ouadhias, *Revue africaine* 98: 14–15.

di Stefano, C. (1991) Masculine Marx, in M. L. Shanley and C. Pateman (eds) *Feminist Interpretations and Political Theory* (Cambridge: Polity Press), pp. 146–63.

Dilthey, W. (1986) The understanding of other persons and their life-expressions, in K. Mueller-Vollmer (ed.) *The Hermeneutics Reader* (London: Blackwell), pp. 152–64.

Donley-Reid, L. (1990) A structuring structure: the Swahili house, in S. Kent (ed.) *Domestic Architecture and the Use of Space* (Cambridge: Cambridge University Press), pp. 114–26.

Doran, J. (1970) Systems theory, computer simulations and archaeology, *World Archaeology* 1: 289–98.

Dormer, P. (1988) The ideal world of Vermeer's little lacemaker, in J. Thackara (ed.) *Design After Modernism* (London: Thames and Hudson), pp. 135–44.

Dormer, P. (1990) *The Meanings of Modern Design* (London: Thames and Hudson).

Dormer, P. (1994) *The Art of the Maker: Skill and its Meaning in Art Craft and Design* (London: Thames and Hudson).

Douglas, M. (1966) *Purity and Danger* (London: Routledge and Kegan Paul).

Douglas, M. (1970) *Natural Symbols: Explorations in Cosmology* (New York: Random House).

Douglas, M. and Isherwood, B. (1980) *The World of Goods: Towards an Anthropology of Consumption* (London: Allen Lane).

Dover, K. J. (1978) *Greek Homosexuality* (London: Duckworth).

Dowson, T. A. (1994) Reading art, writing history: rock art and social change in southern Africa, *World Archaeology* 25 (3): 332–45.

Dowson, T. A. and Lewis-Williams, J. D. (eds) (1994) *Contested Images: Diversity of Interpretation in Southern African Rock Art Research* (Johannesburg: Witwatersrand University Press).

Drickamer, L. (1974) Social rank, observability and sexual behavior of rhesus monkeys, *Journal of Reproduction and Fertility* 37: 117–20.

Droysen, J. G. (1977) *Historik. Band 1: Rekonstruktion der ersten vollständigen Fassung der Vorlesungen (1857) Grundriss der Historik.* Edited by P. Leyh (Stuttgart-Bad Cannstatt: Fromann-Holzboog).

Droysen, J. G. (1986) History and the historical method, in K. Mueller-Vollmer (ed.) *The Hermeneutics Reader* (London: Blackwell), pp. 119–24.

Duberman, M. (1993) *Stonewall* (New York: Dutton).

Dubos, R. (1965) *Man Adapting* (Newhaven, CT: Yale University Press).

Duke, P. (1991) Cultural resource management and the professional archaeologist, *SAA Bulletin* 9(4): 10–11.

Dunbar, R. (1983) Life history tactics and alternative strategies of reproduction, in P. Bateson (ed.) *Mate Choice* (Cambridge: Cambridge University Press).

Dumont, L. (1972) *Homo Hierarchicus* (London: Paladin).

Durkheim, E. (1964) *Rules of Sociological Method* (New York: Free Press).

Durkheim, E. (1976 [1915]) *The Elementary Forms of the Religious Life*, trans. J. W. Swain (2nd edn, London: Allen & Unwin).

Durkheim. E. and Mauss, M. (1963 [1903]) *Primitive Classification*, trans. R. Needham (London: Routledge and Kegan Paul).

Eagleton, T. (1985–86) Marxism and the past, *Salmagundi*, 68–69: 271–90.

Earle, T. and Preucel, R. (1987) Processual archaeology and the radical critique, *Current Anthropology* 28: 501–38.

Eco, U. (1976) *A Theory of Semiotics* (Bloomington, IND: Indiana University Press).

Eco, U. (1981) *The Role of the Reader: Explorations in the Semiotics of Texts* (London: Hutchinson).

Edsforth, R. (1987) *Class Conflict and Cultural Consensus* (New Brunswick: Rutgers University Press).

Ehrenreich, J. (1978) *The Cultural Crisis of Modern Medicine* (New York: Monthly Review Press).

Eisenberg, J., Muckenhirn, N. and Rudran, R. (1972) The relation between ecology and social structure in primates, *Science* 176: 863–74.

Ekeh, Peter P. (1974) *Social Exchange Theory* (Cambridge, MA: Harvard University Press).

Ellison, A. (1981) Towards a socio-economic model for the middle Bronze Age in southern England, in I. Hodder, G. Issacs and N. Hammond (eds) *The Pattern of the Past* (Cambridge: Cambridge University Press), pp. 413–38.

Elverheim, I. (1986) Kvinnofigurer på Hällarna i Tanum, *Adoranten,* Tanumshede, *Scandinavian Society for Prehistoric Art*, 8–13.

Ember, M. (1973) An archaeological indicator of matrilocal versus patrilocal residence, *American Antiquity* 38: 177–82.

Engels, F. (1972 [1884]) *The Origin of the Family, Private Property and the State* (New York: Pathfinder Press; London: Lawrence & Wishart).

English Heritage (1991) *The Management of Archaeological Projects. Historic Buildings and Monuments Commission and Her Majesty's Stationery Office* (London: Her Majesty's Stationery Office).

Eriksen, T. H. (1991) The cultural contexts of ethnic differences, *Man* 26: 127–44.

Eriksen, T. H. (1992) *Us and Them in Modern Societies. Ethnicity and Nationalism in Mauritius, Trinidad and Beyond* (London: Scandinavian University Press).

Eriksen, T. H. (1993) *Ethnicity and Nationalism: Anthropological Perspectives* (London: Pluto Press).

Estioko-Griffin, A. and Griffin, P. (1981) Woman the hunter: the Agta, in F. Dahlberg (ed.) *Woman the Gatherer* (New Haven, CT: Yale University Press), pp. 121–51.

Evans, C. (1989) Archaeology and modern times: Bersu's Woodbury 1938 and 1939, *Antiquity* 63: 36–50.

Evans-Pritchard, E. E. (1940) *The Nuer* (Oxford: Oxford University Press).

Ewen, S. (1976) *Captains of Consciousness: Advertising and the Social Roots of the Consumer Culture* (New York: McGraw-Hill).

Eyo, E. (1977) *2000 Years of Nigerian Art* (Lagos: The Nigerian Museum).

Fabian, J. (1983) *Time and the Other: How Anthropology Makes its Object* (New York: Columbia University Press).

Fardon, R. (1987) 'African ethnogenesis': limits to the comparability of ethnic phenomena, in L. Holy (ed.) *Comparative Anthropology* (London: Basil Blackwell), pp. 168–87.

Farthing, D. (1977) Conference report, *The Funeral Director* 57: 339 45. General Board of Health (1850) *Reports on Extramural Sepulture* (London: HMSO).

Fasham, P. J. (1985) *The Prehistoric Settlement at Winnall Down, Winchester* (Winchester: Hampshire Field Club Monograph No. 2).

Ferguson, L. (ed.) (1977) Historical archaeology and the importance of material things, *Society for Historical Archaeology*, Special Series Publication, 2.

Feyerabend, P. K. (1970) Consolation for the specialist, in I. Lakatos and A. Musgrave (eds) *Criticism and the Wanting of Knowledge* (Cambridge: Cambridge University Press).

Feyerabend, P. K. (1975) *Against Method* (London: Verso).

Feyerabend, P. K. (1988) *Against Method* (revised edition, London: Verso).

Filene, Edward A. (1924) *The Way Out: A Forecast of Coming Changes in American Business and Industry* (New York: Nelson Doubleday).

Finks, R. M. (1979) Fossils and fossilization, in R. W. Fairbridge and D. Jablonski (eds) *The Encyclopedia of Paleontology* (Stroudsburg: Dowden, Hutchinson and Ross), pp. 327–32.

Firestone, S. (1970) *The Dialectic of Sex* (New York: Bantam Books).

Fischer, A., Hansen, P. V. and Rasmussen, P. (1984) Macro and micro wear traces on lithic projectile points, *Journal of Danish Archaeology* 3: 19–46.

Fitting, J. E. (1978) Client orientated archaeology: a comment on Kinsey's dilemma, *Pennsylvania Archaeologist* 48: 12–25.

Fitzpatrick, A. F. (1991) 'Celtic (Iron Age) religion – traditional and timeless?, *Scottish Archaeological Review* 8: 123–8.

Flannery, K. V. (1972) The cultural evolution of civilisations, *Annual Review of Ecology and Systematics* 3: 399–426.

Flannery, K. V. (1973) Archaeology with a capital S, in C. Redman (ed.) *Research and Theory in Current Archaeology* (New York: Wiley).

Flannery, K. V. (ed.) (1976) *The Early Mesoamerican Village* (London: Academic Press).

Flannery, K. V. (1982) The Golden Marshalltown: a parable for the archaeology of the 1980s, *American Anthropologist* 84: 265–78.

Flannery, K. V. and Marcus, J. (1976) Formative Oaxaca and the Zapotec cosmos, *American Scientist* 64: 374–83.

Fletcher, R. (1977a) Settlement studies micro and semi-micro, in D. L. Clarke (ed.) *Spatial Archaeology* (New York: Academic Press).

Fletcher, R. (1977b) Alternatives and differences, in M. Spriggs (ed.) *Archaeology and Anthropology* (Oxford: BAR Supplementary Series 19).

Fletcher, R. (1986) Settlement archaeology: world-wide comparisons, *World Archaeology*, 18: 59–83.

Ford, H. (1929) *My Philosophy of Industry* (New York: Coward-McCann Inc).

Fortes, M. (1969 [1945]) *The Dynamics of Clanship Among the Tallensi. Being the First Part of an Analysis of the Social Structure of a Trans-Volta Tribe* (London: Oxford University Press).

Foster, J. (1974) *Class Struggle and the Industrial Revolution: Early Industrial Capitalism in Three English Towns* (London: Methuen).

Foster, R. J. (1991) Making national cultures in the global ecumene, *Annual Review of Anthropology* 20: 235–60.

Foster, S. M. (1989) Analysis of spatial patterns in buildings (access analysis) as an insight into social structure: examples from the Scottish Atlantic Iron Age, *Antiquity* 63: 40–50.

Foucault, M. (1970) *The Order of Things: An Archaeology of the Human Sciences* (London: Tavistock).

Foucault, M. (1972) The Archaeology of Knowledge (London: Tavistock).

Foucault, M. (1973) *Madness and Civilization* (London: Tavistock).

Foucault, M. (1974) *The Order of Things* (London: Tavistock).

Foucault, M. (1977) Nietzsche, genealogy, history, in D. Bouchard (ed.) *Language, Counter-Memory, Practice* (Ithaca, NY: Cornell University Press), pp. 139–64.

Foucault, M. (1978) *The History of Sexuality* (London: Allen Lane).

Foucault, M. (1980a) Two lectures, in C. Gordon (ed.) *Power/Knowledge* (Brighton: Harvester Press), pp. 78–108.

Foucault, M. (1980b) *Power/Knowledge* C. Gordon (ed.) (Brighton: Harvester Press).

Foucault, M. (1984a) Nietzsche, genealogy, history, in P. Rabinow (ed.) *The Foucault Reader* (Harmondsworth: Peregrine), pp. 76–100.

Foucault, M. (1984b) *The Foucault Reader* P. Rabinow (ed.) (Harmondsworth: Penguin).

Foucault, M. (1988 [1969]) What is an author?, in D. Lodge (ed.) *Modern Criticism and Theory* (London: Longman).

Francis, E. K. (1947) The nature of the ethnic group, *American Journal of Sociology* 52: 393–400.

Frankfort, H. (1951) *The Birth of Civilisation in the Near East* (London: Ernest Benn).

Fraser, D. (1983) *Land and Society in Neolithic Orkney* (Oxford: BAR British Series 117).

Fredsjö. A., Nordbladh, J. and Rosvall, J. (1971) Hällristningar i Kville harad i Bohuslän 1. *Svenneby Socken*. Studier i nordisk arkeologi 7 (Göteborg: Göteborgs Arkeologiska Museum).

Fredsjö, A., Nordbladh, J. and Rosvall, J. (1975) Hällristningar i Kville harad i Bohuslän 2. *Svenneby Socken*. Studier i nordisk arkeologi 13 (Göteborg: Göteborgs Arkeologiska Museum).

Fredsjö, A., Nordbladh, J. and Rosvall, J. (1981) Hällristningar i Kville harad i Bohuslän 3. *Svenneby Socken*. Studier i nordisk arkeologi 14/15 (Göteborg: Göteborgs Arkeologiska Museum).

Freeman, L. (1973) The significance of mammalian faunas from palaeolithic occupations in Cantabrian Spain, *American Antiquity* 38: 3–44.

Freeman, L. and Echegaray, J. (1981) El Juyo: a 14,000-year-old sanctuary in northern Spain, *History of Religion* 21: 1–19.

Freud, S. (1900) *The Interpretation of Dreams*, PFL 4.

Freud, S. (1905a) Fragment of an analysis of a case of hysteria, PFL 8: 31–164.

Freud, S. (1905b) Three essays on the theory of sexuality, PFL 7: 33–169.

Freud, S. (1909) Analysis of a phobia in a five-year-old boy, PFL 8: 167–305.

Freud, S. (1910) Five lectures on psychoanalysis, in *Two Short Accounts of Psychoanalysis*, trans. J. Strachey (London: Penguin 1984).

Freud, S. (1911) Psychoanalytic notes on an autobiographical account of a case of paranoia (dementia paranoides), PFL 9: 131–223.

Freud, S. (1915a) Repression, PFL 11: 145–58.

Freud, S. (1915b) The unconscious, PFL 11: 159–222.

Freud, S. (1917) Introductory Lectures on Psychoanalysis, PFL 1.

Freud, S. (1925) A note upon the 'mystic writing pad', PFL 11: 428–34.

Freud, S. (1926) The question of lay analysis, PFL 15: 279–353.

Freud, S. (1933) *New Introductory Lectures on Psychoanalysis*, PFL 2.

Freud, S. (1954) *The Origins of Psychoanalysis: Letters to Wilhelm Fliess, Drafts and Notes, 1887–1902*, trans. E. Mosbacher and J. Strachey; ed. M. Bonaparte, A. Freud and E. Kris (London: Imago).

Freud, S. (1974) *The Standard Edition of the Complete Psychological Works of Freud*, volume 2 (ed. J. Strachey) (London: Hogarth Press).

Freud, S. and Breuer, J. (1895) *Studies on Hysteria*, PFL 3.

Frey, R. W. (ed.) (1975) *The Study of Trace Fossils* (New York: Springer-Verlag).

Fried, M. H. (1968) On the concepts of 'tribe' and 'tribal society', in J. Helm (ed.) *Essays on the Problem of Tribe* (Seattle: University of Washington Press), pp. 3–20.

Friedman, J. (1989) Culture, identity and the world process, in D. Miller, M. Rowlands and C. Tilley (eds) *Domination and Resistance,* (London: Unwin Hyman), pp. 246–60.

Friedman, J. and Rowlands, M. (1977a) Notes towards an epigenetic model of the evolution of 'civilisation', in J. Friedman and M. Rowlands (eds) *The Evolution of Social Systems*, (London: Duckworth), pp. 201–276.

Friedman, J. and Rowlands, M. (eds) (1977b) *The Evolution of Social Systems* (London: Duckworth).

Fritz, J. M. (1978) Paleopsychology today: ideational systems and human adaptation in prehistory, in C. Redman *et al.* (eds) *Social Archaeology Beyond Dating and Subsistence* (New York: Academic Press).

Fritz, J. M. and Plog, F. T. (1970) The nature of archaeological explanation, *American Antiquity* 35: 405–12.

Frosh, S. (1987) *The Politics of Psychoanalysis* (London: Macmillan).

Fuller, P. (1990) The proper work of the potter, in *Images of God: Consolations of Lost Illusions* (London: Hogarth).

Gadamer, H. G. (1975) *Truth and Method* (London: Sheed and Ward).

Gadamer, H. G. (1977) *Philosophical Hermeneutics* trans., ed. D. Linge (Berkeley, CA: University of California Press).

Gadon, E. (1989) *The Once and Future Goddess* (San Francisco: Harper & Row).

Gage, J. (1838) *The History and Antiquities of Suffolk: Thingoe Hundred* (London: Samuel Bentley).

Galison, P. (1987) *How Experiments End* (Chicago: University of Chicago Press).

Galison, P. (1988) Multiple constraints, simultaneous solutions, in A. Fine and J. Leplin (eds) *Philosophy of Science Association* Vol. 2: (Michigan, East Lansing: Philosophy of Science Association), pp. 157–63.

Gallagher, C. and Laqueur T. (eds) (1987) *The Making of the Modern Body* (Berkeley, CA: University of California Press).

Gallagher, J. (1983) Between realms: the iconography of kingship in Benin, in P. Ben Amos (ed.) *The Art of Power: The Power of Art: Studies in Benin Iconography* Monograph Series 19 (Los Angeles Museum of Cultural History, University of California).

Gamble, C. (1982) Interaction and alliance in Palaeolithic society, *Man* 17: 92–107.

Garfinkel, H. (1967) Studies in Ethnomethodology (Engelfield Cliffs, NJ: Prentice-Hall).

Garrard, R. (1982) English probate inventories and their use in studying the significance of the domestic interior, 1570–1640, *Afdeling Agrarische Bijdragen* 28: 55–77.

Gartlan, J. (1968) Structure and function in primate society, *Folia Primatologica* 8: 89–120.

Gatens, M. (1983) A critique of the sex/gender distinction, in J. Allen and P. Patton (eds) *Beyond Marxism?* (Sydney: Intervention Publications), pp. 142–61.

Gatens, M. (1988) Towards a feminist philosophy of the body, in B. Caine, E. Gross and M. de Lepervanche (eds) *Crossing Boundaries* (Sydney: Allen & Unwin), pp. 59–70.

Gatens, M. (1991a) *Feminism and Philosophy: Perspectives on Difference and Equality* (Cambridge: Polity Press).

Gatens, M. (1991b) Representation in/and the body politic, in R. Diprose and R. Ferrel (eds) *Cartographies: The Mapping of Bodies and Spaces* (Sydney: Allen & Unwin), pp. 79–87.

Gathercole, P. and Lowenthal, D. (eds) (1989) *The Politics of the Past* (London: Unwin Hyman).

Gaudry, M. (1928) *La femme Chaouïa de l'Aurès* (Paris: Geuthner).

Geertz, C. (1973a) *The Interpretation of Cultures* (New York: Basic Books).

Geertz, C. (1973b) Thick description: toward an interpretive theory of culture, in *The Interpretation of Cultures* (New York: Basic Books).

Geertz, C. (1973c) The Balinese cockfight, in *The Interpretation of Cultures* (New York: Basic Books).

Geertz, C. (1983a) Blurred genres: the refiguration of social thought, in *Local Knowledge* (New York: Basic Books).

Geertz, C. (1983b) *Local Knowledge: Further Essays in Interpretative Anthropology* (New York: Basic Books).

Geertz, C. (1983c) 'From the natives' point of view': on the nature of anthropological understanding, in C. Geertz *Local Knowledge: Further Essays in Interpretive Anthropology* (New York: Basic Books), pp. 55–70.

Geertz, C. (1986) The uses of diversity, in S McMurrin (ed.) *The Tanner Lectures on Human Values*, VII (Salt Lake City and Cambridge: University Presses of Utah and Cambridge), pp. 251–76.

Gell, A. (1992) *The Anthropology of Time: Cultural Constructions of Temporal Maps and Images* (Oxford: Berg).

Genevois, H. (1955) *L'habitation kabyle*. Fichier de documentation berbere 46.

Gero, J. (1983) Gender bias in archaeology: a cross-cultural perspective, in J. M. Gero, D. Lacy and M. L. Blakey (eds) *The Socio-Politics of Archaeology* (Amherst, MA: Department of Anthropology, University of Massachusetts). Research Report Number 23.

Gero, J. (1985) Socio-politics of archaeology and the women-at-home ideology, *American Antiquity* 50: 342–50.

Gero, J. (1988) Gender bias in archaeology: here, then, there, now, in S. V. Rosser (ed.) *Resistances to Feminism in Science and the Health Care Professions* (London: Pergamon Press).

Gero, J. (1990) Facts and values in the archaeological eye: discussion or 'Powers of Observation', in S. M. Nelson and A. B. Kehoe (eds) *Powers of Observation: Alternative Views in Archaeology* (Washington, DC: Archaeological Papers of the American Association for Anthropology 2), pp. 113–19.

Gero, J. (1991a) Genderlithics: women's roles in stone tool production, in J. M. Gero and W. M. Conkey (eds) *Engendering Archaeology: Women and Prehistory* (Oxford: Basil Blackwell).

Gero, J. (1991b) Gender divisions of labor in the construction of archaeological knowledge in the United States, in N. Willo and D. Walde (eds) *Archaeology of Gender* (Calgary: University of Calgary, Alberta), pp. 96–102.

Gero, J. and Conkey, M. (eds) (1991) *Engendering Archaeology: Women and Prehistory* (Oxford: Basil Blackwell).

Gero, J., Lacy, D. M. and Blakey, M. L. (1983) *The Socio-Politics of Archaeology* (Amherst, MA: University of Massachusetts Department of Anthropology), Research Report 23.

Geuss, R. (1981) *The Idea of a Critical Theory* (Cambridge: Cambridge University Press).

Giamatti, B. (1988) *A Free and Ordered Space: The Real World of the University* (New York: W. W. Norton).

Gibson, J. J. (1979) *The Ecological Approach to Visual Perception* (Boston: Houghton Mifflin).

Gibson, W. S. (1977) *Bruegel* (London: Thames & Hudson).

Giddens, A. (1972) Elites in the British class structure, *Sociological Review* 20: 345–72.

Giddens, A. (1976) *New Rules of Sociological Method: A Positive Critique of Interpretive Sociologies* (London: Hutchinson).

Giddens, A. (1979) *Central Problems in Social Theory* (London: Macmillan).

Giddens, A. (1981) *A Contemporary Critique of Historical Materialism. Volume 1: Power, Property and the State* (London: Macmillan Press).

Giddens, A. (1982) *Sociology, A Brief but Critical Introduction* (London: Macmillan).

Giddens, A. (1984) *The Constitution of Society: Outline of the Theory of Structuration* (Cambridge: Polity Press).

Giddens, A. (1985) Time, space and regionalisation, in D. Gregory and J. Urry (eds) *Social Relations and Spatial Structures* (London: Macmillan), pp. 265–95.

Giddens, A. (1987) *Social Theory and Modern Sociology* (Cambridge: Polity Press).

Gifford, D. P. (1981) Taphonomy and paleoecology: a critical review of archaeology's sister disciplines, in M. B. Schiffer (ed.) *Advances in Archaeological Method and Theory* Vol. 5: 365–438 (New York: Academic Press), pp. 365–438.

Gifford, J. C. (1960) The type variety method of ceramic classification as an indicator of cultural phenomena, *American Antiquity* 25 (3): 341–7.

Gillispie, C. C. (1959) *Genesis and Geology* (New York: Harper and Row).

Gilman, A. (1984) Rethinking the Upper Palaeolithic revolution, in M. Spriggs (ed.) *Marxist Approaches to Archaeology* (Cambridge: Cambridge University Press), pp. 115–26.

Gilman, C. P. (1966 [1898]) *Women and Economics* (New York: Harper Row).

Gilmore, H. (1980) A syntactic, semantic and pragmatic analysis of a baboon vocalization, PhD thesis, University of Pennsylvania.

Gimbutas, M. (1991) *Civilization of the Goddess* (San Francisco, CA: Harper & Row).

Gittord, D. P. (1978) Ethnoarchaeological observations of natural processes affecting cultural materials, in R. A. Gould (ed.) *Explorations in Ethnoarchaeology* (Albuquerque, NM: University of New Mexico Press).

Glassie, H. (1975) *Folk Housing in Middle Virginia: A Structural Analysis of Historical Artifacts* (Knoxville, TN: University of Tennessee Press).

Glob, P. V. (1969) *Helleristningar i Danmark* (Copenhagen: Jutland Archaeological Society).

Godelier, M. (1977) *Perspectives in Marxist Anthropology* (Cambridge: Cambridge University Press).

Goffman, E. (1959) *The Presentation of Self in Everyday Life* (Harmondsworth: Penguin).

Goldstein, L. (1976) Spatial structure and social organization: regional manifestations of the Mississippian period, PhD, Evanston, IL: North-Western University.

Goldthorpe, J. and Hope, K. (1974) *The Social Grading of Occupations: A New Approach and Scale* (London: Oxford University Press).

Goodwin, B. (1988) Organisms and minds: the dialectics of the animal–human interface in biology, in T. Ingold (ed.) *What is an Animal?* (London: Unwin Hyman), pp. 100–9.

Goody, J. (1962) *Death, Property and the Ancestors: A Study of the Mortuary Customs of the Lodagaa of West Africa* (London: Tavistock).

Gorer, G. (1965) *Death, Grief and Mourning in Contemporary Britain* (London: Cresset).

Gould, P. and White, R. (1974) *Mental Maps* (Harmondsworth: Penguin).

Gould, R. (1978a) Beyond analogy in ethnoarchaeology, in R. A. Gould *Explorations in Ethnoarchaeology* (Albuquerque, NM: University of New Mexico Press), pp. 249–93.

Gould, R. (1978b) From Tasmania to Tuscon: new directions in ethnoarchaeology, in R. A. Gould *Explorations in Ethnoarchaeology* (Albuquerque, NM: University of New Mexico Press), pp. 1–10.

Gould, R. (1980) *Living Archaeology* (Cambridge: Cambridge University Press).

Gould, R. and Watson, P-J. (1982) A dialogue on the meaning and use of analogy in ethnoarchaeological reasoning, *Journal of Anthropological Archaeology*, I: 355–81.

Gouzoules, S. (1984) Primate mating systems, kin associations and cooperative behavior: evidence for kin recognition, *Yearbook of Physical Anthropology* 27: 99–134.

Gramsci, A. (1971) *Selections from the Prison Notebooks* (London: Lawrence and Wishart).

Gray, J. (1995) *Enlightenment's Wake: Politics and Culture at the Close of the Modern Age* (London: Routledge).

Grayson, D. K. (1986) Eoliths, archaeological ambiguity, and the generation of 'middle-range' research, in D. J. Meltzer, D. D. Fowler and J. A. Sabloff (eds) *American Archaeology Past and Future* (Washington, DC: Smithsonian Institution Press), pp. 135–62.

Greengrass, M. (1991) Introduction: conquest and coalescence, in M. Greengrass (ed.) *Conquest and Coalesence: the Shaping of the State in Early Modern Europe* (London: Edward Arnold), pp. 1–24.

Gregory, D. (1978) *Ideology, Science and Human Geography* (London: Hutchinson).

Gregory, D. and Urry, J. (eds) (1985) *Social Relations and Spatial Structures* (London: Macmillan).

Griffin, D. (1981) *The Question of Animal Awareness* (2nd edn, New York: Rockefeller University Press).

Griffin, D. (1984) *Animal Thinking* (Cambridge, MA: Harvard University Press).

Grimshaw, J. (1986) *Feminist Philosophers: Women's Perspectives on Philosophical Traditions* (Brighton: Wheatsheaf Books).

Grint, K. (1991) *The Sociology of Work: An Introduction* (Cambridge: Blackwell Polity).

Guattari, F. (1984) *Molecular Revolution: Psychiatry and Politics*, trans. R. Sheed (London: Penguin).

Guerin, D. (1979) *100 Years of Labor in the USA* (London: Ink Links Ltd.).

Guidino, E. (1975) *Primitive Architecture*, (Milan: Elect).

Guyer, J. (1988) The multiplication of labor: gender and agricultural change in modern Africa, *Current Anthropology* 29: 247–72.

Haaland, G. (1969) Economic determinants in ethnic processes, in F. Barth (ed.) *Ethnic Groups and Boundaries* (London: Allen and Unwin), pp. 58–73.

Habermas, J. (1971) *Knowledge and Human Interests* (Boston: Beacon Press).

Habermas, J. (1986) On hermeneutics' claim to universality, in K. Mueller-Vollmer (ed.) *The Hermeneutics Reader* (Oxford: Blackwell), pp. 294–319.

Hacking, I. (1983) *Representing and Intervening: Introductory Topics in the Philosophy of Natural Science* (Cambridge: Cambridge University Press).

Hacking, I. (1988) Philosophers of Experiment, in A. Fine and J. Leplin (eds) *Philosophy of Science Association* Vol. 2 (Michigan, East Lansing: Philosophy of Science Association), pp. 147–56.

Hall, E. T. (1966) *The Hidden Dimension* (New York: Doubleday).

Hall, K. R. L. (1963) Variations in the ecology of the Chacma baboon, Papio Ursinus, *Symposia of the Zoological Society of London* 10: 1–28.

Hall, K. R. L. and DeVore, I. (1965) Baboon social behavior, in I. DeVore (ed.) *Primate Behavior* (New York: Holt, Rinehart and Winston).

Halperin, D. M. (1995) *Saint=Foucault: Towards a Gay Hagiography* (New York: Oxford University Press).

Hamilton, M. (1984) Revising evolutionary narratives: a consideration of alternative assumptions about sexual selection and competition for mates, *American Anthropologist* 86: 661–2.

Hamilton, W. D. (1971) Geometry for the selfish herd, *Journal of Theoretical Biology* 31: 295–311.

Hamilton, W. D., Buskirk, R. and Buskirk, W. (1975) Chacma baboon tactics during intertroop encounters, *Journal of Mammalogy* 56: 857–70.

Handler, R. (1988) *Nationalism and the Politics of Culture in Quebec* (Wisconsin: University of Wisconsin Press).

Handsman, R. (1980) The domains of kinship and settlement in historic Goshen: signs of a past cultural order, *Artifacts* 9: 2–7.

Handsman, R. (1981) Early capitalism and the center village of Canaan, Connecticut: a study of transformations and separations, *Artifacts* 9: 1–21.

Handsman, R. (1982) The hot and cold of Goshen's history, *Artifacts* 3: 11–20.

Handsman, R. (1983) Toward archaeological histories of Robbins Swamp, *Artifacts* 11: (3): 1–20

Handsman, R. (1985) History and communal class struggles among early gatherer-hunters. Paper read at the annual meeting of the American Anthropological Association, Washington, DC.

Handsman, R. (1986) How histories were made by hunter-gatherers, then disciplined, and finally made to disappear by us. Paper presented at the 4th International Conference on Hunting and Gathering Societies, London.

Handsman, R. (1990) Whose art was found at Lepinski Vir? Gender relations and power in archaeology, in J. Gero and M. Conkey (eds) *Engendering Archaeology* (Oxford: Basil Blackwell), pp. 329–65.

Handsman, R. and Leone, M. P. (n.d.) Living history and critical archaeology and the reconstruction of the past, in V. Pinsky and A. Wylie (eds) *Critical Traditions in Contemporary Archaeology* (Cambridge: Cambridge University Press).

Hanks, W. (1989) Texts and textuality *Annual Review of Anthropology* 18: 95–127.

Hantzschel, W. and Frey, R. W. (1979) Trace fossils, in R. W Fairbridge and Jablonski (eds) *The Encyclopedia of Paleontology* (Stroudsburg: Dowden, Hutchinson and Ross), pp. 813–20.

Haraway, D. (1988) Situated knowledges: the science question in feminism and the privilege of partial perspective, *Feminist Studies* 14: 575–99.

Haraway, D. (1989) *Primate Visions: Gender, Race and Nature in the World of Modern Science* (London: Routledge).

Harding, A. with Lee, G. (1987) *Henge Monuments and Related Sites of Great Britain* (Oxford: BAR British Series), 175.

Harding, S. (1986) *The Science Question in Feminism* (London: Open University Press).

Harding, S. (1987) Introduction: is there a feminist method?, in S. Harding (ed.) *Feminism and Methodology: Social Science Issues* (Bloomington, IND: Indiana University Press), pp. 1–14.

Harries, K. (1993) Thoughts toward a non-arbitrary architecture, in D. Seamon (ed.) *Dwelling, Seeing and Designing* (Albany, NY: State University of New York Press), pp. 41–60.

Harris, E. C. (1979) *Principles of Archaeological Stratigraphy* (London: Academic Press).

Harris, O. (1981) Households as natural units, in K. Young, C. Wolkowjtz and R. McCullagh (eds) *Of Marriage and the Market* (London: CSE Books), pp. 49–68.

Harstrup, K. (1978) The post-structuralist position of social anthropology, in E. Schwimmer (ed.) *The Yearbook of Symbolic Anthropology* 1 (London: Hurst).

Hartmann, H. (1981) The family as the locus or gender, class, and political struggle: the example of housework, *Signs*, 6(3): 366–94.

Harvey, D. (1989) *The Condition of Postmodernity: An Enquiry into the Origins of Cultural Change* (Oxford: Basil Blackwell).

Haselgrove, C. (1989) The later Iron Age in southern Britain and beyond, in M. Todd *Research on Roman Britain 1960–89* (London: Society for the Promotion of Roman Studies) (Britannia Monograph 11), pp. 1–18.

Hasted, R. (1985) Mothers of invention, *Trouble and Strife*, 7: 17–25.

Hastrup, K. (1992) Introduction, in K. Hastrup (ed.) *Other Histories* (London: Routledge), pp. 1–13

Hausfater, G. (1975) *Dominance and Reproduction in Baboons: A Quantitative Analysis. Contributions to Primatology* (Basel: Karger).

Hausfater, G., Altmann, J. and Altmann, S. (1982) Long-term consistency of dominance relations among female baboons, *Science* 217: 752–5.

Hawkes, C. (1954) Archaeological theory and method: some suggestions from the Old World, *American Anthropologist* 56: 155–68.

Hawkes, C. F. C. (1940) *The Prehistoric Foundations of Europe: To the Mycenaean Age* (London: Methuen).

Hawkes, T. (1977) *Structuralism and Semiotics* (Berkeley, CA: University of California Press).

Hayden, D. (1981) *The Grand Domestic Revolution: A History of Feminist Designs for American Homes, Neighborhoods and Cities* (Cambridge, MA: Massachusetts Institute of Technology).

Hebdige, R. (1979) *Subculture: The Meaning of Style* (London: Methuen).

Heidegger, M. (1962) *Being and Time* (New York: Harper and Row).

Heidegger, M. (1971) *Poetry Language Thought*, trans. A. Hofstadter (New York: Harper and Row).

Heller, A. 1984 *Everyday Life* (London: Routledge and Kegan Paul).

Henderson, R. (1972) *The King in Every Man: Evolutionary Trends in Onitsha Igbo Society and Culture* (New Haven, CT: Yale University Press).

Henshall, A. S. (1963) *The Chambered Tombs of Scotland Vol. 1* (Edinburgh: Edinburgh University Press).

Hervey, S. H. A. (1909) *Suffolk in 1568: Being the Return for a Subsidy Granted in 1566* (Suffolk Green Books) 12.

Hervey, S. H. A. (1910) *Suffolk in 1524: Being the Return for a Subsidy Granted in 1523* (Suffolk Green Books) 10.

Hesse, M. B. (1966) *Models and Analogies in Science* (Indiana: Notre Dame University Press).

Higgs, E. (ed.) (1972) *Papers in Economic Prehistory* (Cambridge: Cambridge University Press).

Higgs, E. S. and Vita-Finzi, C. (1972) Prehistoric economies: a territorial approach, in E. S. Higgs (ed.) *Papers in Economic Prehistory* (Cambridge: Cambridge University Press), pp. 27–36.

Hill, J. D. (1989) Rethinking the Iron Age, *Scottish Archaeological Review* 6: 16–24.

Hill, J. D. (1996) Ritual and rubbish: rethinking the Iron Age of Wessex. PhD thesis, Cambridge University Press.

Hill, J. D. (forthcoming) Hillforts and the Iron Age of Wessex, in T. Champion and J. Collis *Recent Research on the Archaeology of Iron Age Britain* (Sheffield: University of Sheffield).

Hill, J. N. (1970) *Broken K Pueblo: Prehistoric Social Organisation in the American Southwest*, Anthropological Papers of the University of Arizona 18.

Hill, J. N. (1971) Report on a seminar on the explanation of prehistoric organisational change, *Current Anthropology* 12: 406–8.

Hill, J. N. (ed.) (1977) *The Explanation of Prehistoric Change* (Albuquerque, NM: University of New Mexico Press).

Hill, J. N. and Gunn, J. (eds) (1977) *The Individual in Prehistory* (New York: Academic Press).

Hillier, B., Leaman, A., Stansall, P. and Bedford, M. (1976) Space, *Syntax Environment and Planning B* 3: 147–85.

Hills, C. (1993) The dissemination of information, in J. Hunter and I. Ralston (eds) *Archaeological Resource Management in the UK: An Introduction* (Dover: Alan Sutton), pp. 215–24.

Hingley, R. (1984) Towards social analysis in archaeology: Celtic society in the Iron Age of the upper Thames valley, in B. Cunliffe and D. Miles (eds) *Aspects of the Iron Age in Central Southern Britain* (Oxford: Oxford Committee for Archaeology Monograph 2), pp. 72–88.

Hingley, R. (1990a) Domestic organisation and gender relations in Iron Age and Romano-British households, in R. Sampson (ed.) *The Social Archaeology of Houses* (Edinburgh: Edinburgh University Press), pp. 125–49.

Hingley, R. (1990b) Boundaries surrounding Iron Age Romano-British settlements, *Scottish Archaeological Review* 7: 96–103.

Hingley, R. (1990c) Iron Age 'currency bars': the archaeological and social context, *Archaeological Journal* 147: 91–117.

Hinton, J. (1972) *Dying* (Harmondsworth: Penguin).

Hirst, P. Q. (1976) *Problems and Advances in the Theory of Ideology* (Cambridge: Cambridge University Communist Party).

Ho, M-W. (1989) Reanimating nature: the integration of science with human experience, *Peshara* 8: 16–25.

Hodder, I. (1979) Social and economic stress and material culture patterning, *American Antiquity* 44: 446–54.

Hodder, I. (1981) Towards a mature archaeology, in I. Hodder, G. Isaac and N. Hammond (eds) *Pattern of the Past* (Cambridge: Cambridge University Press), pp. 1–13.

Hodder, I. (1982a) *Symbolic and Structural Archaeology* (Cambridge: Cambridge University Press).

Hodder, I. (1982b) *Symbols in Action: Ethnoarchaeological Studies of Material Culture* (Cambridge: Cambridge University Press).

Hodder, I. (1982c) The identification and interpretation of ranking in prehistory, in C. Renfrew and S. Shennan (eds) *Ranking, Resource and Exchange* (Cambridge: Cambridge University Press), pp. 150–4.

Hodder, I. (1982d) Theoretical archaeology: a reactionary view, in I. Hodder (ed.) *Symbolic and Structural Archaeology* (Cambridge: Cambridge University Press), pp. 1–16.

Hodder, I. (1982e) Sequences of structural change in the Dutch Neolithic, in I. Hodder (ed.) *Symbolic and Structural Archaeology* (Cambridge: Cambridge University Press), pp. 162–77.

Hodder, I. (1983) Archaeology, ideology and contemporary society, *Royal Anthropological Institute News* 56: 6–7.

Hodder, I. (1984a) Burials, houses, women and men in the European Neolithic, in D. Miller and C. Tilley (eds) *Ideology, Power and Prehistory* (Cambridge: Cambridge University Press).

Hodder, I. (1984b) Archaeology in 1984, *Antiquity* 58: 25–32.

Hodder, I. (1985) Postprocessual archaeology, in M. Schiffer (ed.) *Advances in Archaeological Method and Theory Vol. 8* (New York: Academic Press), pp. 1–26.

Hodder, I. (1986) *Reading the Past: Current Approaches to Interpretation in Archaeology* (Cambridge: Cambridge University Press).

Hodder, I. (1987a) Contextual archaeology: an interpretation of Çatal Hüyük and a discussion of the origins of agriculture, *Bulletin of the Institute of Archaeology, University of London*, 24: 43–56.

Hodder, I. (1987b) *The Archaeology of Contextual Meanings* (Cambridge: Cambridge University Press).

Hodder, I. (1987c) The contextual analysis of symbolic meanings, in I. Hodder (ed.) *The Archaeology of Contextual Meanings*: (Cambridge: Cambridge University Press), pp. 1–10.

Hodder, I. (1987d) The meaning of discard: ash and domestic space in Baringo, in S. Kent (ed.) *Method and Theory for Activity Area Research: An Ethnoarchaeological Approach* (New York: Columbia University Press), pp. 424–48.

Hodder, I. (1987e) Digging for symbols in science and history: a reply, *Proceedings of the Prehistoric Society* 52: 351–5.

Hodder, I. (1987f) The Contribution of the long term, in I. Hodder (ed.) *Archaeology as Long-Term History*: (Cambridge: Cambridge University Press), pp. 1–8.

Hodder, I. (1987g) Reading Bell reading 'Reading the Past', *Archaeological Review from Cambridge* 6: 87–91.

Hodder, I. (1989a) Writing archaeology: site reports in context, *Antiquity*, 63: 268–74.

Hodder, I. (1989b) *The Meanings of Things* (One World Archaeology 6) (London: Unwin Hyman).

Hodder, I. (1989c) This is not an article about material culture as text, *Journal of Anthropological Archaeology* 8: 250–69.

Hodder, I. (1989d) Comments on archaeology into the 1990s, *Norwegian Archaeological Review* 22 (1) 15–18.

Hodder, I. (1989e) Post-modernism, post-structuralism and post-processualism, in I. Hodder (ed.) *The Meanings of Things* (London: Unwin Hyman), pp. 64–78.

Hodder, I. (1990a) *The Domestication of Europe* (Oxford: Blackwell).

Hodder, I. (1990b) Archaeology and the post-modern, *Anthropology Today* 6(5): 13–15.

Hodder, I. (1991a) Interpretive archaeology and its role, *American Antiquity*, 56(1): 7–18.

Hodder, I. (1991b) *Reading the Past* (2nd edition; Cambridge: Cambridge University Press).

Hodder, I. (1991c) Postprocessual archaeology and the current debate, in R. W. Preucel (ed.) *Processual and Postprocessual Archaeologies. Multiple Ways of Knowing the Past*, Occasional Papers No. 10 (Carbondale, IL: Center for Archaeological Investigations, Southern Illinois University), pp. 30–41.

Hodder, I. (1991d) *Archaeological Theory in Europe* (London: Routledge).

Hodder, I. (1992) The post-processual reaction, in I. Hodder, *Theory and Practice in Archaeology* (London: Routledge), pp. 160–8.

Hodder, I. (1999) *The Archaeological Process: An Introduction* (Oxford: Blackwell).

Hodder, I. and Lane, P. (1982) Exchange and reduction, in T. Earle and J. Ericson (eds). *Contexts for Prehistoric Exchange* (New York: Academic Press).

Hodder, I., Shanks, M., Alexandri, A., Buchli, V., Carman, J., Last, J. and Lucas, G. (1995) *Interpreting Archaeology: Finding Meaning in the Past* (London: Routledge).

Homans, G. (1961) *Social Behavior: Its Elementary Forms* (New York: Harcourt, Brace Jovanovich).

hooks, b. (1991) *Yearning: Race, Gender and Cultural Politics* (London: Turnaround Press).

Hopkins, J. W. (1986) Preliminary report on excavations at the State House Inn, Annapolis, Maryland, (1985) MS, Historic Annapolis, Inc.

Horkheimer, M. and Adorno, T. W. (1972) *Dialectic of Enlightenment* (London: Allen Lane).

Horne, L. (1982) The household in space: dispersed holdings in an Iranian village, in R. Wilk and W. Rathje (eds) *Archaeological of the Household: building a prehistory of Domestic Life* (New York: Sage Publications), pp. 677–86.

Hoskins, W. G. (1953) The rebuilding of rural England, 1570–1640, *Past and Present* 4: 44–59.

Hounshell, D. A. (1984) *From the American System to Mass Production 1800–1932: The Development of Manufacturing Technology in the United States* (Baltimore: Johns Hopkins University Press).

Howard, M. (1987) *The Early Tudor Country House: Architecture and Politics 1490–1550* (London: George Philip).

Hugh-Jones, C. (1979) *From the Milk River: Spatial and Temporal Processes in Northwest Amazonia* (Cambridge: Cambridge University Press).

Humphrey, C. (1974) Inside a Mongolian tent, *New Society*, October 21–8.

Humter, J. and Ralston, I. (eds) (1993) *Archaeological Resource Management in the UK: An Introduction* (Dover: Alan Sutton).

Huntingdon, K. and Metcalf, P. (1979) *Celebrations of Death: The Anthropology of Mortuary Ritual* (Cambridge: Cambridge University Press).

Hymes, D. (1970) Comments on analytical archaeology, *Norwegian Archaeological Review* 3: 16–21.

Ihde, D. (1979) *Technics and Praxis* (Dordrecht: D. Reidel).

Illich, I. (1975) *Medical Nemesis: The Expropriation of Health* (London: Calder and Boyars).

Inglis, F. (1977) Nation and community: a landscape and its morality, *Sociological Review* 25: 489–514.

Inglis, W. (1935) *George F. Johnson and His Industrial Democracy* (Endicott, NY: Endicott-Johnson Co.).

Ingold, T. (1986a) *The Appropriation of Nature: Essays on Human Ecology and Social Relationships* (Manchester: Manchester University Press).

Ingold, T. (1986b) *Evolution and Social Life* (Cambridge: Cambridge University Press).

Ingold, T. (1990) An anthropologist looks at biology, *Man* (N.S.) 25: 208–29.

Ingold, T. (1992a) Editorial, *Man* (N.S.), 27: 693–6.

Ingold, T. (1992b) Culture and the perception of the environment, in E. Croll and D. Parkin (eds) *Bush Base: Forest Farm. Culture Environment and Development* (London: Routledge), pp. 39–56.

Ingold, T. (1993) Technology, language, intelligence: a reconsideration of basic concepts, in K. R. Gibson and T. Ingold (eds) *Tools, Language and Cognition in Human Evolution* (Cambridge: Cambridge University Press), pp. 449–72.

Institute of Contemporary Arts (1984) *William Morris Today* (London: Institute of Contemporary Arts).

Institute of Field Archaeologists (1988) *By-Laws of the Institute of Field Archaeologists: Code of Conduct* (Birmingham: Institute of Field Archaeologists).

Institute of Field Archaeologists (1990) *By-Laws of the Institute of Field Archaeologists: Code of Approved Practice for the Regulation of Contractual Arrangements in Field Archaeology* (Birmingham: Institute of Field Archaeologists).

Irigaray, L. (1985a) *This Sex Which Is Not One*, trans. C. Porter with C. Burke (Ithaca, NY: Cornell University Press).

Irigaray, L. (1985b) *Speculum of the Other Woman* (Ithaca, NY: Cornell University Press).

Irvine G. (1959–60) Report on bones and teeth found at St-y-Nyll site, *Transactions of the Cardiff Naturalists' Society* 8: 26–9.

Isaac, G. (1978) The food-sharing behavior of protohuman hominids, *Scientific American* 238 (4): 90–108.

Isaac, R. (1982) *The Transformation of Virginia 1740–1790* (Chapel Hill, NC: University of North Carolina Press).

Isbell, W. H. (1976) Cosmological order expressed in prehistoric ceremonial centres, Paper given in Andean Symbolism Symposium Part 1: Space, time and mythology. Paris, International Congress of Americanists.

Jackson, M. (1989) *Paths Toward a Clearing: Radical Empiricism and Ethnographic Inquiry* (Bloomington, IND: Indiana University Press).

Jameson, F. (1972) *The Prison House of Language* (Princeton, NJ: Princeton University Press).

Jay, M. (1973) *The Dialectical Imagination: A History of the Frankfurt School and the Institute of Social Research 1923–50* (London: Heinemann).

Jay, P. (1968) *Primates: Studies in Adaptation and Variability* (New York: Holt, Rinehart and Winston).

Jeffreys, M. (1936) The divine Umu Ndri: kings of Igbo Land, unpublished PhD thesis, University of London.

Jeffreys, M. (1940) Notes on the Igbo hoard, *Man* 40: 112.

Jeffreys, M. (1951) The winged solar disc, or Igbo Itsi facial scarification, *Africa* 21: 93–111.

Jeffreys, M. (1956) The Umundri tradition of origin, *African Studies* 15: 119–31.

Jochim, M. (1982) Palaeolithic art in an ecological perspective, in G. Bailey (ed.) *Hunter-Gatherer Economy in Prehistory* (Cambridge: Cambridge University Press), pp. 212–19.

Johannessen, K. K. (1985) Tradisjoner og Skoler i Moderne Vitenskaps-filosof (Bergen: Sigma forlag).

Johnsen, H. and Olsen, B. (1992) Hermeneutics and archaeology: on the philosophy of contextual archaeology, *American Antiquity* 57 (3): 419–36. And this volume.

Johnson, G. (1982) Organizational structure and scalar stress, in A. C. Renfrew, M. J. Rowlands and B. A. Segraves (eds) *Theory and Explanation in Archaeology* (London: Academic Press), pp. 389–421.

Johnson, M. H. (1986) Assumptions and interpretations in the study of the Great Rebuilding, *Archaelogical Review from Cambridge* 5: 141–53.

Johnson, W. (1912) *Byways in British Archaeology* (Cambridge: Cambridge University Press).

Jones, S. (1994) *Ethnicity and archaeology: constructing identities in the past and the present*, unpublished PhD thesis, University of Southampton.

Jones, S. (1996) *The Archaeology of Ethnicity* (London: Routledge).

Joukousky, M. (1980) *A Complete Manual of Archaeology* (Englewood Cliffs, NJ: Prentice-Hall).

Just, R. (1989) Triumph of the ethnos, in E. Tonkin *et al.* (eds) *History and Ethnicity* (London: Routledge), pp. 71–88.

Kaiser, T. and Voytek, B. (1983) Sedentism and economic change in the Balkan Neolithic, *Journal of Anthropological Archaeology*, 2: 323–53.

Kapferer, B. (ed.) (1976) *Transactions and Meaning* (Philadelphia: University of Pennsylvania Press).

Kaplan, J. (1978) Fight interference in Rhesus monkeys, *American Journal of Physical Anthropology* 49: 241–50.

Kastenbaum, R. and Aisenberg, R. (1972) *The Psychology of Death* (New York: Springer).

Keene, A. S. (1986) Stories we tell: gatherer-hunters as ideology, paper presented at the 4th International Conference on Hunting and Gathering Societies, London.

Keesing, K. M. (1976) *Cultural Anthropology: A Contemporary Perspective* (New York: Holt, Rinehart and Winston).

Kehoe, A. B. (1984) The myth of the given, paper presented to the Society for American Archaeology, Portland, OR, April.

Keller, E. F. (1985) *Reflections on Gender and Science* (New Haven, CT: Yale University Press).

Kempf, E. (1917) The social and sexual behavior of infra-human primates, with some comparable facts in human behavior, *Psychoanalytic Review* 4: 127–54.

Kent, S. (1990) A cross-cultural study of segmentation, architecture and the use of space, in S. Kent (ed.) *Domestic Architecture and the Use of Space* (Cambridge: Cambridge University Press), pp. 127–52.

Kent, S. (1991) Partitioning space: cross-cultural factors influencing domestic spatial segmentation, *Environment and Behaviour*, 23: 438–73.

Kephart, W. M. (1950) Status after death, *American Sociological Review* 15: 635–43.

Kerr, C. (1964) *The Uses of the University* (Cambridge, MA: Harvard University Press).

Kimes, T., Haselgrove, C. and Hodder, I. (1982) A method for the identification of the location of regional cultural boundaries, *Journal of Anthropological Archaeology* 1: 113–31.

Kinnes, I. (1981) Dialogues with death, in R. W. Chapman, I. Kinnes and K. Randsborg (eds) *The Archaeology of Death* (Cambridge: Cambridge University Press).

Kinnes, I. (1982) Les Fouaillages and megalithic origins, *Antiquity*, 61: 24–30.

Kirk, P. (1969) *Fire Investigation* (New York: John Wiley and Sons Inc.).

Kleiman, D. (1979) Parent-offspring conflict and sibling competition in a monogamous primate, *American Naturalist* 114: 753–60.

Klejn, L. (1977) A panorama of theoretical archaeology, *Current Anthropology*, 18: 1–42.

Knorr, K. and Cicourel, A. (1981) *Advances in Social Theory and Methodology: Towards an Integration of Micro and Macro Sociologies* (London: Routledge & Kegan Paul).

Knorr, K. and Mulkay, M. (1983) *Science Observed: Perspectives on the Social Study of Science* (London and Los Angeles, CA: Sage).

Knorr-Cetina, K. D. (1981) *The Manufacture of Knowledge* (Oxford: Pergamon Press).

Knorr-Cetina, K. D. and Mulkay, M. (eds) (1983) *Science Observed: Perspectives on the Social Study of Science* (London: Sage).

Knudson, R. A. (1989) North America's threatened heritage, *Archaeology* 42: 71–3, 106.

Kohl, P. L. (1981) Materialist approaches in prehistory, *Annual Review of Anthropology* 10: 89–118.

Kohl, P. L. (1993) Nationalism, politics, and the practice of archaeology in Soviet Transcaucasia, *Journal of European Archaeology* 1 (2): 181–8.

Kohl, P. L. and Fawcett, C. (eds) (1995) *Nationalism, Politics and the Practice of Archaeology* (Cambridge: Cambridge University Press).

Kopytoff, I. (1982) Slavery. *Annual Review of Anthropology*, 11: 207–30.

Kopytoff, I. and Miers, S. (1977) African 'slavery' as an institution of marginality, in S. Miers and I. Kopytoff (eds) *Slavery in Africa: Historical and Anthropological Perspectives* (Madison, WI: University of Wisconsin Press), pp. 3–81.

Kosso, P. (1988) Dimensions of observability, *British Journal of Philosophy of Science* 39: 449–67.

Kosso, P. (1989) Science and Objectivity, *Journal of Philosophy* 86: 245–57.

Kostof, S. (1985) *A History of Architecture: Settings and Rituals* (New York and Oxford: Oxford University Press).

Kramer, C. (1982) *Village Ethnoarchaeology: Rural Iran in Archaeological Perspective* (New York: Academic Press).

Kramer, C. and Stark, M. (1988) The status of women in archaeology, *Anthropology Newsletter* 29(9): 1.

Kristeva, J. (1984) *Revolution in Poetic Language*, trans. M. Waller (New York: Columbia University Press).

Kristiansen, K. (1981) A social history of Danish archaeology 1805–1975, in G. Daniel (ed.) *Towards a History of Archaeology* (London: Thames and Hudson), pp. 20–44.

Kristiansen, K. (1993) The strength of the past and its great might: an essay on the use of the past, *Journal of European Archaeology* 1: 3–33.

Kroeber, A. L. (1925) The Yurok, *Handbook of the Indians of California*, Bureau of American Ethnology Bulletin 78.

Kroeber, A. L. O. (1952) Psychosis or social sanction?, in A. L. O. Kroeber *The Nature of Culture* (Chicago: University of Chicago Press).

Kubler, G. (1962) *The Shape of Time: Remarks on the History of Things* (New Haven, CT: Yale University Press).

Kuhn, T. S. (1970) *The Structure of Scientific Revolutions* (Chicago: University of Chicago Press).

Kuhn, T. S. (1977) *The Essential Tension* (Chicago: University of Chicago Press).

Kummer, H. (1967) Tripartite relations in Hamadryas baboons, in S. Altmann (ed.) *Social Communication Among Primates* (Chicago: University of Chicago Press).

Kummer, H. (1973) Dominance versus possession: an experiment on Hamadryas baboons, in E. Menzel (ed.) *Precultural Primate Behavior* (Basel: Karger).

Kummer, H. (1978) On the value of social relationships to nonhuman primates: a heuristic scheme, *Social Science Information* 17: 687–705.

Kummer, H., Goetz, W. and Angst, W. (1974) Triadic differentiation: an inhibitor process protecting pair bonds in baboons, *Behavior* 49: 62–87.

Kussmaul, A. (1981) *Servants in Husbandry in Early Modern England* (Cambridge: Cambridge University Press).

Lacan, J. (1953) Some reflections on the ego, *International Journal of Psychoanalysis* 34: 11–17.

Lacan, J. (1977a) *Ecrits*, trans. A. Sheridan (London: Tavistock).

Lacan, J. (1977b) The mirror stage, in *Ecrits* (London: Tavistock), pp. 1–7.

Lacan, J. (1988) *The Seminar of Jacques Lacan: Book II: The Ego in Freud's Theory and the Technique of Psychoanalysis*, trans. S. Tomasselli (Cambridge: Cambridge University Press).

Laing, D. (1978) *The Marxist Theory of Art: An Introductory Survey* (Brighton: Harvester).

Laing, R. D. (1969) *The Divided Self* (London: Penguin).

Lamberg-Karlovsky, C. C. (ed.) (1989) *Archaeological Thought in America* (Cambridge: Cambridge University Press).

Landau, M. (1984) Human evolution as narrative, *American Scientist* 72: 262–8.

Lane, P. (1987) Recording residues of the past, in I. Hodder (ed.) *Archaeology as Long-Term History* (Cambridge: Cambridge University Press), pp. 54–62.

Langer, S. K. (1953) *Feeling and Form: A Theory of Art* (London: Routledge & Kegan Paul).

Langness, L. (1965) *The Life History in Anthropological Science* (New York).

Laoust, E. (1912) *Etude sur la dialecte berbere du Cheroua* (Paris: Leroux), pp. 12–15.

Laoust, E. (1920) *Mots et choses berberes* (Paris: Maisonneuve-Larose).

Larrain, J. (1979) *The Concept of Ideology* (London: Hutchinson).

Laslett, P. (1965) *The World We Have Lost* (London: Methuen).

Latour, B. (1986a) The powers of association, in J. Law (ed.) *Power Action and Belief: a New Sociology of Knowledge* (Keele: Sociological Review Monograph), pp. 264–80.

Latour, B. (1986b) Visualization and cognition: thinking with eyes and hands, *Knowledge and Society Studies: Past and Present* 6: 1–40.

Latour, B. (1987) *Science in Action: How to Follow Scientists and Engineers Through Society* (London: Open University Press).

Latour, B. and Strum, S. (1986) Human social origins: please tell us another story, *Journal of Sociological and Biological Structures* 9: 169–87.

Latour, B. and Woolgar, S. (1979) *Laboratory Life* (Beverly Hills, CA: Sage).

Lauderie, E. L. (1978) Montaillou: The Promised Land of Error (New York: Vintage Books).

Law, J. (ed.) (1986) *Power, Action and Belief: A New Sociology of Knowledge* (Keele: Sociological Review of Monograph).

Lawrence, D. L. and Low, S. M. (1990) The built environment and spatial form, *Annual Review of Anthropology* 19: 453–505.

Layton, R. (ed.) (1989a) *Conflict in the Archaeology of Living Traditions* (London: Unwin Hyman).

Layton, R. (ed.) (1989b) *Who Needs the Past? Indigenous Values in Archaeology* (London: Unwin Hyman).

Layton, R. (1986) Political and territorial structures among hunter-gatherers, *Man* 21: 18–33.

le Doeuff, M. (1977) Women and philosophy, *Radical Philosophy* 17: 2–11.

le Doeuff, M. (1989) *The Philosophical Imaginary* (London: Athlone).

Leach, E. (1964 [1954]) *Political Systems of Highland Burma: A Study in Kachin Social Structure* (London: Bell and Sons).

Leach, E. (1971) *Rethinking Anthropology* (New York: Humanities Press).

Leach, E. (1973a) Concluding address, in C. Renfrew (ed.) *The Explanation of Culture Change* (London: Duckworth), pp. 761–71.

Leach, E. (1973b) Structuralism in social anthropology, in D. Robey (ed.) *Structuralism: An Introduction* (Oxford: Clarendon Press).

Leach, E. (1974) *Claude Lévi-Strauss* (New York: Viking Press).

Leach, E. (1976) *Culture and Communication* (Cambridge: Cambridge University Press).

Leach, E. (1977) A view from the bridge, in M. Spriggs (ed.) *Archaeology and Anthropology* (Oxford: BAR Supplementary Series 19), pp. 161–76.

Leach, E. (1978) Does space syntax really 'constitute the social'?, in D. Green, C. Haselgrove and M. Spriggs (eds) *Social Organisation and Settlement* (Oxford BAR) 47.

Leakey, R. (1981) *The Making of Mankind* (London: Book Club Associates).

Lee, R. B. and DeVore, I. (eds) (1968) *Man the Hunter* (Chicago: Aldine).

Leitch, J. (1919) *Man to Man: The Story of Industrial Democracy* (New York: Forbes Co.).

Lentricchia, F. (1983) *After the New Criticism* (London: Methuen).

Leone, M. (ed.) (1972) *Contemporary Archaeology: A Guide to Theory and Contributions* (Carbondale, IL: Southern Illinois University Press).

Leone, M. P. (1973) Archaeology as the science of technology: Mormon town plans and fences, in C. Redman (ed.) *Research and Theory in Current Archaeology* (New York: John Wiley and Sons), pp. 125–50.

Leone, M. P. (1977) The new Mormon temple in Washington DC, in L. Ferguson (ed.) *Historical Archaeology and the Importance of Material Things* (Society for Historical Archaeology), Special Series Publication 2.

Leone, M. P. (1978) Time in American archaeology, in C. Redman *et al.* (eds) *Social Archaeology Beyond Subsistence and Dating* (New York: Academic Press).

Leone, M. P. (1981a) Archaeology's material relationship to the present and the past, in R. A. Gould and M. B. Schiffer (eds) *Modern Material Culture: The Archaeology of Us* (New York: Academic Press), pp. 5–14

Leone, M. P. (1981b) The relationship between artifacts and the public in outdoor history museums, in A. M. Cantwell, N. Rothschild and J. B. Griffen (eds) *The Research Potential of Anthropological Museum Collections* (New York: New York Academy of Sciences), pp. 301–13.

Leone, M. P. (1982a) Commentary: Childe's offspring, in I. Hodder (ed.) *Symbolic and structural archaeology* (Cambridge: Cambridge University Press), pp. 179–84.

Leone, M. P. (1982b) Some opinions about recovering mind, *American Antiquity*, 47: 742–60.

Leone, M. P. (1983) Method as message, *Museum News* 62 (1) 35–41.

Leone, M. P. (1984) Interpreting ideology in historical archaeology: using rules of perspective in the Will 16 Paca Garden in Annapolis, Maryland, in D. Miller and C. Tilley (eds) *Ideology, Power and Prehistory* (Cambridge: Cambridge University Press), pp. 25–35.

Leone, M. P. and Potter, P. B., Jr. (1984a) *Archaeological Annapolis: A Guide to Seeing and Understanding Three Centuries of Change* (Annapolis: Historic Annapolis, Inc.).

Leone, M. P. and Potter, P. B., Jr. (1992) Legitimation and the classification of archaeological sites, *American Antiquity* 57 (1): 137–45.

Leone, M. P., Potter, P. B. and Shackel P. A. (1987) Toward a critical archaeology, *Current Anthropology* 28: 283–302. And this volume.

Lerner, J. C. (1975) Changes in attitude toward death: the widow in Great Britain in the early 20th century, in B. Schoenberg, I. Gerber, A. Weiner, A. Kitscher, D. Peretz and A. Carr (eds) *Bereavement: Its Psychosocial Aspects* (New York: Columbia University Press).

Leroi-Gourhan, A. (1965) *Préhistoire de l'Art Occidental* (Paris: Mazenod).

Leroi-Gourhan, A. (1977–8) Résumé des cours et travaux de l'année scolaire 1977–78, *L Annuaire du Collège de France*: 523–34.

Leroi-Gourhan, A. (1982) *The Dawn of European Art* (Cambridge: Cambridge University Press).

Le Roy Ladurie, E. (1978) *Montaillon: The Promised Land of Error* (New York: Vintage Books).

Le Roy Ladurie, E. (ed.) (1979) The 'event' and the 'long term' in social history: the case of the Chouan uprising, in E. Le Roy Ladurie (ed.) *The Territory of the Historian* (Hassocks: Harvester), pp. 111–32.

Lévi-Strauss, C. (1963) *Structural Anthropology*, trans. C. Jacobson and B. C. Schoepf (New York: Basic Books).

Lévi-Strauss, C. (1966) *The Savage Mind* (Chicago: University of Chicago Press).

Lévi-Strauss, C. (1968a) *Structural Anthropology* (London: Allen Lane).

Lévi-Strauss, C. (1968b) *The Scope of Anthropology* trans. S. Ortner and R. A. Paul (London: Jonathan Cape).

Lévi-Strauss, C. (1969) *Totemism* (Harmondsworth: Penguin).

Lévi-Strauss, C. (1970) *The Raw and the Cooked*, trans. J. and D. Weightman (London: Cape).

Lévi-Strauss, C. (1973) *From Honey to Ashes* (London: Cape).

Lewis, G. (1980) *Day of Shining Red: An Essay on Understanding Ritual* (Cambridge: Cambridge University Press).

Lewis-Williams, J. and Loubser, J. (1986) Deceptive appearances: a critique of Southern African rock art, in F. Wendorf and A. Close (eds) *Advances in World Archaeology* (New York: Academic Press), pp. 253–89.

Lewontin, R. C. (1982) Organism and environment, in H. C. Plotkin (ed.) *Learning Development and Culture* (Chichester: Wiley), pp. 151–70.

Lindseth, A. (1981) Forståelsens prosess: et stadig oppgjør med våre for-dommer. Om Hans-Georg Gadamers filoso, *Dyade* 4: 4–28.

Linge, D. E. (1977) Editor's introduction, in H. G. Gadamer *Philosophical Hermeneutics* (Berkeley, CA: University of California Press), pp. xi–lviii.

Llobera, J. (1989) Catalan national identity: the dialectics of past and present, in E. Tonkin *et al.* (eds) *History and Ethnicity* (London: Routledge), pp. 247–61.

Lloyd, G. (1984) *The Man of Reason: 'Male' and 'Female' in Western Philosophy* (London: Methuen).

Lloyd, G. (1989) Woman as other: sex, gender and subjectivity, *Australian Feminist Studies* 10: 13–22.

Lodge, D. (1989) *The Novel as Communication*, Darwin Lecture, Cambridge.

Longacre, W. (1970) *Archaeology as Anthropology*, Anthropological Papers of the University of Arizona, 17 (Tucson, AZ: University of Arizona Press).

Longino, H. (1990a) *Science as Social Knowledge: Values and Objectivity in Scientific Inquiry* (Princeton, NJ: Princeton University Press).

Longino, H. (1990b) Political dimensions of epistemological critiques, Part I of conflicts and tensions in the feminist study of gender and science, in M. Hirsch and E. Fox Keller (eds) *Conflicts in Feminism* (London: Routledge), pp. 165–76.

Lourandos, H. (1980) Change or stability? Hydraulics, hunter-gatherers and population in temperate Australia, *World Archaeology* 11, (3): 245–64.

Lovelock, J. E. (1979) *Gaia: A New Look at Life on Earth* (Oxford: Oxford University Press).

Lowenthal, D. (1985) *The past is a foreign country* (Cambridge: Cambridge University Press).

Lukács, G. (1971) Reification and the consciousness of the proletariat, in *History and class consciousness*, trans. R. Livingstone (Cambridge, MA: MIT Press), pp. 83–222.

Lynch, M. (1985) *Art and Artifact in Laboratory Science: A Study of Shop Work and Shop Talk in a Research Laboratory* (London: Routledge and Kegan Paul).

Lynch, T. F. (1990) Glacial-age man in South America? A critical review, *American Antiquity* 55: 12–36.

Lynd, R. S. and Lynd, H. M. (1929) *Middletown* (New York: Harcourt, Brace and Co.).

Lynton, E. A. and Elman, S. E. (1987) *New Priorities for the University* (San Francisco: Jossey-Bass).

Lyotard, J. F. (1984) *The Postmodern Condition: A Report on Knowledge* (Manchester: Manchester University Press).

Macculloch, D. (1986) *Suffolk and the Tudors: Politics and Religion in an English County 1500–1600* (Oxford: Clarendon Press).

Macherey, P. (1978) *A Theory of Literary Production* (London: Routledge and Kegan Paul).

Machin, R. (1977) The great rebuilding: a reassessment, *Past and Present* 77: 33–56.

Mackenzie, W. (1967) *Politics and Social Science* (Harmondsworth: Penguin Books).

Mackie, E. W. (1977) *Science and Society in Prehistoric Britain* (London: Paul Elek).

Malina, J. and Vasicek, Z. (1990) *Archaeology Yesterday and Today. The Development of Archaeology in the Sciences and Humanities* (Cambridge: Cambridge University Press).

Mallory, J. P. (1989) *In search of the Indo-Europeans: Language, Archaeology and Myth* (London: Thames & Hudson).

Malmer, M. P. (1981) *A Chronological Study of North European Rock Art* (Stockholm: KVHAA handlingar) Antikvariska Serien 32.

Maltby, M. (1985) Patterns in faunal assemblage variability, in G. Barker and C. Gamble (eds) *Beyond Domestication in Prehistoric Europe* (London: Academic Press), pp. 33–74.

Mandel, E. (1978) *Late Capitalism* (London: Verso).

Mandt, G. (1987) Female symbolism in rock art, in R. Bertelsen, A. Lillehammer and J.-R. Ness (eds) *Were They All Men? An Examination of Sex Roles in Prehistoric Society* (Stavanger: Stavanger Archaeological Museum), pp. 35–52.

Marais, E. (1956) *My Friends the Baboons* (London: Methuen).

Marais, E. (1969) *The Soul of the Ape* (London: Anthony Blond).

Marcais, W. and Guiga, A. (1925) *Textes Arabes de Takrouna* (Paris: Leroux).

Marcus, E. (1992) *Making History: The Struggle for Gay and Lesbian Equal Rights, 1945–1990* (New York: Harper Perennial).

Marcus, G. and Cushman, D. (1982) Ethnographies as texts, *Annual Review of Anthropology* 11: 25–69.

Marcus, G. and Fischer, M. (1986) *Anthropology as Cultural Critique: An Experimental Moment in the Human Sciences* (Chicago: University of Chicago Press).

Marshak, A. (1977) The meander as a system: the analysis and recognition of iconographic units in upper Palaeolithic compositions, in P. J. Ucko (ed.) *Form in Indigenous Art* (London: Duckworth).

Marshack, A. (1987) The archaeological evidence for the emergence of human conceptualisation, paper delivered at Santa Fe, April 1987.

Marstrander, S. (1963) *Ostfolds Jordbruksristninger* (Oslo: Institute of Contemporary Research in Human Culture).

Martins, H. (1974) Time and theory in sociology, in J. Rex (ed.) *Approaches to Sociology* (London: Routledge and Kegan Paul).

Marx, K. (1906) *Capital* Vol. 1 (New York: Modern Library).

Marx, K. (1930) *Capital* Vol. 1, trans. E. and C. Paul, from 4th German edn of *Das Kapital* (1890) (London: Dent).

Marx, K. (1950 [1848]) The eighteenth brumaire of Louis Napoléon Bonaparte, in K. Marx and F. Engels, *Selected Works in Two Volumes* (Moscow: Foreign Languages Publishing House).

Marx, K. (1977) The 18th Brumaire of Louis Bonaparte, in D. McLellan (ed.) *Karl Marx: Selected Writings* (Oxford: Oxford University Press), pp. 30–325.

Marx, K. (1983) *Capital* Vol. 1 (London: Lawrence and Wishart).

Marx, K. and Engels, F. (1970) *The German Ideology* (London: Laurence and Wishart).

Maslow, A. (1936) The role of dominance in the social and sexual behavior of infrahuman primates: II an experimental determination of the behavior syndrome of dominance, *Journal of Genetic Psychology* 48: 310–38.

Matthaei, J. A. (1982) *An Economic History of Women in America* (New York: Schocken Books).

Matthews, K. (1994) An archaeology of homosexuality? Perspectives from the Classical World, in S. Cottam, D. Dungworth, S. Scott and J. Taylor (eds) *Theoretical Roman Archaeology Conference* 94 (Oxford: Oxbow Books).

Maunier, R. (1930) Le culte domestique en Kabylie and Les rites de la construction en Kabylie, in *Mélanges de sociologie nord-africaine* (Paris: Alcan).

Maynard Smith, J. (1976) Evolution and the theory of games, *American Scientist* 64: 41–5.

Maynard Smith, J. and Parker, G. (1976) The logic of asymmetric contests, *Animal Behavior* 24: 159–75.

Maynard Smith, J. and Price, G. (1973) The logic of animal conflicts, *Nature* 246: 15–18.

McBryde. I. (ed.) (1985) *Who Owns the Past?* (Oxford: Oxford University Press).

McGimsey, C. R. III and Davis, H. A. (eds) (1977) *The Management of Archaeological Resources: The Airlie House Report. Special Publication* (Washington, DC: Society for American Archaeology).

McGuire, R. and Osterud, N. G., (1980) *Working Lives: Broome County New York: 1800–1930* (Binghamton, NY: Roberson Center for the Arts and Sciences).

McGuire, R. H. (1988) Dialogues with the dead: ideology and the cemetery, in M. P. Leone and P. B. Potter (eds) *The Recovery of Meaning* (Washington DC: Smithsonian Institution Press), pp. 435–80.

McGuire, R. H. (1992) Archaeology and the first Americans, *American Anthropologist* 94: 816–36.

McGuire, R. H. (1988) The dead need not speak: ideology and the cemetery, in M. P. Leone and P. B. Potter, Jr. (eds) *The Recovery of Meaning in Historical Archaeology* (Washington, DC: Smithsonian Institution Press). In press.

McGuire, R. H. and Schiffer, M. (1983) A theory of architectural design, *Journal of Anthropological Archaeology* 2: 277–304.

McGuire, R. H. and C. Woodsong (1990) Making ends meet: unwaged work and domestic inequality in Broome County New York 1930–1980, in J. L. Collins and M. E. Gimenez (eds) *Work Without Wages: Comparative Studies of Housework and Petty Commodity Production* (Albany, NY: State University of New York Press), pp. 169–92.

McMillan, C. (1982) *Women, Reason and Nature* (Oxford: Basil Blackwell).

McOmish, D. S. (1989) Non-hillfort settlement and its implications, in M. Bowden, D. Mackay and P. Topping (eds) *From Cornwall to Caithness: Some aspects of British Field archaeology* (Oxford: British Archaeological Reports) (British series 209), pp. 99–110.

McVicar, J. (1983) Social change and the growth of antiquarian studies in Tudor and Stuart England, *Archaeological Review from Cambridge* 3 (1): 48–67.

Mead, G. H. (1977) [1938]) The process of mind in nature, in A. Strauss (ed.) *George Herbert Mead on Social Psychology* (Chicago: University of Chicago Press), pp. 85–111.

Mead, M. (1949 [1928]) *Coming of Age in Samoa* (New York: Mentor Books).

Megaw, J. V. S. and Simpson, D. D. A. (1979) *Introduction to British Prehistory* (Leicester: Leicester University Press).

Meillassoux, C. (1972) From reproduction to production, *Economy and Society* 1 (1), 93–105.

Meillassoux, C. (1975) Introduction, in C. Meillassoux (ed.) *L'esclavage en Afrique précoloniale* (Paris: Maspero).

Meinig, D. W. (1979a) The beholding eye: ten versions of the same scene, in D. W. Meinig (ed.) *The Interpretation of Ordinary Landscapes* (Oxford: Oxford University Press), pp. 33–48.

Meinig, D. W. (1979b) Introduction, in D. W. Meinig (ed.) *The Interpretation of Ordinary Landscapes* (Oxford: Oxford University Press), pp. 1–7.

Melas, E. M. (1989) Etics, emics and empathy in archaeological theory, in I. Hodder (ed.) *The Meanings of Things* (London: Unwin Hyman), pp. 137–55.

Mellartt, J. (1967) *Çatal Hüyük: A Neolithic Town in Anatolia* (London: Thames & Hudson).

Meltzer, D. (1981) Ideology and material culture, in R. A. Gould and M. B. Schiffer (eds) *Modern Material Culture* (New York: Academic Press).

Meltzer, D. J. (1983) The antiquity of man and the development of American archaeology, *Advances in Archaeological Method and Theory* 6:1–51.

Mercer, E. 1975 *English Vernacular Houses: a Study of Traditional Farmhouses and Cottages* (London: Her Majesty's Stationery Office).

Merleau-Ponty, M. (1962) *The Phenomenology of Perception*, trans. C. Smith (London: Routledge and Kegan Paul).

Merleau-Ponty, M. (1964) The child and his relation to others, in M. Merleau-Ponty *The Primacy of Perception* (Evanston, IL: North-Western University Press), pp. 96–155.

Merriman, N. (1987) Value and motivation in prehistory: the evidence for 'Celtic' spirit, in I. Hodder (ed.) *The Archaeology of Contextual Meanings* (Cambridge: Cambridge University Press), pp. 111–16.

Meskell, L. (1998a) Intimate archaeologies: the case of Kha and Merit, *World Archaeology* 29: 363–79.

Meskell, L. (1998b) Consuming bodies: cultural fantasies of Ancient Egypt, *Body and Society* 4(1): 63–76.

Meyer, S. (1981) *The Five Dollar Day* (Albany, NY: State University of New York Press).

Middleton, A. P. (1953) *Tobacco Coast: A Maritime History of Chesapeake Bay in the Colonial Era* (Baltimore: Johns Hopkins University Press).

Midgley, M. (1985) *The Origin and Function of the Earthen Long Barrows of Northern Europe* (Oxford: British Archaeological Reports International Series) 259.

Miller, D. (1982a) Artefacts as products of human categorisation processes, in I. Hodder (ed.) *Symbolic and Structural Archaeology* (Cambridge: Cambridge University Press), pp. 89–98.

Miller, D. (1982b) Explanation and social theory in archaeological practice, in C. Renfrew, M. J. Rowlands and B. A. Segraves (eds) *Theory and Explanation in Archaeology* (New York: Academic Press).

Miller, D. (1982c) Structures and strategies: an aspect of the relationship between social hierarchy and cultural change, in I. Hodder (ed.) *Symbolic and Structural Archaeology* (Cambridge: Cambridge University Press).

Miller, D. (1985a) *Artefacts as Categories* (Cambridge: Cambridge University Press).

Miller, D. (1985b) Ideology and the Harappan civilization, *Journal of Anthropological Anthropology* 4: 1–38.

Miller, D. (1987) *Material Culture and Mass Consumption* (Oxford: Blackwell).

Miller, D. and Tilley, C. (eds) (1984a) *Ideology, Power and Prehistory* (Cambridge: Cambridge University Press).

Miller, D. and Tilley, C. (eds) (1984b) Ideology, power and prehistory: an Introduction, in D. Miller and C. Tilley (eds) *Ideology, Power and Prehistory* (Cambridge: Cambridge University Press), pp. 1–15.

Miller, J. (1989) *Non-Verbal Communication* Darwin Lecture, Cambridge.

Miller, N. (1995) *Out of the Past: Gay and Lesbian History from 1869 to the Present* (New York: Vintage).

Millett, K. (1972) *Sexual Politics* (London: Granada).

Mitchell, J. (1974) *Psychoanalysis and Feminism* (Harmondsworth: Penguin).

Mitford, J. (1963) *The American Way of Death* (London: Hutchinson).

Miura, D. (1984) *The Forgotten Child*, trans. J. Cuthbert (Henley-on-Thames: Ellis).

Moerman, M. (1965) Who are the Lue? *American Anthropologist* 67: 1215–30.

Moi, T. (1985) *Sexual/Textual Politics* (London: Methuen).

Moller Okin, S. (1991) John Rawls: justice as fairness – for whom?, in M. L. Shanley and C. Pateman (eds) *Feminist Interpretations and Political Theory* (Cambridge: Polity Press), pp. 181–98.

Moore, H. L. (1982) The interpretation of spatial patterning in settlement residues, in I. Hodder (ed.) *Symbolic and Structural Archaeology*, (Cambridge: Cambridge University Press), pp. 74–9.

Moore, H. L. (1986) *Space, Text and Gender: An Anthropological Study of the Marakwet of Kenya* (Cambridge: Cambridge University Press).

Moore, H. L. (1988) *Feminism and Anthropology* (Minneapolis, MN: University of Minnesota Press).

Moore, H. L. (1990a) Paul Ricoeur: action, meaning and text, in C. Tilley (ed.) *Reading Material Culture* (Oxford: Basil Blackwell), pp. 85–120.

Moore, H. L. (1990b) Visions of the good life: anthropology and the study of utopias, *Cambridge Anthropology*, 14 (3): 13–33.

Moore, H. L. (1995) The problem of origins: poststructuralism and beyond, in I. Hodder, M. Shanks, A. Alexandri, V. Buchli, J. Carman, J. Last and G. Lucas (eds) *Interpreting Archaeology: Finding Meaning in the Past* (London: Routledge), pp. 51–3.

Moore, R. C., Lalicker, C. G. and Fischer, A. G. (1952) *Invertebrate fossils* (New York: McGraw-Hill).

Morgan, C. (1973) Archaeology and explanation, *World Archaeology* 4: 259–76.

Morgan, L. (1963) *Ancient Society* (Cleveland: World Publishing Company).

Morley, J. (1971) *Death, Heaven and the Victorians* (London: Studio Vista).

Morphy, H. (1989) From dull to brilliant: the aesthetics of spiritual power among the Yolngu, *Man* (N.S.), 24: 21–40.

Morris, R. and Morris, D. (1966) *Men and Apes* (New York: McGraw-Hill).

Mounier, R. (1972) The question of Man's antiquity in the New World: 1840–1927, *Pennsylvania Archaeologist* 42: 59–69.

Mueller-Vollmer, K. (ed.) (1986) *The Hermeneutics Reader* (London: Blackwell).

Muller, J. (1977) Individual variation in art styles, in J. Hill and J. Gunn (eds) *The Individual in Prehistory* (New York: Academic Press).

Munn, N. (1970) The transformation of subjects into objects in Walbiri and Pitjantjatjara myth, in R. Berndt *Australian Aboriginal Anthropology* (Canberra: Australian Institute of Aboriginal Studies), pp. 141–63.

Munn, N. (1973) *Walbiri Iconography* (Ithaca, NY: Cornell University Press).

Murray, R. (1989) Fordism and post-Fordism, in S. Hall and M. Jacques (eds) *New Times: The Changing Face of Politics in the 1990s* (London: Lawrence and Wishart), pp. 38–53.

Nanda, S. (1993) Hijras: an alternative sex and gender role in India, in G. Herdt (ed.) *Third Sex Third Gender: Beyond Sexual Dimorphism in Culture and History* (New York: Zone Books).

Nash, L. (1976) Troop fission in free-ranging baboons in the Gombe Stream National Park, Tanzania, *American Journal of Physical Anthropology* 44: 63–77.

Navarro, V. (1976) *Medicine under Capitalism* (New York: Prodist).

Navarro, V. (1978) *Class Struggle, the State and Medicine: An Historical and Contemporary Analysis of the Medical Sector in Great Britain* (London: Robertson).

Nelson, D. (1975) *Managers and Workers: Origins of the New Factory System in the United States 1880–1920* (Madison, WI: University of Wisconsin Press).

Nie, N. H., Hull, C. H., Jenkins, J. G., Steinbrenner, K. and Bent, D. H. (1975) *Statistical Package for the Social Sciences* (2nd edn; New York: McGraw-Hill).

Noble, D. (1984) *Forces of Production: A Social History of Industrial Automation* (New York: Knopf).

Norris, W. B. (1925) *Annapolis: Its Colonial and Naval story* (New York: Crowell).

Norton, R. (1997) *The Myth of the Modern Homosexual: Queer History and the Search for Cultural Unity* (London: Cassell).

O'Brien, M. (1982) Feminist theory and dialectic logic, in N. O. Keohane, M. Z. Rosaldo and B. C. Gelpi (eds) *Feminist Theory: A Critique of Ideology* (Brighton: Harvester Press), pp. 99–112.

Okely, J. (1979) An anthropological contribution to the history and archaeology of an ethnic group, in B. Burnham and J. Kingsbury (eds) *Space, Hierarchy and Society* (Oxford: BAR International Series) 59: 81–92.

O'Laughlin, B. (1977) Critique of Meillassoux's *Femmes, Greniers et Capitaux*, *Critique of Anthropology* 8 (2), 3–32.

Ollman, B. (1971) *Alienation* (Cambridge: Cambridge University Press).

Olsen, B. (1986) Norwegian archaeology and the people without (pre-)history: or how to create a myth of a uniform past, *Archaeological Review from Cambridge* 5: 25–42.

Olsen, B. (1989) Comments on archaeology into the 1990s, *Norwegian Archaeological Review* 22 (1): 18–21.

Olsen, B. (1990) Roland Barthes: from sign to text, in C. Tilley (ed.) *Reading Material Culture* (Oxford: Blackwell), pp. 163–205.

Olson, E. C. (1980) Taphonomy: its history and role in community evolution, in A. Behrensmeyer and A. Hill (eds) *Fossils in the Making* (Chicago: University of Chicago Press), pp. 5–19.

Onwuejeogwu, M. (1977) The patterns of population movement in the Igbo culture area, *Odinani Journal* 2: 23–41.

Onwuejeogwu, M. (1981) An Igbo civilisation: Nri kingdom and hegemony, *Ethnographica* (London: Ethnographica).

Onwuejeogwu, M. and Onwuejeogwu, O. (1977) The search for the missing links in dating and intrepreting Igbo-Ukwu finds, *Paideuma* 23: 169–88.

Ortner, S. B. and Whitehead, H. (1981) (eds) *Sexual Meanings: The Cultural Construction of Gender and Sexuality* (Cambridge: Cambridge University Press).

O'Shea, J. (1979) Mortuary Variability: An Archaeological Investigation with Case Studies from the Nineteenth Century Central Plains of North America and the Early Bronze Age of Southern Hungary. PhD thesis, Cambridge University.

Oswald, A. (1991) A Doorway on the past: round-house orientation and its significance in Iron Age Britain, unpublished BA dissertation submitted to the Department of Archaeology, University of Cambridge.

Ottenberg, S. (1975) *Masked Rituals of Afrikpo* (Seattle: Washington University Press).

Oyama, S. (1985) *The Ontogeny of Information: Developmental Systems and Evolution* (Cambridge: Cambridge University Press).

Packer, C. (1979) Male dominance and reproductive activity in Papio Anubis, *Animal Behavior* 27: 37–45.

Packer, C. (1980) Male care and exploitation of infants, *Animal Behavior* 28: 512–20.

Papenfuse, E. (1975) *In Pursuit of Profit: The Annapolis Merchant in an Era of the American Revolution, 1763–1805* (Baltimore: Johns Hopkins University Press).

Parker, G. and MacNair, M. (1978) Models of parent-offspring conflict: I. monogamy, *Animal Behavior* 26: 97–110.

Parker, R. (1975) *The Common Stream* (St Albans: Granada).

Parker Pearson, M. (1982) Mortuary practices, society and ideology: an ethnoarchaeological study, in I. Hodder (ed.) *Symbolic and Structural Archaeology* (Cambridge: Cambridge University Press). And this volume.

Parker Pearson, M. (1984a) Economic and ideological change; cyclical growth in the pre-state societies of Jutland, in D. Miller and C. Tilley (eds) *Ideology, Power and Prehistory* (Cambridge: Cambridge University Press), pp. 69–92.

Parker Pearson, M. (1984b) Social change, ideology and the archaeological record, in M. Spriggs (ed.) *Marxist Perspectives in Archaeology* (Cambridge: Cambridge University Press).

Parker Pearson, M. (1995) Tombs and territories: material culture and multiple interpretation, in I. Hodder, M. Shanks, A. Alexandri, V. Buchli, J. Carman, J. Last and G. Lucas (eds) *Interpreting Archaeology: Finding Meaning in the Past* (London: Routledge), pp. 205–9.

Parker Pearson, M. (1996) Food, fertility and front doors in the first millenium BC, in T. Champion and J. Collis *Recent Research on the Archaeology of Iron Age Britain* (Sheffield: University of Sheffield Press).

Parkes, C. M. (1975) *Bereavement: Studies of Grief in Adult Life* (Harmondsworth: Penguin).

Pateman, C. (1989) *The Sexual Contract* (Cambridge: Polity Press).

Patrik, L. E. (1985) Is there an archaeological record? *Advances in Archaeological Method and Theory,* 8: 27–62. And this volume.

Patterson, O. (1975) Context and choice in ethnic allegiance: a theoretical framework and Caribbean case study, in N. Glazer and D. P. Moynihan (eds) *Ethnicity: Theory and Experience* (Cambridge, MA: Harvard University Press), pp. 305–49.

Patterson, O. (1982) *Slavery and Social Death: A Comparative Study* (Cambridge, MA: Harvard University Press).

Patterson, T. (1984) Exploration and class formation in the Inca state, paper presented to the Canadian Ethnological Society, Montreal, May.

Patterson, T. (1987) History and the post-processual archaeologies, paper presented at the Annual Meeting of the Society for American Archaeology, New Orleans, LA.

Patterson, T. (1989) History and the post-processual archaeologies, *Man* 24: 555–66.

Paynter, R. (1983) Field or factory? Concerning the degradation of archaeological labor, in J. M. Gero, D. M. Lacy, and M. L. Blakey (eds) *The Socio-Politics of Archaeology* (Amherst, MA: Department of Anthropology, University of Massachusetts), pp. 17–30.

Peebles, C. and Kus, S. (1977) Some archaeological correlates of ranked societies, *American Antiquity* 42: 421–8

Peet, R. J. (1975) Inequality and poverty: a Marxist-geographic theory, *Annals of the Association of American Geographers* 65: 564–71.

Peet, R. J. (1977) The development of radical geography in the United States, *Progress in Human Geography* 1: 240–63.

Peet, R. J. and. Lyons, J. V. (1981) Marxism: dialectical materialism, social formation, and geographic relations, in M. E. Harvey and B. P. Holly (eds) *Themes in Geographic Thought* (London: Croom Helm), pp. 187–205.

Peirce, C. S. (1955) Logic as semiotic: the theory of signs, in J. Buchler (ed.) *Philosophical writings of Peirce* (New York: Dover), pp. 98–119.

Perper, T. and Schrire, C. (1977) The Nimrod connection: myth and science in the hunting model, in M. Kare and O. Maller (eds) *The Chemical Senses and Nutrition* (New York: Academic Press).

Petrequin, A. M. and Petrequin, P. (1988) *Les Néolithique des Lacs: préhistoire des lacs de Chalain et de Clairvaux (4000–2000 av jc)* (Paris: Editions Errance), p. 137.

Pettit, P. (1975) *The Concept of Structuralism: A Critical Analysis* (Dublin: Gill and Macmillan).

Phillips, P. (1971) Attribute analysis and social structure of Chassey – Cortaillod – Lagozza populations, *Man* 6: 341–52.

Piaget, J. (1970) *Structuralism*, trans. C. Maschler (New York: Harper and Row).

Piaget, J. (1971) *Structuralism* (London: Routledge and Kegan Paul).

Piaget, J. (1972) *The Principles of Genetic Epistemology* (London: Routledge and Kegan Paul).

Pickering, A. (ed.) (1992) *Science as Practice and Culture* (Chicago: University of Chicago Press).

Piggott, S. (1954) *Neolithic Cultures of the British Isles* (Cambridge: Cambridge University Press).

Piggott, S. (1958) *Approaches to Archaeology* (London: Adam and Charles Black).

Piggott, S. (1959) *Approach to Archaeology* (Harvard: McGraw-Hill).

Piggott, S. (1965) Ancient Europe, *From the Beginnings of Agriculture to Classical Antiquity* (Edinburgh: Edinburgh University Press).

Pittendrigh, C. S. (1958) Adaptation, natural selection and behavior, in A. Roe and G. Simpson (eds) *Behavior and Evolution* (New Haven, CT: Yale University Press), pp. 390–416.

Pitt-Rivers, A. H. L. F. (1875) On the evolution of culture, *Proceedings of the Royal Institute* Vll: 496–520.

Platt, C. (1978) *Medieval England: A Social History and Archaeology From the Conquest to A.D. 1600* (London: Routledge and Kegan Paul).

Pleydell-Bouverie, D. (1980) *The Church of St. Mary Hawkedon* (Hawkedon: Hawkedon Parish Council).

Plog, F. T. (1975) Systems theory in archaeological research, *Annual Review of Anthropology* 4: 207–24.

Podro, M. (1982) *The Critical Historians of Art* (New Haven, CT: Yale University Press).

Polson, C. J. and Marshall, T. K. (1972) *The Disposal of the Dead* (3rd edn; London: English Universities Press).

Popp, J (1978) Male baboons and evolutionary principles, PhD thesis, Harvard University.

Popp, J. and DeVore, I. (1979) Aggressive competition and social dominance theory: synopsis, in D. Hamburg and E. McCown (eds) *The Great Apes* (Menlo Park, CA: W. A. Benjamin).

Pospisil, L. (1963) *Kapauku Papuan Economy* (Yale Publications in Anthropology No. 61). (New Haven, CT: Yale University Press).

Post, D., Hausfater, G. and McCuskey, S. (1980) Feeding behavior of yellow baboons. Relationship to age, gender and dominance rank, *Folia Primatologica* 34: 170–95.

Postone, M., LiPuma, E. and Calhoun C. (1993) Introduction: Bourdieu and social theory, in C. Calhoun, E. LiPuma and M. Postone (eds) *Bourdieu: Critical Perspectives* (Cambridge: Polity Press), pp. 1–13.

Potter, P. B. (1990) The 'what' and 'why' of public relations for archaeology: a postscript to DeCicco's Public Relations Primer, *American Antiquity* 55: 608–13.

Potter, P. B., J. R. and Leone, M. P. (1986) History in museums: a critical capacity in museums versus repeating tradition, in *Education: The Spirit of the American museum*. Edited by M. E. Munley and C. Stapp, *Journal of the Washington Academy of Sciences* 75 (3): 51–61.

Potter, P. B. and Leone, M. P. (1988) Archaeology in public in Annapolis: four seasons, six sites, seven tours, and 32,000 visitors, *American Archaeologist*. In press.

Pound, E. (1961) *The ABC of Reading* (London: Faber and Faber).

Pred, A. (1977) The choreography of existence: comments on Hagestrand's time-geography and its usefulness, *Economic Geography*, 53, 207–21.

Pred, A. (1984) Place as historically contingent process: structuration and the time-geography of becoming places, *Annals of the Association of American Geographers*, 74: 279–97.

Pred, A. (1985) The social becomes the spatial, the spatial becomes the social: enclosures, social change and the becoming of places in the Swedish province of Skane, in D. Gregory and J. Urry (eds) *Social relations and Spatial Structures* (London: Macmillan), pp. 337–65.

Pred, A. (1990) *Making Histories and Constructing Human Geographies* (Boulder, CO: Westview Press).

Preucel, R. (ed.) (1991) *Processual and Post-processual Archaeologies: Multiple Ways of Knowing the Past*. Center for Archaeological Investigations (Carbondale, IL: Southern Illinois University Press).

Price-Beggerly, P. (1976) Edge damage on experimentally used scrapers of Hawaiian basalt, *Lithic Technology* 5: 22–4.

Quiatt, D. and Kelso, J. (1985) Household economies and hominid origins, *Current Anthropology* 26 (2): 207–22.

Raab, L., Klinger, T., Schiffer, M. B. and Goodyear, A. (1980) Clients, contracts, and profits: conflicts in public archaeology, *American Anthropologist* 82: 539–51.

Raab, L. M. and Goodyear, A. C. (1984) Middle-range theory in archaeology: a critical review of origins and applications, *American Antiquity*, 49: 255–68.

Rabinow, P. (1977) *Reflections on Fieldwork in Morocco* (Berkeley, CA: University of California Press).

Rabinow, P. (1986) Representations are social facts: modernity and post-modernity in anthropology, in J. Clifford and G. Marcus (eds) *Writing Culture* (Berkeley, CA: University of California Press).

Radcliffe-Brown, A. R. (1952) *Structure and Function in Primitive Society* (London: Cohen and West).

Ransom, T. (1984) *The Baboons of Gombe* (Lewisburg, PA: Bucknell University Press).

Ransom, T. and Ransom, B. (1971) Adult male-infant relations among baboons (Papio anubis), *Folia Primatologica* 16: 179–95.

Rapoport, A. (1969) The pueblo and the hogan, in P. Oliver (ed.) *Shelter and Society* (New York: Praeger).

Rapoport, A. (1976) Sociocultural aspects of man-environment studies, in A. Rapoport (ed.) *The Mutual Interaction of People and their Built Environment* (The Hague: Mouton), pp. 7–35.

Rapoport, A. (1990) Systems of activities and systems of settings, in S. Kent (ed.) *Domestic Architecture and the Use of Space* (Cambridge: Cambridge University Press), pp. 9–20.

Rasmussen, D. (1979) Correlates of patterns of range use of a troop of yellow baboons: sleeping sites, impregnable females, births and male emigrations, *Animal Behavior* 27: 108–112.

Rawnsley, S. and Reynolds, J. (1977) Undercliffe Cemetery, Bradford, *History Workshop Journal* 1: 215–21.

Redman, C. L. (1991) In defense of the seventies, *American Anthropologist* 93: 295–307.

Reed, E. S. (1988) The affordances of the animate environment: social science from the ecological point of view, in T. Ingold (ed.) *What is an Animal?* (London: Unwin Hyman), pp. 110–26.

Reeder, G. (n.d.) http://www.egyptology.com/niankhkhnum khnumhotep/

Renfrew, C. (1969) Trade and culture process in European prehistory, *Current Anthropology* 10: 151–69.

Renfrew, C. (1972) *The Emergence of Civilisation* (London: Methuen).

Renfrew, C. (1973) *Social Archaeology* (Southampton: Southampton University Press).

Renfrew, C. (1974) Space, time and polity, in M. J. Rowlands and J. Friedman (eds) *The Evolution of Systems* (London: Duckworth), pp. 89–114.

Renfrew, C. (1976) Trade as action at a distance: questions of integration and communication, in J. Sabloff and C. Lamberg-Karlovsky (eds) *Ancient Civilization and Trade* (Albuquerque, NM: University of New Mexico Press), pp. 3–59.

Renfrew, C. (1979) *Investigations in Orkney* (London: Thames & Hudson).

Renfrew, C. (1982a) *Towards an Archaeology of Mind* (Cambridge: Cambridge University Press).

Renfrew, C. (1982b) Explanation revisited, in C. Renfrew, M. J. Rowlands and B. A. Segraves *Theory and Explanation in Archaeology: The Southampton Conference* (New York: Academic Press), pp. 5–23.

Renfrew, C. (1984) *Approaches to Social Archaeology* (Edinburgh: Edinburgh University Press).

Renfrew, C. (1987) *Archaeology and Language: The Problem of Indo-European Origins* (London: Cape).

Renfrew, C. (1989) Comments on archaeology into the 1990s, *Norwegian Archaeological Review* 22: 33–41.

Revell, J. S. (1966) The indefensible status quo, *The Economist*, 15 Jan: 217–19.

Reynolds, P. (1984) *Iron Age Farm* (London: British Museum Publications).

Reynolds, P. (1985) *Iron Age Agriculture Reviewed*, Wessex Lecture 1, Council for British Archaeology Group 12.

Reynolds, P. C. (1993) The complementation theory of language and tool use, in K. R. Gibson and T. Ingold (eds) *Tools Language and Cognition in Human Evolution* (Cambridge: Cambridge University Press), pp. 407–28.

Rhine, R. (1975) The order of movement of yellow baboons, *Folia Primatologica* 23: 72–104.

Rhine, R. and Owens, N. (1972) The order of movement of adult male and black infant baboons entering and leaving a potentially dangerous clearing, *Folio Primatologica* 18: 276–83.

Rhine, R. and Westlund, B. (1978) The nature of the primary feeding habit in dilfferent age-sex classes of yellow baboons, *Folia Primatologica* 30: 64–79.

Rich, A. (1987) *Blood, Bread and Poetry* (London: Virago).

Richards, A. I. (1956) *Chisungu* (London: Faber and Faber).

Richards, C. (1990) The Neolithic house in Orkney, in R. Samson (ed.) *The Social Archaeology of Houses* (Edinburgh: Edinburgh University Press).

Richards, C. (1991) Skara Brae: revisiting a Neolithic village in Orkney, in W. Hanson and E. Slater (eds) *Scottish Archaeology; New Perceptions* (Aberdeen: Aberdeen University Press).

Richards, C. (1993) Monumental choreography: architecture and spatial representation in late Neolithic Orkney, in C. Tilley (ed.) *Interpretative Archaeology* (London: Berg).

Richards, C. (1995) Knowing about the past, in I. Hodder, M. Shanks, A. Alexandri, V. Buchli, J. Carman, J. Last and G. Lucas (eds) *Interpreting Archaeology: Finding Meaning in the Past* (London: Routledge), pp. 216–9.

Richards, C. (in press) *The Neolithic Settlement Complex at Barnhouse Farm.*

Richards, C. and Thomas, J. (1984) Ritual activity and structured deposition in later Neolithic Wessex, in R. Bradley and J. Gardiner (eds) *Neolithic Studies: A Review of Some Current Research* (Oxford: British Archaeological Reports), pp. 189–218.

Richards, P. (1991) Against the motion (2) in T. Ingold (ed.) *Human Worlds are Culturally Constructed* (Manchester: Group for Debates in Anthropological Theory).

Ricoeur, P. (1984) *The Reality of the Historic Past*, The Aquinas Lecture 1984 (Milwaukee: Milwaukee University Press).

Ricoeur, P. (1970) *Freud and Philosophy: An Essay on Enterpretation*, trans. D. Savage (New Haven, CT: Yale University Press).

Ricoeur, P. (1974) *The Conflict of Interpretations: Essays in Hermeneutics*, ed. D. Ihde (Evanston, IL: Northwestern University Press).

Ricoeur, P. (1981) *Hermeneutics and the Human Sciences*, ed. and trans. J. Thompson (Cambridge: Cambridge University Press).

Riley, D. (1988) *'Am I that name?': Feminism and the Category of 'Women' in History* (London: Macmillan).

Riley, E. (1897) *Souvenir Volume of the State Convention of Maryland Firemen Held at Annapolis*, June 9, 1897. Annapolis.

Riley, E. (1901) *Annapolis: Ye Ancient Capital of Maryland* (Annapolis: Annapolis Publishing Company).

Riley, E. (1906) *Pictorial Annapolis, Anne Arundel, and the Naval Academy* (Baltimore: King Brothers).

Riley, E. (1976 [1887]) *The Ancient City: A History of Annapolis in Maryland, 1649–1887* Annapolis, Record Printing Office (Anne Arundel-Annapolis Bicentennial Committee).

Ringer, B. L. and Lawless, E. R. (1989) *Race, Ethnicity and Society* (London: Routledge).

Ritchie, J. N. G. (1976) The Stones of Stennes, Orkney, *Proc. Soc. Antiq. Scot.* 107: 1–60.

Ritchie, J. N. G. (1985) The ritual monuments, in C. Renfrew (ed.) *The Prehistory of Orkney* (Edinburgh: Edinburgh University Press).

Rivers, W. H. R. (1910) The genealogical method of anthropological inquiry, *Sociological Review* 3: 1–12.

Robben, A. (1989) Habits of the home: spatial hegemony and the structuration of house and society in Brazil, *American Anthropology* 91: 570–88.

Roberts, F. H. H., Jr. (1935) A Folsom complex: preliminary report on investigations at the Linden-meier site in Northern Colorado, *Smithsonian Miscellaneous Collections*, 94.

Roberts, M. (1985) Words they are women, and deeds they are men: images of work and gender in Early Modern England, in L. Charles and L. Duffin (eds) *Women and Work in Pre-Industrial England* (London: Croom Helm), pp. 122–80.

Rodman, M. (1992) Empowering place: multilocality and multivocality, *American Anthropologist*, 94: 640–56.

Rorty, R. (1989) *Contingency, Irony and Solidarity* (Cambridge: Cambridge University Press).

Rosaldo, M. Z. (1980) The use of abuse of anthropology: reflections on feminism and cross-cultural understanding, *Signs*, 5 (3): 389–417.

Rosaldo, R. (1986) From the door of his tent: the fieldworker and the inquisitor, in J. Clifford and G. Marcus (eds) *Writing Culture* (Berkeley, CA: University of California Press).

Rose, M. A. (1991) *The Post-modern and Post-industrial: A Critical Analysis* (Cambridge: Cambridge University Press).

Rosen, A. M. (1986) *Cities of Clay: The Geoarchacology of Tells* (Chicago: University of Chicago Press).

Rosovsky, H. (1990) *The University: An Owner's Manual* (New York: W. W. Norton).

Rotherham, W. (1887) *Historical Notices of Hawkedon*. No publisher stated: copy in Suffolk Record Office, Bury St. Edmunds.

Rowell, T. E. (1966) Forest living baboons in Uganda, *Journal of Zoology* 149: 344–64.

Rowell, T. E. (1969) Intra-sexual behavior and female reproductive cycle of baboons, *Animal Behavior* 17: 159–67.

Rowlands, M. J. (1984) Conceptualising the European Bronze Age and Early Iron Age, in J. Bintliff (ed.) *European Social Evolution* (Bradford: Bradford University), pp. 147–56.

Rowlands, M. J. (1980) Kinship, alliance and exchange in the European Bronze Age, in J. Barrett and R. Bradley (eds) *Settlement and Society in the British Later Bronze Age* (Oxford: BAR International, Series) 83[1], pp. 15–46

Rowlands, M. J. (1982) Processual archaeology as historical social science, in C. Renfrew, M. J. Rowlands and B. A. Segraves (eds) *Theory and Explanation in Archaeology* (London: Academic Press), pp. 155–74.

Rowlands, M. J. (1986) Modernist fantasies in prehistory, *Man* 21: 745–6.

Rowlands, M. J. (1987a) The concept of Europe in prehistory, *Man* 22: 558–9.

Rowlands, M. J. (1987b) 'Europe in prehistory': a unique form of primitive capitalism?, *Culture and History* 1: 63–78.

Rowlands, M. J. (1987c) Centre and periphery: a review of a concept, in M. Rowlands, M. Larsen and K. Kristiansen (eds) *Centre and Periphery in the Ancient World* (Cambridge: Cambridge University Press), pp. 1–11.

Rowntree, L. and Conkey, M. (1980) Symbolism and the cultural landscape, *Annals of the Association of American Geographers* 70 (4): 459–74.

Rubin, G. (1975) The traffic in women: notes on the 'political economy' of sex, in, R. R. Reiter (ed.) *Towards an Anthropology of Women* (New York: Monthly Review Press).

Rudwick, M. J. S. (1979) History of paleontology: before Darwin, in R. A. Gould and
  M. B. Schiffer (eds) *Modern Material culture: The Archaeology of us* (New York:
  Academic Press), pp. 375–84.

Rybczynski, W. (1986) *Home: a Short History of an Idea* (New York: Viking Penguin).

Saari, H. (1984) *Re-enactment: A Study in R. G. Collingwood's Philosophy of History* (Abo:
  Abo Akademi).

Sacks, O. (1985) *The Man who Mistook his Wife for a Hat* (London: Picador).

Sahlins, M. (1972) *StoneAge Economics* (London: Tavistock).

Sahlins, M. (1976) *Culture and Practical Reason*, (Chicago: University of Chicago Press).

Sahlins, M. (1985) *Islands of History* (Chicago: University of Chicago Press).

Salmon, M. H. (1975) Confirmation and explanation, *American Antiquity* 40: 459–64.

Salmon, M. H. (1976) 'Deductive' vs. 'inductive' archaeology, *American Antiquity* 41:
  376–81.

Salmon, M. H. (1977) Philosophy for anthropologists, *Teaching Philosophy* 2: 135–38.

Salmon, M. H. (1978) What can systems theory do for archaeology?, *American Antiquity*
  43: 174–83.

Salmon, M. H. (1982a) Models of explanation: two views, in C. Renfrew, M. J.
  Rowlands and B. A. Segraves, *Theory and explanation in archaeology: The Southampton
  Conference* (New York: Academic Press), pp. 35–44.

Salmon, M. H. (1982b) *Philosophy and Archaeology* (New York: Academic Press).

Salt, J. and Elliott, B. J. (1975) *British Society 1870–1970* (Amersham: Hulton).

Sapolsky, R. (1982) The endocrine stress-response and social status in the wild baboon,
  Hormones and Behavior 16: 279–92.

Sapolsky, R. (1983) Individual differences in cortisol secretory patterns in the wild
  baboon: role of negative feedback sensitivity, *Endocrinolgy* 113: 2263–8.

Saussure, F. de (1959) *Course in General Linguistics*, trans. W. Baskin (New York:
  Philosophical Library).

Saussure, F. de (1966) *Course in General Linguistics*, ed. C. Bally, A. Sechehaye and A.
  Riedlinger; originally published 1915; trans. W. Baskin (New York: McGraw-Hill).

Savory, H. N. (1950–52) The excavation of a Neolithic dwelling and a Bronze Age
  cairn at Mount Pleasant Farm, Nottage (Glam.), *Transactions of the Cardiff Naturalists'
  Society* 81: 75–92.

Savory, H. N. (1959–60) The excavation of a Bronze Age cairn at Sant-y-Nyll, St.
  Brides-Super-EIy (Glam.), *Transactions of the Cardiff Naturalists' Society* 89: 9–25.

Savory, H. N. (1972) Copper Age cists and cist-cairns in Wales with special reference
  to Newton, Swansea and other multiple-cist cairns, in F. Lynch and C. Burgess (eds)
  Prehistoric Man in Wales and the West (Bath: Adams and Dart), pp. 117–39.

Savory, H. N. (1980) *Guide Catalogue of the Bronze Age Collections* (Cardiff: National
  Museum of Wales).

Sawicki, J. (1991) Foucault and feminism: toward a politics of difference, in M. L.
  Shanley and C. Pateman (eds) *Feminist Interpretations and Political Theory* (Cambridge,
  Polity Press), pp. 217–31.

Saxe, A. A. (1970) Social dimensions of mortuary practices, PhD thesis, University of
  Michigan.

Sayer, R. A. (1982) Misconceptions of space in social thought, *Transactions of the
  Institute for British Geographers* 7: 494–503.

Schiffer, M. (1972a) Archeological context and systemic context, *American Antiquity* 37:
  156–65.

Schiffer, M. (1972b) Cultural laws and the reconstruction of past lifeway, *Kiva* 37:
  148–57.

Schiffer, M. (1976) *Behavioural Archaeology* (New York: Academic Press).

Schiffer, M. (1983) Toward the identification of formation processes, *American Antiquity* 48: 675–706.

Schiffer, M. (1987) *Formation Processes of the Archaeological Record* (Albuquerque, NM: University of New Mexico Press).

Schiffer, M. (1988) The structure of archaeological theory, *American Antiquity* 53: 461–85.

Schiffer, M. and Rathje W. L. (1973) Efficient exploitation of the archaeological record: penetrating problems, in C. Redman (ed.) *Research and Theory in Current Archaeology* (New York: Wiley- Interscience), pp. 169–79.

Schilder, P. (1978) *The Image and Appearance of the Human Body* (New York: International University Press

Schleiermacher, F. D. E. (1986) General hermeneutics, in K. Mueller-Vollmer *The Hermeneutics Reader* (Oxford: Blackwell), pp. 73–86.

Schoenberg, B., Gerber, J., Weiner, A., Kitscher, A., Peretz, D. and Carr, A. (eds) (1975) *Bereavement: Its Psychological Aspects* (New York: Columbia University Press).

Scholte, R. (1981) Critical anthropology since its reinvention, in J. S. Kahn and J. R. Llobera (eds) *Anthropology of Pre-Capitalist Societies* (London: Macmillan), pp. 148–84.

Scholte, R. (1986) The charmed circle of Geertz's hermeneutics: a neo-marxist critique, *Critique of Anthropology* VI: 5–15.

Scholte, R. (1987) The literary turn in contemporary anthropology, *Critique of Anthropology* VII: 33–47.

Schreber, D. P. (1955) *Memoirs of My Nervous Illness*, trans. I. Macalpine and R. A. Hunter (London: Dawson).

Schubert, G. (1986) Primate Politics, *Social Science Information* 25.3: 647–80.

Schuldenrein, J. (1992) Cultural resource management and academic responsibility in archaeology: a rejoinder to Duke, *SAA Bulletin* 10 (5): 3.

Schwartzman, D. W. and Siddique, M. (1986) How ideology relates to natural science with examples from geology and cosmogony, *Science and Nature* 7/8: 101–11.

Schwimmer, E. (ed.) (1978) *The Yearbook of Symbolic Anthropology* 1 (London: C. Hurst & Company).

Scott, J. (1985) *Weapons of the Weak: Everyday Forms of Peasant Resistance* (New Haven, CT: Yale University Press).

Scott, S. (1984) The baby business, *The Gazette*, B-1, 4. Montreal, 24 April.

Seilacher, A. (1982 [1967]) Fossil behavior, in L. F. Laporte *The Fossil Record and Evolution* (San Francisco: W. H. Freeman), pp. 99–106.

Seyfarth, R. (1976) Social relationships among adult female baboons, *Animal Behavior* 24: 917–38.

Seyfarth, R. (1977) A model of social grooming among adult female monkeys, *Journal of Theoretical Biology* 65: 671–98.

Seyfarth, R. (1980) The distribution of grooming and related behaviours among adult female vervet monkeys, *Animal Behavior* 28: 798–813.

Shackel, P. A. (1986a) The creation of behavioral standardization and social segmentation in Anglo-America, paper presented at the Northeastern Anthropological Meetings Buffalo, NY, 21 March.

Shackel, P. A. (1986b) Archaeological testing at the Thomas Hyde House, 193 Main Street Site, 18 Ap 44, Annapolis, Maryland. MS.

Shanks, M. (1992a) *Experiencing the Past: On the Character of Archaeology* (London: Routledge).

Shanks, M. (1992b) Artefact design and pottery from archaic Korinth: an archaeological interpretation. PhD thesis, Cambridge University.

Shanks, M. (1993) Archaeological experiences and a critical romanticism, in A. Siriaiinen *et al.* (eds) The archaeologists and their reality, *Proceedings of the 4th Nordic TAG Conference* 1992 (Helsinki: Department of Archaeology, University of Helsinki).

Shanks, M. (1995) *Classical Archaeology: Experiences of the Discipline* (London: Routledge).

Shanks, M. and Hodder, I. (1995) Processual, postprocessual and interpretive archaeologies, in I. Hodder, M. Shanks, A. Alexandri, V. Buchli, J. Carman, J. Last and G. Lucas (eds) *Interpreting Archaeology: Finding Meaning in the Past* (London: Routledge), pp. 3–29

Shanks, M. and Tilley, C. (1982) Ideology, symbolic power, and ritual communication: A reinterpretation of Neolithic mortuary practices, in Ian Hodder (ed.) *Symbolic and structural archaeology* (Cambridge: Cambridge University Press), pp. 129–54.

Shanks, M. and Tilley, C. (1987a) *Re-Constructing Archaeology* (Cambridge: Cambridge University Press).

Shanks, M. and Tilley, C. (1987b) *Social Theory and Archaeology* (Cambridge, Polity Press).

Shanks, M. and Tilley, C. (1987c) *Studies in Archaeological Theory Practices* (Cambridge: Cambridge University Press).

Shanks, M. and Tilley, C. (1989a) Archaeology into the 1990s, *Norwegian Archaeological Review* 22(1): 1–12.

Shanks, M. and Tilley, C. (1989b) Questions rather than answers: reply to comments on Archaeology Into the 1990s, *Norwegian Archaeological Review* 22.1: 42–54.

Shanley, M. L. and Pateman, C. (eds) (1991) *Feminist Interpretations and Political Theory* (Cambridge: Polity Press).

Shapere, D. (1982) The concept of observation in science and philosophy, *Philosophy of Science* 49: 485–525.

Shapere, D. (1985) Observation and the scientific enterprise, in P. Achinstein and O. Hannaway (eds) *Observation, Experiment, and Hypothesis in Modern Physical Science* (Cambridge, MA: MIT Press), pp. 22–45.

Shapin, S. (1989) The invisible technician, *American Scientist* 77: 553–63.

Shapin, S. and Schaffer, S. (1985) *Leviathan and the Air Pump* (Princeton, NJ: University of Princeton Press).

Sharples, N. (1985) Individual and community: the changing role of megaliths in the Orcadian Neolithic, *Proceedings of the Prehistoric Society* 51: 59–74.

Sharples, N. (1991) Warfare in the Iron Age of Wessex, *Scottish Archaeological Review* 8: 79–89.

Shaw, T. (1970) *Igbo-Ukwu: An Account of Archaeological Discoveries in Eastern Nigeria* (London: Faber).

Shaw, T. (1977) *Unearthing Igbo-Ukwu* (London: Open University Press).

Shaw, T. (forthcoming) Further light on Igbo-Ukwu, including radio-carbon dates, in P. de Maret, B. Andoh and R. Soper (eds) *Proceedings of the 11th Pan-African Congress on Archaeology and Related Subjects* (Nairobi).

Shennan, S. (1975) The social organization at Branc, *Antiquity* 49: 279–87.

Shennan, S. (1982) Ideology, changes, and the European Early Bronze Age, in I. Hodder (ed.) *Symbolic and Structural Archaeology* (Cambridge: Cambridge University Press), pp. 155–61.

Shennan, S. (1989) Introduction, in S. J. Shennan (ed.) *Archaeological Approaches to Cultural Identity* (London: Unwin and Hyman), pp. 1–32.

Sherratt, A. (1972) Socio-economic and demographic models for the Neolithic and Bronze Ages of Europe, in D. Clarke (ed.) *Models in Archaeology* (London: Methuen), pp. 477–541.

Sherratt, A. (1984) Social evolution: Europe in the later Neolithic and Copper Ages, in J. Bintliff (ed.) *European Social Evolution* (Bradford, University of Bradford), pp. 123–34.

Sherratt, A. (1990) The genesis of megaliths, *World Archaeology* 22, 147–67.

Sherratt, A. (1995) Reviving the grand narrative: archaeology and long-term change, *Journal of European Archaeology* 3, 1–32,

Shibutani, T. and Kwan, K. M. (1965) *Ethnic Stratification: A Comparative Approach* (New York: The Macmillan Company).

Shils, E. (1979) *Tradition* (London: Edward Arnold).

Shipman, P. (1981) *Life history of a Fossil: An Introduction to Taphonomy and Palaeoecology* (Cambridge, MA: Harvard University Press).

Shipman, D. (1986) Scavenging and hunting in early hominids: theoretical framework and tests, *American Anthropologist* 88 (1): 27–43.

Shore, B. (1981) Sexuality and gender in Samoa: conceptions and missed conceptions, in S. B. Ortner and H. Whitehead (eds) *Sexual Meanings: The Cultural Construction of Gender and Sexuality* (Cambridge: Cambridge University Press), pp. 192–215.

Shore, C. (1993) Inventing the 'People's Europe': critical approaches to European Community cultural policy, *Man* 18 (4): 779–800.

Shostak, M. (1990) *Nisa: The Life and Words of a !Kung Woman* (London: Earthscan).

Sigerist, H. E. (1956) *Landmarks in the History of Hygiene* (Oxford: Oxford University Press).

Sigerist, H. E. (1944) *Civilization and Disease* (Ithaca, NY: Cornell University Press).

Silk, J. (1980) Kidnapping and female competition in captive bonnet macaques, *Primates* 21: 100–10.

Slichter, S. H. (1919) *The Turnover of Factory Labor* (New York: B. C. Forbes Co.).

Slocum, S. (1975) Woman the gatherer: male bias in anthropology, in R. Reiter (ed.) *Towards an Anthropology of Women* (New York: Monthly Review Press), pp. 36–50.

Smith, A. (1937 [1776]) *An Inquiry into the Nature and Causes of the Wealth of Nations* E. Canaan (ed.) (New York: (Modern Library) Random House).

Smith, J. W. and Turner, B. S. (1986) Constructing social theory and constituting society, *Theory Culture and Society* 3: 125–33.

Smuts, B. (1982) Special relationships between adult male and female olive baboons, PhD thesis, Stanford University, CA.

Society of Antiquaries of London (1992) *Archaeological Publication, Archives, and Collections: Towards a National Policy* (London: Society of Antiquaries).

Soffer, O. (1985) Patterns of intensification as seen from the Upper Palaeolithic of the central Russian plain, in T. Price and J. Brown (eds) *Prehistoric Hunter-Gatherers: The Emergence of Cultural Complexity* (New York: Academic Press).

Soja, E. (1989) *Postmodern Geographies: The Reassertion of Space in Critical Social Theory* (London: Verso).

Sommer, D. (1988) Not just a personal story: women's testimonies and the plural self, in B. Brodzki and C. Shenck (eds) *Life/Lines: Theorizing Women's Autobiography* (Ithaca, NY: Cornell University Press), pp. 107–30.

Sørensen, M. L. (1987) Material order and cultural classification: the role of bronze objects in the transition from Bronze Age to Iron Age in Scandinavia, in I. Hodder (ed.) *The Archaeology of Contextual Meanings* (Cambridge: Cambridge University Press).

Sorokin, P. A. and Merton, R. K. (1937) Social time: a methodological and functional analysis, *American Journal of Sociology* 42: 615–29.

South, S. (1977) *Method and Theory in Historical Archeology* (New York: Academic Press).

Sparkes, B. (1998) Sex in Classical Athens, in B. A. Sparkes (ed.) *Greek Civilization: An Introduction* (Oxford: Blackwell).

Spears, C. S. (1975) Hammers, nuts and jolts, cobbles, cobbles, cobbles: experiments in cobble technologies in search of correlates, in *Arkansas Eastman Archaeological Project* by C. Baker, with contributions by C. Spears, C. Claassen and M. Schiffer (Fayetteville: Arkansas Archaeological Survey).

Spector, J. D. (1991) What this awl means: toward a feminist archaeology, in J. Gero and M. W. Conkey (eds) *Engendering Archaeology: Women and Prehistory* (Oxford: Basil Blackwell), pp. 388–407.

Spelman, E. (1982) Woman as body: ancient and contemporary views, *Feminist Studies* 8: 109–31.

Spencer, C. (1995) *Homosexuality: A History* (London: Fourth Estate).

Spencer, J. (1989) Anthropology as a kind of writing, *Man* 24: 64.

Spencer, J. (1990) Writing within: anthropology, nationalism, and culture in Sri Lanka, *Current Anthropology* 31 (3): 283–300.

Sperber, D. (1979) Claude Lévi-Strauss, in J. Sturrock (ed.) *Structuralism and Since* (Oxford: Oxford University Press).

Sperber, D. (1975) *Rethinking symbolism*, trans. A. L. Morton (Cambridge: Cambridge University Press).

Spriggs, M. (ed.) (1984) *Marxist Perspectives in Archaeology* (Cambridge: Cambridge University Press).

Stacey, J. and Thorne, B. (1985) The missing feminist revolution in sociology, *Social Problems* 32: 301–16.

Stalio, B. (1968) Naselje i stan neolitskog perioda, in M. Garasanin (ed.) *Neolit Centralnog Balkana* (Beograd: Narodni Muzej), pp. 77–106.

Stanislawski, M. B. (1973) Review of Archaeology as anthropology: a case study by W. A. Longacre, *American Antiquity* 38: 117–22.

Stanislawski, M. B. (1978) If pots were mortal, in R. A. Gould (ed.) *Explorations in ethnoarchaeology* (Albuquerque, NM: University of New Mexico Press), pp. 201–27.

Stea, D. and Turan, M. (1986) Placemaking and production in prehistory: a comparative study in dialectical perspective, in D. Saile (ed.) *Architecture in Cultural Change: Essays in Built Form and Culture Research* (Kansas: School of Architecture and Urban Design, University of Kansas), pp. 91–108.

Stea, D. and Turan, M. (1990) A statement on placemaking, in M. Turan (ed.) *Vernacular Architecture* (Aldershot: Avebury), pp. 102–21.

Stein, D. (1984) *The Sociobiology of Infant and Adult Male Baboons* (Norwood: Ablex Publishing)

Stevens, W. 0. (1937) *Annapolis: Anne Arundel's Town* (New York: Dodd, Mead).

St. George, R. B. (1985) Artifacts of regional consciousness, 1700–1780, in *The great river: Art and Society of the Connecticut Valley, 1635–1820* (Hartford: Wadsworth Atheneum), pp. 29–30.

Stoltz, L. and Saayman, G. (1970) Ecology and behaviour of baboons in the Northern Transvaal, *Annales of the Transvaal Museum* 26: 99–143.

Stone, L. (1957) *The Crisis of the Aristocracy 1558–1641* (Oxford: Oxford University Press).

Stone, L. (1977) *The Family, Sex and Marriage in England 1500–1800* (Oxford: Oxford University Press).

Stopford, J. (1987) Danebury: an alternative view, *Scottish Archaeological Review* 4: 70–5.

Strathern, M. (1987) An awkward relationship: the case of feminism and anthropology, *Signs* 12: 276–92.

Strathern, M. (1988) *The Gender of the Gift* (Berkeley, CA: University of California Press).

Strathern, M. (1996) Cutting the network, *Journal of the Royal Anthropological Institute* 2, 517–35.

Straus, G. (1977) Of deer-slayers and mountain men: Paleolithic faunal exploitation in Cantabrian Spain, in L. Binford (ed.) *For Theory Building in Archaeology* (New York: Academic Press), pp. 41–76.

Strohmeyer, U. and Hannah, M. (1992) Domesticating postmodernism, *Antipode* 24, 29–55.

Struhsaker, T. (1969) Correlates of ecology and social organization among African cercopithecines, *Folia Primatologica* 11: 80–118.

Strum, S. (1975a) Life with the pumphouse gang, *National Geographic* 147: 672–91.

Strum, S. (1975b) Primate predation: interim report on the development of a tradition in a troop of olive baboons, *Science* 187: 755–7.

Strum, S. (1981) Processes and products of change: baboon predatory behavior at Gilgil, Kenya, in G. Teleki and R. Harding (eds) *Omnivorous Primates* (New York: Columbia University Press).

Strum, S. (1982) Agnostic dominance in male baboons: an alternative view, *International Journal of Primatology* 3: 175–202.

Strum, S. (1983a) Why males use infants, in D. Taub (ed.) *Primate Paternalism* (New York: Van Nostrand Reinhold).

Strum, S. (1983b) Use of females by male olive baboons, *American Journal of Primatology* 5: 93–109.

Strum, S. (1983c) Baboon cues for eating meat, *Journal of Human Evolution* 12: 327–36.

Strum, S, (n.d.) Are there alternatives to aggression in baboon society?

Sturrock, J. (ed.) (1979) *Structuralism and Since* (Oxford: Oxford University Press).

Sullivan, A. P. (1978) Inference and evidence in archaeology: a discussion of conceptual problems, in M. B. Schiffer (ed.) *Advances in Archaeological Method and Theory* (New York: Academic Press), vol. 1: pp. 183–222.

Sumner, W. G. (1963) *Social Darwinism: Selected Essays* (Englewood Cliffs, NJ: Prentice-Hall).

Swain, H. (ed.) (1991) *Competitive Tendering in Archaeology Rescue* (Hertford: Publications/Standing Conference of Archaeological Unit Managers).

Sweeney, K. M. (1984) Mansion people, *Winterthur Portfolio* 19: 231–55.

Swidler, A. (1986) Culture in action: symbols and strategies, *American Sociological Review* 51: 273–86.

Sykes, C. (1988) *ProfScam: Professors and the Demise of Higher Education* (Washington, DC: Regnery Gateway).

Tainter, J. (1977) Modelling change in prehistoric social systems, in L. Binford (ed.) *For Theory Building in Archaeology* (New York Academic Press).

Tainter, J. (1978) Mortuary practices and the study of prehistoric social systems, in M. Schiffer (ed.) *Advances in Archaeological Method and Theory*, vol. 1 (New York: Academic Press).

Tambiah, S. (1969) Animals are good to think with and good to prohibit, *Ethnology* 8: 423–59.

Tanner, N. (1971) *On Becoming Human* (Cambridge: Cambridge University Press).

Tasic, N. (1989) Prehistoric migration movements in the Balkans, in N. Tasic and D. Stosic (eds) *Migrations in Balkan History* (Belgrade: Serbian Academy of Science and Arts), pp. 29–38

Taylor, B. (1983) *Eve and the New Jerusalem: Socialism and Feminism in the Nineteenth Century* (London: Virago).

Taylor, T. (1996) *The Prehistory of Sex* (New York: Bantam Books).

Taylor, W. W. (1948) *A Study of Archaeology* (Menasha: Memoirs of the American Anthropological Association) 69.

Tentler, L. W. (1979) *Wage Earning Women* (New York: Oxford University Press).

Therborn, G. (1980) *The Ideology of Power and the Power of Ideology* (London: Verso).

Therkorn, L. (1987) The inter-relationships and materials and meanings: some suggestions on housing concerns in the Iron Age of Noord-Holland, in I. Hodder (ed.) *The Archaeology of Contextual Meanings* (Cambridge: Cambridge University Press), pp. 102–10.

Thevenot, J. P. (1985) Informations archéologiques: circonscription de Bourgogne, *Gallia Préhistoire* 28, 171–210.

Thomas, D. H. (1971) On distinguishing natural from cultural bone in archaeological sites, *American Antiquity* 36(3): 366–71.

Thomas, D. H. (1974) *Predicting the Past* (New York: Holt, Rinehart & Winston).

Thomas, J. S. (1989) The technologies of the self and the constitution of the subject, *Archaeological Review from Cambridge* 8: 101–7.

Thomas, J. S. (1990a) Monuments from the inside: the case of the Irish megalithic tombs, *World Archaeology* 22: 168–78.

Thomas, J. S. (1990b) Same, other, analogue: writing the past, in F. Baker and J. Thomas (eds) *Writing the Past in the Present* (Lampeter: St David's University College), pp. 18–23.

Thomas, J. S. (1991) *Rethinking the Neolithic* (Cambridge: Cambridge University Press).

Thomas, J. S. (1995) Reconciling symbolic significance with being-in-the-world, in I. Hodder, M. Shanks, A. Alexandri, V. Buchli, J. Carman, J. Last and G. Lucas (eds) *Interpreting Archaeology: Finding Meaning in the Past* (London: Routledge), pp. 210–11

Thomas, J. S. (1996) *Time, Culture and Identity: An Interpretive Archaeology* (London: Routledge).

Thomas, R. (1952) Washington's letters in Annapolis, *Picket Post* 37 (July) 40–1.

Thompson, E. P. (1967) Time, work-discipline and industrial capitalism, *Past and Present* 38: 5–97.

Thompson, E. P. (1968) *The Making of the English Working Class* (Harmondsworth: Penguin).

Thompson, E. P. (1977a) *William Morris: Romantic to Revolutionary* (London: Merlin).

Thompson, E. P. (1977b) *Whigs and Hunters: The Origin of the Black Act* (Harmondsworth: Penguin,).

Thompson, E. P. (1978) The poverty of theory: or an orrery of errors, in E. P. Thompson *The Poverty of Theory and Other Essays*, (London: Merlin Press), pp. 193–397.

Thompson, M. (1977) *General Pitt-Rivers: Evolution and Archaeology in the Nineteenth Century* (Bradford-on-Avon: Moonraker).

Thompson, M. (1979) *Rubbish Theory: The Creation and Destruction of Value* (Oxford: Oxford University Press).

Thornton, F. J. (1980) *Space, Time And Culture among the Iraqw of Tanzania* (London: Academic Press).

Thorpe, I. J. (1981) Anthropological orientations on astronomy in complex societies, paper read at the Third Theoretical Archaeological Group Conference, Reading.

Thorpe, I. J. and Richards, C. (1984) The decline of ritual authority and the introduction of beakers into Britain, in R. Bradley and J. Gardiner (eds) *Neolithic Studies: A Review of Some Current Research* (Oxford: BAR British Series) 133.

Tilley, C. Y. (1982) Social formation, social structures, and social change, in I. Hodder (ed.) *Symbolic and Structural Archaeology* (Cambridge: Cambridge University Press), pp. 26–38.

Tilley, C. Y. (1984) Ideology and the legitimation of power in the middle Neolithic of southern Sweden, in D. Miller and C. Tilley (eds) *Ideology, Power, and Prehistory* (Cambridge: Cambridge University Press), pp. 111–46.

Tilley, C. Y. (1989a) Excavation as theatre, *Antiquity* 63: 275–80.

Tilley, C. Y. (1989b) Discourse as power: the genre of the Cambridge inaugural lecture, in D. Miller, M. Rowlands and C. Tilley (eds) *Domination and Resistance* (London: Unwin Hyman).

Tilley, C. Y. (ed.) (1990a) *Reading Material Culture* (Oxford: Blackwell).

Tilley, C. Y. (1990b) On modernity and archaeological discourse, in I. Bapty and T. Yates *Archaeology after Structuralism* (London: Routledge), pp. 127–152

Tilley, C. Y. (1991) *Material Culture and Text: The Art of Ambiguity* (London: Routledge).

Tilley, C. Y. (1993) Interpretation and a poetics of the past, in C. Tilley (ed.) *Interpretative Archaeology* (London: Berg), pp. 1–27.

Tilley, C. Y. (1994) *A Phenomenology of Landscape: Places, Paths and Monuments* (London: Berg).

Tillyard, S. K. (1988) *The Impact of Modernism 1900–1920: Early Modernism and the Arts and Crafts Movement in Edwardian England* (London: Routledge).

Todd, I. (1976) *Çatal Hüyük in Perspective* (Menlo Park, CA: Cummings Publishing Company).

Todorova, H. (1978) *The Eneolithic Period in Bulgaria in the Fifth Millennium BC* (Oxford: BAR International Series) 49.

Todorova, H. (1982) *Kupferzeitliche Siedlungen in Nordostbulgarien* (Munich: Verlag C. H. Beck).

Todorova, H., Vasiliev, V., Ianusevich, I., Koracheva, M. and Valev, P. (eds) (1983) *Ovcharovo* (Sofia: Archaeological Institute of the Bulgarian Academy of Sciences).

Tonkin, E., McDonald, M. and Chapman M. (eds) (1989) *History and Ethnicity* (London: Routledge).

Torrence, R. (1989) *Time, Energy and Stone Tools* (Cambridge: Cambridge University Press).

Tourraine, A. (1974) *The Post-Industrial Society: Tomorrow's Social History: Classes, Conflicts and Culture in the Programmed Society* (London: Wildwood House).

Toynbee, P. (1980) The big funerals come from people living in council houses these days, *The Guardian*, 18 Aug: 8.

Trigger, B. (1980a) *Gordon Childe: Revolutions in Archaeology* (London: Thames and Hudson).

Trigger, B. (1980b) Archaeology and the image of the American Indian, *American Antiquity* 45: 662–76.

Trigger, B. (1989a) Comments on Archaeology into the 1990s, *Norwegian Archaeological Review* 22.1: 28–31.

Trigger, B. (1989b) *A History of Archaeological Thought* (Cambridge: Cambridge University Press).

Trigger, B. C. (1978) *Time and Traditions: Essays in Archaeological Interpretation* (Edinburgh: Edinburgh University Press).

Tringham, R. (1978) Experimentation, ethnoarchaeology and the leapfrogs in archaeological methodology, in R. Gould (ed.) *Explorations in Ethnoarchaeology* (Albuquerque, NM: University of New Mexico Press), pp. 169–99.

Tringham, R. (1990) Conclusion: Selevac in the wider context of European prehistory, in R. Tringham and D. Kristic (eds) *Selevac: A Neolithic Village in Yugoslavia* (Los Angeles, CA: UCLA Institute of Archaeology Press), pp. 567–616.

Tringham, R. (1991a) Men and women in prehistoric architecture, *Traditional Dwellings and Settlements Review*, 111: 9–28.

Tringham, R. (1991b) Households with faces: the challenge or gender in prehistoric architectural remains, in J. Gero and M. Conkey (eds) *Engendering Archaeology: Women and Prehistory* (Oxford: Basil Blackwell), pp. 93–131.

Tringham, R. (1992) Visual images of archaeological architecture: gender in space, paper presented at symposium 'Envisioning the past: visual forms and the structuring of interpretations' at the ninety-first Annual Meeting of the American Anthropological Association, San Francisco: 2–6 December.

Tringham, R. (1993) Review of M. Gimbutas *Civilization of the Goddess*, *American Anthropologist*, 95: 196–7.

Tringham, R., Brukner, B., Kaiser, T., Borojevic, K., Russell, N., Steli, P., Stevanovic, M. and Voytek, B. (1992) The Opovo Project: a study of socio-economic change in the Balkan Neolithic, second preliminary report, *Journal of Field Archaeology* 19: 351–86.

Tringham, R. and Krstic, D. (1990) Introduction: the Selevac Archaeological Project, in R. Tringham and D. Krstic (eds) *Selevac: A Neolithic Village in Yugoslavia* (Los Angeles, CA: UCLA Institute of Archaeology Publications), pp. 1–12.

Tringham, R., Brukner, B. and Voytek, B. (1985) The Opovo Project: a study of socio-economic change in the Balkan Neolithic, *Journal of Field Archaeology* 12: 425–44.

Tringham, R. and Stevanovic, M. (1990) Archaeological excavation of Selevac 1976–78, in R. Tringham and D. Krstic (eds) *Selevac: A Neolithic Village in Yugoslavia* (Los Angeles, CA: UCLA Institute of Archaeology Publications), pp. 57–214.

Trivers, R. (1972) Parent–offspring conflict, *American Zoologist* 14: 249–64.

Trivers, R. and Willard, D. (1973) Natural selection of parental ability to vary the sex ratio of offspring, *Science* 179: 90–1.

Tuan, Y.-F. (1977) *Space and Place: The Perspective of Experience* (Minneapolis, MN: University of Minnesota Press).

Tuan, Y-F. (1979) Thought and landscape: the eye and the mind's eye, in D. W. Meinig (ed.) *The Interpretation of Ordinary Landscapes* (Oxford: Oxford University Press), pp. 89–102.

Turner, V. (1968) *The Forest of Symbols* (London: Cornell University Press).

Turner, V. (1969) *The Ritual Process* (London: Routledge and Kegan Paul).

Ucko, P. J. (ed.) (1995) *Theory in Archaeology: A World Perspective* (London: Routledge).

Ucko, P. J. (1969) Ethnography and archaeological interpretation of funerary remains, *World Archaeology* 1: 262–80.

Ucko, P. J. (1987) *Academic Freedom and Apartheid: The Story of the World Archaeological Congress* (London: Duckworth).

Unger, R. M. (1976) *Law in Modern Society: Toward a Criticism of Social Theory* (New York: Free Press).

Van de Velde, P. (1980) Elsloo and Hienheim: Bandkeramik Social Structure, *Analecta Praehistorica Leidensia* 12.

Vaughan, J. H. (19777) Mafakur: a limbic institution of the Marghi (Nigeria), in S. Miers and I. Kopytoff (eds) *Slavery in Africa: Historical and Anthropological Perspectives* (Madison, WI: University of Wisconsin Press), pp. 85–102.

Vehik, S. (1985) *Lithic Resource Procurement: Proceedings from the Second Conference on Prehistoric Chert Exploitation* (Carbondale, IL: Southern Illinois University, Center for Archaeological Investigations), *Occasional Paper* No. 4.

Vico, G. (1961) *The New Science of Giambattista Vico* (New York: Anchor Books).

von Humboldt, W. (1986) On the task of the historian, in K. Mueller-Vollmer (ed.) *The Hermeneutics Reader* (London: Blackwell), pp. 105–18.

Wainwright, G. (1979) *Gussage All Saints: An Iron Age Settlement in Dorset* (London: Her Majesty's Stationery Office).

Wait, G. (1985) *Ritual and Religion in Iron Age Britain* (Oxford: British Archaeological Reports) (British Series 149).

Walka, J. J. (1979) Management methods and opportunities in archaeology, *American Antiquity* 44: 575–82.

Walker, L. (1984) The deposition of the human remains, in B. Cunliffe (ed.) *Danebury: An Iron Age hillfort in Hampshire* (London: Council for British Archaeology), vol. II, pp. 442–3.

Walkowitz, D. J. (1978) *Worker City, Company Town* (Urbana, IL: University of Illinois Press).

Wallace, M. (1981) Visiting the past: history museums in the United States, *Radical History Review* 25: 63–96.

Wallace, M. (1984) Mickey Mouse history, *Radical History Review* 32: 33–57.

Wallerstein, I. (1960) Ethnicity and national integration in West Africa, *Cahiers d'Etudes Africaines* 1 (3): 129–39.

Wallman, S. (1977) Ethnicity research in Britain, *Current Anthropology* 18 (3): 31–2.

Walsh, K. (1990) The post-modern threat to the past, in I. Bapty and T. Yates (eds) *Archaeology After Structuralism* (London: Routledge), pp. 278–93.

Walsh, K. (1992) *The Representation of the Past: Museums and Heritage in the Postmodern World* (London: Routledge).

Walsh, L. S. (1983) Urban amenities and rural sufficiency: living standards and consumer behavior in colonial Chesapeake, 1643–1777, *Journal of Economic History* 43: 81–104.

Walters, J. (1980) Interventions and the development of dominance relationships in female baboons, *Folia Primatologica* 34: 61–89.

Walters, J. (1981) Inferring kinship from behaviour: maternity determinations in yellow baboons, *Animal Behavior* 29: 126–36.

Warnke, G. (1988) *Gadamer, Hermeneutics, Tradition and Reason* (Cambridge, Polity Press).

Washburn, D. K. (1978) A symmetry classification of Pueblo ceramic designs, in P. Grebinger (ed.) *Discovering Past Behaviour* (New York: Academic Press).

Washburn, S. and DeVore, I. (1961) The social behavior of baboons and early man, in S. Washburn (ed.) *Social Life of Early Man.* (Chicago: Aldine).

Washburn, S. and Hamburg, D. (1965) The study of primate behavior, in I. DeVore (ed.) *Primate Behavior* (New York: Holt, Rinehart and Winston).

Washburn, S., Jay, P. and Lancaster, J. (1965) Field studies of old world monkeys and apes, *Science* 150: 1541–7.

Washburn, S. and Lancaster, C. (1968) The evolution of hunting, in R. Lee and I. Devore (eds) *Man the hunter* (Chicago: Aldine), pp. 293–303.

Wasser, S. (1981) Reproductive competition and cooperation: general theory and a field study of female yellow baboons, PhD thesis, University of Washington, Seattle.

Wasser, S. (1982) Reciprocity and the trade-off between associate quality and relatedness, *American Naturalist* 119: 720–31.

Wasser, S. and Barash, D. (1981) The 'selfish' allowmother, *Ethology and Sociobiology* 2: 91–3.

Waterhouse, R. (1981) *A Heidegger Critique: A Critical Examination of the Existential Phenomenology of Martin Heidegger* (Sussex: Harvester Press).

Watson, P. J. (1979) *Archaeological Ethnography in Western Iran* Viking Fund Publications in Anthropology No. 57 (Washington, DC: Smithsonian Institution).

Watson, P. J. (1986) Archaeological interpretation, 1985, in D. J. Meltzer, D. D. Fowler and J. A. Sabloff (eds) *American Archaeology Past and Future* (Washington, DC: Smithsonian Institution Press), pp. 439–58.

Watson, P. J., Leblanc, S. A. and Redman, C. L. (1971) *Explanation in Archaeology: An Explicitly Scientific Approach* (New York: Columbia University Press).

Watson, R. (1976) Inference in archaeology, *American Antiquity* 41: 58–66.

Weber, M. (1947) *The Theory of Social and Economic Organisation* (Part 1 of *Wirtschaft und Gesellschaft*), trans. T. Parsons and A. M. Henderson, ed. T. Parsons (Oxford: Oxford University Press).

Weeks, J. (1977) *Coming Out: Homosexual Politics in Britain, from the Nineteenth Century to the Present* (London: Quartet).

Weeks, J. (1989a) Against nature, in D. Altman (ed.) *Homosexuality, Which Homosexuality?* (London: Gay Men's Press).

Weeks, J. (1989b) *Sex, Politics and Society: the Regulation of Sexuality since 1800* (London: Longman).

Weiner, A. (1985) Inalienable wealth, *American Ethnologist* 12: 210–27.

Weitzenfeld, J. S. (1984) Valid reasoning by analogy, *Philosophy of Science* 51: 137–49.

Welsh Office (1991) *Planning Policy Guidance Note 16: Archaeology and Planning* (Cardiff: Welsh Office).

Western, J. D. and Strum, S. (1983) Sex, kinship, and the evolution of social manipulation, *Ethology and Sociobiology* 4: 19–28.

Whallon, R. (1973) Spatial analysis of palaeolithic occupation areas, in C. Renfrew (ed.) *The Explanation of Culture Change* (London: Duckworth), pp. 115–30.

White, L. A. (1959) *The Evolution of Culture* (New York: McGraw-Hill).

White, R. (1982) Rethinking the Middle/Upper Paleolithic transition, *Current Anthropology* 23 (2): 169–92.

Whitehead, H. (1981) The bow and the burden strap, in S. B. Ortner and H. Whitehead (eds) *Sexual Meanings: The Cultural Construction of Gender and Sexuality* (Cambridge: Cambridge University Press).

Wiessner, P. (1983) Style and ethnicity in the Kalahari San projectile point, *American Antiquity* 48: 253–76.

Wiessner, P. (1989) Style and changing relations between the individual and society, in I. Hodder (ed.) *The Meanings of Things* (London: Unwin and Hyman), pp. 56–63.

Wikan, U. (1992) Beyond words: the power of resonance, *American Ethnologist* 19: 460–82.

Willey, G. R. (1966) *An Introduction to American Archaeology: North and Middle America*, Vol. 1. (Englewood Cliffs, NJ: Prentice-Hall).

Williams, D. (1974) *Icon and Image* (Harmondsworth: Allen Lane).

Williams, D. (1975) The brides of Christ, in S. Ardner (ed.) *Perceiving Women* (London: J. M. Dent), pp. 105–26.

Williamson, T. and Bellamy, L. (1987) *Property and Landscape: A Social History of the English Countryside* (London: George Philip).

Wilmsen, E. (1965) An outline of early man studies in the United States, *American Antiquity* 31: 172–92.

Wilmsen, E. (1974) *Lindenmeier: A Pleistocene Hunting Society* (New York: Harper and Row).

Wilson, F. (1975) *Sociobiology: The New Synthesis* (Cambridge: Belknap Press).

Winch, P. (1963) *The Idea of a Social Science* (London: Routledge).

Wind, H. (1976) *Filosofisk hermeneutik* (Copenhagen: Berlingske forlag).

Wobst, H. M. (1977) Stylistic behaviour and information exchange, *University of Michigan Museum of Anthropology, Anthropological Paper* 61: 317–42.

Wobst, M. (1976) Locational relationships in Palaeolithic society, in R. Ward and K. Weiss (eds) *The Demographic Evolution of Human Populations*: (New York: Academic Press), pp. 49–58.

Wolf, E. (1982) *Europe and the People Without History* (Berkeley, CA: University of California Press).

Wolf, E. (1984) Culture: panacea or problem? *American Antiquity* 49 (2): 393–400.

Wood, M. (1965) *The English Medieval House* (London: Batsford).

Woodburn, J. (1980) Hunters and gatherers today and the reconstruction of the past, in E. Gellner (ed.) *Soviet and Western Anthropology* (New York: Columbia University Press), pp. 95–117.

Woods, G. (1998) *A History of Gay Literature: The Male Tradition* (New Haven, CT: Yale University Press).

Wormington, H. M. (1957) *Ancient Man in North America* (4th edn, Denver: Denver Museum of Natural History) *Popular Series* No. 4.

Wylie, A. (1982) Epistemological issues raised by a structuralist archaeology, in I Hodder (ed.) *Symbolic and Structural Archaeology* (Cambridge: Cambridge University Press), pp. 39–46.

Wylie, A. (1985a) The reaction against analogy, in M. B. Schiffer (ed.) *Advances in Archaeological Method and Theory* (New York: Academic Press), vol. 8, pp. 63–111.

Wylie, A. (1985b) Putting Shakertown back together: critical theory in archaeology, *Journal of Anthropological Archaeology* 4: 1: 33–47.

Wylie, A. (1986) Matters of fact and matters of interest, paper presented at the World Archaeological Congress, Southampton and London.

Wylie, A. (1987) Comment, *Current Anthropology* 28: 297–8.

Wylie, A. (1988) 'Simple' analogy and the role of relevance assumptions: implications of archaeological practice, *International Studies in the Philosophy of Science* 2.2: 134–50.

Wylie, A. (1989a) Matters of fact and matters of interest, in S. Shennan (ed.) *Archaeological Approaches to Cultural Identity* (London: Unwin Hyman Ltd.), pp. 94–109.

Wylie, A. (1989b) Feminist analyses of social power: substantive and epistemological issues, paper presented at conference on Critical Approaches in Archaeology: material life, meaning and power. Cascais, Portugal.

Wylie, A. (1989c) The interpretive dilemma, in V. Pinsky and A. Wylie (eds) *Critical Traditions in Contemporary Archaeology* (Cambridge: Cambridge University Press), pp. 18–27.

Wylie, A. (1989d) Archaeological cables and tacking: the implications of practice for Bernstein's 'Options Beyond Objectivism and Relativism', *Philosophy of the Social Sciences* 19: 1–18.

Wylie, A. (1991a) Beyond objectivism and relativism: feminist critiques and archaeological challenges, in N. Willo and D. Walde (eds) *Archaeology of Gender* (Calgary: University of Calgary, Alberta), pp. 17–23.

Wylie, A. (1991b) Gender theory and the archaeological record, in J. Gero and M. Conkey (eds) *Engendering Archaeology: Women and Prehistory* (Oxford: Basil Blackwell), pp. 31–56.

Wylie, A. (1992) The interplay of evidential constraints and political interests: recent archaeological work on gender, *American Antiquity* 57: 15–34.

Wylie, A., Okruhlik, K., Thielen-Wilson, L. and Morton, S. (1989) Feminist critiques of science: the epistemological and methodological literature, *Women's Studies International Forum* 12: 379–88.

Yanagisako, S. (1979) Family and household: the analysis of domestic groups, *Annual Review of Anthropology* 8: 161–205.

Yates, T. (1988) Review of the idea of prehistory, *Archaeological Review from Cambridge* 7(2): 264–6.

Yates, T. (1989) Habitus and social space: some suggestions about meaning in the Saami (Lapp) tent *c.* 1700–1900, in I. Hodder (ed.) *The Meaning of Things* (London: Unwin Hyman), pp. 249–63.

Yates, T. (1990a) Jacques Derrida: 'There is nothing outside of the text', in C. Tilley (ed.) *Reading Material Culture* (Oxford: Blackwell), pp. 206–280.

Yates T. (1990b) Archaeology through the looking glass, in I. Bapty and T. Yates (eds) *Archaeology after Structuralism* (London: Routledge), pp. 153–204. And this volume.

Yates, T. (1993) Frameworks for an archaeology of the body, in C Tilley (ed.) *Interpretative Archaeology* (Oxford: Berg).

Yellen, J. (1977) *Archaeological Approaches to the Present* (New York: Academic Press).

Yellen, J. E. (1983) Women, archaeology and the National Science Foundation, in J. M. Gero, D. Lacy and M. Blakey (eds) *The Socio-Politics of Archaeology* (Amherst, MA: Department of Anthropology, University of Massachusetts), Research Report No. 23.

Yellen, J. E. (n.d.) An update on gender differences in funding from the National Science Foundation, paper presented at The Archaeology of Gender: 22nd Annual Chacmool Conference, November 1989.

Yentsch, A. E. (1983) *Salvaging the Calvert House Site*. Final report for the N.E.H. Grant RO–20600–83. MS, Historic Annapolis, Inc.

Yoffee, N. and Sherratt, A. (1993a) Introduction: the sources of archaeological theory, in N. Yoffee and A. Sherratt (eds) *Archaeological Theory: Who Sets the Agenda?* (Cambridge: Cambridge University Press), pp. 1–10.

Yoffee, N., and Sherratt, A. (eds) (1993b) *Archaeological Theory: Who Sets the Agenda?* (Cambridge: Cambridge University Press).

Young, M. (1988) *The Metronomic Society: Natural Rhythms and Human Timetables* (London: Thames and Hudson).

Zahavi, G. (1983) Negotiated loyalty: welfare capitalism and the shoeworkers of Endicott Johnson, 1920–1940, *Journal of American History* 70(3): 602–20.

Zannieri, P. A. (1980) Dancing pilgrims: the dynamics of museum interpretation, MA paper, Department of Anthropology, Brown University, Providence, RI.

Zihlman, A. (1981) Women as shapers of the human adaptation, in F. Dahlberg (ed.) *Woman the Gatherer* (New Haven, CT: Yale University Press), pp. 75–102.

Zimmerman, L. J. (1989) Made radical by my own: an archaeologist learns to accept reburial, in R. Layton (ed.) *Conflicts in the Archaeology of Living Traditions* (London: Unwin Hyman), pp. 60–7.

Zola, I. K. (1975) Medicine as an institution of social control, in C. Cox and A. Mead (eds) *A Sociology of Medical Practice* (London: Collier Macmillan).

Zuckerman, S. (1932) *The Social Life of Monkeys and Apes* (London: Routledge and Kegan Paul).

INDEX